William Nicholson and Sons

Consult me, to know how to cook

William Nicholson and Sons

Consult me, to know how to cook

ISBN/EAN: 9783742838841

Manufactured in Europe, USA, Canada, Australia, Japa

Cover: Foto ©Gila Hanssen / pixelio.de

Manufactured and distributed by brebook publishing software (www.brebook.com)

William Nicholson and Sons

Consult me, to know how to cook

THE BOOK
THAT EVERY FAMILY NEEDS.

CONSULT ME,

TO KNOW HOW TO COOK

Meats, Poultry, Fish, Game, Vegetables, Soups, Gravies, Sauces, Meat Pies, Puddings, Food for the Sick, &c.

CONSULT ME ON CONFECTIONERY;

How to make Biscuits, Cakes, Pies, Tarts, Creams, Cheesecakes, Jellies, &c., to Preserve, &c.,—and the ART OF SUGAR BOILING, Candying, to make Sweetmeats, &c.

CONSULT ME, And I will teach you how to BREW, TO MAKE WINES, CORDIALS, TINCTURES, TO PICKLE, &c.

CONSULT ME ON HOUSEHOLD MANAGEMENT AND ECONOMY;

I will tell you how to Wash, get up Linen, polish Furniture—to keep the House clean and sweet—to beautify the person, &c.

CONSULT ME ON DISEASES AND THEIR REMEDIES,

And I will point out their symptoms, their causes, and their cure; based CHIEFLY ON THE MEDICO-BOTANICAL SYSTEM, so Safe, Effectual, Cheap, and Rational.

How to cure Colds, Coughs, Asthma, Consumption, Aches, Pains, Bruises, Burns, &c., &c. To make Bitters, Decoctions, Extracts, Electuaries, Fomentations, Gargles, Infusions, Injections, Lotions, Ointments, Pills, Plasters, Salves, &c.

CONSULT ME ON THE GAMES OF CHESS, DRAUGHTS, &c.

CONSULT ME HOW TO DYE

In Modern Style, and the Newest Colours.

CONSULT ME ON THE COLD WATER CURE, which has benefited thousands, and which will benefit you.

CONSULT ME ALSO ON A THOUSAND OTHER THINGS.

WAKEFIELD:
WILLIAM NICHOLSON AND SONS.
LONDON: S. D. EWINS JR. AND CO., 22, PATERNOSTER ROW,
AND W. TEGG, PANCRAS LANE, CHEAPSIDE.
MANCHESTER: JOHN HEYWOOD, AND A HEYWOOD & SON.

1872.

TO THE READER.

The design of the author and compiler of the following pages has been to make a useful book,—useful to individuals, to families, and to the public at large; and he presumes that in this purpose he has succeeded; but he will leave the public to determine that matter for him.

The culinary department has been derived from experienced persons, from various authentic sources; nor has he excluded from this work some of the old modes of cookery, which are still in use, and are found to be the best.

The same also may be said of the confectionery department, and of those portions embracing Domestic Economy. For every thing likely to be useful, the author has searched many volumes, European and American, and whatever could be legitimately selected, he has with discrimination, and, in most cases, with great improvements, adopted, and presented to the world—hence the majority of the receipts and recipes in this book are made copyright.

In the medical department, the *treatment of diseases* is very different from that of the allopathists. The barbarous system of bleeding, salivating, cauterizing, and blistering, is abandoned; for such methods often only debilitate the system, and create disease instead of curing it; and it is really surprising with what tenacity they are retained. The author has adopted the *Reformed Practice of Medicine* peculiar to America, and now rapidly obtaining in this country and on the continent. It has a different process from allopathy, and calls to its aid the various plants of the world possessing curative powers; for "*vegetable substances afford the mildest, most efficient, and the most congenial remedies to the human frame. The numerous cures that are now daily performed by the use of vegetable medicines, are sufficient evidence of their super-excellent virtues.*"—Professor Fafinesque.

This department of medicine in this work will doubtless prove a blessing to many families. Many of the receipts are more precious than rubies! They are priceless! The Author confesses his obligations to several of the American botanists; viz.—Thompson, Dunglison, King, Beach, &c. He has derived great pleasure and much information from the "*American Practice of Medicine,*" by Wooster Beach, M. D., the American Edition, in three volumes. The price is high, £5 5s.; but it is worth ten times more.

This volume, treats of *Diseases*, their *Symptoms, Causes,* and *Remedies.* This Book recognizes chiefly

BOTANICAL REMEDIES;

Embracing also whatever is valuable, rational, and innocuous, in Allopathy, Homœopathy, and Hydropathy.

☞ The Botanical Remedies are not sold by the ordinary *Chemists and Druggists;* but there are now, nearly in every town, DEALERS in BOTANICAL MEDICINES, comprising —Herbs, Roots, Cordials Essences, Extracts, Mixtures, Ointments, Pills, Plasters, Powders, Salves, Spirits, Syrups, Tinctures, &c.

These remedies are cheap, innocuous, and most effectual. If properly taken, or applied, they seldom fail to effect a cure.

MAY, 1866.

THE NEW FAMILY GUIDE.

ABDOMINAL RUPTURES, or *Herniæ*, take place at the navel, in females, and the scrotum and groin in males. When the bowel lies quietly in the bag, and admits of being readily put back into the abdomen, the rupture is termed *reducible;* but *irreducible* when the contrary. A hernia is strangulated when the intestine is, as it were, tied round with a string, so as to prevent the contents of the bowels from passing off; in such a case, inflammation is excited, and alarming, and sometimes fatal, symptoms, are manifest.

The causes of ruptures are various; viz. *sedentary habits*, violent exercise, such as *feats of agility, jumping, running, lifting and carrying heavy weights, vomiting, straining, laughing, sneezing,* and whatever induces extreme action of the abdominal muscles. Some parts of the parietes, or enclosure of the bowels, are naturally weaker than others; especially the inguinal and crural rings, and the umbilicus; and it is of these parts that hernia most frequently occurs: or the abdominal walls may be defectively formed. When a hernia takes place suddenly, there is a sensation of something giving way at the part, and some pain; but in many persons it comes on gradually, and almost imperceptibly, particularly in very debilitated constitutions.

The general symptoms of a hernia, when reducible and free from strangulation, are an indolent tumour at some point of the abdomen, frequently descending out of the abdominal ring, or out of the navel, but occasionally from other situations. The swelling often arises suddenly, and is subject to a change of size, being smaller when the patient lies down on his back, and larger when he stands up or holds his breath. It frequently diminishes when pressed, and grows large again when the pressure is removed. Its size and tension often increase after a meal, or when the bowels are flatulent. In consequence of the unnatural position of the bowels, many persons who have rupture are occasionally troubled with colic, costiveness, and vomiting. But sometimes the functions of the intestines suffer little interruption.

But in all cases ruptures are troublesome and dangerous, and therefore ought to be attended to in time. When a rupture is reducible, return the protruded parts to their original cavity, by gently pressing the projecting tumour, which can be best effected when the patient is lying on his back, with the legs bent, so that the knees may be erect; an attitude which he should always preserve as much as possible. An injection should be given made of gruel, butter, salt, and five or six drops of laudanum. Folds of linen dipped in ice-water should be placed upon the tumour, and renewed every fifteen minutes. Ice also may be applied with good effect. If the case has been delayed too long, use flannels dipped in a warm decoction of bitter herbs, as tansy, wormwood, horehound, and hops; these herbs tend to soften the tumour, and facilitate its return. Change the flannels frequently.

Infants are often subject to umbilical hernia, or rupture of the navel. It is cured by applying a proper bandage or truss, which, with increasing strength, effects a cure. Particular attention should be paid to the cure of female infants that are ruptured; that they may be free from the complaint when they become adult and pregnant; for then it often recurs from the too great distension of the abdomen, &c. During pregnancy, it is often troublesome, but after parturition, if the contents have not contracted any adhesion, they will often return into the abdomen, and may be kept there by a proper bandage. Females subject to umbilical rupture, should keep their bowels unconstipated, especially if the navel rupture be *irreducible;* and they should avoid indigestible food.

When the tumour is returned, it should be kept in its place by a bandage or truss. By the permanent pressure of a truss upon the opening, the parts are prevented from descending, and a permanent cure is often effected. A truss may be obtained at a Surgical Instrument Maker's.

Dr. Beach, of America, states; —"Most of the cases of strangulated hernia for which an operation is performed, might be cured by proper treatment. In very many cases, where an operation has been proposed, the patient has recovered by very simple means. I have been called to some, where, at first view, it has seemed impossible to return the protruded viscera without cutting down and dividing the stricture; and yet, by prompt and energetic means, I have succeeded in reducing it." The following directions are founded upon the American practice:—

Commence the treatment by giving a dose of castor oil; avoid strong and irritating purgatives. —Use injections of an oily nature; as *Lobelia inflata*, a sufficient quantity. Infuse in half a pint of hot water, to which add as much milk and treacle, and a gill of olive or sweet oil. Repeat every hour. This is one of the most powerful relaxants that can be used in this disease.

The following *External Applications* are recommended by Dr. Beach:—Steam and foment with bitter herbs (herbs afore mentioned). Put the decoction in a tub or pail, and sit over it by means of a narrow board put across it. Place a blanket over the patient. This will cause perspiration, and reduce the inflammation. In extreme cases, a warm bath should be taken for some time. An alkaline poultice may be applied over the rupture. Mix the slippery elm bark with weak ley, until a poultice of a proper consistence is formed, to be applied tepid, and often renewed. The best effects have been produced by this application.

Dr. Reese, of New York, uses the *sulphuric ether* for the reduction or return of hernia. He wets the tumour with the liquid, and then, in order to produce speedy evaporation, blows upon it with a pair of bellows. He states that he has reduced a number of strangulated herniæ by this method alone, when they had been doomed to undergo an operation.

While these means are being used, manual aid must be used, called *taxis*, (meaning the replacement of parts by the hand). The position of the patient requires care and skill. His legs and buttocks should be elevated as high as possible, forming an angle, if possible, of 45 degrees. This may be effected by placing the back parts of a chair underneath him. His thighs and the body should be a little flexed or bent, in order to relax the muscles. The tumour should then be seized, and moderate pressure made, in order to return the viscera.

The constant application of a solution of alum in a strong decoction of oak bark (two drachms to a pint) has been recommended by some surgeons for the radical cure of rupture in the groin. It is applied by means of soft linen, which should be wetted as soon as it becomes dry. In incipient cases this topical remedy, by constringing the part, may succeed in preventing the escape of intestine or omentum through the abdominal ring. The compress should for some time be kept on the part by a bandage or a truss with easy springs.

ABORTION, *to prevent.*--Women of a weak or relaxed habit should use solid food, avoiding great quantities of tea and other weak and watery liquors. They should go soon to bed and rise early, and take frequent exercise, but avoid being over-fatigued.

If of a full habit, they ought to use a spare diet, and chiefly of the vegetable kind, avoiding strong liquors, and every thing that may tend to heat the body, or increase the quantity of blood.

In the first case, take daily half a pint of decoction of Lignum Guiacum; boiling an ounce of it in a quart of water for five minutes.

In the latter case, give half a drachm of powdered nitre in a cup of water-gruel, every five or six hours; in both cases she should sleep on a hard mattress with her head low, and be kept cool and quiet.

ABSCESS.--They require the application of warm poultices and fomentations, and a cooling aperient medicine. The best fomentation comprises a decoction of marsh mallows, camomile flowers, poppyheads, or hemlock leaves. The poultice may be made of bread and water, or linseed meal. These to be applied till the abscess bursts. When burst, allow the discharge of purulent matter, and after it has ceased, apply moist rags for a day or two; then draw together the edges of the wound by means of diachylon plaster, and to the wound apply Cerate or Spermaceti Ointment. It is necessary sometimes when the bursting is slow and tedious, and the pain great, to open the abscess with the point of a lancet, which prevents much suffering. When the abscess is indolent, and slow in ripening, apply a poultice of oatmeal, and water, and yeast, and a little salt. Let the patient live on nourishing diet. Keep the body open; and if the pain be great, mix with the aperient, about 10 or 12 drops of laudanum.

ABSCESS, *Milk.*--This abscess affects mothers, and requires careful treatment. Apply every two hours warm vinegar to the part. This, if done in time, soon gives relief.

ABSORBENTS, OR ANTI-ACIDS,—Are medicines administered to counteract acidity in the stomach or intestinal canal. In most cases, emetics and aperients are given previous to their being taken; they are; Ammonia, carbonate of, in doses from 5 grains to 1 scruple; Ammonia, liquor of, 10 to 20 drops; Ammonia, aromatic spirit of, 20 to 30 drops; Lime water, 2 ounces to half a pint; Magnesia calcined, 20 to 40 grains; Magnesia, carbonate of, half to 2 drachms; Potass, carbonate of, 10 grains to half a drachm; Potass, solution of, 10 drops to half a drachm! Soda, carbonate of, 10 grains to half a drachm; Soda water, half a pint.

ABSTINENCE.--Disease may oft be cured by abstinence from all food, especially if the disorders have been procured by luxurious living and repletion. The latter overtaxes nature, and it rebels against such treatment. Indigestion, giddiness, headache, mental depression, &c., are often the effects of greediness in meat and drink. Omitting one, two, or three meals, allows the system to rest, to regain strength, and allows the clogged organs to dispose of their burdens. The practice of drug taking *to cleanse the stomach*, though it may give the needed relief, always weakens the system, while *abstinence* secures the good result, and yet does no injury.

Said a young gentleman to a distinguished physician of Philadelphia,—' Doctor, what do you do for yourself when you have headache, or other slight attack?" "Go without my dinner," was the reply. "Well, if that will not do, how do you proceed then?" "Go without my supper," was the answer. "But if that does not cure you, what then?" "Go without my breakfast. We physicians seldom take medicines ourselves, or use them in our families, for *we* know that *starving* is better, but we cannot make our patients believe it."

Hippocrates (the father of medicine) said wisely, that if a man eats sparingly and drinks little, he is nearly certain of bringing no disease upon himself, and that a *moderate* supply of food nourishes the body best. The quantity of food which nature really requires for her support is small, and he that eats and drinks moderately at each meal, stands fair to enjoy sprightliness, vivacity, and freedom of spirits. Bodies governed by temperance and regularity are rarely hurt by melancholy, or any other affection of the mind. To have a clear head, we must have a clean stomach; for this is the grand reservoir in which the food is first deposited, and thence its nutritive power is distributed throughout all parts of the body.

ACETOUS CATAPLASM, OR POULTICE.—This is made with vinegar and bran only, or with the addition of oatmeal, or bread crumbs. It is a simple poultice, but very useful for sprains and bruises. As it becomes dry, it should be moistened with vinegar.

ACHES AND PAINS.—Rub a little opodeldoc upon the part affected, two or three times a day and wear a flannel upon it; or mix Camphorated Spirit, Ammonia, sweet oil, and laudanum: (of the last the least), rub the part well, and then apply a cloth well saturated with the mixture, and cover with a bandage. If this does not give relief, take twenty drops of Volatile Tincture of Guiacum, every night and morning.

ACID DROPS.—Boil 1 lb. of sugar in a cupful of water over a slow fire for half an hour, till half candied; then add lemon juice, or citric acid, or tartaric acid, according to taste. A little dissolved gum Arabic added will make them harder and more wholesome. *Gu.*

ACIDITY, AND FLATULENCY, *in Children.*—It often arises from a mother's impure milk; when it is so she must take the Neutralizing Mixture; and if not effectual, administer it to the infant. Also foment the belly with warm brandy and water, to which add a little salt. Give also the *Carminative Drops*, which see.

ACIDITY of the STOMACH.——The *Neutralizing Mixture*, (which see) is very effectual in curing this disorder.——Or, 10 grains of Calumba, powdered, and 10 grains of magnesia, well mixed. Magnesia and a little finely powdered chalk will be of great service.—See *Absorbents*. *Gu.*

ADHESIVE PLASTER. — Take of common Plaster, half a pound; of burgundy pitch, a quarter of a pound. Melt them together. See *Common Plaster.*

This plaster is principally used for keeping on other dressings.

ADULTERATION OF ALE AND BEER.—They are often adulterated with the most virulent poisons, which in the intemperate, are gradually and constantly undermining the constitution. Ye intemperate ones, just think, ye are drinking *coculus indicus*, a stupefying poison; *tobacco*, a deadly narcotic; *sulphate of iron*, poisonous; *strychnine*, or *nux vomica*, virulent poison; *vitriol*, and many other body-destroying articles.

ADULTERATION OF COFFEE, CHICORY, &c.—Coffee is often adulterated with Chicory, oak or mahogany saw-dust, or roasted corn. In examining 34 specimens of ground Coffee, all, with three exceptions, were more or less sophisticated. Chicory also is often adulterated with ground acorns and roasted wheat, coloured with Venetian Red. Of 36 *Brown Sugars* examined, the Acarus insect was found in all but one, abundance of flour in four, and sand or stone grit in 11 instances.

Mustard was found adulterated with wheaten flour, highly coloured with Turmeric—49 tested loaves of *Bread* contained alum.— Only 8 of 56 specimens of '*Broma*,' '*Soluble*' and '*Homœopathic Cocoa*,' were really such, the rest having variable proportions of sugar, wheat, and potato flour, sago-meal, and red earthy matter. Three other Cocoas were made up of sugar, sago-meal, arrow-root, and potato flour; others with tapioca, starch, sugar, and earthy colouring matter, the latter ingredient being present in 7 of the 9 Rock and flaked articles, the nibs being chiefly mixed with Chicory.

Quassia and Gentian are used instead of Hop, for bitter flavour to *Beer*; and the Sulphate of Copper to beautify *Green Pickles* and bottled fruits.—*Cayenne* and *Curry Powder* are often adulterated with red lead and vermillion.——*Arrow-root* is often adulterated with Potato, Sago, and Tapioca Starches.——*Bread*, by Pea-flour, Bone-dust, and Mashed Potatoes, with Alum, 'Hards,' and 'Stuff.'—— *Butter* with water and lard.—— *Wheat Flour* with Bean and Pea flours, Indian Corn, Bran, and Plaster of Paris.——*Ginger* with Wheat, Sago, Potato Flour, and Mustard Husks.—*Dr. W. Alexander on Adulteration.*

ÆOLIAN HARP, TO MANUFACTURE AN.—Let a box be made of thin deal, the length to correspond exactly to the breadth of the window in which it is to be placed, five inches in depth, and six in width. Glue on it at the extremities of the top two pieces of oak about half an inch high and a quarter of an inch thick, to serve as bridges for the strings, and within-side of each end glue two pieces of beech, about an inch square, and of length equal to the width of the box, which is to hold the pegs. Into one of these bridges fix as many pegs (like those of a violin) as there are to be strings, and into the other fasten as many small brass pins, to which attach one end of the strings. Then string the instrument with first-fiddle strings, fixing one end of them and twisting the other round the opposite peg. These strings, which should not be drawn tight, must be tuned in unison. To procure a proper passage for the wind, a thin board, supported by four pegs, is placed over the strings at about three inches distant from the sounding board. Place the instrument in the window partly open; and, to increase the force of the current of air, open the door of the room or an opposite window. When the wind blows, the strings produce a pleasing admixture of all the notes of the diatonic scale, in the most delightful harmonic combinations.

AGRICULTURE.—The first principles of agriculture are these: make and keep the land perfectly dry and free from weeds. Make and keep the soil which is too adhesive, or too loose, of such a friable nature as will make it receive, retain, and transmit moisture, and thus fit it to produce the most luxuriant state of vegetation. Restore to the soil as a manure, in a state of decay, the produce after it has been consumed by sheep or other stock. Never manure any land till every-weed is exterminated, for weeds grow most luxuriantly in the soil to which they are natural; if any are left they will outgrow the plant cultivated, and take up the greatest quantity of manure laid on the land.

AGRIMONY.—See *Robinson's Herbal*. It is useful in coughs and bowel complaints—In decoction. It is a most valuable plant, having very many medical virtues.

AGUE.—The cause is debility; frequently *marsh miasma*, or the effluvia arising from stagnant water in pools, or on marshy ground. On the attack, the patient should be placed between blankets, and partake freely of water-gruel or barley-water. From 20 to 30 drops of laudanum, or more, should be given just before the commencement of the ague fit. The nails turn blue just before the fit begins. The fit may be moderated also by taking 1 scruple of the carbonate of Ammonia, 8 grains compound powder of Ipecacuanha, mint-water, 1½ ounce. Peruvian Bark, or Sulphate of Quinine, is an efficacious remedy. An emetic before taking it is necessary; about 20 grains of Ipecacuanha powder; then take a small dose of Salts and Senna, and the Peruvian bark in powder; an ounce will make eight doses, one of which should be taken every hour or two. Or, instead of the Peruvian bark, take from 2 to 4 grains of Quinine, with 1 grain of extract of Gentian, made into pills. When the disease is arrested, continue the use of the pill, taking two per day for a few weeks.

AGUE. — Take 30 grains of Snake-root, 40 of wormwood, ½ ounce of Peruvian Bark powdered, and half a pint of Port Wine. Put the whole into a bottle, and shake it well together; divide it into four equal quantities, and take it the first in the morning, and the last at night, when the fit is over. The dose should be often repeated, to prevent a return of the complaint. Or, when the fit is on, take an egg beaten up in a glass of brandy, and go to bed immediately. *Hu.*

AIR.—Impure air is highly charged with noxious gases. It is the chief cause of influenza, cholera, and fevers.—In crowded assemblies, the atmosphere soon becomes injurious. *It is computed* that a man destroys the vital portion of a gallon of air per minute. Fish cannot live in impure *water.* Man cannot live healthfully in an impure atmosphere. Hence houses, chapels, churches, prisons, assembly rooms, &c. ought to be well ventilated.—Persons inhabiting towns should often walk into the country, for the purpose of obtaining pure air.—Pure air is essential to good health; and just in proportion as the air we breathe becomes impure, the system becomes unhealthy. If fresh air be necessary for those in health, it is still more so for the sick who often lose their lives for want of it. The notion that sick people must be kept very hot is so common, that one can scarcely enter the room of the sick, without being ready to faint, on account of the hot suffocating smell. How this must affect the sick any one may judge. No medicine is so beneficial and reviving to the sick as fresh air, if it be administered prudently.— The atmosphere of a sick room may be greatly purified and freshened by sprinkling the floor frequently with vinegar, or any strong vegetable acid.

AIR:—*To purify.*—Powdered nitre and oil of vitriol, six drachms each. Mix, by adding one drachm of vitriol at a time. The vessel must be placed on some hot substance, and the mixture stirred with a glass rod. Place in different parts of the room. This is excellent to prevent infection from Typhus and other fevers.

AIR:—*Country superior to Town Air.*—"If you examine," says M. Pouchet, "the bodies of animals, which live in our towns, and in our houses, you will be astonished at the enormous quantity of starch contained in their respiratory organs. In birds you will find it even in the middle of their bones. Particles of soot, filaments of the different kinds of textures of which our clothes are made, are also found there in great abundance. But the farther the animal lives from a town, the more scarce become these bodies. In animals and birds living in the midst of forests, you will scarcely find any at all of them; in their case the respiratory apparatus is, on the contrary, filled with a large quantity of vegetable *debris chlorophyllæ,* &c. I have found in the lungs of man the same atmospheric corpuscles as in animals. I found two persons who died in one of our Hospitals—a man and a woman— and whose lungs I inspected, a notable quantity of fecula, normal, or after panification, particles of silica, and fragments of glass; fragments of painted wood of a beautiful red colour; *debris* of clothes, and a larvæ of a microscopic *arachnis* still alive."

ALABASTER, *to clean.*—Soap well and wash with hot water. If stained, apply fullers earth, pipe-clay, or whiting, for three or four hours, then wash off. If very dirty and stained, first wash with aquafortis diluted with water.

ALE, FINE WELSH, *to brew.* —Pour forty-two gallons of water hot, but not quite boiling on eight bushels of malt, cover and let it stand three hours. In the mean time infuse four pounds of hops in a little hot water, and put the water and hops into the tub, and run the wort upon them, and boil them together three hours. Strain off the hops, and keep for the small beer. Let the wort stand in a high tub till cool enough to receive the yeast, of which put two quarts of ale, or if you cannot get it, of small-beer yeast. Mix it thoroughly and often. When the worst has done working the second or third day, the yeast will sink rather than rise in the middle, remove it then, and tun the ale as it works out; pour a quart in at a time, and gently to prevent the fermentation from continuing too long, which weakens the liquor. Put a bit of paper over the bung-hole two or three days before stopping up.

ALE, OR STRONG BEER, *to brew.*—Twelve bushels of malt to the hogshead for beer, (or fourteen if you want it of a very good body), eight for ale; for either pour the whole quantity of water hot, but not boiling, on at once, and let it infuse three hours close covered; mash it in the first half-hour, and let it stand the remainder of the time. Run it on the hops previously infused in water; for strong beer three quarters of a pound to a bushel; if for ale, half a pound. Boil it from the wort two hours from the time it begins to boil. Cool a pailful to add three quarts of yeast to, which will prepare it for putting to the rest when ready next day; but if possible put together the same night. Tun as usual. Cover the bung-hole with paper when the beer has done working; and when it is to be stopped, have ready a pound and a half of hops dried before the fire, put them into the bung-hole, and fasten it

up. Let it stand twelve months in casks, and twelve months in bottles before it be drank. It will keep fine eight or ten years. It should be brewed the beginning of March.

Great care must be taken that the bottles are perfectly prepared, and that the corks are of the best sort.

The ale will be ready in three or four months; and if the vent-peg never be removed, it will have spirit and strength to the very last, Allow two gallons of water at first for waste.

After the beer or ale has run from the grains, pour a hogshead and a half for the twelve bushels, and a hogshead of water if eight were brewed; mash, and let it stand, and then boil, &c. Use some of the hops for this table-beer that was boiled for the strong.

When thunder or hot weather causes beer to turn sour, a teaspoonful, or more, if required, of salt of wormwood put into the jug will rectify it.

ALE AND BEER, *to refine.*—Put two ounces of isinglass shavings to soak in a quart of the liquor that you want to clear, beat it with a whisk every day till dissolved. Draw off a third part of the cask, and mix the above with it: likewise a quarter of an ounce of pearl-ashes, one ounce of salt of tartar calcined, and one ounce of burnt alum powdered. Stir it well, then return the liquor into the cask, and stir it with a clean stick. Stop it up, and in a few days it will be fine.

ALE, WINDSOR.—Take 6 quarters of the best pale malt, $\frac{1}{2}$ cwt. hops, 8lbs. of honey, 1 lb. of coriander seed, $\frac{1}{2}$ lb. of grains of paradise, $\frac{1}{2}$ lb. of orange peel, and $2\frac{1}{2}$ lbs. of ground liquorice root. The hops should be of the best kind, and soaked all night in cold liquor. Turn on at 180°; mash thoroughly an hour and a quarter, and stand an hour. Boil one hour. Turn on second liquor at 195°, and stand three quarters of an hour. Boil 3 hours; tun on third liquor at 165°, and mash three quarters of an hour, and stand the same. Pitch the tun at 60° and cleanse at 80°, on the third day. Skim as soon as a close yeasty head appears, until no yeast arises. Half a pound of hops per quarter should be roused in, and the whole left to settle. Also rouse in six ounces of salt, half a pound of finely sifted flour, six ounces of ground ginger, and six ounces of ground carraway seeds.

ALE MULLED.—Place a pint of good ale or beer in a saucepan, with a little grated nutmeg. When it boils take it off the fire, and sweeten. Beat two or three eggs, and mix with a little cold also. Boil, and then add the egg to the hot ale, pouring backwards and forwards from one vessel to the other to prevent curdling. Rum or brandy may be added ad libitum.

ALE OR PORTER, *to ripen.*—Bottle and put a couple of raisins, or a few grains of rice or sugar into each bottle, to generate the required effervescence.

ALL FOURS. — A game at Cards, very amusing; it is played by two, and sometimes by four persons, in two partnerships. This game derives its name from the four chances therein, for each of which a point is scored; namely, "high" (the best trump out) "low" (the smallest,) "Jack" (the knave of trumps) "Game" (the majority of pips) reckoned for the following cards the respective players have in their tricks, viz—

Every ace is counted as four.
Every king is counted as three.
Every queen is counted as two.
Every knave is counted as one.
And each ten counts as ten.

Low is always scored by the person to whom it was dealt, but Jack, being the property of whoever can win or save it, the holder is permitted to revoke and trump with it, and when turned up as a trump, the dealer scores one.

It is also allowable for the player who lays down a high or low trump to inquire at the time whether the same be high or low.

After cutting for deal, at which either the highest or lowest card wins as previously fixed, six cards are to be given to each player, either by three, or one at a time; and the thirteenth turned up for trump; then if the eldest does not like his cards, he may for once in a hand, say "I beg;" when the dealer must either give a point or three more cards to each, and turn up again; but if that should prove of the same suit as the first turn-up, then three cards more must be given, and so on until a different suit occurs.

The cards rank as at whist; and each player should always strive to secure his own tens and court-cards, or take those of the adversary, to obtain which, except when commanding cards are held, it is usual to play a low one, to throw the lead into the opponent's hands. Ten or eleven points constitute game, which may be set up as at whist.

When the dealer shows any of his adversary's cards, a new deal may be demanded; but in showing his own, he must abide by the same.

If discovered previous to playing, that too many cards are given to either party, a fresh deal may be claimed, or the extra cards drawn out. But should even a single card have been played, then there must be a new deal.

With strict players the adversary may score a point whenever his opponent does not trump or follow suit; and each calculates his game without looking at the trick, which, when erroneously set up, must not be taken down; but also the antagonist scores a point instead.

ALMOND CAKES.—Rub 2 ozs. of butter into 5 ozs. of flour, 5 ozs. powdered lump sugar; beat an egg with half the sugar, then put it to the other ingredients. Add 1 oz. blanched almonds, and a little almond flavour; roll them in your hand the size of a nutmeg, and sprinkle with fine lump sugar. They should be *lightly* baked.

ALMOND CAKE.—Bake it in a mould, or baking hoop; bruise 1 lb. of sweet almonds very fine, and 12 bitter almonds, adding a little whites of eggs, to hinder them from oiling; then put to it ½ lb. of fine sugar powder by degrees, two whole eggs, and lemon peel, finely chopped or rasped; when this is properly mixed, add 8 eggs, the yolks and whites first beat up separately: stir it, and mix it all properly: pour into the mould, to bake about an hour; serve it in its natural colour. (Glaze with white of egg, and frost with fine loaf sugar.) *Hu.*

ALMOND CHEESECAKES. —Blanch and pound four ounces of almonds, and a few bitter, with a spoonful of water; then add four ounces of sugar pounded, a spoonful of cream, and the whites of two eggs well beaten; mix all as quickly as possible; put into very small pattypans; and bake in a pretty warm oven under twenty minutes.

ANOTHER WAY.—Blanch and pound four ounces of almonds, with a little orange-flower or rose-water; then stir in the yolks of six and the whites of three eggs, well beaten, five ounces of butter warmed, the peel of a lemon grated, and a little of the juice; sweeten with fine powdered sugar. When well mixed, bake in a delicate paste, in small pans.

ANOTHER WAY. —- Press the whey from as much curd as will make two dozen small ones; then put it on the back of a sieve, and with half an ounce of butter rub it through with the back of a spoon; put to it six yolks, and three whites of eggs, and a few bitter almonds, pounded with as much sugar as will make the curd properly sweet: mix with it the rind of a lemon grated, and a glass of brandy. Put a puff paste into the pans, and ten minutes will bake them.

ALMOND CUSTARD.-Blanch and beat four ounces of almonds fine with a spoonful of water; beat a pint of cream with two spoonfuls of water, and put them to the yolks of four eggs, and as much sugar as will make it pretty sweet; then add the almonds; stir over a slow fire till of a proper thickness; but don't boil. Pour into cups.

ALMOND ICING *for Bridecake and other Cakes.*—Beat the whites of three eggs to a strong froth; beat 1 lb. of Jordan almonds very fine with rose-water; mix them with the eggs lightly together, 1 lb. of common loaf sugar beat very fine, and put in by degrees. When your cake is enough take it out, and lay your iceing on: then put it in to brown. *Rf.*

ALMOND PUDDING, *Small.* —Pound eight ounces of almonds, and a few bitter, with a spoonful of water; mixed with four ounces of butter warmed, four yolks and two whites of eggs, sugar to taste, two spoonfuls of cream, and one of brandy; mix well, and bake in little cups buttered. Serve with pudding-sauce.

ALMOND PUDDING, *Baked*.—Beat fine four ounces of almonds, four bitter, a little wine, yolks of six eggs, peel of two lemons grated, six ounces of butter, a quart of cream, and juice of a lemon. Mix well; bake half an hour; with paste round the dish.

ALMOND PUDDING.—Beat half a pound of sweet and a few bitter almonds with a spoonful of water; then mix four ounces of butter, four eggs, two spoonfuls of cream, warm with the butter, one of brandy, a little nutmeg, and sugar to taste. Butter some cups, half-fill, and bake. Serve with butter, wine, and sugar.

ALOES, *Compound Decoction of*.— Extract of valerian, two drachms; extract of Liquorice, half an ounce; extract of Soccotrine aloes, powdered myrrh, powdered saffron, of each two drachms; subcarbonate of potash, two scruples; aniseed, quarter of an ounce bruised; water, a pint and a half. Boil 20 minutes; add four ounces of compound tincture of cardamoms. This decoction cures constipation, jaundice, mental depression, bilious and nervous affections, female irregularities, &c.—Dose from half an ounce every other morning.

ALTERATIVES.— Medicines adapted to cure a disease without producing any very sensible effect on the human system.

ALTERATIVE PILLS.—Lobelia Seeds, 2 drachms; Mandrake, 2 drachms; Blue Flag, 2 drachms; Blood Root, 2 drachms; Cayenne, Pepper, 1 drachm; Gum Guiacum, two drachms; Extract of Dandelion, 6 drachms; Oil of Peppermint, 3 or 4 drops; Single Syrup to form into Pills.—Dose, two pills twice or thrice a day. These pills are of great service in bilious and liver complaints, diseased joints, boils, carbuncles, cutaneous eruptions, scrofula, syphillis, &c.

ALTERATIVE SYRUP. — Tincture of cayenne, ¼ oz.; tincture of lobelia, and tincture of myrrh, of each, 2 ozs.; treacle, ½ lb. Mix. A tea-spoonful two or three times a day. ☞ Noted for its effectual cure of cutaneous sores; *boils*, indigestion, and some chronic complaints.

ALUM-ROOT.—An American plant, a great remedy in sores, wounds, ulcers, and cancers. It is a powerful styptic in all bleedings; and a great vulnerary, or healer of wounds, sores, cuts, &c. The root is powdered, and applied to bleedings. Made into an ointment with lard, it cures Piles.

ALUM, *to discover in bread*.—Heat a knife, and thrust it into a loaf or cake; if alum be present, it will partially coat the knife.

AMAUROSIS.—A total or partial loss of sight, caused by paralysis of the optic nerve or retina. It first manifests itself by specks floating before the vision, which increase till they become like a cloud; then dilation of the pupil and insensibility to light. It is difficult to cure. The diet must be low, and alcoholic drinks must be avoided. The bowels must be kept gently open by small doses of Black Draught, or by Salts and Senna, or by Rhubarb, Colocynth &c. Electricity may be applied to the eye, to produce a healthy action of the system. Foment the eye with the diluted tincture of Cayenne Pepper. Frequently bathe the head in cold

B

water, and avoid taking cold. Apply blistering or mustard plasters to the back of the ears.

AMBER PUDDING.—Put a pound of butter into a sauce-pan, with three quarters of a pound of loaf-sugar finely powdered; melt the butter, and mix well with it; then add the yolks of fifteen eggs well beaten, and as much fresh candied orange as will add colour and flavour to it, being first beaten to a fine paste. Line the dish with paste for turning out; and when filled with the above, lay a crust over, as you would a pie, and bake in a slow oven. It is as good cold as hot. *Ru.*

ANCHOVIES, *to choose.*—They are preserved in barrels, with bay-salt: no other fish has the fine flavour of the anchovy. The best look red and mellow, and the bones moist and oily; the flesh should be high flavoured, the liquor reddish, and have a fine smell.

ANCHOVIES, *Essence of.*—Take two dozen of anchovies, chop them, and without the bone, but with some of their liquor strained, add to them sixteen large spoonfuls of water; boil gently till dissolved, which will be in a few minutes—when cold, strain and bottle it.

ANCHOVY SAUCE.—Chop one or two anchovies, without washing, put to them some flour and butter, and a little water; stir it over the fire till it boils once or twice. If the anchovies are good, they will dissolve.

ANCHOVY TOAST. — Bone and skin six or eight anchovies; pound them to a mass with an ounce of fine butter till the colour is equal, and then spread it on toast or rusks.

ANOTHER WAY.—Cut thin slices of bread into any form, and fry them in clarified butter. Wash three anchovies, split, pound them in a mortar with some fresh butter, rub them through a hair-sieve, and spread on the toast when cold. Then quarter and wash some anchovies, and lay them on the toast. Garnish with parsley or pickles. *Ru.*

ANDERSON'S PILLS,--Consist of Barbadoes aloes, with a proportion of jalap, and oil of anise seed. In general they are safe, except the patient has piles; and in pregnancy it is better to use other purgatives.

ANIMAL FOOD.—Man is called a carniverous animal. Where animal food is seldom or not allowed, mortality is great, and disease rife. One of the most common forms of disease generated by an exclusively vegetable diet is scrofula, and when traceable to this cause, the most speedy remedy is the addition of animal food to the diet. There are also many other forms of disease produced by the want of animal food, which require for their cure but an abundant supply of the needed material. But it may be eaten too often. It contains much grease, or oil, by which digestion is frequently impaired, the bile vitiated, the blood corrupted, cutaneous and other diseases induced. High-seasoned meat, with condiments, often produce dyspepsia, flatulency, &c. By all, animal food should be eaten sparingly. By frequent participation, the springs of life are hurried on too fast, and often bilious, plethoric, and inflammatory effects follow.

Dr. Beach says, "Among other ill effects of animal food is a temporary fever after eating it, called by the old medical writers, "*the fever of digestion.*" No such effects follow the use of vegetable food."

Dr. Dick considers it incompatible with a state of innocence, to take the life of any sensitive being and feed on its flesh; and that, consequently, no such grant was given to Adam in paradise, or to the antediluvians. He considered it a grant only fitted to the degraded state of man after the flood.

ANISE.—This plant is carminative and pectoral, useful in indigestion and flatulency. It is a component part of the *Cough Drops*. For flatulent and bowel complaints in children and adults, the seeds are used; a tea-spoonful and a half. The oil dropped on sugar (four or five drops) is best. It is a good remedy for coughs. The seeds to be infused.

ANODYNES.— Medicines allaying pain and disposing to sleep.

ANODYNE BALSAM.—Take of white Spanish soap, one ounce; opium, unprepared, two drachms; rectified spirit of wine, nine ounces; Digest them together in a gentle heat for three days; then strain off the liquor, and add to it three drachms of camphor.

This balsam is of service in violent strains and rheumatic complaints, when not attended with inflammation. It must be rubbed with a warm hand on the part affected; or a linen rag moistened with it; and renewed every third hour, till the pain abates. *Bu.*

ANODYNE FOMENTATION.—Take of white poppyheads, two ounces; elder flowers, half an ounce; water, three pints. Boil till one pint is evaporated, and strain out the liquor. *Bu.*

This fomentation relieves acute pain. If the affected part is very painful, add forty drops of Laudanum, and 30 drops of Tincture of Cayenne. *Bu. Al.*

ANODYNE PLASTER.-Melt an ounce of adhesive plaster, or diachlyon, and whilst cooling, add a drachm of powdered Opium, and the same quantity of Camphor, previously dissolved in a small quantity of Olive oil. Spread on leather. This soon relieves an acute local pain. *Bu.*

ANODYNE POWDER.-Opium, ½ oz.; camphor, 3 drs.; valerian, 1 oz.; cayenne pepper, 1 oz. Put the opium and camphor into a close bag; place it on the oven top to harden. Powder and mix. Take a quarter of a tea-spoonful at a time. Most valuable in colic, cramp, and severe pains.

ANTHELMINTICS. — Medicines, destroying or expelling worms.

ANTI - ACIDS. — Medicines, neutralizing acids.

ANTIBILIOUS PILLS.--Extract of Colocynth, 2 drachms; extract of Jalap, 1 drachm; Almond Soap, 1½ drachms; Guiacum, 3 drachms; tartarized Antimony, 8 grains; oil of Juniper, 4 or 5 drops; oil of Carraway, 4 drops; oil of Rosemary, 4 drops. Form into a mass with Syrup of Buckthorn, and divide into pills.

ANTI-CHOLERA DROPS.— Tinctures of capsicum, opium, lobelia, essence of peppermint, of each, 1 oz. Mix. Take when needful, a tea-spoonful in a little coffee. Most efficient in cholera, and affections of the bowels.

ANTI - CHOLERA POWDER.—Ipecacuanha, 3 drachms; ginger, 1 oz.; tormentil root, 1½ ozs.; poplar bark, 1½ ozs.; cayenne, gum myrrh, each 3 drachms; carbonate of soda, 3 drachms; cloves 2 drachms; slippery elm, 5 drachms. Powder and mix. Dose, half a tea-spoonful every half-hour.

ANTIMONIAL WINE.--This may be purchased at the druggists. As an emetic, the dose is from one to two table-spoonfuls. As a febrifuge, sudorific, or relaxant, from twenty to forty drops every three or four hours.—As an Emetic, Ipecacuanha, and Lobelia, stand very high, especially the latter.

ANTISCORBUTIC DRINK.—Take of cream of tartar three ounces, juniper berries four ounces, ginger in powder two drachms, and five pounds of sugar, boil in six gallons of water, after boiling half-an-hour, the whole is poured into a tub and allowed to ferment. It may be drunk in the quantity of from one to three pints daily, as soon as the fermentation commences.

ANTISEPTICS.—Medicines, counteracting putrescency.

ANTISPASMODICS.—Medicines, abating spasm.

ANTISPASMODIC TINCTURE.—Tincture of Lobelia, 1 ounce; Tincture of Cayenne, 1 ounce; Compound Tincture of Lady's Slipper, ½ ounce; oil of Aniseed, 20 drops.—Begin with a teaspoonful. This is an infallible remedy for spasms, fever, ague, and painful flatulence, and colic.

ANTISPASMODIC CLYSTER.—To half a pint of thin gruel, add half an ounce, or an ounce of the Fœtid Tincture, and forty to sixty drops of Laudanum. This is very useful in spasmodic affections of the bowels, in convulsions, or in all hysteric complaints.

ANTS.—A small quantity of green sage, placed where ants infest will cause them to disappear.——Quicklime thrown on their nests, and then watered, will destroy them.——Or a strong solution of alum water.——Or gas tar;—or lime from gas-works.—Gas tar painted round a tree an inch or two broad, will prevent ants and other insects from climbing trees, and will preserve the fruit.

APERIENT MIXTURE.—Senna leaves, 2 drachms; infuse in a quarter of a pint of boiling water, for half an hour, and add Epsom salts, half an ounce; compound Tincture of Senna, an ounce. Three table-spoonfuls to be taken every three hours.

APERIENT ELECTUARY.—Senna, one ounce, *powdered;* flour of sulphur, half an ounce; ground ginger, two drachms; treacle, or honey, four ounces. Mix well. Dose about the size of a nutmeg morning and night. If not strong enough, add a small quantity of jalap.

APERIENT FOR CHILDREN.—Infusion of senna, one ounce; mint water, half an ounce; calcined magnesia, one scruple; manna, three drachms; syrup of roses, two drachms; (a solution of sugar will do). Mix and give in doses of one or two tea-spoonfuls at a time.

APERIENT, INFANTS'.—Take of rhubarb, five grains; magnesia, three grains; white sugar, a scruple; manna, five grains; mix. Dose, varying from a piece half the size of a sweet-pea to a piece the size of an ordinary pea.

APERIENT MIXTURE, *Abernethy's.*—Epsom Salts, half an ounce; infusion of Senna, six drachms; tincture of Senna, two drachms; spearmint water, an ounce; distilled water, two ounces; best manna, two drachms. Mix; and take three or four table-spoonfuls every morning, or every other morning.—This is a valuable mixture.—A decoction of Peruvian Bark will render it a Tonic Aperient.

APERIENT PILLS.—Compound Rhubarb Pill, a scruple; extract of Colocynth, half a drachm; castile soap, ten grains; oil of juniper, three drops. Beat into a mass; make into *ordinary sized* pills. Take one at bed-time.

APERIENT PILLS, *to promote Digestion.*——Aloes, forty grains; extract of gentian, twenty-four grains; extract of colocynth, one drachm; oil of aniseed, sufficient to make into pills. Take from one to three when necessary.

APERIENT TONIC MIXTURE.—Boil two ounces of bruised dandelion roots, and one ounce of powdered liquorice, in one quart of water down to one pint; then add Epsom Salts, four drachms; Sulphate of Iron, four grains; Elixir of Vitriol, thirty-five drops. This mixture is aperient, and does not debilitate.

APERIENT, TONIC.—Take of Epsom salts one ounce, diluted sulphuric acid, one drachm, infusion of quassia chips, half an imperial pint, compound tincture of rhubarb, two drachms. Half a wine-glassful for a dose—to be taken twice a day.

APOPLEXY.—It is a sudden deprivation of all the senses, and of voluntary motion, generally the effect of compression of the brain; which, when produced by an effusion of blood, or a distension of the internal vessels of the head, from an accumulation of blood, is termed *Sanguineous Apoplexy*; and when caused by an effusion of *serum*, which occurs chiefly in dropsical habits, *Serous Apoplexy*.

APOPLEXY, SANGUINEOUS.—The short necked, the indolent, great eaters and great drinkers, are its victims! The fit is generally preceded by a sense of weight in the head, and giddiness; frequent head-ache; bleeding at the nose; redness of the eyes; imperfect vision; ringing in the ears; numbness in the extremities; weakness of the knees; faltering of the voice; drowsiness, and disturbed sleep. It is brought on by whatever hurries the circulation, so as to increase the afflux of blood into the vessels of the head; such as violent exercises; passions of the mind; much straining; whatever impedes the free return of blood from the head; as a tight ligature, or handkerchief round the neck; or lying with the head lower than the chest.

If the fit has lasted long, i. e. two or three days; if the breathing is very laborious and loud; if the patient is far advanced in life; it is probable that the disease will prove fatal. A second attack is always of more danger than a first; and when apoplexy comes upon a patient who has had frequent attacks of epilepsy, it very commonly proves fatal.

Treatment:—Remove the cause, that is, pressure upon the brain—apply blisters to the head, and also between the shoulders—and lessen the determination of the blood to the head by increasing the circulation in the extremities; i. e. stimulating the feet and hands by Mustard Poultices, and by emptying the lower intestines by a clyster, made of Epsom salts, castor oil, salt, and aloes. Also give sudorifics, or medicines to promote sweat. If the attack takes place soon after a full meal, an emetic should be given; *Lobelia*. See my Herbal under that article;—*Robinson's Herbal*. Keep the body nearly in an erect posture to promote the return of the blood from the head.

APOPLEXY, SEROUS.—Compression of the brain, producing apoplexy, is seldom caused by an effusion of the serous part of the blood. When it occurs in a dropsical person, it may be referred to an effusion of serum, which will require the aforesaid means. Cordials are proper and may be given. It is in consequence of extreme debility of the system, and generally terminates in death. Give emetics of Ipecacuanha and tartarized antimony—blisters to the head—mustard poultices to the legs and feet—-sharp purges—-diffusive stimulants of Ammonia, castor oil, assafœtida, valerian, and electricity passed through the head.

Prevention of Apoplexy.—Avoid intoxicating drinks, keep the feet dry and warm, take plenty of exercise, eat sparingly, sleep with the head higher than the trunk, prevent constipation, wash the head and sponge the chest every morning in cold water.

For the treatment of Apoplexy, the following hints have been collected from the works of the most eminent physicians:—

Remove all compression from every part of the body.—Immerse the legs in warm water and mustard for twenty minutes, applying friction at the same time.—Bathe the whole surface with the diluted tincture of Cayenne.—Avoid bleeding.—Put a mustard plaster between the shoulders. If possible, let a brisk purgative be administered, for evacuation is necessary to unload the bowels and stomach, and therefore the pressure on the brain.—Blood-letting in Apoplexy aggravates the cerebral congestion. —Professor Recamier says, "I have not the least evidence that blood letting has the smallest power to diminish the violence or duration of an apoplectic paroxysm; nay, I have every reason to believe that it so far weakens the powers of reaction as to prove fatal, or greatly to retard the cure."—Apply cold water to the head, and hot water to the feet, if slight symptoms begin to appear. At first do it slightly, and increase the application gradually. This will force back the blood from the upper to the lower extremities through the heart, and remove the disease.— The whole secret of treatment consists in equalizing the circulation.

APOTHECARIES' WEIGHT.
20 Grains *(gr.)* make 1 Scruple, *sc.*
equal to 20 grains Troy.
3 Scruples ....1 Dram, *dr.*,
equal to 60 grains.
8 Drams ....1 Ounce, *oz.*,
equal to 480 grains or 24 scruples.
12 Ounces..........1 Pound, *lb.*,
equal to 5760 grains, or 288 sc., or 96 drams.

By this weight medicines are mixed; but drugs are bought and sold wholesale by avoirdupois.

APOTHECARIES' MEASURE.—
60 Minims make 1 Fluid Dram.*dr.*
8 Fluid Drams 1 Ounce......*oz.*
16 Fluid Ounces 1 Pint.......*pt.*
8 Pints........1 Gallon....*gal.*

APPLES, *to keep.*—Let them be well dried, and pack in a hamper, or box without lid, wrapped in straw, or covered with saw-dust in layers. Keep in a cool place, and not exposed to frost. Apples should always be plucked when the weather is fine; and when packed they should not touch one another.

The Americans preserve apples and pears by cutting them into eighths, without the core, and dry them in a kiln till quite hard; they will keep for two or three years. When used, they steep in hot water.

APPLE, CURRANT, *or* DAMSON DUMPLINGS, *or* PUDDINGS.— Shred very fine about 5 or 6 ounces of suet, and roll it into 8 or 10 ounces of flour; add a little salt, and make into a paste with water. Line a basin with the paste, and cover it with the same; tie a cloth over it tightly, and boil till the fruit is enough.

Some add eggs and milk in

making the paste, but the above is more wholesome.   *A. N.*

APPLE EGG PUDDING.—Beat an egg well; then add a gill of water or milk, seven or eight table spoonfuls of flour, and half a spoonful of salt; mix well together. Pare and cut into pieces three apples, and stir them into the batter. Boil the whole in a cloth an hour and a quarter, if in a basin, a little longer. Serve with melted butter flavoured with lemon.

APPLE FOOL.—Stew apples as directed for gooseberries, and then peel and pulp them. Prepare the milk, &c., and mix as before.

APPLE FRITTERS.—Take one pint of milk, three eggs, salt just to taste, and as much flour as will make a batter. Beat the yolks and whites separately, add the yolks to the milk, stir in the whites with as much flour as will make a batter; have ready some tender apples, peel them, cut them in slices round the apple; take the core carefully out of the centre of each slice, and to every spoonful of batter lay in a slice of apple, which must be cut very thin. Fry them in hot lard to a light brown on both sides.

APPLE GINGER.—To 4 lb. of apples add 4 lb. of sugar, 1 quart of water, and 2 oz. of the best essence of ginger. First pare the fruit, cutting out every particle of core; then shape it so as to resemble the small kind of preserved ginger. Boil the sugar and water together for twenty-five minutes until it is a nice syrup; then put in the apple, but be sure and do not stir it too much. Add the essence of ginger; if 2 oz. be insufficient, add more. It will take nearly an hour to boil, until it becomes yellow and transparent. There will be some pieces that will not clear; put them by themselves, as they will spoil the appearance of the rest. It will require skimming. American or Ribstone apples are the best to use. This is an excellent substitute for preserved foreign ginger.

APPLE JAM.—Fill a wide jar nearly half full of water; cut the apples, unpeeled, into quarters, take out the core, then fill the jar with the apples; tie a paper over it, and put it into a slow oven. When quite soft and cool, pulp them through a sieve. To each pound of pulp put three-quarters of a pound of crushed sugar, and boil it gently until it will jelly. Put it into large tart dishes or jars. It will keep for five or more years in a cool, dry place. If for present use, or a month hence, half a pound of sugar is enough.

APPLE JELLY.—Prepare twenty golden pippins; boil them in a pint and a half of water from the spring, till quite tender; then strain the liquor through a colander. To every pint put a pound of fine sugar; add cinnamon, grated orange or lemon; then boil to a jelly.

ANOTHER.—Prepare apples as before, by boiling and straining; have ready half an ounce of isinglass boiled in half a pint of water to a jelly; put this to the apple-water and apple, as strained through a coarse sieve; add sugar, a little lemon-juice and peel; boil all together and put into a dish. Take out the peel.

APPLE MARMALADE.—Scald apples till they will pulp from the core; then take an equal weight of sugar in large lumps, just dip them in water, and boil it till it can be well skimmed, and is a thick syrup, put to it the pulp, and simmer it on a quick fire a quarter of an hour. Grate a little lemon-peel before boiled, but if too much it will be bitter.   *Ru.*

APPLE PIE.—Pare and core the fruit, having wiped the outside, which with the cores boil in a little water till it tastes well; strain and put a little sugar, a bit of bruised cinnamon, simmer again, in the mean time place the apples in a dish, a paste being put round the edge; when one layer is in sprinkle half the sugar, shred lemon peel, squeeze some lemon juice in, or a glass of cider if the apples have lost their flavour, put in the rest of the apple, sugar, and the liquor that you have boiled, cover with paste.

APPLE PRESERVE.—Take 20 fine apples; peel and core them; grate them into a pulp, and strain through a colander; allow ½lb. of fine sugar to 1lb. of pulp. Clarify the sugar by adding water, and the beaten white of an egg. Then boil the fruit in the syrup, till sufficiently done. Add cinnamon, or ginger, according to taste. *A. N.*

APPLE PUFFS.— Pare the fruit, and either stew them in a stone jar on a hot hearth, or bake them. When cold, mix the pulp of the apple with sugar and lemon-peel, shred fine, taking as little of the apple-juice as you can. Bake them in thin paste, in a quick oven; a quarter of an hour will do them, if small. Orange or quince-marmalade, is a great improvement. Cinnamon pounded, or orange-flour water, in change. *Ru.*

APPLE PUDDING, *American.*—Peel and core one dozen and a half of good apples; cut them small; put them into a stew-pan with a little water, cinnamon, two cloves, and the peel of a lemon; stew over a slow fire, till soft; sweeten and strain, add the yolks of four eggs and one white, a quarter of a pound of butter, half a nutmeg, the peel of a lemon grated, and the juice of a lemon: beat well together; line the inside of a pie-dish with good puff paste; put in the pudding, and bake half an hour.

APPLE PUDDING, BAKED.-- Pare and quarter four large apples; boil them tender with the rind of a lemon, in so little water, that when done, none may remain; beat them quite fine in a mortar; add the crumb of a small roll, four ounces of butter melted, the yolks of five, and whites of three eggs, juice of half a lemon, and sugar to taste; beat all together, and lay it in a dish with paste to turn out. *Ru.*

APPLE PUDDING, BOILED. —Suet, 6 ozs.; flour, 8 ozs.; chop the suet very fine, and roll it into the flour. Make it into a light paste with water. Roll out. Pare and core 8 good sized apples; slice them; put them on the paste, and scatter upon them ¼ lb. of sugar; draw the paste round the apples, and boil two hours, or more, in a well floured cloth. Serve with melted butter sweetened. *A. N.*

APPLE PUDDING *Swiss.*— Butter a deep dish; put into it a layer of bread crumbs; then a layer of finely chopped suet; a thick layer of finely chopped apples, and a thick layer of sugar. Repeat from the first layer till the dish is full, the last layer to be finger biscuits soaked in milk. Cover it till nearly enough; then uncover, till the top is nicely browned. Flavour with cinnamon, nutmeg, &c., as you please. Bake from 30 to 40 minutes. *A. N.*

APPLE SAUCE, *for Goose or Roast Pork.*—Pare, core, and slice some apples, and put them in a strong jar, into a pan of water. When sufficiently boiled, bruise to a pulp, adding a little butter, and a little brown sugar. *Ru.*

APPLES, *Baked.*—Put the apples on a baking-dish, with a sprinkle of sugar, and a drop of cider or water, and set them in the oven to bake. Baked apples or pears, with bread, form a cheap and wholesome supper for children.

APPLE SNOWBALLS.—Swell rice in milk, and strain it off, and having pared and cored apples, put the rice round them, tying each up in a cloth. Put a bit of lemon peel, a clove, or cinnamon in each, and boil them well.

APPLES *(Red) in Jelly.*—Pare and core some well-shaped apples; pippins, or golden rennets, if you have them, but others will do; throw them into water as you do them; put them in a preserving pan, and with as little water as will only half cover them; let them coddle, and when the lower side is done, turn them. Observe that they do not lie too close when first put in. Mix some pounded cochineal with the water, and boil with the fruit. When sufficiently done, take them out on the dish they are to be served in, the stalk downwards. Take the water and make a rich jelly of it with loaf-sugar, boiling the thin rind and juice of a lemon. When come to a jelly, let it grow cold, and put it on and among the apples; cut the peel of the lemon in narrow strips, and put across the eye of the apple.

APPLE SYRUP. — Take 2 pounds of good ripe apples, pare and slice; place in a jar with about half a pint of water, and 1 lb. of sugar. Place the jar in a pan of water and boil two or three hours. When cold flavour with orange flower water, or lemon, cinnamon according to taste. Place in jars or bottles for use.

APPLE-TREES, *New mode of Planting.*—A horticulturist in Bohemia has a beautiful plantation of the best apple-trees, which have neither sprung from seeds, nor grafting. His plan is to take shoots from the choicest sorts, insert them in a potato, and plunge both into the ground, having put an inch or two of the shoot above the surface. The potato nourishes the shoot, whilst it pushes out roots; and the shoot gradually springs up, and becomes a beautiful tree, bearing the best fruit, without requiring to be grafted.

APPLE, OR GOOSEBERRY TRIFLE.—Scald such a quantity of either of these fruits, as, when pulped through a sieve, will make a thick layer at the bottom of your dish; if of apples, mix the rind of half a lemon grated fine; and add to both as much sugar as will be pleasant.

Mix half a pint of milk, half a pint of cream, and the yolk of one egg; give it a scald over the fire, and stir it all the time; don't let it boil; add a little sugar only, and let it grow cold. Lay it over the apples with a spoon; and then put on it a whip made the day before, as for other trifle. *Ru.*

APPLE WATER.—Cut four large apples in slices, and pour upon them a quart of boiling water; let them remain for two or three hours, and then strain and sweeten them according to your palate. Put in lemon juice. *Hu.*

APPLE WINE.—Pure cider made from sound, dry apples, as it runs from the press. Put sixty pounds of brown sugar into fifteen gallons of the cider and let it dissolve, then put the mixture into a clean barrel, and fill the barrel up to within two gallons of being full with clean cider; put the cask in a cool place, leaving the bung out forty-eight hours, then put in the bung with a small vent, until fermentation wholly ceases, and bung up tight, and, in one year, the wine will be fit for use. This wine requires no racking; the longer it stands upon the lees the better.

APRICOTS, *to preserve.*—When ripe, choose the finest apricots; pare them as thin as possible, and weigh them. Lay them in halves on dishes, with the hollow part upwards. Have ready an equal weight of good loaf sugar finely pounded, and strew it over them; in the meantime break the stones, and blanch the kernels. When the fruit has laid twelve hours, put it, with the sugar and juice, and also the kernels, into a preserving pan. Let it simmer very gently, till clear; then take out the pieces of apricots singly as they become so; put them into small pots, and pour the syrup and kernels over them. The scum must be taken off as it rises. Cover with brandy-paper.

APRICOT CAKES.—Scald 1 lb. of ripe apricots, peel and take out the stones as soon as you find the skin will come off. Beat them in a mortar to a pulp; boil ½ lb. of refined sugar, with a spoonful of water, and skim it well. Then put in the pulp of the apricots; simmer a quarter of an hour over a slow fire, and stir gently all the time. Pour into shallow flat glasses, turn them out upon glass plates, put them into a stove, and turn once a day till dry. *Far.*

APRICOT JAM.—Pare the ripest apricots, and cut them thin. Infuse them in an earthen pan till they are tender and dry. To 1½ lb. of apricots, put 1 lb. of refined sugar, and 3 spoonfuls of water. Boil the sugar to a candy height and put it upon the apricots. Stir over a slow fire till they look clear and thick; but they must only simmer, and not boil. Put them into glasses. *Far.*

APRICOT JELLY.—Peel and stone 20 fine apricots. Grate them to a pulp, and put them into a pan with a small cupful of water, and 1 lb. of fine sugar. Add lemon juice, and stir in the white of one egg thoroughly. Boil it till it will jelly when put to cool.

Apples, grapes, and damsons, may be jellied in the same way, and in summer they make fine effervescing drinks.—The jelly may be boiled down to make elegant *Fruit Candy.* *Gu.*

APRICOT PUDDING.—Halve twelve large apricots, give them a scald till they are soft; meantime pour on the grated crumbs of a penny loaf a pint of boiling cream; when half cold, add four ounces of sugar, the yolks of four beaten eggs, and a glass of white wine. Pound the apricots in a mortar with some or all of the kernels; then mix the fruit and other ingredients together; put a paste round a dish, and bake the pudding half an hour.

APRICOTS, OR PEACHES *in Brandy.*—Wipe, weigh, and pick the fruit, and have ready a quarter of the weight of fine sugar in fine powder. Put the fruit into an ice pot that shuts very close; throw the sugar over it, and then cover the fruit with brandy. Between the top and cover of the pot, put a piece of double cap-paper. Set the pot into a sauce-pan of water till the brandy is as hot as you can possibly bear to put your finger in, but it must not boil. Put the fruit into a jar, and pour the brandy on it. When cold, put a bladder over, and tie it down tight.

APRICOT MARMALADE.—Apricots that are not fit for preserves, or too ripe for keeping, will answer this purpose. Boil them in syrup till they will mash, then beat them in a mortar to a paste. Take half their weight of loaf sugar, and water enough to it to dissolve it. Boil and skim it till it is clear, and the syrup thick like a fine jelly. Put it into sweetmeat glasses, and tie up close. *Far.*

APRICOTS, *to dry in half.*—Pare thin and halve four pounds of apricots, weighing them after; put them in a dish; strew among them three pounds of sugar in the finest powder. When it melts, set the fruit over a stove to do very gently; as each piece becomes tender, take it out, and put it into a china bowl. When all are done, and the boiling heat a little abated, pour the syrup over them. In a day or two remove the syrup, leaving only a little in each half. In a day or two turn them daily, till quite dry, in the sun or a warm place. Keep in boxes, with layers of paper.

APRICOTS, *to preserve in Jelly.*—Pare the fruit very thin, and stone it; weigh an equal quantity of sugar in fine powder, and strew over it. Next day boil very gently till they are clear, move them into a bowl, and pour the liquor over. The following day pour the liquor to a quart of codlin-liquor, made by boiling and straining, and a pound of fine sugar; let it boil quickly till it will jelly; put the fruit into it, and give one boil, skim well, and put into small pots. *Ru.*

APRICOTS, *to preserve Green.*—Lay vine or apricot leaves at the bottom of your pan, then fruit, and so alternately till full, the upper layer being thick with leaves; then fill with spring water, and cover down, that no steam may come out. Set the pan at a distance from the fire, that in four or five hours they may be only soft, but not cracked. Make a thin syrup of some of the water and drain the fruit. When both are cold, put the fruit into the pan and the syrup to it; put the pan at a proper distance from the fire till the apricots green, but on no account boil or crack; remove them very carefully into a pan with the syrup, for two or three days; then pour off as much of it as will be necessary, and boil with more sugar to make a rich syrup, and put a little sliced ginger into it. When cold, and the *thin* syrup has all been drained from the fruit, pour the thick over it. The former will serve to sweeten pies. *Ru.*

APRICOT TART.—Use puff paste, see page 333, and put in Apricot Jam, Jelly, or Marmalade. Ornament with little bars of paste. *A. N.*

ARDENT SPIRITS.—Water is the natural beverage of man. Strong alcoholic liquors were formerly kept and sold in Apothecaries' shops, and were by physicians prescribed as medicines merely. Spirituous liquors and wines, more or less, inflame the blood, and induce gout, stone, rheumatism, fevers, pleurisies, &c. They scorch and shrivel the solids, destroy digestion, dry up the juices, and bring on rapidly premature old age, gray hairs, &c. Nothing has a greater tendency to destroy the coats of the stomach, to impair the digestion, destroy the appetite, and produce diseases, as inflammation of the liver, dropsy, jaundice, apoplexy, palsy, and madness. Ardent spirits, &c. produce imbecility and often insanity.

AROMATIC TINCTURE.—Infuse two ounces of Jamaica pepper in two pints of brandy, without heat, for a few days; then strain off the tincture.

This simple tincture will sufficiently answer all the intentions of the more costly preparations of this kind. It is rather too hot to be taken by itself; but is very proper for mixing with such medicines as might otherwise prove too cold for the stomach.

ARROW-ROOT BLANC-MANGE.—Put two tablespoonfuls of arrow-root to a quart of milk, and a pinch of salt. Scald the milk, sweeten it, and stir in the arrow-root, which must first be wet up with some of the milk. Boil up once. Orange-water, rose-water, or lemon-peel may be used to flavour it. Pour into moulds to cool. *A. N.*

ARROW-ROOT CUSTARD.—Arrow-root, one tablespoonful; milk, 1 pint; sugar, 1 tablespoonful, and one egg. Mix the arrow-root with a little of the milk, cold; when the milk boils, stir in the arrow-root, egg, and sugar, previously well beaten together. Let it scald, and pour into cups to cool. To flavour it, boil a little ground cinnamon in the milk.
A. N.

ARROW-ROOT JELLY. — To a dessert-spoonful of the powder, add as much cold water as will make it into a paste, then pour on half a pint of boiling water, stir it briskly and boil it a few minutes, when it will become a clear smooth jelly; a little sugar and sherry wine may be added for debilitated adults; but for infants, a drop or two of essence of carraway seeds or cinnamon is preferable, wine being very liable to become acid in the stomachs of infants, and to disorder the bowels. Fresh milk, either alone or diluted with water, may be substituted for the water.
Dr. Reece.

ARROW-ROOT AND TAPIOCA GRUELS.—Make a thin paste as before, and put into boiling water, adding sugar, salt, nutmeg, and a little lemon-juice.

Tapioca may be soaked 10 hours in twice the quantity of water; then add milk and water. Boil till it is soft. Flavour the same as Arrow-root. *A. N.*

ARROW-ROOT PUDDING.—Take 2 tea-cupfuls of arrow-root, and mix it with half a pint of cold milk. Boil another half pint of milk, flavouring it with cinnamon, nutmeg, or lemon-peel. Stir the arrow-root and milk into the boiling milk. When cold, add the yolks of 3 eggs beaten into 3 ozs. of sugar. Then add the whites beat to a stiff froth, and bake in a buttered dish an hour. Ornament the tops with sweetmeats, or citron sliced. *A. N.*

ARROW-ROOT PUDDING, as used in a West Indian family.- Two table-spoonfuls of arrow-root, one egg beaten, yolk and white together; sweeten to taste, add any seasoning agreeable; a pint of milk; mix well together, boil, put in a shape, when cold and stiff, turn out. Sauce, melted butter, and wine, cold. This preparation is very suitable for invalids, who often take a dislike to it, prepared in the ordinary way, if medicinally ordered.

ARROW-ROOT, *to make for Invalids.*-Put into a saucepan half a pint of water, grated nutmeg, and fine sugar, boil up once, then mix into by degrees a dessert spoonful of Arrow-root, previously rubbed smooth, with two spoonfuls of cold water. A glass of sherry, or a table spoonful of brandy, may be added when the patient has no tendency to inflammatory action.

ARTICHOKES, *to dress.*—Trim a few of the outside leaves off, and cut the stalk even. If young, half an hour will boil them. They are better for being gathered two or three days first. Serve them with melted butter, in as many small cups as there are artichokes, to help with each. *Ru.*

ARTICHOKE BOTTOMS.—If dried, they must be soaked, then stewed in weak gravy, and served with or without forcemeat in each.

Or they may be boiled in milk, and served with cream sauce; or added to ragouts, French pies, &c. *Ru.*

ARTICHOKES, JERUSALEM.—They must be taken up the moment they are done, or they will be too soft. They may be boiled plain, or served with white fricassee sauce.

ARTICLES IN SEASON.
JANUARY.

Poultry. — Game: Pheasants, Partridges. Hares. Rabbits. Woodcocks. Snipes. Turkeys. Capons. Pullets. Fowls. Chickens. Tame Pigeons.

Fish.—Carp. Tench. Perch. Lampreys. Eels. Crayfish. Cod. Soles. Flounders. Plaice. Turbots. Thornback. Skate. Sturgeon. Smelts. Whitings. Lobsters. Crabs. Prawns. Oysters.

Vegetables.—Cabbage. Savoys. Colewort. Sprouts. Brocoli. Leeks. Onions. Beets. Sorrel. Chervil. Endive. Spinach. Celery. Garlic. Scorzonera. Potatoes. Parsnips. Turnips. Brocoli, white and purple. Shalots. Lettuces. Cresses. Mustard. Rape. Salsafy. Herbs, dry, and green. Cucumbers. Asparagus and Mushrooms, though not in season.

Fruit.—Apples. Pears. Nuts. Walnuts. Medlars. Grapes.

FEBRUARY AND MARCH.

Meat, Fowls and Game, as in January, with the addition of Ducklings and Chickens; which last are to be bought in London, most, if not all the year, but very dear.

Fish.—As the last two months; except that Cod is not thought so good from February to July, but may be bought.

Vegetables.—The same as the former months, with the addition of Kidney-beans.

Fruit—Apples. Pears. Forced Strawberries.

SECOND QUARTER: APRIL, MAY AND JUNE.

Meat.—Beef. Mutton. Veal. Lamb. Venison in June.

Poultry. — Pullets. Fowls. Chickens. Ducklings. Pigeons. Rabbits. Leverets.

Fish..—Carp. Tench. Soles. Smelts. Eels. Trout. Turbot. Lobsters. Chub. Salmon. Herrings. Crayfish. Mackerel. Crabs. Prawns. Shrimps.

Vegetables.—As before; and in May, early Potatoes. Peas, Radishes. Kidney-beans. Carrots. Turnips. Early Cabbages. Cauliflowers. Asparagus. Artichokes. All sorts of Salad forced.

Fruits.--In June; Strawberries. Cherries. Melons. Green Apricots. Currants and Gooseberries for Tarts.—In July; Cherries. Strawberries. Pears. Melons. Gooseberries. Currants. Apricots. Grapes. Nectarines; and some Peaches. But most of these are forced.

THIRD QUARTER: JULY, AUGUST, AND SEPTEMBER.

Meat as before.

Poultry.-Pullets. Fowls. Chickens. Rabbits. Pigeons. Green Geese. Leverets. Turkey. Poults. Two former months, Plovers. Wheatears. Geese in September.

Fish.—Cod. Haddock. Flounders. Plaice. Skates. Thornback. Mullets. Pike. Carp. Eels. Shellfish; except Oysters. Mackerel the first two months of the quarter, but not good in August.

Partridge-shooting begins on the 1st of September; what is therefore used before is poached.

Vegetables.-Of all sorts, Beans, Peas, French Beans, &c., &c.

Fruit.-In July; Strawberries. Gooseberries. Pine-apples, Plums. various Cherries. Apricots. Raspberries. Melons. Currants. Damsons.

In August and September; Peaches. Plums. Figs. Filberts. Mulberries. Cherries. Apples. Pears. Nectarines. Grapes. Latter months; Pines. Melons. Strawberries. Medlars and Quinces in the latter month. Morello Cherries. Damsons. Plums.

OCTOBER.

Meat as before, and Doe-venison. *Poultry and Game.*—Domestic Fowls, as in former quarter. Pheasants, from the 1st of October. Partridges. Larks. Hares. Dotterels. End of the month; Wild-ducks. Teal. Snipes. Widgeon. Grouse.

Fish.—Dories. Smelts. Pike. Peach. Halibuts. Brills. Carps. Salmon-trout. Barbel. Gudgeons. Tench. Shell-fish.

Vegetables.—As in January; French-beans, last crops of beans. *Fruit.*—Peaches. Pears. Figs. Bullace. Grapes. Apples. Medlars. Damsons. Filberts. Walnuts. Nuts. Quinces. Services.

NOVEMBER.

Meat.—Beef. Mutton. Veal. Pork. House-Lamb. Doe-venison. Poultry, Game, Fish, as in last month.

Vegetables.—Carrots. Turnips. Parsnips. Potatoes. Skirrets. Scorzonera. Onions. Leeks. Shalots. Cabbage. Savoys. Colewort. Spinach. Chard-beets. Cardoons. Cresses. Endive. Celery. Lettuces. Salad. Herbs. Pot-herbs.

Fruit.—Pears. Apples. Nuts. Walnuts. Bullace. Chestnuts. Medlars. Grapes.

DECEMBER.

Meat.—Beef. Mutton. Veal. House-Lamb. Pork and Venison. *Poultry and Game.* — Geese. Turkeys. Pullets. Pigeons. Capons. Fowls. Chickens. Rabbits. Hares. Snipes. Woodcocks. Larks. Pheasants. Partridges. Sea-fowls. Guinea-fowls. Wild-ducks. Teal. Widgeon. Dotterels. Dun-birds. Grouse. *Fish.*—Cod. Turbot. Halibuts. Soles. Gurnets. Sturgeon. Carp. Gudgeons. Codlins. Eels. Dories. Shell-fish.

Vegetables. — As in the last month. Asparagus forced, &c. *Fruit* as the last. *Hu.*

ARSENIC. *Remedies for Poisoning by.*—Mustard and water; and other emetics, or milk, lime water, and white of an egg, as much as can be got down. Also Glauber's or Epsom salts; chalk and water, or in linseed tea, if at hand. In case of inflammation, give a clyster of gruel, Epsom salts, and treacle.

ASAFŒTIDA, *Tincture of.*—This strong solution of asafœtida gum in proof spirit, in the quantity of thirty to fifty drops, in a glass of pennyroyal or peppermint water, is much and successfully employed as a remedy for lowness of spirits, hysteric and fainting fits; different nervous complaints, spasmodic colic and asthma. The addition of ten drops of sal volatile to each dose will render it more pleasant to the palate, and at the same time coincide with its virtues.

A mixture of one-third of tincture of asafœtida, and two of paregoric elixir, taken in the dose of a teaspoonful, has been found particularly serviceable in relieving asthma in languid constitutions, and chronic difficulty of breathing, by expelling air from the stomach promoting expectoration, and allaying irritation. (see Asthma.) In the hooping-cough, unattended with fever, it will prove equally beneficial, in doses proportioned to the age of the patient, viz. to a child of two years old, six drops, increasing two drops for every year.

ARTIZAN'S WAGES TABLE.

	s.	d.	s.	d.	s.	d.	s.	d.	s.	d.	s.	d.	s.	d.
Per Week	2	6	3	0	3	6	4	0	4	6	5	0	5	6
Per Day, 6 to Week	0	5	0	6	0	7	0	8	0	9	0	10	0	11
Per Hour, 10 to Day	0	0½	0	0½	0	0½	0	0¾	0	1	0	1	0	1
	s.	d.	s.	d.	s.	d.	s.	d.	s.	d.	s.	d.	s.	d.
Per Week	6	0	6	6	7	0	8	0	9	0	10	0	11	0
Per Day, 6 to Week	1	0	1	1	1	2	1	4	1	6	1	8	1	10
Per Hour, 10 to Day	0	1¼	0	1¼	0	1½	0	1½	0	1¾	0	2	0	2¼
	s.	d.	s.	d.	s.	d.	s.	d.	s.	d.	s.	d.	s.	d.
Per Week	12	0	13	0	14	0	15	0	16	0	17	0	18	0
Per Day, 6 to Week	2	0	2	2	2	4	2	6	2	8	2	10	3	0
Per Hour, 10 to Day	0	2¼	0	2½	0	2¾	0	3	0	3	0	3¼	0	3½
	s.	d.	s.	d.	s.	d.	s.	d.	s.	d.	s.	d.	s.	d.
Per Week	19	0	20	0	21	0	22	0	23	0	24	0	25	0
Per Day, 6 to Week	3	2	3	4	3	6	3	8	3	10	4	0	4	2
Per Hour, 10 to Day	0	3¾	0	4	0	4	0	4¼	0	4½	0	4¾	0	5
	s.	d.	s.	d.	s.	d.	s.	d.	s.	d.	s.	d.	s.	d.
Per Week	26	0	27	0	28	0	29	0	30	0	31	0	32	0
Per Day, 6 to Week	4	4	4	6	4	8	4	10	5	0	5	2	5	4
Per Hour, 10 to Day	0	5	0	5¼	0	5½	0	5¾	0	6	0	6	0	6¼

ASCARIDES, *or Seat-worms, to destroy.*—A tea-spoonful of flowers of sulphur, in a wine-glassful of Gin, or Brandy, in a morning fasting. The addition of a small quantity of Aloes will render it more effectual.

ASPARAGUS, *Officinalis.*—Asparagus is one of the most wholesome and nutritious of our culinary vegetables; it is both a diuretic and a sedative, and is recommended in cases of dropsy, stone, and affections of the chest and lungs. For the latter complaint the following extract will be found serviceable:—Boil the asparagus in water for several hours, then strain, and evaporate the liquor gradually over a very slow fire until it becomes exceedingly thick; then add a wineglassful of brandy to each pint, and put by in bottles. Take a tablespoonful night and morning in warm milk.

ASPARAGUS, *to boil.*—Scrape the asparagus; tie them in small bunches; boil them in a large pan of water with salt in it; before you dish them up toast some slices of bread, and then dip them in the boiling water; lay the asparagus on the toasts; pour on them rich melted butter, and serve hot. *Rf.*

ASPARAGUS, *ragout of.*—Cut small asparagus like green peas; the best method is to break them off first; then tie them in small bunches to cut, boil them till half done; then drain them, and finish with butter, a little broth, herbs, two cloves, and a sprig of savory. When done, take out the cloves, herbs, &c., mix two yolks of eggs, with a little flour, and broth, to garnish a first course dish. But if you intend to serve it in second course mix cream, a little salt, and sugar. *Hu.*

ASPARAGUS AMULET.—Beat up six eggs with cream, boil some of the largest and finest asparagus, and when boiled cut off all the green in small pieces. Mix them with the eggs, and add pepper and salt. Heat a slice of butter, put them in, and serve on buttered toast. *Far.*

ASPARAGUS OMELET.—Boil a dozen of the finest asparagus, cut off the green portion, and chop into thin slices; season with salt and cayenne pepper; (soluble is best); beat an egg in cream, and melt four ounces of butter in a frying pan; pour half the batter into the middle of the pan, when the butter is hot; then place the asparagus tops upon the eggs, and cover with the rest of the batter. Serve on buttered toast.

ASTHMA.—This disease is well known. It manifests itself in temporary fits of difficult breathing, is accompanied with wheezing, cough, a sense of suffocation, and constriction of the chest. The *cause;* hereditary predisposition; cold and moist atmosphere; sudden changes of temperature; intense study: suppression of long accustomed evacuations; certain fevers: irritation of the air cells of the lungs, by aerial acrimony, or other causes; irritation of the stomach, &c.

When this disease is attended with expectoration, it is called *humoural Asthma;* and when there is no discharge, it is named *dry Asthma*. It is remarkable, that what will excite the disease in one patient, will often prove a means of relieving it in another. This peculiarity is shown in the eight pair of nerves, branches of which go to the lungs and stomach. When these branches are in a state of morbid excitement, or irritation, the muscles concerned in conveying air from the lungs become contracted so as to limit the expansion of the chest, and by retarding the circulation of the blood through the lungs, the blood becomes surcharged with carbon, causing a dark appearance of the lips, &c.

Asthma may be distinguished from Pulmonary Consumption, by the former being attended not only with fits of difficult breathing, but with violent fits of suffocation; whereas in consumption the patient has only shortness of breath on motion. Ashma also more generally attacks persons in advanced life.

If the system is much debilitated, so that swelling of the legs, great oppression of breathing, and florid countenance, are predominant symptoms, a more powerful tonic is requisite:—Tincture of Rhatany, 6 ounces; Ammonia, 2 scruples; Compound Spirit of Juniper, 2 ounces; Tincture of Squills, half an ounce. Mix. Three table-spoonfuls to be taken every four hours, with the following Pills:—

Precipitated Iron, 2 grains; Extract of Hemlock, 3 grains; Gum Ammoniac, 4 grains; Oil of Aniseed, two drops. Mix, and divide into two or three Pills.

Keep the bowels open by any of the aforementioned Aperients. But if the patient is affected with Diarrhœa, a frequent attendant on the last stage of this malady, the following may be substituted for the preceding tonic mixture:—Compound Tincture of Rhatany, 1 ounce; Lime water, 6 ounces; Laudanum, 30 drops. Mix. Three table-spoonfuls to be taken every three hours; if it does not restrain diarrhœa, add to the above 1 or 2 ounces of Decoction of Logwood.

Should a distressing pain affect the integuments of the head, or the back of the head, a small blister will give relief. Or, take Ammoniated Tincture of Valerian, two drachms; Tincture of Castor, a drachm; Laudanum, thirty drops; Camphor Mixture, one ounce; Syrup of Tolu, one drachm. Mix. This is most valuable for spasmodic affections.

ASTHMA, *Treatment of.*—For its cure or relief, see my *Herbal*, under the following articles; they are first-rate remedies for this disease;—Assafœtida, Black Byrony, Butter-Bur, Chervil, Coffee, Colt's foot, Foxglove, Garlic, Horse-radish, Lobelia in two places, Meadow Saffron, Hedge Mustard, Myrrh, Thorn Apple, Thyme, and Skunk Cabbage.

The smoking of *Stramonium*, known as *Thorn Apple*, is particularly recommended, the vapour, if possible should be inhaled. It wonderfully allays morbid irritability, and the caloric which is taken with it, during the operation of smoking, powerfully promotes the secretion of mucus, and thus often speedily terminates the fit. If the patient is unable to smoke it, the vapours of a strong decoction of it may be inhaled, by breathing over it as soon as it is taken off the fire. Boil an ounce in a pint of water; as soon as it boils, take it off the fire; it should be made in a close vessel.

Hedge Hyssop is an excellent remedy. It powerfully allays the morbid irritation of the lungs, promotes expectoration, obviates costiveness, strengthens the stomach, and increases the secretion of urine, and perspiration of the skin. A strong decoction of it, combined with Carraway, or Aniseed, is the best form of administration.

Before and during the fit the patient should immerse his feet in warm water, and drink warm simple beverages, as balm tea, barley water, &c., with two or three tea-spoonfuls of Æther, or of aromatic spirit of Ammonia. Whatever tends to quiet the nervous system, is of the greatest service; though active remedies should be applied with the greatest caution. Washing the head with warm water has been of very great service; and sometimes sneezing, produced by snuff, made of Asarabacca, has suddenly terminated the paroxysm. If the chest be much pained, forment with hot flannels, or apply a bran or oatmeal poultice. Very strong Coffee is much recommended if the attack is violent; combine with it 10 or 15 drops of laudanum, half a drachm of Æther, and two drops of oil of mint. This mixture may be taken several times during the day. The following pills are valuable in Asthma:—Ipecacuanha powder, 6 grains; James's Powder; 12 grains; Camphor, 15 grains; Extract of Henbane, or Syrup, to form into 10 or 12 Pills. One or two may be taken every hour, or less frequently.

Asthmatics are very subject to an accumulation of inflammable air in the intestines which renders an aperient necessary. Distension of the stomach or intestines from any cause is a source of great distress to the patient, by mechanically preventing the motion of the diaphragm. Therefore, take of Compound Colocynth Pill, 1 drachm; prepared Calomel, 8 grains; Assafœtida half a drachm. or more. Divide into 15 or 20 Pills; take two or three occasionally. But probably the best Aperient is Castor Oil given in Peppermint, or weak Brandy and Water.

To hasten the termination of the Paroxysm, rubbing the scalp with Camphorated Sal Volatile, and immersing the feet in warm water are often useful. Vomiting excited in the evening will sometimes, by unloading the stomach, promoting expectoration, and increasing perspiration, prevent the accession of a paroxysm. For this purpose, take 20 grains of Ipecacuanha powder :--Or, Ipecacuanha powder, 15 grains; sulphate of zinc, 4 grains; oxymel of squill, 2 drachms; peppermint water, 1 ounce. Mix:--Or, Tincture of Lobelia is good in obstinate cases; dose 1 drachm. *Lobelia* is now declared by the most eminent physicians to be the *king* of all remedies for Asthma. See my *Herbal on Lobelia*. I shall now subjoin a few other remedies, and some advice, the value of which has been confirmed by my medical experience, and that of others.

Æther is a good remedy during the fit. Dr. Graham directs its use thus; "Heat a common teapot with boiling water--let it stand three or four minutes; pour the water entirely out, and then put one or two tea-spoonfuls of Ether into the pot, close the lid, and inhale the fumes through the spout in the mouth, breathing in that way for several minutes.--Strong Brandy and Water, and Gin and Water, have been found very serviceable *during the fit*, especially the latter, with two or three drops of the Oil of Juniper added.

The following receipts for asthma have been found very useful:—

Take of the Milk of Gum Ammonia, six ounces; syrup of squills, four ounces and a half; mix. A spoonful to be taken when relief is required. It promotes copious expectoration.

Or, Gum Ammoniac, one drachm; gum Assafœtida, squill pill, of each half a drachm; oil of Cinnamon, six drops; form into 24 pills, with common syrup. Take twice a day.

Or, Powdered Senna, 1 ounce; flour of Sulphur, ½ ounce; powdered ginger, 2 drachms; powdered saffron, ½ drachm. Size of a nutmeg to be taken night and morning, in treacle or honey. Or two ounces of best honey, and one ounce of castor oil mixed. A tea-spoonful or two to be taken night and morning.

Carraway and Sweet Fennel seeds of each half an ounce; boil in a pint of vinegar about twenty minutes; take it off the fire, and add three ounces of sliced Garlic. Cover up, and when cold, squeeze and strain, and by gentle heat, mix with it a pound and a quarter of good honey. A tea-spoonful or two to be taken night and morning.

To relieve the breathing, steep some blotting paper in a strong solution of saltpetre; dry it, and light a portion when going to bed, lay it on a plate. Many have experienced much relief from this.

ASTHMA.—The Rev. John Wesley recommends the following: —A pint of cold water every morning, and wash the head in cold water, and using the cold bath once in two weeks.——Or a decoction of liquorice often gives relief. ——Or half a pint of tar water twice a day. Or *live a fortnight chiefly on boiled carrots*. It SELDOM FAILS. Many have been cured by this diet.——Or take from ten to sixty drops of Elixir of Vitriol in a glass of spring water three or four times a day.——Or into a quart of boiling water put a tea-spoonful of Balsamic Æther; receive the steam into the lungs, through a fumigator, twice a day.

☞ Balsamic Æther is made thus:—Put 4 ozs. of Spirits of Wine, and one ounce of Balsam of

Tolu, into a phial, with one ounce of Æther. Keep it well corked. It will not Keep above a week or two.——Or, vomit with warm water, and always keep the body open.— *Wesley.*

To prevent a return of a fit of Asthma, or to relieve Asthma.—Keep the bowels gently open with Rhubarb, or some other mild aperient, and strengthen the tone of the stomach by bitter infusions, as Camomile, Gentian, and Quinine. When the chest is constricted, apply mustard, or blistering plasters, and take an emetic occasionally to clear out the phlegm from the bronchial passages—avoid everything difficult of digestion—wear flannel next the skin—avoid a bleak damp air, easterly winds, and take constant exercise. An animal diet, rather light, is preferable to a vegetable diet.

ASTHMATIC COUGH.——Take Spanish liquorice, two ounces, salt of tartar, half an ounce; boil the liquor in three pints of water to a quart: add the salt to it when it is blood warm. Drink two spoonfuls of this every two hours. It seldom fails. I have known this cure an inveterate moist asthma.   *Wesley.*

ASSAFŒTIDA. —— Sold by Druggists. It is stimulant, antispasmodic, expectorant, and laxative. Its action is quick, giving relief in spasmodic, flatulent, and nervous affections, especially when they arise from costiveness. It is useful in cough, hooping cough, and difficult breathing, and senile constipation. Dose, from 10 grains in powder; Tincture from half drachm to two drachms.

For Pills, it may be combined with aloes, and a little ginger.

ASTRINGENTS. — Medicines which contract the living fibre. Their more immediate effect is to diminish excretion and secretion, acting subsequently as a tonic; they are remedies for debility, inward or external hæmorrhage, injurious secretions from the glands, fluxes, &c. The following is a *List of Astringents* :—

ALUM, POWDERED	dose 8 grains to 1 scruple.
AROMATIC CONFECTION..	,, 12 to 30 grains.
BISTORT, ROOT OF	,, 11 grains to 2 scruples.
CATECHU, TINCTURE OF..	,, 1 to 2 teaspoonfuls.
CHALK, PREPARED	,, 8 to 16 grains.
CINNAMON, TINCTURE OF	,, 2 to 5 drachms.
ELIXIR OF VITRIOL	,, from 6 drops in water.
GALLS	,, 1 to 12 grains.
GALLS, TINCTURE OF..	,, 20 grains to 1½ drachm.
IRON, SULPHATE OF	,, ½ grain to 4 grains.
IRON, FILINGS OF	,, 3 grains to 2 drachms.
IRON, TARTARIZED	,, 10 grains to ½ drachm.
IRON, SUBCARBONATE OF..	,, 1 to 12 grains.
KINO, POWDER OF	,, 8 grains to ½ drachm.
KINO GUM, TINCTURE OF	,, 1 to 2 drachms.
LOGWOOD, DECOCTION OF	,, from ½ to 1 wineglassful.
LOGWOOD, EXTRACT OF..	,, 10 grains to 1½ scruple.
OAK, POWDERED BARK OF	,, ½ drachm to 1 drachm.
PERUVIAN BARK..	,, 10 grains to ½ oz.
ROSE WILLOW, DECOCTION OF	,, A cupful three times a-day.
RASPBERRY LEAVES, INFUSION OF..	A cupful.

ROSES, RED, THE PETALS OF	dose 1 scr.	to 1 drachm.
ROSES, DAMASK	,, 1 ,,	to 1 ,,
QUICKSILVER, NITRATE OF	,, 1-8 grain	to 2 grains.
SAGE, LEAVES OF	,, 10 grs.	to 1 drachm.
SIMAROBAR, BARK OF	,, 1 ,,	to ½ ,,
SAUNDERS, RED, THE WOOD	,, 1 ,,	to ½ ,,
TANIN	,, 5 ,,	to 10 grains.
TORMENTIL, THE ROOT	,, 10 ,,	to 1 drachm.
WORTLEBERRY; USE THE LEAVES	,, 10 ,,	to 1 drachm.

ATROPHY.—The word is derived from the Greek *a*, not, and *trophe*, nourishment; *not nourishment*, and the want of that nourishment induces emaciation, and loss of strength. The *symptoms* are a gradual consuming or wasting away, impaired digestion, loss of appetite, depression of spirits, and general languor; in the later stages hectic fever, cough, and difficult breathing. In young persons of scrofulous habit, there is enlargement of the mesentreic glands, indigestion, costiveness or diarrhœa, uncertain appetite, flushed or pallid cheeks, remittent fever, swelling of the abdomen, emaciated limbs, and eruptions of the skin on the shoulders, arms, thighs, &c. I have seen the vessels so attenuated as to be scarcely able to contain the blood, and, in some cases, the smaller ones congested.

The *cause* may be hereditary, damp houses, rooms, and beds, unwholesome foul air, close and bad ventilated sleeping rooms, excessive evacuations, worms, mental anxiety, excessive indulgence in venery, or spirituous liquors. It is induced in females by giving suck too long.

Treatment. —— Many diseases are accompanied by Atrophy to a greater or less extent. In those cases, therefore, it is but an effect of a disease, and that disease must be prescribed for. There are cases, however, in which the most careful and repeated scrutiny fails to detect any serious disease of the vital organs, though some important viscus may be affected. If the glands are affected, apply the Tincture of Iodine by means of a Camel Hair brush, or the Ointment of the same. The following formula has been recommended:—

Iodine of Potassium, 1 drachm; Compound Infusion of Gentian, 6 ounces; Aromatic Spirit of Ammonia, 2 drachms; mix, and take a table-spoonful three times a day; with the following Aperient at bed-time;—Compound Rhubarb Pill, 4 grains; Sulphate of Quinine, 4 grains; Cayenne Pepper, 2 grains; make into 3 or 4 pills.

In this disease, fresh air should be obtained, and abundant exercise in the open air. Keep the bowels regular, and always combine a tonic with a purgative. The diet must be light and nutritious. If the disease arises from a venereal taint, (alas! how many monstrous parents thus infect their children!) then Sarsaparilla will be useful. See article *Venereal*, in Robinson's *Herbal;* the same course will, in a great measure, be applicable to *Atrophy*. If the disease proceeds from worms, then Anthelmintics must be administered.

Sometimes Atrophy is produced by suckling too long, which must be abondoned, or it will cause wasting, and ultimately consumption. The child should be weaned immediately, and out-door exercise in a pure atmosphere, and a course of tonics should be taken immediately.

AUNT NELLY'S PUDDING.—Half a pound of flour, half pound of treacle, six ounces of chopped suet, the juice and peel of one lemon, 4 table-spoonfuls of cream, two or three eggs. Mix and beat all together. Boil in a basin, (previously well buttered) four hours.—For sauce, melted butter, a wine-glassful of Sherry, and two or three table-spoonfuls of apricot jam.

AVENS.—This plant is astringent, styptic, tonic, febrifuge, stomachic, and it is very applicable to all fevers, and promotes digestion. This plant is useful in dysentery, a lax state of the bowels, asthma, colics, debility, sore throat, &c., &c. It is the opinion of an eminent physician, that its continued use restores strength to the most shattered and enfeebled constitutions. Decoction, sweetened with sugar and milk, makes a very pleasant beverage, having much of the taste of coffee or chocolate. Take half a pint of the decoction at a time; and about forty or fifty grains of the powder daily.—See *Robinson's Herbal*.

AVOIRDUPOIS WEIGHT.
16 Drams	.. ..	1 Ounce.
16 Ounces	.. ..	1 Pound.
14 Pounds	.. ..	1 Stone.
28 Pounds, or 2 stones		1 Quarter.
4 Quarters or 8 stone or 112 pounds		1 Hundred
20 Hundreds	..	1 Ton.

By this weight nearly all the necessaries of life are weighed; bread, cheese, butter, meat, groceries, coal, &c.

BACHELOR'S CAKE.—One pound of flour, half a pound of sugar, quarter of a pound of butter or lard, four wine-glassfuls of milk, half a pound of Sultana raisins, quarter of a pound of currants, the same of candied peel, a quarter of a nutmeg, two teaspoonfuls of ground ginger, one of cinnamon, and one of carbonate of soda. These ingredients being well mixed, and slowly baked for an hour and a half, will form a very nice cake.

BACK, STRAIN IN THE.—The first thing is rest; take night and morning 15 or 20 drops of the balsam of capiva. If the part is inflamed, apply cold water cloths. Let the bowels be kept gently open by aperients. When the inflammation is gone, rub the part with the Stimulating Liniment, page 405.——The application of the Plaster for the Stomach, or the Warm Plaster, page 317, will be found useful. *Gu.*

BACKGAMMON.—This game is played by two persons, with a box and dice upon a table divided into two parts, upon which there are twelve black and twelve white points. Each player has fifteen men, black and white, to distinguish them, which are thus placed:—If you play into the right-hand table, two upon the ace point in your adversary's table; five upon the six-point in the opposite table; three upon the cinque point of the nearest table; and five on the six point in your own table.

The grand point is to bring the men round into your own table; all throws that contribute towards it, and prevent your opponent doing the like, are advantageous to you, and vice-versa. The best throw upon the dice is the aces, as it stops the six point in the outer table, and secures the cinque in your own; whereby the adversary's two men upon your ace point cannot get out with either four, five, or six.

When you carry your men home, in order to lose no points, carry the most distant men to your opponent's bar-point, as the first stage you are to place it on; the next stage is six points further, namely, in the place where your opponent's five men are first placed out of his tables; the next stage is upon the sixth point in your tables. Pursue this method till your men are brought home, except two, when by losing a point, you may often save your gammon, by putting it in the power of two fives or two fours to save it.

If you play to win a hit only, try to gain either your own or your adversary's cinque point; if that fails by your being hit, then you must throw more men into his tables, thus: put a man upon your cinque or bar point, and if he hit it, you may then gain a forward instead of a back game, but if he hits you, play for a back game; and the greater number of men which are taken up makes your game the better, because by that you preserve your game at home; and must then always endeavour to gain both your adversary's ace and trois points, or his ace and deuce points. At the beginning of a set, do not play for a back game; that is, running the risk of a gammon to win a single hit.

If you play three up, your principal object is, either to secure your own or your opponent's cinque point; when that is effected, you may play a pushing game, and endeavour to gammon him by so doing. The next best point, after having gained your cinque point, is to make your bar point; thereby preventing him running with two sixes. Then prefer making the quatre point in your own tables, rather than the quatre point out of them. Then you have a chance to gammon the adversary if he is very forward; for if his tables are broke at home, it will be your interest to open your bar point, to oblige him to come out of your tables with a six, and having your men spread, you not only catch that man your opponent brings out of your tables, but may also take up the man left in your table, (supposing that he had two men there.) And if he should have a blot at home, it will then be your interest not to make up your table, because if he enter upon a blot, which you are to make purposely, you may get a third man; which, if accomplished, will give you four to one of the gammon. If you play for a hit only, one or two of your opponent's men taken up, makes it surer than a greater number, providing your tables are made up.

To play for a gammon you are to make blots purposely, the odds being that they are not hit; but should it happen, in such cases you will have three men in your adversary's tables; you must then try to secure your adversary's cinque, quatre, or trois point, to prevent a gammon; and do not suffer him to take up a fourth man.

If your opponent is greatly before you, never play a man from your quatre, trois, or deuce points, in order to bear that man from the point where you put it, because nothing but high doublets can give you any chance for the hit; therefore, instead of playing an ace or a deuce from any of the aforesaid points, always play them from your highest point; by which means throwing two fives or two fours, will, upon having eased your six and cinque point, be of great advantage. But, had your six point remained loaded you might be obliged to play at length those fives and fours.

As soon as he enters one, compare his game with yours; and if you find your game equal, or better, take the man if you can, because it is twenty-five to eleven against his hitting you; which, being so much in your favour, you ought always to win that risk when you have already two of his men up; except you play for a single hit only.

Never be deterred from taking any one man of your adversary's, by the apprehension of being hit by double dice; it is five to one against it. If you should happen to have five points in your tables, and to have taken up one of your adversary's men, and are obliged to have a blot out of your tables, rather leave it upon the doublets than any other, because doublets are thirty-five to one against his hitting you; any other chance is seventeen to one against his doing so.

Two of your adversary's men upon your tables are better for a hit than any greater number, providing your game is the most forward; because having three or more men on your tables, gives him more chances to hit you than if he had only two men.

If you have a blot upon entering a man upon your adversary's tables, and have your choice where, always chose that point which is most disadvantageous to him.

CRITICAL CASES FOR A BACK GAME.

Question.—Suppose A plays the fore game and that all his men are placed in the usual manner; for B's game suppose that fourteen of his men are placed upon his adversary's ace point, and one on his deuce point, and that B is to throw, which game is the likeliest to win the hit?

Answer.—A's is the best by twenty-one to twenty, because if B misses an ace to take his opponent's deuce point, which is twenty-five to eleven against him, A is in that case to take up B's men in his tables, either singly or to make points; and if B secures either A's deuce or trois points, then A is to lay as many men down as possible, in order to be hit, and so get a back game.

DIRECTIONS FOR PLAYING AT SETTING OUT THE 36 CHANCES OF THE DICE.

1. Two aces to be played upon your cinque point and bar point, for gammon or hit.

2. Two sixes to be played on your adversary's bar point, and on your own, for a gammon or hit.

3. Two trois to be played on your cinque point and the other two in your trois point, in your own tables, for a gammon only.

4. Two deuces to be played on your quatre point in your own tables, and two to be brought over from the five men placed in your adversary's tables; this also for a gammon only.

5. Two fours to be brought over from the five men placed in your adversary's table, and to be put upon the cinque point in your own tables, for a gammon only.

6. Two fives, to be brought over from the five men placed in your adversary's tables, and put on the trois point in your own, for a gammon or hit.

7. Six ace, now take your bar point for a gammon or hit.

8. Six deuce, a man to be brought from the five, in your adversary's tables, and placed on the cinque point in your own, for a gammon or hit.

9. Six and three, bring a man from your opponent's ace point as far as he will go, for a gammon or hit.
10. Six and four, exactly the same as last.
11. Six and five, ditto.
12. Cinque and quatre, ditto.
13. Cinque-trois, makes the trois point in your own tables for a gammon or hit.
14. Cinque-deuce, play two men placed in your adversary's outer table in the five, for a gammon or hit.
15. Cinque-ace, bring one man from the five in your adversary's tables for the cinque, and play one down on the cinque-point in your own tables, for the ace, for a gammon or hit.
16. Quatre-trois, bring two men from the five in your adversary's tables, for a gammon or hit.
17. Quatre-deuce, make the quatre-point in your own tables, for a gammon or hit.
18. Quatre-ace, play a man from the five, in your adversary's tables for the quatre; and for dice, a man down on the cinque point in your tables, for a gammon only.
19. Trois-deuce, bring two men from the five in your adversary's tables, for a gammon only.
20. Trois-ace, make the cinque point in your own tables, for a gammon or hit.
21. Deuce-ace, play one man from the five in your adversary's tables, for the deuce; and for the ace, play a man down upon the cinque point in your own tables, for a gammon only.

LAWS OF BACKGAMMON.

1. If you take a man or men from any point, that man or men must be played.
2. You are not understood to have played any man till placed upon a point, and quitted.
3. If you play with 14 men only, there is no penalty attending it, because with a lesser number you play to a disadvantage, by not having the extra man to make up your tables.
4. If you bear any number of men, before you have entered a man taken up, and which consequently you were obliged to enter, such men, so borne, must be entered again in your adversary's tables, as the man taken up.
5. If you have mistaken your throw, and played it, and if your adversary has thrown, it is not in your choice nor his to alter it, unless both sides agree to do so.

BACON, YORKSHIRE.—Yorkshire Bacon is first-rate, equal to that of Wiltshire, Cumberland, &c. The peculiarity of flavour depends upon curing, which is conducted in the following manner:—After killing, the pig must hang for twenty-four hours, before being cut up. Take saltpetre, six ounces to the cwt., and rub it well in; and 10 lbs of common salt to the cwt; well rub it in, and place in the salting-tub. After having been in salt twelve or fourteen days, it must be turned over, and a few pounds of fresh salt applied, and left for ten days longer. Then take out, wipe well, and hang up in a cool, dry place in a linen or cotton bag, or wash over with lime and water, to prevent rancidity, and the attack of the bacon-fly. Hams especially should be preserved in this way.

Some people make their bacon thus: Take off all the inside fat of a side of pork, and lay it on a long board or dresser, that the blood may run from it. Rub it well on both sides with good salt, and let it lie a day. Then take a pint of bay-salt, a quarter of a pound of saltpetre, and beat them both fine; two pounds of coarse sugar, and a quarter of a peck of common salt. Lay your pork in something that will hold the pickle, and rub it well with the above ingredients. Lay the skinny side downwards, and baste it every day with the pickle for a fortnight. Then hang it on a wood-smoke, and afterwards hang it in a dry place, but not in a hot place. Observe, that all hams and bacon should hang clear from everything, and not touch the wall. Take care to wipe off the old salt before you put it into the pickle, and never keep bacon or hams in a hot kitchen, or in a room exposed to the rays of the sun, as all these matters contribute to make them rusty. *Far.*

BACON, *to cure as in Wiltshire.*—Sprinkle each flitch with salt, and let the blood drain off for twenty-four hours; then mix a pound and a half of coarse sugar, the same quantity of bay-salt, nearly half a pound of saltpetre, and a pound of common salt. Rub this mixture well into the bacon, turning it every day for a month, then hang it to dry, and afterwards smoke it ten days. This quantity of salts is sufficient for the whole hog.

BACON, *to choose.*—If the rind is thin, the fat firm and of a red tinge, the lean tender, and of a good colour, and adhering to the bone, you may conclude it good and not old. If there are yellow streaks in it, it is going, if not already, rusty. *Ru.*

BACON, *Excellent.* — Divide the hog, and take the chine out; it is common to remove the spareribs, but the bacon will be preserved better from being rusty if they are left in. Salt the bacon six days, then drain it from that first pickle; mix as much salt as you judge proper with eight ounces of bay-salt, three ounces of saltpetre, and a pound of coarse sugar, to each hog, but first cut off the hams. Rub the salts well in, and turn it every day for a month. Drain, and smoke it a few days; or dry without, by hanging in the kitchen, not near the fire.

BAD SMELLS.—When a person is so much affected by a pungent smell, as to cast him down, instantly convey him to a place where there is fresh air, dash cold water upon his head, face, and chest. Then let a person press upon his breast bone, and push his bowels up to his chest, and suddenly let them go, producing the same action as breathing, which must be continued some minutes. Rub the chest and limbs with brandy or ammonia, mixed with oil, as a stimulant. Hold ammonia, or strong smelling salts to the nose, tickle the throat to cause sickness. If cold, put him to bed, put bottles of hot water to his feet, thighs, and arm-pits; and if possible, get some brandy, or other spirit, and water, down his throat; or put him into a warm bath, and use the flesh brush while in it.

BAKING POWDER.—Take 6 oz. carbonate of soda, 4 oz. tartaric acid, 2 oz. sugar (very finely sifted,) 1 oz. salt. Mix well together, and after the flour has been made into dough (with water for bread, or milk for rolls,) add one teaspoonful of the powder to every pound of flour, and knead it well. By this powder hot rolls may be had to breakfast every morning, as its action is so rapid. Keep the powder in a well corked-bottle.

BALDNESS.— The cause of baldness is defect in the hair follicles, from which the hair is developed. Sometimes it is the result of disease; and it is frequently hereditary. Those who perspire much about the head are generally bald. If the hair falls off after fever, shaving a few times will tend to promote the growth. Keeping the head closely wrapped prevents the growth of hair. A drachm of the Tincture of Cantharides mixed with an ounce of lard, is a good application. An infusion of the *Asarum Europeum* Asarabacca, (see Robinson's Herbal) may be used as a lotion for the scalp.

Rub the bald part frequently with the juice of an onion till it looks red.—Or, water, 1 pint; pearlash, half an ounce; onion juice, 1 gill; rum, half a gill; oil of rosemary, 20 drops. Rub the head hard with a rough linen towel dipped in the mixture.—Or, take 4 ounces of castor oil, 8 ounces best rum, 30 drops oil of lavender, apply occasionally to the head, shaking the bottle well.—Or, beef marrow, well washed, melted, and strained, half a pound; tincture of cantharides, one ounce; oil of bergamot, 12 drops.—Wash the head frequently with warm water and Windsor soap; or with a decoction of rosemary and southernwood.

BALDNESS.—Rub the part morning and evening with onions, till it is red, and afterwards with honey.—Or wash it with a decoction of boxwood.—Or electrify it daily.—*Wesley.*

BALDNESS.—Infuse for a few days, 1 drachm of powdered cantharides in 1 ounce of proof spirit; beef marrow, half pound, soak in several waters, lastly in weak salt and water; melt, strain, and mix, adding 10 or 12 drops of oil of bergamot, or lavender.

BALM.—It is diaphoretic. It makes an excellent drink in colds, fevers, and influenza. *See Robinson's Herbal.*

BALM OF GILEAD, *Decoction of, and Tincture of.*—These form excellent remedies for cough, asthma, wheezing, &c. Populus balsomefera, or balsom poplar, belongs to America; but it may be obtained by applying to the Medical Botanists. For the decoction, simmer 1 ounce of the buds in a quart of soft water, down to half a pint. Take a wine glassful or more, when the cough is troublesome.—For the *Tincture*, infuse 2 ounces of the buds in a quart of good rum, and 4 ounces of sugar. Digest for four days. Take two or three tea-spoonfuls at a time. It greatly relieves cough, pains in the chest, and other pulmonary affections.

BALMONY.——An American plant. It is a good tonic, antibilious and stimulant. It is very bitter, and purgative. Hence it may be used in constipation, indigestion, loss of appetite, and general debility, with great effect; also in complaints of the liver, and in jaundice. It is a good anthelmentic, soon ridding children of worms. Take in a weak infusion; and in powder from four to eight grains.

BALM TEA.—Balm leaves, 1 ounce, fine sugar, 1 spoonful, lemon juice, 1 ounce, infused in a pint of boiling water, for twenty minutes. This forms a useful drink in colds, or fevers. (See Robinson's Herbal, under *Balm.*

Or it may be made just like common tea, without the lemon. Let the patient drink it frequently, especially the last thing at night, and keep himself warm during the perspiration.

BALM WINE.—Take 40 lbs. of sugar, and 9 gallons of water, boil it gently two hours, skim it well, and put it into a tub to cool.

Take 2½ lbs. of the tops of balm, bruised, and put them into a barrel with a little new yeast; and when the liquor is cold, pour it on the balm. Stir it well together, and let it stand twenty-four hours, stirring it often. Then close it up, and let it stand six weeks. Rack it off, and put a lump of sugar into each bottle. Cork well; it will be better the second year than the first. *Far.*

BALSAMIC MIXTURE.—Balsam of Capivi, 3 ozs.; oil of juniper, 30 drops; gum arabic, dissolved in water, a sufficient quantity; a cupful of spring water, and 1 oz. each of proof spirit, and syrup of marshmallows. Mix. Good for urinary affections.

BALSAM, *Locatilla's*.—Olive-oil, one pint; oil of turpentine and yellow wax, of each half a pound; red saunders, six drachms. Melt the wax with part of the oil over a gentle fire, then add the remainder of the oil of turpentine; afterwards mix in the saunders, reduced to powder, and stir till the balsam is cold.

This balsam is recommended in erosions of the intestines, the dysentery, hæmorrhages, internal bruises, and in some complaints of the breast. Outwardly it is used for healing and cleansing wounds and ulcers. The dose, internally, is two scruples to two drachms.

BALSAM FOR COUGHS AND COLDS.—Tincture of tolu, and compound tincture of benzoin, of each, one ounce; rectified spirit, two ounces; syrup of blood root, a table-spoonful. (*See Blood-root Syrup.*) Mix. Dose, a tea-spoonful.

BANBURY CAKES.—Roll out puff paste about a quarter inch thick, and place *Banbury Composition* in the middle of the piece of paste you are to use; fold the other side over it and press it into an oval shape, flatten it with your hand at the top, letting the joining be at the bottom. Rub the top over with white of egg, and dust with powdered sugar.—*Banbury Composition*:—Beat up well a quarter pound of butter, mix with it half a pound of candied orange and lemon cut small, one pound of currants, and quarter ounce each of ground cinnamon, and allspice. Mix all together with eight ounces of sugar. Keep in a jar for use. Bake fifteen minutes.

BANBURY CAKES.—Take 3 lbs. of flour, 1 lb. of butter rubbed into the flour, mix it with milk and a little balm; about two ounces for a penny; roll them round, then put sugar, currants, and a little of the essence of lemons in the middle; take them up long and bake them in a hot oven.

BANDOLINE FOR THE HAIR.—This fixature is best made a little at a time. Pour a table-spoonful of boiling water on a dozen quince seeds; and repeat when fresh is required.

Or a solution of Gum Arabic; scented with otto of Roses.

BANNOCK.—Meal, 2 cupfuls; Flour, 2 cupfuls; a teaspoonful of salt; one of ginger; two table-spoonfuls of treacle; sufficient buttermilk; half a teaspoonful of soda. Bake an hour.

BARBERRIES, *for Tartlets.*—Pick barberries that have no stones, from the stalks, add to every pound weight three quarters of a pound of lump sugar; put the fruit into a *stone* jar, and either set it on a hot hearth or in a saucepan of water, and let them simmer very slowly till soft; put them and the sugar into a preserving-pan, and boil them gently fifteen minutes.—Use no metal but silver.

BARBERRIES, *to preserve.*—This fruit must first be boiled in water twenty minutes, drained, and then preserved with sugar like other fruit.

BARBERRY JAM, *to make.* Pick the barberries from the stalks; bake them in an earthen pan; when baked, pass them through a sieve with a large wooden spoon; weigh the berries, and put their weight of powdered sugar; mix well together; put it in your pans and cover it up; set it in a dry place; when you have filled the pans, sift powdered sugar over the tops. *Hu.*

This fruit is cooling, antiscorbutic, and deobstruent, containing malic and citric acid. They are very useful in all inflammatory fevers, especially typhus, and bilious disorders, and scurvy. In the form of jam, the fruit is very refreshing. *Gu.*

BARCLAY'S ANTIBILIOUS PILLS.—Extract of colycinth, 2 drachms; extract of jalap, 1 drachm; almond soap, 1 drachm and a half; guiacum, 3 drachms; tartarized antimony, 8 grains; oil of juniper, 4 drops; oil of caraway, 4 drops; oil of rosemary, 4 drops; Form into a mass with syrup of buckthorn, and divide into pills.

BARK, *Decoction of.*——Boil an ounce of the Peruvian bark, grossly powdered, in a pint and a half of water, to one pint, then strain the decoction. If a teaspoonful of the weak spirits of vitriol be added to this medicine, it will render it both more agreeable and efficacious.

BARK, *Compound Decoction of.* ——Take of Peruvian bark, and Virginia snake-root, grossly powdered, each three drachms. Boil in a pint of water to one half. To the strained liquor add one ounce and a half of aromatic water.

BARK, *Tincture of.*—Peruvian Bark, 2 ounces; of Cinnamon and Orange peel, ½ ounce each; Cayenne Pepper, 4 teaspoonfuls. Infuse all in 1½ pint of Brandy, for six days in a close vessel.—Very useful in agues, remittent fevers, and the slow, nervous, and putrid kinds, especially at their decline. A table-spoonful at a time in any suitable liquor, sharpened with a few drops of Elixir of Vitriol.

BARK, *Electuary of.*—Take of Peruvian bark, in powder, three ounces; cascarilla, half an ounce; syrup of ginger, enough to make an electuary.

In the cure of obstinate intermitting fevers, the bark is assisted by the cascarilla. In hectic habits, however, it will be better to leave out the cascarilla, and put three drachms of crude sal ammoniac in its stead. *Bu.*

BARLEY GRUEL.—Take of pearl barley 3 ozs.; boil in two quarts of water, till reduced to about one; a little cinnamon or ginger may be added; strain, and return into the saucepan; and then add, according to your palate, three quarters of a pint of port wine. *Hu.*

BARLEY MILK.—Boil half a pound of pearl barley in three pints of milk; when sufficiently boiled, add one quart of cream, a stick of cinnamon, and sugar to taste; when nearly cold, pour in a pint of sherry wine, beat it into a froth, and serve.

BARLEY PUDDING.—To 6 eggs well beaten put a quart of cream, half the whites, sweeten to your palate, a little orange flower or rose water, and 1 lb. of melted butter. Then put in six handfuls of barley, boiled tender in milk. Butter the dish, and put it in. Bake it a light brown. *Far.*

BARLEY SUGAR, *Common.*—Boil three pounds of coarse raw

sugar in three tea-cupfuls of water, over a slow fire for half an hour. Dissolve a little gum in hot water; and put it in to clear; keep scumming while any scum rises; when ready it will snap like glass; cut it into long sticks.

BARLEY SOUP.—Take a gallon of water, and half a pound of barley, a blade or two of mace, a large crust of bread, a small piece of lemon-peel; let it boil till it comes to two quarts; then add half a pint of sherry wine, and sweeten to your palate. *Hu.*

When boiled to 3 quarts, chopped chicken and bacon may be put in, and salt; omitting the sugar.

BARLEY SUGAR.—Boil one pound of very fine sugar in a teacupful of water, over a slow fire for half an hour; keep skimming it as often as any scum arises on the surface, till enough. Before it comes to the crack, take it off, and pour it on a stone. You must not pull this but make it into long sticks, and clear it with vinegar.

Flavour with lemon juice, or oil of lemons; rub a little fresh butter over a stone or marble slab, and pour sugar along it in narrow strips; twist it to a spiral form while warm; and when it becomes cold, mark it across with a knife, and it will break into any lengths desired.

BARLEY WATER.—Carefully clean two table-spoonfuls of pearl barley, put it into a quart jug, adding a very little salt, and lump sugar to taste. Fill up with boiling water, and keep stirring for ten minutes. Cover, and let cool. It will be fit for use in ten or twelve hours. Finely shred lemon peel, or a little calf's feet jelly, greatly improves it.

To make Barley-water *pectoral*, add to the above, sliced figs, bruised liquorice root, raisins, stoned; the quantity of each according to taste; distilled water, 1 pint; boil awhile, and strain. These drinks are useful in fevers, and diseases of the chest. The barley should be well washed, then boiled a few minutes to extract its colouring matter. Then boil in fresh water to a proper consistence.

Or, take a tea-spoonful of pearl barley, two ounces of loaf sugar of the ordinary size, half a lemon, and enough isinglass to clear it. Pour half a gallon of spring water on these ingredients, and let it stand till cold.

Or, add the juice and rind of one lemon to a table-spoonful of honey, and two teacupfuls of barley, pour a quart of boiling water upon it.

BARONESS'S PUDDING.—Suet, flour, raisins, of each, three quarters of a pound, and a little salt, and cinnamon. This is a real good pudding.

BASILICON OINTMENT, *Yellow.*—Yellow Wax, 8 ounces; Burgundy Pitch, 3 ounces; Venice Turpentine, 4 ounces; Linseed Oil, 10 ounces. First melt the Rosin, to which add the Wax, and the Burgundy Pitch. When the whole is melted, remove from the fire, and slowly put in the Oil, stirring well till it is cold.

For the *Black Basilicon*, Yellow Wax, and Yellow Rosin, 10 ounces; Common Pitch, 5 ounces. Melt as before, and add 10 ounces of Linseed Oil when taken from the fire.

For the *Green Basilicon*, Yellow Wax, and Yellow Rosin, of each, 3 ounces; Venice Turpentine, 6 ounces; Powdered Verdigris, 1 ounce; Lard, 6 ounces. Melt first the Rosin, &c., as before.

These ointments are very efficacious in healing cuts, abscesses, and local affections of any kind.

BATH, BATHING.—See under their descriptive Names, as *Cold Bath, Warm Bath, Vapour Bath, &c.*

BATH BUNS.—Take 1 lb. of flour, put it in a dish, and make a hole in the middle, and pour in a dessert spoonful of good yeast; pour upon the yeast half a cupful of warm milk, mix in one-third of the flour, and let it rise an hour. When it has risen, put in 6 ozs. of cold butter, 4 eggs, and a few carraway seeds; mix all together with the rest of the flour. Put it in a warm place to rise. Flatten it with the hand on a paste-board. Sift 6 ozs. of loaf sugar, half the size of a pea; sprinkle the particles over the dough; roll together, to mix the sugar; let it rise, in a warm place about 20 minutes. Make into buns, and lay on buttered tins; put sugar and 9 or 10 comfits on the tops, sprinkle them with water; bake in a pretty hot oven. *A. N.*

BATH CAKES.—-Take six pounds of flour, three quarters of a pound of butter, and three pounds of raw sugar, rub the butter and sugar well into the flour, after crushing the sugar small; take a little volatile salts dissolved in milk, mix the sugar and milk together, and then put the other things in: roll it thin, and cut it into round cakes with a tin mould, and bake them in a slow oven; they must not be browned much. Some persons prefer them with a few carraway seeds.

BATHING *the feet and legs in warm water at night.*—Excellent for colds, coughs, hoarseness, pains headaches, and fevers. It prevents determination of blood to the head, excites the blood downwards, and promotes perspiration. The patient should go to bed immediately.

BATH PIPE.—Take powdered white sugar, 16 parts: Italian juice, dissolved in a little water, 2 parts; powdered gum Arabic, 1 part. Make them into a stiff mass with warm water, and roll it into the usual form.

BATTER PUDDING.—-Rub three spoonfuls of fine flour extremely smooth by degrees into a pint of milk: simmer till it thickens; stir in two ounces of butter: set it to cool; then add the yolks of three eggs; flour a cloth that has been wet, or butter a basin, and put the batter into it; tie it tight, and plunge it into boiling water, the bottom upwards. Boil it an hour and a half, and serve with plain butter. If approved, a little ginger, nutmeg, and lemon-peel may be added. Serve with sweet sauce.

BATTER PUDDING WITH MEAT.--Make a batter with flour, milk and eggs; pour a little into the bottom of a pudding-dish; then put seasoned meat of any kind into it, and a little shred onion; pour the remainder of the batter over it; bake in a slow oven.

BATTER, *to be used with all sorts of roasting meat.*—Melt good butter; put to it three eggs, with the whites well beat up, and warm them together, stirring them continually. With this you may baste any roasting meat, and then sprinkle bread crumbs thereon; and so continue to make a crust as thick as you please.

BATTER, *for frying Fruit, Vegetables, &c.*—Cut four ounces of fresh butter into small pieces, pour on it half a pint of barley water, and when dissolved, add a pint of cold water; mix by degrees with a pound of fine dry flour, and a small pinch of salt. Just before it is used, stir into it the whites of two eggs beaten to a solid froth; use quickly, that the batter may be light.

BAY-BERRY.--The American kind of this plant is the best. It is very astringent and stimulant, and is judged to be the most valuable and astringent medicine ever discovered. As a stimulant it is very powerful, and preferred by some to cayenne, and other stimulants. It removes canker, or morbific matter from the mucous membranes of the stomach and bowels. It is a wonderful cleanser. In cold phlegmatic systems, it generates heat, and it is sometimes combined with cayenne in all cases of cold clamminess, where there is much morbific matter in the system; in such cases it may be given strong and frequently. Being an alterative it is a good remedy for bowel complaints, and effects a radical change in the secretions. The bark is the strongest. The powdered leaves, or the bark of the root, make an excellent poultice for ulcers, cancerous and scrofulous sores, &c.

BEANS, *to dress.*—Boil tender, with a bunch of parsley, chopped to serve with them. Bacon or pickled pork must be served to eat with, but not boiled with them.

BEANS, FRENCH, *to boil.*—Cut the ends of your beans off, then cut them slantways: put them in strong salt and water as you do them; let them stand an hour; boil them in a large quantity of water, with a handful of salt in it, they will be a fine green; when you dish them up pour on them melted butter. *Rf.*

BEANS, FRENCH, *a la Poulette.*—Choose the beans small and tender; clean them, and take out the fibers, and throw them into fresh water; cut them all to one size; put them upon a hot fire, in a pot or stew pan, with water, and a handful of salt; let them be well done and very green; throw them into cold water, drain, and put them into a stewpan with a bit of butter, cut onions in little dice, do them white in butter, dust in a little flour, let them cook a little without browning; add a spoonful of soup; mix it well with hashed parsley and scallions; salt and pepper; when done enough put in the beans, give them a boil; thicken the sauce with two or three yolks of eggs; finish with the juice of a lemon and butter. *Beau.*

BEANS, FRENCH, *to preserve for Winter.*—Pick them young, and throw into a little wooden keg a layer of them three inches deep; then sprinkle them with salt, put another layer of beans, and do the same as high as you think proper, alternately with salt, but not too much of this. Lay over them a plate, or cover of wood, that will go into the keg, and put a heavy stone on it. A pickle will rise from the beans and salt. If they are too salt, the soaking and boiling will not be sufficient to make them pleasant to the taste. *Ru.*

BEANS, *Ragout of.*—Boil your beans, so that the skins will slip off, take about a quart, season them with pepper, salt, and nutmeg; then flour them, and have ready some butter in a stewpan, throw in some beans; fry them of a fine brown, then drain them from the fat, and lay them in your dish; have ready a quarter of a pound of butter melted, and half a pint of the blanched beans boiled, beat in a mortar, with a very little pepper, salt, and nutmeg: then by degrees, mix them to the butter. *Hu.*

BEANS, FRENCH.—String, and cut them into four or eight; the last looks best. Lay them in salt and water, and when the sauce-pan boils put them in with some salt. As soon as they are done, serve them immediately; to preserve the green colour. *Ru.*

BEANS, *French a la Creme.*—Slice the beans and boil them in water with salt. When soft, drain. Put into a stew-pan two ounces of fresh butter, the yolks of three eggs, beaten up into a gill of cream, and set over a slow fire. When hot, add a spoonful of vinegar, and the bones, simmer for five minutes.

BEANS, FRENCH, *Pickled.*—Put small young beans into strong salt and water for three days, and stir now and then. Put them into a sauce-pan with vine leaves, under and over them, and fill with salt and water; keep on the fire till they are a fine green; drain; place in jars, and cover them with vinegar, allspice, cayenne, ginger, boiled six minutes; pour on hot.

BEANS, FRENCH. *as Salad.* Boil the beans in salt and water, drain them, season with cayenne pepper, cream and vinegar; cover them; to stand three hours. Drain again, and mix salad of any kind, seasoning in the usual way.

BEANS AND BACON, *to dress.*—When you dress beans and bacon, boil the bacon by itself, and the beans by themselves, for the bacon will spoil the colour of the beans. Always throw some salt into the water, and some parsley nicely picked. When the beans are done enough, which you will know by their being tender, throw them into a colander to drain. Take up the bacon and skin it; throw some raspings of the bread over the top, and if you have a salamander, make it red hot, and hold it over it. to brown the top of the bacon; if you have not one, set it before the fire to brown. Lay the beans in the dish, and the bacon in the middle, on the top, and send them to table, with butter in a tureen.

BEANS, *Windsor, Fricasseed.*—When grown large, but not mealy, boil, blanch, and lay them in a white sauce ready hot; just heat them through in it, and serve. If any are not of a fine green, do not use them for this dish. *Ru.*

BEAUTY, *personal, to promote.*—Labour to be cheerful. Do not give way to trouble. If you have misfortunes, bear them with submission; for brooding, maundering, &c. do no good. Above all be *good-tempered.* For the state of the mind has great influence upon the facial appearance, and bodily attitude.

BECHAMEL SAUCE.—Put a few slices of ham into a stew-pan, a few mushrooms. two or three shalots, two cloves, also a bay leaf and a bit of butter. Let them stand a few hours. Add a little water, flour, and milk or cream; simmer forty minutes. Scalded parsley, very fine, may be added.

BEDS, *to detect dampness in.*—After having warmed the bed with the pan, place between the sheets a wine or beer glass; if after a few minutes, the glass collects no vapour, it is safe, and *vice versa.* In all doubtful cases, sleep between the blankets.

BED SORES.—The white of an egg beaten to a strong froth; then drop in gradually, whilst you are beating, two table-spoonfuls of spieits of wine; put it into a bottle, and apply occasionally with a feather.——*Soap Plaster,* sold by the Druggists, protects the affected part from friction or rubbing.

BEECH WOOD, *to stain Mahogany colour.*—Put two ounces of dragon's blood in small pieces into a quart of spirits of wine; let it stand in a bottle, in a warm place, and shake it frequently.

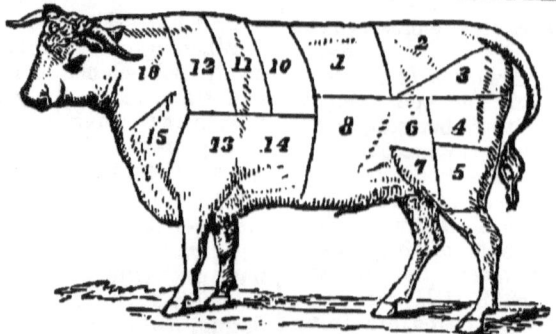

BEEF.

Hind-Quarter.
1. Sirloin.
2. Rump.
3. Edge-Bone.
4. Buttock.
5. Mouse-Buttock.
6. Veiny Pice.

7. Thick Flank.
8. Thin Flank.
9. Leg.
10. Fore Rib; 5 Ribs.

Fore-Quarter.
11. Middle Rib; 4 Ribs.
12. Chuck; 3 Ribs.

13. Shoulder, or Leg of Mutton Piece.
14. Brisket.
15. Clod.
16. Neck or Sticking-Piece.
17. Shin.
18. Cheek.

BEEF, *to choose.*—If the flesh of ox-beef is young, it will have a fine smooth open grain, be of a good red, and look tender. The fat should look white rather than yellow; for when that is of a deep colour, the meat is seldom good; beef fed by oil-cakes is in general so, and the flesh is flabby. The grain of cow-beef is closer, and the fat whiter, than that of ox-beef; but the lean is not of so bright a red. The grain of bull-beef is closer still, the fat hard and skinny, the lean of a deep red, and a stronger scent. Ox-beef is the reverse. Ox-beef is the richest and largest, but in small families, and to some tastes, heifer-beef is better, if finely fed. In old meat there is a streak of horn in the ribs of beef: the harder this is, the older; and the flesh is not finely flavoured.

BEEF *a-la-mode.*——Choose a piece of thick flank of a fine heifer or ox. Cut into long slices some fat bacon, but quite free from yellow; let each bit be near an inch thick: dip them into vinegar, and then into a seasoning ready prepared of salt, black pepper, allspice, and one clove, all in fine powder, with parsley, chives, thyme, savory and knotted majoram, shred as small as possible, and well mixed. With a sharp knife make holes deep enough to let in the larding; then rub the beef over with the seasoning, and bind it up tight with tape. Set it in a well-tinned pot over a fire, or rather, stove; three or four onions must be fried brown and put to the beef, with two or three carrots, one turnip, a head or two of celery, and a small quantity of water; let it simmer gently ten or twelve hours, or till extremely tender, turning the meat twice.

Put the gravy into a pan, remove the fat, keep the beef covered, put them together, and add a glass of port wine. Take off the tape and serve with the vegetables; or you may strain them off, and send them up cut into dice for garnish.

D

Onions roasted and then stewed with the gravy are a great improvement. A tea-cupful of vinegar should be stewed with the beef.

BEEF, *Brisket of, to stew.*—Put the part that has the hard fat into a stew pot, with a small quantity of water, let it boil up, and skim it thoroughly; then add carrots, turnips, onions, celery, and a few pepper-corns. Stew till extremely tender; then take out the flat bones, and remove all the fat from the soup. Either serve that and the meat in a tureen; or the soup alone, and the meat on a dish, garnished with some vegetables. The following sauce is much admired, served with the beef:—Take half a pint of the soup, and mix it with a spoonful of ketchup, a glass of port wine, a teaspoonful of made mustard, a little flour, a bit of butter, and salt; boil all together a few minutes, then pour it round the meat. Chop capers, walnuts, red cabbage, pickled cucumbers, and chives or parsley, small, and put in separate heaps over it.

BEEF BROTH.——Put two pounds of lean beef, one pound of scrag of veal, one pound of scrag of mutton, sweet herbs, and ten pepper-corns, into a nice tin saucepan, with five quarts of water; simmer to three quarts; and clear from the fat when cold. Add one onion if approved.

Soup and broth made of different meats, are more supporting as well as better flavoured.

To remove the fat, take it off, when cold, as clean as possible; and if there be still any remaining, lay a bit of clean blotting or cap-paper on the broth when in the basin, and it will take up every particle.

BEEF-COLLOP. — Cut thin slices of beef from the rump, or any other tender part, and divide them into pieces three inches long; beat them with the blade of a knife, and flour them. Fry the collops quick in butter two minutes; then lay them into a small stew-pan, and cover them with a pint of gravy; add a bit of butter rubbed in flour, pepper, salt, the least bit of shalot shred as fine as possible, half a walnut, four small pickled cucumbers, and a teaspoonful of capers cut small. Take care that it does not boil; and serve the stew in a very hot covered dish.

BEEF, *to collar.*—-Choose the thin end of the flank of fine mellow beef, but not too fat; lay it into a dish with salt and saltpetre, turn and rub it every day for a week and keep it cool. Then take out every bone and gristle, remove the skin of the inside part, and cover it thick with the following seasoning cut small: a large handful of parsley, the same of sage, some thyme, marjoram, and pennyroyal, pepper, salt, and allspice. Roll the meat up as tight as possible, and bind it, then boil it gently for seven or eight hours. A cloth must be put round before the tape. Put the beef under a good weight while hot, without undoing it: the shape will then be oval. Part of a breast of veal rolled in with the beef, looks and eats very well.

BEEF, *to cure.*—Take 28 lbs. of good beef and rub it thoroughly with salt and saltpetre; then make a pickle of 4 ozs. of bay salt, ¼ oz. of saltpetre, and 4 ozs. of coarse sugar, and 50 ozs. of common salt. Rub this well in every day for 3 or 4 weeks. Take out and roll in bran or sawdust and hang it in a wood smoke for six or 8 days. Hang in a dry place near the chimney for a week; then keep it by covering it with bran.

Spiced Beef is done the same way, adding mace, cloves, and pepper. All rubbed well into the beef. Spiced beef is not smoked, and it is generally boiled—slowly.

BEEF COOKED IN A FRENCH MANNER.—Procure six pounds of beef, and a pound of fat bacon in thin strips; roll each strip separately, in a seasoning of parsley and pepper, and cover the beef thickly over with them. Place some veal bones at the botttom of a pan, with a cover, tie the larded beef round, and place it upon the bones. Then slowly pour over it two tablespoonfuls of rum, so as to penetrate the beef. Place a thin slice of bacon at the top, and vegetables: viz. a few carrots, an onion, half a turnip, and one head of celery. Put these into the pan, with pepper-corns, and a bunch of sweet herbs in a bag, and pour over the whole a cupful of good gravy. Cover the pan well. Bake in a oven slowly for four hours; garnish, when cold, with jelly, and with the vegetables stewed with the meat.

BEEF, *called Sanders, to dress.*—Mince beef, or mutton, small, with onion, pepper, and salt; add a little gravy: put it into scallop-shells, or saucers, making them three-parts full, and fill them up with potatoes, mashed with a little cream; put a bit of butter on the top, and brown them in an oven, or before the fire.

BEEF CAKES.—Pound some beef that is underdone with a little bacon, or ham; season with pepper, salt, and a little shalot, or garlic: mix them well; and make into small cakes three inches long; and half as wide and thick; fry them a light brown, and serve them in a good thick gravy.

BEEF, *to salt, Dutch way,*—Take a lean piece of beef; rub it well with treacle or brown sugar, and let it be turned often. In three days wipe it, and salt it with common salt and salt-petre beaten fine; rub these well in, and turn it every day for a fortnight. Roll it tight in a coarse cloth, and press it under a large weight; hang it to dry in a wood-smoke, but turn it upside down every day.

BEEF *en Miroton.*—Cut thin slices of cold roast beef and put them into a frying-pan with a $\frac{1}{4}$lb. of butter, and six onions, and a few cloves, turn the pan frequently, then mix a little broth and some salt, pepper, and after a few boils, serve up hot. This dish is excellent and economical.

BEEF, *Fricandeau of.*—Take a nice bit of lean beef; lard it with bacon seasoned with pepper, salt, cloves, mace, and allspice. Put it into a stew-pan with a pint of broth, a glass of white wine, a bundle of parsley, all sorts of sweet herbs, a clove of garlic, a shalot or two, four cloves, pepper and salt. When the meat is become tender, cover it close; skim the sauce well, and strain it; set it on the fire, and let it boil till it is reduced to a glaze.

Glaze the larded side with this, and serve with sorrel-sauce.

BEEF, *Fricassee of cold Roast Beef.*—Cut the beef into very thin slices, shred a handful of parsley very small, cut an onion into quarters, and put all together into a stewpan, with a piece of butter, and some strong broth: season with salt and pepper, and simmer very gently a quarter of an hour: then mix into it the yolks of two eggs, a glass of port wine, and a spoonful of vinegar; stir it quick, rub the dish with shalot, and turn the fricasse into it.

BEEF, *to hash.*—Do it the same as in the last receipt; only the meat is to be in slices, and you may add a spoonful of walnut-liquor or ketchup.

Observe, that it is owing to *boiling* hashes or minces that they get hard. All sorts of stews, or meat dressed a second time, should be only simmered; and this last only hot t'rough.

BEEF, *Hunters'*.—To a round of beef that weighs twenty-five pounds, take three ounces of saltpetre, three ounces of the coarsest sugar, an ounce of cloves, a nutmeg, half an ounce of allspice, three handfuls of common salt, all in the finest powder.

The beef should hang two or three days; then rub the above well into it, and turn and rub it every day for two or three weeks. The bone must be taken out at first. When to be dressed, dip it into cold water, to take off the loose spice, bind it up tight with tape, and put it into a pan with a tea-cupful of water at the bottom, cover the top of the meat with shred suet, and the pan with a brown crust and paper, and bake it five or six hours. When cold, take off the paste and tape.

The gravy is very fine; and a little of it adds greatly to the flavour of any hash, soup, &c.

Both the gravy and beef will keep some time.

The meat should be cut with a very sharp knife, and quite smooth, to prevent waste.

BEEF, *to keep*.—The kernels should be removed from the neck pieces. As the butchers seldom attend to this matter, the cook should do it, and then rub the salt well into such beef as is designed for boiling, and slightly sprinkle that which is for roasting.

BEEF, *to mince*.—Shred the underdone part fine, with some of the fat; put it into a small stewpan, with some onion or shalot, (a very little will do,) a little water, pepper, salt; boil it till the onion is quite soft, then put some of the gravy of the meat to it, and the mince. Don't let it boil. Have a small hot dish with sippets of bread ready, pour the mince into it, but first mix a large spoonful of vinegar with it: if shalot-vinegar is used, there will be no need of the onion, nor the raw shalot.

BEEF, *to mince*.—Shred the meat fine, and boil with onion, or shalot, pepper, &c.; add a little of its gravy, or some butter. Garnish with toast. *A. N.*

BEEF-OLIVES, *or to dress meat that has not been done enough.*—Cut slices half-an-inch thick, and four inches square; lay on them a forcemeat of crumbs of bread, shalot, a little suet, or fat, pepper, and salt. Roll them, and fasten with a small skewer; put them into a stew-pan with some gravy made of the beef-bones, or the gravy of the meat, and a spoonful or two of water and stew them till tender. Fresh meat will do.

BEEF OR PORK *to salt for immediate use.*—The piece should not weigh more than five or six pounds. Salt it very thoroughly just before you put it into a pot; take a coarse cloth, flour it well, put the meat in, and fold it close. Put it into a pot of boiling water, and boil it as long as you would any other salt beef of the same size, and it will be as salt as if done four or five days.

BEEF-PALATES. — Simmer them in water several hours, till they will peel; then cut the palates into slices, or leave them whole, as you choose; and stew them in a rich gravy till as tender as possible. Before you serve, season them with Cayenne, salt, and ketchup. If the gravy was drawn clear, add also some butter and flour.

If to be served white boil them in milk, and stew them in a fricassee sauce; adding cream, butter, flour, and mushroom powder, and a little pounded mace.

BEEF, *to Pot.*—Take two pounds of lean beef, rub it with saltpetre, and let it lie one night; then salt with common salt, and cover it with water four days in a small pan. Dry it with a cloth and season with black pepper; lay it into as small a pan as will hold it, cover it with coarse paste, and bake it five hours in a very cool oven. Put no liquor in.

When cold, pick out the strings and fat; beat the meat very fine with a quarter of a pound of fine butter just warm, but not oiled, and as much of the gravy as will make it into a paste; put it into very small pots, and cover them with melted butter.

ANOTHER WAY.—Take beef that has been dressed, either boiled or roasted; beat it in a mortar with some pepper, salt, a few cloves, grated nutmeg, and a little fine butter, just warm.

This eats as well, but the colour is not so fine. It is a good way for using the remains of a large joint.

BEEF, *to Roast.*—Beef may be roasted before the fire, though this method is not now so common. It is mostly roasted in the oven. If before the fire, it is a good plan to put a little salt and water in the dripping-pan; baste the meat a little with it; let it dry; then dust it well with flour; baste it with good butter, to give the meat a better colour. Place at a proper distance from the fire, and baste it often; let the thickest part of the beef have the most fire. If you allow it to scorch, it makes the meat hard, and prevents the heat from penetrating to the centre; besides it will appear enough when it is only about half done. When the steam draws near the fire it is a sign of its being enough. Never salt your meat much before you lay it to the fire, as salting brings out the gravy, and forms brine. This caution applies to beef for immediate eating.

If you roast in the oven, have it hot before you put in the beef; keep the oven door open five or six minutes after putting the beef in, to get rid of the steam. Baste it occasionally. *A. N.*

BEEF, *Corned.*—Make the following pickle:—Water, 2 gallons; salt, 2½ lbs.; treacle, ¼ lb.; sugar, 1 lb.; saltpetre, 1½ ozs.; pearlash, ¼ oz. Boil all together; skim, and pour the pickle on about 25 lbs. of beef. Let it stay in a few days. Boil in plenty of water when cooked to remove the salt, and eat with it plenty of vegetables. It is nice to eat cold, and makes excellent sandwiches. *Gu.*

BEEF, *Rolled.*——Hang three ribs three or four days; take out the bones from the whole length, sprinkle it with salt, roll the meat tight, and roast it. Nothing can look nicer. The above done with spices, &c., and baked as hunters' beef is excellent.

BEEF, *Rolled to equal Hare.*—Take the inside of a large sirloin, soak it in a glass of port wine and a glass of vinegar mixed, for forty-eight hours; have ready a very fine stuffing, and bind it up tight. Roast it on a hanging spit; and baste it with a glass of port wine, the same quantity of vinegar, and a tea-spoonful of pounded allspice. Larding it improves the look and flavour; serve with a rich gravy in the dish; currant-jelly and melted butter in tureens.

BEEF, *Round of.*—Should be carefully salted and wet with the pickle for eight or ten days. The bone should be cut out first, and the beef skewered and tied up to make it quite round. It may be stuffed with parsley, if approved, in which case the holes to admit the parsley must be made with a sharp pointed knife, and the parsley coarsely cut and stuffed in tight. As soon as it boils, it should be skimmed, and afterwards kept boiling very gently.

BEEF, *to salt red.*—Choose a piece of beef with as little bone as you can (the flank is most proper), sprinkle it, and let it drain a day; then rub it with common salt, saltpetre, and bay-salt; but only a small proportion of the saltpetre, and you may add a few grains of cochineal, all in fine powder. Rub the pickle every day into the meat for a week, then only turn it. It will be excellent in eight days. In sixteen drain it from the pickle; and let it be smoked at the oven-mouth when heated with wood, or send it to the baker's. A few days will smoke it. A little of the coarsest sugar may be added to the salt. It eats well, boiled tender with greens or carrots. If to be grated as Dutch, then cut a *lean* bit, boil it till extremely tender, and while hot, put it under a press. When cold, fold it in a sheet of paper, and it will keep in a dry place two or three months,—ready for serving on bread and butter. *Ru.*

BEEF SAUSAGES.—Take 2 lbs. of nice lean tender beef, and one pound of beef suet. Cut and chop them fine. Mix powdered sage and sweet herbs with the meat. Season pretty high with pepper, salt, nutmeg, &c.; also the finely shred rind of a small lemon. Skins may be dispensed with, if they be rolled well in a beaten egg, fried in hot butter, and rolled about in the pan. *A. N.*

BEEF, *Sirloin, to dress.*—Cut out all the meat and fat in little pieces as thick as your finger, and two inches long; dredge it with flour; and fry in butter, of a nice brown; drain the butter from the meat, and toss it up in a rich gravy, seasoned with pepper, salt, anchovy, and shalot. Do not let it boil on any account. Before you serve, add two spoonfuls of vinegar. Garnish with crimped parsley. *Ru.*

BEEF SOUP.—Put into ten pints of water, eight pounds of beef, cut into two or three pieces, one pound of mixed green vegetables, four teaspoonfuls of salt, half a teaspoonful of cayenne pepper, a few shalots, and three cloves. Boil gently three hours.

BEEF-STEAKS should be cut from a rump that has hung a few days. Broil them over a very clear fire, or in the oven; put into the dish a little minced shalot, and a table-spoonful of ketchup; and rub a bit of butter on the steak the moment of serving. It should be turned often, that the gravy may not be drawn out on either side.

This dish requires to be eaten so hot and fresh done, that it is not in perfection if served with any thing else. Pepper and salt should be added when taking it off the fire.

BEEF-STEAK, *with Potatoes.*—Cut thin slices of beef, beat and season them with pepper and salt, dip them into a little melted butter and broil them. When done, put them into a dish before the fire, and fry potatoes to a fine brown colour, serve with parsley chopped fine, a small piece of butter, pepper and salt.

BEEF-STEAKS, *Rich.*—Cut

a fine large steak from a rump that has been well hung, or it will do from any tender part; beat it, and season with butter, pepper, salt, clove, and onion; lay it in a dish that has a cover to fit quite close, and set in the oven with water. In two or three hours it will be quite tender, and then serve with its own gravy.

BEEF, *Stewed Rump*.—Wash it well; and season with pepper, cayenne, salt, allspice, cloves, and mace, in fine powder. Bind it up tight, and lay it in a pot that will just hold it. Fry three large onions sliced, and put them to it, with three carrots, two turnips, a shalot, four cloves, a blade of mace, and some celery. Cover the meat with good beef-broth, or weak gravy. Simmer it very gently for several hours, till quite tender. Clear off the fat, and add to the gravy half a pint of port wine, a glass of vinegar, and a large spoonful of ketchup; simmer half an hour, and serve in a deep dish. Half a pint of table-beer may be added. The herbs to be used should be parsley, thyme, basil, savoury, marjoram, pennyroyal, and chives.

Garnish with carrots, turnips, or truffles and morels, or pickles of different colours, cut small, and laid in little heaps separate; chopped parsley, chives, beet-root, &c. If, when done, the gravy is too much to fill the dish, take only a part to season for serving, but the less water the better; and to increase the richness add a few beef-bones and shanks of mutton in stewing.—A spoonful or two of made mustard is a great improvement to the gravy. Rump *roasted* is excellent; but in the country it is generally sold whole with the edge bone, or cut across instead of lengthways.

ANOTHER WAY.—Half roast it; then put it into a large pot with three pints of water, one of small beer, one of port wine, some salt, three or four spoonfuls of vinegar, two of ketchup, a bunch of sweet herbs of various kinds (such as burnet, tarragon, parsley, thyme, basil, savoury, pennyroyal, marjoram, knotted morjoram, and a leaf or two of sage,) some onions, cloves, and cayenne; cover it close, and simmer till tender. When done lay it into a deep dish, set it over hot water, and cover it close. Skim the gravy; put in a few pickled mushrooms, truffles, morels, and oysters if agreeable, but it is good without; thicken the gravy with flour and butter, and heat it with the above, and pour over the beef. Forcemeat balls of veal, anchovies, bacon, suets, herbs, spices, bread, and eggs, to bind, are a great improvement.

BEEF, *boiled*.—Boil the thick end of a brisket of beef, some carrots, turnips cut in small balls, and some celery, for two hours. Let it simmer for six hours longer, taking care to fill up the pot as the water decreases. An hour before the meat is done, take out as much broth as will fill your soup dish, and boil in it turnips and carrots, cut in small pieces, with some celery, and season it with salt and pepper; serve the beef in one dish, and the soup in another. Add toasted bread to the soup. *Hu.*

BEEF GRAVY.—According to the quantity wanted, cut slices of lean gravy beef, which place in a stew-pan upon a slice of ham or lean bacon, sliced onions, a carrot, two or three cloves, and a head of celery; add a little good fat broth, and a pint of water; put on a slow fire for about half an hour, stirring it a few times. Then add boiling water as you think proper. Get it to the proper colour. It should be frequently skimmed, and at last strained.

BEEF HASH.—Take the bones of the joint to be hashed, break them small; then stew them in very little water, with two onions, pepper, salt, a few sweet herbs, and a little butter; then add some slices of underdone beef with fat. If you like, add gravy, ketchup, and a glass of sherry. Put it into a small stew-pan with a little water, an onion, pepper, and salt. Simmer it till hot through, and serve with dried parsley.

BEEF, HASHED, *American.*—Put nearly a pint of boiling water into a small saucepan, and make a thin paste with a dessert spoonful of flour, and a tablespoonful of cold water. Stir it in, and boil three minutes. Add half a teaspoonful of black pepper, and one of salt. Gently simmer 10 minutes. Cut the beef into half-inch pieces, and add as many pieces of boiled potatoes and turnips, and two or three ounces of butter, and, if you like, a table-spoonful of tomato ketchup. Simmer again 5 or 10 minutes; add gravy, port wine, and lemon juice, if you like.

BEEF-HEART.—Wash it carefully; stuff as hare; roast, and serve with rich gravy, and currant-jelly sauce. Hash with the same, and port wine.

BEEF, SIRLOIN, *to force.*—Split it; cut off the skin and fat; bone it; chop the meat fine with beaten mace, shalots, an anchovy, half a pint of port, pepper and salt; lay the bones, fat, and skin on; skewer and pepper it well. Serve with sauce made of port wine, shalot, anchovy, and horseradish. *Rf.*

BEEF-STEAKS AND OYSTER SAUCE.—Strain the liquor from the oysters, and throw them into cold water to take off the grit; simmer the liquor with mace and lemon-peel; put the oysters in, stew a few minutes, add a little cream, and butter rubbed in flour; boil up once; and have rump-steaks, well-seasoned, and broiled, ready for throwing the oyster-sauce over, when you serve.

BEEF-STEAKS, *Fried.*—Cut your steaks as for broiling; put them into a stewpan, with butter; set them over a slow fire, turning them t'll the butter becomes a thick white gravy; add a little pepper and salt, pour it into a basin, and add more butter; when they are almost enough, pour all the gravy into the basin, and put more butter into the pan; fry them a light brown over a quick fire; put them in a hot dish; slice a shalot among them; put a little in the gravy drawn from them, and pour it hot upon them. *Rf.*

BEEF-STEAKS, *Staffordshire.*—Beat them well; flour and season; then fry with sliced onions of a fine light brown; place in a stew-pan, and pour as much boiling water over them as will serve for sauce; stew very gently half-an hour, and add a spoonful of ketchup, or walnut-liquor.

BEEF PATTIES.—Use the best beef, half roast it, cut it very small, season with pepper, salt, and onion, or shalot, put it into thin paste, close up, and bake to a brown.—Underdone beef may be used instead of fresh.

BEEF STEAK PIE.—Take fine rump steaks; beat them with a rolling pin; then season them with pepper and salt, according to your palate; make a good crust; lay in your steaks; fill your dish; then pour in as much water as will half fill the dish. Put on the crust, and bake it well. If the pie be intended to be eaten cold, more seasoning must be put in than if intended to be eaten hot. An onion, finely sliced, is a great improvement to it. *Hu.*

BEEF-STEAK PIE.—Prepare the steaks as stated under *Beefsteaks*, and when seasoned and rolled with fat in each, put them in a dish with puff paste round the edges; put a little water in the dish, and cover it with a good crust.

BEEF-STEAK PUDDING.—Take some fine rump steaks; roll them with fat between; and if you approve a little *shred* onion. Lay a paste of suet in a basin, and put in the chopped steaks; cover the basin with a suet paste, and pinch the edges to keep the gravy in. Cover with a cloth tied close, let the pudding boil slowly for two hours. *Ru.*

BEEF-STEAK PUDDING, *baked.*—Make a batter of milk, two eggs and flour, or, which is much better, potatoes boiled and mashed through a colander; lay a little of it at the bottom of the dish; then put in the steaks very well seasoned; pour the remainder of the batter over them, and bake it. *Ru.*

BEEF-STEAK, *Stewed.*—Peel and chop two Spanish onions, cut into small parts four pickled walnuts, and put them at the bottom of a stewpan; add a tea-cupful of mushroom ketchup, two teaspoonfuls of walnut ditto, one of shalot, one of Chile vinegar, and a lump of butter. Let the rump-steak be cut about three quarters of an inch thick, and beat it flat with a rolling-pin, place the meat on the top of the onions, &c., let it stew for one hour and a half, turning it every twenty minutes. Ten minutes before serving up, throw in a dozen oysters with the liquor strained.

BEEF SOUP.—See *Soup and Bouille*, page 397.

BEEF STOCK.—Cut a piece of good beef into pieces, and boil with water just to cover it. Keep skimming, and add parsley, thyme, carrot, onion, turnip, celery, and a little salt; boil till the meat is tender, and strain it fine.

BEEF TEA.—Cut a pound of fleshy beef in thin slices; simmer with a quart of water twenty minutes, after it has once boiled, and been skimmed. Season, if approved. *Ru.*

BEER. See *Ale.*

BEER, *Excellent Table.*—On three bushels of malt pour of hot water the third of the quantity you are to use, which is to be thirty-nine gallons. Cover it warm half an hour, then mash, and let it stand two hours and a half more, then set it to drain. When dry, add half the remaining water, mash, and let it stand half an hour, run that into another tub, and pour the rest of the water on the malt, stir it well, and cover it, letting it infuse a full hour. Run that off, and mix all together. A pound and a half of hops should be infused in water, and be put into the tub for the first running.

Boil the hops with the wort an hour from the time it first boils. Strain off and cool. If the whole be not cool enough that day to add the yeast, a pail or two of wort may be prepared, and a quart of yeast put to it over night. Before tunning, all the wort should be added together, and thoroughly mixed with the lade-pail. When the wort ceases to work, put a bit of paper on the bung-hole for three days, when it may be safely fastened close. In four weeks the the beer will be fit for drinking.

Note. Servants should be directed to put a cork into every barrel as soon as the tap is taken out, and to fasten in the vent-peg, the air causing casks to become musty.

BEETLE, *House.*—Take some small lumps of unslacked lime and put into the cracks or holes from which they issue; it will effectually destroy them: or it may be scattered on the ground.

Another method, is to sprinkle the floor at night with coarse red wafers, which they will greedily devour, and the red lead will act upon them as poison.

Another method. Those who cannot procure a regular beetle trap, may make a very good substitute, by placing a bell-lipped tumbler upon the ground near their haunts, and run up a conical surface with sand to the lip of the glass; then, after filling the glass about half-way up with beer, or sugar and water, suspend a little sugar itself in a thimble over the glass, horizontally with its margin, and in the centre: you will find in their eagerness to get at the sugar, which is not within their reach, they will overstretch themselves, and falling into the liquor, which will attract them, you will destroy thousands. *Hu.*

Or make a cake of sugar, dripping, flour, and any poison, as arsenic, powdered phosphorus, &c. Be careful to keep the poison out of the way of children, and domestic animals.—See *Cockroaches.*

BEET ROOTS, *to pickle.*—Beet Roots are a very pretty garnish for made dishes, and are thus pickled. Boil the roots till they are tender, then take off the skins, cut them in slices, gimp them in the shape of wheels, or what form you please, and put them into a jar. Take as much vinegar as you think will cover them, and boil it with a little mace, a race of ginger sliced, and a few slices of horse-radish. Pour it hot upon your roots, and tie them down. *Far.*

BETHROOT.—An American plant. It stops inward bleeding from the kidneys, bladder, urethra, &c. It is good in fevers, coughs, asthma, consumption, taking a teaspoonful of the powdered root at a time; or it may be infused and taken. United with bloodroot, and made into a poultice, it is effectual in gangrene, or incipient mortification, ulcers, and sores. It restrains profuse menstruation, the whites, and it is an excellent astringent taken after child-birth for the uterine organs, employed as an enema. It may be obtained at the Medical Botanists.

The powdered root is used a teaspoonful at a time; or it is infused, to be drunk freely. This powder united with raspberry leaves, and made into tea is most effectual in diarrhœa, or laxity of the bowels.

BIRD'S EYE, *or Chile Vinegar.*—Nearly fill a bottle with cayenne pepper pods, then pour in the best white vinegar, cork, and put on the hob for five or six days, then cork tightly. It improves with age. It is a first-rate seasoner.

BISCUITS, *Plain.* — Make a pound of flour, the yolk of an egg, and two ounces of sugar, and some milk into a very stiff paste; beat it well, and knead till quite smooth; roll very thin, and cut into biscuits. Bake them in a slow oven till quite dry and crisp. *Ru.*

BISCUITS, *American.*— Rub half a pound of butter into four pounds of flour, and a full pint of milk or water. Well wet them up. Break your dough well, and bake them in a hot oven. They will be better with two ounces of sugar added. Cut out with the top of a wine-glass. These biscuits are made light by dissolving a quarter of a teaspoonful of salt of tartar in half a cupful of water, and adding to the mixture.

BISCUITS, *a la duchesse.*—

They are made with rice flour, sifted as fine as possible; dried orange flour, preserved and powdered very fine; rasped lemon-peel; a quarter of a pound of flour, to one pound of sugar; six yolks, and twelve whites of eggs, well beat up; finish as other biscuits. Add fruit or marmalade if you like.

BISCUITS, *Buttered.* — Dissolve a pound of butter in a quart of warm milk, and with eight pounds of flour make up a stiff smooth paste, roll thin and stamp out the biscuits, prick them, and bake on tins in a quick oven.

BISCUIT CAKE.—One pound of flour, five eggs well beaten and strained, eight ounces of sugar, a little rose or orange-flower water: beat well, bake one hour. *Ru.*

BISCUIT CAKE.—Rub into 1 pound of flour six ounces of butter, and three large spoonfuls of yeast, and make into a paste, with a sufficient quantity of new milk; make into biscuits, and prick them with a clean fork. *Ru.*

BISCUITS, *Drop.*—Beat the yolks of 10 eggs, and the whites of 6, with one spoonful of rose water, half an hour; then put in 10 ozs. of loaf sugar beat and sifted; whisk them well for half an hour, then add 1 oz. of carraway-seeds crushed a little, and 6 ozs. of fine flour; whisk in the flour gently, drop them on wafer-papers, and bake in a moderate oven. *Rf.*

BISCUIT, *French.*—Flour 6 lbs.; milk, 1½ pint; butter, 6 ozs.; sugar, 1¼ cupful; salt, a teaspoonful; 6 eggs, and half a pint of good yeast. Melt the butter in the milk, and beat the eggs. Add all the ingredients, set it to rise, and when very light, mould it into small biscuits, and bake in a quick oven. *Mrs. Dr. C.*

BISCUIT, *Spanish.*—Beat the yolks of 8 eggs near half an hour, then beat in 8 spoonfuls of sugar; beat the whites to a strong froth, then beat them very well with yolks and sugar near half an hour; put in 4 spoonfuls of flour, and a little lemon cut very fine, and bake them on papers. *Rf.*

BISCUITS, *Ginger.*—Take half an ounce of pounded ginger, the weight of seven eggs in sugar, and half the weight in flour; pound the sugar and sift it through a silk sieve; beat up the yolks of the eggs with the sugar until it is quite thick, then beat up the whites until they are stiff; put them together, add the flour, stirring it lightly in, and bake them in a slow oven.

BISCUITS, *Hard.*—Warm two ounces of butter in as much skimmed milk as will make a pound of flour into a very stiff paste, beat it with a rolling-pin, and work it very smooth. Roll it thin and cut it into round biscuits; prick them full of holes with a fork. About six minutes will bake them.

BISCUIT JELLY.——White biscuit, 1 pound; white sugar, 3 pounds; water, 2 gallons. Boil to one-half, strain and evaporate to a proper consistence, then add wine, 1 pint; cinnamon, ½ oz.

BISCUIT, *Light Lemon.*—For eight eggs put eight spoonfuls of sugar in a basin, and a little rasped lemon; put six yolks into the sugar, and beat them well; then beat the whites of eggs to snow, and add them; mix well three spoonfuls of flour; drop them into paper cases, and sift sugar over them. Bake in a slow oven.

BISCUITS, *Naples and Savoy.*—To one pound of loaf sugar, grated fine, add nine eggs, (take the whites out of two,) add one pound of flour, beat your eggs very well, and then whisk your sugar and eggs together with a little rose water, add the flour and bake them long or round.

BISCUITS OF FRUIT.—Take fruit of any kind, scald it, and to the pulp, put an equal quantity of the finest sugar, beat it an hour or two, then place in little white paper forms, dry in a cool oven, turn the next day, and in a few days box them.

BISCUITS, *Orange Heart.*—Put three quarters of a pound of powderd sugar into a basin, and thirty yolks of eggs; take seven preserved orange peels pounded very fine; add a handful of sweet and half a handful of bitter almonds pounded fine, and then mixed with a little orange flower water. Then put four eggs into the basin with the other ingredients, mixing them well, and beating until a fine froth arises. Then add half a pound of sifted flour to mix with the batter very lightly. Butter the moulds, fill them and sift a little powdered sugar over the top. Place in a quick oven, and empty the tins while hot.

BISCUITS, PIC NIC.—Into a pound of flour, work very small two ounces of butter, mix well with half a salt-spoonful of the finest carbonate of soda, two ounces of sugar, mix these thoroughly with the flour, and make up the paste with a few spoonfuls of milk, not more than quarter of a pint. Knead it very smooth and roll it quarter of an inch thick.

BISCUIT POWDER.—Dry your biscuits in a slow oven, roll them, and grind them with a rolling-pin on a clean board, till reduced to powder. Sift it through a close hair sieve, and it is fit for use.

BISCUITS, *Rice.*—Six ounces of fine sugar, half a pound of ground rice, six ounces of butter, six ounces of flour, and mix it into a paste with two eggs. Add a little lemon juice. Be careful in the baking.

BISCUITS, *Richmond.*—Flour, 2 lbs.; Butter, ¼ lb, two eggs, and milk sufficient to make a thick paste; a little sugar, and a few currants. Make the biscuits round, and half an ounce in weight. Bake in a quick oven; they will be brown in a minute or two. Previously steep the currants in hot water. Season if you like with cinnamon, &c.

BISCUITS, *Seed.*—Flour, 1 lb; sugar, 4 ozs; carraway seeds, as many as you like; half a tea-spoonful of carbonate of soda; with milk and cream, or buttermilk, mix well, roll thin, and with the top of a wine-glass cut them out, and bake quickly.

BISCUITS, *Spice.*—Take three pounds of flour and three pounds of sweet almonds cut in half; add three ounces of cinnamon and mace pounded, and one pound of fine sugar. Mix. Take three pounds of loaf sugar, boil slightly in some water, and mix with the other ingredients, and pound to the consistency of paste, heat the oven very hot, cover a plate with three sheets of clean paper. Roll the paste to a form like a large rolling-pin, place it on the paper, and press it down, letting it bulge slightly in the middle. When baked, and, while hot, cut into slices across, about the eighth of an inch in thickness, in the form of a rusk.

BISCUITS, *Spicy.*—Pound candied lemon in a mortar with some orange-flowers crisped; add two spoonfuls of apricot marmalade, four ounces of loaf sugar, and the yolks of four eggs. Mix well, and rub it through a sieve; then add the whites of the eggs beaten to a froth, and put the biscuits, in an oblong form on white paper; sift sugar over, and bake. These biscuits are very rich. The sweetmeat may be varied according to fancy.

BISCUIT, *American*.—Buttermilk, 1½ pint; a little salt, 2 spoonfuls of carbonate of potash dissolved in 4 table-spoonfuls of hot water. Mix flour enough to be stiff. Add shortening. Form and bake immediately.

BISCUITS, *Yarmouth*.—Take six ounces of well washed and picked currants; dry them well, and rub a little flour among them to make them white; add half a pound of powdered sugar, twelve ounces of sifted flour, and half a pound of the best fresh butter. Break three eggs and mix the whole together until it becomes of the consistence of paste; then roll and cut into shapes. The oven must be hot, and paper must be used. Bake to a slight brown colour.

BITE OF A MAD DOG.—Mr. Hildebrand, Veterinary Surgeon of Germany, says: *Bathe* the bitten place in *hot water*. He has ascertained, by experience, that hot water has the effect of decomposing the virus, and if applied in time renders cauterization unnecessary. In that case, all that is to be done after well bathing the part, as stated, is, to apply the solution of caustic potash to the wound with a brush, and afterwards anoint it with antimony ointment.

Apply ice to the Spinal column. This is *effectual*.——Or, wash well with a strong decoction of tobacco, and then bind wetted tobacco on the wound.——Or, take a pound of salt, dissolve in a quart of water. Squeeze, bathe, and wash the wound with this liquid for one or two hours; then bind some salt upon it for ten or twelve hours.——Or, mix powdered liverwort, four drachms; black pepper, two drachms. Divide this into four parts, and take one in warm milk for four mornings, fasting. Dr. Mead affirms he never knew this fail. WESLEY.

BITTER, *an excellent Family*.—Two ounces of gentian root, half ounce of Virginian Snake root, a pint of water, and a pint of brandy. Infuse for three days, strain, and bottle for use. This bitter is excellent for the stomach.

BITTER INFUSION.—Take gentian root, cut into pieces, half an ounce; dried Seville orange peel, bruised, one drachm; coriander seeds, bruised, half a drachm; spirits of wine, four ounces; water, one pint. First pour on the spirits of wine, and in three hours the water; then macerate for twelve hours, and strain. Take three spoonfuls between meals to promote digestion.

BITTER TONIC. — Gentian root, one ounce; the yellow rind of a fresh lemon; put into a jar or bottle with hot water; let it stand. A cupful in the morning promotes appetite.

BITTERSWEET OINTMENT. — Bark of Bittersweet Root, 2 ounces; cover with spirits of wine, and add, unsalted butter, 8 ounces. Simmer and strain. Excellent for swelled breasts, tumours, ulcers, &c. It may be applied twice a day.

BITTERSWEET.—See Robinson's Herbal, page 193; *Nightshade, Woody*.—It is a valuable plant, on account of its detergent, tonic, and healing qualities. Useful in scrofula, skin diseases, bad ulcers, syphilis, &c.

BLACK BALL FOR LEATHER.—Beeswax, 2 pounds; tallow, ¼ pound; gum arabic, ¼ pound; lamp-black, ¼ of a pound. Melt the tallow and wax; then cool a little and stir in the black and gum, previously mixed.

BLACKBERRY.—See Robinson's Herbal. Of the Blackberry, Dr. Chapman says, "Of the vegetable astringents, I believe that the blackberries are amongst the most efficacious. To check the inordinate evacuations which attend the protracted stages of cholera infantum, no remedy has ever done so much in my practice."

BLACKBERRY BRANDY.— To half a gallon of blackberry juice put one pound and a half of lump sugar, half an ounce of cinnamon, half an ounce of grated nutmeg, quarter of an ounce of cloves, and one ounce of allspice. Boil it a few minutes and when cool, add one pint of brandy. This is an invaluable remedy for diarrhœa.

BLACKBERRY CORDIAL. —To one gallon of blackberry juice put four pounds of lump sugar. Boil and skim off. Then add one ounce of cloves, one ounce of cinnamon, ten grated nutmegs; boil down till sufficiently rich. Let it cool and settle. Then drain off and add one pint of brandy.

BLACKBERRY AND WINE CORDIAL. — The following is recommended as a delightful beverage, and an *infallible specific* for diarrhœa, or diseases of the bowels:—To half a bushel of blackberries, well mashed, add a quarter of a pound of allspice, two ounces of cinnamon, two ounces of cloves; pulverize well, mix, and boil slowly until done; then strain the juice through flannel, and add to each pint of the juice one pound of loaf-sugar; boil again for some time, take it off, and, while cooling, add half a gallon of best Cognac brandy.—*Dose*: for an adult, a wine-glassful; for a child, a teaspoonful or more, according to age.

BLACKBERRY JAM.—Gather the fruit in dry weather. Boil or bake it for three-quarters of an hour, with half its weight of coarse sugar. Pot it, and keep it air tight, and it will be excellent. The fruit must be used when fresh gathered.

BLACKBERRY JELLY.— Bruise two quarts of Blackberries; add 2 quarts of water; and when they boil, run them through a linen bag; boil the syrup five minutes; then to every pound of juice, add a pound of sugar; boil 15 minutes, skim well, and pot, and put brandy papers over them. The addition of a little isinglass, and stewing them in a slow oven till a little candied, is a great improvement, especially if half of the water be left out. *A. N.*

BLACKBERRY SYRUP, *for Cholera and Summer Complaints*.— Blackberry juice, 1 quart; fine sugar, ½ lb.; nutmegs, cinnamon, allspice, of each, ¼ oz.; cloves, 1½ drachms, cayenne pepper, ½ dr. Powder them all, and gently boil them in the juice for about twenty miuutes. When cold, add half a pint of brandy. It relieves inward pains, cramp, and diarrhœa. *Gu.*

BLACKBERRY SYRUP.— Make a syrup of a pound of sugar, to each pint of water; boil until it is thick; add as many pints of the expressed juice of blackberries as there are pounds of sugar; put half a nutmeg grated to each quart of the syrup; boil fifteen or twenty minutes, then add half a gill of best French brandy for each quart of syrup; bottle it for use. A tablespoonful for a child, or a wineglass for an adult, is a dose.

BLACKBERRY WINE.—To make a wine equal to port. Take ripe blackberries, press the juice from them, let it stand thirty-six hours to ferment (lightly covered) and skim well; then, to every gallon of the juice, add one quart of water and three pounds of sugar; let it stand in an open vessel for twenty-four hours; strain, and barrel it. Let it stand six months, then bottle and cork close. It improves by age.

BLACK CAP PUDDING.—Make a batter with milk, flour, and eggs; butter a basin; pour in the batter, and 5 or 6 ounces of well cleaned currants. Cover it with a cloth well floured, and tie the cloth very tight. Boil nearly one hour. The currants will have settled to the bottom; therefore dish it bottom upwards. Serve with sweet sauce and a little rum. *A. N.*

BLACK CUPS.—Halve and core some fine apples, put them in a shallow pan, strew white sugar over, and bake them. Boil a glass of wine, the same of water, and sweeten it for sauce.

ANOTHER WAY.—Take off a slice from the stalk end of some apples, and core without paring them. Make ready as much sugar as may be sufficient to sweeten them, and mix it with some grated lemon, and a few cloves in fine powder. Stuff the holes as close as possible with this, and turn the flat end down in a stew-pan; set them on a very slow fire, with half of raisin wine, and the same of water; cover them close, and then baste them with the liquor.

BLACK CURRANT JAM.—See *Currant*, p. 136.

BLACK CURRANT JELLY.—See *Currant*, p. 137.

BLACK CURRANT LOZENGES.—Boil the fruit in a jar stopped close. Strain the juice through a coarse sieve. Measure the juice, and boil briskly half an hour. The more the juice has evaporated before adding the sugar, the better. For every full quart of juice (as first measured into the pan,) allow—Fine loaf sugar, 5 oz.; best gum arabic, finely powdered, 3 drachms, cream of tartar, 3 drachms. Mix these well in a basin with a very small quantity of the boiling juice, stirred briskly to it till smooth, then stir in the whole. Boil the mass till it is stiff and candies on the sides of the pan. Pour it on plates turned upside down; the thickness should not exceed one-eighth of an inch. Dry in the sun, or in front of a fire, but at some distance. When quite dry, cut out in lozenges. A sharp tin cutter is the best instrument. The form should be either square, diamond, or hexagonal, that the pieces may be cut close to another without waste. Shake among the lozenges a little magnesia to prevent sticking. Keep them in a wide-mouthed bottle, with a glass stopper. N.B—These lozenges may be made with the entire fruit.

BLACK CURRANTS, *to preserve.*—Get the currants when they are dry, and pick them; to every 1¼ lb of currants, put 1 lb. of sugar into a preserving pan, with as much juice of currants as will dissolve it; when it boils, skim it, and put in the currants, and boil them till they are clear; put them into a jar, lay brandy paper over them, tie them down, and keep in a dry place. A little Raspberry juice is an improvement. *Hu.*

BLACK CURRANT PUDDING, *to bake.*—Make a puff paste crust, roll it thin, line a basin with it, put three parts full of the currants, fill up with sugar, and put a paste cover over on the top, well closed; bake on a tin in a moderate oven 50 or 60 minutes. When served turn out upon a dish. Serve with cream, &c.

When boiled, use a suet crust,

and proceed as above, boiling two hours. *A. N.*

BLACK CURRANT WINE.—Take six gallons of ripe currants and put them into a large jar. Boil nine or ten gallons of water with four pounds of loaf sugar. Skim well, and let it stand for forty-eight hours. Then strain through a flannel bag into another vessel, return it into the jar, and let it stand three weeks to settle, and then bottle off.

BLACK DRAUGHT.—Infuse 2 ozs. of Senna leaves, and a ¼ oz. of Ginger in hot water (not boiling) for eight hours. Strain, and to the liquor add six ounces of Epsom Salts, 1 oz. of Liquorice; gently simmer till the Salts are dissolved. When cold, add ¼ oz. of Sal Volatile and six drops of the Oil of Cloves. Cork tightly. In order to keep it for a length of time, 2 ozs. of Tincture of Senna should be added.

BLACK EYE.—This is caused by a blow or bruise. If attended with inflammation and pain, wash the eye often with very warm water, in which is dissolved a little carbonate of soda; or with equal parts of tincture of opium and water. If the pain be acute, foment with a decoction of stramonium leaves, simmered in spirits. Wash the eye, and bind on the leaves; often repeat. Perhaps the best application is a poultice of Slippery Elm-bark. Mix with milk, and put it on warm.

To remove the black colour of the eye, bind on a little raw meat; or a poultice made of the root of Solomon's seal. Culpeper says, "It is available for bruises, falls, or blows, to dispel the congealed blood, and to take away the pains, and the black and blue marks that abide after the hurt." The blackness may be concealed by painting the part with flesh-coloured paint.

BLACKING BALLS, (*to make*)—Take of mutton suet, four ounces; bees' wax, one ounce; sugar-candy, or gum arabic and coarse sugar, one drachm, in fine powder. Melt these well together, over a gentle fire, and add about a spoonful of turpentine, and lamp-black sufficient to give it a good black colour. While hot enough to run, make it into a ball, by pouring the liquid into a tin mould; or let it stand till almost cold, or it may be moulded by the hand. *Hu.*

BLACKING, *real Japan.*—Take three ounces of ivory-black, two ounces of coarse sugar, one ounce of sulphuric acid, one ounce of muriatic acid, one lemon, one table-spoonful of sweet oil, and one pint of vinegar. First mix the ivory-black and sweet oil together, then the lemon and sugar, with a little vinegar to qualify the blacking; then add the sulphuric and muriatic acids, and mix them all well together.

The sugar, oil, and vinegar, prevent the acids from injuring the leather, and add to the lustre of the blacking. *Hu.*

BLACKING CAKE *for Boots and Shoes.* — Gum Arabic, one ounce; a pint of soft water, or more; ivory black, two ounces; a tablespoonful of sweet oil; treacle, or brown sugar, one ounce. Boil till of a proper thickness, and mould into cakes. These cakes, when used, must be dissolved in vinegar, or vinegar and water.

BLACKING, *Cheap.*—Take of ivory-black, one pound; lamp-black, half an ounce; treacle, one pound; sweet oil, one ounce and a half; coarse gum-arabic, half an ounce; and stale vinegar, three pints and a half; mix well: first dissolve the gum in a little water;

then add gradually half an ounce of oil of vitriol. Let the mixture stand two days.

BLACKING, *Matchless.*—Take a quarter of a pound of ivory black, two ounces of the coarsest brown sugar, three pints of sour table beer; mix it well together, then throw in about a small tablespoonful of sweet oil, and as much vitriolic acid; stir it well together, and in a few hours bottle.

BLACKING, *Oil Paste.*—Ivory black, 2 lbs; treacle, 4 or 5 ounces; oil of vitriol, 2 ounces; tanner's oil, 5 ounces; (if this cannot be obtained, then use 4 ounces of best tallow, gum arabic, 1 ounce. Mix the oil and vitriol together, and let it stand 24 hours; dissolve the gum in a cupful of warm water; then add three table spoonfuls of best vinegar; heat it and mix with the oil; &c., and then add the Ivory Black, Treacle and white of two eggs. A superior Blacking.

BLACKING, *Another.* — A quarter of a pound of ivory black, a quarter of a pound of moist sugar, a table-spoonful of flour; a piece of tallow the size of a walnut; and a small piece of gum arabic.

Make a paste of the flour; and, while hot, put in the tallow; then the sugar; and, afterwards, mix the whole well together in a quart of water. *Hu.*

BLACK LACE, *to clean.*—Wind the lace round a board four inches wide. Make a lather of white soap and water, and then wash the lace with great care and a gentle hand; rinse away the soapy water with clean, milk-warm water; then let it gently dry. Next day make some good strong tea—black tea is best—and dissolve in it a little gum arabic, using about as much gum as one would sugar. Rinse the clean lace in this gum-tea several times. The tanning principle will restore the colour of the lace, the gum will impart stiffness. Before the lace is quite dry it must be folded backwards and forwards between the alternate leaves of an old book, and then pressed.

BLACK LACE, *to clean.*—Pass the lace through a warm liquor of bullock's gall and water; afterwards rinse in cold water; then take a small piece of glue, pour boiling water on it, and again pass the lace through it; clap it with your hands, and frame it to dry.

BLACK PAPER *for transfer.* —Mix well together fine lamp black and sweet oil, and a drop or two of turpentine. Apply it to soft sheets of paper with a flannel or a soft sponge.

BLACK REVIVER. — First dip the cloth in, or apply to the article with a sponge, a solution of bichromate of potass. Then do in the same way with a decoction of logwood, and lastly with a little solution of copperas; this makes a capital black. Cloth is best dyed when it is boiled a little. *Gu.*

BLACK SALVE, or, *Healing Salve.*—Olive Oil, 1 pint; Common Resin, ½ ounce; Bees' wax, ¼ ounce; Venice Turpentine, ¼ ounce. Melt, raising the oil nearly to the boiling point; then gradually add two or three ounces of powdered red lead while on the fire; do not burn it; boil slowly till it becomes a dark brown; remove from the fire, and add one drachm of powdered Camphor when it is nearly cold.—This is a first-rate healing salve, superior to most, is wonderful in burns, scalds, scrofulous, fistulous, and all other ulcers. Spread on linen, and renew daily.

BLACK STAIN FOR WOOD. —Pour one quart of boiling water on half an ounce of commercial extract of Logwood; when the solution is effected, add half a drachm of Yellow Chromate of Potash, and let the whole be well stirred.

BLADDER, *Inflammation of.* It manifests itself by pain and tightness in the lower part of the abdomen; the pain increases by pressure, there is a constant desire to pass urine, and great difficulty in passing a few drops; sometimes there is complete retention; the bladder may become enlarged, caused by the inflammatory action. In old people the chronic form occurs, and it is frequently caused by stone. In the decline of life, the common symptom is the difficulty of making water.

In painful retention of urine, hot fomentations of herbs, as hops, wormwood, tansy, camomile flowers, and a little valerian root, may be applied over the region of the bladder. Use also the warm foot-bath. Parsley tea with a little spirits of nitre and *best* gin may be taken. Take also the *Diuretic Infusion*, which see. Should these fail, use the hip-bath, temperature from 86 to 96, for half an hour; take also a tablespoonful of castor oil, and, if the pain is severe, twelve drops of laudanum. Warm injections are also serviceable. Add to the injections a little Tincture of Lobelia.

The following is an excellent remedy in affections of the bladder, particularly in old age:—

Solidified Copaiaba, Alcoholic Extract of Cubebs, equal parts. Mix and make into three or four grain pills, and give one or two three times a day. It has been known to act like a charm. It is invaluable in all urinary affections, and especially those which affect old people. It allays pain and irritation about the neck of the bladder, of the prostrate gland, and in the kidneys. In case of extreme pain apply the Irritating Plaster (which see) over the pubic region.

To strengthen the bladder, avoid all intoxicating drinks, exposure to wet, damp, and cold; sponge the lower parts of the abdomen with salt and water, and occasionwith vinegar. See *Urine*, or *Urinary*.

BLANC-MANGE, A RICH. —Simmer an ounce and a quarter of fine isinglass in a pint and a half of new milk; add the rind of half a lemon, shred very fine, two blades of mace, a stick of cinnamon, and sweeten to taste with loaf-sugar. Blanch and pound with a spoonful of rose-water, half an ounce of sweet almonds, eight or ten bitter; put them to the milk, and mix. When the isinglass is dissolved, strain through a new flannel, to half a pint of rich cream, and stir well. When it has stood an hour, pour it off into another basin, leaving the sediments at the bottom, and when nearly cold, pour it into moulds, jelly glasses, or custard cups. Two tablespoonfuls of noyeau will answer the purpose of the almonds. And the isinglass may be dissolved in a pint of water and half a pint of milk.

ANOTHER WAY.—Put one ounce and a half of isinglass into a basin, and pour over it a quart of boiling milk; cover it over with a plate, and let it stand till the next day; put it into a saucepan with the rind of a lemon, a bit of cinnamon, and a little loaf sugar; let it boil till the isinglass is dissolved, then add to it some orange flour and rose-water, and a little Sherry wine; strain and cool a little, wet the moulds in cold water, and pour it into them. Sweet and bitter almonds blanched, and beat in a mortar with a little rose-water, may be added, if agreeable.

BLANC-MANGE, *Arrow-root.*—Put two tea-cupfuls of arrow-root to a quart of milk. Flavour it with an ounce of sweet almonds, and fifteen or sixteen bitter, blanched and pounded; or with noyeau. Moisten the arrow-root with a little cold milk, and pour to it the boiling milk, stirring all the time. Then put it in the saucepan, and boil it a minute or two, still stirring. Dip the moulds in cold water. Turn it out when cold.

BLANC-MANGE, *Isinglass.*—One ounce of Isinglass dissolved in 1 pint of boiling milk, and flavoured with bitter almonds, lemon-peel, &c. If boiled for some time together, it will be fit for moulding. Stir occasionally while cooling. It is an excellent diet for an invalid.

BLANC-MANGE, *Oswego.*—Four tablespoonfuls or three ounces of Oswego Prepared Corn to one quart of milk. Dissolve the corn to some of the milk. Put into the remainder of the milk, four ounces of sugar, a little salt, a piece of lemon rind, or cinnamon stick, and heat to *near* boiling. Then add the mixed corn, and boil (stirring it briskly) four minutes: take out the rind, and pour into a mould or cup, and keep until cold. When turned out, pour round it any kind of stewed or preserved fruits, or a sauce of milk and sugar.

BLANC-MANGE, RICE.—Swell four ounces of rice in water; drain and boil it to a mash in good milk, with sugar, a bit of lemon-peel, and a stick of cinnamon. Take care it does not burn, and when quite soft pour it into cups, or into a shape dipped into cold water. When cold turn it out, garnish with currant jelly, or any red preserved fruit. Serve with cream or plain custard.

BLANC-MANGE, RICE.—Steep a tablespoonful of rice in ½ pint of cold milk for eight hours, adding more milk as it dries up, to keep it moist and soft. Boil half an hour. Flavour with almonds, or lemon-peel, cinnamon, or nutmeg. When the rice becomes pulp, place it in moulds till cool, when it will turn out.

BLEEDING AT THE NOSE.—Use wheaten flour; it forms a good styptic; snuff it up the nose. Tighten the garters; apply ligatures to the arms, and put the feet into warm water, to bring the blood downwards. To apply a cold wet cloth to the privities is effectual. When it arises from constipation, the bowels should be moved immediately.——Or plug the nostrils up with lint steeped in strong vinegar, and apply cloths dipped in cold water. The application of ice to the back, temples, &c. is also serviceable.——Or dissolve two scruples of Nitre in half a pint of water, and take a cupful every hour.——Or apply to the neck behind, and on each side, a cloth dipped in cold water.——Or wash the temples, nose, and neck, with vinegar.——Or snuff up vinegar and water.——Or foment the legs and arms with it.——Or dissolve an ounce of powdered alum in a pint of vinegar; dip a cloth in it, and apply it to the temples, steeping the feet in warm water.—WESLEY.

BLEEDING OF A WOUND.—Make two or three tight ligatures toward the lower part of each joint: slacken them gradually.——Or, apply tops of nettles bruised.——Or, strew on it the ashes of a linen rag dipped in sharp vinegar and burnt.——Or, take ripe puff balls, break them warily, and save the powder. Apply it to the wound, and bind it on. This will stop it speedily.——Or, take two ounces of Brandy; two drachms of Castile Soap; Potass, one drachm; scrape the soap fine, and dissolve it in the Brandy, add the Potass, mix, and keep well corked. Apply a little of this to a bleeding wound, and the blood will immediately congeal.—WESLEY.

BLESSED THISTLE. — See Robinson's Herbal.

BLISTERS, *Management of.*—Spread the plaster thinly on paper, or linen, and rub over it a few drops of olive oil. In this way the blister acts speedily, and with less irritation than usual.

BLISTERED FEET.—Before and after walking, wash the feet well in a solution of Sal Ammoniac—half an ounce in two quarts of water. Let not the stocking be wrinkled, or much mended, when you walk. Easy boots and shoes should be worn, and very smooth next to the sole of the foot.——Or, the best remedy for this is to rub the feet, when going to bed, with spirits mixed with tallow, dropped from a lighted candle into the palm of the hand.

BLOOD-ROOT; *Sanguinaria Canadensis.*—An American plant. It has great emetic and expectorant influence. It is tonic, narcotic, stimulant, emetic, according to the dose and form in which it is administered. In a large dose it produces nausea, &c. In small doses, it acts as a stimulant and tonic. Like digitalis, it calms the pulse. It is an invaluable remedy in diseases of the chest, lungs, and liver.

Dr. Beach, of America, says, " In plethoric constitutions, when respiration is very difficult, the cheeks and hands livid, the pulse full, soft, vibrating, and easily compressed, the Blood-root has done more to obviate the symptoms and remove the disease than any other remedy used. It is most useful in bleeding at the lungs, influenza, hooping-cough, and croup. It should be given in quantity to cause vomiting."

Thirty drops of the saturated alcoholic solution taken three times a day, cured a bad case of rheumatism in a gouty person. It is also of great benefit in Asthmatic affections, scarlet fever, jaundice, and female obstructions. In Water of the Chest, (hydrothorax,) doses of fifty or sixty drops should be given until nausea follows each dose. It is excellent in chest complaints, and excessive expectoration.

Externally, Blood Root is a great healer of the worst sores, ulcers, ringworms, tumours, (and taken as snuff, of Polypus;)—used as a powder, or as a wash. The roots are generally used; but the leaves have similar virtues. It is given in the form of syrup, extract, infusion, decoction, and tincture.

As an emetic it should be combined with Lobelia. If infused in vinegar, its effects, as a wash, are more powerful in sores, ulcers, tetters, and ringworms.

Dr. Tully asserts that in the subacute form of inflammation, which often precedes a rapid phthisis, or consumption, the cure may, in general, be trusted to *Sanguinaria,* (*Blood-root*) and Opium, after the previous use of aperients. In confirmed phthisis, it is of more value, he says, in combating and palliating symptoms than any other remedy.

Dr. Stevens, of Ceres, (1850) has seen the most marked benefit result from it in *hæmoptysis,* (spitting of blood.) For this symptom it was employed by Dr. N. Smith, and others, with remarkable success, some years ago.

As an expectorant in the first and second stage, its action is said to be certain to arrest the cough and freely empty the bronchial tubes. In the second and third stages, it is a remedy of some importance, that can be relied on.

I gave it in three cases of that condition of body, preceding the deposition of tubercle, although there was cough, short and feeble inspiration, and a general phthisical aspect. In one, a girl of ten years, there was an hereditary predisposition, and many symptoms of phthisis in the first stage were present, but no physical signs of the disease. She had taken cod-liver oil and other remedies without benefit, and was extremely weak and emaciated. After attending to the secretions, I put her on the compound sanguinaria powder nightly, which permitted me subsequently to give her steel, and to resume the cod-liver oil. Her health improved; the cough diminished and disappeared; she gained strength and flesh, and was restored to perfect health. In a girl of ten years, with a sluggish liver, jaundice, cough, but no deposition of tubercle, the same good result ensued, although the time was longer.

In the first stage of phthisis, wherein actual deposition of tubercle was going on, with all the symptoms well marked, in which cod-liver oil alone was not agreeing, I have combined with it small doses of the compound sanguinaria powder twice a day, with relief to shortness of breath, and improvement of the general health; and all the improvement has been attributed by the patients to the sanguinaria.

In the second stage, the tincture in moderate doses may be combined with other expectorants with great advantage, and will assist other remedies to cure; whilst, in the third, the relief afforded in a ready expectoration and complete emptying of the bronchial tubes is really marvellous. The expectoration becomes more easy, the breathing clearer, the spasmodic efforts at coughing less; and much improvement will result for a time in the last stage of this malady. Some bitter infusion may be combined with the sanguinaria, with decided good effect in the dyspepsia, or loss of appetite sometimes present. I believe the sanguinaria in moderate doses will be found a remedy of much service in the pretubercular and first stages of phthisis, either alone or combined with other substances; and that as an expectorant, in the second and third, it cannot be surpassed. It materially helps to prolong life even in very hopeless cases.

Bronchitis. In the chronic form, it is in general use all over America, as one of the most active expectorants. Dr. Leonard observes, that its acrimony renders it powerful in removing the tenacious phlegm, and which it is our object to get rid of. Dr. Wood, of Philadelphia—a name honoured in America, and well known in Europe—recommends the tincture, among other remedies, as well adapted for this complaint, four to six times a day, kept just within the nauseating point. It is used extensively in the various hospitals in Canada, and is found truly valuable as a remedy. Its value in bronchitis I have known for some years, and have found it more serviceable than many other expectorants, and one that promotes the expulsion of mucus in such a manner as to afford very great relief, with a feeling of warmth and comfort to the patient.

Catarrh, is much benefited by

this remedy. Equal parts of the tincture and of paregoric were found by Dr. Tully to afford most marked relief. It produces a warmth about the chest, which the patients find agreeable. It is much employed in cold in the head, promoting the discharge of mucus, and imparts a pleasing sense of warmth to the whole head. Dr. R. P. Stevens speaks highly of its virtues in this affection, combined with cloves and camphor, and taken as snuff. As a gargle it is very efficacious.

Asthma. The paroxysms of asthma are much relieved by it. I gave it with advantage to a female aged 57, who had been asthmatic since the change of life in 1850, and who suffered from frequent diarrhœa and dyspnœa, or difficult breathing. It completely dispelled an asthmatic cough in a female of 30, who had aborted a few weeks before. Among other cases, was a girl of 13, with hereditary asthma, and symptoms of stone in the bladder. She passed her water in bed, was fretful and irritable, and the urine was loaded with lithates. She rapidly improved under a suitable pectoral mixture and the compound sanguinaria powders, and in a little while was restored to perfect health. Its efficacy in asthma is confirmed by other observers, and amongst them may be mentioned Dr. Eberle, who speaks well of it. —It is most valuable in Hooping Cough. It should be combined with camphorated tincture of Opium.

Croup. Dr. Nathan Smith and others speak of it as a *sovereign* remedy in this disease. Dr. Bird recommends its use in the membranous stage, as an emetic, in the form of decoction. It expels the false membrane, and produces a stimulating effect upon the mouth and fauces. Dr. Barton pronounces it an excellent remedy in malignant sore throat, croup, and similar affections, in the form of an emetic and stimulating expectorant. Dr. Ives recommends it as highly useful in the first stage of croup, and must be given so as to produce vomiting. He observes, that many physicians have relied, for years, wholly upon it as a remedy for croup.

Diphtheria. Of the three forms of this disease, the simple, croupal, and malignant, it is in the two last that the sanguinaria will be found especially useful. In my own practice, I employ this substance as an emetic in the *croupal* form; it acts with energy, and produces a thrilling effect upon the entire mucous membrane of the fauces and respiratory tract, with a feeling of warmth. It alone, seems to impart vitality to the suffering throat, and I recommend it with the very greatest confidence.

In the *malignant* form of diphtheria, besides the most active treatment, as hydrochloric acid to the throat, &c., a gargle, of a warm decoction of sanguinaria in vinegar, is invaluable.

Scarlatina. Dr. Tully has used the decoction as a gargle with benefit, and Dr. Stevens, of Ceres, derived great benefit from full emetic doses of the decoction in the malignant form of scarlatina. It removes the morbid secretions of the mucous membrane of the stomach, œsophagus, and fauces, and tends to break up the morbific influence of the disease. In an epidemic of scarlatina, with symptoms of the most alarming character, Dr. R. G. Jennings, of Virginia, after the failure of almost every thing else, including nitrate of silver, found gargles of the infusion of sanguinaria in vinegar most efficacious. They effectually cleansed the throat of viscid secretion, and afforded much comfort to the suffering patients, allaying all irritation.

Rheumatism has been treated by Professors Smith and Ives, in the acute form, with the tincture or decoction, given till its operation upon the skin and system generally becomes manifest. Very many other physicians speak of its use in the chronic form. I have cured some cases of chronic rheumatism by the tincture and compound powder. In one, a female of 29, the subject of leucorrhœa and rheumatism, all the pains disappeared in a fortnight, and even the leucorrhœal discharge diminished.

Hepatic or Liver Diseases. In the Southern States of America, yellow fever, jaundice, inactivity of the liver, &c. from the nature of the climate, prevails, but the Sanguinaria has been found by Dr. Macbride, of Charleston, of utility in torpor of the liver, with colic and yellowness of the skin. Jaundice he submitted to frequent trials of the medicine with advantage. Dr. A. D. Wilson cured a case of enlargement of the liver and spleen in a girl of 16, by the tincture and extract. The evidence of its value in jaundice, is favourable by a host of careful American writers.

Amenorrhœa. It is an emmenagogue of some importance and power. Indeed, its first known use among the native Indian women was for this purpose. If the patient is plethoric and of full habit, large doses are necessary; and if combined with aloes, shortly before the usual monthly period, it will scarcely or never fail to produce menstruation.

Powder. The usual dose of this as an emetic is from ten to twenty grains suspended in water. It is preferable sometimes to administer it as a pill, to avoid the irritation of the fauces. Dr. Leonard frequently combines it with ipecacuan; the dose is from one to five grains, repeated according to the effect desired. Grain doses will produce a diaphoretic and expectorant effect; if given every one or two hours, it will then exert a sedative action, and reduce the frequency of the pulse.

Compound Powder. Powdered Blood-root, two scruples; opium, powdered, one scruple; sulphate of potass, powdered, seven scruples. Mix. Dose is from three to fifteen grains. It is probably the least irritating of all the preparations.

The Powder of Sanguinaria with Camphor. Take of Sanguinaria powdered, one scruple; powdered camphor, eight grains; powdered cloves, thirty-two grains. Mix. This is used in cold in the head, and proves very efficacious.

Infusion of Sanguinaria. Sanguinaria bruised, five drachms; boiling water, a pint. Macerate for four hours, and strain. The emetic dose is from half an ounce to an ounce, at short intervals, till its effects are produced.

Decoction of Sanguinaria. Sanguinaria bruised, six drachms; distilled water, a pint and a half. Boil down to a pint, and strain. Dose same as the infusion.

Extract of Sanguinaria. This and the powder, can be obtained of the Medical Botanists. The dose is from an eighth to half a grain per day. It is best to commence with a sixteenth, according to the strength of the patient.

Tincture of Blood-root. This, also can be bought. Will prove emetic in a dose of two to four drachms; but is rather intended to act as a stimulant to the stomach, expectorant, or alterative, for which purpose twenty to sixty drops may be given every two or three hours in acute cases, and three or four times a day in chronic.

BLOOD-ROOT SYRUP.—Bruised Blood-root, 2½ ounces; Lobelia, ¼ ounce; White Sugar, 1½ ounce; water, 1½ pint; gently simmer half an hour, till it thickens; when cool, add a teaspoonful of paregoric elixir. Take a tablespoonful occasionally; a child a teaspoonful, or less. This Syrup is very valuable in chest complaints, bronchial affections, coughs, and difficult breathing.

BLOODY FLUX. — Feed on rice, sago, and beef-tea. To stop it, take a spoonful of suet melted over a slow fire. Do not bleed.

A person was cured in one day by feeding on rice-milk, and sitting a quarter of an hour in a shallow tub, having in it warm water, three inches deep.

BLOTCHES.--Blotches or pimples on the face and neck are often the effect of some functional derangement of the liver or stomach. Lotions, in that case, do more harm than good. If they proceed from a disordered liver, take the compound colocynth and blue pill, (which a druggist will supply,) night and morning, for two or three days; then purge off with two or three doses of Epsom salts and senna. If they proceed from derangement of the stomach, take fifteen grains of carbonate of soda, six grains of rhubarb, and two of ginger, or cayenne pepper in water twice a day, and a compound colocynth pill every other day. Last thing at night rub the blotches with tallow, and in the morning apply fullers earth about half an hour, wash off with warm water and soap; and during the day several times with elder-flower water. Take also extract of sarsaparilla to purify the blood.

BLUE FIRE.—Nitre, 2 parts; sulphur, 3 parts; zinc, 3 parts; meal gunpowder, 4 parts. Mix.

BLUE FIRE FOR ROCKETS.—Fine zinc filings, 1 part, antimony, 2 parts; nitre, 4 parts. Mix.

BLUE FLAME.—Gunpowder, 1 part; king's yellow, 1 part; sulphur vivum, 2 parts; crude antimony, powdered, 4 parts; nitrate of potash, 14 parts. Mix, and sift through lawn.

BLUE FLUID FOR MAKING BLUE WRITING INK—OR BLUE BLACK.—Prussian Blue in fine powder, 1 oz., placed in a common phial, and concentrated Hydrochloric Acid, 2 ozs. poured over it. Effervescence ensues, and the mixture soon assumes the consistence of a thin paste. After 24 hours it may be diluted with 8 or 9 ozs. of water, and preserved in a glass bottle. The intensity of this colour may be lessened by water. It forms an excellent Blue Writing Fluid.

BLUE WRITING FLUID.--Pure Prussian Blue, 6 parts; oxalic acid, one part; triturate with water to a perfectly smooth paste, then dilute. Add a little gum.

BOARDS, *to scour.* — Brush well with soft soap, and soda, adding a small quantity of washing salts. To kill vermin wash again with salt, or alum, or with chloride of lime. *A. N.*

BOARDS, *to remove stains and grease from.*—Make a ley of pearl ashes, unslacked lime, and soft water. Let it settle and bottle it. When used, dilute it with water, and wash it very quickly, that it may not discolour the boards.

Should the first application not succeed, the operation must be repeated two or three times, or as often as may be necessary for its removal. To *remove Ink spots* apply strong muriatic acid, or spirits of salts.

BOILS.—Poultice the boil, and paint it with aqueous Extract of Opium, or Tincture of Iodine, or the *Rheumatic Liquid*, (which see) frequently. Renew the process every two or three hours. A piece of lint soaked in olive oil may be strapped over the boil, if the person is necessitated to do business. An aperient may be proper, except in weakness, when it is best to give weak Elixir of Vitriol and Quinine. Or, give two of the *Alterative Pills* night and morning, and the Compound decoction of Sarsaparilla. If a boil breaks, apply the *Black Salve*.

BOILS.—Apply a little Venice Turpentine.——Or, an equal quantity of soap and brown sugar well mixed.——Or, a plaster of honey and flour.——Or, of figs.——Or, a little saffron in a white bread poultice.——Or, a tablespoonful of yeast in a glass of water twice a day. Take an aperient.-WESLEY.

BONESET.——An American plant, and in America it is a regular family medicine. It possesses emetic, expectorant, and sudorific properties. As a laxative it acts gently without irritating the bowels. In fevers it is very valuable, relaxing the bowels and subduing the febrile symptoms. In rheumatism and influenza it has a good effect. The cold infusion is an excellent tonic. To produce a vomit, take one ounce of the powdered leaves, and infuse in a pint of hot water. Drink a cupful every fifteen minutes until it takes effect. To promote perspiration, take small doses frequently.

The root of the *purple* Boneset infused is most excellent for gravel, stone in the bladder, and all obstructions in the kidneys, &c.

BORAGE.——*See Robinson's Herbal.* All parts of this plant contain much mucilage; the stem and leaves contain the nitrate of potassa, and other saline qualities. It is tonic, demulcent; it is good in rheumatic affections, promoting perspiration. It is very cooling in fevers, &c. The flowers are sometimes made into a healing ointment.

BOTTLES, *to purify*.—Rinse with lime water, or water and powdered charcoal.

BOTTLE SEALING WAX. —Rosin and Linseed oil, and any colour boiled together, and then moulded. Boil over a slow fire, and carefully, to prevent ignition.

BOWEL COMPLAINT.—— Tincture of Rhubarb, 1 oz.; Syrup of Rhubarb, 1½ oz.; Laudanum, ¼ oz.; Essence of Peppermint, ¾ oz.; mix in half a quartern of the best brandy, and cork tightly. When required for use, take two teaspoonfuls in half a glass of warm water, and the pain will be almost instantly remedied. Sometimes sicknesss and vomiting are present. In that case take a wine-glassful of soda water, with two teaspoonfuls of brandy every hour or oftner. One drachm of the tincture of assafœtida, 20 or 30 drops of laudanum, aromatic powder, 2 drachms; oil of peppermint, 6 drops; prepared chalk, 1 ounce, will remove the pain and griping in the stomach and bowels. If not, add a quarter of a teaspoonful of cayenne pepper.

For bowel complaints in children, give tincture of kino, from 6 to 30 drops in a little warm water sweetened.

BOWELS.—*Keep them regular.*

—Neglect of them brings on all sorts of diseases, and many persons are apt to neglect them. Many years ago, an old gentleman at Greenock, left, at his death, a number of sealed packets to his friends, and opening them, they found a Bible, £50, and a box of Pills, with the words, "*Fear God, and keep your bowels open.*" It was good advice, though it might have been more decorously worded. If you were a doctor, you would be astonished how many violent diseases of the mind, as well as of the body, are produced by irregularity of the bowels. The old Greeks, who were always seeking after wisdom, but did not always find it, showed their knowledge and sense in calling depression of the mind melancholy, which means black bile.

BRAIN, *Inflammation of.*—It begins with inflammatory fever, a flushed countenance, redness of the eyes, pain in the head, disturbed sleep, dryness of skin, constipation, restlessness, irritability, pain in the stomach, a tendency to delirium.

It is caused by hard study, intemperance, grief, anxiety, stopping of evacuations, exposure to the heat of the sun, external injuries, &c., respiration deep and slow, and sometimes difficult.

The disease is a dangerous one, and often proves fatal in a few days, if not speedily arrested.

CURE.—Promote the evacuations. Remove constipation by purgatives, clysters, and mix nitre with tea and other beverages. Divert the blood from the head by restoring the circulation in the extremities—equalize the circulation. Bathe up the knees in warm water. In excessive inflammation, apply cups to the temples, and the nape of the neck. Perspiration should also be promoted as much as possible. Should the disease appear obstinate, put a mustard plaster between the shoulders, and to the feet at night. Frequently apply vinegar cloths to the head and temples. The less irritation, noise, light, and the better it will be for the patient. "Cold water to the head," says an eminent physician, "and tepid or hot water to the surface of the body, have a powerful effect in forcing the congested blood from the head, and restoring an equilibrium in the circulation.

The food must be simple and light, as panado, water-gruel, toast and water, or lemonade, light jellies, barley-water. Nothing stimulating must be taken.

BRAN BEER.—Good bran, 1 bushel; water, (to produce,) 18 gallons; hops, ¼ pound. Mash with hot water, and ferment in the usual way. This beer will cost about three-pence per gallon; two or three pounds of sugar, or four or five of treacle, improve it.

BRANDRETH'S FAMOUS PILLS.—Aloes, 4 ounces; Gamboge, 2 ounces; Extract of Colocynth, ½ ounce; Castile Soap, 2 ounces; Peppermint, ½ drachm; Cayenne Pepper, ½ drachm. Mix and form into pills.

BRANDY BITTERS.—Bruised gentian, 8 ounces; orange-peel, 4 ounces; cardamoms, 3 ounces; cassia, 1 ounce; cochineal, ¼ ounce; spirit, 1 gallon. Digest for one week, then decant the clear, and pour on the dregs, water, 5 pints. Digest for one week longer, decant, and mix the two tinctures together.

BRASS AND COPPER, *to clean.*——Gently rub the article with sweet oil, and then with finely powdered rotten stone; clean, and polish with fine leather.

American method.——Powder rotten stone, and put it into a pint of water, intimately mix, and add a teaspoonful of sulphuric acid. Apply, then rub off, and polish with the finest whiting. ——Or, wash in a hot solution of alum, and when dry polish with Tripoli powder.

BRASS WORK, *to clean.*——Rub the article first with fine emery powder and oil, using a piece of felt; then rub the article well with Bath brick, and lastly with fine whiting. Then rub well with wash-leather alone. This plan answers well. *A. N.*

BRASS ORNAMENTS.—Dilute one part of sulphuric acid with three parts of water. Apply it to the article; and then polish with rotten stone and whiting. ——Or, rub them with powdered sal ammoniac moistened with water, first heating the article; then rub fine rotten stone, or tropoli. Rub with a piece of felt hat, and good wash leather to finish with.

BRAWN.—Clean a pig's head, and rub it over with salt, and a little saltpetre, and let it lie two or three days; then boil it until the bones will leave the meat; season with salt and pepper, and lay the meat hot in a mould, and press and weight it down for a few hours. Boil another hour, covering. Be sure and cut the tongue, and lay the slices in the middle, as it much improves the flavour.

BREAD, *Making and Baking.* Currants should be well washed, dried, and set before the fire. If damp they will make cakes or puddings heavy. Before they are added, dredge them with dry flour, and a shake given to them which causes the cakes, &c., that they are put to, to be lighter. Eggs should be well beaten, whites and yolks apart, and always strained.

Sugar should be rubbed to a powder on a clean board, and sifted through a fine hair sieve. Lemon-peel should be pared thin, and with a little sugar beaten to a paste, and then mixed with a little wine, or cream, so as to divide easily among the other ingredients. After all the articles are put into the pan, they should be very well beaten, as the lightness of the cake depends on their being well incorporated.

Whether black or white plumcakes, they require less butter and eggs for having yeast, and eat equally light and rich. If the leaven be only of flour, milk and water, and yeast, it becomes tougher, and is less easily divided, than if the butter be first put with those ingredients, and the dough set to rise by the fire.

The heat of the oven is of great importance for cakes, especially those that are large. If not pretty quick, the batter will not rise. Should you fear its catching by being too quick, put some paper over the cake to prevent its being burnt. If not long enough lighted to have a body of heat, or if it is become slack, the cake will be heavy. To know when it is soaked, take a broad-bladed knife that is very bright, and plunge it into the centre, draw it instantly out, and if the least stickiness adheres, put the cake immediately in, and close the oven.

If the heat was sufficient to raise, but not to soak, I have had fresh fuel quickly put in, and kept the cakes hot till the oven was fit to finish the soaking, and they turned out well. But those who bake ought to be careful that no mistake occur from negligence when large cakes are to be baked.

BREAD, TO MAKE.—Put half a bushel of good flour into a kneading-tub; mix with it between four and five quarts of warm water, and a pint and a half of good yeast, put it into the flour, and stir it well with the hands till it becomes tough. Let it rise an hour and twenty minutes, or less if it rises fast; then, before it falls, add four quarts more of warm water, and half a pound of salt; work it well, and cover it well with a cloth. Put the fire then into the oven; and by the time it is warm enough the dough will be ready. Make the loaves about five pounds each; sweep out the oven clean and quick, and put in the bread; shut it up close, and two hours and a half will bake it. In summer the water should be milk warm, in winter a little more, and in frosty weather as hot as you can well bear your hand in, but not scalding, or the whole will be spoiled. If baked in tins, the crust will be very nice.

Rolls, muffins, or any sort of bread, may be made to taste new when two or three days old, by dipping them uncut in water, and baking afresh or toasting.

BREAD, *Adulteration in.*—See *Adulteration.*

BREAD CAKE.—Take the quantity of a quartern loaf from the dough, when making white bread, and knead well into it two ounces of butter, two of sugar, and eight of currants. Warm the butter in a tea-cupful of good milk. By the addition of an ounce of butter or sugar, or an egg or two you may make the cake the better. A tea-cupful of raw cream improves it much. It is best to bake it in a pan, rather than as a loaf, the outside being less hard.

BREAD, FRENCH.—With a quarter of a peck of fine flour mix the yolks of three and whites of two eggs, beaten and strained, a little salt, half a pint of good yeast that is not bitter, and as much milk, made a little warm, as will work into a thin light dough. Stir it about, but don't knead it. Have ready three quart wooden dishes, divide the dough among them, set to rise, then turn them out into the oven, which must be quick. Rasp when done.

BREAD, ITALIAN.—Make a stiff dough, with two pounds of fine flour, six of white powdered sugar, three or four eggs, a lemon-peel grated, and two ounces of fresh butter. If the dough is not firm enough, add more flour and sugar. Then turn it out, and work it well with the hand, cut it into round long biscuits, and glaze them with white of egg.

BREAD PUDDING.—Pour boiling milk over grated bread, and cover it close. When soaked sufficiently, beat it fine, and mix with it two or three eggs, well beaten. Put into a basin that will just hold it, and cover it with a flowered cloth, and put it into boiling water. To be eaten with melted butter and sugar, or preserves.

BREAD PUDDING.—Boil half a pint of milk with a bit of cinnamon; take four eggs, and the whites well beaten, the rind of a lemon grated, half a pound of suet chopped fine, and as much bread crumbs as are necessary. Pour your milk on the bread and suet, keep mixing it till cold, then put in the lemon-peel, eggs, a little sugar, and some nutmeg grated fine. This pudding may be either baked or boiled. *Far.*

BREAD AND BUTTER PUDDING.—Slice buttered French rolls, scatter over them two ounces of well-washed currants; beat up three eggs in half a pint of new milk, and quarter of a pint of cream, and four ounces of sugar. Put in the dish a layer of currants; then a layer of bread and butter, and so on till the dish is full; pour the milk and eggs over the whole, and add nutmeg; bake forty minutes.

BREAD, *Rice and Wheat.*—Simmer a pound of rice in two quarts of water till soft; when it is of a proper warmth, mix it well with four pounds of flour, and yeast, and salt as for other bread; of yeast about four large spoonfuls; knead it well; then set it to rise before the fire. Some of the flour should be reserved to make up the loaves. If the rice should require more water, it must be added, as some rice swells more than others.

BREAD CUP PUDDINGS.—Steep bread crumbs in a pint of warm milk; beat it with 6 eggs, 2 ozs. of butter; sugar, brandy, nutmeg, and a cupful of cream. Beat well; bake in tea-cups. *Ru.*

BREAD, SAGO.—Boil two lbs. of sago in three pints of water until reduced to a quart, then mix with it half a pint of yeast, and pour the mixture into fourteen lbs. of flour. Make into bread in the usual way.

BREAD SAUCE.—Grate some old bread into a basin; pour boiling new milk upon it; add an onion with five cloves stuck in it, with pepper and salt to taste. Cover it, and simmer in a slow oven. When enough, take out the onion and cloves; beat it well, and add a little melted butter. The addition of cream very much improves this sauce. *A. N.*

BREAD, *Unfermented.*—Take fine flour, five pounds; bicarbonate of soda, one ounce; pure muriatic acid, one ounce; water, one quart; salt, half an ounce; mix the bicarbonate of soda and the salt with the flour, and put the muriatic acid into the water, and then blend the whole in the usual way of making dough; bake it either in tins or not. Bread thus made has an agreeable natural taste; keeps much longer than fermented bread, and is more digestible, and less liable to turn sour or mouldy. The chemical action of the acid on the soda disengages gas, which, though it makes the bread "light," disappears in the oven; the result of this action is to produce nothing but common table-salt, which can be proved by mixing a similar proportion of the acid and soda in an appropriate vessel, when the taste of salt will be recognised.

BREAD AND FLOUR.

	lbs.	oz.	dr.
A peck loaf weighs ..	17	6	1
A half peck	8	11	0¼
A quartern	4	5	8¼
A peck (or st.) of flour	14	7	0
A bushel of flour ..	57	12	0
A barrel of American flour	196	0	0
A sack, or 5 bushels of flour, ...	288	12	0

BREAKFAST RELISH.—Roast fowl, cold, the same quantity of tongue, half the quantity of nice ham, and boiled egg, salt, cayenne pepper, and a small portion of powdered mace and nutmeg, all chopped fine, and then beat in a mortar. Pot, and pour lard over the same; but in potting leave out the egg, and use butter instead.

BREAST, *Inflammation of.*—The breasts of females are sometimes inflamed, swelled, and subject to abscess. In mothers these affections are painful, and prevent the flow of milk. A swelling in the breast may be reduced by applying the Bitter-sweet Ointment, and the Adhesive Strengthening Plaster. If there be chill, it must be removed by perspiration. For this purpose take the *Sudorific Powder*. Also, take a teaspoonful of best Rum, a teaspoonful of ginger, quarter of a teaspoonful of cayenne pepper; boil four or five minutes, and thicken with coarse flour, or ground elm bark, or slippery elm; put a little oil upon the breast, then apply the poultice, and repeat three or four times. It generally cures. If the pain be excessive, add a small quantity of Laudanum to the poultice. This generally cures.

In hard swellings of the breast, rub with sweet oil, or friction with Soap Liniment; a drachm of Compound Tincture of Iodine to each ounce will render it more effectual. The bowels should be kept gently open, to subdue the fever.

When matter has formed, it is best to let it break and discharge spontaneously; or it may be punctured with a lancet. An abscess in the breast will discharge a long time. The diet therefore should be nutritious, light and strengthening. A warm bread poultice is good for an abscess; it should be changed every four or five hours, and covered with oiled silk. When the discharge has nearly ceased, simple warm water dressings may be substituted, and then apply the *Black Salve*, which see.

BREASTS, *Hard.*——Apply turnips roasted till soft, mashed and mixed with a little oil of roses. Change twice a day, keeping the breast warm with flannel.

BREASTS, *sore and swelled.*—Boil a handful of Camomile, and as much Mallows in milk and water. Foment with it between two flannels, as hot as can be borne, every twelve hours. This also dissolves any knot or swelling in any part. WESLEY.

BREATH, *Fœtid.*—The smell may proceed from the lungs or the stomach, but in nine cases out of ten it originates in the stomach, and the following is a simple and prompt remedy:—Three hours after a meal take a large teaspoonful of a solution of six parts of chlorate of potash in 120 parts of sugared water, and at the same time rinse out the mouth well with the same solution. When the breath is tainted with onions, eat parsley and vinegar, or orris root, or gum kino.

Or, take a dose of rhubarb and magnesia occasionally; finely powdered charcoal has been recommended; also a decoction of camomile and wormwood. For impure breath caused by decaying teeth, chew Orris root, and Peruvian bark, or use the same as a powder. Or take charcoal powder, powdered myrrh, powdered cuttle-fish, carbonate of soda, and a drop or two of oil of cloves. Keep the mixture in the mouth as long as possible.

BREATHING, *Difficult.*——Vitriolated Spirits of Ether, 2 ounces; Camphor, 15 grains; Paregoric, ¼ ounce; Ipecacuanha wine, a tablespoonful; water, half a pint. Mix, and cork well. Take a teaspoonful when the breathing is laborious. It relieves at once.

BREAST PANG.—Called *Angina Pectoris*. This is a sudden and most violent pain across the chest, particularly about the breast bone extending towards the arms, attended with difficulty of breathing, and a sense of suffocation, seeming to threaten immediate dissolution. In the young, it arises from nervous irritability of the heart, or internal muscles of the chest; but, in old persons, it is generally accompanied with some organic disease of the heart or the coronary arteries.

Effectual relief may be obtained by quiet, rest, opium, and cordials. The part should be well rubbed with antispasmodics, as the ammoniated tincture of guiacum; or cause an eruption by rubbing the chest with the tartar emetic ointment. The bowels should be kept open by a laxative, as salts and senna. Take foetid spirits of ammonia, half ounce; solution of morphia, three drachms; camphor mixture, six ounces; mix, and take a table-spoonful every half hour till relieved.

If the paroxysm be violent, 30 drops of ether, and ten or twelve of laudanum, may be taken immediately in a little brandy and water. The *tincture of Lobelia* also is an efficacious remedy. (See Robinson's Herbal, article *Lobelia*) Take twenty or thirty drops, and gradually increase. The bowels must be kept regular; and if there be irritability and want of sleep take 15 or 20 drops of laudanum, or 6 or 8 grains of the extract of henbane at bed-time. Let the diet be light and sparing, the exercise gentle, the mind be kept easy, and avoid all spirituous and heating liquors.

Dr Beach says, 'Nothing is so well calculated to remove this affection permanently, as a long-continued course of purgation; even where it arises from disease or ossification of the coronary arteries of the heart. All mental exertion, violent exercise, overeating, ardent spirits, and excessive venery—indeed, all excesses, must be carefully avoided—cold and wet should especially be guarded against. The diet should be light, and easy of digestion."

BRENTFORD ROLLS.—Mix with two pounds of flour a little salt, two ounces of sifted sugar, four ounces of butter, and two eggs, beaten with two spoonfuls of yeast, and about a pint of milk. Knead the dough well, and set it to rise before the fire. Make twelve rolls, butter tin-plates, and set them before the fire to rise, till they become of a proper size; then bake half an hour.

BREWER'S BITTERS.—Quassia, 2 parts; cocculus indicus, 1 part; Italian juice, 1 part; water, 25 parts. Boil until reduced to 20 parts, then add copperas, 1 part. Boil to a syrup. Or, Extract of quassia, extract of cocculus indicus, extract of liquorice, sulphate of iron, equal parts. This preparation is used for the same purpose as the last, and also to give an appearance of strength to weak liquor.

BRIDE CAKE.—Take 4 lbs. of fine flour well dried, 4 lbs. of fresh butter, and 2 lbs. of loaf sugar. Pound and sift fine $\frac{1}{4}$ oz. of mace, and the same of nutmeg; and to every pound of flour, put eight eggs well beaten. Wash 4 lbs. of currants, pick them well, and dry before the fire. Blanch 1 lb. of sweet almonds, and cut them lengthways very thin, take 1 lb. each of citron, candied orange, and candied lemon, and half a pint of brandy. First work the butter to a cream with your hand, then beat in the sugar a quarter of an hour, and work up the whites of the eggs to a strong froth. Mix them with the sugar and butter, beat the yolks half an hour at least, and mix them with your other ingredients.—Then put in the flour, mace, and nutmeg, and beat it well till the oven is ready; put in the brandy, and beat in lightly the currants and almonds. Tie three sheets of paper round the bottom of the hoop, to keep it from running out, and rub it well with butter. Then put in the cake, and place the sweetmeats in three layers, with some cake between every layer. As soon as it is risen and coloured, cover it with paper and bake it in a moderate oven. Three hours will bake it.

BRITANNIA METAL, *to clean.*—If very dirty, rub them gently with finely powdered Bath brick or rotten stone and water; then with oil and turpentine and whiting; finish off with dry whiting. *A. N.*
Some persons only moisten with oil, and polish with fine whiting, or finely powdered rotten stone.

BRITISH CHAMPAGNE, *to make.*—Take gooseberries before they are ripe, crush them with a mallet in a wooden bowl, and to every gallon of fruit put a gallon of water; let it stand two days, stirring it well; squeeze the mixture thoroughly with the hands, through a loop sieve; then measure the liquor, and to every gallon put three pounds and a half of loaf sugar; mix it well in the tub, and let it stand one day; put a bottle of the best brandy into the cask, which leave open five or six weeks, taking off the scum as it rises; then make it up, and let it remain one year in the barrel before it is bottled.

The proportion of brandy is one pint to seven gallons. *Hu.*

BROCCOLI, *to boil.*—Peel the thick skin of the stalks, and boil for nearly a quarter of an hour, with a little bit of soda, then put in salt, and boil five minutes more. Broccoli and savoys taste better when a little bacon is boiled with them.

BRONCHIAL TROCHES.—Powdered Extract of Liquorice, 4 ounces; Sugar, 2 ounces; Powdered Cubebs, 1 ounce; Gum Arabic, ½ ounce; Powdered Hemlock, 1 drachm. Mix.

BRONCHITIS.—This disease is very prevalent in the English climate, and often proves fatal. The acute affection often passes into the chronic form. *Bronchitis* is derived from the Greek *Bronkos,* the wind-pipe, and has a reference to the *bronchia,* the ramifications of the trachea. It is an inflammation of the lining membrane of the passages of the throat, through which respiration is carried on.

The first symptoms are running at the nose, eyes watering, frequent sneezing, shivering, dulness, and sometimes pain in the head. The chest is affected, there is a roughness of feeling in the trachea, or wind-pipe, which causes frequent attempts to clear the throat. The fever runs high, there is great weakness, a troublesome cough, and difficult breathing, hoarseness, tightness and pain across the chest. The cough is soon accompanied with expectoration of a thin fluid, having a saline taste, possessing an irritating quality. As the expectoration thickens and increases, the pain begins to abate, and the breathing to be relieved. The pulse is not so violent and the fever abates. These are favourable symptoms; and especially so when the phlegm changes from a glairy liquid to a tenacious phlegm, and decreases in quantity.

The unfavourable symptoms are, feeble, frequent, and irregular pulsation, palid countenance, cold sweats, increased mucous, and the prostration of strength through the cough in efforts to remove it; the cough becomes less effectual to expectorate; wheezing comes on, and next a rattling in the large air-tubes, delirium, and suffocation. Frequently, the collapse is very rapid, inducing dissolution in two or three days.

CURE.—The loss of vitality in the system has caused a diminished temperature, chills, coldness of the surface and extremities, imperfect cutaneous functions and the effusion of impure blood on the mucous membrane of the bronchia; followed by irritation and congestion, and the secretion of mucous hinders the breathing. Nature requires the removal of these obstructions. Place the feet in warm water, and administer warm and mucilaginous drinks; as, linseed tea, barley water, with a little lemon juice; balm tea; gentle aperients, if required; foot-baths, and hot bran poultices to the chest. The surface of the body should occasionally be bathed with warm water and carbonate of soda. The vapour bath also is recommended.

Nothing is so effectual as nauseating medicines. The design of all remedies in this disease is to dislodge the tenacious and viscid secretion which lines the air-tubes, and the impure blood must be corrected and returned to the surface. Emetics have a specific action on the respiratory organs, dislodging the bronchial phlegm, and removing the tension of the parts.

Take 4 grains of Ipecacuanha powder, in a little warm water, every twenty minutes, till vomiting takes place. Repeat if necessary. Or take the following emetic:—

Lobelia, 6 drachms; Skunk Cabbage, 3 drachms; Ipecacuanha, 4 drachms; Cayenne Pepper, half a drachm. Powder and mix. A teaspoonful in camomile tea, every twenty minutes till it operates. It is most effectual in clearing the lungs from accumulated matter.*

Laborious breathing may be relieved by inhaling steam from a decoction of bitter herbs, or even hot water. Gentle perspiration must be promoted, and medicines employed to allay the cough, if troublesome. The following is a good mixture:—

Ipecacuanha wine, 1 drachm; Aromatic Spirit of Ammonia, 2 drachms; Carbonate of Potash, 1 drachm; water, 8 ounces; and if the cough be irritable, add a grain of Acetate of Morphia—take two table-spoonfuls every four hours.

Or, take Almond Oil, half ounce; Solution of the Carbonate of Soda, half drachm; Syrup of Tolu, one ounce; Syrup of Poppies, one ounce; Water, six ounces. Mix, and take two table spoonfuls every two or three hours.

Perspiration may be promoted by taking the Sudorific Powder. *See Sudorific Powder.*

Counter-irritants are sometimes effectual, as mustard plasters; and in extreme cases, small blistering plasters to the chest.

Dr. Beach recommends flannels dipped in a decoction of hops and wormwood, boiled in vinegar; the flannels to be gently wrung, and applied as hot and as often as possible over the bronchial tubes, or the upper part of the chest. If it produces an eruption, it is favourable.

The bowels must not be neglected, but kept open by gentle aperients, as castor oil, a weak infusion of salts and senna, according to the strength of the patient. This tends to cool the system, and di-

---

*These Herbs are sold by the Medical Botanists. Not many Druggists keep them.

nuisance, much care is necessary to get rid of them. Bedsteads should be taken to pieces at the beginning of the year, and each part washed with a strong solution of corrosive sublimate, or the joints and crevices may be filled with soft soap. If the walls are infested, the paper should be removed, and the walls washed with the corrosive sublimate. The floor, in inveterate cases, may be painted all round the skirting-board to the extent of four inches. As the corrosive sublimate is a strong poison, the bottle containing it should be marked, and a caution given to those who apply it.

Coal oil is said to be a sure destroyer of bed-bugs. Apply plentifully, with a small brush or feather, to the places where they most do congregate. The cure is effectual and permanent. Gilt frames, chandeliers, &c., rubbed slightly over with coal oil, will not be disturbed by flies.

BUGS, *to destroy*.—1. Corrosive sublimate, 1 ounce; muriatic acid, 2 ounces; water, 4 ounces; dissolve, then add turpentine, 1 pint; decoction of tobacco 1 pint; mix. For the decoction of tobacco boil two ounces in a pint of water. This mixture must be applied with a paint brush. This wash is *a deadly poison!*

2. Dissolve camphor in spirits of wine, then add nearly the same quantity of turpentine. Apply it with a brush to the bed, furniture, &c., infested by the vermin. The smell of this is very wholesome, but death to the bugs.—

3. Arsenic, one ounce; soft soap, two ounces; camphor, nearly half ounce, dissolved as above, made into a paste, and applied.

4. Use a strong solution of alum water.—Or spirits of naptha applied with a brush.—Or apply turpentine and creasote, or oil of tar.

BUGLE.—A plant growing in woods, ditches, swamps. copses, &c. *(See Robinson's Herbal.)* It is of great use in coughs, and the first stages of consumption, spitting of blood, &c. Amongst the doctors of America it is in high repute. Like Digitalis, though not so powerful, it allays irritation, cough, regulates the pulse, and equalizes the circulation. It has been described as "one of the mildest and best narcotics in existence." Administered by *infusion*, or decoction.

BUNIONS.——A plaster of Burgundy pitch should be kept over a bunion. Or, a piece of lint or linen rag wetted with a strong solution of Sal-ammoniac, to be kept on constantly wet.— Poultice them with housleek and ground ivy, dipped in strong vinegar.—Some recommend the application of caustic to the part; and also the application of leeches, and the Burgundy Pitch and Soap Plasters, spread upon soft leather. To be free from bunions and corns, especially avoid pressure from tight boots, shoes, and stockings; the last are very injurious, as they compress the feet by their elasticity.

BURDOCK. — *See Robinson's Herbal*. It has been successfully employed in scurvy, rheumatism, gout, and pulmonary complaints. It is a great diuretic.

BURNS AND SCALDS. *See Spanish Flies.*—If the clothes have caught fire, wrap the person in a shawl, coat, blanket, &c. very tightly, to extinguish the flames; or when these are not at hand, roll the person on the floor. Then gently disengage the clothes from around the burned surface. If any parts of the dress should stick to the burned part, do not remove them, but cut the clothes from around that part. The treatment for burns is applicable to scalds. *If the injury is merely superficial*, saturate a piece of cotton wool, or wadding, &c. with Tincture of Spanish Flies, *largely diluted with water*, and apply it over the burned or scalded part, and cover it with folded cotton or linen, &c. to exclude the atmospheric air. Saturate with the liniment as the cloth dries.——*If the wound is deep,* use the Arnica Lotion, (See plant Leopard's Bane,) instead of Cantharis. When the burning pain ceases, apply simple cerate spread on a linen rag, and cover well up. Liniments are better than Lotions, as they contain soap dissolved in spirits of wine, both curative of burns, &c. The Arnica Lotion may be obtained from any Homœopathic Chemist.

When the afore-mentioned liniments are not at hand, Cotton Wool, or a linen rag may be well saturated in oil and soap lather, and applied.

'A most primititve, yet very effectual remedy in the treatment of burns and scalds is *cow-dung ;* and from its being so rich in phosphorus, it must exert a specific, and a mechanical action to cure injuries resulting from fire.'

Apply a poultice of Elm Bark and milk, and when the inflammation has left, apply Black Salve. For very slight burns, the Black Salve alone will cure. The Slippery Elm poultice is a sovereign remedy, and has effected the greatest cures. Dr. Beach relates the case of a girl dreadfully scalded by falling into a large pan of boiling water, which scalded, and actually burnt or disorganized the parts from the back nearly to the feet. A poultice of Slippery Elm Bark, and Olive Oil alone, very soon arrested the inflammation and acute sufferings of the patient, to the astonishment of all. *The Elm Bark may be bought of the Medical Botanists.*

In all cases of burns and scalds, it is necessary to observe, that if fever should ensue, gentle laxative medicines ought to be given; as castor oil, or salts and senna.

In cases of scalding the mouth with hot liquids, gargle with a solution of borax, and then hold in the mouth a mucilage of slippery elm, swallowing it slowly, if the throat also has been scalded ; the slippery elm bark may be mixed with olive oil. Some recommend soap liniment, which is made by dissolving soap in spirits.

When a burn is only trifling, and causes no blister, it is sufficient to apply a compress of several folds of soft linen upon it, dipped in cold water, in which has been dissolved a little carbonate of soda ; to be renewed every 15 minutes, until the pain is removed.

Dr. Tissot says, In cases of blisters, beat up an egg with two table-spoonfuls of olive oil, or linseed oil, spread it on soft linen, and apply it to the affected part.

For very slight burns or scalds, the *Black Salve* alone is sufficient to remove the pain and inflammation; page 65.

If the skin is not broken, cover the part with a layer of flour or starch, place cotton wool over it, or a linen rag, and bind it over lightly.

If a blister has been burst or cut, use a cerate.

Where the skin has been burnt off, wet applications may be used ; the best is lime water and linseed oil ; one part of the former to two of the latter, well mixed.

Milk may be used to advantage

out and wash well. Boil in soft water till they are tender. Then make syrup of loaf sugar and water, and boil till they are candied. Add sugar, as required. You may regulate the taste, by adding cinnamon, mace, and cloves. When candied, dust them with fine sugar.

CAPERS, *to keep.*—Scald some vinegar, when cold, pour it upon the capers; tie close, to keep out the air. *Hu.*

CAPER SAUCE.—Melt some butter, chop the capers fine, boil them with the butter. An ounce of capers will be sufficient for a moderate sized sauce-boat. Add, if you like, a little chopped parsley, and a little vinegar. More vinegar, a little cayenne, and essence of anchovy, make it suitable for fish. *A. N.*

As a substitute for capers, some use chopped pickled gherkins.

CAPILLAIRE.—Take 2½ lbs. of loaf sugar, 2 eggs well beaten, 1 quart of water. Simmer it one hour, skim it, let it cool; boil and skim, and add 2 ozs. of orange flower water and 4 tablespoonfuls of brandy. Strain and bottle for use. A spoonful in a tumbler of water makes a pleasant beverage.

CARBUNCLE.—A carbuncle is a species of boil, but larger, and much more painful. It shows debility in the constitution.—Give a mild aperient, rendered tonic by the addition of quinine. Foment the part with bitter herbs, or steam it with the same. Linseed meal, and slippery elm bark, well boiled, make an excellent poultice. Or of poplar bark and slippery elm, and a few drops of tincture of myrrh. When the poultice is taken off, wash well with a decoction of bayberry. The *Vegetable Caustic,* and the *Black Salve,* are good remedies. Every time the place is dressed, it should be well washed with soap and water, or weak tincture of myrrh and water. The diet must be light and nourishing; the patient must take exercise in the open air. When the tongue indicates no fever, give tonic bitters.

CARMINATIVES.—Rind of Seville oranges, 3 drachms; fresh lemon peel, 2 drachms; ginger, in powder, ½ drachm; boiling water, 8 ozs. Infuse 2 hours, and strain. Then take of the above, ½ oz.; spirit of peppermint, ½ drachm; spirit of lavender, ½ drachm.

Antiflatulent mixture.—Oil of aniseeds, 10 drops; refined sugar, 1 drachm. Beat up together, and add, tincture of ginger, 2 drachms; peppermint water, 6 ozs. Mix; three tablespoonfuls when needful.

Another.—Assafœtida, 6 grains; rhubarb, 4 grains; oil of aniseeds, 5 drops. Make two pills, and take every five or six hours.

CARMINATIVE DROPS; *for expelling wind.*—Angelica, 2 ounces; Lady's Slipper, 1 ounce; Sweet Flag, ¼ ounce; Anise, 1 ounce; Fennel Seed, ½ ounce; Catnep Flowers, 1 ounce; Motherwort, 1 ounce; Pleurisy Root, 2 ounces. Infuse in a pint of Spirits of wine for three or four days, oft shaking, keeping it in a warm place; then add a pint of water, and a table-spoonful of Tincture of Cayenne. Excellent in flatulency, colic, nervous affections, promoting perspiration, and refreshing sleep.

Another Receipt.—Anise, Dill, Fennel Seed, of each ½ ounce, Catnep Flowers, and Motherwort, of each, 1 ounce; Pleurisy root, 4 ounces. Infuse in Brandy for 22 hours, and then strain; To children, give from five to fifty drops; and to adults, from one to four teaspoonfuls, every three or four hours.—It eases pain, produces perspiration and sleep, removes flatulency, colic, and is an excellent nervine.

CARMINATIVE PURGATIVE.—Tincture of senna, 1 oz.; powder of aloes, 10 grains; peppermint water, 3 ozs.; syrup of ginger, 1 oz. Two table-spoonfuls for a dose, repeated in three hours if necessary.

CARNATION LIP SALVE.—Olive oil, ½ lb; alkanet root, ½ oz. macerate with heat, until the oil is well coloured; then add white wax, 3 ozs.; spermaceti, 3 ozs.; oil of lavender, 15 drops; essence of bergamot, 15 drops.

CARP OR TENCH.—Clean and scale; wash and dry them; dredge them well with flour; fry them in lard, or dripping, until of a light brown; then put them into a saucepan with gravy, port wine, and a little water if requisite; add a table-spoonful of browning, the same of walnut ketchup, and cayenne pepper to taste. Stick an onion all over with cloves; add it and two bay leaves to the rest of the ingredients. Stew gently over a slow fire until the gravy is reduced to a sufficient quantity to cover the fish when they are served; take the fish out and place carefully upon the dish for table; put the gravy again upon the fire, and thicken it with flour and butter; boil for a few minutes, and strain it over the fish. A sprig of myrtle placed in the mouth of each fish forms a pretty garnish.

CARP, *to fry.*—Split a carp at the back, flatten the back bone, and marinate it about two hours, with a glass of vinegar and water, parsley, shalots, a clove of garlic, two of spices, thyme, whole pepper, and salt; drain, and flour it over, fry on a smart fire, and serve with fried parsley. *Hu.*

CARPETS, *to clean.*—Take up the carpet, and let it be well beaten; then laid down, and brushed on both sides with a hand brush, turn it the right side upwards, and scour it with ox gall, and soap and water, very clean, and dry it with linen cloths; then lay it on grass, or hang it up to dry.

Newly-cut grass is much better than tea-leaves for sweeping carpets. *Hu.*

CARPETS, *Soiled.*— Beat all the dust out. Then take 2 gallons of water, ½ lb. of soft soap, well dissolved in it, and 4 ozs. of liquid ammonia. Dip in it a flannel, and rub the carpet well with it, and afterwards with a dry cloth.

CARRAWAY BRANDY, *to make.*—Steep an ounce of carraway seeds, and six ounces of loaf sugar, in a quart of brandy; let it stand nine days, and then draw it off. *Hu.*

CARRAWAY CAKES.—Sift 2 lbs. of fine sugar, 2 lbs. of flour; mix, and sieve into the bowl; butter, 2 lbs.; 18 eggs, leaving out 8 of the whites; add 4 ozs. candied orange, and 2 ozs. carraway seeds; work the butter with rose-water; then put in flour and sugar gradually, and the eggs with a glassful or two of sherry wine; beat constantly, till you put into the hoop for the oven. Buttered paper must be placed underneath. You may add allspice, ginger, and nutmeg, as you like. Sift fine sugar upon them.

CARRAWAY SEED BISCUITS.—Make as other biscuits, adding carraway seeds.

CARRIER SAUCE.-Chop fine 6 shalots; boil with ½ pint of good gravy, a little vinegar, salt, and pepper.

CARROTS BOILED.-Scrape, wash, and clean them; if large, cut them into two or four pieces, set them over the fire in boiling water with some salt in it. and boil them for two or three hours. Very young carrots will only require one hour.

CARROTS, *to prepare.*—Scrape clean, put them into the pan, when enough, take out, rub them in a cloth. Slice them into a plate, and pour melted butter, pepper, and salt over them. If young carrots, boil half an hour, if large, an hour; old carrots will take two hours boiling. Some cooks mash them, and add milk or cream. *Far.*

CARROT PUDDING.—Boil a large carrot tender; then bruise it in a marble mortar, and mix with it a spoonful of biscuit-powder, or three or four sweet biscuits without seeds, four yolks and two whites of eggs, a pint of cream either raw or scalded, a little ratafia, a large spoonful of orange or rose-water, a quarter of a nutmeg, and two ounces of sugar. Bake it in a shallow dish lined with paste, and turn it out to serve with a little sugar dusted over. *Ru.*

CARROT SOUP.—Put some beef-bones, with four quarts of the liquor in which a leg of mutton or beef has been boiled, two large onions, a turnip, pepper and salt into a saucepan, and stew for three hours. Have ready six large carrots, scraped and cut thin, strain the soup on them, and stew them till soft enough to pulp through a hair-sieve or coarse cloth, then boil the pulp with the soup, which is to be as thick as peas-soup. Use two wooden spoons to rub the carrots through. Make the soup the day before it is to be used. Add Cayenne. Pulp only the red part of the carrot, and not the yellow. *Ru.*

CARROT SOUP.—The liquor in which you have boiled mutton or veal, or a gravy drawn from beef bones, will make a sufficient foundation to this excellent soup; put a couple of quarts of either of these into a stewpan, then scrape six large carrots, and cut off the red portion; put that, with a head of celery and onion both cut up, into the stew-pan, cover down close, and set it near the fire, or in a very slow oven, for two hours and a half; if you do not find the carrots quite soft by this time, give them another half hour's simmering; force the vegetables through a sieve by the aid of a wooden spoon, and if you find the pulp mixed with the liquor, is too thick for soup, add more broth; season with salt and pepper to your taste. Warm before sending to the table. Serve with toasted bread.

CARROTS, *Stewed.*—Half boil, then nicely scrape, and slice them into a stew-pan. Put to them half a tea-cupful of any weak broth, some pepper, and salt, and half a cupful of cream; simmer them till they are very tender, but not broken. Before serving rub a very little flour with a bit of butter, and warm up with them. If approved, chopped parsley may be added ten minutes before the carrots are served. *Ru.*

CASCARILLA, *Tincture of.*—Cascarilla bark, powdered, 2 ozs; proof spirit, 1 pint; digest with a gentle heat for seven days, and strain. A valuable stimulant of great use in gout; it gives tone and system to the stomach. Two drachms three times per day.

CASKS, *to sweeten.*—To scour casks effectually rinse them with a solution of vitriol and water, which will entirely deprive them of their foulness.

CASTOR OIL.—A valuable and safe aperient. It acts speedily, effectually cleanses the bowels, without leaving any tendency to constipation. The dose is one or two table-spoonfuls. To most it is disagreeable, and it requires to be disguised. A good way is to take it in meal and water, or barley water, or brandy and water, or in milk well mixed, or in coffee, or in orange juice. Some eat a little orange or lemon peel, previously to taking it.

CASTOR OIL, *French way of giving it to Children.*—Pour the oil into a pan over a moderate fire; break an egg into it, and stir up; when it is done, add a little salt or sugar, or some currant jelly. The sick child will eat it agreeably, and never discover the disguise.

CASTS OF PLASTER, *to harden*—Immerse them in a solution of alum to about 84° Fah., for about five hours; 1lb. of alum dissolved in 4 or 5 gallons of water will form the solution.

CATARRH.—This comprises *a cold in the head, or influenza.*—Both begin with chilliness, sneezing, bad appetite, running at the nose, red and watery eyes, fever, &c. It is inflammation of the mucus membrane of the nostrils, or bronchial passages. Sometimes there is a slight cough only, and sometimes a harrassing one. It is caused by exposure to cold or wet, damp, epidemic poison. To cure, let the diet be low, drink toast and water, warm gruel, or barley water acidulated with a little lemon or cream of tartar. Bathe the feet at bed-time in hot water. Use the vapour bath, or wrap hot bricks in cloths or flannels dipped in vinegar and water, to the feet and sides. Should the cough be troublesome, take a cough pill or the pulmonary syrup.

CATECHU-An extract obtained from an acacia tree, growing in Hindostan.—It is a most valuable astringent in looseness, dysentery, or flux, bleeding from the anus or womb, the whites, and obstinate coughs. It makes an excellent gargle for relaxation of the uvula, or the body which hangs down from the soft part of the palate. It may be sucked in the mouth for that purpose, and for curing sponginess of the gums. It makes an excellent dentrifice, combined with Peruvian bark and myrrh. The extract, say $2\frac{1}{2}$ ozs.; 2 ozs. resin; 10 ozs. of olive oil, with a very little water; is most efficacious in ulcers. Melt and mix.

CATERPILLARS, *to destroy.* Syringe the trees with decoction of tobacco, or a solution of alum, or dust the tree with dust from the common road, and in a day or two wash off with clean water.

CATHARTICS. — Medicines increasing the discharge from the bowels.

CATHARTIC POWDER.—Best senna, ginger, camomile flowers, of each 1 oz.; jalap, $\frac{1}{2}$ oz. Powder fine, and mix well. Take from half to a teaspoonful in warm water or tea. This is a valuable aperient; it is powerful, and yet mild; effectually cleanses the bowels, and produces a healthy action in them, and also upon the liver.

CATNEP.-An American plant. —It is carminative, diaphoretic, and refrigerant. It produces perspiration effectually, and is most useful in colds; throwing off fever, and restoring to health rapidly. It is good for nervous complaints, indigestion, wind, colic, and is very suitable for infants and children in belly-ache, flatulency, &c. Dose; infuse a small quantity in a pint of boiling water. It is a good fomenter in swellings.

CATTLE, TO ASCERTAIN THE WEIGHT OF.—Measure the girt close behind the shoulder, and the length from the fore part of the shoulder-blade along the back to the bone at the tail, which is in a vertical line with the buttock, both in feet. Multiply the square of the girt, expressed in feet, by five times the length, and divide the product by 21; the quotient is the weight, nearly, of the four quarters, in stones of 14 lbs. avoirdupoise. For example, if the girt be $6\frac{1}{2}$ feet, and the length $5\frac{1}{4}$ feet, we shall have $6\frac{1}{2}$ multiplied by $6\frac{1}{2}$ equal to $42\frac{1}{4}$, and $5\frac{1}{4}$ multiplied by 5 equal to $26\frac{1}{4}$; then $42\frac{1}{4}$ multiplied by $26\frac{1}{4}$ is equal to 1,109 1-16th, and this divided by 21, gives 52 4-5ths stones nearly, or 52 stones 11lbs. It is to be observed, however, that in very fat cattle the four quarters will be about one-twentieth more, while in those in a very lean state they will be one-twentieth less than the weight obtained by the rule. The four-quarters are little more than half the weight of the living animal; the skin weighing about the eighteenth part, and the tallow about the twelfth part of the whole.

CAULIFLOWERS, *to boil.*—Strip the leaves which you do not intend to use, and put the cauliflowers into salt and water some time to force out snails, worms, &c. Boil them twelve minutes on a drainer in plenty of water, then add salt, and boil five or six minutes longer. Skim well while boiling. Take out, and drain. Serve with melted butter, or a sauce made of butter, cream, pepper, and salt.

CAULIFLOWER, *to fry.*—Wash as before. Boil twenty or thirty minutes; cut it into small portions, and cool. Dip the portions twice into a batter made of flour, milk, and egg, and fry them in butter. Serve with gravy.

CAULIFLOWER, *with Parmesan.*—Prepare the cauliflower as before, and cut the stalk, so that the flower will stand upright two inches above the dish. Put it into a stew-pan with a little white sauce; stew till done enough, a few minutes; then dish it with the sauce round, and grate parmesan over it. Brown it with a salamander.

CAULIFLOWERS, *to pickle.*—Take the best and firmest cauliflowers. Separate the flowers into small parts, spread them on a dish, sprinkle salt over them for a few days. Then put them in jars, and pour boiling salt and water upon them, and let them stand all night; then drain them on a hair sieve, and jar them again, and fill up with the best vinegar, in which you have simmered mace, long pepper, white pepper-corns, &c.

CAULIFLOWER, *with Queen's Sauce.*—Make the sauce with a bit of ham, fillet of veal, cut into small dice, a little butter, chopped parsley, shallots, and a clove of garlick; soak this for a time on the fire; then add a few spoonfuls of jelly broth, and half a pint of cream; pour part off into the table-dish; place the cauliflower therein, boiled properly, and the remainder of the sauce over it; garnish with bread crumbs, and colour it in the oven with a little butter on it.

CAULIFLOWER, *with white Sauce.*—Parboil it; then cut into nice pieces, and lay them in a stew-pan with a little broth, a bit of mace, salt, pepper; simmer half an hour; then add a little cream, butter, and flour; shake; simmer a few minutes; serve.

CAYENNE, *good Soluble.*—All cooks acknowledge the supremacy of Cayenne among the peppers. It is thus made:—Infuse 1 oz. of genuine Cayenne in boiling water, enough to cover it; let it stand on the hob for a couple of hours, and then pour the liquor through a fine sieve upon 1 oz. of salt in a soup plate; cover this down, and let it cool. The new crystals have absorbed the liquid, which can be rubbed up to any size required, and placed in a cruet-stand. These new grains will dissolve, and be free from the husk and seed of the pepper-pod.

CELERY, *Essence of.*—Soak the seeds in spirits of wine or brandy; or infuse the root in the same for 24 hours, then take out, squeezing out all the liquor, and infuse more root in the same liquor to make it stronger. A few drops will flavour broth, soup, &c.

CELERY SAUCE. — Wash well the inside leaves of three heads of celery; cut them into slices quarter inch thick, boil for six minutes, and drain; take a table-spoonful of flour, two ounces of butter, and a tea-cupful of cream; beat well, and when warm, put in the celery, and stir well over the fire about twelve minutes. This sauce is very good for boiled fowl, &c.

CELERY VINEGAR. — Infuse the root in best vinegar for 48 hours, near a fire, and renew, as needful.—Cress, Mustard, Parsley, &c., vinegar, may be made in the same way.

CEMENT.—Asphaltum and a small quantity of india-rubber dissolved in refined naptha, make an adhesive cement, not affected by water.

CEMENT. —A little ground borax mixed with plaster of Paris makes an excellent cement for many purposes. It is simply mixed up into a plastic consistency, then applied with a trowel. It soon hardens.

CEMENT, *a strong repairing.* —Professor Edmund Davy proposes as an excellent cement for repairing gutters, drain-pipes, pumps, &c., two parts of common pitch melted with one part of gutta percha. This compound is in many cases preferable to gutta percha alone, and may be dryed and preserved for use. To apply it to metal gutters or pipes, they should be warmed with a hot iron, and the cement be poured upon the leaky places. It is equally applicable to wood, glass, porcelain, ivory, leather parchment, and a number of other substances.

CEMENT, *durable.*—Common clay well dryed and powdered, then mixed with oil; it will last years.

CEMENT, *for Glass to resist heat.*—Equal parts of wheat flour, finely powdered glass, and powdered chalk; add half as much brick dust, scraped lint, and white of eggs.

CEMENT, FOR ROOMS.— M. Sorel has recently discovered a property possessed by oxychloride of zinc, which renders it superior to plaster of Paris for coating the walls of rooms. It is thus applied;—"A coat of oxide of zinc mixed with size, and made up like a wash, is first laid on the wall, ceiling, or wainscot, and over that a coat of chloride of zinc is applied, being prepared in the same way as the first wash. The oxide and chloride effect an immediate combination, and form a kind of cement, smooth and polished as glass, and possessing the advantages of oil paint, without its disadvantages of smell, &c." The inventor further suggests the employment of oxychloride of zinc as a paint for iron, and also to stop hollow teeth, for which its plasticity and subsequent hardness and impenetrability to the moisture of the mouth, render it particularly applicable.

CEMENT, *for joining marble, stone, &c.*—Hold the fractured

part to the fire, and then apply shellac and sulphur, melted together. This holds firmly.

CEMENT, *for joining Steam-Pipes.*—Boiled linseed oil, litharge, and white lead, mixed up to a proper consistence, and applied to each side of a piece of flannel, or linen, and placed between the pieces before they are joined. This will effectually join broken stones, and the seams of a water cistern, &c.

CEMENT, *for joining Steam Joints.*—Sublimed sulphur, 1 oz.; sal-ammoniac, 2 ozs.; fine cast-iron turnings, 1 lb. Mix, and keep dry. When it is to be used, mix with it twenty times its bulk of clean iron turnings or filings, and grind all in a mortar. Mix to a proper consistence with water.

CEMENT, *for repairing Copper Boilers.*—Mix powdered lime and ox-blood intimately, and apply while fresh.

CEMENT, *for mending broken Vessels.*—To half a pint of milk put a sufficient quantity of vinegar, in order to curdle it; separate the curd from the whey, and mix the whey with the whites of four eggs, baking the whole well together; when mixed, add a little quicklime through a sieve until it acquires the consistency of a paste. With this cement broken vessels or cracks can be repaired; it dries quickly, and resists the action of fire and water.

CEMENT, JAPANESE.—Intimately mix the best powdered rice flour with a little cold water, then gradually add boiling water until a proper consistence is acquired, being careful to keep it well stirred all the time; lastly, it must be boiled for one minute in a clean saucepan. This glue is beautifully white, and nearly transparent, for which reason it is well adapted for fancy paper work, which requires a strong and colourless cement.

CEMENT, *never yielding.*—Calcine oyster shells, pound and sift them through a sieve, and grind them on a flat smooth stone with a muller till reduced to the finest powder, then take the whites of eggs and form the whole into a paste. With it join the pieces of china or glass, and press them together for six or eight minutes. This cement will stand both heat and water, and will never give way, even if the article should fall to the ground.

CEMENT *to mend Stones.*—Mix ground white lead with as much powdered red lead to make it as thick as putty. Or, mix equal weights of red lead and white lead with boiled linseed oil, to a proper consistence. Effectual, however large the stone.

CENTAURY.—See *Robinson's Herbal.* It is a valuable tonic, promoting digestion, appetite, destroying fever, and worms. Infuse in warm water, or in brandy.

CEPHALIC SNUFF.—Take half an ounce each of rosemary, sage, lilies of the valley, and the tops of sweet marjoram, with a drachm each of asarabacca root, lavender flowers and nutmeg. Reduce the whole to a fine powder, and take it like common snuff for the relief of the head, &c.

CERATE, *White.*—Take of olive oil, ¼ pint; white wax, 4 ozs.; melt them together, and stir till the cerate is quite cold. This is a good soft dressing for blisters, cuts, &c., where the drawing plaster generally employed for that purpose is too irritating. *Ball.*

CHALK OINTMENT.—It is good for burns. Powder some chalk, and mix with lard.

CHAMPAGNE.——Raisins, 8 lbs.; sugar, 20 lbs.; water, 9 or

10 gallons; citric acid, 1 oz.; honey 1 lb. Boil the water and sugar half an hour. Ferment with good yeast. When the fermentation is nearly over, add 2 quarts of brandy. Bung well for 2 months. Then bottle, and put a lump of white sugar into each bottle.

Cider will resemble champagne, if you put a teaspoonful of carbonate of soda, 2 teaspoonfuls of fine sugar, and a table-spoonful of brandy in a tumbler, and fill it up with sharp cider.

CHANTILLY TRIFLE.—Bake a rice cake in a mould. When cold, cut it round about two inches from the edge with a sharp knife, taking care not to perforate the bottom, put in a thick custard, and some tea-spoonfuls of raspberry jam, and then put on a high whip.

CHAPPED HANDS.——Rub them night and morning with raw Linseed Oil.

CHAPPED HANDS.—Rub a little Glycerine, (which can be bought at any Chemists,) with a little Borax, upon your hands at night, and wear gloves in bed.

CHAPPED HANDS, &c.—— Wash with soft soap, mixed with red sand.—Or, wash them in sugar and water.—Or apply a little sal prunello.—WESLEY.

CHAPPED LIPS.——Clarified honey, a table-spoonful; pour a few drops of rose or lavender water into it. Apply it to the lips often.——Or, honey, 1 oz.; litharge and myrrh, each ½ oz.; melt, and perfume; cork well. *Hu.*

CHARCOAL, *useful properties of.*—All sorts of glass vessels and other utensils may be purified from bad smells by rincing them out with charcoal powder, after the grossest impurities have been scoured off with sand and potash. Rubbing the teeth, and washing out the mouth with charcoal powder will render the teeth beautifully white, and the breath perfectly sweet. Putrid water is immediately deprived of its smell by charcoal.

CHARCOAL MEDICINE.— It is much used in Mexico, and in South America, where few drugs are procurable, save those "simples" which the ingenuity and experience of the *Indian Herbalists* have devised. Freshly-burnt Charcoal, reduced to powder and given in water, is in great repute. It immediately removes offensive odours from intestinal and renal discharges, and purifies the breath, it removes offensive exhalations from any part of the body, either given in water, or in the form of pills, made up in wheat flour, or gum mucilage. It removes pains about the right shoulder caused by obstructions of the liver. As an antiacid, either alone, or combined with rhubarb, and carbonate of soda, it speedily and permanently removes heartburn. Charcoal is a powerful antiseptic, removing, or checking decay, and must be very valuable in the incipient stages of consumption.

CHEESE, *as iced* BUTTER.— Boil a pint of good cream a few minutes with rasped lemon-peel, and a table-spoonful of orange flower water; when taken off the fire, add 12 yolks of eggs, well beaten up; mix all together; sift, and put into an icing pot to freeze; whisk it like ices; ice it so that you may take it up with a spoon to serve like pats of butter stamped, and bits of clean ice appear between as crystals.

CHEESE, *to stew.*—Cut best Cheshire cheese very thin; lay it in a toaster; set it before the fire; pour a glass of ale over it; let it stand till it is like a light custard. Serve on toasts hot.

CHEESE, *to stew.*——Cut a

plateful of best cheese; pour upon it a glass of port wine; grate upon part of it light biscuit unsugared; pour over it two or three spoonfuls of hot port; then put the rest of the cheese upon it.

CHEESE *to toast.*——Cut the cheese fine, and put it with a little butter into the oven, or before the fire in a dutch oven; salt, pepper and mustard as you like it.

It is nice with finely chopped onions mixed with it. Better still with finely chopped onions and nice ham.

CHEESECAKES.—Strain the whey from the curd of two quarts of milk; when rather dry, crumble it through a coarse sieve, and mix with 6 ozs. of butter, 1 oz. of pounded blanched almonds, a little orange-flower water, half a glass of raisin wine, a grated biscuit, 4 ozs. of currants, some nutmeg, powdered fine, and beat all with three eggs, and half a pint of cream till quite light; then fill the tins three parts full.

CHEESECAKES.—Butter, 4 ozs.; powdered sugar, 4 ozs.; potatoes boiled, and floured through a sieve, 6 ozs.; three eggs, and 25 drops of essence of lemon. Line the moulds with a light puff paste, and fill them.—This makes a cheap cheesecake.

CHEESECAKES. —— Put a quart of new milk near the fire with a spoonful of rennet; when it is broken, drain the curd through a coarse cloth, breaking the curd gently with the fingers; rub into the curd ¼ lb. of butter, ½ lb. of sugar, a nutmeg, and two Naples' biscuit grated, the yolks of four eggs, and the white of one, 1 oz. of almonds well beaten, two spoonfuls of rose-water, and two of sherry wine; add 6 ozs. of currants. Line the moulds with light paste, pour the mixture into each, and bake in a slow oven from 15 minutes.

CHEESECAKES, ALMOND.—Almonds, 4 ozs., blanch and beat them with a little orange-flower water; add the yolks of eight eggs, the rind of a lemon grated, ½ lb. of melted butter, and sugar to taste; lay thin puff paste at the bottom of the tins; and little slips across. Add 6 bitter almonds.

CHEESECAKES, BREAD.—Slice a penny loaf very thin, pour on it a pint of hot cream, and let it stand two or three hours; then take eight eggs, ½ lb. of butter, and a nutmeg grated; beat well, and mix them into the cream and bread, with ½ lb. of currants, well washed and dried, and a spoonful of white wine, or brandy, bake them in moulds, or raised crusts.

CHEESECAKES, LEMON.—Boil the peelings of two large lemons till they are tender; pound them well in a mortar, with ¼ lb. of loaf sugar, the yolks of six eggs, with ½ lb. of fresh butter; lay puff paste in the moulds; and pour half full, and bake them.

CHEESECAKES, ORANGE.—Blanch ½ lb. of almonds, beat them very fine, with orange-flower water, and ½ lb. of fine sugar sifted, 1 lb. of butter melted carefully without oiling, and nearly cold; then beat the yolks of ten, and whites of four eggs; pound two candied oranges, and a fresh one with the bitterness boiled out, till as tender as marmalade, without lumps; and beat the whole together, and put into moulds.

CHEESECAKES, RICE.—Boil 4 ozs. of rice till it is tender, and then drain; mix it with four eggs well beaten up, ½ lb. of butter, half a pint of cream, 6 ozs. of sugar, a grated nutmeg, and a glass of brandy. Beat them well together, put into raised crusts, and bake in a moderate oven.

CHEESE SANDWICHES.—Take Cheshire cheese 3 parts, butter, 1 part, ham and veal 1 part each, and two eggs, a little salt, pepper, and mustard. Powder well in a mortar. Make into sandwiches.

It may be *potted* in a similar way, either with or without the meat; the eggs would require to be well boiled.

CHEESE SOUP.——Bread crumbs, ½ lb. sifted; 1 lb. of good Cheshire Cheese; simmer these together in a stew pan with some good broth; in another pan mix well together four yolks of eggs, and four spoonfuls of broth. Mix both when ready to serve.

CHEMICAL SOAP.—Fullers Earth, 1 oz. powdered; moisten with a little spirit of turpentine; salt of tartar, ½ oz.; potass, 1 oz. Work the whole into a paste with a little soft soap. Form into squares. - Moisten grease, and with a little water rub the soap well on till it lathers; the spot will disappear.

CHERRIES, *iced.*—Bruise 2 lbs. of cherries, put to them a pint of water; strain, and add sugar sufficient. See *ice.*

CHERRIES, *to jar.*—Stone 12 lbs. of cherries; put them into the pan, with 3 lbs. of double refined sugar; and a quart of water; put on the fire till they begin to boil; take off to cool a little; then boil till they are tender; sprinkle with ½ lb. of refined sugar, afterwards, skim clean. Put all in a china bowl; let them stand in the syrup three days, then drain, and take them singly, with the holes downwards, on a wicker sieve, and set them on a warm stove to dry, turning them upon clean sieves. When dry enough, put a white sheet of paper in the pan, and all the cherries, with another sheet at the top; put them on the fire till they sweat; cool, and put in boxes or jars to keep.

CHERRY BRANDY.—Cherries, 36 lbs; half red and half black; squeeze them with the hands, and add 1½ gallons of brandy. Let them infuse 24 hours; then put the bruised cherries and liquor into a canvass bag, a little at a time, and press it as long as it will run. Sweeten with fine sugar, and let it stand a month; bottle off, putting loaf sugar into every bottle.

Another.—To every gallon of brandy put 4 lbs. of red cherries, 2 lbs. of black, 1 quart of raspberries, with a few cloves, a stick of cinnamon, a little orange peel; closely stop for a month in a barrel; bottle off as before.

CHERRY JAM. — Pick and stone 4 lbs. of May-duke cherries; press them through a sieve; then boil together half a pint of red currant or raspberry juice, and ¾ lb. of white sugar, put the cherries into them while boiling; add 1 lb. of fine white sugar. Boil quickly 35 minutes, jar, and cover well.

CHERRY JELLY.—Cherries, 5 lbs.; stone them; red currants, 2 lbs.; strain them, that the liquor may be clear; add 2 lbs. of sifted loaf sugar; and 2 ozs. of isinglass.

CHERRY MARMALADE.—Take some very ripe cherries, cut off the stalks, and take out the stones; crush them, and boil them well; put them into a hand sieve, and force them through with a spatula, till the whole is pressed through and nothing remains but the skins; put it again upon the fire to dry; when reduced to half, weigh it, and add an equal weight of sugar; boil again; and when it threads between the fingers, it is finished. *Hu.*

CHERRY PIE.——Having made a good crust, lay a little of

it round the sides of your dish, and throw sugar at the bottom. Then lay in your fruit, and some sugar at the top. A few red currants put along with the cherries make an agreeable addition. Put on the lid; bake in a slack oven. *Far.*

CHERRY PUDDING.—Make a paste of flour, beef suet chopped small, and water. Butter a basin, and line with paste. Put in the cherries, and sugar; cover with crust, tie in a cloth, boil 1½ hour. *A. N.*

CHERRY WINE.—Pick and press out the juice of good cherries, White or Black Hearts, or May Dukes, without breaking the stones. (This wine is much improved by adding rasps, and red currants; an addition of black currants causes it to resemble port). To every gallon put 2 lbs. of fine loaf sugar. Put in a cask till the fermentation ceases, stop it close. In three or four months, bottle it, and in five or six weeks it will be fit to drink.

CHESS.—This is a very scientific game. The reader is referred to *Hoyle*, *Walker*, and *Lewis* on *Chess*. Each player has a force of 16 men, viz., a king, queen, 2 bishops, 2 knights, 2 castles, or rooks, and 8 pawns. They all have different moves. The King can only move one square at a time, forwards, backwards, diagonally, &c. The Queen is the most powerful of all the pieces; can move in straight lines, either forwards, backwards, or sideways, to the extent of the board, or she can move diagonally within the same range. The Rook moves same as the Queen, except diagonally. The Bishop moves either forwards or backwards diagonally, the full extent of the board, keeping on his own square. The Knight moves one square, and one diagonally, or one diagonally, and one square, forwards, or sideways, &c. He is the only piece that leaps over the head of another piece. The Pawn moves one square at once straight forward; but it takes a piece diagonally. If a Pawn reaches the other side of the board, it claims a superior piece, instead of itself, except the king.

LAWS OF CHESS.—1. The chess-board must be so placed that each player has a white corner square nearest his right hand.

2. If a piece or pawn be misplaced, it must be rectified, if perceived before four moves have been made.

3. If a player on commencing the game omit to place all his men on the board, he may correct the omission before making his fourth move.

4. Should a player, who undertakes to give the odds of a piece or pawn, neglect to move it from the board after four moves, the adversary may continue or recommence the game.

5. When no odds are given the players must take the first move of each game alternately, drawing lots who shall begin the first game.

6. The player who gives the odds has the right of moving first in each game, unless agreed otherwise. Whenever a pawn is given it is to be the king's bishop's pawn.

7. If a piece or pawn be touched, it must be played, unless at the moment of touching it, the player exclaims, "J'adoube" (I adjust).

8. While a player holds the piece or pawn he has touched, he may play it to any square but the one he took it from, but if he quit the piece, he cannot recall the move.

9. If a player takes one of his adversary's pieces or pawns without saying "J'adoube," or words to that effect, his adversary may compel him to take it; but if it

cannot be legally taken, he may oblige him to move his king; if the king cannot be legally moved, no penalty can be inflicted.

10. If a player move one of his adversary's men, his antagonist may compel him either to replace the piece or pawn, and move his king, or to replace the piece or pawn, and take it, or to let the piece or pawn remain on the square to which it had been played.

11. If a player takes one of his adversary's men, with one of his own, that cannot take it without making a false move, his antagonist may either compel him to take it with a piece or pawn that can legally take it, or to move his own piece or pawn which he touched.

12. Should any player by mistake take one of his own men with another, his adversary can compel him to move either.

13. If a player make a false move, that is, plays a piece or pawn to any square to which it cannot legally be moved, his opponent may compel him to take the piece or pawn to a correct square, or let it remain on the square to which he had moved it, or to replace the piece or pawn, and move his king.

14. Should a player move out of his turn, his opponent may choose whether both moves shall remain, or the second be retracted.

15. When a pawn is first moved in a game, it may be played one or two squares, but in the latter case the adversary has the privilege of taking it as it is named "en passant," with any pawn which could have taken it had it been moved only one square; a pawn cannot be taken en passant by any other piece but a pawn.

16. A player cannot castle in the following cases:—1st. If the king or rook have been moved. 2nd. If the king be in check. 3rd. If there be any piece between king and rook. 4th. If the king pass over any square attacked by one of the adversary's pieces or pawns.

17. If a player touch a piece or pawn that cannot be moved without leaving the king in check, he must replace it, and move his king; but if the king cannot be moved, no penalty can be inflicted.

18. If a player attack the adverse king without saying "check," the last player must retract his last move and free his king from check, but if moves be made subsequent to the attack being known, they must be retracted.

19. Should any player say check without giving it, and his adversary, in consequence, moves his king; or touch a piece to protect it, he may retract such moves.

20. If the king has been in check for several moves, and it cannot be ascertained how it occurred, the player whose king is in check must retract his last move, and free his king from check; but whatever moves made, previous to the check being known, must remain.

21. Every pawn which has reached the eighth square of the chess-board, may be immediately exchanged for a queen, or any other piece the player may think proper.

22. If a player remain at the end of a game with a rook and a bishop against a rook, or with both bishops only, or knight and bishop only, &c., he must check-mate his adversary in fifty moves on each side at most, or the game will be considered drawn.

23. If a player agrees to checkmate with a particular piece or pawn, or on a particular square; or engages to force his adversary to stale-mate or check-mate him, he is not restricted to any number of moves.

24. A stale-mate is a drawn game.

25. If a player makes a false move, castles improperly, &c., the opponent must notice it before he touches a piece or pawn, or he will not be allowed to inflict any penalty.

CHESTNUTS.——Roast them well, depriving them of husks. Mix four ounces of sugar in a cupful of water, and the juice of a lemon; put all together in a saucepan over a slow fire for ten minutes; serve in a dish and grate sugar over it.

CHICKEN BROTH.—Skin a small chicken, and split it in two; boil in a quart of water, or more, with three blades of mace, and a small crust of white bread, over a slow fire till reduced to half the quantity. Skim.

CHICKEN CURRY.——Remove the skin; cut up raw, slice onions, and fry both in butter to a light brown. Lay the joints cut into two or three pieces each, into a stew-pan, with a veal or mutton gravy, and two cloves of garlick. Simmer till tender; and before serving, take a spoonful or two of curry powder, a spoonful of flour, and 1 oz. of butter, and four table-spoonfuls of cream, and add them to the stew; salt to taste. Squeeze in a little lemon. A dish of rice, boiled dry must be served.

CHICKEN *and* HAM PATTIES.—Take the white meat from the breast of chickens, and 4 ozs. of ham cut small; put them into a stewpan, with 1 oz. of butter rolled in flour, half a gill of cream, half a gill of real stock, a little nutmeg, lemon-peel, cayenne pepper, salt, and a spoonful of lemon juice. Stir over the fire some time, but do not burn.

CHICKEN *and* HAM *potted.*— Bake the chicken in a close covered pan with a little water for about 30 minutes, adding, as you like, salt, pepper, cloves, mace. Broil or fry some ham, and pound both chicken and ham small, moistening with butter: place in alternate layers when you pot them, and press tightly.

CHICKEN PANADA.—Boil a chicken in a quart of water, till three parts done; skin it, cut off the white meat, and pound it to a thick paste with a little of the water it was boiled in; season it with salt, nutmeg, and lemon-peel; boil gently for a few minutes; let it not be so thick. It is very nourishing. *Ru.*

CHICKEN PIE.——Cut the chickens in pieces, and boil nearly tender. Make a rich crust with an egg or two to make it light and puff. Season the chicken and slices of ham with pepper, salt, mace, nutmeg, and cayenne. Put them in layers, first the ham, chicken, forcemeat balls, and hard eggs in layers. Make a gravy of knuckle of veal, mutton bones, seasoned with herbs, onions, pepper, &c. Pour it over the contents of the pie, and cover with a paste. Bake an hour.

CHICKEN POX.—-This is a mild eruptive disease, and seldom occurs more than once in a person's life-time. The eruption is attended with but little indisposition. There is a slight chilliness, weariness, cough, fever, bad appetite, &c. a day or two before the eruption appears, which resembles the small-pox. Treatment is simply plenty of cooling drinks acidulated, some cooling and aperient medicine, to keep the bowels gently open. Let the patient also be kept warm till the pox die away.

CHICKEN PUDDING.—Cut half a pound of good ham very fine, and a couple of chickens. Season with salt, pepper, thyme, nutmeg, and mace. Stew them gently, and in ten minutes, add a lump of butter. When half stewed, take them out, and cool. Reserve the gravy to serve with the pudding. Then take a pound of flour, a quart of milk, four eggs, well beaten, and salt. This will form the batter. Put a layer of chicken in a dish, and pour over it a portion of the batter, and so alternately till the dish is full. Bake it brown. Put an egg to the gravy preserved; give it a boil, and put in a sauce-boat to serve with the pudding.

CHICKENS, *boiled*.—Fasten the wings and legs to the body by thread tied round. Steep them in skim milk two hours. Then put them in cold water, and boil over a slow fire. Skim clean. Serve with white sauce or melted butter sauce, or parsley and butter. —Or melt 1 oz. of butter in a cupful of milk; add to it the yolk of an egg beat up with a little flour and cream; heat over the fire, stirring well.

CHICKENS, *to broil*.—Slit down the back, and season with pepper and salt; put them before a clear fire, at a distance, the inside next the fire, till half-done; turn them, and mind the fleshy side does not burn, rasp bread over it, and nicely brown. Let the sauce be good gravy, with mushrooms; garnish with lemon, and the livers broiled, the gizzards cut, slashed, and broiled with pepper.

Or, take a handful of sorrel, dip it in boiling water; drain; have ready half a pint of good gravy, a shallot chopped fine, and boiled parsley, thickened with a piece of butter rolled in flour; add a glass of port; lay the sorrel round the fowls; pour the sauce over them; garnish with lemons.

CHICKENS, to *braise*.—Bone them and fill them with forcemeat; lay the bones and any other poultry trimmings into a stewpan, and the chickens on them. Add a few onions, herbs, mace, a pint of stock, and a glass or two of sherry. Cover the chickens with slices of bacon, and white pepper; cover, and boil *slowly* two hours. Take up, strain, skim off the fat; then boil very quick to a glaze, and do the chickens over it with a brush. Serve with a brown fricassee of mushrooms.

CHICKENS *to fatten quickly*. —Make a paste with ground rice scald with milk, mixed with treacle. Give it warm in the daytime as much as they will eat, leaving none. It fattens in a short time.

CHICKENS, *to fricassee*.— Skin and cut in small pieces; wash in warm water, and dry; season with pepper and salt; put into a stew-pan with water, and a large piece of butter, a little lemon, a glass of white wine, one anchovy, mace and nutmeg, an onion stuck with cloves, a bunch of lemon thyme, and sweet marjoram. Stew till the chickens are tender; then dish. Thicken the gravy with flour and butter; strain it; beat the yolks of three eggs in a large cupful of cream, and put it in the gravy; shake over the fire; do not boil, pour over the chickens.

CHICKENS *to roast*.—Pluck carefully, draw and truss them, and put them to a good fire; singe, dust, and baste them with butter. Cover the breast with a sheet of buttered paper; remove it ten minutes before it is enough, that it may brown. A chicken will take 15 or 20 minutes. Serve with butter and parsley.

CHILBLAINS.—To cure chilblains, simply bathe the parts affected in the water in which potatoes have been boiled, as hot as can be borne. On the first appearance of this ailment, indicated by inflammation and irritation, this bath affords relief. In the more advanced stages, repetition prevents breaking out, followed by a certain cure; and an occasional adoption will prevent a return.

CHILBLAINS.—Take 1 oz. of white copperas; dissolve in a quart of water, and apply it occasionally to the affected parts. Let this be used before the chilblains break. ——Or, apply a poultice of roasted onions.——Or, wash with a decoction of horseradish made with vinegar and water.——Or, with a little camphorated brandy.

Or rub into them before the fire, a solution of white vitriol and sugar of lead. If the chilblains are broken it must not be used.—Or, take lard, 2 ozs.; turpentine, ½ oz.; camphor, ¼ oz.; melted together.

If the parts have been frost bitten, keep from the fire; immerse the parts in snow or cold water; then apply brisk friction, and a little camphorated spirits. To ease the pain, apply an elm bark poultice, or a poultice made of wheat bran, soft soap, and table salt. Apply afterwards the black or healing salve.

If unbroken, take sal ammoniac, 1 oz.; vinegar, ½ pint; bathe the part.—Alum and salt will do, but not so effectually—mix in vinegar and water.—If the chilblains are old, use the Stimulating Liniment.

CHILBLAIN LINIMENT.— One ounce of camphorated spirit of wine, half an ounce of liquid sub-acetate. Mix, and apply in the usual way three or four times a day. Some persons use vinegar as a preventive, its efficacy may be increased by the addition of one-fourth of its quantity of camphorated spirit.

CHILBLAIN LOTION.—Get one drachm of sugar of lead, two ditto of white vitriol, reduce them to a fine powder, and add four ozs. of water. Before using this lotion, it is to be well shaken, then rubbed well on the parts affected, before a good fire with the hand. The best time for application is in the evening. It scarcely ever fails curing the most inveterate chilblains by once or twice using. It is not to be used on broken chilblains.

CHILI VINEGAR.—Infuse half an oz. of cayenne pepper and six cloves in a pint of vinegar.

CHINA, to mend.—Burn oyster shells in the fire, and then reduce them to fine powder. Mix the powder with the white of egg, and lay it thickly on the edges of the broken article, and dry before a hot fire.—Some persons combine with the above white lead.

Common lime finely sifted and the white of an egg, make an excellent cement. The Chinese use finely ground flint glass with the white of an egg, and it is very adhesive. The pieces to be united should be well heated. Or, mix plaster of Paris with a thick solution of gum arabic.

CHIMNEYS ON FIRE.— Shut all the doors and windows; stop up the bottom of the chimney with a piece of water-saturated sacking, wraping, &c., throwing first salt, or sulphur, upon the fire.

CHINE OF BACON, to boil. —Soak a chine, salted and dried, in cold water several hours. Take a handful of parsley, a few sprigs of thyme, and a little sage; chop them very fine; stuff these into the chine, both in the fat and in the lean; skewer it close in a cloth. Boil slowly for two or three hours.

CHINE OF PORK.—Boil it half an hour; then make holes in

it; stuff them with shred parsley; rub it all over with the yolks of eggs, and strew over it bread crumbs, baste it, and set in a Dutch oven; when it is done enough, lay round it dried spinach.

CHINESE FIRE, *for Sky-rockets.*—1. If three quarter inch or under, nitre, 16 parts; charcoal, 4 parts; sulphur, 8 parts; east-iron borings, 4 parts. Mix.

2. If over 1 inch and under 2 inches bore, nitre, 16 parts; charcoal, 4 parts; sulphur, 4 parts; iron borings, 5 parts. Mix.

CHINTZ, *to wash.*—Use only a little white soap. Or boil sago, or rice to a *perfect pulp*, and use it instead of soap; the article may afterwards be washed in the pulp well diluted with warm water, and this will stiffen it beautifully.

This will be found useful for printed dresses whose colours are likely to give way by the use of alkaline soaps.

CHLORIDE OF LIME.— Scatter chloride of lime on a board in a stable, to remove all kinds of flies, but more especially biting flies. Sprinkling beds of vegetables with even a weak solution, effectually preserves them from caterpillars, slugs, &c. A paste of one part powdered chloride of lime and one half-part of some fatty matter placed in a narrow band round the trunk of the tree, prevents insects from creeping up it. Even rats, mice, cockroaches, and crickets flee from it.

CHLORIDE OF LIME.— *It is* a great purifier. One pound requires three gallons of water; use the clear solution. To purify rooms, sprinkle on the floor; and if needful, on the bed-linen. Infected clothes should be dipped in it and wrung out, just before they are washed. It purifies night commodes, water closets, &c.

CHOCOLATE CREAM.— Scrape into a quart of thick cream 1 ounce of the best chocolate, ¼ lb. of sugar; boil and mill it; when quite smooth, cool, then add the whites of new eggs. Whisk, and take up the froth on sieves, and serve it in glasses, to rise above some of the cream.

CHOLERA.—A compound of two greek words, *chole*, bile, and *rein*, to flow. Its literal meaning is, a discharge of bile. But the word *cholera* designates that dreadful Asiatic disease which is so very fatal. In this disease, the secretion of bile is suspended, and the evacuations are entirely free from it. Therefore there are two species of Cholera—the *English*—and the *Asiatic*.

The *English Cholera*, or Bilious Diarrhœa, attacks suddenly, with nausea, purging and vomiting; sometimes painful colicky griping in the bowels. The evacuations are thin and watery, and at last become very bilious, the colour sometimes green, at other times approximating to black, indicating vitiated bile caused by unhealthy secretions during its passage through the alimentary canal. If the disease is not restrained, the vomiting, retching, and spasmodic pain, increases, accompanied with cramp in the legs, and muscles of the abdomen. Coldness of the extremities, cold sweats, and fainting sometimes occur. Sometimes this disease ends in death, especially with old and delicate subjects. But in this country it is seldom fatal.

It is caused by intemperance, by a vitiated atmosphere, by eating unwholesome food, and unripe fruits. In the treatment of it, it is necessary to neutralize the acid, vitiated or acrid bile, and produce a determination to the surface. As soon as the symptoms appear, give the *Neutralizing Mixture*, (which see). If vomited, repeat the dose, and it will soon produce a beneficial effect, subduing the irritation, nausea, vomiting, and passing through the alimentary canal, changing its contents to the most healthy state. It is useful to bathe the feet in hot water and salt, and when the disease is violent, to give a vapour bath; and to check the vomiting, salt in vinegar or brandy. To allay the pain, foment the belly and breast with the following;—Cayenne pepper, ½ oz., spirits of wine, ½ a pint, vinegar a gill. Simmer a few minutes; then add a tea-spoonful of tincture of opium, and two table-spoonfuls of turpentine. Apply flannnels dipped in it warm to the stomach. Hops and camomile flowers simmered in vinegar, make an excellent fomentation. The drink should be toast and water. Milk thickened with arrow-root, tapioca sago, or slippery-elm, may be taken as food.

In the ASIATIC CHOLERA, there is a total suppression of bile, and a profuse cold, clammy sweat over the body; the cramps become fearful, the stomach and bowels are emptied by vomit, &c.—and exhaustion becomes apparent, giddiness, deafness, sinking of the eyes and nostrils, blueness of the skin, lips and nails; weakness of voice, &c., are often fatal symptoms.

To cure the same, as for English Cholera, but more active. Give the *Neutralizing Mixture;* and this injection;—Bogberry, 3 drachms; Scullcap, 1 drachm; Slippery-Elm, 1 drachm; Boiling water, ½ a pint. Infuse ten minutes; then add two tea-spoonfuls of tincture of Myrrh, eight drops of Laudanum, and a tea-spoonful of Carbonate of Soda. Foment as in English Cholera, or with the *Rheumatic Liniment*. Apply as hot as possible. Apply also friction to the limbs; or apply hot bricks, wrapped in vinegar cloths, to the feet, legs, and sides. Give a tea-spoonful of the *Anti-Cholera Drops* every half hour, which see at the end of the book.

The following *Anti-Cholera Mixture* is a sovereign remedy:—Tormentil Root, 1 ounce; Bayberry Bark, 1 ounce; Cayenne Pepper, ¼ ounce; Carbonate of Soda, ¼ ounce. Simmer forty minutes in three pints of water down to 1 quart. Strain, and add Tincture of Myrrh, 2 ounces, and 1 drachm of Camphor, dissolved in spirits of wine. In the first attack of Cholera, give a wine-glassful; place the feet in hot salt and water, or mustard and water, and repeat the mixture every twenty minutes, and apply mustard plaster, and the hop poultice to the stomach. Rub freely the cramped and drawn parts of the body with boiled Cayenne Pepper and Vinegar; and the effects will in most cases appear like magic. Such treatment has cured thousands upon thousands.

CHOLERA IN INFANTS is treated in the same way as English Cholera, but in a milder, and more restricted manner.

CHRISTMAS PUDDING.—Suet, 1½ lbs., minced small; currants, 1½ lbs.; raisins, stoned, ¼ lb.; sugar, 1 lb.; ten eggs, a grated nutmeg; 2 ozs. of citron and lemon peel; 1 oz. of mixed spice, a tea-spoonful of grated ginger, ½ lb. of bread crumbs, ½ lb. of flour, 1 pint of milk, and a wine-glassful of brandy. Beat first the eggs, add half the milk, beat all together, and gradually stir in all the milk, then the suet, fruit, &c., and as much milk to mix it very thick. Boil in a cloth six or seven hours.

Another.—Flour, suet, currants, raisins, of each 1 lb.; nine eggs; 2 ozs. of candied peel; almonds and spices, according to taste. Boil in a cloth six or seven hours.

CIDER CUP.—Grate nutmeg and ginger; put it in a cup with a well-browned toast; on these pour two glasses of sherry, or one glass of pale brandy; then add cider. A few fresh borage leaves add to the refreshing appearance of the cup.

CINNAMON.—This valuable spice comes chiefly from Ceylon. It is a most useful aromatic. Its effects are stimulating, carminative, tonic, and warming; but it is used rather as an adjunct to other remedies than as a remedy itself. The *oil* is a most powerful stimulant, and is used in cramps of the stomach, and in syncope, or in paralysis of the tongue.

CINNAMON CORDIAL.—Take 8 lbs. of cinnamon, broken; 17 gals. of rectified spirit, and 2 gals. of water. Digest in the still 24 hours by a gentle heat; draw 16 gallons by a stronger heat. *Hu.*

CINNAMON CAKE.—Put 6 eggs, and 3 table-spoonfuls of rose-water into a pan; whisk well together; add 1 lb. of fine sugar, a large spoonful of ground cinnamon, and flour to make it into paste; roll, form, and bake on white paper.

CINNAMON SOAP.—Good tallow soap, 10 lbs; palm-oil soap, 7 lbs; essence of cinnamon, 3 ozs.; essence of sassafras, ½ oz.; bergamot, ½ oz.; colour, 4 ozs. of yellow ochre.

CINNAMON WATER.—Take of cinnamon bark, one pound; proof spirit and common water, of each one gallon. Steep the cinnamon in the liquor for two days, then distil off one gallon.

Or, Cinnamon, 2 ozs. in 3 qrts. of brandy, with a quart of water, the rind of two lemons, and 2 or 3 ozs. of liquorice root; infuse five days, distil, and add 2 lbs. of fine sugar, and 3 pints of water.

CISTERNS, *to measure*.—Multiply the diameter of the bottom in inches by the diameter of the top; then multiply that product by the height in inches, and that product by 7, 854; divide the last obtained number by 231, cut off four figures at the right hand, and the quotient will be the answer in gallons.

CITRIC ACID.—It is cooling, allays inflammation, and is a substitute for lemon juice; in fact, it is the same.

CLARIFIED SUGAR.—Put 2 lbs. of finest sugar into a tinned stewpan with a pint of cold spring water to dissolve. Beat half the white of an egg; put it to the sugar, and stir; put on the fire, and boil gently till no scum rises, and it is perfectly clear; strain through a cloth, and closely bottle.

CLEAVERS.—The American plant is the best. It is a good diuretic, perhaps one of the best for curing all suppressions of urine, and gravelly complaints, scurvy, and spitting of blood. Infuse 2 ounces in a pint of *cold* water, and drink a wine-glassful occasionally. See Robinson's Family Herbal.

CLOTH, *to Raise the Nap on*.—When woollens are worn threadbare the part of the dress must be soaked in cold water for half an hour, then put on a board, and the threadbare parts rubbed with a half-worn hatter's "card" filled with flocks, or with a prickly thistle, until a sufficient nap be raised. If faded, apply the *Black Reviver*, which see. Then hang the coat to dry, and with a brush lay the nap the right way.

COCKIE LEEKIE.—A fa-

H

vorite Scotch dish. Take a scrag of mutton or knuckle of veal, and 3 quarts of liquor in which some meat has been boiled. Get a fowl, and a fine leek cut in pieces, with salt and pepper. Boil an hour and a half, then add five more leeks, and boil 1 hour more. Beef liquor is the best.

COCKLE KETCHUP.—Open the cockles, scald them in their own liquor; add a little water when the liquor settles; strain; season with pepper, mace, cloves, and other spices; if for brown sauce, add port, anchovies, and garlick.

COCKROACHES, *to destroy.*—Mix bread crumbs, sugar, and corrosive sublimate, and place it near their haunts.—Or mix sugar, laudanum, and water together.—They are very fond of beer, which might be substituted for water.—Some persons have found a mixture of plaster of Paris, sugar, and oatmeal, effectual.——Powdered phosphorous, oatmeal, and sugar, form a sure remedy.

COCOA SAUCE.—Scrape a portion of the kernel of a Cocoa Nut, adding the juice of three lemmons, a tea-spoonful of the tincture of cayenne pepper, a tea-spoonful of shallot vinegar, and half a cupful of water. Gently simmer for a few-hours.

COD, *to boil.*—If boiled fresh, it is watery; but it is excellent if salted, and hung for a day, to give it firmness. Wash and clean the fish well, and rub salt inside of it; tie it up, and put it on the fire in cold water; throw a handful of salt into the fish-kettle. Boil a small fish 15 minutes; a large one 30 minutes. Serve it without the smallest speck and scum; drain. Garnish it with lemon, horse-radish, the milt, roe, and liver. Oyster or shrimp sauce may be used.

Another way.—After cleaning well, put into the boiling water a handful of salt, a small cupful of vinegar; boil as above, as to time. Take it up; strip off the skin, put before a brisk fire, dredge with flower, and baste with butter; when the froth begins to rise, throw over it fine white bread crumbs; baste on to make it froth well, when a fine brown, dish it up, and garnish it with sliced lemon, horse-radish, oysters, &c.

COD'S HEAD AND SHOULDERS, *to boil.*—Wash it well, dry, and tie it up. Put in salt and a glass of vinegar. Frequently skim it. Boil half an hour. Half boil the milt and roe. Cut thin slices, fry, adding gravy, and a little port wine. For sauce, oysters, eggs, or butter and parsley.

COD *broiled.*—Clean as before. Cut into slices an inch thick; rub them with thick melted butter. Sprinkle a little salt and pepper over them. Place on the gridiron, and broil on both sides. Serve with parsley sauce, or melted butter and anchovy sauce.

COD'S HEAD, *to bake.*—Clean well; put in a dish rubbed with butter. Put in sweet herbs, an onion stuck with cloves, three blades of mace, pepper, nutmeg, lemon peel, horse radish, and 1 quart of water; dust and grate flour and nutmeg over it, and put bits of butter in various parts, and place in the oven. When done, place in the serving dish. Pour all the liquor out of the dish in which it was baked into a saucepan, and boil three minutes; strain, and add a gill of red wine, two spoonfuls of ketchup, a pint of shrimps, half a pint of oysters, a spoonful of mushroom pickle, and 4 ozs. of butter rolled in flour. Garnish with toasted bread, parsley, lemon, and horse-radish.

COD, *to fry.*—Cut the cod in slices about 1½ inch thick, and dry and flour them well. Make a good clear fire; rub the gridiron with a piece of chalk, and place it high from the fire. Turn often till they are enough, and of a fine brown. Be careful, or they will break.— Or do them in a dish in the oven, with a little butter, vinegar, or lemon, and salt and pepper. Serve with lobster or shrimp sauce. A.N.

COD, *Egg Sauce for Salted.*— Boil the eggs hard; half chop the whites, put in the yolks, and chop all together, but not very small; put them into ½ lb. of good melted butter, and boil up; then put it on the fish. *Rf.*

COD LIVER OIL. — This is very good in debility, in wasting diseases, in the incipient stages of consumption, in chest diseases, rheumatism, gout, rigid limbs, &c. It should be taken freely. Yet some people are unable to retain and digest this useful remedy. In such cases, it should be taken in milk, or orange wine, bitter ale, cinnamon water, cold coffee, &c.

COFFEE.—It is a tonic and stimulating beverage, of a wholesome nature.—*To make Coffee.* Use the best. For eight cups, use nearly eight cups of water; put in coffee as much as you like; a solution of isinglass; boil a minute, take off, and throw in a cup of cold water to throw the grounds to the bottom; in five minutes it will be very clear.

Or, beat one or two eggs, which mix with ground coffee to form a ball; nearly fill the pot with cold water, simmer gently for half hour, having introduced the ball; *do not boil*, or you will destroy the aroma.

COFFEE ICE.—Pour some of this coffee into a bowl, and sufficient sugar-candy and cream, and place it in an ice pail till quite frozen. Serve in proper glasses. This is a delightful refreshment in hot weather.

COFFEE MILK.—Boil a tablespoonful of ground coffee in a pint of milk 15 minutes, put in a little isinglass; clear it; boil a minute; throw in a little cold water to precipitate the grounds. Let it stand on the rib ten minutes.

COHOSH, *Black.*—An American plant, astringent, diuretic, alterative, &c. It restrains diarrhœas, and is much used by the American Indians in rheumatism and parturition. In incipient consumption, it prevents febrile symptoms, the hectic flush, and reduces pulsation. It promotes the menstrual flux; it has rarely failed to cure hooping-cough. It is most valuable in rheumatism, using the saturated tincture, from six to forty drops, and first cleansing the bowels. A strong decoction or powder united with slippery elm forms a valuable poultice for all kinds of inflammation. The powdered root made into a syrup is effectual in coughs. The tincture may be made by infusing one ounce of the powdered root in half a pint of spirits.

COLCHICUM, *Oxymel of.*— This preparation has been found beneficial in asthma and winter cough. Dose from two teaspoonfuls to a dessert-spoonful, three times a day in barley-water. It effectually allays fever and irritation about the wind-pipe.

COLD.—Never neglect a cold. It may be the forerunner of some disease difficult to cure. Consumption is often followed by a neglected cold. A cold is caused by the loss of heat, and a decrease of nervous energy, causing an obstruction of the perspiration.

To remove a cold restore the perspiration. Take a decoction of the sudorific herbs, as catnep, pennyroyal, yarrow, or angelica. Take the composition powder (which see). Place the feet in warm water before going to bed, and put a bottle of water to the feet, wrapped in cloth wet with vinegar and water. Give a basin of hot gruel, and let the patient oft drink of the herb tea. Repeat this treatment, if necessary. If the throat is sore, wet some hops in hot vinegar, put in cloth, and wrap round the neck. If the cough is troublesome, use some of the Cough Remedies. *See Cough.*

Or, take linseed, a cupful; rasins, 4 ozs.; liquorice in stick, two pennyworth; soft water, 2 quarts; simmer till reduced to 1 quart; add 4 ozs. of sugar candy, a table-spoonful of old rum, and one of good vinegar, or lemon-juice. Add the rum and vinegar as the decoction is taken. Take a cupful two or three times a day—the patient should lie in bed a day or two.

COLD IN THE HEAD.—M. Farn, a Belgian physician, says, a cold may often be arrested by a brisk friction of the back of the head with some stimulant lotion, as lavender water, sal volatile, &c. And also a similar rubbing, two or three times a-week will prevent the "catching" of a cold by those who are liable to do so from slight causes.

COLD TO AVOID CATCHING.—Accustom yourself to the use of sponging with cold water every morning on first getting out of bed, followed with a good deal of rubbing with a wet towel. It has considerable effect in giving tone to the skin, and maintaining a proper action in it, and proves a safeguard to the injurious influence of cold and sudden change of temperature. Sir Astley Cooper said, "The methods by which I have preserved my own health are—temperance, early rising, and sponging the body every morning with cold water, immediately after getting out of bed; a practice which I have adopted for thirty years without ever catching cold."

COLD, A, TO CURE.—The following plan is very effectual in curing most colds, but not all:— Let a man eat next to nothing for two days, provided he is not confined to bed, for by taking no carbon into the system by food, and by consuming the surplus which caused his disease, by breath, he soon carries off his disease by removing the cause. This will be found more effectual if he adds copious water draughts to the protracted fasting. By the time a person has fasted one day and night, he will experience a freedom from disease, and a clearness of mind, in a delightful contrast with mental stupor, and physical pain caused by colds.

Or take one handful of Yarrow, half an ounce of Ginger root, bruised, or a teaspoonful of Cayenne Pepper, and about three pints of water. Boil to one pint. Add a little sugar if you like. Take a good dose at bed-time, and your cold will be cured by the next morning; if not, repeat the dose.

COLD BATHING.—It is useful in some fevers, chronic rheumatism, hysterics, hypochondriac, and paralytic affections, rickets, scrofulous complaints, debility, obstructed perspiration, langour and weakness of circulation, &c. It requires great prudence in using, and should be of short duration. In some cases it would be best to commence with tepid bathing, and proceed to the use of the cold bath, which should be from 40° to 65° Fahrenheit. Sea-water is preferable, from the stimulating effects of the salt.

The most suitable time for bathing is morning; because in the latter part of the day the body becomes too enfeebled to bear the cold shock. A dose of cayenne, ginger, or any of the pure stimulants, taken before the cold bath, will keep up the heat of the body, and promote the reaction and determination of blood to the surface, which causes a refreshing glow.

Cold bathing is inadmissible in inflammatory diseases, fluxes, diseases of the breast, difficult breathing, short and dry coughs, pregnancy, palsy, diseases of the skin, &c. The Cold Bath is injurious in all cases where immediate reaction does not follow its use. If it produces chills, depression, langour, headache, and blueness of the lips, it should not be used. After leaving the bath, the body should be rubbed with a flesh-brush, or coarse towels. Cold bathing is never beneficial unless followed by a warm glow of the skin.

COLD CREAM. — Take the juice of house-leek, a few drops of camphorated spirit; melt spermaceti, white wax, and olive oil; then beat in the spirit and juice. Excellent for sore lips. *Gu.*

COLD PUNCH, or COOL CUP.—Loaf sugar, 9 ozs.; rub each lump over a lemon to collect the flavour of the lemon rind; then squeeze the lemon juice over it, and add half a pint of rum or gin, and grated nutmeg. Infuse twenty minutes, and add 3 pints of cold spring water. Add a lump of ice.

COLIC.—This is a spasmodic affection of the bowels, especially of the colon. It begins with great pain in the bowels, especially just under the navel, nausea, retching, and vomiting. The pain is of a sharp twisting character, very distressing. This affection is caused by wind, disagreeing food, acrid bile, obstinate costiveness, worms, noxious metallic vapours, &c.

Flatulent Colic. Give a tea-cupful of the *Anti-Spasmodic Tincture*, in a cupful of pepper-mint tea; or a teaspoonful of Turkey rhubarb, and one of magnesia, with a pinch of Cayenne pepper; this will often afford relief. Apply fomentations or friction to the abdomen. If the bowels are not operated upon, give castor oil, from half an ounce; add also a simple injection.

The *Bilious Colic* is more severe. It is known from the former by a bitter taste in the mouth, great thirst, fever, vomiting of bilious matter, headache, and great costiveness. The remedies must be the same, but stronger and brisker. The Neutralizing Mixture must not be forgotten; give also the Stimulating Injection.

COLIC, *Bilious.*—Drink warm lemonade. I know nothing like it. Or, give a spoonful of sweet oil every hour. This cured one at the point of death.—*Wesley.*

COLIC.—Drink strong Camomile and Ginger Tea.—Or, from 30 to 40 drops of Oil of Aniseed.—Or, apply outwardly a bag of hot oats, or bran.—Or, steep the legs in hot water.—Or, take as much Daffy's Elixir as will purge. Very effectual. *Wesley.*

COLIC *Ball for Horses.*--Powdered opium, half a drachm; Castile soap and camphor, of each 2 drachms; of cayenne pepper, 1 drachm; ginger, 1 drachm. Make into a ball with liquorice powder and treacle. If the horse is constipated as well, add to the ball 5 or 6 drops of croton oil.

COLLEGE PUDDING. — Grate the crumb of a two-penny

loaf; shred suet, 8 ozs.; and mix with 8 ozs. of currants, one of citron mixed fine, one of orange, sugar, 4 ozs.; half a nutmeg, three eggs beaten, yolk and white separately. Mix and make into the shape and size of a goose-egg. Put ½ lb. of butter into a frying-pan; and, when melted and quite hot, stew gently in it over a stove; turn them two or three times till of a fine light brown.. Mix a glass of brandy with the batter. Serve with pudding-sauce.

COLONEL PUDDING.-Pour a pint and a half of boiling milk and cream upon some of the choicest biscuits grated; they must be very light; add the yolks of four eggs and the whites of two, some grated nutmeg, a spoonful of flour, some fine sugar, a little brandy, some candied lemon, and lemon juice according to taste. Butter a basin, boil 1 hour; serve it with melted butter, wine, and sugar.

COLOURINGS FOR JELLIES, ICES, OR CAKES.— For a beautiful *red*, boil fifteen grains of cochineal in the finest powder, with a dram and a half of cream of tartar, in half a pint of water, very slowly, half an hour. Add in boiling a bit of alum the size of a pea. Or use beet-root sliced, and some liquor poured over.

For *white*, use almonds finely powdered, with a little drop of water; or use cream.

For *yellow*, yolks of eggs, or a bit of saffron steeped in the liquor and squeezed.

For *green*, pound spinach-leaves or beet-leaves, express the juice, and boil in a tea-cupful of water in a saucepan, in order to take off the rawness.

COLOURING MATTER. — A chemist of Lyons states that the colouring matter of any tree may be known by the colour of its fruit; and advises the boiling of the bark with lime, when a precipitate will be formed of the same colour as its fruit. Several of the new vegetable dyes have thus been discovered.

COLTSFOOT.—This plant is well known. The leaves are the basis of the British herb tobacco. It has demulcent bitter qualities, and is slightly tonic and stomachic. The leaves smoked are useful in asthma. Dr. Cullen found a strong decoction of the leaves beneficial in scrofula cases—and to succeed where sea-water had failed. It should be persevered in. Dr. Percival found it useful in hectic diarrhœa. A decoction with wormwood has done wonders in gravel and stone.

COLTSFOOT SYRUP.-Coltsfoot, 5 ozs.; balm and hyssop, 1 oz. each; horehound, ½ oz. Boil in 2 quarts of water down to 1 quart; strain, add 1 lb. or more of sugar; boil till as thick as honey. For cough or shortness of breath, take a teaspoonful occasionally.

COLTSFOOT LOZENGES.— To a pint of water add one handful of coltsfoot leaves; boil down to a gill, strain it, when cold, and add ¼ lb. of sugar. Boil to a syrup. Strain again and put to it as much common liquorice as will give it consistency. Then form it into any shape you please.

COMFITS.—Take 1 lb. of raw sugar, and make it into syrup with water; then take 1 lb. of coriander seeds, and dip them in the syrup; then put the seeds into a sieve with a little flour, shake them well in it, and place them to dry. Keep steeping them in the syrup, adding flour, and drying them till they are of the size you want them to be. CARAWAY

COMFITS are made the same way. The colouring for comfits is rose or Dutch pink.

COMMON PLASTER.—Yellow resin, ½ lb.; beeswax, 2 ozs.; cayenne pepper, 1 oz.; spirits of wine, half a pint or more. Simmer carefully till the spirits are almost evaporated. When nearly cold, add camphor, 1 oz.; oil of sassafras, 1½ drachm; opium, 1 drachm. As a strengthening plaster, it always gives relief.

COMPOSITION POWDER; *Thompson's. See Robinson's Family Herbal*, page 341.—Take bayberry, 8 ounces; ginger, 8 ounces; poplar bark, 4 ounces; white oak bark, 4 ounces; cayenne pepper, 3¼ ounces; cloves, ½ ounce. Powder and mix intimately. Dissolve a teaspoonful in a cup of boiling water, sweetened. Valuable to remove colds, influenza, fever, relax, pain in the bowels, cold extremities. For promoting perspiration, and morbific matter, the cause of disease, it is invaluable. When taken, the patient should go to bed, and apply the hot brick, &c.

COMPLEXION, to improve it.—Be cheerful; get as much fresh air in-doors and out-doors, as possible. Keep in health; promote a good digestion, and regular evacuations; avoid alcoholic drinks: a milk and vegetable diet makes a fair complexion; plain living, without condiments and hot seasonings, &c., makes the fairest face. It is good to rise early in the morning, drink a cup of milk, walk into the fields, wash the face in sparkling dew, gaze on creation, below, above, and all around you, till mental pleasure beams forth on your face in radiant smiles. Check the effects of grief, disappointments, embarrassment, &c.

Dissolve flowers of sulphur in milk, and strain. With the clear milk, wash the face.—Or infuse sifted bran in best vinegar; add, well beaten, the yolks of 3 or 4 eggs, and 1 grain of ambergris. Distil. Bottle, and cork well.—Or, Castile soap, 4 ozs.; Fuller's earth water, 1 quart. Dissolve, Add ¼ oz. of spirits of wine, and ½ drachm each of oil of lavender and rosemary. Fuller's earth water is made by merely dissolving it in water, stirring well, and then let it settle. This earth alone is good for the complexion.

CONSTIPATION, *Costiveness.*—A sluggish state of the lower bowel, causing the retention of the fæces. It is a very common disease. It may be caused by food hard to be digested, by ardent spirits which have a very constipating influence, and debilitate the lower bowel; frequent excessive purges have the same effect. Sedentary employments, the want of exercise, and fresh air, and not drinking water in sufficient quantity, lead to costiveness. It is often attended with many distressing symptoms, and is the cause of various dangerous diseases; as piles, fistula, indigestion, hernia, colic, cholera. And it is also the effect of many diseases.

Constipation is to be removed by an attention to diet, by adopting a vegetable diet, and by eating bread made of unsifted flour; that is, no bran, sharps, &c., taken away. Also, by taking much exercise, and a more copious supply of diluents, especially toast and water. Make a regular habit of evacuating once a day at a fixed hour, and always make an effort whether successful or not. Assist the bowels by an injection of warm water, about half a pint; if very obstinate, add to the water a little castor oil. For several nights take one or two of the Dyspeptic Pill;

or one or two of the following:—

Powdered aloes, jalap, gamboge, colocynth, extract of gentian, mandrake, cayenne pepper, of each, ½ oz.; castile soap, ¼ oz.; oil of peppermint, ¼ drachm. Mix well, and form into pills. It purges without griping and weakening. Dose:—two or three pills. *Beach.*

Sulphur is a good remedy, especially when there is a tendency to piles. If there is a deficiency of bile, take Blood-root (which see,) with a little powdered dandelion root. The flesh brush, cold sponging, and the shower-bath, are excellent remedies

CONSTIPATION OR COSTIVENESS.--Professor Phœbus, of Giessen, refers habitual costiveness to the following causes:—

1. The too spare use of articles of diet which promote the action of the bowels. Water is placed first. It is taken by many in insufficient quantity. In sedentary occupations the sensation of thirst is too seldom excited, and the habitual frequency of such sensation may be diminished if the satisfaction of the call be neglected. To this class of aliments belong fruits, salads, sour milk, honey, and fat. Many country people, who sell all their produce, eat little of these things, and the poorer inhabitants of towns get them in insufficient quantity. Those persons who can procure them, eat salads and fats in too small quantities. 2. Too little bodily exercise. 3. Want of exercise of the powers of the large intestine. This is the most influential of all the causes. It is an error to suppose that the power of the will extends only over the sphincter; for it prevails much higher, only it requires more time for its exertion. Several minutes, or a quarter of an hour, may be required to initiate the evacuatory movement. By exercising it, we increase the disposition of the intestine to act, but this is rarely the case in less than five minutes.

Numerous remedies have been recommended for constipation; but the action of medicinal substances in so chronic an affection may become prejudicial, especially such as exert a chemical action, as salts or drastics. If a stool is desired, the patient must earnestly practice the necessary gymnastic, which consists in alternate movements of the rectum as during actual evacuation, and in rapidly drawing in and then expanding the abdominal muscles. Such movements may be commenced in the chamber and completed in the closet, several minutes, a quarter of an hour, or even more, being required. If evacuation has commenced, but has not proved productive enough, the movements must be continued, the person resolving not to quit the closet until the aim has been attained. The movements are the same as those normally employed; but they are more rapid, and continued for a longer time. Kneading and rubbing the abdomen, may be useful, but they are unnecessary; and may be reserved for those not able to follow the above directions, such as children, &c.

An adult should compel a stool every day. In from four to eight weeks a complete mastery may be acquired over the intestine, so that a stool may be always secured once in the twenty-four hours. This powerful agency acts more efficiently when conjoined with articles of diet favourable to an open state of the bowels. A large quantity of water will be more easily drank if at first carbonic acid gas be added. An adult, during winter, should take from fifty to seventy ounces daily (deducting from this the equivalent of any artificial drinks he may take), a larger quantity still during great bodily exertion, and from one-and-a-half to twice the quantity in a summer. When raw fruit gives rise to flatulence, it may be taken cooked with spices, and especially when dried and cooked. With greater regularity of stools, flatulence becomes less, the food being retained for a less time within the canal. Exercise is of great service; but it exerts no sudden effect, and at first may even induce constipation.

Trying the plan upon himself when a student, the author has, during his twenty-eight years of practice, recommended it to an immense number of persons, and in the great majority of cases with complete success. He has attained the power of procuring a daily stool at any convenient time between four o'clock a.m. and mid-day, the average time required being a quarter of an hour. Only on one occasion during thirty years has he failed in his object. The plan is not so suitable for the aged; and is inapplicable to women during advanced pregnancy, or in organic disease or prolapsus of the uterus. When from insufficient perseverance the means does not succeed, cold water clysters form the best supplement; and, exceptionally, salt and oil, with camomile tea, etc., may be thrown up. The author never gives purgatives by the mouth in chronic constipation, believing it to be most impolitic to irritate the stomach and small intestine, disturbing chylopœsis, and introducing into the blood materials that are always more or less injurious.

CONSUMPTION.—The word is derived from the Latin verb *consumo*, to consume or to waste away. It is also called phthisis, from the Greek verb *phthio*, to waste away. Consumption is the most frequent and most fatal of all pulmonary diseases. It often begins with a slight dry cough, so slight and painless as not to attract notice. By and by the cough increases, and expectoration gradually becomes copious, thick, yellow, and tinged with blood. Sometimes the appetite remains tolerable, but the breathing is more difficult, especially during and after bodily exertion, and the pulsation is become accelerated. There is a gradual emaciation of the body, debility, night sweats, interrupted rest, the hectic flush, or a bright scarlet spot on the cheek, especially after eating, tightness of the chest, and acute pains under the breast-bone. In the last stage emaciation rapidly increases, and the patient has alternations of hope and fear as to recovery. Hope, however, the most prevails.

As to the *treatment of consumption*, Dr. Beach says, "If the pathology of phthisis consists in a *diseased state of the blood*, all former treatment is wrong, or very inefficient. We presbribe for the *symptoms* instead of the cause. If the elements of this disease circulate in the blood, as in scrofula, syphilis, and other complaints, and are thrown by the efforts of the system to the lungs, and these develope tubercles then is it not obvious that we must prescribe *alteratives*, or such medicines as will eradicate its morbid condition?" It is evident from these rational remarks, that the nature of this disease, and that of others, depends upon a morbid and diseased condition of the blood. Hence then there must be an attempt *to alter* the quality of the blood. Remove all the causes which have produced this disease, as obstructed perspiration, evacuations, and secretions, a cold and damp residence, insufficient warmth and clothing, intemperance, venery, and self-pollution; the last habit is a most prolific cause of consumption.

In the first stage of consumption, special attention must be given to the skin and bowels, by adopting the vapour bath, stimulating liniments, *(See Stimulating Liniment)* and also injections, to equalize the circulation, reduce all feverish symptoms, and prevent night sweats. A *medicated vapour bath* is the best; which see. Put the patient to bed, and place to the feet and sides hot bricks wrapped in cloths dipped in vinegar, and half wrung out, and give an emetic; repeat this process once or twice a week, and sponge morning and evening with the aforenamed Liniment, and occasionally in the morning with a decoction of poplar bark. Rub very dry with a towel. This will prevent night sweats. To improve the appetite, if bad, give the *tonic bitters*, (see *Tonic* Bitters). If the patient is constipated, give an injection of half a pint of warm water, or thin gruel, with a little butter, or sweet oil, or castor oil, adding one or two teaspoonfuls of tincture of myrrh. Sometimes a lax state of the bowels prevails; in that case give from 10 to 15 drops of laudanum; or mix finely pulverized charcoal, 2 parts, and magnesia, 1 part; a table-spoonful occasionally, or give the *Neutralizing Mixture*, (which see.) Let the *Cough Syrup* be taken two or three times a day, to promote expectoration, ease pain, &c. Let the patient's diet be light, nourishing, and easy of digestion.

In consumption, the celebrated Dr. Beach, of America, highly extols the use of *Sanguinaria Canadensis*, or *Blood-root*. It is a sedative and alterative of great power; in reducing the pulsation it is superior to digitalis, and it does not debilitate at all. It promotes the secretions of the liver, and therefore promotes the appetite; it is a powerful tonic, and when it is taken properly nothing tends more to check morbific influence, to promote the secretions, appetite, and digestion, and to improve the muscular power, and facial appearance. In restraining spitting of blood, and especially in females where the menses are substituted by the effusion of blood from the lungs, no medicine is so efficacious as *blood-root*, (which see.)

As to the benefit to be derived from cod liver oil, the matter is dubious. It is feeding, but not antiseptic. It may prevent, to some extent, emaciation; but to prevent the formation of tubercles, and, consequently, decay, it is a matter of doubt. Much benefit may be derived from gentle emetics, tonics, the *Irritating Plaster*, (which see); and for pain in the side the *Rheumatic Liquid*. Also constant fresh air in a genial atmosphere. The following syrup is a fine expectorant and alterative; —Blood-root, 4 ozs.; bruise and simmer in a quart of water, down to a pint nearly; add 1 lb of sugar; simmer again to form a syrup; and ½ oz. of solution of iodide of iron; take a teaspoonful two or three times a day.

Many have derived much benefit from Tar-water, and some have been completely cured by it. "In *Dr. John William's Legacy to the World*," this recipe is given,—common tar, a table-spoonful; honey, three table-spoonfuls; three yolks of hen's eggs; wine, half a pint. Mix, and bottle for use. A teaspoonful thrice a day.

Should the bowels be extremely relaxed, take a grain of powdered alum, and a grain of sulphate of iron, as a powder. This has performed wonders. Drink much barley-water, taking occasionally five or six drops of the oil of aniseeds to relieve the cough. Chlorodyne also affords much relief to a cough.

With regard to *climate* for the consumptive it is not only as uniform a climate as can be found that is wanted, but the same means of eradicating the disease as the patient had in his own country, but where he was prevented by fitful weather from making use of them. Occupation for his mind and body is essential to recovery. His object should be to remain as much as possible in the open air; to enjoy moderate daily exercise for several hours; to partake of a mixed and wholesome nourishing diet; to be refreshed by undisturbed repose during the night; to cleanse the body by daily ablutions; and to have his mind diverted by new and cheerful scenery, from home-longings, and from dwelling too much upon the nature of his malady.

Dr. Richardson, in his treatise on pulmonary consumption, says, " I shall recommend no particular place as a resort for consumptives. It should be near the sea coast, and sheltered from the northerly winds; the soil should be dry; the drinking-water, pure; the mean temperature about 60°, with a range of not more than about 10° or 15° on either side. It is not easy to fix any degree of humidity; but extremes of dryness or of moisture are alike injurious. It is of importance, in selecting a locality, that the scenery should be enticing, so that the patient may be the more encouraged to spend his time out of doors in walking, or riding exercise; and a town where the residences are isolated, and scattered about, and where drainage and cleanliness are attended to, is preferable to one where the houses are densely packed, however small the population.

A sea-voyage is sometimes recommended in *incipient* consumption. This is often followed by a total suspension, or removal of the disease, in cases where it is judiciously recommended. Short voyages are often more injurious than beneficial. To a delicate person going out to India, a voyage round the Cape is of great benefit; but the most serviceable voyage is one to Australia, New Zealand, and back again.... the great advantage is the enjoyment of a perpetual summer, which may be effected by leaving this country about the beginning or middle of October, and returning before the cold weather sets in at the antipodes.

CONSUMPTION.—One in a deep consumption was advised to drink nothing but water, and eat nothing but water gruel, without salt or sugar. In three months time he was quite well.——Take no food but new buttermilk, churned in a bottle, and white bread. I have known this successful.—Or, use as common drink, spring water and new milk, each a quart, and sugar candy 2 ozs.——Or, boil two handfuls of sorrel in a pint of whey, strain it, and drink a glass thrice a day.

Or, turn a pint of skimmed milk with half a pint of small beer. Boil in this whey about twenty ivy-leaves, and two or three sprigs of hyssop. Drink half over night, the rest in the morning. Do this, if needful, for two months daily.

This has cured in a desperate case. Tried.——Or every morning, cut a little turf of fresh earth, and laying down, breathe in the hole for a quarter of an hour.——Or, take in for a quarter of an hour, morning and evening, the steam of white resin and bees' wax boiling on a hot fire shovel. This has cured one who was in the third stage of a consumption.——-Or, take morning and evening a tea-spoonful of white resin powdered and mixed with honey. This cured one in less than a month, who was near death.—— Or, drink thrice a-day two spoonfuls of juice of water-cresses. This has cured a deep consumption. In the last stage, suck a healthy woman daily. This has cured my father. For diet, use milk and apples, or water gruel made with fine flour. Drink cider-whey, barley water, sharpened with lemon-juice, or apple water. So long as the tickling cough continues, chew well, and swallow a mouthful or two of a biscuit or crust of bread twice a-day. If you cannot swallow it spit it out. This will always shorten the fit, and would often prevent a consumption. *John Wesley.*

CONSUMPTION, *Useful drink for.*—Coltsfoot, two ounces; horehound, rue, of each one ounce; and blood-root, three drachms. Boil in three quarts of water down to two quarts. Strain, and to the liquor, add of figs and sugar, of each four ounces, and boil fifteen minutes. Take a wine-glassful three or four times a day.

CONVULSIONS, *in Children.*—They originate in some derangement or irritation of the bowels, stomach, brain, or from teething. Give an aperient, as magnesia and rhubarb, and a warm bath at about 90°, and apply to the head linen dipped in the water. The following powder is useful:—Rhubarb in powder, 8 grains; super-sulphate of potash, 12 grains. Mix. Give also a little syrup of poppies. If aperients cannot be taken, give a mild injection; as a little epsom salts in barley gruel, with a little butter; or a weak solution of salt and water, with a few drops of oil, or butter.

Convulsions often arise from over-feeding; this must be avoided. If indigestible food has been taken, give an emetic,—the wine of ipecacuanha; or if the patient cannot be sufficiently roused from sleep, so as to take the emetic, tickle the back part of the mouth with a feather to produce the effect. If the convulsions are obstinate, apply friction along the spine, when in the bath; or out of it, rub the spine with an anodyne composed of 10 drops of laudanum, 10 drops of oil, and 6 drops of tincture of cayenne. Mustard plasters may be applied a minute or two to the legs and feet. If convulsions are caused by teething, the gums must be lanced a little.

COOL TANKARD.—Mild ale, 1 quart; port, or sherry wine, 1 glassful; the same of brandy; one of capilaire; the juice of a lemon; a little of the peel pared thin, with ¼ oz. of cream of tartar. Strain it.

COPPER, *to detect in Pickles or Tea.*—Into a beer glass put a portion of the pickles or tea; add a little liquid ammonia, with nearly as much water; stir well, and if the liquid become blue, it indicates the presence of copper.

COPPER OR BRASS PANS. Always put away dry, or they will generate verdigris, which is very poisonous.—If tinged with dye, clean with oil of vitriol and water, and a little fine sand. Wipe quite dry.

COPYING INK.—Powdered

galls, 2 lbs.; sulphate of iron, 8 ozs.; gum, 6 ozs.; logwood, 6 ozs.; sugar, 4 ozs.; vinegar, 2 quarts; water, 1½ gallon. Stir often for a fortnight. A few drops of oil of cloves will prevent mould.

Another.—Add ¼ oz. of gum arabic, and 1 oz. of fine brown sugar, to every pint of good black ink.

COPYING PAPER, *Black*— Mix well and stiff, lamp black and lard, or butter. Spread evenly over fine printing paper with a soft brush or flannel. Dry in a warm room. It is used for transferring drawings, &c., or for multiplying copies.—Place a sheet of white paper upon it; place the pattern upon it to be copied, and trace with a style.

CORNS.—When small, they may be removed by stimulants or escharotics; as nitrate of silver, (lunar caustic,) by wetting the corn, and touching it with a pencil of the caustic every evening; previously soften the skin by immersing the feet in warm water.—Or apply a blister the size of a sixpence. —Or the following remedies:—

1. Apply fresh every morning, the yeast of small beer spread on a rag.—Or, after paring them close, apply bruised ivy-leaves daily, and in fifteen days they will drop out. ——Or, apply chalk powdered and mixed with water This also cures warts. Some corns are cured by a pitch plaster.——All are greatly eased by steeping the feet in hot water wherein oatmeal is boiled. This also helps dry and hot feet. *Wesley.*

2. Four ounces of white diachlyon plaster, four ounces of shoe-maker's wax, and fifty drops of muriatic acid, or spirits of salt. Boil these ingredients for a few minutes in an earthen pipkin, and when cold, roll the mass out between the hands, or upon a marble slab, slightly moistened with olive oil.

3. Rub together in a mortar, 2 ozs. of powdered savine leaves; ½ oz. of verdigris, and ¼ oz. of red precipitate. Mix, and put some of it in a linen bag; apply to the corn at bed-time.

4. Some people roast a clove of garlic, and fasten it on with a piece of cloth at the time of going to bed. It softens the corns, and removes the core in two or three nights' using. When the garlic is taken off, wash the foot with warm water; in a little time the indurated skin that forms the horney tunic of the corn will disappear.

Avoid tight shoes, boots, and stockings, to be devoid of corns.

5. Bathe the feet for twenty or thirty minutes in strong soda water and soft soap. After repeating a few times, the corn may be easily drawn out.—If the corn be soft, apply a rag dipped in turpentine. —Corns should never be cut without being softened in warm water and soap.

6. Sir Astly Cooper gives the following receipe as an infallible cure:—Gum Ammonia, 2 ozs.; yellow wax, 2 ozs.; verdigris, 6 drachms. Melt them together, and spread the composition on a piece of soft leather, or linen; cut away as much of the corn as you can with a knife, before you apply the plaster; renew in a fortnight, if the corn is not gone.

7. A *hard* corn should be soaked night and morning in hot water, and scraped. Tincture of Iodine, laid on with a camel's hair brush twice a day will remove a *hard* corn. For a *soft* corn, the solution of potass should be well rubbed in.

8. Tincture of Iodine, 4 drachms; Iodide of iron, 12 grains; chloride

of antimony, 4 drachms. Mix and apply, after paring the corn.

After bathing the feet and cutting the corns, apply to them a leaf of houseleek, or one of ground-ivy, or of purslane, well steeped in vinegar. Renew every evening for a few days.

CORN SOLVENT, *Sir H. Davy's*:—Potash, 2 parts; Salt of Sorrel, 1 part: Mix in fine powder. Lay a small quantity on the corn for four successive nights, binding it on with rags.

CORPULENCY.—Mr. Alfred William Moore, sent the following communication to the *Medical Times*:—"Fat is a necessary ingredient of the body. Nature is sometimes too liberal in its supply; it then becomes burdensome, and subjects the objects of its prodigality to ridicule. The discovery of a certain remedy may prove a boon. The following systematic plan of treatment, adopted by myself, who am constitutionally fat, will clearly show that abstaining from bread and fermented liquors will remedy this inconvenience:—Weighing 15½ stones, I reduced myself in three months to 12½ stones by strictly adhering to the following plan of dieting myself: Breakfast early, consisting of 2 oz. of biscuit, 1 egg, two cups of tea or coffee; then fasted till five; my dinner consisting of animal food, &c., but no bread: likewise avoiding bread at my tea or supper."

Abstain as much as possible from the use of butter, sugar, and fat meat, and take plenty of exercise every day.

COSMETICS.—It is said that Pimpernel water is a great beautifier of the countenance.—Or, melt 1 lb. of soft soap, and half a pint of sweet oil, and add a tea-cupful of very fine sand, and three or four drops of camphorated spirit.

COSTIVENESS.—See *Constipation*.

COSTIVENESS.—Rise early every morning. Or boil in a pint and a half of broth, half a handful of mallow leaves, strain, and drink it before you eat any thing else. Do this frequently, if needful. Or, take daily, two hours before dinner, a small tea-cupful of stewed prunes. Or, live upon bread made of wheat flour with all the bran in it. Or, boil an ounce and a half of tamarinds in three pints of water to a quart. In this, strained, when cold, infuse all night two drachms of senna, and one drachm of red rose leaves; drink a cupful every morning.—An infusion of senna, with Epsom salts, with gentian root, and camomile flowers, may be taken every other day.

COUGHS.—The following are the best recipes for Coughs. Some of them are of rare excellence;—

1. *To allay a tickling Cough.*—Six table-spoonfuls of treacle; the juice of half a lemon; simmer over the fire till well incorporated. Take off, and add one table-spoonful of paregoric, and about the size of a horse-bean of refined nitre. Take two tea-spoonfuls when the cough troubles.

2. Take 4 ozs of sugar candy, powdered, ½ oz. of citric acid, or lemon juice; mix by heat; add a few drops of oil of aniseed. If the cough is not a dry one, add 20 drops of laudanum, or a dessert spoonful of paregoric. Take a teaspoonful at a time, when the cough is troublesome.

3. Two table-spoonfuls of Linseed, four ounces of Liquorice root, or Spanish Juice, four ounces of Elecampane root, water three quarts; boil down to three pints. Dose, a wine-glassful four or five times a day.

4. Powder of tragacanth, one

drachm; syrup of white poppies, two drachms; laudanum, forty drops; water, four ounces. Shake the powder in the water till it is dissolved, then add the others. Dose:—A teaspoonful three times a day.

5. *Asthmatic Cough.*——Take two good handfuls of Coltsfoot leaves, one ounce of Garlic, and two quarts of water. Boil down to three pints. Strain, and to the liquor add eight ounces of sugar, boil gently for ten minutes. Take half a cupful occasionally.

6. *Consumptive Cough.* — The following is a most valuable recipe: —Of Sanctuary, Horehound, Bayberry Bark, two pennyworth of each; and of Agrimony, Raspberry Leaves, Clevers, and Ground Ivy, one pennyworth; Extract of Liquorice, 4 ozs.; and half a teaspoonful of Cayenne pepper. Gently simmer in two gallons of water for an hour.

7. The following has cured most *obstinate* coughs:—Take a pint of milk, warm it, and when it comes to the boiling point, add as much made mustard as will turn it to a posset. Take away the curd, and into half a pint of the posset put one ounce of brown sugar candy, to dissolve. Take the posset as hot as you can at night, when in bed, and renew it for three or four times. This has given relief in asthma.

8. *A dry cough.*—Disolve ½ oz. of gum arabic, ½ oz. of Spanish juice, and two table-spoonfuls of treacle, in a little warm water; add 3 drachms of the syrups of squills, and 2 drachms of syrup of poppies. Cork and shake well. Take a teaspoonful when the cough is annoying; drink linseed tea, sweetened with sugar-candy. *Gu.*

9. Chew a little Peruvian Bark constantly swallowing the spittle. It seldom fails to cure a dry cough. —*Wesley.*

10. Two or three table-spoonfuls of Linseed, a small bunch of horehound; boil to a jelly, and strain. Add ½ lb. of Sugar Candy, ¼ lb. of Honey, ¼ lb. of loaf Sugar. First boil the horehound in a quart of water; then add the strained Linseed and the other articles. Simmer for two hours. When cold, add of Chlorodyne to the value of 1s. Bottle it and cork tight. A small quantity of spirits of wine or Brandy to keep it. When the cough is troublesome, take a table-spoonful. *This Recipe is invaluable.*

11. Balsam of Tolu, ½ ounce; gum storax, ¼ drachm; opium, 8 grains; best honey, 2 ounces; spirits of wine, half a pint. Digest for 6 days, and strain. If the cough is fast, add ¼ ounce of Ipecacuanha in powder.

12. An old remedy is to dissolve two ounces of mutton suet in a quart of milk, and drink it warm. This relieves a violent cough.

13. Beat well the yolk of an egg, put it in a mortar, and add half a drachm of powdered spermaceti, a little fine sugar, and a table-spoonful of paregoric elixir. Take a table-spoonful when the cough is troublesome.

14. Dr. James recommends a mixture of vinegar and treacle in equal quantities; a teaspoonful to be taken when required—Or take half a pint of vinegar, ½ oz. Spanish juice, 1 oz. each, sugar candy, and spirits of wine. A table-spoonful at a time. *Gu.*

15. Take honey and treacle, of each 4 ozs.; best vinegar, 5 ozs. Mix, and slowly simmer them in a common pipkin for fifteen minutes. When the mixture is cold, add a dessert-spoonful of paregoric elixir. Dose—a table-spoonful three or four times a day.

This is very useful in the coughs of children, as it has a very pleasant taste. Dose, one or two teaspoonfuls.

16. Or, peel and slice a large turnip, spread coarse sugar between the slices, and let it stand in a dish till all the juice drains down. Take a spoonful of this when you cough.

17. Or, take a spoonful of syrup of horehound morning and evening.

18. Or, take from ten to twenty drops of elixir of vitriol, in a glass of water, twice or thrice a-day. This is useful when the cough is attended with costiveness, or a relaxation of the stomach and lungs.

19. For a *tickling Cough*, drink water whitened with oatmeal four times a-day.

Or, keep a piece of barley-sugar or sugar-candy constantly in the mouth.

COUGH DROPS.—Gum Guiacum, 2 drachms; Camphor, 2 scruples; Castile, Soap, 1 scruple; Laudanum, 40 drops; Spirits of Wine, 2 ounces; Balsam, of Peru, 24 drops. Mix. Dose—10 or 15 drops three or four times a day.

COUGH DROPS.—Linseed half a cupful; olive oil, half a pint; treacle or honey, half a pint; spirits of turpentine, balsam of fir, ½ oz. each; extract of liquorice, ¼ oz. Mix and simmer. Take from 10 to 20 drops two or three times a day.

COUGH LOZENGES.—Best Spanish Liquorice, one ounce; refined sugar, 2 ounces; gum arabic finely powdered, 2 drachms; and extract of opium, 1 scruple. Well beat, or pound the whole together; then with mucilage of gum tragacanth, make into small lozenges, to be dissolved in the mouth when the cough is troublesome.

COUGH LOZENGES.—Laudanum, 1 ounce; balsam of tolu, one ounce and a half; liquorice, three and a half ounces; ipecacuanha powder, two ounces; oil of aniseeds, half an ounce; starch, one pound; sugar, three pounds; mucilage to mix.

COUGH, *For*.--Lobelia, 2 oz.; Cayenne, ¼ oz.; Vinegar 1 pint; Sugar, 2 ozs.: Boil the vinegar, and pour it hot upon the herb, &c. into a stone bottle; cork close for a few days. Dose for a cough, half a tea-spoonful, or a piece of loaf sugar moistened with it

Or take of Lobelia, 2 drachms; Blood root, 1 drachm; Skunk Cabbage, 1 drachm; Pleurisy root, 1 drachm. Make into pills with treacle, honey, or Balsam of Peru. Dose, one or two, twice a day.

COUGH PILL.—Extract of Henbane, ¾ ounce; Ipecacuanha, ½ ounce; Extract of Balm of Gilead Buds, ½ ounce; Cayenne, 2 grains; Oil of Mint, 3 drops. Form into pills. Take one or two when needful. In bronchitis, catarrh, &c., these pills are invaluable for Cough.

COUGH PLASTER.—Castile Soap, 1 ounce; Lead Plaster, 2 drachms; Powdered Sal Ammoniac, ½ drachm. Mix the soap and lead plaster together, and when the mass has cooled, add the sal ammoniac, and 1 drachm of Cayenne pepper.

COUGH, PLASTER FOR.— Bees wax, Burgundy-pitch, and Rosin, of each an ounce, melt them together, and stir in three quarters of an ounce of common Turpentine, and half an ounce of oil of mace. Spread it on leather, grate some nutmeg over, and apply quite warm to the pit of the stomach.

COUGH SYRUP.— Hyssop and Rue, of each 1 ounce; Horehound, 1 ounce; Acid Tincture of Lobelia, 3 ounces; Essence of

Pennyroyal, 1 drachm; Essence of Spearmint, 2 drachms.—Boil the Hyssop, Rue, and Horehound till the strength is obtained; strain, add sugar and treacle; boil to a syrup, and when nearly cold, add the tincture and essences.

COUGH SYRUP.——Sage, 1 ounce, Johnswort, 1 ounce, Iceland Moss, 2 ounces; White Poppy heads, 2 ounces; Pearl Barley, 2 table-spoonfuls; water, 2 quarts. Boil to a quart and sweeten with sugar candy, adding a little lemon juice. If the cough is obstinate, add ¼ ounce of Ipecacuanha. If the patient is asthmatical, add 1 ounce of Sulphuric Ether.

COUGH SYRUP.—Tincture of Lobelia, 1 oz.; Iceland Moss, 2 ozs.; White Poppy Capsules, bruised, 2 ozs.; Pearl Barley, 2 table spoonfuls; water, 2 quarts; treacle, 2 ozs. Boil down to three pints, and strain. Dissolve in it from 4 to 8 ozs. of sugar-candy. It effectually allays a tickling cough. A table-spoonful when the cough is troublesome. It does not constipate like laudanum and paregorie.

Or, take Lobelia herb, Horehound, Boneset, of each 1 oz.; Comfrey root, Spikenard, St. Johns wort, Poppy Capsules, of each, ½ oz. Infuse in three pints of boilng water for three hours. Strain and add ¼ lb. of loaf sugar boiled to a syrup. Add a wineglassful of best rum. A table-spoonful is a dose. This is a valuable receipt for cough, hoarseness, &c.

COURT PLASTER. — Isinglass, ½ oz.; Friar's balsam, 1 drachm. Melt the isinglass in 1 oz. of water, and boil the solution till a great part of the water is consumed; add it gradually to the balsam, and mix well. Keep a little longer on the fire, and brush it evenly over silk.

Or, isinglass, 4 ozs.; water, 3 ozs. Dissolve; then add tincture of benzoin, 1 oz. Heat. Apply warm.

COWHAGE. — An effectual remedy for round and other worms. It is made into an electuary with treacle; a tea-spoonful to be taken at a time; and to be followed by a brisk purge with rhubarb and jalop, or salts and senna.

COW-HEEL BROTH. — Put a cow-heel into a pan with three quarts of water, and boil; skim it well, season with peppercorns, thyme, parsley, and salt; boil gently for two hours; skim well, and serve the broth with the glutinous part of the heel in it. It is very strengthening.

COWSLIP WINE.—To two gallons of water, put six pounds of powdered sugar, boil 40 minutes, take off the scum as it rises, pour into a tub to cool, and add the rinds of two lemons; when it is cold, add four quarts of cowslip flowers to the liquor, with the juice of two lemons, let it stand in the tub two days, stirring it every two or three hours, then put in the barrel and let it stand three weeks or a month, then bottle it, and put a lump of sugar into every bottle. The addition of brandy improves it much.

CRABS, *to choose*.—They must feel heavy in the hand; the very large ones are seldom good; those of the middle size are the sweetest. If light they are watery; the joints of the legs are stiff, and the body has an agreeable smell.

CRABS, *to butter*.—Boil two crabs; when cold, take all the meat out; mince it small; put it into a pan, with a glass of sherry, two spoonfuls of vinegar, and a nutmeg grated; boil till it is thoroughly hot. Take ½ lb. of butter, melt with an anchovy; mix with the same the yolks of two eggs; mix all together after shaking the pan round all quite hot. Serve.

CRAB, *dressed cold.*—Empty the shells and mix the flesh with butter, vinegar, salt, white and cayenne pepper. Put the mixture into the large shell, and serve.

It may be served *hot* by putting it into a Dutch Oven before the fire, adding a few crumbs of bread and nutmeg. Brown it nicely.

CRAB, *to stew.*—Put the meat into a stew-pan, with half a pint of sherry, pepper, nutmeg, salt, a few crumbs of bread, the yolk of an egg well beaten, and a spoonful of vinegar. Put on a slow fire, shaking up. Serve on a plate.

CRACK NUTS.—Mix 8 ozs. of flour, and 8 ozs. of sugar; melt 4 ozs. of butter in two spoonfuls of rasin-wine: then, with four eggs beaten and strained, make into a paste; add caraways; roll out as thin as paper, cut with the top of a glass, wash with the white of an egg, and dust sugar over.

CRACKNELS.—Mix with a quart of flour, half a nutmeg grated, the yolks of four eggs beaten, with four spoonfuls of rose-water into a stiff paste, with cold water; then roll in a pound of butter, and make them into a cracknel shape; put them into a kettle of boiling water, and boil them till they swim, take out, put into cold water; when hardened, lay them out to dry, and bake them on tin plates.

CRAMP. — Employ friction, rubbing the part affected with the hands. A draught of camphor-jalap at night is strongly recommended. Stretch the heel out as far as possible, bending the toes slightly upwards. Persons subject to cramp should sleep on a mattress, slightly declined at the foot, and exercise caution in eating and drinking, for cramp often arises from a weak or imperfect digestion.

A towel dipped in hot water applied to the part, will afford immediate relief. But rubbing with the Stimulating Ointment is more effectual. Persons subject to cramp should keep the lower limbs warm; occasionally bathe the feet in warm water before bed-time. Keep the bowels open.

CRAMP IN THE STOMACH. —Apply friction over the stomach immediately; bathe the feet in hot water; give the Anti-Cholera Mixture, described under *Asiatic Cholera;* p. 112 Sometimes strong peppermint tea is effectual; if not, apply a hot brick wrapped in cloths dipped in vinegar to the stomach. Or take a tea-spoonful of sal-volatile in warm water immediately.

CRAMP, PILLS FOR.—Camphor, 1 dr.; spirits of wine, 1 dr.; dissolve, and add opium, 10 grains; confection of roses to form a mass. Mix, and divide into 24 pills. Take one every night.

CRANBERRY JELLY.—— Make a very strong isinglass-jelly. When cold, mix it with a double quantity of cranberry juice, sweeten it and boil up; then strain it into a shape.

The sugar must be good loaf, or the jelly will not be clear.

CRANBERRY AND RICE JELLY.—Boil and press the fruit, strain the juice, and by degrees mix into it as much ground rice as will, when boiled, thicken to a jelly; boil it gently, stirring it, and sweeten to your taste. Put it in a mould, and serve to eat with milk or cream.

CRANBERRY TART.--Wash the cranberries well; put them into the dish with the juice of half a lemon; ½ lb. of moist sugar to each quart of cranberries. Cover with a good paste, and then bake it 45 minutes. Five minutes before it is done, take from the oven, and ice it. It is best served cold.

CRANESBILL.—It is a fine plant. It strengthens the stomach and bowels, restraining all excessive evacuations, and preventing internal mortification. In bowel complaints, and fluxes, it is of great use. A decoction of the root forms a valuable gargle in quinsy, sore mouth and throat. For bleeding wounds it is a sovereign styptic. The root bruised and saturated with cold water should be applied to the wound. Dose. Powdered root, from twelve grains. Decoction, Boil an ounce in a pint of water; a table-spoonful.

CRAYONS.—Take shellac, 6 parts; spirits, 4 parts; turpentine, 2 parts; colour, 12 parts; pale clay, 12 parts. Mix.

CREAM, *Almond.*—Beat 4 ozs. of blanched sweet almonds, and a few bitter, with a teaspoonful of water, to prevent oiling. Put a paste to a quart of cream, and the juice of three lemons sweetened; beat it to a froth, which take off; then fill glasses with the liquor and froth. *Ru.*

CREAM, *an excellent.*—Whip up three quarters of a pint of rich cream to a strong froth, with finely scraped lemon peel, a squeeze of the juice, half a glass of sweet wine, and sugar to taste; lay it in a form, and next day put it on a dish, and ornament with light puff-paste biscuits, the length of a finger, and about two thick, over which sugar may be strewed, or a little glaze with isinglass. Or, use macaroons, to line the edges of the dish.

CREAM — *Brandy Cream.* — Boil 12 blanched and 12 bitter almonds, pounded, in a little milk. When cold, add the yolks of five eggs well beaten in a little cream; add sugar, and quarter of a pint of brandy. Mix well, and pour to it a quart of thin cream: gently simmer on the fire till it thickens; do not let it boil. Pour into cups or low glasses. A ratafia drop may be added to each.

CREAM CAKES.—Beat the whites of 9 eggs to a stiff froth and keep it up; grate the rinds of two lemons to each white of egg. Sprinkle in a spoonful of fine sugar, lay a wet sheet of paper on a tin, and drop it on in little lumps, a little distance from each other. Sift sugar over them. When put in the oven the froth will rise. As soon as coloured, they are baked; take out, and put two bottoms together; put on a sieve, and dry in a slow oven.

CREAM CHEESE.—Put five quarts of the last milking of a cow, called "*strippings,*" into a pan with two spoonfuls of rennet. When the curd is come, strike it down with the skimmer to break it. Let it stand two hours; spread a cheese cloth on a sieve and drain upon it; break the curd a little with your hand; put it into a vat with a 2 lb. weight upon it. After standing 12 hours bind a fillet round. Turn every day till dry; cover with green leaves, and let them gradually ripen on a pewter plate.

CREAM COOKIES.-One teacupful of cream turned; ½ lb. of sugar; one or two eggs, a teaspoonful of carbonate of soda dissolved; sufficient flour to make into dough. Add spices and seeds if you like.

CREAM, *Sack.*—Boil a pint of raw cream, the yolk of an egg well beaten, two or three spoonfuls of white wine, sugar, and lemon-peel; stir it over a gentle fire, till it be as thick as rich cream, and afterwards till cold; then serve it in glasses, with dry toast. *Ru.*

CREAM FOR THE HAIR.—Lard, two parts; oil of almonds, one part. Melt and scent with jessamine or bergamot.

CREAM, *Italian*.—One quart of good cream, and a quart of new-milk, the grated rind of two or three lemons, and strain the juice; take also eight ounces of fine sugar powdered, a little ground cinnamon, and three grains of salt. Boil till the milk is reduced one-third; then take five or six eggs thickened with a little fine flour, well beaten, and gradually add to the milk, stirring well; strain through a fine sieve into the dish for the table; place it in a hot bath on the hob till the cream is set. Grate a little nutmeg over the top, and brown.

CREAM PUDDING.—Cream, 1 pint; the yolks of seven eggs, seven table-spoonfuls of flour, 2 table-spoonfuls of sugar, salt, and a small bit of soda. Rub the cream with the eggs and flour; add the rest, the milk last, just before baking, and pour the whole into the pudding dish. Serve with sauce of wine, sugar, butter flavoured as you like.

CREAM AND SNOW.—Make a rich boiled custard, and put it in the bottom of a dish; take the whites of eight eggs, beat with rose water, and a spoonful of fine sugar, till it be a strong froth; put some milk and water into a stew-pan; when it boils, take the froth off the eggs, and lay it on the milk and water; boil up once; take off carefully, and lay it on the custard.

CRIBBAGE is considered to be the next most scientific game to whist. It is played by four or two partners, with a whole pack of cards, and is termed five, six, or eight-card cribbage, according to the number dealt to each person; but five-card cribbage is the usual game.

The parties cut for deal, and he that cuts the lowest card, deals out five cards to each player, one at a time; each player then lays out one card for crib, which always belongs to the dealer: one opponent then cuts the cards, and the dealer takes the uppermost card, and lays it face upwards on the four cards composing the crib. If it should happen to be a knave it counts two to the dealer; the card thus turned up is included in the counting, by both parties, when counting their hands; the crib is counted by the dealer alone.

For every two cards of one sort that can be made, the person playing the second, that is, making the pair, counts two.

Should the third player play another card the same as the two former, it is called a Pair Royal, and counts six.

And should the last player also possess a similar card to the previous three, it is called a double Pair Royal, and scores twelve.

Any four cards, of any suits, reckon a double Pair Royal, either in hand or in crib; such as four deuces, kings, sevens, nines, in short four of any number or description. Same with pair royals and pairs.

All sequences count of any suits, according to the number. All flushes count, that is, your hand being composed of any four cards of the same suit.

If you hold the knave of the suit turned up, you score one for his nob, as it is termed. Should you hold four hearts, clubs, or any other suit, in your hand, and the turn-up card is of the same suit, you count a flush of five.

Pair-hand Cribbage is more generally played than four-hand, from which it only varies in each of the players putting out two cards for the crib, retaining only three in their hand. First, the two cut for deal, which belongs to the person cutting lowest, the non-dealer securing three points as equivalent to the crib; the dealer must give one card alternately to his opponent and himself, until each has five. In laying out for the crib, study your hand, for what might be correct in one instance, would be dangerous in the other.

When you hold a pair royal, or three cards of one sort, put out the other two for either crib; unless those two others be fives, or a two and a three, or seven and eight, or a ten and a five; in which cases it is better if it is your opponent's crib, to spoil your hand by keeping these cards, and chance a card turning up to your advantage.

Laws of Cribbage. The dealer may discover his own cards during the deal if he pleases; but if he shows any of his opponent's, that opponent may call a fresh deal, and also add two to his score.

Should too many cards be dealt to either hand, the non-dealer may demand another deal, and also add another two points to his score; but if not, the surplus cards must be drawn; and when any player, after the game has commenced, has more than his proper number of cards in hand, then the adverse party may add four to their score, and demand a new deal.

If any player touch or interfere with the cards, after dealing, until cutting them, for the turn-up card, his adversary shall score two points.

When either player scores more than he is justly entitled to, the adverse party cannot only put him back as many holes as he has overmarked, but he may score the same extra number for himself.

If either party by mistake should take out his front peg, he must place it back, behind the other.

If either party touches even his own peg, without occasion, his opponent may score two points.

Either party putting down a less number of points than are due to him, incurs the loss of those points. Each player, when he has taken his hand and scored it, has a right to place his own cards on the pack.

CRICKETS, *to destroy.*—See *Cockroaches,* for the same directions are applicable to Crickets.——Or put a little chloride of lime and powdered tobacco in their holes. ——Or a little snuff.——The smoke of charcoal destroys both them and cockroaches.—Loud vibrating sounds drive away crickets.

CRIMSON DYE FOR SILK. —For each lb. of cloth, or stuff, dissolve in boiling water $2\frac{1}{2}$ ozs. of alum, and $1\frac{1}{2}$ ozs. of white tartar. Boil two minutes; put in the goods, and boil $1\frac{1}{2}$ hour. Take out and add fresh water; when it boils, put in $1\frac{1}{2}$ oz. of cochineal powdered; boil 1 hour. The shade may be lighter by using less of the ingredients.

CRIMSON FLAME. — Take alcohol, any quantity, and dissolve a little of one of the salts of strontia in it.

CROSS BUNS.—To $2\frac{1}{2}$ lbs. of flour add 1 lb. of powdered sugar, and a little coriander seed, cassia, and mace, powdered fine; make a paste with $\frac{1}{4}$ lb. of butter dissolved in half a pint of hot milk; work in three table-spoonfuls of yeast and a little salt; set it before the fire for an hour to rise; make it into buns; and place before the fire on a tin for half an hour; lastly brush them over with warm milk, and bake to a nice brown in a slow oven.

CROUP.—This is a dangerous disease. It is common to infancy, and rarely occurs to adults. It is an inflammation of the larynx, treachea, and contiguous tissues. It derives its name from the peculiar sound of the voice and breathing, being of a whistling or crowing character, owing to a contraction of the glottis. It generally commences with a common cold and catarrh, hoarseness, cough, and increased difficulty of breathing, and the crowing already spoken of. It demands prompt treatment.

The great object is to diminish the inflammation and irritation, and to relax the spasmodic state of the muscles in the parts diseased. The vessels in those parts are overcharged with blood, by an imperfect action of the exhalents. Place the feet in warm water, and give an *emetic*. After bathing, rub the legs and feet well with flannel. Then give a vapour bath, if the patient can bear it. (See *Emetic Powder—-Expectorant Tincture*.) Repeat the process, if needful. The perspiration will be greater by applying to the feet and each side hot bricks, and wrapped in flannel saturated with vinegar and a little water. At the same time give an aperient to produce a free action on the bowels. Apply this tincture to the throat, viz:— Half a tea-spoonful of cayenne pepper, nearly a cupful of vinegar; simmer ten minutes, and strain. This tincture may be diluted with warm water, according to the strength of the patient. Rub it well on the throat for five or ten minutes; and next saturate a flannel with it, and apply it to the throat. This application tends to relieve the internally congested blood-vessels. Repeat the application, as necessary.

Mustard plasters may be applied to the feet, the upper part of the chest, and between the shoulders alternately. It has been recommended to steep hops in hot vinegar, and the patient to inhale the vapour. Even a large sponge dipped in as hot water as the hand can bear, squeezed half dry, and renewed before it is cool, is of great advantage. Keep the atmosphere of the room at a regular temperature. Aid the perspiration by warm drinks, as balm tea, &c.

To prevent a return of this disorder, keep the child warm, avoid wet feet, cold, damp, easterly winds, &c. Children whose constitutions dispose them to croup, ought to have their diet properly regulated, and be kept from all crude, raw, and trashy fruits.

CRUMPETS.—Beat well two eggs, and put them into a quart of warm milk and water, with a table-spoonful of yeast; beat in as much fine flour to make them rather thicker than a common batter pudding. Heat the bakestone very hot, rub it with a little butter on a cloth; have a tin ring the size and thickness of a crumpet, into which pour the batter. Turn them quickly with a thin broad knife.

CRUMPETS, *Orange*.—Cream and new milk, of each 1 pint; warm and put to it a little rennet to break it, then stir it gently; drain on a cloth six hours; take the rind of three oranges, boiled, as for preserving, in three waters; pound fine, and mix with the curd and 8 eggs, in a mortar, some nutmeg, the juice of a lemon, and sugar to taste. Bake as above. Some persons add slices of orange.

CRUMPETS, *Royal*. — Three cups of raised dough; work 4 table-spoonfuls of melted butter in the dough; a cup of sugar and 3 eggs beaten; put in buttered tins; bake 20 minutes. When served too many should not lie on each other, as it destroys the crispness, and makes them soft.

CRUMPETS, *Scotch.*—Milk, 1 pint; two or three eggs; a little butter; four table-spoonfuls of yeast, salt; as much oatmeal, or unsifted flour, as will make a batter. Melt the butter in the milk made hot; and when the batter is just warm, beat the eggs, and mix them well in. Let it stand to rise. Butter them, and serve hot.

CRUSHES. — Take 1 lb. of flour, and ¼ lb. of butter, rubbed in; mix with cold water, and a little yeast; stamp it with a butter print, and lay the paste on the mould; lay on tins, to bake a fine brown.

CRUST, *a short one.*—Make 2 ozs. of pounded and sifted white sugar dry; mix it with 1 lb. of flour well dried; rub into it 3 or 4 ozs. of butter, so fine as not to be seen —into some cream put the yolks of two eggs, beaten, and mix the above into a smooth paste; roll it thin, and bake it in a slow oven.

CRUST FOR APPLE PIES, &c.—Rub 6 ozs. of butter in 9 of flour, mix it into a stiffish paste, with as little water as possible, beat it well, and roll it thin; bake it in a moderate oven.

CRUST FOR RAISED MEAT PIES, &c.—Boil water with a little fine lard, and an equal quantity of fresh dripping, or of butter. While hot, mix this with as much flour as you will want, making the paste as stiff as you can to be smooth, which is to be made by good kneading and beating it with the rolling pin. When quite smooth, put a lump into a cloth to soak till nearly cold.

Those who are not clever at raising crust, may roll the paste of a proper thickness, and cut out the top and bottom of the pie, then a long piece of the sides. Cement the bottom to the sides with egg, bringing the former rather further out, and pinching both together; put egg between the paste to make it adhere to the sides. Fill your pie and put on the cover, and pinch it and the side-crust together. The same way of uniting the paste is to be observed if the sides are pressed into a tin form, in which the paste must be baked, after it shall be filled and covered; but the tin should be buttered, and carefully taken off when done enough; and as the form makes the sides of too light a colour, the paste should be put in the oven again for 15 minutes. With a feather, put egg over as at first.

CRUST, *for Sweet Pastry.*— Work ½ lb. lightly of butter into 1 lb. of flour, breaking it small; add salt, 2 ozs. of finely powdered sugar, and sufficient milk to make it into a smooth paste. Bake slowly, and keep it pale.

CRUST FOR TARTS.—Beat an egg till quite thin, have ready 10 ozs. of butter, melted without being oiled; when cold mix the egg with it and stir it into 1 lb. of flour well dried; make the paste very thin, line the patty pans quickly; as you put them in the oven, brush them over with water, and sift sugar over them.

CUCUMBERS, *for immediate use.*—Slice, sprinkle with salt; let them stand several hours, drain, and then put to them sliced onions, vinegar to cover them, with salt, pepper, &c. Cayenne pepper and ground mustard render them wholesome.

CUCUMBERS, *to pickle in slices.*—Cut into slices; sprinkle salt over them, and lay with them sliced onions; let them stand twenty-four hours; then drain them; boil two quarts of vinegar, with cayenne pepper, large mace, ginger, and a table-spoonful of ground mustard. Mustard renders them *wholesome*. Put the cucumbers into a jar, and pour the vinegar boiling hot upon them. Cover well; after standing two days, boil the pickle again until they are green. Cucumbers keep best unpared.

CULVER'S ROOT.—A valuable American plant. The root is a good purgative, tonic, diaphoretic, antiseptic, &c. Its operation is mild, without producing weakness or prostration, and is most effective in fevers, to remove black and morbid matter from the bowels. Good for indigestion, to purify the blood, and acts powerfully on the absorbent system, Valuable in dropsy. Dose, one or too spoonfuls in a small cupful of water sweetened.

CUMMIN PLASTER.—Take cummin seeds, caraway seeds, bayberries, of each, 3 ozs.; burgundy pitch, 3 lbs.; yellow-wax, 3 ozs.; melt the pitch and wax together, and the other ingredients, powdered; make into rolls. To be spread on leather. To be applied to the lower part of the abdomen for expelling flatulence, and colicky pains.

CURDS AND WHEY may be made by putting half a drachm of citric acid into a pint of milk.

CURD CHEESECAKES.—Half a pint of good curds; beat them with four eggs, some rich cream, half a nutmeg, a spoonful of ratafia, rose, or orange flower water; add 4 ozs. of sugar; 8 ozs. of currants, well washed and dried. Bake in patty-pans, with a good crust under them.

CURD PUDDING.—Rub the curd of two gallons of milk, well drained through a sieve; mix it with six eggs, a little cream, two spoonfuls of orange flour water, half a nutmeg; flour and bread crumbs, three spoonfuls each; currants and raisins, half a pound each. Boil one hour in a thick, well floured cloth.

CURLING *of the Hair.*—Use no oil; curl it when wet, and allow it to dry in that state. Use a weak solution of isinglass, which secures a permanent form. *A. N.*

CURRANT BISCUITS.—Sugar, 1½ lb.; flour, 2 lbs.; butter, 1¼ lb.; currants, 1½ lb.; 1 teaspoonful each of cinnamon and nutmeg; five eggs. Beat the butter and sugar together, whisk the eggs, and add to the other ingredients, mix well. Roll out the dough in sheets, cut into cakes, place them on tins, strew white sugar on the top, and bake in a moderate oven.

BLACK CURRANT *Water Ice.*—Put a table-spoonful of black currant jelly into a basin; add the juice of two lemons, a gill of black currant syrup, and half a pint of water; strain, and freeze.

CURRANT CAKES.—Take 2 lbs. of flour, and 1 lb. of butter rubbed into the flour; mix it to a paste with cold water, and two tea-spoonfuls of yeast; take 10 ozs. of currants, 4 ozs. of sugar, a little clove pepper, and a little cinnamon: mix, and put a little into the inside of every cake; roll your cakes thin, and cut into different shapes with a tin mould; bake them in a sharp oven.

CURRANT DROPS.—Put 1 lb. of pounded loaf sugar upon a plate; then the juice of black or red currants; make into a paste of thickish consistency; drop on fine paper, and dry.

CURRANT JAM, *black, red or white.*—Let the fruit be very ripe, pick it clean from the stalks, bruise it, and to every pound put three quarters of a pound of loaf-sugar;

stir it well, and boil half an hour.

CURRANT JELLY, *red or black*.—Strip the fruit, and in a stone jar stew them in a sauce-pan of water, or on the fire; strain off the liquor, and to every pint weigh 1 lb. of loaf-sugar; put the latter in large lumps into it, in a stone or China-vessel, till nearly dissolved; then put it into a preserving-pan; simmer and skim. When it will jelly on a plate, put it in small jars or glasses.

CURRANTS, *to preserve for Tarts*.—Let the currants be ripe, dry, and well picked. To every 1¼ lb. of currants, put 1 lb. of sugar into a preserving pan with as much juice of currants as will dissolve it; when it boils skim it, and put in the currants; boil till clear; jar, and put brandy-paper over; tie down; keep in a dry place.

CURRANT SHRUB.—To every quart of juice, add 1 lb. of fine white sugar, and a quarter of a pint of brandy. Bottle and cork.

CURRANTS, *Syrups of Black*.—Half a pint of strained juice of black currants; fine sugar, 12 ozs. Dissolve the sugar in a pint of water, and boil to make a syrup. It is valuable for sore throats; it cleanses from phlegm, and abates thirst and fever.

CURRANT WINE.—Gather the currants when ripe, strip them, and squeeze out the juice; to one gallon of the juice put two gallons of cold water and two spoonfuls of yeast; let it ferment two days, strain through a hair sieve; and to every gallon of liquor add 3 lbs. of loaf-sugar, stir it well together, put it in a good cask; to every 10 gallons of wine put one quart of brandy; close well up and let it stand four months, then bottle it; a few raspberries will improve the flavour.

CURRY, *Indian way of dressing*.—Stew your meat in water enough to cover it. Mix the curry powder with milk, salt, and lemon juice; add this to the meat liquor; fry a few onions to a light brown, and put them in just before dishing.

CURRY POWDER. — Take 3 ozs. of coriander; 1 oz. black pepper; mustard and ginger, of each, ½ oz.; lesser cardamoms, cayenne, and cummin seed, of each, ¼ oz. Dry them well, and powder fine; mix, and keep in a well-stopped bottle. *Hu.*

CURRY STEW.—Cow-heel is the best material for a dish of curry. Being mucilaginous, it absorbs the nature of the curry, and gives a better flavour to the meat. If a rabbit or fowl, cut into small bits, add butter, or rich gravy to the meat, and onion in thin slices; put into a stew-pan. Stew over a gentle fire for twenty minutes. Mix a table-spoonful of flour with one of salt, in water, half a cupful of cream, if you like, and three or four tea-spoonfuls of curry powder, and the juice of a lemon. Stir all well together, and boil from ten to twenty minutes.

CURRY, *to dress*. — Cut up fowls or rabbits; put ¼ lb. of butter into a stew-pan, and when melted put in the meat, with two onions sliced; brown well, and add ½ pint of gravy; simmer 20 minutes; mix in a basin a table-spoonful of curry powder, one of flour, and a little salt, mix it smooth with water; simmer all in the pan 20 minutes; add lemon juice, and a bit of butter. *Hu.*

CUSTARDS, *Almond*. — Take of almonds, ¼ lb., blanch and beat them very fine, put them into a pint of cream, with two spoonfuls of rose-water. Sweeten it to your palate; beat up the yolks of four eggs, very fine, and put them in. Stir all together one way over the fire, till it is thick, and then pour it into cups.

CUSTARDS, *Baked.*—Boil a pint of cream with some mace and cinnamon: and when it is cold, take four yolks and two whites of eggs, a little rose and orange-flower water, sack, nutmeg, and sugar to your palate. Mix them well, and bake it in cups.

Or, pour into a deep dish, with or without lining or rim of paste; grate nutmeg and lemon peel over the top, and bake it in a slow oven about thirty minutes.

CUSTARDS, *Beast.*—Set a pint of beast over the fire with a little cinnamon, and three bay leaves, and let it be boiling hot. Then take it off, and have ready mixed a spoonful of flower, and the same of thick cream. Pour the hot beast upon it by degrees, mix it well together, and sweeten it to your taste. You may bake it either with crust or in cups.

CUSTARD, *Cheap and good.*— Boil three pints or new milk with a little lemon peel, a little cinnamon, three bay leaves, and sweeten it; rub down a large spoonful of rice flour into a cup of cold milk, and mix it with two yolks of eggs well beaten; take a basin of boiling milk and mix with the cold, then pour that to the boiling, stirring it one way till it begins to thicken, and is just going to boil up, then add a large spoonful of peach water, and a little ratafia; marbles boiled in custard or any thing likely to burn, will, by shaking them in the saucepan, prevent its catching.

CUSTARD FRITTERS.—Beat the yolks of 8 eggs with a spoonful of flour, half a nutmeg, a little salt, and a glass of brandy; add a pint of cream; sweeten; bake in a dish; when cold, cut into quarters; dip them in batter made of ½ pint of cream, ¼ pint of milk, 4 eggs, a little flour, and ginger grated; fry in good lard or dripping, then strew over them grated sugar. *Hu.*

CUSTARD, ORANGE.—Boil the juice of 12 oranges with a little of the rinds and sugar to your taste. Strain it, and when cold add a pint of cream and the yolks of 12 eggs. Stir over a slow fire until it thickens.

CUSTARD OSWEGO, *Boiled.* —Two tablespoonfuls of Oswego Prepared Corn to one quart of milk; mix the corn with a small quantity of the milk, and flavour it; beat up two eggs. Heat the remainder of the milk to *near* boiling,—then add the mixed corn, the eggs, four table-spoonfuls of sugar, and a little butter and salt. Boil it two minutes, stirring it briskly.

CUSTARD PIE.—Boil a quart of milk with the rind of a lemon. Strain it, and then boil. Mix a table-spoonful of flour smoothly with two of milk, and stir it into the boiling milk. Boil a minute, constantly stirring; take off, and when cool, add three beaten eggs; sweeten to your taste; bake in a quick oven.

CUSTARD PUDDING.-Half-pint of cream; pint of new milk, boiled; stir in a little finely sifted flour; add three or four table-spoonfuls of white sugar, quarter of a nutmeg grated, a tea-spoonful of lemon-peel finely cut; the yolks of two eggs. Beat well and mix. Add brandy according to taste. Then place some light puff paste round the sides of a dish, pour in the custard, and bake about half an hour.

CUSTARD PUDDING, *Boiled.*—Boil a stick of cinnamon and lemon peel in a quart of thin cream, with ¼ lb. of sugar; when cold, add the yolks of six eggs well beaten, and mix; set over a slow fire, and stir one way, till it is thick; but do not let it boil; let it cool; butter a cloth; dredge it with flour, tie up the custard; boil three quarters of an hour. When out, turn it upside down on the dish; take the cloth off carefully.

CUSTARDS, *Rice.*-Put a blade of mace and quarter of nutmeg into a quart of cream; boil, strain, and add to it some whole rice boiled, and a little brandy. Sweeten to your palate, stir it over the fire till it thickens, and serve it up in cups, or a dish. It may be used either hot or cold.

CUSTARD, RICH. — Boil a pint of milk with lemon peel and cinnamon; mix a pint of cream and the yolks of five eggs well beaten. When the milk tastes of the seasoning, sweeten it enough for the whole; pour it into the cream, stirring it well; then give the custard a simmer till of a proper thickness. Don't let it boil; stir the whole time one way; season as above. If to be extremely rich, put no milk, but a quart of cream to the eggs.

CUTS.—All that is required in cases of incised wounds or cuts, is to clear away the surrounding blood, &c., and bring the lips of the wound closely together, retaining them in that position by slips of adhesive plaster, and if the cut be deep and extensive, supporting it and the surrounding parts by proper bandages.

In all large wounds, interstices should be left between each slip of plaster, to facilitate the escape of secreted matter, or effused blood. The first dressing should remain for three or four days, and if much pain or inflammation follows the accident, gentle purgatives should be taken.

The bleeding consequent upon wounds may be stopped by pressure and rest. The application of cobweb will arrest the flow of blood.

For light cuts with a knife, or any sharp instrument, the Riga balsam usually stops the bleeding immediately.

CUTS. — After closing the wound, bind on toasted cheese.— Or pounded grass; shake it off after twelve hours.—*Wesley.*

DAFFY'S ELIXIR.—Take of the best senna, guiacum, liquorice sliced small, aniseeds, coriander seeds, and elecampane root, of each half an ounce; raisins of the sun, stoned, a quarter of a pound: let them all be bruised and put into a quart of brandy. Let it stand by the fire for a few days, and then strain it. Good for flatulence.

DAINTY BISCUITS. — A cupful of flour, the whites of four eggs, well beaten, 3 or 4 ozs. of beef suet, chopped fine; bitter almonds, blanched, and chopped, $\frac{1}{2}$ oz.; mix the yolks with six ounces of fine sugar; mix all with lemon to flavour. Bake in small tins quickly.

DAINTY BREAD. — Flour, 6 lbs.; butter, 6 ozs.; 5 or 6 eggs well beaten; $1\frac{1}{2}$ pint of milk, and sufficient yeast. Mix into a paste, and form into rolls or cakes. When risen, bake. When cool, dip in milk, and dry in a Dutch oven before the fire.

DAMP WALLS.—Cover with this mixture:—Boil 1 quart of linseed oil, 3 ozs. of litharge, and 4 ozs. of resin, and put on four or five coats.——Or, line the wall with sheet lead, the thickness of tea lead, and fasten with copper nails.

DAMP WALLS. — Boil two quarts of tar, with two ounces of kitchen grease, for a quarter of an hour, in an iron pot. Add some of this tar to a mixture of slaked lime and powdered glass, passed through a flour-sieve, two parts of lime and one of glass, till the mixture is like thin plaster. It must be used immediately after being mixed, and no more of it should be mixed than will coat one square foot of wall, as it quickly becomes too hard for use. For a wall merely damp, a coating one eighth of an inch thick is sufficient; but if the wall is wet, there must be a second coat. Plaster made of lime, hair, and plaster of Paris, may afterwards be laid on as a cement.

DAMSON DUMPLINGS. — Line a basin with suitable crust, rolled thin, fill with damsons, and sugar, cover it with paste; boil in a cloth for an hour. Sauce;—melted butter, milk or cream.

DAMSON JELLY.—Proceed as in *Cherry Jelly*, which see.

DAMSON PIE.—The same as *Cherry Pie*, which see.

DAMSON PRESERVES. — Cut the damsons into pieces, and put them on the fire, with as much water as will cover them. When they are boiled, and the liquor strong, strain, and add to every pound of the damsons 1 lb. of refined sugar. Put one third of it into the liquor, put on the fire, and when it simmers, put in the damsons. Give one good boil, and take off for half an hour covered close. Set them on again, and simmer over the fire after turning them. Then put them in a basin, strew all the sugar that was left on them, and pour the hot liquor over them. Cover; let them stand till the next day, and then boil them up again till they are enough. Then put them in pots; boil the liquor till it jellies, and pour it upon them when almost cold. Put paper over them, and tie them up close. *Far.*

DAMSON PUDDING.—Four or five table-spoonfuls of flour, three eggs beaten, a pint of milk, made into batter. Stone 1½ lbs. of damsons, put them and 6 ozs. of sugar into the batter, and boil in a buttered basin for one hour and a half.

DAMSON WINE.-Take seven or eight pounds of fruit to a gallon of water. Bruise the damsons, and pour the water boiling upon them. Let it stand two or three days. Draw off the liquor, and to every gallon of liquor, add three pounds of sugar. Barrel, and stop it close. It should be kept several months before using it.

DANDELION.-——This very valuable plant is well known. It is diuretic, tonic, and aperient, and has a direct action in removing obstructions of the liver, kidneys, and other viscera. It is peculiarly valuable in all liver complaints, derangement of the digestive organs, and in dropsical affections. Had not this plant been so common and so cheap, it would be *prized like gold!* An infusion or decoction may be made of the roots and leaves. But the extract is the best, thus prepared:—Take up the roots in September, clean them; bruise in a mortar, and press out the juice; strain, and put it upon a plate in a warm room to evaporate, and render it thick and solid. Dose; from a scruple to a drachm three times a day.

Dandelion has cured liver complaints when all other means have failed. "The more dandelion is used, the more certain proof will it afford of its utility." *Dr. J. Johnson.*

DANDELION BEER.—Dandelion root, ½ lb. to 1 gallon of water; boil well, and when cooled new milk warm, add 1 lb. sugar, 1 oz. ginger, a lemon, and 1 oz. cream of tartar. Add a little yeast. It is very good for the liver and digestion.

Young nettles, balm, or any other herb may be treated the same way.

DANDELION COFFEE.—Good colonial coffee, 3 parts; hard extract of dandelion, 1 part; chicory, 1 part. Reduce them to coarse powder, and mix, and grind them together. Good for digestion and affections of the liver.

DEAFNESS.-Fox-glove leaves well bruised; mix the juice with double the quantity of brandy. Keep for use. Drop one drop into the ear once a day, and place in the ear constantly a piece of cotton saturated with it.——Or, clean the ear well out with warm water, dry it, and then soak cotton in glycerine, and put it into the ear, moving it backwards and forwards, to lubricate it thoroughly——Or, syringe the ears well with warm milk and oil; then take opodeldoc, and oil of almonds, of each, ¼ oz., and apply with cotton wool.

Or, fill a clean stone bottle with hot water; lay the ear on the bottle as hot as it can be borne, so that the steam may ascend into it every night when going to bed, for five or ten minutes.

Or, take fine black wool, dip it in *Camphorated Oil*, and put it into the ear; as it dries, dip it again; and keep it moistened in the ear for two or three weeks.

Be electrified through the ear.——Or, put a little salt in the ear mixed with sweet oil.——Or, three drops of onion juice at lying down, keeping it in with wool.——Or, mix brandy and sweet oil; dip black wool in this and put it into the ear. When it grows dry, wash it well in brandy; dip it and put it in again.—If attended with headache, peel a clove of garlic, dip it in honey. Apply it with black wool. Previously drop into the ear a few drops of the juice.—A mixture of ten drops of spirit of turpentine with 1 oz. of almond oil, using black wool, will tend to the cure of deafness arising from diseased ceruminous glands.—If deafness arises from wax, syringe the ear with warm water, applying the night before a little glycerine.

DEAFNESS CURED BY ETHER.—A poor French governess, Madlle Cleret, has succeeded in partially curing several persons afflicted with deafness and loss of speech. The French Academy have awarded the Monthyon Prize for the discovery, which has been proved innocuous. The method consists in introducing sulphuric ether into the aural conduit, in doses of two to eight drops a day for twenty days, when the application is suspended for a short time, and again commenced. A gunner's mate, aged 51, had been attacked six months before with acute rheumatism, which became chronic and complicated, with deafness in the left ear, and difficulty of hearing in the right one. There was frequent singing in both ears, and the deafness increased or diminished with the rheumatic pains. At the first, a few drops of ether were instilled into both his ears, when he immediately experienced a feeling of expansion within, with a slight pain, and from that moment he could distinguish sounds less confusedly. On the following morning he declared he could hear with his right ear quite as well as before his illness; the installation was therefore only repeated in the left ear, and on the fourth day he declared himself quite cured. Another case, similar to this, is reported by Dr. Berlemont, of Joncourt; and Dr. Coursier, of Honnecourt, announces that he has been treating six patients, between five and fifteen years of age, for some time with ether, to their manifest advantage.

An eminent physician says,— "Take sassafras oil, five drops; sweet oil, ½ oz. Mix, and drop into the ear once or twice a day." He says that this seldom fails.— —Or, saturate a little cotton wool with tincture of Lobelia, and insert twice a day.

DELIRIUM TREMENS.— This is the disease of drunkards, and those who take narcotics, as opium, &c. It may be called "the *brain fever of drunkards.*" The person is tremulous, has nausea, vomiting, and wakefulness, restlessness; he raves, and imagines snakes, demons, &c., are about him. This disease doubtless arises from extreme stimulus of the brain.

To cure.—First allay the paroxysm, calm and support the nervous system, by giving brandy and other spirits. The redness of the face, and the pulsation of the arteries, heart, &c., indicate determination of blood to the head. Equalize the circulation by bathing the feet and legs in warm leywater; then apply mustard plasters to the feet and nape of the neck. Give a purge; and now and then a cupful of valerian scullcap, or strong hop tea, or from 10 to 20 drops of laudanum. Emetics are very useful, and may be given in the same kind of spirits the patient has been accustomed to take. A strong decoction of wormwood is successfully used in American hospitals.

DEMULCENTS. — Medicines moistening, softening, and abating irritation in a part.

DENTIFRICE, *Indian.*—Procure six betel nuts from a drysalter's, and place them in a charcoal fire, until they become white hot. When they are cold, place them in a mortar, and reduce them to fine powder. Deposit in boxes for use. It may be scented with orange flower water or extract of orris root. This tooth powder is prized for its antiseptic efficacy, dispelling all impurities of the teeth and gums, and preserving the enamel from corrosion.

DENTRIFICE, *Invaluable.*— Dissolve nearly a tea-spoonful of finely powdered borax in half a pint of tepid water; add to it 10 drops of tincture of myrrh.——Or prepared chalk, 1 oz.; camphor, 1 drachm. Mix. Dissolve the camphor in a little spirits of wine.—— Or, Cuttlefish, 3 ozs.; cream of tarter, ½ oz.; orris root, ¼ oz. Powder all fine. Mix, and add 10 drops of tincture of myrrh.

DEPILATORY. — *To remove superfluous Hairs*, satuarate the part well with fine oil. In about an hour, wipe it off; then take finely powdered quick lime, 1 oz.; powdered orpiment, 1 drachm; mix with white of egg; and apply with a small brush.

DETERGENTS. —— Deterge means to cleanse. Detergents remove unwholesome matters adhering to, and obstructing the vessels; usually applied to foul ulcers, &c., as tincture of myrrh, honey, alum, water, turpentine, &c.

DEVONSHIRE SOUP—Lean beef, 2 lbs.; six onions, six potatoes, one carrot, one turnip, half a pint of split peas, one gallon of water, a head of celery, and a British herring, with salt and pepper. When boiled, pass through a sieve; add spinach and celery boiled, dried mint, and toasted bread.

DIABETES. — An excessive discharge of urine.

Sassafras, 2 oz.; guiacum, 1 oz.; liquorice root, 3 ozs.; coriander seeds, bruised, 6 drachms; infuse in one gallon of cold lime water for two days. Take a cupful three or four times a day.——Or, 4 ozs. of alum whey may be taken three times a day. Made thus—Boil two quarts of milk over a slow fire, with three drachms of alum till turned into whey.

Or, take the *Diuretic Drops*—Give the Bitter Vapour Bath occasionally, and rub the body well with the Stimulating Liniment. If the bowels are constipated, give the Cathartic Powder.

A DIABETES.—Drink wine, boiled with ginger, as much and as often as your strength will bear. Let your drink be milk and water. All milk meats are good.——Or, drink three or four times a-day a quarter of a pint of alum posset, putting three drachms of alum to four pints of milk. It seldom fails to cure in eight or ten days.—*Dr. Mead.*——Or, infuse half an ounce of cantharides in a pint of elixir of vitriol. Give from ten to thirty drops in Bristol water twice or thrice a-day.—*Wesley.*

DIAMOND CEMENT.—Take isinglass, soak it in water until it becomes soft, then dissolve it in proof-spirit, and add a little resin varnish. Used for joining china, glass, &c., and, under the name of "Armenian cement," for joining and fixing precious stones.

DIAPHORETICS. - Medicines producing perspiration, or gentle sweat.

DIAPHORETIC POWDER.—Ipecacuanha powder, 2 grains; purified opium, ½ grain; nitrate of potass, or saltpetre, 10 grains. Take at bed-time in a severe attack of influenza, or bronchitis, in gruel. ☞ Henbane is preferable to opium.

DIAPHORETIC DECOCTION.—Simply 2 or 3 ounces of Pleurisyroot, boiled in two or three pints of water. A tea-cupful. A good remedy for pleurisy, and inflammation of the lungs.

DIARRHŒA.——From the Greek, *dia, rheo*, to flow through. It is an undue relaxed state of the bowels, as induced by improper food, drunkenness, cold; or it may be a symptom of another disease, as consumption, &c.

The *Neutralizing Mixture* will be found efficacious in this complaint.——Or, take a tea-spoonful of *Composition Powder*, and one of tincture of myrrh, and keep the patient warm. The following are good remedies:—

To one quart of blackberry juice add one pound of white sugar, one table-spoonful of cloves, one of allspice, one of cinnamon, and one of nutmeg. Boil all together fifteen minutes; add a wineglassful of whiskey, brandy, or rum. Bottle while hot, cork tight and seal. This is almost a specific in diarrhœa. Dose:—a wineglassful for an adult—half for a child—will often cure diarrhœa. Take three or four times a day if the case is severe.

Or, Confection of catechu, 2 drs.; cinnamon water, 4 ounces; syrup of white poppies, 1 ounce; mix together. One or two table-spoonfuls to be taken twice or thrice a-day as required; for children under ten years of age, a dessert spoonful to be used; under two years, a tea-spoonful, also two or three times a-day, as above stated.

Draught for Diarrhœa. Take tincture of opium, 30 drops; prepared chalk, 2 drachms; powdered gum, 4 drachms; tincture of catechu, 2 drachms; rose-water, 2 ounces. Mix, and take a table-spoonful three or four times a day.

Or fill a small basin with dry flour, tightly cover it with a greased cloth; boil it three hours.

Then let it cool. For use, grate a dessert spoonful of it into peppermint water; more for an adult.—— Or make a strong tea of blackberry leaves, or raspberry leaves. I have known the latter superior to all physicians. Follow it with a little port wine, grated nutmeg and ginger.

Or, take of poplar bark, $\frac{1}{2}$ oz.; prickly ash berries, $\frac{1}{4}$ oz.; fleabane, $\frac{1}{2}$ oz.; slippery elm, 1 drachm; pour on them a pint of boiling water; infuse two or three hours. ——Tonics must be given after the cessation of the relax.

DINING TABLES, *to polish*.—Put a little cold-drawn linseed oil in the middle of a table, and then with a piece of *linen* rub it well over the table; repeatedly change the linen till the table is dry. The table, by repeating this process, will assume a beautiful polish.

DINNER PILLS.—Aloes and Jalap, of each 2 ozs.; Rhubarb, $\frac{1}{2}$ oz. Make into three grain pills with Syrups of Wormwood. Take from one to four during the day.

DIPHTHERIA.—"I have had the treatment of several cases, and have uniformily been successful; the remedy is very simple. It is the external application of water to the throat, at degrees of temperature alternating from the highest that the human skin will bear, down to almost zero. I am prepared to verify that by proof. A. HENDERSON, M.R.C.S., Eng. 13, Upper Seymour St., Portman Square, London, 1858.

M Roche mentions in *L'Union Medicale* that he had saved six patients in six cases of Diphtheria by the following mode of treatment. The false membranes were first freely cauterized with lunar caustic, and injections then made every hour against the fauces with a solution of common salt, the strength of the solution being such as not to create nausea. Chlorate of Potash was also given internally; and Tincture of Iodine as a topical application, was used in half the cases; but M. Roche considers that the irrigations with the solution of common salt were the chief agents in the case.

DIPHTHERIA, *American remedy for*.—Make two small bags to reach from ear to ear, and fill them with wood ashes and salt; dip them in hot water, and wring them out so that they will not drip, and apply them to the throat; cover up the whole with a flannel cloth, and change them as often as they become cool, until the throat becomes irritated, near blistering. For children it is necessary to put flannel cloths between the ashes and the throat to prevent blistering. When the ashes have been on a sufficient time take a wet flannel cloth and rub it with castile soap until it is covered with a thick lather; dip it in hot water, and apply it to the throat, and change as they cool; at the same time use a gargle made of one tea-spoonful of cayenne pepper, one of salt, one of molasses, in a tea-cupful of hot water, and when cool, add one-fourth as much cider, vinegar, and gargle every 15 minutes, until the patient requires sleep. A gargle made of castile soap is good to be used part of the time."

A correspondent in Maine, in sending the above remedy, says there had been a number of deaths from diphtheria until this remedy was used, since then all had recovered.

DIPHTHERIA.—A gentleman who has administered the following remedy for diphtheria says that it has always proved effectual: Take a tobacco pipe, place a live coal in the bowl, drop a little tar upon the coal, and let the patient draw smoke into the mouth, and discharge it through the nostrils. The remedy is safe and simple.

DISCOUNT TABLE.

per cent				s.	d.	
2½ is	..	..	..	0	6	per £
3 ,,	..	..	..	0	7¼	,,
4 ,,	..	..	..	0	9¾	,,
5 ,,	..	..	..	1	0	,,
6 ,,	..	..	..	1	2¼	,,
7½ ,,	..	..	..	1	6	,,
10 ,,	..	..	..	2	0	,,
12½ ,,	..	..	..	2	6	,,
15 ,,	..	..	..	3	0	,,
17½ ,,	..	..	..	3	6	,,
20 ,,	..	..	..	4	0	,,
22½ ,,	..	..	..	4	6	,,
25 ,,	..	..	..	5	0	,,
30 ,,	..	..	..	6	0	,,
35 ,,	..	..	..	7	0	,,

DISCUTIENT OINTMENT.—Deadly Night shade, Bark of Bitter-sweet root, Cicuta leaves, Stramonium leaves, of each 3 ozs.; lard, 1½ lb. Bruise and simmer the roots in spirits; then add the lard, and simmer till the ingredients are crisp, and strain. A great disperser of scrofulous and glandulor swellings.

DISEASE, *Indications of.*—Disease sometimes attacks suddenly; sometimes it comes on slowly. Irritation and inflammation make themselves understood at once. Mental depression is often a sign of failing health. Fevers have four stages:—

1. The *forming* stage, characterised by a feeling of weariness, aching of the limbs, pain in the back, loss of appetite and sleep, and depression of spirits.

2. The *cold* stage. A chill over the entire body is felt, with drowsiness, prostration, and sometimes by sickness.

3. The *hot* stage, when heat follows the chilness, and the skin becomes flushed and dry. Great headache prevails, restlessness, intense thirst, nausea, and light and sound give pain.

4. The *last* stage, in favourable cases, is marked by perspiration and by some relief from pain.

The state of the tongue indicates health or disease. Florid redness is a sign of dyspepsia; a livid or purple tongue, shews obstruction in the circulation, or lungs; a white tongue denotes a weak and impoverished state of the blood; a furred tongue is common to some people even when in health, but when there are bright red points perceptible beneath the fur, fever is present; a tongue with red edges and furred in the middle is a sign of intemperance, or brain disorder.

DISINFECTANTS.—— The most effectual and agreeable is *Coffee.* Even the smell of musk and castor, which cannot be overpowered by any other substance, is completely dispelled by the fumes of coffee. Powder the beans well in a mortar, and strew the powder over a heated shovel or iron plate. Carry it up and down the house to neutralize all offensive smells.

Or, in a quart of water dissolve three ounces of sugar of lead, and then add three ounces of aquafortis. Shake up well. It is efficacious, in removing offensive smells from *chamber* utensils. Sprinkle the place or room infected, or hang up cloths dipped in it. See *Chloride of Lime.*——Or, saltpetre, 6 drachms, sulphuric acid, 1 oz.; add the acid very slowly. Stir oft, that it may be diffused.—It prevents infection in fevers.

DIURETICS.—Medicines increasing the secretion of the urine.

DIURETIC DECOCTION.—Queen of the Meadow, Wild Carrot Seed, Spearmint, Milkweed, Dwarf Elder, Juniper-berries, of each, 2 ozs. Bruise, and boil a short time in two quarts of water. Very useful in gravel and dropsy. A cupful to be taken occasionally.

DIURETIC DROPS.—Tincture of Kino, ½ oz.; Balsam of Copaiba, Spirits of Turpentine, of each 1 oz.; Sweet Spirits of Nitre, 2 ozs.; Queen of the Meadow, 1 oz. Mix, and add 1 scruple of Camphor. Take nearly a teaspoonful in mucilage. Most valuable for scalding urine, inflammation of the kidneys, &c.

DIURETIC INFUSION.— Parsley seeds, ¼ oz.; Cleavers, ¾ oz.; Burdock seeds, ¾ oz.; Coolwort, ¾ oz.; Spearmint, ½ oz.; Juniper berries, ¾ oz.; Linseed, ½ oz.; Gum Arabic, ¼ ounce. Pour upon these two quarts of boiling water; infuse two or three hours, covering the vessel. Strain, and add half a pint of best gin, 4 ounces of honey, and three table-spoonfuls of Slippery Elm. This is a most valuable diuretic; it is cooling, and allays all urinary affections, gravel, scalding of urine, and it causes an easy and sufficient flow of the same.

DIURETIC PILLS.—Calcined Magnesia, 1 drachm; Solidified Copaiba, 2 ozs.; Extract of Cubebs, 1 oz.; Oil of Turpentine, 4 drops; Oil of Juniper, 6 drops; form into 3 grain pills. Take one or two a few times a-day. A *sovereign remedy* for diseases of the kidneys, bladder, urethra, gravel, whites, and venereal complaints.

DOMESTIC RULES.—Have a place for every thing—and every thing in its place, when wanted.—Do everything in its proper time.—Keep every thing to its proper use.—Keep your temper, and be forbearing.—Be economical, and not extravagant.——Avoid luxuries; plain living is best for bodily health, and mental comfort.—

Avoid intemperance, as you would the fiercest tiger.

DOUGH-NUTS. — Make into dough, 1 lb. of flour, ¼ lb. of butter; ¾ lbs. of fine sugar; a nutmeg grated, a little cinnamon, a table-spoonful of yeast, and milk sufficient to mix. Let it rise an hour; form in squares, diamonds, twists, and bake, or fry.

DOVER'S POWDER.—Ipecacuanha, in powder, 1 drachm; powdered opium, one drachm; powdered saltpetre, 1 oz. All well mixed. Dose, from 8 to 20 grains.

DRAUGHTS. —- Each player alternately moves one of his men forward at a right angle to the next white square; and when a man is moved to a square adjoining an enemy, and the square behind that man angularly is unoccupied or becomes so, that man must be captured by the adversary by leaping over with his own man to the vacant square, and the man leaped over is removed from the board.

When any man gets to the other end of the board, he becomes a king, and is crowned by placing one of the captured men upon him, he then can move and take either forwards or backwards in an angular direction; and when any player neglects to capture the adversary when he has the opportunity, he then is said to stand the "Huff." The following are the Laws of the Game:—

1. The first move of each game to be taken alternately.

2. Pointing over the board, or otherwise interrupting the view is not permitted.

3. Whoever touches a man must play him somewhere; and if a man is removed into another square, he must remain there.

4. In case of standing the "huff," it is optional with the

adversary to take the man or insist upon him taking his omitted by the "huff."

5. If either party, when it is his turn to move, hesitates for a longer period than three minutes, the other may call upon him to play; and if, after so calling upon him, he delay longer than five minutes, he loses the game.

6. During a game neither party must leave the room without the permission of the other; and a third person should decide the time of absence.

6. When the draws are given to an inferior player, the game must be played in a more advanced state; and when the situations become so equal that no advantage can be gained, then he who gives the draws shall either force the other out of his strong position, or he must be considered to have lost the game.

DRINK, STRENGTHENING.— Put to a cupful of pearl barley, with three pints of cold water, the rind of a lemon, and a small piece of cinnamon. Boil gently till the barley is tender; add ¼ oz. of extract of sarsaparilla, and boil gently five minutes more. Strain, and sweeten with honey, or sugar. You may add ginger or cayenne, if flatulent, or, phlegmatic.

DRINK FOR THE SICK.— Take half an ounce of sugar-candy, quarter of an ounce of cream of tartar, and a few lemon and orange chips; pour upon them one quart of boiling water. When cold pour off.

DRIPPING, *to clarify.*—Put water in a pan, boil, and pour your dripping in; cool, and the dripping will swim at the top, while all impurities will sink into the water. Repeat the process, if it is needful.

DROPSY.—From the Greek, *udor,* water, and *opsis,* an appearance. It denotes the effusion of water, or rather serous fluid into any cavity of the body, or into the cellular tissue under the skin.

It is indicated by distension of the belly, difficult breathing, dry skin, immoderate thirst, a dry cough, swelling of the feet and legs, deficient urine, and deficient perspiration.——*Observe;* Dropsy is a symptom of disease, rather than itself a disease, and generally the original cause is a morbid change in one or more of the principal organs of the body, the heart, liver, or kidneys. It is caused by a loss of vitality in the capillary exhalents of the blood vessels, by which they are deprived of their elasticity or contractility, consequent upon the loss of the electric fluid, or the nervous energy upon which their contractility chiefly depends; and from a deficiency of iron in the blood.

Give a vapour bath made of bitter herbs. (See Vapour Bath) Drink the Composition Powder tea, sweetened. Give diuretics, and a pill made of cayenne, colocynth and rhubarb; and also the *Diuretic Infusion.* Keep up the perspiration when deficient; and foment the body daily with the *Stimulating Liniment.* The compound extract of jalap is very effective in evacuating the water.

Or, mustard, ½ oz.; juniper berries, milkweed root, horse radish root; black alder bark, mandrake root, bitter-sweet bark, of each, 1 oz. Bruise them, and infuse in 3 quarts of hot water, adding the juice of a lemon. A wineglassful two or three times a-day.

Or, take as much as lies upon a sixpence of powdered laurel leaves, every second or third day. It works both ways.——Or, make tea of roots of dwarf elder. It works by urine. Every twelve or fourteen minutes (that is, after every discharge) drink a tea-cupful. I have known a dropsy cured by this in twelve hours' time.——Or, one was cured by taking a drachm of nitre, every morning, in a little ale.——Or, Tar-water drank twice a-day has cured many; so has an infusion of juniper berries, roasted, and made into a liquor like coffee. ——Or, three spoonfuls of the juice of leeks, or elder leaves.—Tried. This cured the windy dropsy.

Or, half a pint of decoction of butcher's broom, (intermixing purges twice or thrice a-week.) The proper purge is ten grains of jalap with six of powdered ginger. It may be increased or lessened according to the strength of the patient.

Or, of the decoction of the tops of oak boughs. This cured an inveterate dropsy in fifteen days.

Or, take senna, cream of tartar, jalap, half an ounce of each. Mix them and take a drachm every morning in broth. It usually cures in twenty days. This is nearly the same as Dr. Ward's powder; He says it seldom fails, either in the watery or windy dropsy.--*Rev. John Wesley.*

DYSENTERY, *or Bloody Flux.*—From the Greek; *dus*, painful, and *enteron*, the bowels. It is inflammation of the mucous membrane of the large intestines, especially the colon. It is attended by frequent bloody stools, straining, nausea, long attempts at evacuation, and often great pain. There is loss of appetite, strength, and great lowness of spirits. The evacuations increase, and become more fœtid. It often ends in death. It is *caused* by obstructed perspiration, morbid humours, unwholesome diet, night air, damp beds, wet clothes, intemperance, and infection, in close habitations, prisons, cells, &c. It is very prevalent in tropical climates.

To *cure*, give gentle emetics; and mild purgatives, if needful. The *Neutralizing Mixture* (which see) is of great efficacy—a tablespoonful per hour. It will neutralize the acidity of the stomach, relieve the spasms, &c., and effect a wondrous change. Should inflammation continue, give an injection; as, milk, half a pint; mucilage of slippery elm bark, half a pint; treacle, quarter pint, olive oil, half a wine glassful; and a tea spoonful of salt. This affords great relief. Keep up a gentle perspiration by the Sudorific Powders, or by the application of hot bricks, as before stated. See also *Diaphoretic Powder.* If there be local pain, foment with a decoction of vinegar, hops, tansy, horehound, and catnep. Give warm diluents, and mucilaginous drinks, and if putresence appears, give yeast in a decoction of logwood. The following has been recommended :—

Prepared chalk, $\frac{1}{2}$ drachm; compound powder of gum dragon, $2\frac{1}{2}$ drachms, aromatic confection, 1 drachm; tincture of catechu, and of kino, 2 drachms each; laudanum, $\frac{1}{2}$ drachm; aromatic spirit of ammonia, $1\frac{1}{2}$ drachm; and cinnamon water 3 or 4 ozs. Dose two table spoonfuls every three hours.

Or, simmer 1 oz. of blackberry root bark, and two ounces of Raspberry leaves in a quart of water for 40 minutes, strain and add $1\frac{1}{2}$ ozs. of tincture of myrrh, and a little sugar. Take a wine glassful every half hour. It seldom fails.

Butter just churned is said to be a sure cure; it must be unsalted, and clarified over the fire. Two table-spoonfuls several times a day.

The following is said to be an unfailing remedy; good vinegar, and as much salt as it will dissolve.

Give as many teaspoonfuls till it becomes purgative.

The diet must be light and easy of digestion, as sago, arrow-root, mutton and beef-tea.

DRUNKENNESS, *to cure a fit of.*—Take an ounce of minderus spirit in a cupful of water. Repeat the dose every fifteen minutes.

DUCKS, *to choose.*—A young duck should have supple feet, breast and belly hard and thick. A tame duck has dusky yellow feet. They should be picked dry, and ducklings scalded.

DUCK *boiled.*—A duck boiled and smothered in onions, is an excellent dish, and fit for a monarch. Boil twenty-five minutes. The onions should be twice boiled before being made into a sauce. Serve them as follows:—To the onion sauce add chopped parsley, a cupful of good gravy, a spoonful of lemon juice, and a wine glassful of port wine. Pour the whole upon the ducks.

DUCK PIE.—Make a stiff paste crust; clean well a couple of ducks; scald them; cut off the feet, pinions, neck, and head, all clean picked and scalded, with the gizzard, liver and hearts; pick out all the fat of the inside; lay a crust all over the dish; season the ducks with pepper and salt, inside and out; lay them in the dish, and the giblets at each end, seasoned; cover the meat with water; lay on the crust, and bake.

DUCKS, *to roast.*—Carefully pick, and clean the inside. Boil two or three onions in two waters; chop them very small. Mix the onions with about half the quantity of sage leaves, bread crumbs finely powdered, a spoonful of salt, and a little cayenne pepper; beat up the yolk of an egg, and rub the stuffing well together. With a brisk fire roast about 35 minutes. Serve with gravy sauce.

DUCK, *to stew.*—Lard two young ducks down each side the breast; dust with flour; brown before the fire; put into a stew-pan with a quart of water, a pint of port wine, a spoonful of walnut ketchup, the same of browning, one anchovy, a clove of garlick, sweet herbs, and cayenne pepper. Stew till they are tender, about half an hour; skim, and strain, and pour over the duck.

DUCK, *to stew with peas.*—Half roast the ducks. Then put them into a stew-pan with a pint of good gravy, a little mint, and six sage leaves chopped small, salt, &c., cover, and stew half an hour: boil a pint of green peas, as for eating, and put them in after you have thickened the gravy. Dish up the ducks, pour the gravy and peas over them.

DUSTING POWDER FOR CHILDREN.——Mix prepared chalk, rice, starch, and fullers earth equally. First wash the part in cold water.

DUTCH CAKE.—Take 5 lbs. of flour; 2 ozs. of carraway seeds; ¼ lb. of sugar; better than a pint of milk, and ¾ lb. of butter; make a hole in the middle of the flour; put in a pint of good yeast; pour in the butter and milk; make into a paste; rise, roll into thin cakes; bake 15 minutes. *Hu.*

DUTCH SAUCE.——Slice an onion, put into a stew-pan, with a little scraped horseradish, 2 anchovies, some elder vinegar, and some second stock; boil for ten minutes; strain; return it into the stew-pan, and beat up two eggs, put it to the sauce, and set it on the fire till it comes to a boil.

DYEING.—BLUE; first dip the article in a solution of alum; and then in a solution of extract of Indigo. Wash out. If not bloomy enough, pass it through a weak solution of Archil.——BUFF; use annotta, ground down, and boiled in water, with potass added, to give the requisite colour. Boil and stir it well ten or twelve minutes. Wash out.——BROWN; Saffron, or Persian Berry liquor, and soda, or bichromate of potass. ——BLACK; logwood and copperas, or shumac and copperas, or galls, logwood, and copperas.——GREEN; Persian Berry liquor, and extract of Indigo; or quercitron bark, extract of indigo, and alum.—— GREY; by diluting down the black dye.——LILAC; logwood, first dipping the article in a weak solution of alum;—or use archil. ——PINK; from safflower and alum; or brazil wood, and quercitron bark, or Persian berry liquor. ——PURPLE; from archil, or logwood and roche alum.——SCARLET; Cochineal and Persian berry liquor. Or dye in a soap lather with Annotta, boiling hot, for an orange bottom. Wash the article; then dye with Cochineal and a little Nitrate of tin.——RED; from Brazil wood and madder.——NANKEEN from annatto and pearl ash. ——ORANGE; from Brazil wood and quercitron bark, or young fustic, or Persian berry liquor, and alum.——LAVENDER; Extract of Indigo, alum, a little Plum liquor. The shade may be altered by decreasing the indigo.——BLUE BLACK; Steep in Nitrate of Iron for about one hour; then wash, make a soap lather, and add logwood liquor; dip the article into the liquor.

DYSPEPSIA. See *Indigestion*. Pure water, 6 ozs.; carbonate of ammonia, 2 drachms; syrup of orange peel, 1 oz. Mix.

DYSPEPTIC PILL. — Colocynth, Castile Soap, Gamboge, of each 2 ozs.; Socotrine Aloes, 4 ozs.; Oil of Cloves, 2 drachms; Extract of Gentian, 4 ozs. Mix and form into pills. Most valuable for indigestion, and cleansing the stomach, and giving it tone.

EAR-ACHE.—Place in the ear cotton wool moistened with sweet oil and laudanum. A flannel bag of salt, or camomile flowers, made very hot and applied to the ear at bed-time, will often give relief.—— Or, wet a rag with laudanum, and cover the ear with it. A bag of hops, a roasted onion, and hartshorn and oil, are household remedies. If it arises from heat, frequently apply wet cloths.—If from cold, boil rue, or rosemary, and steam the ear through a funnel. EAR-ACHE. — Rub the ear hard for a quarter of an hour.— Tried.——Or, be electrified.—— Or, put in a roasted fig, or onion, as hot as may be.——Or, blow the smoke of tobacco strongly into it. But if the ear-ache is caused by an inflammation of the uvula, it is cured in two or three hours by receiving into the mouth the steam of bruised hemp-seed boiled in water.—*Wesley.*

EAR-ACHE, *from Worms.*— Drop in warm milk, which brings them out.——Or, juice of wormwood, which kills them.

EAR-ACHE, *Indian Cure for.* —Take a piece of the lean of mutton, the size of a large walnut, put it into the fire and burn it for some time till it is reduced almost to a cinder; then put it into a piece of clean rag, and squeeze it until some moisture is expressed, which must be dropped into the ear as hot as the patient can bear it.

EAU DE COLOGNE.—Alcohol, 1 gallon; neroli, 50 drops; essence of cedrat, 50 drops; essence of orange, 50 drops; essence of lemon, 50 drops; essence of bergamot, 50 drops; essence of rosemary, 50 drops; lesser cardamons, 2 drachms. Distil, or macerate and filter.

EAU DIVINE.—Spirit of wine, 1 quart; essence of lemons, and essence of bergamot, each. ¼ dr. Distil in a bath heat; add 1 lb. of sugar, dissolved in two quarts of water, and 4 ozs. of orange flower water.

EAU SUCRE.—Dissolve fine loaf sugar in boiling water; add a little cinnamon, or ginger, &c.

EBONY, *Imitation of.*—Wash the wood over several times with a strong decoction of logwood, and then with a solution of copperas. When dry, polish with Furniture Paste.

EELS, *to stew.*-Clean them well. Cut in pieces two or three inches long, and fry till quarter cooked. Put thin slices of butter into the stew-pan, then the fish, with salt, pepper, a little shred lemon-peel, mace, cloves, and nutmeg; a gill of sherry wine, with marjoram, thyme, savory, and an onion partly boiled, and chopped. Stew gently till tender; take them out, and put an anchovy into the sauce; thicken with the yolk of an egg, or butter rolled in flour. Boil, and pour on the eels.

EELS, *to boil.*—Remove the gut, skin, blood, and heads; dry them well; and boil in salt and water. Serve with parsley sauce.

EELS, *to broil.*—Skin, gut, and clean well; rub them with the yolk of an egg; strew over them bread crumbs, chopped parsley, sage, pepper, and salt; baste them well with butter in the dripping-pan, roast or broil them on a gridiron, or in a dutch oven.

EEL PIE.—Skin and wash clean, cut in pieces 1½ inch long, season them with pepper, salt, and sage rubbed small, mace, bread crumbs and parsley. Place the fish in a pie-dish; (if you have any veal stock it will improve them.) Cover with a light paste, and bake for an hour. Before sending it to table, make an opening at the top, and pour in a tea-cupful of veal stock in which a glass of sherry and the juice of a lemon have been mixed. The pie may be made plainer by omitting some of the articles.

EEL SOUP.—A pound of eels will make a pint of good soup.— To every pound of eels, put a quart of water, three blades of mace, cayenne, an onion, and sweet herbs, as lemon thyme, and winter savory, and a little parsley; boil till half the liquor is wasted, skimming well. When boiling, cover close. Strain, toast some bread; cut it small, and pour the soup over it boiling. A piece of carrot may be put in to brown it.—A rich soup.

EFFERVESCING BEVERAGES.—These may be made by taking any fruit syrup, as apricot, cherry, raspberry, &c., &c. About half a pint, filtered; add half an oz. of tartaric acid, and a little brandy, to keep it, bottle and cork well. To half a tumbler of water, put two tablespoonfuls of syrup, and nearly half a teaspoonful of carbonate of soda, stir well, and drink while effervescing.

EGGS.—In making bread, confectionery, &c., the eggs should be added, if possible, after all the other articles are well mixed. By this method, two eggs will enrich the cake and make it as light as three eggs used at the first.

EGGS, *to have in winter.*—To cause hens to lay all winter, give them flesh meat to supply the place of insects which they eat in summer. Let them have a sufficiency of fresh water, and sheltering places when the weather is inclement. Put a small portion of lime or ground oyster shell, or chalk into their food; also give them potatoes and bran, cabbage leaves, &c. This plan will produce a harvest of eggs in winter.

EGG FLIP.—Beat up four or five new laid eggs, omitting two of the whites; add 3 ozs. of fine sugar, and rub these well in the eggs: pour in *boiling* water, half a pint at a time, and when the pitcher is nearly full throw in two glasses of brandy, and one of Jamaica rum.

Or, 1 quart of ale, 1 of porter; mix, and place over the fire till it creams only. Add half a pint of gin, and two wine-glasses of good rum, and five eggs well beaten; add sugar to taste. Mix the ale, &c., with the egg and spirit, pouring backwards and forwards; return it to the fire, but do not boil. Use a little nutmeg or cinnamon.

EGGS, *to fricassee.*—Boil the eggs rather hard; cut in round slices. Make a sauce of butter, parsley, shalots, pepper, &c. Boil, and when ready, add cream in proportion to the eggs used, and a little flour to thicken the same; pour all upon the eggs. *A. N.*

EGGS AND BACON.—Toast some cutlets of fine streaked bacon in a dutch oven; they will be done in about ten minutes; then put the fat and some dripping into a frying-pan, and when hot, break the eggs into it; do not turn while frying, but keep pouring fat over them; when the yolk looks white, they are enough; turn, and serve with the bacon.

EGG PICKLE.—Boil from two to three dozen fresh eggs quite hard; then set a sufficient quantity of good vinegar over the fire, ginger, white pepper, mustard seed, and a clove or two of garlic. Having placed the eggs without shells into broad mouthed jars, pour the vinegar, &c., over them. When cold, tie them down. The pickle will be ready in a month. It forms a pretty garnish when cut in slices, and constitutes a piquant relish with cold meat.

EGGS, *to poach.*—They must be fresh. Put a little vinegar and salt into the water, and break the eggs into it when boiling; boil three minutes; turn them with a skimmer. When you take them out, immerse them in warm water, to free them from froth, &c. Eat with pepper, salt, and butter. Or serve on toast. They are nice served on greens, as spinach, &c.

EGGS, *to preserve.*-Apply with a brush a solution of gum arabic to the shells, or immerse the eggs therein, let them dry, and pack them in dry charcoal dust. This prevents their being affected by any alterations of temperature.

EGG PUDDING.—It is made chiefly of eggs. It is nice made thus:—beat well seven eggs; mix well with 2 ozs. of flour, pint and a half of milk, a little salt; flavour with nutmeg, lemon juice, and orange flour water. Boil 1¼ hour in a floured cloth. Serve with wine-sauce sweetened. *A. N.*

EGG SAUCE.—Boil two eggs hard, half chop the whites, put in the yolks, chop them together, but not very fine; put them with ¼ lb. of good melted butter.

EGGS IN SNOW.—Take 1½ pint of cream; 3 ozs. of sugar, and the pulp of an onion. Take six whites of eggs and whip them well; put in a little salt, 2 ozs. of sugar and some drops of orange flower water; whisk well. Take a spoonful of the whites; poach them in cream; turn them, that they may be equally done; arrange them when done, as if they were poached eggs; dilute four yolks with a little cream which has cooled; thicken it over the fire,—without boiling.

ELDER FLOWERS.—They are alterative and cooling. The infusion is recommended for erysipelas, fever, gout, &c. As an external application, it is very useful in inflammations and painful swellings.

ELDER BUDS *to pickle.*—Put the buds into a strong brine for nine days, stirring well; then boil them in the water slowly, covered with vine leaves, till they are quite green; drain. Then pour over them in jars hot vinegar in which has been boiled mace, ginger, cloves, cayenne, &c.

ELDER FLOWER OINTMENT.—Very cooling and healing. It is made by simmering the fresh flowers in butter or good lard, with one eighth the proportionate quantity of spermaceti.

ELDER FLOWER WATER.—To a ½ oz. of elder flowers put 3 pints of boiling water; infuse for two hours, and strain. A good wash for sunburn and freckles.—But the distilled water is the best. Steep a peck of the flowers in two quarts of water all night; put in a cold still, and let the water come cold off the still, and it will be very clear. Cork well; it will keep a year.

ELDER FLOWER WINE.—Spring water, 6 gallons; sugar, 12 lbs.; raisins, chopped, 6 lbs.; boil these one hour. When this liquor is cold, put into it ½ peck of elder flowers, and the next day the juice of three lemons, and four spoonfuls of good yeast. Cover for two days. Strain; to every gallon of wine, put a half pint of brandy. Bung for six months. A splendid wine, equal to *Frontignau.*

ELDER RAISIN WINE.—To every gallon of water, put 6 lbs. of Malaga raisins, chopped small; pour the water upon them boiling hot; let it stand 9 days, stirring well. Put the elderberries in a moderate oven all night; strain them through a coarse cloth, and to every gallon of liquor add 1 quart of juice; mix well; toast a slice of bread, and spread yeast on both sides; put it in, and ferment a day or two. Barrel it, bung close, and let it stand from 6 to 12 months. Brandy may be added, *ad libitum.*

ELDER WINE.—Put the berries into a jar, and put them all night in a slow oven; then mix one quart of the juice with three quarts of water; add 4 lbs. of sugar, a little ginger and cloves; boil three quarters of an hour, and when cool ferment it with yeast, spread upon toast, and let it work two days, then put it into the cask, and bung lightly till the fermentation is over.

Another.—To every quart of berries, put two quarts of water; boil half an hour; run the liquor, and break the fruit through a hair sieve; to every quart of juice, put nearly 1 lb. of sugar. Boil 15 minutes with Jamacia pepper, cloves, and ginger. Pour into a tub, and ferment with toast and yeast. After fermentation, put a quart of brandy to eight gallons, and barrel it; bung well for a few months; then bottle off.

In America they flavour elder wine with hops, which renders it a more wholesome beverage—about 1 oz. of hops to every gallon of wine.

ELECAMPANE.—This plant is tonic, astringent, diuretic, and expectorant. It is good in colds, coughs, pulmonary irritation, consumption, and indegestion. It may be given in powder, decoction, or infusion.

ELECTUARY FOR COUGH.

— Take syrup of horehound, ground-ivy, and white poppies, of each one ounce, and spermaceti, half a drachm. Mix and beat these very fine, and take a little spoonful when your cough is troublesome, and at going to rest.

ELM BARK.—See Slippery Elm.

EMBROCATION *for Sprains and Bruises.*—Vinegar, 1 pint; distilled water, ½ pint; rectified spirits, 1½ pint; camphor, 2 ozs.; Dissolve the camphor in the spirits of wine, and put all together.

Another.—Carbonate ammonia, 2 ozs.; vinegar, 2 pints; proof spirits, 3 pints. Mix the ammonia and vinegar; when the effervescence ceases, add the spirit. For inflammation of the joints, of some standing, mix with aniseed meal, and use as a poultice twice a day. It is also valuable for sprains, bruises, and other injuries.

Another for LUMBAGO, GOUTY PAINS, AND RHEUMATISM.—Soap Liniment, 2 ozs.; spirit of camphor, 1 oz.; oil of thyme, 2 drachms; tincture of opium, 1 drachm. Mix, and rub well over the part affected. It is good for toothache.

EMBROCATION, *Valuable.*—Take half an ounce of camphor, cut it into small pieces, and dissolve it in half a pint of spirits of wine, in a closely corked bottle; when completely dissolved, add one pint of ox-gall, (which can be had of any butcher's) and about forty or fifty drops of laudanum; shake it well and bottle it for use. Apply lint dipped into it.

EMBROIDERY, *Articles of, to clean.*—Gold and silver fancy-work may be cleaned with a little spirit of wine, diluted with an equal weight of water. Alkalies and Acids destroy the beauty of the articles instead of cleaning them.

EMERGENCIES. — *Recovery of persons apparently drowned, or dead.*—1. Lose no time. 2 Avoid all rough usage. 3. Never hold the body up by the feet. 4. Nor roll the body on casks. 5. Nor rub the body with salt and spirits. 6. Nor inject tobacco smoke, or infusion of tobacco.

RESTORATIVE MEANS, IF APPARENTLY DROWNED. — Send quickly for medical assistance; but do not delay the following means:—

I. Convey the body CAREFULLY, with the head and shoulders supported in a raised condition, to the nearest house.

II. Strip the body and rub it dry; then wrap it in hot blankets, and place it in a warm bed in a warm chamber.

III. Wipe and clean the mouth and nostrils.

IV. In order to restore the natural warmth of the body;

1. Move a heated covered warming pan over the back and spine. 2. Put bladders, or bottles of hot water, or heated bricks, to the pit of the stomach, the armpits, between the thighs, and to the soles of the feet. 3. Foment the body with hot flannels; but, if possible, 4. Immerse the body in a warm bath as hot as the hand can bear without pain. 5. Rub the body briskly with the hand; but do not suspend the use of the other means at the same time.

V. To restore breathing, introduce the pipe of a common bellows, into one nostril, carefully closing the other and the mouth; at the same time drawing downwards, and pushing gently backwards, the upper part of the wind pipe, to allow the free admission of air; blow the bellows gently, in order to inflate the lungs, till the breast be a little raised; the mouth and nostrils should then be set free, and a moderate pressure made with the hand upon the chest. Repeat this process till life appears.

VI. Electricity to be employed early by a medical assistant.

VII. Inject into the stomach, by means of an elastic tube and syringe, half a pint of warm brandy, or wine and water.

VIII. Apply sal-volatile to the nostrils.

IF APPARENTLY DEAD FROM INTENSE COLD.—Rub the body with ice, snow, or cold water.—Restore warmth by slow degrees; and, after some time, if necessary, employ the means recommended for the apparently drowned. It is HIGHLY DANGEROUS to apply heat too early.

IF APPARENTLY DEAD FROM HANGING. — In addition to the means recommended for the apparently drowned, BLEEDING should early be employed by a Medical Assistant.

IF APPARENTLY DEAD FROM NOXIOUS VAPOURS, LIGHTNING, &c.—1. Remove the body into a cool fresh air. 2. Dash cold water on the neck, face, and breast frequently. 3. If the body be cold, apply warmth, as recommended for the apparently drowned. 4. Use the means for inflating the lungs in Direction V. 5. Let Electricity (particularly in accidents from lightning) be early employed by a Medical Assistant.

IF APPARENTLY DEAD FROM INTOXICATION.—Lay the body on a bed, with the head raised: remove the neckcloth and loosen the clothes. Obtain instantly medical assistance; in the mean time apply cloths soaked in cold water to the head, and bottles of hot water, or hot bricks, to the calves of the legs and to the feet.

GENERAL OBSERVATIONS.—On restoration to life, a teaspoonful of warm water should be given; and then, if the power of swallowing be returned, small quantities of weak brandy and water, warm; the patient should be kept in bed, and a disposition to sleep encouraged, except in cases of apoplexy and intoxication. Great care is requisite to maintain the restored vital actions, and to prevent undue excitement. The treatment is to be persevered in for *three or four hours*. It is an erroneous opinion that persons are irrecoverable because life does not soon make its appearance.

EMETIC MIXTURE.—Ipecacuanha wine, $\frac{1}{2}$ oz.; water, 1 oz.; simple syrup, $\frac{1}{2}$ oz. Mix.—For a child, 20 drops, or more, every quarter of an hour until vomiting ensues. An adult may take from half to one oz.

EMETIC POWDER.—Ipecacuanha and Lobelia, of each 2 ozs.; Blood-root 1 oz. Powder, and mix well. Take half a teaspoonful every twenty minutes till it operates.

EMMENAGOGUES. — Medicines exciting the womb to secretion of the menses.

ENGRAVINGS, TO TRANSFER TO PAPER.—Place the engravings a few seconds over the vapour of iodine. Dip a slip of white paper in a weak solution of starch, and, when dry, in a weak solution of oil of vitriol. When again dry, lay a slip upon the engraving, and place both for a few minutes under the press. The engraving will thus be reproduced in all its delicacy and finish. The iodine has the property of fixing the black parts of the ink upon the engraving, and not on the white. This important discovery is yet in its infancy.

EPILEPSY, or *Falling sickness*.—A sudden deprivation of

sense, with violent convulsions of the whole system. Previous to the fit, there is a peculiar sensation felt by the patient; a scream or cry is then uttered, and he falls heavily to the ground. The eyes are fixed and reverted, and the convulsive agitations are violent; the teeth gnash against each other, the tongue projects, and is sadly bitten; the patient froths at the mouth, and is quite unconscious. "The period of recurrence of epileptic fits is very variable. Death sometimes occurs in the first; or, though rarely, recovery taking place, the disease never returns. Years may intervene, or an irregular period of months, weeks, or days, may separate the attacks." Epilepsy is more common in the night than in the day. As it becomes more firmly rooted in the system, the fits recur more frequently.

Treatment.--Prevent the patient from injuring himself during the fit. A piece of wood, india rubber, &c., should be placed between the teeth to prevent injury to the tongue. Remove all tight clothing especially about the neck. Elevate the head and shoulders. If the fit does not depart, give one or two tea-spoonfuls of the antispasmodic tincture. When the fit subsides, give a vapour bath, and an emetic two or three times a week. After the bath, rub the body over with the Stimulating Liniment. Gentle aperients should also be given now and then. Sponge the body every or every other morning with cold salt and water. Let the diet be very light and digestible. As it is a disease of debility, tonics should be employed; as Peruvian Bark, Snake Root, Lady's Slipper, and Peony, which may be obtained of the Medical Botanists. Boil them till strong; add sugar, and best Madeira wine. Dr. Beach says, that salt is very efficacious. "As soon as there are any premonitory symptoms, give a tea-spoonful of salt, in a little water; and, if practicable, repeat it in twenty minutes; it shortens the fit, and may be taken twice or thrice a day. The shower bath may also be used. If the disease proceeds from worms, use the remedies in that case prescribed. A pill made of equal parts of Scullcap, Lobelia seed, and Cayenne, and mucilage is very useful in this disease.

EPPING SAUSAGES. — Six pounds of good pork, free from skin and gristle, cut it small, and beat it fine in a mortar. Chop 6 lbs. of beef suet very fine, powder a handful of sage leaves, which sprinkle over the meat; shred the rind of a lemon very fine, and with sweet herbs, scatter it on the meat, and two nutmegs grated, a spoonful of pepper, (less if cayenne) and salt. Mix the suet and all together; when used, roll it up with as much egg as will make it smooth.

EPSOM SALTS, are distinguished from Oxalic Acid, which is poison, thus:—Epsom Salts have a *bitter taste;* Oxalic Acid has a very *acid,* or *sour taste.*

ERRORS IN SPEECH.—Never use a verb plural to a singular nominative; as, Thomas *were* there..should be *was*..... Never use a verb singular to a plural nominative; as, The things *has* come—the cows *was* in the field..should be *have* and *were.*

I *expect* the books were sent.. say, I *think; expect* refers to the future..... Give me both *of them* apples,..should be, both *those* apples..... Mr. Smith *learned* me Grammar,..*taught*..... I *propose* to offer a few hints,..*purpose,* or *intend*..... I never omit walking out when*ever* the weather is fine, ..leave out *ever*..... I *seldom or* *ever* see her,..*seldom or never,* or *seldom, if ever*.....You have *sown* the seam badly,..*sewed*.....I shall *summons*,..*summon*.....This *here* is my farm,..leave out *here*.....*Without* you study, you will not learn,..*Unless* you study, &c.....The *observation* of the sabbath is a duty, .. *observance.* .... Add *one more* reason,..*one reason more*....Be *sharp*, and get your work done,..*quick*.....Who finds Tom *in* money,..leave out *in*.....I admire such *an one*,..*a one*.....*An* Europeon,..*a*.....*An* University,..*a*.....A *quantity* of men, or horses,..a *number of*, &c.....*Lots* of money, *lots* of friends, *lots* of learning,..*plenty of money, many friends, much learning*.....Galileo *discovered* the telescope,..*invented*.....I rose *up*, and put on my clothes,..leave out *up*.....It *lays* on the floor,..*lies*.....I intend to *stop* at home,..*stay*.....No man has *less* enemies,..*fewer*.

A *couple* of men,..*two* men.....Tom was in *eminent* danger,..*imminent*.....The *two first* pages,..*first two*.....He came last of *all*,..leave out, *of all*.....I plunged *down* into the water,..leave out, *down*.....He was *exceeding* industrious,..*exceedingly*.....I did it *conformable* to your wishes,..*conformably*.....Little grows there *beside* a coarse kind of grass,..*except*.....He ascended *up* into heaven,..leave out, *up*.....It is not *as* large as I expected,..*so*.....A *young beautiful boy*,..*beautiful young* boy.....The *latter* end of the pious is peace,..leave out, *latter*.....On *either* side of the river,..*each*.

I will think *on* thee, friend,..*of*.....Take hold *on* it; I knew nothing *on* it; He was made much *on* in London,..*of*.....No need *for* that,..*of*.....Free *of* blame,..*from*.....He is resolved *of* going to America,..*on*.....I had *rather not*,..*would rather not*.....We prevailed *over* him to come,..*upon*.....He ran *again* me,..*against*.....I put it *in* my pocket,..*into*.....He was accused *for* neglecting his duty,..*of*.....I am ruler *over* my house,..*of*.....She reads *slow*,..*slowly*.....*At* best,..*at the* best.....A few weeks *back*,..*ago*.....Harvey *invented* the circulation of the blood,..*discovered*.

I am very *dry* to-day,..*thirsty*.....No *less* than twenty persons,..*fewer*.....Opposite *the* town-hall,..*to the*.....Tell me *the reason* why he is dejected,..leave out, *the reason*.....Edwin speaks *bad* grammar..*speaks ungrammatically*.....His character is *undeniable*,..*unquestionable*.....Before you go you must *first* finish your work,..leave out, *first*.....That was his *principle* reason,..*principal*.....The Board of *ordinance*,..*ordnance*.....The horse is full of *metal*...*mettle*.....A *new pair* of boots,..*a pair of new boots*.....*Direct* the letter to me, at, &c.,..*Address*.....It *militates* against my business,..*operates*.....He lifted *up* his arm to strike me,..leave out, *up*.....His case was heard *pro and con*,..*on both sides*.

Take two *spoonsful* of, &c.,..*spoonfuls*.....Bring me *them* books,..*those*....They are coming to see Charles and *I*,..*me*.....*These* sort of entertainments,..*this*.....It is I who *is* to do it,..*am*.....The money was divided *between* fifty,..*among*.....He *was* no sooner departed, than they expelled his officers,..*had*.....That is *him*...*he*.....At some time, or another,..*other*.....You are *mistaken*,..*you mistake*.....She has such a bad temper,..*a temper so bad*.....The fellow was *hung* last week,..*hanged*.....This is my *oldest* sister,..*eldest*.

☞ *Leave out the superfluous words printed in Italics.* :—
She fell *down* upon her knees.... More than you think *for*..... Who has *got* my inkstand..... What are you doing *of*..... Missing his way, he returned *back*..... You may enter *in*..... Her conduct was approved *of*..... I can*not* by no means allow it...... The fellow *again* repeated the assertion..... Such conduct admits *of* no excuse. ....I can do it *equally* as well as he..... They combined *together*, and covered it *over*..... Nobody else..... As soon as *ever*..... I have *not* had no dinner yet..... Please give me both *of* those books..... Our cat caught a great *big* rat.... It is a *wonderful* phenomenon.... Has Alfred returned *back* from his journey?....It is four months *ago* since I had a letter..... The *verdant* green field..... It is *very* true.

ERUPTIONS ON THE FACE. --After washing, the eruptions, foment with camphor-spirit, two or three times per day.

ERYSIPELAS--Dr. Baumann employs Collodion in all cases, and has found it, even in several cases of Erysipelas of the face, and in one case of phlegmonous Erysipelas of the thigh, highly useful. He first gives an emetic, and then daily applies Collodion to the parts. The recovery is rapid, and no ill consequences have been observed.

Bathing the legs and feet in warm water is very serviceable. Some recommend the part to be covered with meal, or flour, or yeast. Some persons recommend a poultice of cranberies powdered fine, in a raw state.

A decoction of elder-leaves will promote perspiration; applying to the part a cloth dipped in lime-water. Or take gentle purgatives, as senna, manna, cream of tartar, with a little fennel seed, to prevent griping. The *vapour bath* is very beneficial. The Marshmallow ointment is very serviceable; also the Elder ointment. Wash the parts oft with the following liquid or tincture:—Infuse 1 oz. of celandine leaves in a pint of whiskey a few hours. Apply it when there is much itching. But the best application is a poultice made of slippery elm bark. Mix the bark with milk, buttermilk, or cream. Should there be ulceration, add brewer's yeast to the poultice. The diet should be cool and nourishing.

Dr. Beach referring to a case, says, "The patient was so bad that he had to sit in a chair five or six months, day and night," and the most eminent allopathic docters could do him no good. "I used the pulverized *willow bark*, commonly called *pussy willow*; it was mixed with cream, under which it grew better; it sloughed in several places nearly to the bone. When the pain almost subsided, I applied the slippery-elm bark and milk, and then the *Black Salve*, which effected a cure in a few months."

ESPRIT DE ROSE.—Otto of roses, ½ oz.; Spirits of wine, 1 pint; mix, and bottle. Shake frequently. Put the bottle in a warm bath till it is warm. Take out and shake up till cold. If not bright, filter rapidly through fine linen.

ESSENCES, &c., *To extract from wood, barks, roots, herbs, &c.* —Take balm, mint, sage, or any thing you please; put into a bottle, and pour upon them a spoonful of ether; keep in a cool place a few hours, and then fill the bottle with cold water; the essential oil will swim on the surface, which may be easily separated.

EVERTON TOFFEE. -- Fine sugar, 1 lb.; butter, 2 oz.; water.

a wine-glassful, and a small lemon. Boil the butter, sugar, water, and half the rind of a lemon together. Drop a little into cold water; if crisp, it is done. When the boiling has ceased stir in the juice of the lemon. Pour it into a buttered dish about a quarter of an inch thick.

Or to 1 lb. of fine sugar, add 2 ozs. of butter. When boiled to the crackled degree, grain it, and pour into buttered tins. It may be flavoured with ginger, peppermint, cloves, &c., as you like, by adding a drop or two of the respective essential oil.

EVE'S PUDDING.—Take six large juicy apples; pare, core, and chop them fine; six ounces of bread crumbs; six ounces of currants; six eggs, and three or four ounces of sugar, and the rind of half a lemon shred very fine. Mix well, and boil in a mould or closely-covered pan for three hours; serve with sweet sauce.

EXCORIATIONS, *chafing.*—Apply Fullers earth.--Wash with a strong raspberry leaf tea.--Apply a weak solution of brandy and salt.--The celandine ointment is very efficacious.

EXPECTORANTS. — Medicines increasing the secretion from the lungs.

EXPECTORANT SYRUP.—St. John'swort, 1 oz.; Sage, 1 oz.; Lobelia, 1 drachm. Form a syrup by using sugar, or treacle. For a child six months old, a small teaspoonful, and increase by age.

EXPECTORANT TINCTURE.—See *Antispasmodic Tincture,* page 20, which is the same.

Another. — Blood-root, lobelia seed, ipecacuanha, of each, ½ oz.; 1 pint of spirits. Infuse for a week. Take in water. Useful in coughs, inflammation of the lungs, pleurisy, asthma, hooping cough.

EXPLOSIVE COMPOUND.—Nine parts of well-dried and finely powdered chlorate of potash, mixed with three parts of finely powdered galls, will make a highly explosive compound. Do not mix it in a mortar, as it would explode, but by means of a bone spatula, or passing through a brass sieve. The strength of common gunpowder may be increased by working up with the powdered meal about 12 per cent. of powdered galls, and re-granulating it.

EXTRACTS, *to make.*—Take of the plant, root, or leaves you wish to make the extract from, any quantity, add sufficient water, and boil them gradually, then pour off the water and add a second quantity; repeat the process until all the virtue is extracted, then mix the several decoctions, and evaporate at as low a temperature as possible, to the consistence of an extract. Extracts are better made in a water-bath, and in close vessels, and for some very delicate articles, the evaporation may be carried on at a very low temperature, in a vacuum, by surrounding the vessel with another containing sulphuric acid. Manufacturing druggists usually add to every seven pounds of extract, gum arabic, 4 ounces; alcohol, 1 ounce; olive oil, 1 ounce. This mixture gives the extract a gloss, and keeps it soft.

EXTRA PUDDING. — Cut light bread into thin slices. Form into the shape of a pudding in a dish. Then add a layer of any preserve, then a slice of bread, and repeat till the dish is full. Beat four or five eggs, and mix well with a pint of milk; then pour it over the bread and preserve, having previously dusted the same with a coating of rice flour. Boil twenty-five minutes.

EYE, *Blood Shot.*—Apply linen

rags dipped in cold water for two or three hours.——Or, apply boiled Hyssop as a poultice. Very efficacious.--*Wesley.*

EYE-BRIGHT. — This plant is useful in affections of the eyes, as it improves the vision, especially in old age. See *Robinson's Herbal.*

EYES, *bruised.* — Frequently bathe in water with a little carbonate of soda dissolved in.—Or apply bread poultices pretty warm, change often.—Or foment with a decoction of stramonium leaves, and then bind them on the eye.—Or use slippery elm poultices. *Gu.*

EYE-SALVE.—White or yellow wax, ½ oz.; red precipitate, 3 drachms; prepared tutty, or pure zinc powdered, 1 drachm; lard, 4 ozs. Melt and mix. Add 1½ drs. of camphor dissolved in oil.

EYES, *Inflammation of.*—Mix bread crumbs with the white of an egg, three drops of laudanum, three drops of brandy, and a very little salt. Apply in a bag of thin soft linen or muslin. It is better to apply it at night when lying down. It always affords relief.—Drink also eye-bright tea, and wash the eyes with it.

EYE, *Films.*—Mix juice of Eye-bright, and juice of Ground Ivy with a little honey, and 2 or 3 grains of Bay Salt. Drop it in morning and evening.

EYE, *Hot Humours.* — Apply a few drops of double refined sugar melted in brandy.——Or, boil a handful of bramble leaves with a little alum in a quart of spring water, to a pint. Drop this frequently into the eye. This likewise speedily cures cancers or any sores.

EYE, *or* EYELIDS *inflamed.*—Apply as a poultice, boiled, roasted, or rotten apples warm.—Or, wormwood tops with the yolk of an egg.

This will hardly fail.——Or, beat up the white of an egg with two spoonfuls of white rose-water into a white froth. Apply this on a fine rag, changing it so that it may not grow dry till the eye or eye-lid is well.—Tried.

Or, dissolve an ounce of fine gum arabic in 3 spoonfuls of spring water; put a drop into the inner corner of the eye, from the point of a hair pencil, four or five times a-day. At the same time take as much saltpetre as will lie upon a sixpence, dissolved in a glass of water, three or four times a-day; abstaining from all liquors till cured. White bread poultices applied to the eyes in an inflamed state often occasion blindness.

EYE-LID, *Removing foreign bodies from beneath the.*—M. Renard, in the case of small moveable bodies which become entangled beneath the upper eyelid, recommends the following simple procedure, which will often dispense with all others. Take hold of the upper eyelid near its angles with the index finger and thumb of each hand, draw it gently forwards and as low down as possible over the lower eyelid, and retain it in this position for about a minute, taking care to prevent the tears from flowing out. When, at the end of this time, you allow the eyelid to resume its place, a flood of tears washes out the foreign body, which will be found adhering to, or near to, the lower eyelid.

EYE POULTICE. — Stir two drachms of powdered alum in the powdered whites of two eggs till a coagulum be formed. Place it between a piece of soft linen rag, and apply it. Very applicable for inflamed eyes attended with a purulent discharge, and for chilblains.

EYES, *good for the.*—To give brilliancy to the eyes, shut them early at night, and open them early in the morning; let the mind be constantly intent on the acquisition of benevolent feelings. This will scarcely ever fail to impart to the eyes an intelligent and amiable expression.

EYE-SIGHT, *to preserve.*—Never sit long in absolute *gloom*, or exposed to a *blaze of light.*—*Avoid reading* SMALL PRINT.—Do not strain the eyes by looking at *minute* objects.—Do not read in the dusk, nor by candle-light or gaslight, if the eyes be disordered.—Do not permit the eyes to gaze on glaring objects, as the sun, or bright day-light, especially on opening the eyes in the morning.—Do not let the curtains, walls, &c., be white; green is the best for curtains, &c.—Avoid much exposure to cold easterly winds; especially avoid intemperance, and excessive venery, which are awfully destructive to eye-sight.

EYE WATER.—Boil lightly a spoonful of white copperas, and 3 spoonfuls of salt, in 3 pints of spring water. When it is cold, bottle it without straining. Put a drop or two in the eye morning and evening.

It takes away redness and soreness; it cures pearls, rheums, and often blindness. If it makes the eye smart, add more water to it.

Another.— Stamp and strain ground ivy, celandine, and daisies, an equal quantity; add a little rose-water and loaf-sugar. Drop a drop or two at a time into the eye; it takes away all the inflammation, smarting, itching, spots, webs, &c.

Or take 2 table-spoonfuls each of brandy, and rain water, and about the size of a horse-bean of camphor. Dissolve the last in the first. Valuable.

EYE WATER.--Take of white vitriol, ten grains; rose, or elder flower water, eight ounces. Mix.

EYE WATER.—Half a pint of the best brandy, two pints of spring water, and sugar of lead, one ounce; mix. This is a good eye-water.——Or, take six ounces of Rectified Spirits of Wine, dissolve in it one drachm of Camphor, then add two small handfuls of dried Elder Flowers; infuse twenty-four hours. Bathe the forehead, over your eyes, and each temple, several times a day; meantime, dip a soft rag in stale small beer, new milk warm, and bathe each eye a few times gently morning and evening. If it is a watery humour, wet the eyelids two or three times, but be sure to shut your eyes, or it will make them smart and burn excessively.

It is also a good remedy for the toothache, or swelled face, bruises, &c., used as a rubefacient.

EYES, *Weak*.--May be relieved by washing them in cold water; or dissolve four grains of sugar of lead, and crude sal ammoniac, in eight ounces of water, to which add a few drops of laudanum. With this mixture bathe the eyes night and morning. Rose water is also good for the eyes.

If lime gets into the eyes, a few drops of vinegar and water will dissolve and remove it. Almond or olive oil will do away with any hot fluid that may reach the eye. *Styes* should be bathed with warm water, and it is as well to take an aperient. A little ointment of citron and spermaceti may be used when the stye is broken.

FACE-ACHE &c.--The jaws, teeth, and face, often swell, and become painful. It proceeds from cold.—Poultice the parts with bread or bran poultice hot. For neuralgiac pains, take half a

K

drachm of sal-ammoniac in water three times a day.——Or steam the parts over bitter herbs. If the swelling be great apply a ley poultice.——Or bathe the parts with the Rheumatic Liquid. For jaw and tooth-ache, apply tincture of cayenne on cotton lint between the cheek and the teeth.

FACE BURNING.—It arises from acidity of the stomach. Take one or two tea-spoonfuls of magnesia in milk.

FAINTING FITS.—Remove the patient to the open air, and lay him in a horizontal position, with nothing tight left upon him. Should the case be obstinate, immerse the feet and legs in warm water, and apply spirits of hartshorn to the nostrils; and give a few drops in a glass of water, or hot brandy and water. *Hu.*

FAMILY WINE.——Equal parts of black, red, and white currants, cherries, and raspberries. Bruise and mix with soft water,— 4 lbs. of fruit to 1 gal. of water. Press, strain, and add 3 lbs. of sugar to each gallon of liquid. After standing two or three days, skimming it, barrel it, and let it ferment for a fortnight. Add brandy, and bung. It gets rich with age.

FEATHERS, *to clean.*—Feathers may be cleansed from their animal oil by steeping them in lime water—1 lb. of lime to a gallon of water; stir well, and then pour the water from the lime.

To *cleanse feathers from dirt*, make a strong lather of white soap and hot water. Put in the feathers and rub them for five minutes. Rinse in clean hot water.

FEATHERS TO CURL.—Heat them slightly before the fire, then stroke them with the back of a knife, and they will curl.

FEATHERS TO DYE.—Steep them a few hours in warm water. ——*Blue* may be dyed by extract of indigo and boiling water. Simmer over the fire a few minutes. ——*Green*; Verdigris and Verditer, 1 oz. each; and gum water; dip the feathers. Or mix the indigo liquor with Persian berry liquor. —— *Lilac.* Use cudbear and hot water. —— *Red.* Brazil wood, a little vermilion and alum, and vinegar; boil 30 minutes; and then dip the feathers.——*Yellow* by turmeric.——*Scarlet*, by cochineal, cream of tartar, and muriate of tin.

FEBRIFUGES.——Medicines abating heat and fever.

FEBRIFUGE.—Take houseleek; place in a coarse cloth, and squeeze out the juice, and strain; to 1 lb. of which add 1 lb. of loaf sugar; simmer a short time to form a syrup. Give a table-spoonful every two hours. In fevers this acts like magic—in all kinds of fever.

FELON, *or* WHITLOW.—A very painful inflammation of the fingers, thumb, or hand. A whitlow resembles a felon, but it is not so deeply seated. It is often found at the root of the nail. Immerse the diseased finger in strong ley as long and as hot as can be borne several times a day. Constantly poultice it with a mixture of strong ley and elm bark, or elm bark and powdered linseed, and one poppy head softened in the ley. Or steam it well with the bitter herbs, which may be used several times; about twenty minutes at a time. Continue till well, or when it begins to suppurate; then will appear a white spot, which when fully ripe, may be opened with a fine needle, Should gangrenous matter appear, apply a little Vegetable Caustic, which see. Apply the Black Salve to heal it. Keep the bowels open, and take now and then the Composition Powder.

FEMALE PILL.—Aloes and Lobelia, 1 drachm each; Black Cohosh, Gum Myrrh, Tansy, Unicorn Root, 1 oz. each; Cayenne, ½ oz. Mix, and form into pills with solution of gum.—These pills remove female obstructions, and are good for head aches, lowness of spirits, nervousness, and sallowness of the skin.

Or Aloes, Red Oxide of Iron, White Turpentine, 1 oz. each. Melt the turpentine, and strain; mix well; form into pills with mucilage. Take two or three per day.

FENNEL SAUCE.—Soak four sliced onions, in two spoonfuls of oil, a cup of gravy, two cloves of garlick; simmer an hour; skim off the fat, and sieve; add chopped parsley, fennel, pepper and salt; boil a moment.

FERMENTATION, *to check.*—The least bit of sulphate of Potass. It is applicable to liquors, syrups, preserves, &c.

FERMENTATION, *to promote.*—Put into the wort some powdered ginger.——Or fill a bottle with boiling water, and sink it into the worts.——Or heat a small quantity of the worts, and put it to the rest, with a little yeast.——Or beat up the whites of two eggs with some brandy, and put it into the wort. Do not disturb the wort.

FERNS, *to copy.*—Dip them well in common porter, and then lay them flat between white sheets of paper, with slight pressure, and let them dry out.

FERTILITY, IMMENSE.—A single plant may produce:—

	No. of flowers.	Seeds to a flower.		total.
Groundsel.	130	× 50	=	6,500
Chickweed.	500	× 10	=	5,000
Shepherd's Purse.	150	× 30	=	4,500

FEVER DRINKS.—The juice of a lemon, cream of tartar, 1 teaspoonful; water, 1 pint. Sweeten with loaf sugar. When the patient is thirsty, let him drink freely.

FIG PASTE, *for Costiveness.*—Chop small 1 lb. of figs, and mix with them 2 ozs. of best senna, cut small, and a cupful of treacle; stew and stir it till it becomes stiff and firm. Take a piece about the size of a walnut.

FININGS FOR BEER.-Isinglass, 4 ozs.; dissolve it in two quarts of stale beer; simmer it till thick as a syrup, put into it a handful of salt, and half a pint of powdered oyster-shells; mix them with one gallon of strong beer or ale, stir till it ferments; cover it up close. The quantity will be sufficient for a butt of beer.

FIRE IRONS, *to prevent rusting.*—Apply sweet oil, and dust them with unslaked lime powdered.——If rusted, oil them, and in two or three hours, polish with fine emery, lime, or powdered pumice stone.——Tripoli and sulphur, equal parts, combined, will remove rust.

FIRE TO LIGHT.—Clear the grate, and place at the bottom a few coals about the size of a walnut, place the fuel (shavings and wood split) upon them, then cinders, and lastly coals. This method speedily produces a good fire.

FIRE KINDLERS.—Tar, 1 quart; rosin, 3 lbs.; melt them. When not quite cool, add 1 gill of spirits of turpentine, and mix as much saw-dust, with a little charcoal, as can be worked in; spread out while hot on a board; divide into pieces. They will instantly ignite, and briskly burn long enough to ignite coal, or wood.

FIRE, *to revive.*—Strew on a dull fire powdered nitre, or saltpetre.

FIRE, *to extinguish.*—Dissolve pearlash, soda, wood-ashes or common salt in the water, before it is put into the engine, and direct the jet on the burning wood work. The proportion may be 20 pounds to every 50 gallons; the more, however, the better.——Or throw sulphur on the fire. A solution of 5 ozs. of ammonia in one gallon of water, will extinguish a large fire.

FIRE, *to prevent, escape.*—Washing linen, dresses, &c., in a solution of alum prevents them taking fire.——If in a house or room on fire, crawl with your face as near the ground as you can.——Wet a blanket, and throw it upon things on fire.——Or dip a blanket in water and beat the flames, putting a handkerchief over your mouth and nose if there is much smoke.——If a lady's clothes take fire, roll on the floor, or wrap her in a carpet tightly.——Throw a solution of pearl-ash upon the flames.

FIRE-PROOF STUCCO.—Take moist gravelly earth (previously washed), and make it into stucco with the following composition: Pearlashes, 2 parts; water, 5 parts; common clay, 1 part. Mix. This costs about one shilling and sixpence per hundred square feet. It has been tried on a large scale and found to answer.

FISH, *to choose.*—CARP. They have the same signs of freshness as other fish.——COD. Gills should be very red, the neck thick, flesh white, firm; eyes fresh.——EELS. Except the middle of summer, they are always in season. Those taken in ponds are not good—a flowing river is the best for them.——FLOUNDERS. Should be thick, firm, bright eyes.——GUDGEONS are best in running streams.——HERRINGS. Gills red; eyes bright; flesh firm.——MACKEREL. Season, May, June, July; they keep worse than any fish.——MULLETS. The sea ones are the best. Season, August.——PERCH. River Perch are the best.——PIKE. The best as Perch—rather a dry fish.——SALMON. Flesh and gills, fine red, scales bright, and the fish stiff and firm. Small heads, and thick in the neck, are the best.——SKATE. When good, very white and thick.——SMELTS. If good, a fine silvery hue, firm.——SOLES. If good, thick; belly, cream colour.——TENCH. Gills red, and hard to open, eyes bright, body stiff.——TURBOT. If good, thick; belly a yellowish white. WHITINGS. Firm, smell fresh. SHELL FISH.—CRABS. The heaviest are best; middling size, sweetest; joints of the legs, stiff.——LOBSTERS. The heaviest are the best. If fresh, will have a strong motion, when you press the eyes.——OYSTERS. The Pyefleet, Colchester, and Milford, are the best. The native Milton are fine, being white and fat. When alive and strong, the shell closes on the knife.——PRAWNS AND SHRIMPS. If fresh, they have a sweet flavour, are firm, bright in colour.

FISH, *to keep sound.*—To prevent meat, fish, &c., going bad, put a few pieces of charcoal into the sauce-pan wherein the fish or flesh is to be boiled.

FISH, *to render boiled firm.*—Add a little saltpetre to the salt in the water in which the fish is to be boiled; a quarter of an ounce to one gallon.

FISH PIE.—Pike, perch, and carp may be made into savory pies if cut into fillets, seasoned, and baked in paste, sauce made of veal broth, or cream put in before baking.

FISH SAUCE.—Indian Soy,

1 gill; Shalot Vinegar, a wine-glassful; mixed mushroom and walnut ketchup, ½ pint in equal proportions, the juice of a lemon, with its peel chopped fine, two anchovies boned, three tea-spoonfuls of soluble cayenne pepper, two table-spoonfuls of horse-radish vinegar, and a tumbler of port wine. Bottle, and for two or three weeks shake frequently.

FISHING-ROD VARNISH. —Equal parts of Canada balsam and fine turpentine, warmed together for several hours, make an excellent varnish.——Or, alcohol, one pint; Venice turpentine, a quarter of a pint; gum sandarach, 4 ozs.; gum mastic in tears, 1 oz.; resin, 2 ozs.; heated by ether till dissolved.

FISTULA.—-This disease is seated near the anus and rectum, in the form of abscess, or ulcer, emitting an offensive discharge. It may be caused by derangement of the liver, costiveness, or great laxity, high living, intemperance, bruises, piles, &c. It is first known by a painful swelling near the rectum, inflammation, a pressure upon the bladder, or urethra, supression of urine, great pain in passing the fœces.

The treatment generally is by the knife; but we prefer the reform practice of America; for cures by the knife are very rare indeed. Dr. Beach says, "Moderate excessive inflammation; diminish painful symptoms; promote suppuration; if the swelling cannot be discussed. Apply to the swelling the *Discutient Ointment*, which see; afterwards foment with bitter herbs, tansy, wormwood, horehound, catnep, hops, a handful of each—make a decoction. Put into a vessel, and add half a pint of soft soap. Put a board across the vessel, or tub, and let the patient sit over it for twenty minutes, covered with a blanket, except the head, to retain the steam. Repeat several times a day." It often relieves the most painful cases.

Apply the Discutient Ointment as often as possible; also a poultice made of linseed meal, and powdered slippery elm bark, renewing it every day. If the pain prevents sleep, take a little of the Diaphoretic Powder at bed-time. Promote perspiration by bathing the feet daily, drinking balm and hyssop tea. The bowels must be kept open by emollient purgatives; but if internal medicines cause pain, injections must be given; of warm water mixed with butter, or castor oil. This treatment will ripen the abscess; it is the best to let it break spontaneously; after which the Black Salve will be found of great service, introduced into the ulcer by means of small tents of lint. Inject also into the anus a *weak* solution of carbonate of potash; or castile soap and water. It renders the discharge more healthy. Wash the fistula twice a day with salt and water. After the painful symptoms are gone, the patient can scarcely tell whether he is improving or not, though the fistula may be daily decreasing.

FISTULA.—Use a sitz-bath as often as you can bear it.

Wash muscle shells clean, burn them to powder, sift them fine, mix them with hog's lard, spread it on clean wash-leather, and apply it. This cured one who was thought to be at the point of death.

N.B. This also cures the piles.

FISTULA LACHRYMALIS. This is a swelling, and inflammation in the inner corner of the eye, caused by an obstruction of the tear-duct. Steam over the vapour of camomile and groundsel tea, for thirty minutes twice a day.

Snuff up the nostril near the affected eye, powdered lobelia herb, mixed with a little blood-root. Should the eye swell, use eye-waters and the brown Ointment—

FITS.—If a person falls in a fit, let him remain on the ground, provided *his face be pale;* for should it be fainting or temporary suspension of the heart's action, you may cause death by raising him upright, or by bleeding; but if the face be *red or dark coloured*, raise him on his seat, throw cold water on his head immediately, and send for a surgeon, and get a vein opened, or fatal pressure on the brain may ensue.

FIXED STARS. — Nitre, 12 parts; sulphur, 6 parts; meal gunpowder, 12 parts; antimony, 1 part. Mix. The bottom of the rocket must be stuffed with clay; one diameter of rocket composition must be then introduced, and the remainder filled with the above mixture; the case is then to be tied up, and the paste-board pierced with five holes for the escape of the luminous rays.

FLANNEL.—Before it is made up, flannel should be immersed in hot water.

FLANNELS, *to wash.*—Do not use boiling water, but as hot as the hands can bear. Wash with good brown soap and a little pearl-ash, or soda, and blue.

FLANNEL, *to wear.*—Put it on at once, winter and summer—nothing better can be worn next to the skin than a loose red flannel shirt—"loose," for it has room to move on the skin, thus causing a titillation, which draws the blood to the surface and keeps it there, and when that is the case no one can take cold; "red," for white flannel creases up, mats together, and becomes tight, stiff, heavy, and impervious. Cotton wool merely absorbs the moisture from the surface, while woollen flannel conveys it from the skin and deposits it in drops on the outside of the shirt, from which the ordinary cotton shirt absorbs it, and by its nearer exposure to the air it is soon dried without injury to the body. Having these properties, red woollen flannel is worn by sailors even in the midsummer of the hottest countries. Wear a thinner material in summer.

FLANNEL, *Beware how you lay aside.*—Never be in a hurry to put off woollen garments. Flannel protects against the sudden changes of temperature. When perspiration flows freely, the quick evaporation carries with it much heat from the body, and a chill may be produced, and that may be followed by derangement of some function, as cold in the head, or unnatural discharge from the bowels.

Flannel is a slow conductor of cold or heat, and evaporation proceeds from it more slowly than from cotton or linen; hence its excellence for clothing.

Many persons wear flannel next to the skin all the year round, and find it a shield against prevalent complaints in the summer.

Much depends of course upon the constitution and employment of the individual, but in all cases flannel should not be laid aside till the weather is settled permanently warm, and the change should be made in the morning, not in the after-part of the day, when the energies are somewhat abated, and the air is usually cooler. Many a delicate person has sown the seeds of consumption in undressing for an evening party.

FLATULENCY.—See *Carminatives*, and *Colic*.

FLATULENCY, *griping, &c., in Children.*—It proceeds from indigestion. Give an emetic to produce a vomit. In two hours after, give a little rhubarb and magnesia, and occasionly a little castor oil, in aniseed water. Also a warm bath now and then.

FLEAS AND LICE, *on animals, to destroy.*—Solution of camphor—the camphor first dissolved in spirits of wine.—The root of the tail, and most of the back of dogs may be rubbed with Scotch snuff. —— Or apply oil of turpentine.

FLIES. —- Horses, cows, and oxen may be relieved from the annoyance of flies and the stings of venomous insects, by rubbing their legs and stomachs with train oil, which drives those unwelcome visitors away.

FLIES *annoying Working Horses.*—An infusion of walnut leaves, applied occasionly between the ears, and on other sensitive parts of the horse, is successful.

FLIES, *to destroy.*--A teaspoonful of laudanum, and two table-spoonfuls of water, strongly sweetened with sugar, placed in a saucer.——Or dissolve quassia chips in boiling water, and sweeten.—— Or a strong infusion of green tea, well sweetened. —— Or ground black pepper and sugar, diluted in milk, and put on plates, &c.

FLIES, *to keep off.*—Dust meat over with pepper, or powdered ginger, or fasten to it a piece of paper on which camphor has been well rubbed, or a few drops of creosote.

FLIP.—Put a quart of ale on the fire; beat 3 or 4 eggs, with 4 ozs. of sugar, a tea-spoonful of grated nutmeg or ginger, and a gill of good old rum or brandy. When the ale is about to boil, put it into one pitcher, and the eggs, rum, &c. into another; then pour it from one vessel to the other till it is as smooth as cream.

FLOUNDERS, *to fry.*—Rub with salt inside and out; let them stand two hours to give them firmness; dip them into egg, cover with crumbs and fry.

To boil. Open and clean; boil in salt and water; make either gravy, shrimp, cockle, or mussel sauce, and garnish with red cabbage.

FLOUR, *to detect adulterated.* —Take a little in the hand, and squeeze it for half a minute; if good, it can be put out of the hand in a lump; if adulterated, it will fall apart as soon as it leaves the hand.

FLOUR CAUDLE.--Into five large spoonfuls of pure water rub smooth a dessert-spoonful of fine flour. Set over the fire five spoonfuls of new milk, sweetened; the moment it boils, pour into it the flour and water; and stir it over a slow fire twenty minutes. It is a nourishing and gently astringent food--an excellent food for babies with weak bowels.

FLOWERS, *a hint to lovers of.* —A beautiful show of evergreens may be had by a very simple plan. If geranium branches, taken from luxuriant and healthy trees just before the winter sets in, be cut as for slips and immersed in soap-water, they will, after drooping for a few days, shed their leaves, put forth fresh ones, and continue in vigour all winter. By placing a number of bottles thus filled in a flower-basket, with moss to conceal them, a show of evergreens is insured for the whole season. They require no fresh water.

FLOWER BULBS AT ANY SEASON IN THREE WEEKS. —Fill a flower pot half full of quick lime, fill up with good earth, plant the bulb, and keep the earth damp.

FLOWERS, *to extract essence from.* — Take any flowers you choose; place a layer in a clean earthen pot, and over them a layer of fine salt. Repeat the process until the pot is filled, cover closely, and place in the cellar. Forty days afterwards, strain the essence from the whole through a crape by pressure. Put the essence thus expressed in a clear bottle, and expose for six weeks in the rays of the sun and evening dew to purify. One drop of this essence will communicate its ordour to a pint of water.

FLOWERS, *to preserve in water.*—Mix a little saltpetre or a little carbonate of soda with water, and it will preserve the flowers for a fortnight.

FLOWERS, *when faded to revive.*--Put one-third of the stalk in hot water till it is cold. Then cut off the end of the stalk, and put in cold water in which a little saltpetre has been dissolved. It acts like magic.

FLUMMERY.--Put 1 oz. each of bitter and sweet almonds into a basin; pour boiling water upon them to remove the skins; place the kernels in cold water a little; then beat in a mortar with rosewater; afterwards put them into a pint of calf-feets' stock; sweeten with loaf sugar. When it boils, strain; cool, and add a pint of thick cream, and stir till it is thick and cold; wet the mould and pour in the flummery. In five or six hours turn out. Constant stirring is essential to preserve the figures of the moulds, and the clearness of the flummery.

FLUMMERY, *French.*-Cream, 1 quart, isinglass, ½ oz., beat it fine, and stir it into the cream; boil gently over a slow fire 15 minutes, stirring all the time; take off; sweeten to taste; add a spoonful each of rose and orange-flower water; pour into a glass or mould, and when cold, turn it out.

FLUX.--Castor oil, 4 ozs.; gum arabic, two table-spoonfuls; gum kino, 1 table-spoonful; laudanum, 1 tea-spoonful; water, 1 pint; mix, and take a table-spoonful three or four times a-day. It is unfailing in most cases.

FLY PAPERS.--Melt 4 ozs. of resin with 2 ozs. of treacle, and 1 drachm of venice turpentine. Spread on sheets of paper.

FOMENTATION, *Decoction for.*—Take tops of wormwood, and oak bark, and camomile flowers dried, each, two ounces. Boil in two quarts of water. Pour off the liquor, and then add French brandy, or spirit of wine, as the case may require. *Hu.*

FOMENTATION, *Aromatic.*—Take of Jamaica pepper, half an ounce; red wine, a pint. Boil them a little, and then strain the liquor. This is intended not only as a topical application for external complaints, but also for relieving internal parts. Pains of the bowels which accompany dysenteries, and diarrhœas, flatulent colics, uneasiness of the stomach, and retching to vomit, are frequently abated by fomenting the abdomen and region of the stomach with a warm liquor.

FOMENTATION, *Soothing.*--Take 3 ozs. each of Hops, Horehound, Tansy, Wormwood, and 2 ozs. of Poppy Heads. Make a decoction by boiling in equal parts of vinegar and water.—Excellent for removing pain, caused by dislocations, contusions, sprains, and other causes. It may also be usefully employed in inflammation of the bowels, and all inflammations.

FOOT SPRAINS.—Slide the fingers under the foot, and having greased both thumbs, press them successively with increased force over the painful parts for about a quarter of an hour. Repeat the application several times, or until the patient is able to walk. This is a simple remedy for a very common casualty, and can be performed by the most inexperienced.

FORCEMEAT.—Take a pound of fresh lean veal, and the same weight of beef suet, and a bit of bacon or ham; shred all together; beat it in a mortar very fine; then season it with sweet herbs, pepper, salt, cloves, mace, and nutmegs; add the yolks of two or three eggs well beaten. A few oysters may be added; or marrow, if the forcemeat is intended to be rich. This may be made into balls about the size of a walnut. *Hu.*

ANOTHER, *to force Fowls or Meat.*—Shred a little ham, some cold veal, or fowl, or beef-suet; a small quantity of onion, parsley, a little lemon-peel, salt, nutmeg, or pounded mace, and white pepper, or Cayenne, and bread crumbs. Pound it in a mortar, and bind it with one or two eggs beaten and strained.

FOUL AIR IN WELLS.—To remove the gas before a descent is made into any well, a quantity of burned but unslacked lime should be thrown down. This, when it comes in contact with whatever water is below, sets free a great amount of heat in the water and lime, which rushes upward, carrying all the deleterious gases with it; after which descent may be made with safety. The lime also absorbs the carbonic acid in the well.

FOWLS, *to boil.*—Truss as in page 170. Put in a pan of cold water; cover; skim; boil slowly twenty minutes; take off, cover close, and the heat of the water will stew them enough in half an hour; it keeps the skin whole, white, and plump. Pour over them white sauce.

FOWLS, *to dress cold.*—Peel off all the skin, and pull the flesh off the bones in large pieces; dredge with flour; fry it a nice brown in butter; toss it up in a rich gravy, well seasoned; thicken it with a piece of butter rolled in flour; before serving; squeeze in the juice of a lemon.

FOWLS, *to fatten.*—Mix a little unsifted flour, ground rice, scalded with milk; add a *little* butter and coarse sugar, and a little chopped meat. Make it thick, and feed them several times a-day. This soon fattens them. Give them also now and then barley meal and water mixed thin.

FOWL, *to hash.*—Cut up the fowl as for eating; put it into a stew-pan with half a pint of gravy, a tea-spoonful of lemon pickle, a little mushroom ketchup, a slice of lemon, and a chopped shalot or two. Thicken with flour and butter; before it is dished, add a table-spoonful of thick cream; lay sippets round the dish, and serve.

FOWL, *Roasted.*—When the fowl is about half done, skewer pieces of fat bacon to it. It serves for larding, and saves time and trouble for the same. The bacon will serve to garnish the dish. Make a gravy of the necks and gizzards; strain, and put in a spoonful of browning. Serve with egg sauce.

FOWLS, *to roast a la Servante.*—Prepare a fowl for roasting, and make a forcemeat with the liver, parsley, shalots, butter, pepper, salt, and basil. Stuff the fowl with this; roast it, wrapped in slices of lard and paper. When three parts done, take off the lard and paper; baste it all over with the yolks of eggs beaten up with melted butter; freely sprinkle bread crumbs over it; roast to a fine yellow. Make a sauce with butter, a chopped anchovy, a few capers, flour, three spoonfuls of broth, nutmeg, pepper, and salt; make like a white sauce.

FOWLS, *to truss*.--Pluck them; cut off the neck close to the back; take out the crop, liver, and entrails; cut off the vent, draw it clean, and beat the breast-bone flat. *If for boiling*, cut off the nails of the feet, and tuck them close to the legs; put your finger into the inside, and raise the skin of the legs; then cut a hole in the top of the skin, and put the legs under; put a skewer in the first joint of the pinion, bring the middle of the leg close to it, put the skewer through the middle of the leg, and through the body, and do so on the other side. Take the filth from the gizzard; put it and the liver in the pinion; turn the points on the back, and tie a string over the tops of the legs to keep them in their place. *If to be roasted*, put a skewer in the first joint of the pinion, bring the middle of the leg close to it; put the skewer through the middle of the leg, and through the body;-- put a skewer in the small of the leg, and through the sidesman and one through the skin of the feet. Cut off the nails of the feet.

FOWL, *the best for the Winter.* --Cochins are the only birds to lay all the winter; and by their willingness to sit almost at any time in the summer, you may get pullets which will lay late in the autumn.

FOWL SOUP.—Cut up two fowls and some nice ham in small pieces, with sliced onions and celery; fry them in butter till brown; then boil them in water, thicken with fresh cream, and season with pepper, salt, and mace. Boil all together; and before serving add port wine. *A. N.*

FOXGLOVE INFUSION.--- Foxglove leaves, 1 dr.; boiling water, ½ pint; tincture of cinnamon, 1 fluid oz. Infuse the leaves in the water for five hours, strain, and add the tincture. A dessert spoonful twice a day. Valuable in water of the chest, and palpitation of the heart. *See Robinson's Family Herbal.*

FRAGRANT ODOUR, *to diffuse a.*--A few drops of oil of sandal wood dropped on a hot shovel, will diffuse a most agreeable balsamic perfume through the room.

FRECKLES.—Take 1 oz. of lemon-juice, a quarter of a drachm of powdered borax, and half a drachm of sugar; mix, let them stand a few days in a glass bottle, then rub it on the hands and face occasionally.——Or, mix two-teaspoonfuls of muriatic acid with 2 ozs. of spirits of wine; and 1½ pint of distilled water.——Or, 2 drs. of muriatic acid in 1 pint of water, and a teaspoonful of spirits of lavender. Apply with a camel hair pencil, or linen.——Or, Horseradish steeped in sour milk for 12 hours, and a drop or two of tincture of myrrh. Wash two or three times per day.

FREEZING MIXTURES.-- If ice cannot be obtained, water may be cooled to the freezing point by the following mixtures:---Sal Ammoniac, 5 parts; Nitre, 5 parts; Glauber Salts, 8 parts; Water, 16 parts.——Or, Nitrate of Ammonia, 1 part; Carbonate of Soda, 1 part; Water, 1 part.——Or mix 1 part of Muriate of Ammonia, or sal-ammoniac powder, with 2 parts of Nitrate of Potash, or Salt-petre:— this forms *one powder*. The powder to be mixed with it is formed of Barilla, or the best Scotch Soda, powdered. This must be kept in a cool place, well corked, as must the first powder. For use put an equal quantity of these two powders into the ice pail, and pour on them as much cold spring water as will dissolve them.

FRENCH BEANS. — See *Beans*.

FRENCH BEANS *for winter use.*—Put into boiling water for a minute, then into cold, drain, and dry them. Put at the bottom of a large earthen vessel, a two inch layer of salt, then a layer of beans, and so proceed till it is filled, the top layer always to be salt. Cover well. When you take out, fill the vacancy with salt. In cooking, soak them all the previous night, and add a little carbonate of soda.

FRENCH BEANS, *Pickled.* See page 47.

FRENCH BREAD.—Mix the yolks of three, and the whites of two eggs with a quarter of a peck of flour, a little salt, half a pint of good yeast, as much milk, warm, as will work it into a thin light dough. Do not knead it, but stir it about; put into dishes or tins, to rise; then turn them out into a quick oven; rasp when done.

FRENCH BREAD.—See page 76.

FRENCH BROWN BREAD. —Sour milk, 1 quart; salt, 1 teaspoonful; carbonate of soda, 1 teaspoonful; and half a tea-cup of treacle put into the milk. Thicken with unsifted or ground-down flour, and bake immediately.

FRENCH POLISH, *and the art of Staining and Graining.*— Take 2 ozs. of wood naptha, ½ oz. of best shellac, 1 drachm gum benzoin; crush the gums, mix them with the naptha in a bottle; shake them frequently till dissolved; it is then ready for use. This is the clear polish. Take a little cotton wool, apply a little of the polish to it, cover it tightly with a linen rag, to which apply a drop of linseed oil, to prevent it from sticking to the wood; use your rubber gently, polishing from a centre in a circular manner; finish with a drop of spirits of wine on a clean rubber, which will extract the oil. Wood may be stained or grained any colour or design, by mixing it with the polish, or dipping the rubber in the colour (finely powdered), at the time you apply the polish with the cotton. To produce a red: dip the cotton into dragon's blood (finely powdered), immediately applying the polish; then cover with the linen, and polish. For yellow: use the best chrome yellow. For blue: ultramarine blue, or indigo. For black; ivory, or lamp-black, &c. Graining is produced by touching or streaking the wood with the colour, as above, in irregular lines or marks, and in such shapes as the fancy may suggest, then finishing it with a coat of clear polish.

FRENCH ROLLS.—Rub 1 oz. of butter into 1 lb. of flour, mix one egg, well beaten, a little yeast, not bitter, as much milk as will make a dough of a middling stiffness; beat it well, but do not knead, let it rise; bake on tins quick.

FRIAR'S BALSAM. --- Gum Benzoin, 3½ ozs.; strained Storax, 2½ ozs.; Balsam of Tolu, 10 drs.; aloes, 5 drs.; rectified spirit, 2 pints; let it stand for 14 days, shaking oft before using. A good application for wounds and cuts; and such was very effectual in the hands of the old friars. *Internally,* it is stimulant, expectorant, and antispasmodic, and is useful in asthma, catarrh, consumption, and languid circulation. *Dose,* ½ a drachm on loaf sugar.

FRENCH POMADE.—Pomade (any) 8 ozs.; white wax, 1 oz.; spermaceti, ½ oz.; oil of almonds, 3 ozs. Mix.

FRENCH PUDDING.—Milk, 1 quart; flour, a cupful, or more, 8 or 9 eggs. Beat the eggs, and add them to the milk, with the flour. Butter a dish, and bake. Serve with sweet sauce.

FRITTERS.—Make them of any of the batters directed for pancakes, by dropping a small quantity into the pan; or make the plainer sort, and put pared apples sliced and cored into the batter, and fry some of it with each slice. Currants or sliced lemon as thin as paper, and orange flower water make an agreeable change.

FRITTERS, *common.*—Half a pint of ale and two eggs, beat in 2 or more table-spoonfuls of flour, with nutmeg and sugar to taste; let it rise four minutes; then drop them into a pan of boiling lard; fry a light brown; serve with sugar grated upon them.

It may be varied by adding cream, sweatmeat, marmalade, jam, currants, &c.

FRITTERS *Spanish.*—Cut the inside of a French roll into lengths as thick as your finger, in what shape you will. Soak in some cream, nutmeg, sugar pounded, cinnamon, and an egg. When well soaked, fry to a nice brown; and serve with butter, wine, and sugar sauce.

FROST BITES.—Keep from the fire, and rub well with snow, and then with cold water.

FROTH, *to set on cream, custard, or trifle.*—Sweeten ½lb. of the pulp of damsons, or any other scalded fruit, put to it the whites of four eggs beaten, and beat the pulp with them until it will stand as high as you choose; and being put on the cream, &c., with a spoon, it will take any form; it should be rough, to imitate a rock.

FRUIT, *to bottle.*—Currants, gooseberries, and other fruits may be thus preserved:—After having been well cleaned, put them into wide-mouthed glass bottles, shaking them so that each bottle may be full. Place them, slightly corked, in an oven nearly cold, for four or five hours; when the fruit contracts or wrinkles, take out, cork well down rapidly and cover with leather and wax. Keep in a dry place.

FRUIT, *to candy.*—After apricots, peaches, plums, nectarines, &c. have been preserved, take the fruit from the syrup; drain; to 1 lb. of loaf-sugar put half a teacupful of water; when dissolved set it over a moderate fire; when boiling hot put in the fruit; stir it continually until the sugar is candied about it; then take it upon a sieve and dry in a warm oven, or before a fire; repeat this two or three times if necessary.

FRUIT PIE *for invalids and children.*—The rich crusts generally made are not fit for invalids and children. Therefore divide into two slices each, as many sponge cakes as will be required for the size of your dish; put a layer of these, with the brown side downwards, at the bottom of the pie-dish, then fill with currants and raspberries, plums, damsons, or whatever fruit the season affords; sprinkle well with fine Lisbon sugar, and pour in water nearly to the brim; place a portion of the cut cakes upon the fruit as an upper crust, and let the dish be put in the oven for forty minutes.

FRUIT STAINS, *to remove from linen.*—Rub each side of the stained part with soap; then steep it in a strong solution of pearl-ash; soak well in hot water, or boil.

Dry in the sun.——Or, saturate the cloth with a little water, and hold the part over a lighted match, at a little distance. The spots will be removed by sulphureous gas.

FRUIT TART.—-Spread puff paste with a rolling pin; cut a piece the size of the dish, and out of the trimmings cut some strips; brush the edge of the dish with egg-wash and stick the strips on it: then put the fruit into the dish with sugar and a little water; roll the paste on the rolling pin and lay it over the fruit. Before you put the paste on brush the strips with egg-wash to make them stick. When you have trimmed the dish all round brush white of egg over the tart and sift sugar over it: then dip the paste brush into water and shake it over the tart. Bake it properly and serve up cold.

FRUMENTY.—To a quart of ready boiled wheat put two quarts of new milk, and a ¼ lb. of currants, or raisins, boil and stir till done; beat the yolks of 3 eggs, a little nutmeg, with four spoonfuls of milk; add this to the wheat; stir over the fire a little; then sweeten.

FUEL, *cheap*.—One bushel of small coal or saw-dust, or both mixed together, two bushels of sand, one and a half bushels of clay, made into balls, or bricks, and allowed to set firmly, will supply an excellent fuel, and effect a great saving in coals.

FUEL *to save*.—Take 4 lbs. of chalk in lumps, not above ½ lb. each. Make a clear fire of coal, and place the lumps of chalk in the grate, as coal is laid. The chalk becomes red hot, so as to be scarcely distinguishable from burning cinders. A few ashes or small coal thrown lightly on from time to time, will keep up a clear bright fire all day. The same chalk may be used three or four days, when it becomes lime, and manure for gardens or allotments, or for whitewashing. Half-a-peck of coal used thus with chalk, will give a capital fire for fourteen hours. The saving in coal is one-half. In grates the chalk should be kept behind, and coals in front; because chalk will not burn unless it has coal or heat on all sides of it.

FULMINATING SILVER.—Put into a small-necked bottle, resting on a little sand, one part of fine silver filings and three parts of nitro-muriatic-acid. When the silver is dissolved, pour the solution into a glass, add five times the quantity of water, then take spirit of sal-ammoniac, and pour it into the solution drop by drop, until the silver is precipitated to the bottom; decant the clear liquor, and wash it several times in warm waters, dry and place it on paper, to absorb the moisture. If a grain of this powder is put into an iron spoon, and exposed to the flame of a candle, it will explode with a loud report. The crackers are made with this powder, a small quantity being placed in a bit of paper with a pea and a bit of sand twisted up.

FUNERAL BISCUITS. —-Take twenty-four eggs, three pounds of flour, and three pounds of lump sugar grated, which will make forty-eight finger biscuits for a funeral.

FUNERAL BUNS.——Take two stones of flour, one pound of butter, and one pound of sugar, rubbed together, three pounds of currants, ginger, seeds, cinnamon, and a little rose-water, mixed up with milk. The above will make forty-eight cakes, at threepence per cake, each weighing one pound before they are baked. Make them round, and bake them a fine brown. They will take one pint of yeast.

FURNITURE CREAM. — Linseed oil, 1 pint; spirits of wine, 2 ozs.; vinegar, 1 oz.; butter of antimony, ½ oz.

FURNITURE POLISH. — The cheapest is a mixture of linseed oil and turpentine, laid on in a thin coat, rubbed off with a soft cloth and polished.

Furniture in constant use is greatly improved by washing with vinegar and water, and afterwards applying cold drawn linseed oil, rubbing it very much. It should be rubbed again in a day or two afterwards.

Or, linseed oil, 1 pint; spirits of wine, half a gill. Mix well. Apply with a linen rag. Rub dry with a soft cotton cloth. Rub last and hard with a piece of old silk. In time it will have a most beautiful gloss. Or,

Linseed oil, bees wax scraped into, and gradually dissolved in turpentine, to the thickness of cream. Apply as above, and rub well.

Or, 1 pint of linseed oil, 1 oz. of finely powdered rose pink, 1 oz. of shell-lac; beat well 1 oz. of alkanet root, and add it to the other. Keep the vessel in a warm place for a week, stirring now and then. This is excellent for darkening new wood, and removing marks, &c. Apply, and rub as before. Chamois leather is the best to rub with.

FURNITURE POLISH. — Spirits of wine, 1 pint; gum shellac, and gum lac, of each ½ an oz.; gum sandarac, ¼ oz. Melt with very gentle heat, frequently shaking the bottle. Double or treble a piece of cloth; put a little polish upon it; cover that with a piece of soft linen rag lightly touched with cold-drawn linseed oil. Rub the furniture or wood in a circular direction. Afterwards, rub in the same way spirits of wine, with a little of the polish added to it; and a very brilliant polish will be produced. Some furniture requires previous scraping with fine glass paper, on account of having been polished with wax.

Or, linseed oil, 1 pint; treacle, 8 ozs.; add a glass of gin; stir well; apply with a rag; rub till dry, and it will produce a splendid gloss.

FURS, *to keep moths from.* — Sprinkle them, and the drawers in which they are kept with spirits of turpentine.

FURS, *to improve.* -- Warm bran in an oven. Rub it well into the fur several times. Shake and brush till free from dust. Rub light furs with magnesia.

GAME PIE. — Divide the birds, if large, into pieces or joints. They may be pheasants, partridges, &c. Add a little bacon or ham. Season well. Cover with puff-paste, and bake carefully. Pour into the pie half a cupful of melted butter, the juice of a lemon, and a glass of sherry, when rather more than half baked.

GAME SOUP. — Cut in pieces a partridge, pheasant, or rabbit; add slices of veal, ham, onions, carrots, &c. Add a little water; heat a little on a slow fire, as gravy is done; then add some good broth; boil the meat gently till it is done. Strain, and stew in the liquor what herbs you please.

GANGREEN, OR MORTIFICATION. — See *Logwood.*

GARDENING, *Directions for each month in the year.*

January. — Trench and manure; prepare hot-beds for asparagus, cucumbers, mint, potatoes, and the small salads. Sow the brown, Dutch, and grand admiral cabbages, curled parsley for transplanting: frame peas, horn carrots, mazagan beans, onions (to be allowed to grow large); plant out cabbage plants to succeed those which have been planted out in autumn.

February.-All the ground which is destined for early crops must now be prepared, and hot-beds be multiplied for cucumbers and early melons. Celery may be sown on a moderate hot-bed; also sow cabbages, horn carrots, lettuces, leeks, parsnips, and in fact most of the table vegetables. Those plants, such as cabbages, chives, garlic, shalots, underground onions, and horseradish, which are fit, should now be transplanted.

March.—In open borders sow asparagus, cabbages, carrots, and Hamburgh parsley, Neapolitan kale, parsnips, onions, &c.; plant out such vegetables as have been already sown. Before sowing, dig carefully, and make the ground level and fine. Main crops may be sown in this month, such as early long-pod beans, peas, celery, turnips, and, indeed, most other vegetables. Mustard, cress, lettuce, spinach, and radishes, may be sown every week or fortnight, for succession. Chives, shalots, garlic, &c., may be planted; also rhubarb, potatoes, Jerusalem artichokes. Cuttings, or slips of sweet herbs may be planted.

April.—Planting the vegetables which have been sown is now the chief business. Make hot-beds for cucumbers and melons; force kidney beans and Victoria rhubarb. Plant out artichokes and potatoes; sow asparagus, beets, cabbages, celery, garden and kidney beans, Dutch turnips, lettuces, peas, radishes, small salading.

May.—Sow carrots, lettuce, capsicums, cauliflowers, spinach, Knight's marrow-fat peas, campions, &c. Transplant cabbages, winter greens, lettuces, and celery. Hoe and stake peas, water newly planted crops, and propagate aromatic plants by slips and cuttings. Protect from wind and rain choice tulips, ranunculuses, and anemonies. Propagate herbaceous plants by dividing the roots; wallflowers, sweet-williams, and rockets, by slips; and China roses, heliotropiums, &c., by cuttings.

June.—Sow Cape brocoli, kidney beans, peas, lettuces, Campions, spinach, small salading, &c. The best peas for sowing now are Knight's marrow-fat peas; they will bear till October. Hoe the table vegetables, and pick out the most curled plants of curled parsley, cress, and chervil, for seed. Watering the freshly-planted crops must now be attended to in dry weather in the evenings, or very early in the mornings. Weeding and thinning out are also of importance, as well as hoeing, particularly with potatoes, cabbages, and peas.

July.—Plant cabbages, savoys, coleworts, brocoli, lettuce, celery, &c. Train and regulate the summer shoots both of wall trees and standards; prune vine and fig-trees, and shade ripe currants that are exposed to the full blaze of the sun. Place nets on the cherries to protect them from birds. Take up garlic, onions, and shalots, as their leaves begin to decay.

August.—Both cabbages, brocoli, endive, spinach, Welsh onions, turnips, and radishes should now be sown. The celery sown should be planted, and that already planted, as well as cardoons, should be earthed up.

September.—Sow vegetable seed for a spring crop. Prick out cabbage plants, and gather ripe seeds. Endive and lettuce may be planted out on beds sloping to the southwest, and fenced round to drain off water. Hoe and clear the ground about turnips. Cabbage for collards in November, and German greens may be planted early in the month.

October.—Sow magazan beans, and frame peas on a warm southern border; lay into the ground purple and white brocoli, within a few inches of their lower leaves, letting their heads face the north; transplant cauliflowers and purple brocoli under frames and handglasses; cabbages, garlic, lettuces, and shalots, under frames.

November.—Force seakale, rhubarb, and asparagus; take up endive, brocoli, and cauliflower, and lay them flat in dry ground; transplant suckers taken from the roots of the pear and codling plum, and prepare them for budding and grafting different fruits upon.

December.—Celery should now be earthed up, and in so careful a manner as not to require the operation again; force asparagus, also rhubarb, and seakale; lay in as early as possible this month the brocoli, purple, and white.

GENERAL HINTS, *Operating on the soil.*—Trenching should always follow draining, or the latter will act but partially. Unless the ground be stirred pretty deeply, half the effect of draining will be lost. Both must be done in the autumn or early part of the winter, and the ground will then be in a good state, for cropping in spring. Manuring may be done in early winter when the ground is somewhat frozen, as the material can then be wheeled on with greater ease, and the grounds and paths will be less cut up.

LIGHT.—Want of light is often the real cause of evils which are ascribed to want of air, though both combined may occasionally be acting. Light may, however, be prejudicial to plants in certain stages, as after fresh planting or potting, when it stimulates them more than their crippled roots will bear. Dull weather is, therefore, best both for potting and planting, and a little shade after either process may often be beneficial.

GARGLE.—A gargle of yeast and milk is good for a sore throat.
——Also a decoction of Cohosh has the same effect——Sage and Hyssop, 1 oz. each. Infuse in 1 quart of water. Cool, strain, and add 1 drachm of borax. Good for thrush, quinsy, or sore throat.

GARGLE, *Cooling.*—Nitre, 2 drachms; honey, 4 drachms; rose water, 6 ozs. Mix.

Gargle for Sore Throat.—Decoction of bark, 7 ozs.; tincture of myrrh, 2 drachms; purified nitre, 3 drachms. Mix. This will disperse tumefied gland, or common sore throat. A little nitre alone put into the mouth now and then, and swallowing the saliva, often prevents or cures throat affections.

Gargle for putrid Sore Throat.—Decoction of bark, 6 ozs.; diluted vitriolic acid, 1 drachm; honey of roses, or yeast, 1 oz. Mix with the same quantity of port wine. Use oft.

Or, Cayenne pepper, 2 drachms; tincture of myrrh, 2 drachms; water, half a pint; vinegar, 1 oz. Mix. At first using, it may be diluted.

GARLIC SAUCE.—Pound two cloves of garlic with fresh butter the size of a nutmeg, rub it through a double hair-sieve, and stir into it half a pint of beef gravy, or melted butter, or it may be made with garlic vinegar.

GARLIC VINEGAR.—Peel and chop 2 ozs. of garlic; pour upon it the best vinegar; cover the jar, and shake it frequently; infuse ten days, then strain off the liquor.

GEESE, *to choose.*—The largest are esteemed the best; also the white and the grey; the dark coloured are not so good. A young goose has a yellow bill; if the bill be red, it is a sign of age: if fresh, the feet will be pliable, but, when stale, stiff and dry.

GENTIAN.—The root is a most valuable bitter tonic, proper for all cases of debility, and indigestion. It strengthens the stomach, promotes digestion, and prevents acidification of the food.

GENTIAN, *Compound Infusion of.*—The root, cut in pieces, ½ oz.; dried Seville orange peel bruised, 1 drachm; coriander seeds, bruised, half a drachm; spirits of wine, 4 ozs.; water, 1 pint; infuse first in the alcohol three hours; then add the water, and macerate 12 hours without heat. The dose is 2 or 3 drachms three times a day.

GENTIAN, *Tincture of.*—Gentian, 1¼ oz.; orange peel, 4 drs.; cardamoms, 2 drachms; spirits of wine, 1 pint. Macerate for 15 days. Dose, one teaspoonful.

GHERKINS, *to pickle.*—Put them into strong salt and water, and stir twice a day; take out and place in a jar with vine leaves, and pour boiling vinegar over them. When cold heat the vinegar again, cover the gherkins with fresh vine leaves, and pour it upon them; repeat till of a good colour. Then add to it as much vinegar as is necessary, suppose two quarts, ¼ oz. of mace, 6 cloves, ½ oz. ginger, ¼ oz. of black pepper, and a tablespoonful of salt. Boil five minutes, and pour upon the pickle.

Another Receipt.—Put them into a jar, and cover them with boiled vinegar; add a little salt; place them near the fire; boil the vinegar every day for five or six days; cover to keep in the steam; then take fresh vinegar, with black, white, or cayenne pepper, and ginger; put in the gherkins; simmer slowly till they look green. When cool, cover, and keep in a dry place.

GIBLET PIE.—Clean the giblets well; stew with a little water, onion, pepper, salt, sweet herbs till nearly done. Cool, and add beef, veal or mutton steaks. Put the liquor of the stew to the giblets. Cover with paste, and when the pie is baked, pour into it a large tea-cupful of cream.

GILDING, *for Books, &c.*—Screw a quantity of pages strongly into a press. After being cut and scraped as smooth as possible, size them with isinglass glue mixed up with spirits of wine, and then apply the gold leaves, let them dry, then burnish with a blood-stone.

GILDING, *to preserve from fly-dirt.*—Cover over with gauze or tissue paper, till the flies are gone.——Or boil a few leeks in a pint of water; with a very soft brush wash over the glasses and frames with the liquid—flies do not like it, and will not alight.

GILDING, *to renew.*—Give the wood a coating of size made of the white of an egg, well beaten, and diluted with water, or isinglass dissolved in a weak spirit. Apply the size, and when half dry, apply the gold, and when *completely dry,* polish with an agate.

GINGER, *to candy.*—Put 1 lb. of loaf sugar finely powdered into a pan with as much water as will dissolve it, and 1 oz. of race ginger powdered; stir over a slow fire till the sugar begins to boil: then stir in 1 lb. more sugar, and stir till it becomes thick, and falls in a mass from the spoon; take off, and dry it in cakes upon earthen dishes; put in a warm place, and

L

they will be white, hard and brittle. Colour with a little saffron.

GINGER, *Syrup of.*—Macerate 1½ oz. of beaten ginger in a quart of boiling water, closely covered for twenty-four hours; then strain the infusion, make it into a syrup by adding at least two parts of fine loaf sugar, dissolved and boiled up in a hot water bath.

GINGER, *Tincture of.*—Ginger, 1 oz.; proof spirits, 1 pint. Digest in a gentle heat seven days, and strain. A good stimulant, and expellant of wind; used as a corrective to purgative draughts.

GINGER BEER, *Cheap.*—Sugar, 1 lb.; boiling water, 1 gallon; ginger, ¼ oz., and a lemon sliced thin. Stir till all is mixed. Cool, and add a table-spoonful of yeast. Let it stand 20 hours, then strain, bottle, and tie down the corks. Will be prime in a few days.

Another Receipt.—To every gallon of spring water, add 1 oz. of sliced white ginger, and 1 lb. of white sugar, or 1¼ lb., if you like. Boil nearly an hour. Then add ½ oz. of lemon juice to every gallon; strain, cool, and add yeast, 1 table-spoonful or rather more to a gallon. In 48 hours, add a little isinglass, and the white of one or two eggs. Put into the cask, and let it stand 24 hours longer. Bottle and cork well.

Another Receipt.--Ginger 3 ozs.; sugar, 4 lbs.; cream of tartar, ½ oz.; essence of lemon, ¼ oz.; the juice and peel of two lemons; brandy, ½ pint; yeast, quarter of a pint; water, 4 gallons. Bruise the sugar and ginger; boil 25 minutes; pour it boiling upon the lemon, tartar, essence, &c. Stir well; nearly cool, and add the yeast; let it work three days, skimming well; then strain into a cask; add the brandy; bung down close; and in a fortnight, draw off, and bottle.

Receipt for six gallons.—Bruised ginger, 8 ozs.; cream of tartar, 6 ozs.; loaf sugar, 6 lbs.; water, 6 gallons; three unpeeled lemons sliced. As soon as the water boils pour it on the ingredients, and stir well. Add a small portion of yeast. Some prefer the addition of 1 lb. of honey. After fermentation, strain, and bottle. Or strain, and bottle, without previously adding yeast.

GINGER BEER, *Common.*—Brown Sugar or Treacle, 1¼ lb., Water, 1½ gallon, 1 oz. of Ginger, ground, and a lemon, if preferred. Boil, and then add yeast.

Ginger Beer instantly made.—Sugar, 1½ lb.; bruised ginger, 1¼ oz.; water, 1 quart. Boil down to a syrup. When cool, strain, and add the juice of a lemon, or ¼ oz. of citric acid, and a little brandy. Keep this always by you in a bottle. It is to be used along with Carbonate of Soda and Tartaric Acid. First dissolve in water a quarter of a tea-spoonful of Tartaric Acid, into which put Ginger Syrup according to taste; then dissolve half a tea-spoonful of carbonate of soda in water; unite the two mixtures, and you will have a grateful beverage.

Another, quickly made.—Dissolve 4 ozs. of candied ginger in 2¼ gallons of boiling water, add 2 lbs. of sugar; add ¼ oz. of citric acid, powdered when nearly cold, and two table-spoonfuls of yeast.

GINGER BEER POWDERS *For the white paper;*—Loaf sugar, powdered, 2 drachms; ginger powdered, 6 or 7 grains; carbonate of soda, 26 grains. Mix well.—— *For blue paper;*—Citric Acid, 30 grains, or tartaric acid, 28 grains (which you please). Dissolve each powder in *nearly* half a tumbler of water, and mix together.

GINGER BISCUITS.-Grated

ginger, ½ oz.; sugar, 12 ozs.; flour, 6 ozs.; beat the yolks 7 eggs; till thick, then the whites stiff; stir the flour into the whole. Bake in a slow oven. *A. N.*

GINGERBREAD BUTTONS, *Snap.*—Treacle 3 lbs.; sugar, 1 lb.; ginger, 1½ oz.; seeds, &c.; butter, ¼ lb. rubbed in 2 lbs. of flour; mix and drop them on tins.

Ginger Bread Buttons, Best.—Treacle, 7 lbs., warmed; sugar, oatmeal, 2 lbs. each; butter, 2 lbs. rubbed in 7 lbs. of flour; candied lemon peel, 1 oz. cut very thin; carraway, cinnamon, or clove, according to taste; mix stiff, and bake in small balls on a tin in a slow oven.

GINGERBREAD, *fine.*--Flour, 2 lbs.; sugar, 8 ozs.; orange peel, or candied lemon, cut very thin, 8 ozs.; ground ginger, 1 oz.; carraway seeds, ½ ozs.; cloves, mace, allspice, according to taste; mix with these, 1½ lb. of treacle, and ¼ lb. melted butter, and 2 drachms of carbonate of soda. Mix well, and let it stand 2 or 3 hours. Use flour in rolling out. Cut into shapes.

GINGERBREAD NUTS.— Treacle, 3 lbs.; sugar, 1 lb.; butter, 1 lb. rubbed into 4 lbs. of flour; essence of lemon, 2 tea-spoonfuls; ginger, seeds, &c., according to taste. Mix; drop on buttered tins: bake in a slow oven.

These may be varied by the addition of candied lemon, brandy, and a couple of eggs well beaten.

GINGERBREAD, *Superior.* —Flour, 2 lbs.; carbonate of magnesia, ½ oz.; mix, and add treacle, 1 lb.; powdered sugar, ¼ lb.; melted butter, 2 ozs.; tartaric acid in solution, 2 drachms. Make a stiff paste; add grated nutmeg and cinnamon, of each 2 drachms; grated nutmeg, 1½ oz. Mix well. Let it stand 1 hour, and then bake slowly.

Another Receipt.—Flour, 3 lbs.; sugar, 1 lb.; butter, 1 lb.; treacle, 1½ lb.; ginger, ½ oz.; cloves, ¼ oz. and the peel of a good sized lemon; form into cakes and bake.

GINGERBREAD, *Victoria.*— Flour, 3½ lbs.; fine sugar, 2¼ lbs.; honey, 1½ lb.; ½ lb. each of sweet almonds blanched, and chopped small, and candied lemon or orange peel; the rinds of two lemons; cinnamon, 1 oz.; nutmeg, ½ oz.; powdered cloves, mace, and cardamoms, according to taste, and 3 tablespoonfuls of water. Melt the sugar, and honey in the water over the fire. Mix well the other articles in the flour, and pour in the syrup from the fire. Mix well. Do not bake till the day after. Mix the white of an egg and sugar, and brush it over the gingerbread.

A good sort without butter.— Treacle, 2 lbs. 4 ozs. of orange, lemon, citron, and candied ginger, all thinly sliced; 1 oz. each coriander seeds, carraways, and bruised ginger; as much flour as will make a soft paste; bake in a quick oven on tin plates.

GINGERBREAD, *White.*-— Flour, 6 lbs.; white sugar, 3 lbs.; rub 1 lb. of butter into the flour, and ½ oz. carraway seeds; mix well with milk. Make it light the same as *Bath Cakes*, page 46.

GINGER CAKES.-Beat 3 eggs in ½ pint of cream; stir in a saucepan till warm; add butter, 1 lb.; loaf sugar, ¼ lb.; ginger, 2½ ozs. Stir these ingredients over the fire to melt and mix; make into a good paste with 2 lbs. of flour; roll out, cut into forms half an inch thick. Lay on papers, and bake in a hot oven.

GINGER DROPS.—Beat 2 ozs. of soft candied orange in a mortar with a little sugar to a paste; mix with 1 oz of powdered white ginger, with 1 lb. of loaf sugar. Wet the sugar with a little water, and boil all together to a candy, and drop on paper.

GINGER POP.—This is made by adding strong ale to the Ginger Beer ingredients, and fermenting.

GINGER WINE.—Fine loaf sugar, 12 lbs.; powdered ginger, 6 ozs.; water, 6 gallons. Boil for an hour. Whisk the whites of 6 eggs, to mix with the liquors. When cold, put into a barrel, and 6 lemons cut into slices, and a cupful of yeast; ferment 3 days, then bung. In eight days, bottle it. It is improved by adding a pint of brandy.

GLASS, *to cut*, &c.—Glass may be easily filed, sawed, cut, drilled, or turned, by keeping the edge of the tool constantly wet with spirits of turpentine.

GLASS, *to draw on*.—Grind lamp black with gum water, and common salt; draw the design with a pen or hair pencil.

GLASS, *to frost*.—This may be done by sugar of lead, Glauber's Salts, Epsom Salts. Dissolve in hot water, and apply with a brush.

GLASS, *to join*.—Melt a little isinglass in spirits of wine, and add a little water. Gently warm the mixture over the fire. When thoroughly melted, it forms a transparent glue, which will unite broken glass firmly, and so that the joining will not be seen.

Lime mixed with the white of an egg forms a very strong cement for joining glass, porcelain, &c.

GLASS, *to paint gold colour*.—Silver, 1 oz.; antimony ½ oz.; mix in a crucible; then pound the mass to powder, and grind it on a copper plate, adding yellow-ochre, or brick dust calcined again, 15 ozs., and grind them well together with water.

GLASS, *to paint red*.—Take jet, 4 ozs.; litharge of silver, 2 ozs.; red chalk, 1 oz. Powder fine, and mix.

GLASS, *to remove crust from*.—Wash with sulphuric or muriatic acid diluted with water, and mixed with coarse sand.

GLASSES, *to clean*. — Wash with warm water and soap, then rinse in clean cold water; wipe the wet off with a cloth, and finish with a dry one. Sifted Fullers Earth is excellent for cleaning glasses. It restores the *lustre of glass*.

GLASS STOPPLES, *to loosen*. —Drop a little hot oil round the stopple, close to the top of the neck of the bottle, and place before the fire so as not to crack. In about half an hour apply more oil, and then gently try to work it about, occasionally gently beating it against the soft part of your hand, or gently strike it with a very light wooden instrument.

If this does not succeed, apply more oil, and a cloth dipped in hot water wrapped round the neck only.

Gloves to clean.—Wash in soap and water; then stretch them on wooden hands, or pull them out in their proper shape. Dry. If wanted yellow, rub with yellow ochre; if white, with pipe clay; or mix the two.

GLOVES, *to cleanse*.—Lay the gloves upon a clean board, pass over them with a brush a mixture of fullers earth and powdered alum; sweep off, and rub well with dry bran and whiting; and dust them well. But if they are greasy and soiled, take out the grease with crumbs of toasted bread, and burnt bone powdered, then take a clean woollen cloth, and rub them over with the first-named powder.

GLOVES, *Perfume for*.—Extract of ambergris, 4 drops, spirits of wine, 1 oz. Rub the inside with cotton saturated with it.

GLUE, *Liquid.*—Glue, water, vinegar, each 2 parts. Dissolve in a water bath; then add alcohol, 1 part. An excellent cement.

GLUE, *Liquid.* — Shellac, 2 parts; borax, 1 part. Boil till the shellac is dissolved.

Shellac dissolved in naptha will unite glass, china, wood, iron, &c.

GLUE, MOUTH.—Dissolve 4 ounces of fine Russian glue, or gelatine, in water, adding two ounces of sugar. Boil till it is of a consistence to become solid when cool. Then mould it to any size you like. It may be wet with the tongue, and applied to paper, silk, &c.

GLUE, *Portable for Draughtsmen,* &c.—Glue, 5 parts; sugar, 2 parts; water, 8 parts. Melt in a water-bath and cast it in moulds. For use, dissolve in warm water.

GLUE, *to resist water.*—Boil 1 lb. of glue in two quarts of skimmed milk.

GLUE, *Waterproof.*—1. Glue, 2 parts; skimmed milk, 8 parts. Melt, and evaporate in a water bath to the consistence of strong glue.

2. Glue, 12 parts; water sufficient to dissolve it. Then add yellow resin, 3 parts, and when melted, add turpentine, 4 parts. Mix thoroughly together. This should be done in a water-bath.

GOLD LIQUID.—Honey and gold leaf in equal parts. Grind *intimately* together upon a slab; agitate with thirty times its weight of hot water; settle, and pour off; repeat the agitation. Dry the gold. Mix up with gum water for use.

GOOSE, *(a la mode).*—Skin and bone the goose; boil and peel a dried tongue, also a fowl; season with pepper, salt, and mace, and then roll it round the tongue; season the goose in the same way, and lay the fowl and tongue on the goose, with slices of ham between them. Beef marrow rolled between the fowl and the goose, will greatly enrich it. Put it all together in a pan, with two quarts of beef gravy, the bones of the goose and fowl, sweet herbs, and onion; cover close, and stew an hour slowly; take up the goose; skim off the fat, strain, and put in a glassful of good port wine, two table-spoonfuls of ketchup, a veal sweet bread cut small, some mushrooms, a piece of butter rolled in flour, pepper, and salt; stew the goose half an hour longer; take up and pour the ragout over it. Garnish with lemon.

GOOSE PIE.-Bone two young green geese, of a good size, but first take away every plug, and singe them nicely. Wash them clean; and season them high with salt, pepper, mace, and allspice. Put one inside the other; and press them as close as you can, drawing the legs inwards. Put a good deal of butter over them, and bake them either with or without crust: if the latter, a cover to the dish must fit close to keep in the steam. It will keep long.

GOOSE, *to roast.*—After it is picked, the plugs of the feathers pulled out, and the hairs carefully singed, let it be well washed and dried, and a seasoning put in of onion, sage, and pepper and salt. Fasten it tight at the neck and rump, and then roast. Put it first at a distance from the fire, and by degrees draw it nearer. A slip of paper should be skewered on the breast-bone. Baste it very well. When the breast is rising, take off the paper; and be careful to serve it before the breast falls, or it will be spoiled by coming flatted to table. Let a good gravy be sent in the dish.—Gravy and apple sauce: goose-berry sauce for a green goose.

GOOSE SAUCE.—*For Roasted Goose, Duck, or Pork.*.—Mix a tea-spoonful of made mustard, a salt-spoonful of salt, and a few grains of cayenne pepper, in a large wine-glassful of claret, or good port wine; pour it into the goose just before serving up. *Hu.*

GOOSEBERRIES, *to Bottle.*—Gooseberries picked green from the trees into bottles, corked tightly, and buried in the earth, the corks downwards, are as good at Christmas as if freshly picked from the trees. The old *Red Rough* and the *Warrington* (both red) are best for preserving; the white or green are best for bottling.

GOOSEBERRIES, *to preserve.*—The old English boiling berry, and the rough reds are the best. Take 8 lbs of fruit, and 6 lbs. of loaf sugar. Boil 40 or 50 minutes, skimming well. Some prick each berry with a needle. Jar the same as other fruits.

GOOSEBERRY CREAM.—Boil them in milk till soft; beat them, and strain the pulp through a coarse sieve. Sweeten cream with sugar to your taste; mix with the pulp; when cold, place in glasses for use.

GOOSEBERRY FOOL.—Put the fruit into a stone jar, and some good sugar; set the jar in a saucepan of water over the fire. When it is done enough to pulp, press it through a colander; have ready a sufficient quantity of new milk, and a tea-cupful of raw cream, boiled together, or two or three eggs, instead of the latter, and left to be cold; then sweeten it pretty well with fine sugar, and mix the pulp by degrees with it.—A tablespoonful of orange-flower water, a seasoning of cloves, cinnamon, or nutmeg, greatly improve it.

GOOSEBERRY JAM.—Put 12 lbs. of the ripe red hairy gooseberries gathered dry, into a preserving pan with a pint of currant juice; boil quick, beat them with the spoon; when they begin to break, put to them of sugar 6 lbs. and simmer slowly to a jam; it requires long boiling or it will not keep. It is not expensive, but it is excellent for tarts or puffs. Do not burn the bottom.

Another.—Gather your gooseberries, (the clear white or green sort when ripe; top and tail, and weigh them; a pound to three quarters of a pound of fine sugar, and half a pint of water; boil and skim the sugar and water; then put in the fruit, and boil gently till clear; then break and put into small pots.

GOOSEBERRY JELLY. — Make as currant jelly; or it may be made of green gooseberries, the same as apple jelly.

GOOSEBERRY PIE. — Pick and wash the gooseberries; dry them well; let the dish be three parts full of the gooseberries; fill up with sugar; cover with a nice puff paste. Put in a small cup inverted, to prevent the syrup escaping. Some line the dish with puff paste; but a cover is generally sufficient. Bake in a moderate oven 40 minutes. *A. N.*

GOOSEBERRY PUDDING, *to bake.*—Scald the gooseberries till they are soft; drain; when cold, squeeze the juice through a sieve with a wooden spoon; add ¼ lb. of sugar, ¼ lb. of butter, 4 ozs. of Naples biscuits; beat well six eggs; mix all together, beat 15 minutes; pour into an earthen dish with or without paste.

GOOSEBERRY PUDDING.—Chop fine ¼ lb. of beef suet; roll it well into about 1 lb. of flour; then mix with cold water till it be-

comes a nice paste; add a little salt. Line a buttered basin with the paste, and let it be three parts full of gooseberries; fill up with fine sugar, and cover with paste. Bake 1½ hour. Sauce, melted butter, sweetened, or with fresh cream.
A. N.

GOOSEBERRY OR APPLE TRIFLE.-Scald as many of either of these fruits, as, when pulped through a sieve, will make a thick layer at the bottom of your dish; if of apples, mix the rind of half a lemon grated fine; add to both as much sugar as will be pleasant.

Mix half a pint each of milk and cream, and the yolk of one egg; give it a scald over the fire, and stir it all the time; do not let it boil; add a little sugar, and cool. Lay it over the apples with a spoon; and then put on a whip made the day before, as for other Trifles.

GOOSEBERRY VINEGAR.—Bright yellow English Gooseberries, ripe, 1 quart; stamp them small; water, 3 quarts; stir well together, and let them stand 48 hours; strain, and add 1¼ lb. of sugar. Let it remain in the cask for 9 or 10 months.

GOOSEBERRY AND CURRANT WINE.—Six gallons of cold soft water; four gallons of gooseberries; four gallons of currants; ferment; mix raw sugar, 13 lbs.; honey, 2 lbs.; citric acid, 1 oz. Brandy, 6 pints. This will make 12 gallons.

Another.—Water, 5½ gallons; gooseberries and currants, 4 gals.; ferment; sugar, 13 lbs.; tartar, in fine powder, 1 oz.; ginger, do. 3 ozs.; sweet marjoram, half a handful. Brandy, 1 quart, or more. Will make nine gallons.

GOUT.—Supposed to be a disease of the blood. It is generally produced by luxurious living, beer and wine drinking, and the want of exercise; also by too free a use of animal food, and intoxicating drinks. These cause deficient secretionary action, deficient perspiration and urine, so as to corrupt the blood with uric acid and other matter, which should have been ejected from the body, but which are thrown upon some debilitated part of the body, causing inflammation and great pain. Gouty inflammation does not terminate in suppuration or gangrene, but by an effusion of chalky liquid deposited at the joints, causing a stiffness of them; the deposit is called *chalk-stones.*

A fit of the gout attacks suddenly, without warning, generally in the night; often with a severe pain in the ball of the great toe, the heel, or perhaps the whole foot. The inflammation may also attack the knee, hand, wrist, elbow, &c., or change from one joint to another. It is attended with a quick pulse, fever, hot skin, confined state of the bowels, urine high colour, with dense deposits. Hard malt liquor tends to produce uric acid, even in spite of regular exertions and labour.

Treatment.—First restore the deficient secretions, and cleanse the stomach and bowels. If there be much fever, nausea, &c., give an emetic, say 15 grains of ipecacuanha powder. Give purgatives; as small doses of rhubarb, about 10 grains, and bicarbonate of potash, 15 grains. The following are very useful internal remedies: Infusion of gentian, 3 ozs.; tincture of columba, 2½ drachms; liquor potassa, 25 drops. Mix; and take in four doses, two per day. Or,

Dissolve 1 oz. of gum guiacum in a pint of the best French Brandy; infuse a day, then add half a pint of water. Two table-spoonfuls to be taken every morning fasting, followed by a cup of tea. Or,

Rhubarb, saltpetre, milk of sulphur, mustard, of each, $\frac{1}{2}$ an oz.; powdered coriander seed, powdered gum guiacum, of each $\frac{1}{4}$ an oz. Mix; take a tea-spoonful every other night in a wine-glassful of weak peppermint water.

Meadow-saffron, or colchicum, is said to exert a wonderful influence over gouty affections:—Calcined magnesia, 16 grains; vinegar or wine of meadow-saffron, 1 drachm; mix with 3 table-spoonfuls of peppermint water for a draught. Of the wine alone, (colchicum) take 30 or 40 drops for several days.

Pain arising from inflammation may be relieved by saturating a piece of lint in spirits of wine and camphor, applied to the part and covered with oiled silk.——Or steam the part several times a-day over the vapour of bitter herbs, after which rub with the tincture of cayenne; in severe pain, add a little opium. Occasionally apply a poultice of bran and vinegar.

If gout of the stomach arises from indigestible food, take an emetic. On recovery, sponge the body every morning with cold salt and water, drying well and using the flesh brush freely. Take also exercise in the open air freely. The food must be plain—be sparing of malt liquors—promote the evacuations—be sparing of animal food, avoiding it at supper—use unsifted flour, and vegetables, cooling fruits—milk preparations—tea and coffee should not be taken strong.

GRAPES, *to prevent dropping off.*—Make a circular incision in the wood, cutting a ring of bark, about the breadth of the twelfth of an inch. The wood acquires greater size about the incision, and the operation accelerates the maturity, and also of the fruit.

GRAPES, *to pickle.*—Lay grapes not too ripe, in a stone jar; then a layer of vine leaves, alternately till the jar is full. Then take 2 quarts of water, common salt, $\frac{1}{2}$ lb. and bay salt, $\frac{1}{2}$ lb.; boil 30 minutes; skim; take off to settle; pour the liquor, milk warm, upon the grapes, and lay plenty of vine leaves upon the top; cover close; stand two days; then drain, and dry the grapes. Put in flat bottomed stone jars with vine leaves in layers, and plenty on the top. Boil a quart of hard water, and 1 lb. of white sugar 15 minutes; skim well, and add 3 blades of mace, a nutmeg, and two quarts of the best vinegar; when cold, pour upon the grapes. Tie up with bladders.

GRAPES, *to preserve.*—Into an air-tight cask put a layer of bran dried in an oven; upon this place a layer of grapes, well dried, and not quite ripe, and so on alternately till the barrel is filled; end with bran, and close air-tight; they will keep 9 or 10 months. To restore them to their original freshness, cut the end of each bunch stalk, and put into wine, like flowers. Or,

Bunches of grapes may be preserved through winter by inserting the end of the stem in a potato. The bunches should be laid on dry straw, and turned occasionally. —— Or they may be kept in layers of Cotton, as the Americans do.

GRAPES, *to preserve in brandy.*—Take close bunches of grapes, not too ripe; put them into a jar with 4 ozs. of sugar candy, and fill the jar with brandy. Tie close with bladder. Morello cherries are done the same way.

GRAPE JAM.—Stew grapes to a soft pulp, and strain. To 1

lb. of pulp add 1 lb. of sugar. Boil 25 minutes slowly, stirring well.

GRAPE JELLY.—Mix equal quantities of the juice of ripe grapes, and dissolved isinglass; add sugar as you like. Add two glasses of Madeira, strain and put into moulds.

GRAPE WINE.—Bruise a gallon of white grapes into a gallon of water, to stand a week without stirring; pour off the liquor fine. To each gallon, add 3 lbs. of lump sugar; after it ceases hissing, stop it close, and in six months it will be fit to bottle. Less water used, and better the wine.

GRATES, *bright to clean.*—Use rotten stone and sweet oil.

GRAVEL.—A collection of sand or small particles of stone in the kidneys, ureters, or bladder. The urine oft gives the deposit of a brick-dust appearance, *uric acid.* The symptoms are shivering, pain in the loins, generally felt more severely on one side, and passing downwards—towards the bladder, a frequent desire to make water, which is passed in small quantities, sometimes with blood, or for a time not passed at all, irritation about the neck of the bladder. As the irritating matter passes from the kidneys into the ureter, it produces pain so great as to cause faintings and convulsive fits. The transit of this matter may be made in a few hours, or it may last for several days.——The following are good remedies:—

Dissolve 3 drachms of prepared natron or carbonate of soda, in a quart of cold soft water, and take half during the day. Continue as the case may require. The greatest martyrs have been relieved by this simple remedy. Or,

Take one ounce of the spirits of sweet nitre, two drachms of liquid laudanum, and half an ounce of the oil of juniper. Take a tea-spoonful in a cup of linseed tea sweetened with honey. This has performed wonders. Or,

Take dandelion and marshmallow roots, of each two ounces, agrimony, a small handful, to three quarts of water; boil to two quarts. Dose—a wine-glassful every three or four hours.

A gentle aperient may at times be given, and warm injections are very soothing. Take also the Diuretic Infusion. Flannels dipped in hot Tincture of Cayenne, and wrung out, or the Stimulating Liniment may be applied to the pained part. Hops simmered in vinegar, to which add 20 or 30 drops of laudanum. Drink at the same time a strong infusion of spearmint, and bathe the feet in warm water. The vapour bath now and then is very useful.

Dr. Beach advises the following:—Acetate of potash, 2 drachms; honey, ½ oz.; spirits of turpentine, ½ drachm; carbonate of soda, ½ a drachm; mint water or tea, 8 ozs. Mix. Dose, two tablespoonfuls three times a day.

Eat largely of spinach.——Or, drink largely of warm water sweetened with honey.——Or, of pellitory of the wall tea so sweetened.——Or, infuse an ounce of wild parsley-seeds in a pint of white wine for twelve days. Drink a glass of it, fasting, three months. To prevent its return, breakfast for three months on agrimony tea. It entirely cured me twenty years ago, nor have I had a symptom of it since.—*Wesley.*

Red onion juice, and horse-mint tea, as much as the patient can take morning and night, is a fine remedy, and will dissolve stone.

GRAVY.—If richness be wanted in any gravy, a lump of butter, given for candying fruit; some may be done each way.

GREEN GAGE JAM.— Peel and take out the stones. To 1 lb. of pulp put ¾ lb. of loaf sugar; boil half an hour; add lemon juice. *A.N.*

GREEN GAGE TART.—Select fruit not quite ripe, but sound; fill a pie-dish; beat up ¼ lb. of powdered sugar, in as much water as will dissolve it; pour over the fruit, cover with puff paste, and bake in a moderate oven. Lay on a coating of yolk of egg with a brush over the crust; put the tart back in the oven for a few minutes; sprinkle powdered sugar over the top before serving.

GREEN GOOSEBERRY JELLY.—Place the berries in hot water on a slow fire till they rise to the surface; take off; cool with a little water, add also a little vinegar and salt to green them. In two hours drain, and put them into cold water a minute; drain, and mix with an equal weight of sugar; boil slowly 20 minutes; sieve, and put into glasses.

GREEN OINTMENT.—One ounce each chickweed, tansy, wormwood, horehound, hops, and a pinch of salt, finely powdered. Bruise, put into a kettle, cover over with lard and some spirits of wine. Infuse a week or two, and then simmer a little over the fire. Add from 8 to 12 ozs. of venice turpentine.—This salve is very healing, applied to wounds, sores, and ulcers. It is useful in contusions, sprains, swellings, &c.

GRETNA BUNS.—Flour, 1 lb.; yeast, 1 gill; butter, ¼ lb.; which rub into the flour; add the yeast, and flour sufficient to form the dough; rise, and make into cakes; bake them on greased tins in a quick oven.

GROUND IVY. See *Robinson's Herbal.*—It is a purifier of the blood, beneficial to the lungs and kidneys. It is stimulant and tonic. Taken in decoction and infusion. Made into an ointment, it cures inflammation of the eyes.

GROUND RICE MILK.——Boil a spoonful of ground rice, rubbed down smooth, with better than a pint of milk, a bit of cinnamon, lemon peel, and nutmeg. Sweeten.

GROUND RICE PUDDING. —Boil rather more than a tablespoonful of ground rice in a pint of new milk with lemon-peel and cinnamon. When cold, add sugar, nutmeg, and two eggs well beaten. Bake with a crust round the dish. ——Some incorporate currants or raisins.

GROUNDSEL.—United with chickweed, and slippery elm, it makes an excellent poultice for inflammations and all painful swellings.

GROUSE PIE.—May be made as most fowl pies, seasoning with cayenne, salt, cloves, stock, brown gravy, and a glass of port wine.

GROUSE, *to roast.*—-Roast them like fowls; twist the head under the wing. Roast carefully half an hour. Serve with a rich gravy with bread sauce, or on buttered toast, the underside saturated with gravy.

GRUEL.—-Mix intimately a table-spoonful of oatmeal or patent groats in three or four of cold water; add a pint of boiling water, and boil 8 or 10 minutes.

GUM ARABIC STARCH.— Make a solution of the finest Gum Arabic with hot water. Strain. Put a little into the ordinary starch; mix well. It will give to muslin, lawn, &c., a much improved appearance.

GUMS, *Tincture for the.*—Infuse 1 oz. of Peruvian bark, grossly powdered, in ½ a pint of brandy for two or three weeks. Gargle the mouth every morning and night with a teaspoonful of this tincture diluted with an equal quantity of rose-water. The addition of a little tincture of myrrh will render it more effectual as a tonic for the gums.

H.—This Letter is often *aspirated* when it should not be, and *not aspirated* when it should be.

Aspirated.	Not to be aspirated.
Heart	Art, *skill.*
Hand	And, *a conjunc.*
Hall	All, *every one.*
Halter	Alter, *to change.*
Hale	Ale
Ham	Am, *(to be).*
Hat	At, *prep.*
Hare	Are, *(to be).*
Hell	Ell, *a measure.*
Hedge	Edge.
Her	Err, *to do wrong.*
Hill	Ill, *unwell.*
Hear	Ere, Ear.
Hard	Ardor.
Cow*herd*	Cow*ard.*

Words in which the h is not aspirated, or is dropped :—

Spelt	Pronounced
Heir	air
Herb	erb
Historian	istorian
Historical	istorical
Honest	onnest
Honour	onnur
Hour	our
Humble	umbl.

Common words in which the h is often wrongly dropped. ☞ PRONOUNCE THE h STRONGLY :—Horse, house, happy, heaven, head, home, holy, hurt, heat, habit, hospital, hostler, humour, &c.

Words which are often wrongly aspirated :—Angel, amiable, am, anecdote, animal, appetite, earth, enemy, elegant, eloquent, elephant, ever, image, imitate, infant, opulent, odd, oracle, oratory ugly.—*Never pronounce these with* h, *as* hangel, hamiable, *&c.*

HADDOCKS, *or Whitings, to broil.*—Gut and wash them; dry them; rub a little vinegar over them, to keep the skin on; dust well with flour; rub the gridiron with butter; let the gridiron be very hot; turn the fish two or three times. When served, lay pickles round them, melted butter, or cockle sauce. *Rf.*

Another way.—Having cleaned them, put them in a Dutch oven before a quick fire; when the skins rise, take them off; rub egg over them, and strew them with a few bread crumbs, dredge with flour; when you have turned them, rub butter over them; turn till they are done enough; lay round them cockles, muscles, or red cabbage. Use shrimp sauce, or melted butter, as you please. *Rf.*

HADDOCK, *to boil.*—*The same as for Cod.*—*Haddocks cured and dried,* &c., you may buy cheaper than you can do them.

HAIR-BRUSHES AND COMBS, *to clean.*—Dissolve potash in boiling water, and rub the brush with soap; dip the brush into the solution, and draw it through the comb frequently, taking care to keep the wood dry! Lastly, rinse the hair in cold water, and dry.

HAIR, *to dye.*—Hair may be changed from a red, gray, or other colour, to a brown or deep black, by a solution of silver. The silver is dissolved in aquafortis, and then largely diluted with water—rain-water is the best. An eminent physician says that the hair will assume a darker hue by having it cut close, and passing a leaden comb through it every morning and evening.

HAIR OILS.—Olive oil, 2 ozs.; oil of lavender 1 drachm; otto of roses, ½ drachm; apply morning and evening.——Or, Palma Christi oil, 2 ozs.; oil of lavender, oil of rosemary, oil of nutmeg, 1 drachm each.——Or, olive oil, 1 oz.; oil of origanum, 1 drachm; oil of rosemary, 2 drachms.——Or, oil of sweet almonds, 2 ozs.; spermaceti, ¼ oz.; melt over the fire. Cool, and add a few drops of oil of bergamot.

HAIR WASHES.—A weak infusion of tea, with a small quantity of rum, is a good application. Apply with a sponge—If the person can bear it, wash the head in cold water, morning and night, and then brush the head until of a warm glow; then apply twice a day this mixture;—tincture of cantharides, ¼ oz.; eau de Cologne, ½ oz.; rose water or distilled water, 2 ozs.——Or, wash the hair with Windsor soap suds twice a week, rub well in, wash with clean soft water, and then apply a little rum, brandy, or weak camphor water.——Or, to 1 oz. of borax, add ½ oz. of camphor; dissolve in a little spirits of wine; then mix with a quart of boiling water; cool, and it will be ready for use. It cleanses and strengthens the hair effectually.——Or, boil in water, 3 ozs. of sassafras wood, and ¾ oz. of pearl-ash.——Or, honey, 4 lbs.; tendrils of vines, 1½ lb.; rosemary, 1 lb. Put into a still, and distil slowly.——Or, take rosemary, maiden-hair, southernwood, myrtle berries, and hazle bark, 2 ozs. each; burn them to ashes, and with the ashes make a ley, and wash the hair with it. It cleanses and strengthens the hair.

HALIBUT, *to fry*.—Cut into thin slices; rib it with a knife; fry it almost brown with butter; take it up; drain it from the butter; clean the pan, and put it in again with port wine, sliced ginger, nutmeg, anchovy, salt, and saffron beaten; fry a little more; add a little butter; shake well together with a minced lemon.

HAMS, *to choose*. — Stick a skewer or sharp knife under the bone; if it comes out with a pleasant smell, the ham is good; but if the knife be daubed, and has a bad scent, do not buy it. Hams short in the hock are best. Choose not long-legged pigs.

HAMS, *to cure*.—If the weather be cool, hang it up two days before it is salted. Beat it with a rolling-pin. Take plenty of common salt, ½ lb. of course sugar, and 4 ozs. of saltpetre; mix; warm; rub the ham with it well, and lay the rest of the salt upon it; in two days turn it; rub it well with brine; baste it several times a-day for a month, for a large ham; drain, wash off the salt with cold water; dry with a cloth; rub black pepper over the inside and in at the knuckle; hang in a warm room to dry.

Another way.—Hang two days as before; if large, use 1 lb. of bay salt; 4 ozs. saltpetre; 1 lb. coarse sugar, and a handful of common salt, all finely powdered. Rub in the mixture thoroughly. Lay the rind downwards, and cover the fleshy parts with the mixture. Baste it often for four weeks, turning every day; proceed as before.

To give a high flavour.—Hang as before. Sprinkle it with salt; let it drain; make a pickle of 1 quart of strong beer, ½ lb. of treacle, 1 oz. of coriander seeds, 2 ozs. juniper berries; pepper, allspice, saltpetre, 1 oz. each; salprunella, ¼ oz.; a handful of salt, and a head of shalot, sliced; boil all together five minutes, and pour over the ham. Rub and turn every day for a fortnight. This is for a ham weighing 10 lbs.

HAMS, *to keep.* — The most effectual way is to tie them closely in cotton or canvass bags. Hang in a dry, cool, and well ventilated room when bagged.

HAM AND EGGS FRIED.— Cut thin slices, place in the pan, and fry carefully. Do not burn. When done, break the eggs into the fat; pepper slightly; keep them whole; do not turn them. Ham Rashers may be served with spinach, and poached eggs.

HAMS, *to cook.*-Scrape it clean. Do not put into cold nor boiling water. Let the water become warm; then put the ham in. Simmer or boil lightly for five or six hours; take out, and shave the rind off. Rub granulated sugar into the whole surface of the ham, so long as it can be made to receive it. Place the ham in a baking-dish with a bottle of champagne or prime cider. Baste occasionally with the juice, and let it bake an hour in a gentle heat. A slice from a nicely cured ham thus cooked is enough to animate the ribs of death.—*American Receipt.*

Or, having taken off the rind, strew bread crumbs or raspings over it, so as to cover it; set it before the fire, or in the oven till the bread is crisp and brown. Garnish with carrots, parsley, &c. The water should simmer all the time, and never boil fast.

HAM EXTRACT.--Cut away from a ham all the skin and fat; then take the meat from the bone and put it into a large saucepan, having plenty of water; add two large carrots, and three onions sliced, a handful of sweet basil and parsley, three cloves, and a tablespoonful of mushroom powder; stew over the fire for an hour, then take out the bone, and put in the meat. Set the saucepan, well covered, on a slow fire, for two hours: stir the ingredients well, taste the flavour, and judge of the thickness. Stew till the liquor, when cold, is a very stiff jelly. It must be put through a sieve, to clear it from the vegetables and meat. A table-spoonful of this extract is sufficient to flavour a tureenful of winter pea or carrot soup, and a tea-spoonful in melted butter makes an admirable sauce for a roast fowl. To keep it some time, add salt.

HAM AND CHICKEN PATTIES.—Mince finely 1½ lb. of cold boiled or roasted chicken, and 1 lb. of lean ham. Put some good gravy to the minced meat, (see *Gravy*) with a little cayenne, or white pepper, grated lemon peel, and a squeeze of lemon. Stir till hot. Fill the moulds lined with paste, cover with crust, and bake. *Ham and Veal Patties* may be made the same way. Some mix a little cream with it.

HAM PIE.—Slice cold boiled ham half inch thick; make a good crust; cover the dish, and put a layer of ham; clean a young fowl; put pepper and salt in the belly, and rub a little outside; lay the fowl on the ham; boil eggs, put in the yolks, cover all with ham; put on pepper, and cover with crust. Bake, and when done, fill with rich beef gravy.

HAM POTTED.—Take 2 lbs. of cold lean ham; 1 lb. of cold roast veal. Cut, and pound very fine, adding 12 ozs. of butter, ground mace, nutmeg, and a little cayenne pepper. Pot, and cover with butter.—Chicken may be potted with ham in the same way.

HAM SAUCE.—When a ham is almost done with, pick the remaining meat from the bone; beat the meat and bone to a mash with the rolling-pin, put it into a saucepan with three spoonfuls of gravy, set it over a slow fire, and stir it all the time; when it has been on some time, put to it a small bundle of sweet herbs, some pepper, and half a pint of veal gravy, and stew over a gentle fire; when it has the flavour of the herbs, strain. A little of this is an improvement to all gravies.

HAM TOAST,--Ham, ½ lb., minced fine; the yolks of two eggs; cream, two table-spoonfuls; season with salt, and a very little cayenne. Boil all together. Pour it upon toast; cover with fine bread, and brown it nicely.

HANDS, *to whiten.*—Take a wineglassful of eau de Cologne, half a cupful of lemon-juice, scrape two cakes of Windsor soap to a powder; mix well, then add a tea-spoonful of sulphuric acid. Mould it, and let it harden.

HARE, *broiled.*—The flavour of broiled hare is very fine. The legs and shoulders must be seasoned first, rubbed with cold butter, and served very hot.

HARE, *to jug.*—Cut it up; season with pepper, salt, allspice, pounded mace, and nutmeg. Put it into a jar with an onion, a clove or two, a bunch of sweet herbs, a piece of coarse beef, or good beef steak, and the bones of the hare at the top. Tie the jar down with bladder or strong paper. Put into a saucepan up to the neck. Keep the water boiling four hours. The jar will also do well in an oven in two or three hours. When it is to be served, boil the gravy up with a piece of butter and flour. Add a little stock gravy, and a glass or two of port wine. Pour it over the hare. A little bacon is an improvement.

HARE, *to pot.*—Season and bake with butter; when cold beat the meat in a mortar with some nice cold ham, a little parsley, thyme, &c. If not high enough, add salt, mace, pepper, a little butter melted in a spoonful of gravy that came from the hare. Pot, and cover with butter.

HARE, *roasted.*—After skinning, wash well. Stuff with bread crumbs, the liver half boiled, an anchovy, or bacon, parsley, grated lemon-peel, nutmeg, salt, cayenne, the yolks of three eggs, and a little lemon-thyme. Fasten all tight. Boil half an hour. Take out and roast it for one hour or more. Baste it with milk till half done, then with butter. Do not place too near the fire. Serve with rich gravy, melted butter, and currant jelly sauce. The gravy may be improved by ketchup, port wine, and a little flour.

HARE SOUP.—Cut the hare into pieces, and 1½ lb. of good beef; put into a jar with 3 blades of mace, two large onions, three anchovies, a little bacon or ham, a bunch of sweet herbs, cayenne, and a pint of port wine. Stew in the oven three hours; strain into a stew-pan; put in ¼ lb. of French barley, or the crumbs of two penny rolls, ready boiled; scald the liver, rub it through a sieve into the soup; place on the fire till near boiling. Put toasted bread in the tureen, and pour the soup upon it.

HARE, *Stewed.*—Cut to pieces; put into a stew-pan, with mace, pepper, an onion stuck with cloves, an anchovy, 1 lb. of beef, ½ lb. of bacon, sweet herbs, salt, nutmeg; cover with water; stew till the hare is tender; strain the sauce into a clean pan, and put in the hare again with the sauce; take butter the size of a walnut, rolled in flour, a table-spoonful of ketchup, and two of red wine. Stew till it is thick and smooth.

HARNESS, *to clean.*—Free it from all dirt, sweat, and grease. Then use Bristol-brick, or rotten stone, and pulverized charcoal, and a little Galipoli oil. Apply it with a soft brush, wipe off, and polish off with charcoal dust.

The Brass Ornaments may be cleaned with half ounce of oxalic tin, half pint of water, and half pint of naptha. Then polish off with sal-ammoniac powdered, before a hot fire, and then with fine whiting.

When the harness is faded, it may be restored by a mixture of logwood and bichromate of potass, or aleppo galls, powdered, with a little alum.

HARNESS POLISH.—Take 2 ozs. of mutton suet, 6 ozs. of bees' wax, 6 ozs. of powdered sugar-candy, 2 ozs. of soft soap, and 1 oz. of indigo or lamp black. Dissolve the soap in a quarter of a pint of water; then add the other ingredients; melt and mix together; add a gill of turpentine. Lay it on the harness with a sponge, and polish off with a brush.

HARROGATE WATER, *Artificial.*—Dissolve half drachm of liver of sulphur, and 1 oz. of tartarised kali in 1 quart of pure soft water. It is as good as the real Harrogate water. Take a wineglassful now and then. Useful in chronic rheumatism, skin diseases, and piles.

HARTSHORN JELLY.—Simmer 8 ozs. of hartshorn shavings with two quarts of water to one; strain, and boil it with the rinds of four oranges and two lemons pared thin; when cool, add the juice of both, ¼ lb. of sugar, and the whites of six eggs beaten to a froth; let the jelly have three or four boils without stirring, and strain it through a jelly-bag.

HASTY PUDDING.——Rub down a table-spoonful of flour in a little cold milk, then stir it into a pint of boiling milk; sweeten with sugar, and serve hot.

Another is made by stirring flour into boiling water, into which a little salt has been put. It is served with treacle, or sugar, or sugar and butter. It is good for a lax state of the bowels, without treacle.

HASTY PUDDING, *baked.*—Into a pint of cold milk stir ¼ lb. of flour, and boil up; let it stand till cold; then add two eggs beaten; mix well with sugar to sweeten, and spices; put into cups and bake.

HATS.—When silk hats are wetted by the rain, shake it off, and wipe round frequently with a silk handkerchief, and when dry with a soft brush.

HAY, *to ascertain the weight of.*—Measure the length and breadth of the stack; then take its height from the ground to the eaves, and add to this last one third of the height from the eaves to the top. Multiply the length by the breadth, and the product by the height, all expressed in feet; divide the amount by 27, to find the cubic yards, which multiply by the number of stones supposed to be in a cubic yard (viz: in a stack of new hay, six stones; if the stack has stood a considerable time, eight stones; and if old hay, nine stones), and you have the weight in stones. For example, suppose a stack to be 60 feet in length, 30 in breadth, 12 in height, from the ground to the eaves, and 9 (the third of which is 3) from the eaves to the top; then 60 multiplied by 30 and by 15, is equal to 27,000; 27,000, divided by 27, is equal to 1,000; and 1,000, multiplied by 9, is equal to 9,000 stones of old hay.

HEADACHE.—Take a small handful of Centaury, and as much

Feverfew, and one ounce of Camomile Flowers, to two quarts of water; boil to one quart; then add while hot half an ounce of rhubarb, and stir well. Dose—a wineglassful three times a day.— Wear the hair short, often wash the head in cold water, rub the hair dry, and keep the head uncovered as much as possible. Sometimes head-ache proceeds from a torpid liver; in that case, take extract of colocynth and blue pill, of each ½ a drachm, and 4 drops of the oil of cloves. Make into 12 pills. Dose, two to four. ——Bathing the crown of the head every morning in cold water has been found of singular use. Should the pain be extreme, apply mustard plasters between the shoulders, and on the soles of the feet.

HEADACHE.—Rub the head for a quarter of an hour.—Tried. ——Or, be electrified.—Tried.—— Or, apply to each temple the thin yellow rind of a lemon newly pared off.——Or, pour upon the palm of the hand a little brandy and some zest* of lemon, and hold it to the forehead; or a little æther. ——Or, snuff up the nose camphorated spirits of lavender.——Or a little of horse radish.

Take of white-wine vinegar and water, each three spoonfuls, with half a spoonful of Hungary water. Apply this twice a-day to the eyelids and temples.—*Wesley.*

HEADACHE, *Chronic.*—— Keep your feet in warm water a quarter of an hour before you go to bed, for two or three weeks.— Tried.——Or, wear tender hemlock leaves under the feet, changing them daily.——Or, order a tea-kettle of cold water to be poured on your head every morning, in a slender stream.——Or, take a

* Zest is the juice of the peel squeezed out.

large tea-cupful of carduus tea without sugar, fasting, for six or seven mornings.— *Wesley.*

HEADACHE, *from heat.*— Apply to the forehead cloths dipped in cold water.

HEALTH, *Preservation of.*— Adopt the plan of rising early, and never sit up late at night.

Wash the whole body every morning with cold water, by means of a large sponge, and rub it dry with a rough towel, or scrub the whole body for ten or fifteen minutes with flesh brushes.

Those who use cold water regularly, either with a sponge or as a bath, are able to bear exposure to the weather much better than without its aid.

Drink water generally, and avoid taking spirits, wines, and all fermented liquors.

Sleep in a room which has free access to the open air, and is well ventilated.

Keep the head cool by washing it with cold water when necessary, and abate feverish and inflammatory symptoms when they arise, by preserving stillness.

Symptoms of plethora and indigestion may be corrected by eating and drinking less per day for a short time.

Never eat a hearty supper, especially of animal food. Never indulge in luxuries; guard against intemperance; and never sit in a draught, or in wet clothes, nor lie in a damp bed.

Exercise regularly taken tends to preserve the health. Walk one or two miles a day, regardless of weather, unless very bad indeed. Even a lady with stout walking boots, a large thick cloak, and an umbrella, may defy bad weather.

In taking exercise in very severe weather, keep your mouth close and walk rapidly; the air can only reach the lungs by a circuit of the nose and head, and becomes warm before reaching the lungs, thus causing no derangement. Brisk walking throws the blood to the surface of the body, thus keeping up a vigorous circulation, making a cold impossible if you do not get into a cold bed too quickly after reaching home. Neglect of these precautions brings sickness and death to multitudes every year.

The amount of exercise necessary for health is variable, depending upon natural constitution, education, sex, and age. For men from twenty to fifty, eight or ten miles a day of walking exercise may be taken as the average; and for women of the same age, about half this quantity will suffice. Less than this will go a great way, but for keeping up high health, the above amount, omitted only on thoroughly wet days, may be considered necessary.

By all means avoid a morbid desponding feeling, for scarcely anything is more injurious to health.

Mental as well as bodily exercise is essential to the general health and happiness; therefore, labour and study should succeed each other.

The plainest food is the best, taken in quantities so small as not to oppress the stomach. A man should never know that he has a stomach except when he is hungry.

To increase muscular power, food should be taken which does not produce fat; for fat is frequently a sign of disease. A race-horse is brought to his prime condition by a system of training. So with man, if he wishes to see the full developement of all his muscular power, he must restrict himself in diet, and exhaust his fat by having a good sweating every day, but not to take cold.

Lying too long in bed is injurious to health. The want of expansion of the chest through exercise, will aggravate or create consumptive tendencies, which all more or less have; and the constant heat of the back or one side, occasioned by cushioning, disturbs healthy action.

When food rises in the stomach, the stomach is speaking to us, and we ought to listen to it, or health will suffer. In due time headaches will be the result; the liver is oppressed, and cannot fulfil its functions. There has been more introduced into the body than can be conveniently disposed of. Every part receives some of the obtrusive matter; it is forced into the absorbents; the blood is unwillingly compelled to take a part of it; the brain feels the effect of the poisonous infusion; the circulation is impeded; the heart feels it, and labours hard to do its allotted work. By persisting in the habit, life will be shortened.

Too little food has its symptoms as well as too much. The body will flag for want of stimulus; it will lose warmth and energy; and if it be found that more food restores both, and brings comfort, then more food is wanted. Every one should endeavour to discover his own maximum and minimum allowance, and adhere to it.

Those who think most, require the most sleep. The time "saved" from necessary sleep is destruction to mind, body, and estate. Give yourself, children, and servants, the fullest amount of sleep by compelling them to go to bed at some early hour, and to rise in the morning the moment they awake of themselves, and within a fortnight nature will unloose the bonds of sleep the moment enough repose has been secured.

Rise and retire at a fixed hour; take a gentle walk before breakfast; and take your meals at the same hours daily.

The less quantity of fermented liquors you drink the better.

Nothing conduces more to health and long life than abstinence and plain food, with due labour.

Where water does not disagree, value the privilege, and continue it.

Late hours and anxious pursuits exhaust the nervous system; therefore avoid them as much as possible.

In order that digestion may take place, the food should be well chewed. The stomach will not deal with it in lumps. It must be thoroughly masticated and well mixed with the saliva which flows into the mouth during mastication.

Do without medicine if possible; but in case of real indisposition, immediately consult a competent medical man.

HEARTBURN.—Drink a pint of very cold water.—Tried.——Or, drink slowly decoction of camomile flowers.——Or, eat four or five oysters.—*Wesley.*

HEARTBURN.——"If acidity of the stomach occasions the heartburn, absorbents are the proper medicines. Take 1 oz. of powdered chalk, ½ oz. of fine sugar, and ¼ oz. of gum arabic may be mixed in a quart of water, and a tea-cupful of it taken when necessary. But the best absorbent is *magnesia alba.* It acts also as a purgative. This powder is not disagreeable; it may be taken in a cup of tea, or a glass of mint water." *Buchan.*

If it arises from wind, take a teaspoonful of spirits of lavender, or the *Neutralizing Mixture.*

HEARTBURN LOZENGES. —Powdered lump sugar, 100 parts; prepared chalk, 15 parts; subcarbonate of soda, 5 parts; mucilage to mix.

HEARTBURN, *Pills for.*—Carbonate of ammonia, extract of gentian, of each half a drachm; mix, and divide into twelve pills; take two twice or thrice a day.

HEARTBURN POWDER.—Quassia, powdered rhubarb, of each ½ scruple; and calcined magnesia, 1 scruple. Mix, and make into 12 powders. Take 3 per day.

Spanish liquorice has been found a very good palliative in heartburn. Neutralize the acid which produces heartburn; take of carbonate of soda, half a teaspoonful; half a teaspoonful of peppermint plant powdered, in a table-spoonful of brandy, and a little cold water; take it for a dose.

HEAT, *to moderate.*—To moderate the intensity of heat during the summer, where slated or tiled roofs are in close proximity with bed-rooms; let the roof, (i. e. the slates) be whitewashed; and the temperature in the room underneath, which before was almost insupportable, will be not only tolerable, but very agreeable. The materials to use are whiting, size, or thin glue, and a little linseed oil. This mixture has a good body, and will not be very soon washed off by rain.

HEMLOCK LINIMENT. — Oil of Hemlock, ½ oz.; Camphor, in gum, ¼ oz.; opium, ¼ oz.; spirits of wine, 1 pint. Mix. It is a first-rate rubefacient in inflammatory rheumatism, gout, quinsy, inflamed breast, white swellings, &c.

HERBS.—They make the best medicines, and the completest cures. For their Medical Properties, see *Robinson's Herbal.*

HERBS. — *For dyspepsia, or indigestion.*——Camomile, agrimony, betony, thistle, (blessed,) carraway seeds, sweet flag, fennel, garlic, horehound, hyssop, lavender, masterwort (the root), mint, mustard seed, pennyroyal, horse radish, rue, wormwood.

Decoctions of the above are made by pouring boiling water on them. A little should be taken in the morning fasting.

For purging the bowels.—Class 1. The powerful are the following: common dock, hellebore, (white), in doses not exceeding four grains; black hellebore, from two to five grains; marshmallow leaf decoction, and mountain flax.

Class 2. more moderate; buckthorn berry, broom, and dandelion.

For worms.—Bear's-foot, cowhage, camomile, garlic, fern root, savin, and wormwood.

Astringents, which serve to correct excessive discharges. Logwood, red roses, sage, and tormentil root.

Carminatives, or those herbs which allay pain, or dispel wind from the stomach; aniseed, caraway seed, peppermint, spearmint, ginger, and dill root.

Demulcents; those herbs which soften, or which lessen acrimony, or the effects of stimulus on the solids; as, colt's-foot, liver-wort, mallows, liquorice root, comfrey, &c.

Diaphoretics, or those which promote perspiration; burdock, centaury, bay tree, betony, balm, germander, lovage, and rue.

Tonics, or those which give strength and vigour to the body; bistort, balm, bog-bean, camomile, centaury (lesser), logwood, gentian, southernwood, tansy, tormentil, valerian, and wormwood.

To heal ulcers.—Adder's tongue, agrimony, archangel, arse-smart, cuckoo pint, blue bottle, burdock, bryony, soapwort, celandine, centaury, chickweed, cinquefoil, comfrey root, mugwort, cudweed, dog grass, water dock, figwort, flaxweed, foxglove, glass wort, ground ivy, ground pine, tormentil, tansy, bugle, scurvy grass, and nightshade.

Either made into ointments with hog's-lard, or washes made of them, and daily applied to the parts.

To purify the blood.—Agrimony, borage, burdock (sea,) chickweed, chervil, fennel, fir tree, fumitory, garden cresses, wild water cresses, ground pine, hops, maiden hair, sorrel, and tansy.

Made into decoctions with hot water, and taken every morning.

HERRINGS, *fresh, to broil*, or *roast*.—Scale, gut, and wash; cut off the heads; steep them in salt and vinegar ten minutes; dust them with flour, and broil them over or before the fire, or in the oven. Serve with melted butter and parsley.

Herrings are nice *jarred*, and done in the oven, with pepper, cloves, salt, a little vinegar, a few bay leaves, and a little butter.

HERRINGS, *fresh, to fry.*—Slice small onions, and lay in the pan with the herrings; add a little butter, and fry them. Perhaps it is better to fry the onions separately with a little parsley, and butter, or drip.

HERRINGS, *to pot.*—Clean, cut off the heads, and lay them close in an earthen pot. Strew a little salt between every layer; put in cloves, mace, whole pepper, cayenne, and nutmeg; fill up the jar with vinegar, water, and a quarter of a pint of sherry, cover, tie down; bake in an oven, and when cold pot it for use.—A few anchovies and bay leaves intermixed will improve the flavour much.

HICCUP.—One drop of chemical oil of carraway on a small

lump of sugar, which must be kept in the mouth till dissolved, and then gently swallowed.——If you press firmly on the end of the collar-bone next the throat, the hiccuping will be stopped.——Or hold your breath as long as you can. If it should prove obstinate, and become spasmodic, a teaspoonful of ether, 8 drops of laudanum, in a glass of cold water, is the best remedy.—It is often removed by startling a person.

HICCUP.—Swallow a mouthful of water, stopping the mouth and ears.—Tried.——Or, take any thing that makes you sneeze.—— Or, three drops of oil of cinnamon on a lump of sugar.—*Wesley.*

HIPS, *Conserve of.*—Cut off the stalks of ripe Hips; take out all the seeds; throw hot water upon them, and let them stand till soft enough to be sieved; mix the pulp with the same weight of sugar, without boiling. Good for consumptive coughs, hoarseness. Where the cough is very troublesome, with mental depression, add a few drops of laudanum, and of tincture of valerian.

HOARSENESS.——Rub the soles of the feet, before the fire, with garlic and lard well beaten together, over night. The hoarseness will be gone next morning.—

Or, take a pint of cold water, lying down.

Or, swallow slowly the juice of radishes.

Or, dry nettle roots in on oven; then powder them finely, and mix with an equal quantity of treacle. Take a teaspoonful twice a-day.

Or, boil a large handful of wheat bran in a quart of water, strain, and sweeten it with honey. Drink frequently.—*Wesley.*

HOARSENESS.—Frequently gargle with a decoction of sage. ——Or, a solution of alum.——Or, a solution of gum kino.——Or chew catechu.——Or take two or three times a day a teaspoonful of sweet spirits of nitre in a wine-glassful of weak ginger and water.——Or take occasionally a tablespoonful of the decoction of horse-radish. ——Or dip a piece of flannel in brandy, or in brandy and salt; and apply to the chest; cover with a dry flannel; wear it all night.—— Boiled onions are sometimes useful in colds, hoarseness, &c.——Or, take spermaceti and sugar candy, equal parts, and make them into a fine powder.——A piece of anchovy has been known to restore the proper tone of the voice.

HOARSENESS OF SINGERS.—A celebrated singer states, that the greatest benefit is derivable from taking, during five or six days, twice a-day, five or six drops of nitric acid in a glass of sugared water. If from use the acid loses its efficacy, the dose may be increased to ten or twelve drops.

HONEY *balsam of.*—To 1 lb. of honey add a teacupful of vinegar; boil and skim; when cold stir in 1 oz. of elixir of paregoric, and bottle. This is first-rate for a cough: *dose,* one table-spoonful three times a day.

HONEY OF ROSES.—Dried red rose buds, 4 ozs.; clarified honey, 5 lbs.; distilled boiling water, 3 pints; macerate the rose leaves in the water for 6 hours; then mix the honey with the strained liquor, and boil to a syrup. Good for sore mouths, &c.

HONEY OF VIOLETS.— Violet flowers, the bottoms chipped off, 2 lbs.; infuse in 2 quarts of water; boil up, and add 2 lbs. of honey; boil to a syrup; press the liquid part through a linen cloth.

HONEY WATER.—Powder 2 ozs. of volatile salts; dissolve it

in a pint of water for use. It is a good cosmetic. Add a little lavender water.

HOOPING COUGH.--Use the cold bath daily.——Or, rub the feet thoroughly with hog's lard, before the fire, at going to bed, and keep the child warm therein.——Or, rub the back at lying down with old rum. It seldom fails.——Or, give a spoonful of the juice of pennyroyal, mixed with brown sugar-candy, twice a-day.—*Wesley*.

HOOPING COUGH.-Dissolve a scruple of salt of tartar in a quarter of a pint of water; add 8 drops of laudanum, sweeten it with sugar. Give to an infant a teaspoonful four times a day; two years old, two spoonfuls; for four years, a table-spoonful. —— Or, take flower of Benjamin, and strained opium, of each 2 drachms, camphire, 2 scruples, essential oil of aniseeds, half a drachm, rectified spirit of wine, one quart, 4 ozs. of powdered liquorice, and 4 ozs. of honey: digest and strain.—— Or, take of musk julep, 6 ozs.; paregoric elixir, ½ oz., volatile tincture of valerian, 1 drachm; mix, and take two spoonfuls three or four times every day.——Or, take ipecacuanha, 14 grains; warm water ½ a pint. Infuse. Take a teaspoonful now and then.

HOOPING COUGH, *Embrocation for.*—Olive oil eight ounces, oil of amber, four ounces, oil of cloves, sufficient to scent it strongly; croton oil, 3 drops; mix, rub on the chest.——Or, oil of amber, and spirits of hartshorn, equal parts. Mix. Apply to the soles of the feet, and to the palms of the hands, morning, noon, and night.

HOPS.—The extract of tincture of hops may be used instead of opium in most cases; it is not narcotic, but very anodyne. In consumption it gives ease without any deleterious effects. Its valuable medicinal properties are but little known. In jaundice, indigestion, melancholy, nervous depression, &c., it has been of singular use. A strong infusion or decoction, is a cure for indigestion, attended with nervous irritation, weakness of the stomach and bowels; and for typhoid fevers, and twitching of the tendons. It is of vast service in the after pains of child-birth. It may be taken in tincture, decoction, infusion, or pills made of the extract.

HOPS, *Infusion of.*—Hops, 2 ozs.; boiling water, 1 quart. Infuse a day. Dose; a wineglassful.—The *Tincture* is made by macerating 1 oz. of the hops in quarter of a pint of proof spirits; dose, ½ a drachm to 1 drachm. The *Extract* is made by boiling the strength of it obtained by infusion or decoction, to a thin syrup, and then evaporating till it becomes thick. Cover close. Dose, in pills, from four to ten grains.

Hops heated, in a flannel bag, are a good remedy for the toothache, and neuralgic pains. A bag of hops warmed, and put under the head, allays nervous excitement, and procures sleep. Dr. Beech says, he has "given it with success in inflammation of the bowels." A strong decoction, half a pint at a time, is drunk by the Spaniards for venereal.

HOREHOUND.—The plant is very stimulant, diaphoretic, pectoral, and tonic. It is good for coughs, asthma, and female weakness. Very beneficial in consumption--See *Pulmonary Balsam, or Syrup.*

HOREHOUND, *to candy.*—Boil some horehound till the juice is extracted. Boil some sugar till feathery; (See *Sugar*); add the juice to the sugar, and boil till it is again the same height, stir till it is thick; pour into a paper case dusted with fine sugar, and cut into squares.

HOREHOUND CAKES.—Boil 3 lbs. of raw sugar in one pint of water, till candied; then rub a little dried horehound into the pan while boiling. Pour it on buttered paper.

HOREHOUND SYRUP.—Dried horehound, 2 ozs.; honey, ¼ lb.; boiling water, ½ pint; spirits, ½ pint; honey, 4 oz.; laudanum, 20 drops; essence of lemon, 1 teaspoonful. Infuse the horehound in the spirits and water for 2 days; then add the other ingredients.

HORSE RECIPES. — The following Recipes are very useful:—*Horse Ointment.*—Resin 4 ozs.; bees' wax, 3 ozs.; hog's lard ½ lb.; common turpentine, 6 ozs; dissolve in a pipkin with a gentle heat; then add 2 ozs. of fine verdigris, stir well together, and strain the whole through a coarse cloth: cool for use. This is a good ointment for a wound, or bruise in flesh or hoof, broken knees, galled backs, bites, cracked heels, mallenders, or, when a horse is gelded, to heal and keep off the flies.

Purge for a horse.—Aloes, 1 oz; rhubarb, 2 drs.; oil of mint, 4 drops, made into a ball with honey.

Cordial for a horse.—If the horse is weak through travel, give him a pint of warm ale, with 1 oz. of diapente in it. Diapente will comfort his bowels, drive out cold and wind, and may cause him to carry his food the longer.—Diapente is composed of gentian root, bay berries, bay leaves, birthwort, mint, and myrrh.

Sore back.—If the saddle bruises his back and makes it swell, a greasy dishcloth laid on hot, and a cloth over it, bound on fifteen minutes, (with a surcingle), and repeated once or twice, will sink it flat. If it is slight, wash it with a little salt and water only. Alter the saddle, that it may not press upon the tender part, for a second bruise will be worse than the first.

Splint.—The splint is a fixed, callous, bony excrescence, growing upon the flat of the inside or outside, of the shark bone; a little under, and not far from the knee, and may be seen and felt.—*Cure.* To take it off, first cut the hair close, then gently beat it with a round rule until it appears hot to the touch, then rub hard soap all around the edge of the splint, to prevent the blister affecting any other part, and apply on the splint the following blister ointment: mercurial ointment, 1 oz.; Spanish flies, 2 drs., mixed well together; a little of this may be applied once a week until the splint is removed.

Spavin.—The Spavin is of the same nature, and appears, in like manner, on the instep bone behind, not far below the hough.—*Cure.* The same blister as recommended for splints: if it fails, firing and turning the horse to grass for three months, is the best method.

HORSES, *to water.*—Water is as necessary to a horse as food, and horses are found to thrive better by having water *ad libitum* than by being stinted. The best way is to have the manger divided, so that corn may be in one half and the water in the other: by this plan the horse takes the water as he wants it, and not when it is offered to him. The plan of having the water in the manger has been tried by a great number of the London merchants, and found to answer admirably.

HORSERADISH SAUCE.—Grate very small a stick of horseradish; then with two tablespoonfuls of it, mix a little salt, and four tablespoonfuls of cream; stir briskly, and add gradually a wineglassful of vinegar, and a little sherry wine. Excellent with cold roast beef.

Another.—Grate horseradish into a basin, then add three tablespoonfuls of cream, a teaspoonful of mustard, and a little salt. Mix well with half a cupful of vinegar, to which has been put a little melted butter, a little gravy, and some mushroom, or walnut ketchup. Season with clove, black, or cayenne pepper. *A. N.*

HORSERADISH VINEGAR —To 3 ozs. of scraped horseradish, put a quart of best vinegar, 1 oz. of minced shalot, and 1 dr. of cayenne. Let it stand a week.

HOSIER BISCUIT. — One pint of new milk. Stir in a teaspoonful of salt, and flour, until it becomes a stiff batter; add two table-spoonfuls of yeast; let it rise in a warm place as much as it will. Then stir in a teaspoonful of bicarbonate of potass dissolved in hot water; beat up three eggs; stir them, and flour with the batter till it becomes thick dough; let it rise; knead again; cut to biscuit shape; bake in a quick oven.

HOTCH-POTCH.—Stew peas, lettuce, and onions in a little water with a beef or ham bone. While these are doing, fry mutton or lamb steaks brown; forty minutes before dinner put the steaks into a stew-pan, and the vegetables over them; stew, and serve in a tureen.——A knuckle of veal and scrag of mutton, stewed with vegetables, as above, will make a nice hotch-potch.

HOTCH POTCH, *of different kinds.*—Take a brisket of beef, or mutton steaks or pigeons, rabbits cut in quarters, or veal, or poultry; boil long over a slow fire in a little liquid, with onions, carrots, parsnips, turnips, celery, parsley, shalots, spices, a laurel leaf, thyme, sausages, and thin broth or water. When done, drain.

Fowl may be done in the same way, pickled pork, a little ham, &c. *Pigeons* also with bacon, broth, a little butter, nutmeg, ginger, a little lemon, &c.

HOT WATER PIPES, *to stop leakage in.*—Iron borings and filings, mix them with vinegar and a little sulphuric acid; let the mixture stand till it becomes a paste; with this fill up the cracks, where the leakage is; and if the pipe has been previously dried, and is kept dry till the paste hardens, it will effectually stop the leakage, and will last a long time.

HOUSELEEK.—It is used as a cooling application to sores, ulcers, &c. The juice mixed with cream is good for inflammation of the eyes, and erysipelas. Taken inwardly it is good for fevers, cooling them down wonderfully. *First give a purgative to cleanse the stomach and bowels; then bruise the houseleek; adding to the juice its weight in fine sugar to form a syrup. A tablespoonful every two hours. Drink balm or catnep tea.* This receipt is worth gold. See *Robinson's Family Herbal.*

HUNTER'S PUDDING.-Mix 1 lb. each of suet, flour, currants, rasins stoned, and cut; the rind of half a lemon shred fine; 6 Jamaica peppers finely powdered, 4 eggs, a glass of brandy, salt, and a little milk to make it of a proper consistence; boil it in floured cloth 8 or 9 hours. Serve with white sauce. This pudding will keep 6 months, if tied up in the same cloth.

HYDROGEN GAS, *to make.*— Procure granulated zinc, put it into a bottle, and pour over it 1 pint oil of vitriol (sulphuric acid) to 5 or 6 pints of water; to collect the gas you must have a pipe inserted through the cork leading to a pneumatic trough or bladder.

HYDROPHOBIA. See *Bite of a Mad Dog.*

HYDROPHOBIA.— Immediately wash the bitten part with clear water; then take good tobacco, (leaf tobacco, if possible; if not, strong manufactured cut tobacco) and make a suitable poultice for the place, changing it three or four times a day for a week. This effectually absorbs every thing poisonous——A strong decoction of the roots of the white ash will cure the bite of a mad dog.——At Ulina, in Friula, a man suffering under the agonising tortures of hydrophobia, was cured by draughts of vinegar given him by mistake. A physician at Padua hearing of it, tried the same remedy upon a patient at the hospital, giving 1 lb. of vinegar in the morning, another at noon, and a third at sunset, and the man was speedily and perfectly cured.

CURE FOR HYDROPHOBIA —Dr. Buisson, of Lyons, claims to have discovered a remedy. In attending a female patient in the last stage of canine rabies, the doctor imprudently wiped his hands with a handkerchief impregnated with her saliva. He had a slight abrasion on the index finger of the left hand, and confident in his own curative system, the doctor merely washed the part with water. However, he was fully aware of the imprudence he had committed, and gives the following account of the matter afterwards:— "Believing that the malady would not declare itself until the 40th day, and having numerous patients to visit, I put off from day to day the application of my remedy— that is to say, *vapour baths.* The ninth day, being in my cabinet, I felt all at once a pain in the throat, and a still greater one in the eyes. My body seemed so light that I felt as if I could jump to a prodigious height, or that, if I threw myself out of a window I could sustain myself in the air. My hair was so sensitive that I appeared able to count each separately without looking at it. Saliva kept continually forming in the mouth. Any movement of the air inflicted great pain on me, and I was obliged to avoid the sight of brilliant objects; I had a continual desire to run and bite, not human beings, but animals, and all that was near me. I drank with difficulty, and the sight of water distressed me more than the pain in the throat. I believe that, by shutting the eyes, any one suffering under hydrophobia can always drink. The fits came on every five minutes, and I then felt the pain start from the index finger and run up the nerves to the shoulder. In this state, thinking that my course was preservative and not curative, I took a vapour bath, not with the intention of cure, but of suffocating myself. When the bath was at a heat of 52 Centigrade (93 3 5 Fahrenheit), all the symptoms disappeared, as if by magic, and I have never felt any thing more of them. I have attended more than 80 persons bitten by mad animals, and I have not lost a single case." When a person has been bitten by a mad dog he must for seven successive days take a vapour bath *a la Russe*, as it is called, of 57 to 63 degs. This is the preventive remedy. When the disease is declared, it only requires one vapour bath, rapidly increased to 37 Centigrade, then slowly to 63; the patient must confine himself to his chamber until the cure is complete. Dr. Buisson mentions other curious facts. An American had been bitten by a rattlesnake, about eight leagues from home; wishing to die in the bosom of his family, he ran the greater part of the way home, and going to bed perspired profusely, and the wound healed as any simple cut. The bite of the tarantula is cured by the exercise of dancing, the free perspiration dissipating the virus. If a young child be vaccinated and then be made to take a vapour bath, the vaccine does not take. *Galignani.*

When first bitten, or when the symptoms are manifest, give a dessert-spoonful of the anti-spasmodic tincture, and a mild injection. Then proceed to the vapour bath, as hot as the patient can bear it. After the bath, give an emetic. The wound should be cupped, and caustic potash applied afterwards. Apply a yeast poultice, and keep up the discharge. Add a little powdered charcoal to the poultice. Repeat the vapour bath and the injection every ten or twelve hours. The diet should be light and unstimulating; the drink sudorific, or promoting perspiration. Drink oft a decoction of skullcap, and at night take sulphur and cream of tartar.

HYPOCHONDRIA or *Melancholly.* — A disordered state of mind caused by the debility of the nervous system. It is manifested by lowness of spirits, inactivity, shunning and dreading effort, foreboding of evil, fears without cause; —*physically* by flatulency, eructations, costiveness, pale urine, palpitations, spasmodic pains in various parts of the body, &c.

Treatment.—First ascertain the causes of the disease, and try to remove them. As to medicine, give an emetic; if the disease is obstinate, repeat it; give also anodyne aperients and injections. For an hypochondriac, the *Dyspeptic Pill* is very efficacious, taken at night. Also the *Nervous Pill.* Treat the patient kindly and encouragingly. Harshness will aggravate the disease. The great thing is to arouse the nervous energy from its lethargy; and this must be effected as above, and also by giving tonics, light and digestible food, open air exercise, sea air, change of scenes, travelling and lawful amusements. An aged minister once said that "weak nerves are the devil's fiddle strings, and he always plays well on them."

Should this disease arise from affections of the liver, he must be treated for that disease also. The following is a good pill for melancholy;—Lobelia Seed, 1 drachm; Extract of Dandelion, 3 drs.; Bloodroot, 1 dr.; Senna, powdered, 2 drs.; Cayenne, 1 dr.; valerian powdered, 2 drs.; butternut powdered, 3 drs. Form into pills with syrup and oil of mint. Two or three, three times a-day.

☞ *These ingredients may be obtained at the Medical Botanists.*

HYSSOP.—It is very useful in colds, coughs, catarrhs, influenza, and affections of the lungs; as a gargle for sore mouth. See *Robinson's Herbal.*

HYSTERICS. — This disease mostly affects young, nervous, single women. It manifests itself by fits, often preceded by nervous lowness, difficult breathing, sickness at the stomach, palpitations, and a pain at the left side, a rumbling noise in the bowels, the sensation of a ball ascending to the throat, with the feeling of suffocation, convulsions, laughing and crying without any apparent cause. Almost every part of the nervous system is liable to this affection. The disease seldom proves fatal. It is caused by menstrual irregularities, indolence, irregular living, costiveness, indigestion, worms, obstructed perspiration, &c.

An *hysteric fit* may be easily distinguished from fainting; for, in fainting the pulse and respiration are entirely stopped; in hysterics, they are both perceptible.

Treatment. First loosen the dress, and dash cold water in the face. It is of the greatest importance to put the feet and legs in warm water as soon as possible. Give an emetic. The *Expectorant Tincture* must be given to remove the rising in the throat, the sense of suffocation, collected phlegm, &c. If the patient cannot swallow, pour it into the mouth, and it will relax the jaws, &c., and cause the patient to swallow; it will send the blood to the surface and extremities, affect the brain and nervous system so as to end the attack even by a single dose.

The vapour bath should be given as soon as possible.——Or, put the patient to bed, and apply hot bricks or bottles of hot water to the feet and sides; the bottles to be folded in cloths wet with vinegar and water. Should these means fail give the *Anodyne Powders;* (see Appendix.) Give also gentle aperients; and above all, do not neglect to give the *Nervous Pill* which is wonderfully efficacious. The aperients may be assisted by injections of gruel, ½ oz. of the tincture of assafœtida, or a table-spoonful of spirits of turpentine; sweeten with treacle. Tonics, as quinine, should be freely given. If the disease arises from obstructed menses, worms, &c., the case must be treated as directed under those complaints.

ICE, *to procure.*—(See *Freezing Mixture.*)—Nearly fill a gallon stone bottle with hot spring water (leaving room for about a pint), and put in 2 ozs. of refined nitre; the bottle must be stopped very close, and let down into a deep well. After three or four hours it will be completely frozen; but the bottle must be broken to procure the ice. If the bottle is moved up and down, so as to be sometimes in and sometimes out of the water, the consequent evaporation will hasten the process.

ICE CREAM.—Put into a bucket 1 lb. of ice broken very small; throw two handfuls of salt, among it, and have it in the coolest place you can find. Put the cream into an ice-pot, and cover it; immerse it in the ice, and draw the ice round the pot, so as to touch every part. In a few minutes put a spatula or spoon in, and stir the parts that ice round the edges to the centre. Stirring quickly increases the cold. There should be holes in the bucket to let out the ice as it thaws.

The cream for icing is thus made:—New milk, 1 quart; yolks of 6 eggs; fine sugar, 4 ozs. Mix. Strain. Heat gently, and then cool.

ICEING, *for Cakes.*—Beat the whites of two eggs to a solid froth, add 8 ozs. of finely powdered white sugar; mix in the juice of a quarter of a lemon. Place the cakes before the fire; pour over them the icing, and smooth over the sides and tops with a knife. Set them to dry at the mouth of a cool oven.

ICEING, *for Tarts.*—Beat the yolk of an egg, and some melted butter well together; wash the tarts with a feather, and sift sugar over them as you put them in the oven.

Ice Waters.—Rub some fine sugar upon lemon or orange, to give the colour and flavour, then squeeze the juice of either on its respective peel; add water and sugar to make a fine sherbet, and strain it before it be put into the ice-pot. If orange, the greater proportion should be of the China juice, and only a little of Seville, and a small bit of the peel grated by the sugar.

Currant or Raspberry Water Ice.—The juice of these, or any other sort of fruit, being gained by squeezing, sweetened and mixed with water, will be ready for iceing.

Ice Creams.—Mix the juice of the fruits with as much sugar as will be wanted, before you add cream, which should be of a middling richness.

ICELAND MOSS.—It derives its name from the country in which it is found. As an article of food for invalids, it is very light, and nutritious. It has tonic, and demulcent properties, and it forms a very suitable diet for the consumptive. It allays the tickling cough, relieves the breathing, and improves the digestion. The decoction is the most medicinal. It is bitter; but that may be obviated by previous washings.

ICELAND MOSS JELLY.—Moss, ½ oz. to 1 oz.; water, 1 qrt. Simmer down to ½ pint. Add fine sugar, and a little lemon juice. It may be improved with ¼ ounce of isinglass. The moss should first be steeped in cold water an hour or two.

IMPERIAL.—Cream of tartar, 2 ozs.; citric acid, 1 oz.; orange or lemon peel, 3 ozs.; fine sugar, 6 or 8 ozs.; boiling water, 2 qrts. Mix; cover the vessel to cool. Very suitable for hot weather. It might be bottled by adding a little yeast.

IMPERIAL CREAM.—Boil a quart of cream with the thin rind of a lemon; stir till nearly cold; have ready in a dish to serve in, the juice of three lemons strained with as much sugar as will sweeten the cream; pour it into the dish from a large tea-pot, holding it high, and moving it about to mix with the juice. It should be made from 6 to 12 hours before it is served.

INDELIBLE INK.—*German Receipt.*—Dissolve 20 grains of sugar in 30 grains of water, and the addition to the solution of a few drops of concentrated sulphuric acid; the mixture is then heated, when the sugar is carbonized by the action of the acid. It is said that the writing is not only of a solid black colour, but that the acid resists the action of chemical agents.

INDELIBLE INK.—Add a little nitrate of silver to ordinary writing ink.

INDIA PICKLE.—Strong vinegar, 3½ quarts; salt, ½ lb.; shallots, ¼ lb.; ginger, 2 ozs.; white pepper, 1 oz.; mustard seeds, 2 ozs.; cayenne pepper, half a table spoonful. Boil all together; put into a jar; add 2 ozs. of ground mustard. You may put in kidney beans, cauliflower, &c., as you like.

INDIAN PUDDING.—Indian meal, a cupful, a little salt, butter, 1 oz.; treacle, 3 ozs.; 2 teaspoonfuls of ginger, or cinnamon. Put into a quart of boiling milk. Mix a cup of cold water with it; bake in a buttered dish 50 minutes.

INDIGESTION.—It may be the effect or symptom of some disease, as nervous debility of the stomach, affections of the liver, inflammation of the stomach, costiveness, obstructed perspiration, want of exercise, especially in the open air, deficiency or vitiation of the gastric juice, gluttony, alcoholic drinks, depressing passions; intense study, onanism, or self-abuse, &c. Tea, coffee, and tobacco are most fruitful causes of this disease.

Treatment.—Abandon, if possible, the causes which produce the effect. Give occasionally an emetic. If necessary, gentle aperients. Injections are often of great use. These methods may be repeated about once a week, till the disease abates. Emetics serve to remove morbid matter, impart new tone to the stomach, and give healthy action to the secretions. Dr. Beach recommends *lobelia* combined with *mandrake*, as the best emetic. The bowels are best regulated by always eating *brown bread;* for the *bran* gives a more natural stimulus to the liver and alimentary canal than any medicine which can be given.

The use of the *Dyspeptic Pill* tends very much to improve the tone of the stomach. The *Restorative Wine Bitters* cannot be too much recommended. If indigestion arises from affections of the liver, treat for the same; especially take the *Liver Pill* with the aforesaid medicines. If, from a disordered stomach, there is acidity, &c., take the *Neutralizing Mixture.*

In fine, be choice in your diet; and eat the unsifted flour, by some called ground down, or brown bread—a better name would be—*ground altogether.* It is the grand *panacea* for indigestion. The dyspeptic must avoid or take little of fat meat, butter, cheese, pastry, strong coffee, green tea, and ardent spirits, which *harden the food* in course of digestion, and cause the feculent matter difficult and painful to be evacuated. Eat sparingly, take open air exercise as much as possible; use cold sponging.

INDIGESTION —— *Prescriptions.*—Dr. Babington's. —Infusion of Columba, 6 ozs.; carbonate of potass, 1 dr.; compound tincture of gentian, 3 drs. Mix. Three table-spoonfuls to be taken every day, at noon.——Or, take Gentian and Columba roots (bruised) and camomile flowers, of each 1 oz., to three quarts of water; boil to three pints. Dose—two or three tea-cupfuls a day.——Or, take one ounce each of hops and carraway seeds; 24 cloves; ¼ oz. of senna, and 24 black peppers. Boil the whole in 3 pints of water till it is reduced to 2 pints. A wine-glassful of the infusion to be taken twice a day, at eleven and three o'clock.

Pain in the Stomach from bad digestion.—Take fasting, or in the fit, half a pint of camomile tea. Do this five or six mornings.—— Or, drink the juice of half a large lemon, or sweet orange, immediately after dinner every day.—*Dr. Mead.*——Or, from ten to twenty drops of elixir of vitriol in sage tea, twice or thrice a-day.——Or, in the fit a glass of vinegar.—— Or, take two or three tea-spoonfuls of stomachic tincture, in a glass of water, thrice a-day.

☞ The tincture is made thus:— Gentian root, sliced, 1 ounce; orange peel, dried, half an ounce; cochineal, fifteen grains; proof brandy, one pint; in three or four days it is fit for use.—This is useful in all disorders that arise from a relaxed stomach.—*Wesley.*

INFANTS, *Management of.*— A child, when born, should be laid, for the first month, upon a thin mattress, which the nurse may sometimes keep on her knee, that the child may always lie, and only sit up as the nurse slants the mattress. Keep it as dry as possible. At the end of a month, the nurse may set it up, and dance it by degrees.

The clothing should be light, and not much longer than itself, that the legs may be readily reached and rubbed, for rubbing takes off scurf, and causes the blood to circulate. Rubbing the ankle-bones and inside of the knees will strengthen those parts, and make the child stretch its knees, and keep them flat.

Do not keep a child too long in the arms, lest the legs should be cramped, and the toes turned inwards. The oftener the posture is changed the better.

During the first fortnight the child should sleep on a bed, except when taken up to supply its wants, which will give it early habits of cleanliness. It is injurious to be laid always asleep on a person's knee.

By slow degrees the infant should be accustomed to exercise, within doors, and in the open air. It should be carried about, and *gently* dandled in the nurse's arms. Exercising a child in the open air, in fine weather, is of the greatest service.

Endeavour to harden the body, but without violent means. A child is constitutionally weak and irritable; hence we should try to strengthen the child, and diminish this irritability, in order to procure it the greatest blessing,—a firm body, which may resist all influence of air and weather. The cold bath may be used too much, and bodily exercise may be too violent.

Infants should by imperceptible degrees be inured to the cool, and then to the cold bath. If they have been accustomed to an effeminate treatment, and should be suddenly subjected to an opposite extreme, such a change would be attended with danger.

The child's skin is to be kept perfectly clean, by washing its limbs morning and evening; begin with warm water, till, by degrees, it will bear, and like, to be washed with cold water. After carefully drying the whole body, head, and limbs, another dry soft cloth, a little warmed, should be used gently, to take all the damp from the wrinkled and fat parts of the body. Apply gentle friction to the body, but do not press upon the stomach and bowels. If the skin is chafed, hair powder, or violet powder, is to be used, or a thin mixture of fullers earth. For the head, a small soft brush is safer than a comb. It should have clean linen, &c. every day.

Some females in dressing an infant are very rough, and must harass and fatigue it much. The most tender deliberation should be observed. Never let the clothes be tight. Never use pins, for they are dangerous. The strings must be tied so slack that one might get two fingers between. Many instances of idiotism, fits, and deformity, are owing to tight bandages.

Never expose an infant to open doors or windows, especially in winter. The extreme of a summer day should also be avoided. Excessive heat or cold will injure an infant. Infants should not be kept too near the fire.

The wisest course in treating infants, is to follow the simple dictates of nature; yet some people are so devoid of consideration as to give them wine, spirits, spices, sugar, and other things too strong for their tender stomachs. The first milk a baby can draw from its mother's breast is medicine and nourishment for it, and if she is too ill to give it, it is better to let it wait a few hours, than to give it any kind of food. But if it is very craving, mix milk with soft boiled water, and give it half a teaspoonful at a time, only warm, for its mouth cannot bear much heat. Let it swallow one little portion before another is offered, and raise its head that it may pass the gullet easily. Do not overload the stomach, which may greatly disorder the infant, and become the foundation of gluttony.

If a mother cannot suckle the child, get a healthy cheerful woman, with young milk, who is fond of infants. After the first six months, broths, and simple food, may do as well as living wholly upon milk.

If milk cannot be had, a teaspoonful of the yolk of a fresh egg, well beaten and mixed with two table-spoonfuls of soft boiled water will do instead. Three inches square of lean veal, and one inch thick, will make soup for a baby for two or three days. Boil only half at once, in a pint of soft water, down to two-thirds. Strain. When cold, take off the scum. Warm a little as wanted. A thin gruel also may be made from rice flour.

In the latter part of the first year, pure water may occasionally be given. Those parents who accustom their children to drink water only, bestow on them a benefit, the value of which will be sensibly felt through life. Habits of intemperance, the curse of after life, are often laid in infancy.

Rising early in the morning is good for all children, provided they awake of themselves, which they generally do; they ought not to be waked out of their sleep. Children, till they are two or three years old must never be allowed to walk long enough to be weary.

In laying a child to sleep, place it upon the right side oftener than on the left, but twice in the twenty-four hours it should be changed to the left side. Laying it on its back when it awakes, is enough of that posture, in which alone it can move its legs and arms with freedom. Place the cradle so that the light may come equally on both eyes, to prevent squinting.

Infants cannot sleep too long. Sleep promotes a more calm and uniform circulation of the blood, and facilitates assimilation of the nutriment received. Mothers and nurses should try to accustom infants, from the time of their birth, to sleep in the night, preferably to the day.

To awaken children from sleep with a noise, or in an impetuous manner, is unwise and hurtful; also to carry them from a dark room immediately into a glaring light, for the sudden impression of light debilitates the organs of vision, and lays the foundation of weak eyes from infancy.

Infants are sometimes very restless at night, caused by either cramming them with too much food, by tight night clothes, or by being overheated with blankets, &c.

Never give an infant wine, spirits, or any drug, to make it sleep. Milk, water, or both mixed, whey or thin gruel; these are the fittest for infants. The more simple and light their diet and drink, the more they will thrive.

A bed-room or nursery, ought to be spacious and lofty, dry, airy, and not inhabited through the day. Feather beds should be banished from nurseries, as they are an unnatural and debilitating contrivance. The windows should never be opened at night, but left open the whole day, in fine clear weather.

Nurses ought never to conceal any accident befalling a child. All violent impressions on the senses and bodies of children should be avoided. It is injurious to toss them about rapidly and violently in their arms. Loud crying, or shouting in their ears, presenting glittering objects to their view, and sudden and too great a degree of light; such practices are very injurious.

INFECTION, *to prevent.*—Sprinkle a room, &c. with a solution of chloride of lime; or sprinkle dissolved camphor in spirits of wine upon your handkerchief; it may be diluted with acetic acid.

Or, smoke this mixture:—Tobacco, 4 ozs.; cascarilla bark, ½ oz.; unburnt coffee, ground, 1 oz.; mix, and smoke occasionally.

INFECTION, *to prevent.*—See *Disinfectants.*

INFLAMMATION *of the Bowels.* See *Intestines, Diarrhœa, Bowels.*

INFLUENZA.—See *Catarrh.*

INK.—This will keep for very many years. Boil 4 ozs. of logwood chips in a gallon of water for 15 minutes, and pour it boiling hot upon 12 ozs. of galls coarsely powdered. Stir during four or five days. Pour off the liquor clear, and add to it 4 ozs. each of copperas and gum arabic. To prevent moulding, add bruised cloves, or oil of cloves.

Another.—Water, 1 quart; best Aleppo galls in coarse powder, 4 ozs., and 1 oz. each of rasped logwood, green vitriol or copperas, and gum arabic. Stir or shake four or five times a day, for 12 or 14 days, when it will be fit for use. Vinegar instead of water makes a deeper coloured ink, but it is not fit for steel pens.

Another Receipt for a Gallon.—Aleppo galls, 1 lb., slightly bruised; rain-water, 1 gallon, nearly boiling. Let them stand mixed together for 14 days. Then add 4 ozs. of green copperas; 4 ozs. of logwood chips; 1 oz. each of alum and sugar-candy, and 4 ozs. of gum arabic. Cover over, and agitate for 14 days in a warm place. Strain, and bottle, pouring a little brandy on the top of the ink in each bottle.

INK, *invisible.*—See *Sympathetic Ink.*

INK, *Permanent.*—Best galls, and logwood, each 6 ozs.; copperas, 3 ozs.; gum arabic, 1½ oz.; pomegranate bark, 1 oz. (sold by druggists); rain water, cold, 3 pints; cloves, 2 or 3 ozs. Stir for several times a day for 2 or 3 weeks.

INK, *to erase.*—Press a little emery paper over the finger, and rub out the ink-spot, or writing, or wrong figure. This method is better than that of the erasing knife.

INK, *to prevent moulding.*—Put a few cloves into each bottle.——Or add to the ink before boiling, spirits of wine and oil of cloves.

INK, *to take out of marble.*—Unslaked lime, and strong soap ley; make it thick, and lay it on with a painter's brush; let it remain on a week, wash it off, and apply again, and wash it off with soft soap and water.

INK POWDER. — Copperas, four ounces; nutgalls, powdered, six ounces; common salt, three quarters of an ounce; powdered gum arabic, one ounce and a half. Mix and keep dry. A small quantity of this powder, stirred up with a table-spoonful or two of hot water, will make good ink, ready for use in a few minutes, and will keep good for years in any climate.

INK SPOTS, *to remove.*—Apply a solution of salts of lemon, or wet with strong acetic acid.——Or, apply a solution of muriate of

N

tin.——Or, muriatic acid. On the ink disappearing, rub it over immediately with a rag wetted with cold water, to prevent a white mark.

INSECTS *on plants to destroy.*—Tie up sulphur in a muslin bag, and dust the leaves of young shoots and plants. A dredging-box may be used. Sulphur increases verdure. A weak solution of alum sprinkled upon plants is not relished by insects.——Or, a thin mixture of soft soap and oil of turpentine painted on the stems of trees.—Painting the walls behind rose trees, fruit trees, &c., prevents the visits of spiders, earwigs, caterpillars, &c. The best paint for this purpose is gas tar.

INTERMITTENT FEVER. See *Ague.*

INTESTINES, *Inflammation of.*—See *Bowel Complaint;* page 73. The mucous membrane is generally the seat of this disease. The stomach and intestines are lined with a membrane which secretes a liquid termed "mucous." This disease is often caused by exposure to cold and wet, especially while in a state of perspiration; the suppression of customary evacuations, indigestible food, mercury, frequent drastic purges, feculent accumulation in the intestines, strangulated rupture, and over-feeding, giving nature more than it is able to do; *drunkenness* is an awful thing for the bowels, gradually, by its extreme terrible friction, lessening the secretion of the mucous. When that ceases, farewell to life.

It manifests itself by acute pains in the bowels, pains shooting around the navel, which increase by pressure. There is great constipation, and vomiting of bilious matter, fever, debility, mental depression. It is a dangerous disease, and requires prompt attention. The object is to remove the inflammation. Let all exciting food and drinks be abandoned. Avoid severe purgatives. Give a table-spoonful, or rather more of castor-oil every two hours until it acts on the bowels. Bathe the feet and legs in warm water. If the oil takes no effect, give the following injection;—Lobelia herb, $\frac{1}{2}$ dr.; slippery elm, $\frac{1}{2}$ dr.; valerian root, 1 dr.; boiling water, half a pint. Infuse ten minutes, strain, and give warm. If the pain is severe, make a decoction of bitter herbs, with a trifle of cayenne and opium, and flannels dipped in it, and applied to the abdomen. To allay vomiting, take infusion of spearmint, half a pint; bicarbonate of potash, half a tea-spoonful. Give a tablespoonful every hour. As soon as the bowels are relieved, give a vapour bath, and then the Diaphoretic Powder. Should the extremities become cold, repeat the vapour bath.

IODINE LOTION.—Tincture of Iodine, $\frac{1}{2}$ fluid oz.; iodide of iron, 12 grains; chloride of antimony, $\frac{1}{2}$ oz. Mix for a wash. It is a remedy for corns. Apply with a small brush.

Or Iodine, $1\frac{1}{2}$ grains; spirits of wine, 3 teaspoonfuls. Dissolve, and add a pint of water. A most excellent wash for scrofulous sores.

IPECACUANHA.—It is emetic, stimulant, tonic, and sudorific. It is useful in bleeding from the lungs, and indigestion, if taken in small doses, so as not to produce nausea; also in fluxes, diarrhœa, hooping cough, and in some fevers. From 25 to 30 grains form a good emetic, without causing debility. In doses of 2 or 3 grains, it forms a tonic, giving tone to the stomach, and promoting digestion. It is valuable in bilious and liver complaints.—See *Robinson's Herbal.*

IRISH STEW.—Cut off the fat of part of a loin of mutton, and cut it into chops. Pare, wash, and slice very thin some potatoes, two onions, and two small carrots; season with pepper, and salt. Cover with water in a stew-pan, and stew gently till the meat is tender, and the potatoes are dissolved in the gravy. It may be made of beefsteaks, or mutton and beef mixed.

IRON-MOULD, *to remove.*—Rub the iron-mould part with a little oxalic acid, or salts of lemon, dissolved in warm water. After remaining ten minutes, rinse well in warm and then in cold water.- Or apply a mixture of milk and salt.

IRON AND STEEL, *to prevent from rusting.*—Fat oil varnish, one part, and rectified spirits of turpentine, three parts, intimately mixed, and applied with a sponge. ——Camphor, lard, and black lead, mixed, applied, and after two days wiped off will preserve from rust. ——Or smear over the iron, or metal, hardware, &c. with melted mutton-suet, and dust with powdered unslaked lime.

Brown paper is a good preservative from rust. Hence all Sheffield and Birmingham Hardware, Cutlery, &c., are wrapped in Brown Paper.

IRRITABLE.—Physically denotes a habit of body prone to tonic inflammation, but without strength to form it perfectly, or to bear the remedies proper to subdue it.—*Irritation* signifies an imperfect inflammation. Many infantile diseases partake more of irritation than inflammation. A state of irritability is present in most diseases, and is very trying both to the patients and their attendants, and one for which every allowance and consideration ought to be made.

IRRITATING LINIMENT. Tincture of Cayenne, ½ oz.; spirits of turpentine, 1 oz.; croton oil ¼ oz.; olive oil, 1½ oz. It produces eruptions, and removes the severest pains.

IRRITATING PLASTER.—Burgundy-pitch and beeswax, ¼ lb. each; thick tar, ½ lb.; Venice turpentine, ½ oz. Melt well and mix on a slow fire. When cold, mix with them powdered blood-root, poke-root, and a little cayenne. Spread on linen or soft leather. This plaster is counter-irritant, causes eruptions, and is a good curative for old sores and ulcers. It is highly recommended.

ISINGLASS JELLY.—Boil 1 oz. of isinglass in a quart of water, with ¼ oz. of Jamaica pepper-corns, or cloves, and a crust of bread, till reduced to a pint. Add sugar. It keeps well, and may be taken in wine and water, milk, tea, soup, &c.

ISINGLASS PLASTER. — Dissolve isinglass in a little hot water, and brush it over silk or fine linen, to form a glaze upon it. Dry, and when wanted cut strips, and moisten them. I. is an elegant plaster for abrasions of the skin.

ISSUE OINTMENT. — Mix half an ounce of Spanish flies, finely powdered, in six ounces of yellow basilicon ointment. This ointment is chiefly intended for dressing blisters, in order to keep them open during pleasure.

ITALIAN PUDDING.—Lay puff paste at the bottom and round the edge of the dish; over which pour a pint of cream, French rolls enough to thicken it, ten eggs beaten fine, a nutmeg grated, 12 pippins sliced, orange peel, sugar, and half a pint of red wine. Half an hour will bake it.

ITALIAN SAUCE, *Brown.*—Chop a few mushrooms and shalots; put them into a stewpan, with some stock, and a glass of sherry; boil up; add clove, nutmeg, a little lemon, and the juice of parsley, thyme; add a little sugar.

ITALIAN SAUCE, *White.*—Put some chopped mushrooms, and shalots into a stew-pan with a slice of ham minced very small, and put in a little stock; simmer 15 minutes; add bechemel, (which see). Boil a minute; if it loses its colour, add a spoonful of cream; strain; season with salt, a few drops of garlic vinegar, a squeeze of lemon, and a bit of sugar.

ITCH.—It is a skin disease, infectious. Sometimes it is caused by poor living, unwholesome food, bad air, unventilated and dirty houses, dirty beds and clothes. The itch begins with small eruptions on the joints of the fingers, on the wrists, thighs, &c. They cause a most intolerable itching, the scratching of which only spreads the disease.

Remedies:—Sweet oil, 1 lb.; suet, 1 lb. Melt and macerate; then add powdered nitre, 3 ozs.; powdered alum, 3 ozs.; powdered sulphate of zinc, 3 ozs.; oil of aniseed, oil of spike, and oil of origanum, to perfume.——Or, mix 2 ozs. of lard with 1 oz. of sulphur-vivum, and a few drops of essence of lemons. Before going to bed rub this well into the affected parts. In the morning wash with soap and warm water; change the linen and clothes. Repeat the application, if necessary. Take at the same time flour of sulphur and cream of tartar, in milk, beer, or treacle.

FREQUENTLY take a WARM BATH. The *greatest cures have been effected by it.*

Wash the parts affected with strong rum.—-Tried.——Or, anoint them with black soap, but wash it off soon.——Or, steep a shirt half an hour in a quart of water mixed with half an ounce of powdered brimstone. Dry it slowly, and wear it five or six days. Sometimes it needs repeating.— Tried.——Or, mix powder of white hellebore with cream for three days. Anoint the joints for three mornings and evenings. It seldom fails.—— Or, beat together the juice of two or three lemons, with the same quantity of oil of roses—Anoint the parts affected. It cures in two or three times using.

The following is said soon to effect a cure:—Sulphur-vivum, Venice turpentine, 1 oz. each; lard, ½ oz. Melt the lard and turpentine; add the sulphur. Apply several times a day.

Or, wash the body well in warm water, and rub it with the following preparation:—Lime, 2 ozs.; sulphur-vivum, 2 ozs. Mix in 1 quart of water. Pour off, and use it when clear.

A decoction of white hellebore, with a little lavender water, has been recommended.

IVORY, *to polish.*—Ivory is polished with putty and water, by means of a rubber made of hat, which in a short time produces a fine gloss.

IVORY AND BONE, *to stain.* —*Black*;—Rub over with diluted oil of vitriol; wash, and then steep in nitrate of silver and good ink.——*Blue*; steep in a strong solution of extract of indigo and a little potash.—— *Green;* dissolve copper in nitric acid, and steep the ivory in it.—Steep in oxalic tin, and then in a strong decoction of Brazil wood, or lac dye, and alum. ——*Purple;* nitric acid, 2 parts; sal ammoniac, 1 part; mix, and steep the ivory in it.

JALAP.—It is the resin of a Mexican plant. It is one of our common and most valuable purgatives; it acts upon the whole alimentary canal, chiefly on the small intestines, increasing the peristaltic action, the secretions, and exhalations; and it is useful in bilious and dropsical complaints; in low spirits, melancholy, worms, &c. It is given in doses of ten to thirty grains. For worms it is combined with calomel; and for dropsy, with cream of tartar. Mixed with sugar in small doses, it is a safe purge for children.

JAPAN INK.—Aleppo galls, ½ lb; logwood chips, and copperas, of each 4 ozs.; gum arabic, 3 ozs.; sugar, 1 oz.; blue vitriol, and sugar-candy, of each ½ oz. Boil the galls and logwood in 6 quarts of water till reduced one half; strain; add the other ingredients. Stir, until dissolved. Clear, and bottle. If it does not shine enough, add more gum; also a few cloves to prevent mould.

JAPANNER'S COPAL VARNISH.—Copal, picked, 5 pounds; linseed oil, 20 ounces. Melt and digest until dissolved, then withdraw it from the fire and add oil of turpentine, 6 pounds. Well mix.

JAPANNER'S GOLD SIZE. —Gum ammoniac, 1 pound; boiled oil, 8 ounces; spirits of turpentine, 12 ounces. Melt the gum, then add the oil, and lastly the spirits of turpentine.

JARGONEL PEARS, *to preserve.*—Pare the fruit very thin, simmer them in a thin syrup. In two days make the syrup richer; simmer again, and repeat till they are clear; drain, and dry in the sun, or in a cool oven a very little time. They may be kept in a syrup, and dried as wanted.

JAUNDICE.—From the French word, *jaune, yellow*. This disease is known by the yellow colour of the eyes, skin, and urine. The stools are either white or grey, caused by the absence of bile; and there is often pain in the right side, arising from the state of the liver; also, mental depression, constipation, headache, drowsiness, nausea, vomiting. Jaundice is caused by obstructed secretion, or by a reabsorption of the bile. Hence it appears that the yellowness of the skin is produced by bile taken up into the circulation, the effect of those causes. When large gallstones get into the gall-ducts, they cause jaundice, and very severe pain. When they pass away, a cure soon takes place. Should the colour of the skin become very dark-coloured, it is an indication of some incurable organic disease of the liver.

Treatment.—Those means must be used which will promote the secretions, and the regular flow of bile. Give an aperient composed of senna, camomile flowers, ginger, and powdered jalap, of each 1 oz. Mix. Take half a teaspoonful in a little warm tea. After it has operated, give the common *Emetic*, page 155. Keep the bowels always gently open; and give the *Liver Pill*.

Dr. Beech says, 'In obstinate cases, the barberry root, cut up, and infused in cider, may be taken, and the purgative repeated, and the emetic also, if necessary. Common soot (he must mean woodsoot, peculiar to America) scraped from the chimney, enclosed in linen, and boiled in water, makes a liquid which will be found very efficacious; it may be taken alternately with the other medicines."

If the pain on the right side is severe, use fomentations of the decoction of hops. Use the vapour bath, and take some of the Sudorific Powder; for such means tend to relax the biliary duct, that the gall-stones may pass away. Let the diet be light and nourishing. The following decoction is useful: —Burdock root, one ounce, Agrimony, one ounce, water, two qrts.; boil down to three pints. Dose, a wine-glassful two or three times a day.

Dr. A. Hunter recommends eggs. He states that the *yolk* of an egg is the most salutary of all animal substances. In jaundice no food is equal to it. "When the gall is too weak, or by accidental means, does not flow sufficiently into the duodenum, our food which consists of watery and oily parts, cannot unite so as to become chyle. The yolk of an egg unites the water and oil into a uniform substance, thereby supplying the deficiency of natural bile."

Or, take a small pill of Castile soap every morning for eight or ten days.—Tried.——Or, beat the white of an egg thin; take it morning and evening in a glass of water. ——Or, half a pint of strong decoction of nettles, or of burdock leaves morning and evening.——Or, boil three ounces of burdock root, in two quarts of water to three pints. Drink a tea-cupful of this every morning.—*Wesley.*

The plant *Bitter-sweet* has been very useful in this disease. See *Robinson's Herbal*, for that plant, and also for *Jaundice*.

JELLY, *Stock*.-Put a sufficient number of calves' feet into a stewpan, with 3 pints of water to each foot; boil gently for 4 or 5 hours; then take out the meat part, and put it into cold water. When cold, trim it for any use it is designed for; throw the trimmings back into the stock, and let it boil to a proper strength. Four feet to produce two quarts of stock.

JELLY FOR THE SICK.— Mix 1 oz. each of rice, pearl barley, sago, and hartshorn shavings, in three pints of water; boil till reduced to one, and strain. When required for use, dissolve in milk, wine or broth.

JELLY of GOOSEBERRIES. —Bruise gooseberries, and strain out the pulp. To every pint of juice put ¾ lb. of sugar; boil up well together, so that if a little is laid upon a plate, it will not stick, but come clean off. Strain off, and keep to put into tarts with pears, apples, &c., to make them taste like gooseberries. Other fruits may be done in a similar way.

JELLY, *Savoury Meat.*—Chop a knuckle of veal and a scrag of mutton, so that one bone may be placed on the other. Scrape and slice 3 carrots and 2 turnips, cut small a stick of celery, butter the bottom of a small jar or well-tinned saucepan. Place the meat and vegetables in alternate layers, closely together. Sprinkle with a little salt, cover the jar, and place it in a slow oven for half an hour; pour in as much hot water as will cover the contents. Place in the oven hotter than before, for five hours. Strain the liquor from the meat and vegetables; when cold, remove the fat from the surface, and the sediment. The jelly will then be ready for use.

JONQUILLE PERFUME.— Oil of sassafras, 1 part; oil of orange, 1 part; oil of carraway, 2 parts; oil of lavender, 3 parts; essence of lemon, 8 parts; essence of bergamot, 8 parts. Mix.

JUMBALLS.—Flour, 1 lb.; sugar, 1 lb.; make into a light paste with whites of eggs beaten fine; add ½ pint of cream; ¼ lb. of butter, melted; and 1 lb. of blanched almonds, well beaten; knead all together, with a little rose-water; cut into any form; bake in a slow oven. A little butter may be melted with a spoonful of white wine, and throw fine sugar all over the dish.

JUNIPER BERRIES.--Very diuretic, and pleasant, as it is (or should be) a principal ingredient in Hollands or Geneva Gin. The oil is the best for dropsical and urinary diseases. The dose is from 10 to 15 drops three times a day.

KERNELS, *to blanch.*—Simply put them into boiling water a minute or two; rub them between a clean cloth, and the brown skins will soon peel off. *Almonds* and other kernels may thus be blanched.

KETCHUP. See *Mushroom Ketchup, Walnut Ketchup, &c.*

KETCHUP, *to keep twenty years.*—Take a gallon of strong stale beer, 1 lb. of anchovies, washed from the pickle; 1 lb. of shalots; ½ oz. of mace; ½ oz. of cloves; ¼ oz. of whole pepper; ½ oz. of ginger; 2 quarts of large mushroom flaps, rubbed to pieces; cover all close, and simmer till it is half wasted; strain; cool; then bottle. A spoonful of this ketchup is sufficient for a pint of melted butter.

KETTLES, *incrustation or furring to prevent.*—Keep in the vessel a clean marble, a cockle, or oyster shell; these will attract the particles of sand.

KID GLOVES, *to clean.*—Rub with very slightly damped bread crumbs. If not effectual, scrape upon them dry fullers earth, or French chalk, when on the hands, and rub them quickly together in all directions. Do this several times.—— Or put gloves of a light colour on the hands, and wash the hands in a basin of spirits of hartshorn :—Some gloves may be washed in a strong lather made of white soap and warm water, or milk; or wash with rice pulp.—Or sponge them well with turpentine. Alum powder and fullers earth well mixed may be usefully used.

KIDNEY BEANS.—String them; cut down the middle, and across; boil in salt and water till tender, and serve with melted butter.

Another way.--Cut in small dice two onions; put them in a stewpan with a little butter; when they begin to brown put in a little good gravy; flour them; give them and the flour a fine brown colour: if gravy is not used, put in a spoonful of soup, season with salt and pepper; reduce this sauce; put in the beans already cooked; simmer till enough; dish, and serve. *French.*

Another way.—Cut two onions in half rings, and put them into a frying-pan with butter; when they begin to brown, put in the beans which have been cooked; fry with the onions; put in hashed parsley, scallions, salt and pepper; give a turn or two more, and dish: boil a little vinegar in the pan, and pour it over them. *French.*

KIDNEY BEANS *in Salad.*—Take haricots already cooked, put them in a salad-dish; garnish them with strips of anchovy, onions, roasted in the ashes, beet root, or any thing properly hashed; season with salt, pepper, oil, and vinegar, and serve.

KIDNEY, *(beef,) Broiled.*—Cut the kidney lengthways. Season with nutmeg, pepper, and salt. Pass a wire skewer through them to prevent them curling. Have a brisk clear fire, and place on the gridiron for about ten minutes, turning them often. When dished, rub them over with butter, and serve with parsley fried crisp, and a little sherry, butter, salt, and pepper.

Kidneys may be minced by a similar seasoning, and be done in the oven, or in a dutch oven before the fire.

KIDNEY, (beef,) Fried.—Chop the kidney with a little veal and ham, and butter or lard. Season as you like with white pepper, cayenne, and salt. To make them into balls add rice flour and yolk of egg. Fry in lard or butter. Dish; pour the gravy upon them, and serve with toasted bread. A.N.

KIDNEY PUDDING.—If kidney, split and soak it, and season that or the meat. Make a paste of suet, flour, and milk; roll it, and line a basin with some; put the kidney or steaks in, cover with paste, and pinch round the edge. Cover with a cloth and boil a considerable time.

KIDNEY, VEAL, to fry.—Chop veal kidney, and some of the fat; also a little leek or onion, pepper, and salt; roll it up with an egg into balls, and fry them.

Calf's heart, stuff and roast as a beast's heart, or sliced, make it into a pudding, as directed for steak or kidney pudding. *Run.*

KIDNEYS, inflammation of.—It is indicated by chilliness and fever, with severe piercing pains, sometimes dull, with a sense of weight over the kidney inflamed. The urine is very high coloured, and is partially or wholly suppressed, and sometimes it is bloody. Sometimes faintness, nausea, vomiting, hiccup, and relax are present. It may be caused by calculus, external blows, falls, hard riding, &c. Persons of intemperate habits are very liable to diseases of the kidneys. Gin drinkers, on account of the admixture of turpentine with that spirit, often pay dear for their tippling.

Treatment.—In severe cases the patient should lie in bed. The bowels should be cleared by gentle aperients and injections. If there is coldness of the surface and extremeties, bathe the feet in warm water. Drink decoctions of the diuretic plants; as, horsemint, marsh-mallow, broom tops, parsley, pennyroyal, &c. Take also the diuretic drops. Diluents may also be drunk; the best is common barley-water. Make a strong infusion of parsley, two parts; of pennyroyal, 1 part, and half a cupful of best Hollands gin, and $\frac{1}{2}$ oz. of sweet nitre, all mixed; take at three times; it often acts effectually. Externally, apply cayenne pepper simmered in vinegar, and add 30 drops of laudanum. The Rheumatic Liniment will be of great service. To prevent vomiting, drink peppermint tea, with a little bicarbonate of potass.

KING'S CAKE.—The finest flour, 5 lbs.; salt, $1\frac{1}{2}$ teaspoonful; cinnamon, $\frac{1}{2}$ oz.; nutmeg, $\frac{1}{4}$ oz.; mace, 1 drachm; all finely powdered. Add 14 ozs. of sugar, and gradually work well into the mass $1\frac{1}{2}$ lb. of fresh butter. Then add 6 eggs, a quart of cream, half a pint of good yeast, a $\frac{1}{4}$ pint of sherry wine, and two table-spoonfuls of orange water. All must be mixed and kneaded well together. After it has stood a little, knead in 2 lbs. of clean-picked raisins stoned and chopped, and 2 or 3 lbs. of currants. Bake for three hours in a gentle oven; when baked, rub the surface with white of an egg and rose-water, and sift over it finely powdered sugar.

KING'S EVIL.—See *Scrofula.*

KINO.—It is the concrete juice of an Indian tree. It is a powerful astringent similar to catechu. It is applied externally to ulcers, and is used as a gargle for relaxed uvula, sore throat, &c. It is good for relax, whites, and internal bleedings. The dose of the gum is from 10 grains to half a drachm;

of the tincture from one to two drachms.

KISSES.—Boil the same as barley sugar, and flavour with lemon juice and a few drops of essence of lemon; after which let it boil a little. Drop it on a slab, nearly the size of a shilling. When cold, put them into sifted white sugar in a dish; shake them, and fold them singly in papers, with mottoes, if you like.

Another.—Beat the whites of five eggs till they stand alone. Mix gradually with this 1¼ lb. of the finest sifted white sugar, and 15 drops of essence of lemon; beat the whole well. Lay a sheet of stiff writing paper at the bottom of a baking tin; drop upon it at equal distances, a small teaspoonful of stiff raspberry, currant, apricot, or pine apple jelly, and then cover the same over with the white of egg and sugar. Do it so evenly that the kisses may be quite smooth and compact. Place in a cool oven, and when coloured, take out, and place the flat parts of each together. Put lightly on a sieve, and dry in a cool oven.

KITCHEN PEPPER.—Mix in the finest powder one ounce of ginger; of cinnamon, cayenne pepper, black pepper, nutmeg, and Jamaica pepper, half an ounce each; ten cloves, and six ounces of salt. Keep it in a bottle; it is an agreeable addition to any brown sauces or soups.

KITCHENER'S RELISH.—Cayenne pepper, ginger, black pepper, and salt, of each 1 oz.; ground allspice, 1½ oz.; horseradish and shalots, 1 oz. each, well minced; walnut pickle, and mushroom ketchup, 1 pint each. Add ground mace and cloves, ¼ oz. each. Infuse for 15 days.

KNIFE BOARD.—Cover a smooth board with thick buff leather on both sides. For one side melt sufficient mutton suet; apply it hot to the leather, and sprinkle it with fine emery and bath brick, smoothing it down with a knife. Use the other side for polishing off, using three parts of powdered charcoal, and one part of Bath brick, or rotten-stone. *Gu.*

To clean steel forks, fill a small oyster barrel with fine gravel, brick-dust, or sand, mixed with a little hay or moss: make it damp, press it well down, and always keep it damp. By running the prongs of the forks a few times into this, they will be cleaned and polished. To polish between the prongs have a small stick shaped like a knife, covered with leather, and use emery powder. Emery powder might be mixed with the sand in the barrel to render it more efficient in knife cleaning.

KNIVES, HANDLES OF, *to fasten.*—Melt resin, add brick-dust and mix well together. This is a very good cement for this and other purposes.—-Shellac, and prepared chalk, intimately mixed, answer well. Heat the part to be inserted, and fill the aperture with the mixture. Press it in.

KRINGLES.—Beat well the yolks of eight, and whites of two eggs, and mix with 5 ozs. of butter warmed; with this knead 1 lb. of flour, and 5 ozs. of sugar to a paste. Roll into thick biscuits, prick and bake them on tin plates.

LACE, *White, to wash.*—Wash it the same way as Chintz. See *Chintz.*

LACQUER FOR BRASS.—Seed-lac, 6 ozs.; amber, or copal, well ground, 2 ozs.; dragon's blood, 40 grains; extract of red sandal wood, 30 grains; saffron, 36 grains; pounded glass, 4 ozs.; pure alcohol, 40 ozs. Expose the article to a gentle heat, and dip it into the varnish two or three times. This varnish is durable, beautiful in colour, and may be cleaned with water and a bit of dry rag.

LACQUER, *Pale, for Tin-plate.*—Best alcohol, 8 ozs.; turmeric, 4 drs.; hay saffron, 2 scs.; dragon's blood, 4 scs.; red sanders, 1 sc.; shell lac, 1 oz.; gum sandarach, 2 drs.; gum mastic, 2 drs.; Canada balsam, 2 drs.; when dissolved add spirits of turpentine, 80 drops.

LACQUERED ARTICLES.—*Ormolu, candelabra, mosaic gold, gilt, jewelry, &c. to clean.*—Wash or brush them with soap and hot water. Dry and rub with wash leather. Acids must not be used.

Or, take rotton stone, 1 oz., finely powdered; oil, a teaspoonful; oxalic acid, 2 drachms; water sufficient to make into a paste.

LACQUER, *for philosophical instruments.*—Alcohol, 80 oz.; gutta percha, 3 ozs.; gum sandarach, 8 ozs.; gum elemi, 8 ozs.; dragon's blood, 4 ozs.; seed lac, 4 ozs.; terra merita, 3 ozs.; saffron, 8 grs.; pulverized glass, 12 ozs.

LAMB, *to choose.*—If the hind quarter and the knuckle be flexible, it is stale. If the neck-vein of a four quarter be of an azure colour, it is fresh; but if greenish or yellowish, the meat is nearly tainted. If the eyes are sunk, the head is not fresh.

LAMB, *Breast of, and Cucumbers.*—Cut off the chine-bone from the breast, and set it on to stew with a pint of gravy. When the bones will draw out, put it on the gridiron to grill; and then lay it in a dish on cucumbers nicely stewed.

LAMB CHOPS, *en casserolle.*—Cut a loin of lamb into chops; do them with yoke of egg on each side and stew them with bread crumbs, cloves, pepper, salt, mace, mixed; fry them of a light brown, and put them round in a dish very close; leave a hole in the middle to put the sauce in, made of sweet herbs and parsley shred fine, and stewed in good thick gravy. Garnish with parsley.

LAMB, *fore quarter of, to roast.*—Roast it either whole, or in separate parts. It should be roasted before a brisk fire, or done in the oven. While roasting baste well with butter. If left to be cold, chopped parsley should be sprinkled over it. The neck and breast together are called a scoven.

LAMB, *fore quarter of, to ragout.*—Take off the knuckle bone, and cut off all the skin. Lard well with bacon, and fry it to a nice brown; put it into a stewpan, and just cover it with gravy, sweet herbs, pepper, salt, ground mace, and a little whole pepper; cover and stew half an hour; strain off the gravy, and have ready half a pint of fried oysters; pour off the fat, and put them into the gravy with two spoonfuls of port wine, a few mushrooms, and a little butter rolled in flour. Boil all together with the juice of half a lemon. Pour the sauce over the lamb.

LAMB'S FRY.—Should be scalded a moment; then soaked one hour in vinegar, pepper, and salt, with parsley and shalots; then dip them in a thick batter, and fry to a good colour; serve with fried parsley.

To ragout, put them into a light braise, with small onions, thin slices of lard, sweet herbs, half a bay leaf, thyme, a glass of sherry, sufficient broth, pepper, and salt. Serve with any sauce, with fried bread round the dish.

To fricassee, Take the marrow out of the small bladders, and prepare a cream thus—a little flour, an egg, a chestnut pounded, rasped lemon, sugar and cream; make small paste cases; place the fry in them, and put them a moment into the oven. Boil the cream a moment before filling the bladders with it, and baste them over with eggs and cream.

LAMB'S HEAD *and* HINGE.—This part is best from a house-lamb; but any, if soaked in cold water, will be white. Boil the head separately till very tender. Have ready the liver and lights, three parts boiled and cut small; stew them in a little of the water in which they were boiled, season and thicken with flour and butter, and serve the mince round the head.

LAMB, LEG OF.—Should be boiled in a cloth to look as white as possible. The loin fried in steaks and served round, garnished with dried or fried parsley; spinach to eat with it; or dressed separately, or roasted.

LAMB, LEG OF, *to boil.*—Steep it half an hour in cold soft water, a cupful of vinegar, and a handful of salt having been mixed with the water; flour a thin white cloth, and wrap the leg in it, and boil it; add a bundle of sweet herbs. It will require boiling 1½ hour. Serve with spinach, or French beans. Garnish with parsley, and thin slices of lemon.

LAMB, *Leg of, to force.*—Slit the leg on the wrong side, and take out as much meat as possible, without cutting or cracking the outward skin. Pound this meat well with an equal weight of fresh suet; add 12 large oysters, and two anchovies boned, with salt, black pepper, mace, and nutmeg, and a little thyme and parsley, finely shred; beat all well together, and mix it up with the yolks of three eggs. Having filled the skin tight with this stuffing, sew it up very close. Fry the remainder of the stuffing to garnish the loin of lamb, which is to be fricasseed as chickens are done. Tie the stuffed leg with packthread to the spit, and roast. In the fricassee of lamb, add a little oyster liquor, and fried oyster.

LAMB, *a nice dish of.*—Take the best end of a neck of lamb, cut it into steaks, and chop each bone so short as to make the steaks almost round. Egg and strew with crumbs, herbs and seasoning; fry them of the finest brown: mash some potatoes with a little butter and cream, and put them into the middle of the dish raised high. Then place the edge of one steak on another with the small bone upward, all round the potatoes.

LAMB PASTY. — Bone the lamb, cut it into square pieces; season with salt, pepper, cloves, mace, nutmeg, and minced thyme; lay in some beef suet, and the lamb upon it, making a high border about it; then turn over the paste close, and bake it. When it is enough, put in some claret, sugar, vinegar, and the yolks of eggs, beaten together. To have the sauce only savoury, and not sweet, let it be gravy only, or the baking of bones in claret.

LAMB PIE.—Make a good puff paste; cut the meat into pieces; it is best from the loin, neck, or breast; some prefer the leg; lightly season with pepper, salt, mace, cloves, and nutmeg finely ground; place in the crust, with a few sweetbreads seasoned like the meat, (and, if you like, some oysters and forcemeat balls, hard yolks of eggs, and the tops of asparagus, first boiled green). Butter all over the pie, put on the lid, and place in a quick oven one hour and a half. Take a pint of gravy, and the oyster liquor, a gill of port wine, a little grated nutmeg, with the yolks of two or three eggs well beaten; stir one way all the time. When it boils pour it into the pie.

LAMB SAUCE.—Mix a little butter with shred parsley, shalots, and crumbs of bread, grated fine. Put the whole into a stew-pan with a cupful of good stock, and one of sherry; season with pepper, salt, &c. and squeeze a lemon into it.

LAMB, SHOULDER OF.—Bone a shoulder of lamb, and fill it up with forcemeat; braise it two hours over a slow stove. Take it up, glaze it; or it may be glazed only, and not braised. Serve with sorrel-sauce under the lamb.

LAMB STEAKS.—Fry them of a beautiful brown; when served, throw over them a good quantity of crumbs of bread fried, and crimped parsley.

Mutton or lamb steaks, seasoned and broiled in buttered capers, either with crumbs and herbs, or without, are a genteel dish, and eat well.

LAMB STEAKS, *to dress white*.—Stew them in milk and water till very tender, with a bit of lemon-peel, a little salt, pepper, and mace. Have ready some veal gravy; put the steaks into it; mix some mushroom-powder, a cup of cream, and a bit of flour; shake the steaks in this liquor, stir, and get hot. Just before taking it up, put in a few white mushrooms.

LAMB STEAKS, *to dress brown*.—Season with pepper, salt, nutmeg, grated lemon-peel, and chopped parsley; but dip them first into egg: fry them quick. Thicken some good gravy with a bit of flour and butter; and add to it a spoonful of port wine, and some oysters; boil it up, and then put in the steaks warm: let them heat up, and serve. You may add palates, balls, or eggs, if you like.

LAMB-STONES, *fricasseed*.—Skin and wash, then dry and flour them; fry brown in hog's lard. Lay them on a sieve before the fire till you make the sauce: thicken half a pint of veal gravy with a little flour and butter, adding a slice of lemon, a large spoonful of mushroom ketchup, a tea-spoonful of lemon pickle, a grate of nutmeg, and the yolk of an egg beaten in two large spoonfuls of thick cream. Put this over the fire, and stir till it is hot, and looks white; but don't let it boil, or it will curdle. Then put in the fry, and shake it about near the fire for a minute or two. Serve in a hot dish and cover.

LAMB-STONES, *and Sweet breads*.—Blanch some lambstones, parboil, and slice. Flour two or three sweetbreads; if very thick, cut them in two. Fry all together with a few oysters, of a fine brown. Pour the butter off; and add a pint of good gravy, some asparagus-tops, a little nutmeg, pepper, and salt, two shalots shred fine, and a glass of white wine. Simmer ten minutes; then put a little of the gravy to the yolks of three eggs well beaten, and by degrees mix the whole. Turn the gravy back into the pan, and stir it till of a fine thickness without boiling. Garnish with lemon.

LAMB'S SWEETBREADS—Blanch them, and put a short time into cold water. Put them into a stew-pan with a cupful of broth, pepper, salt, a bunch of small onions, and a blade of mace; stir in it a bit of butter and flour, and stew half an hour. Have ready two or three eggs well beaten in cream, and a little minced parsley and nutmeg. Put in some boiled asparagus-tops. Do not boil after the cream is in; but make it hot, and stir all the while. Take great care it does not curdle. Young French beans or peas may be added, first boiled of a beautiful colour.

LAMB'S HEAD and PLUCK.—Wash clean; take the black part from the eyes, and the gall from the liver. Put into warm water, boil the heart, liver, &c.; serve.

LAMPREYS, *to stew.*—Clean the fish, remove the cartilage which runs down the back, and season with a little clove, mace, nutmeg, pepper, and allspice; put it into a stew-pot with strong beef-gravy, port, and an equal quantity of Madeira, or sherry. Cover close: stew till tender, take out the lamprey and keep hot, while you boil up the liquor with three anchovies chopped, and some flour and butter; strain the gravy, and add lemon juice, and mustard. Serve with sippets of bread and horse radish.

Eels done in the same way, are much like the lamprey. When there is spawn it must be fried and put round.

LANDLORD AND TENANT.—A yearly tenant must give notice to quit his premises half a year before the time of the expiration of the current year of his tenancy. If by agreement, a quarter's notice is to be sufficient, such notice must always expire with the tenancy if that is yearly.—If a landlord neglects to repair the premises, according to his covenant, the tenant may maintain an action against him; but such neglect does not absolve the tenant from payment of the rent.—A landlord can legally dispose of goods taken under a distress for rent, by appraisement, without putting them up by auction.—A landlord may take possession of the goods of his tenant's lodger which have been distrained under distress for rent; or he may maintain an action for pound breach.——A landlord can be compelled, according to the Small Tenement Act, to pay the poor rates, if the rent is under £10 per annum.—If a landlord agrees to make repairs, and neglects to do so, the tenant may do it, and deduct the amount from the rent. But the tenant must give previous notice of these repairs to the landlord; the notice to be signed by himself and a witness.—If the landlord has to pay the rates, an agreement properly witnessed and signed, should be drawn up to that effect.—The payment of the rent of a house, or building of any kind is absolute, if the landlord demands it; even though the house fall down, be blown, or burnt down, the tenant is bound to pay the rent; and the tenancy can only cease by giving the proper Notice to Quit, just as if the house continued in a perfect state. When the rent is paid, the landlord is bound to give the tenant a *receipt;*—thus,—— *Received of* Mr. John Thomas *the sum of* (here insert the amount) *for half year's rent due on the First day of May last, for the House, No,* ——*Street.* £— (Stamp) Robert Southey.

Landlord's Notice to Tenant to Quit;—Sir, I hereby give you Notice to quit the house (or workshop, warehouse, as the case may be) and appurtenances, which you, as tenant, now hold of me, situate No.—, ——Street, on or before ——next.

(Signed) T. C. landlord.
To Mr. W. S.

Notice to Quit of Tenant to Landlord:—Sir, I hereby give you notice, that on or before the—— day of——next, I shall quit and deliver up possession of the house and premises (or workshop, or warehouse, as the case may be) I now hold of you, situate at―――― in the parish of―――― in the county of――――.

Dated the――day of――, 186
Witness, Job Clark.   P. R.
To Mr. C. S.

☞ If the rent is payable quarterly, or half yearly, six month's notice to quit must be given; the notice to expire on the same day of the year when you took the house, warehouse, &c. Suppose you took a house the first day of May; then you must give notice a day or two before the first of November, for then the six months' notice will expire on the same day of the year on which you took it, viz. on the first day of May.

Leases for less than three years are often made by word of mouth. But in all cases it is best to have a written agreement; for sometimes the words of a mutual agreement may be forgotten, or be misconstrued on account of imperfect remembrance.

All Leases for terms above three years must be by deed of agreement, upon stamped paper, and properly signed and witnessed. It is best to have this deed made by a solicitor. The tenant should specially inquire if the landholder is the freeholder, or if he is merely a *tenant by lease*, and is about only to *sub-let* it. If so, he should inquire if the rent has been regularly paid, and also the rates and taxes, either by himself, if he has it on lease, or by the previous lessee.

In cases where a landlord leases or lets a furnished house, it is sometimes customary to receive from the tenant, and his surety, a bond for the due performance of the covenant or agreement, stipulations, and for the payment of rent:—for, being a furnished house, he cannot enforce the payment of the rent by distraint.

When a house is let from year to year, and then sublet, the incoming sub-tenant must inquire if the rent to the chief landlord, the queen's taxes, and the local rates, have been duly paid, for he will be answerable for any arrears.

If a lessee holds possession after the expiration of his term, he is, until he has paid rent subsequently due, merely a tenant by sufferance, and may be dispossessed at any moment; but as soon as he has paid, and the landlord has received any such rent, he constitutes himself a tenant from year to year, and can legally give, and must legally receive, a proper notice to quit.

In respect to Lodgers, any goods taken upon the premises by the Lodger will be liable for rent, taxes, and rates; and he should therefore be very careful to inquire whether all due up to the time of his taking have been duly paid. The Landlord has power to distrain upon the goods of his Lodger, and has also a perfect right to break open any of his Lodger's doors to seize and execute distress upon his goods—he cannot without such regular distraint detain the property of his Lodger. The keeper of an inn, hotel, or public-house has a legal right to, and may detain the goods of a Lodger till the rent is paid.

If the lodgings be taken monthly, a month's notice is required on either side; if three months, or six months, then a three or six month's notice will be required.

A Lodging-house keeper cannot forcibly eject, or by a policeman, a lodger who is determined to remain after the expiration of his term, or the expiration of the time properly specified in a notice to quit. But, during his Lodger's temporary absence, he may fasten up the doors of the rooms he occupied, to prevent his occupation of them; but the Landlord is bound, on the return of the tenant, to deliver any property he has left there. But if a Lodger leave his rooms without paying all demands upon him the Landlord may sell any property the Lodger may have left behind him, after giving the owner sufficient notice of his intention to do so. A fortnight's notice is sufficient.

All chattels and personal effects found on the demised premises may be distrained, whether they belong to the tenant or a stranger.

Fixtures cannot be distrained, though the tenant may have fixed them; yet the landlord may claim those which are incorporated with the building.

Cloth sent to a tailor's to be made into clothes, or old clothes sent to be repaired, warps and weft sent to be woven, dresses to make or alter, a horse sent to be shod, books to bind, paper to print, corn to grind, watches to be repaired, shoes to mend, &c., &c.; these are not to be distrained.

No distress can be made till the day after that on which the rent falls due; it cannot be made between sunset and sunrise; nor after the rent has been tended. Goods removed to avoid distraint, may be followed and seized within thirty days, wherever they may be found, unless *really* bought by some person ignorant of the fraud. Goods fraudulently secreted, the landlord may with a peace officer, break open any house, warehouse, &c., where they are secreted, and distrain the said property.

A landlord cannot legally distrain for more rent than is due to him; but if the amount of the first distraint does not cover the amount of rent due, he can distrain again. Or should the distraint be postponed by mutual agreement, the landlord can still distrain.

The outer door of the house, except where goods have been fraudulently removed, cannot be broken open. But if the outer door has been passed, the inner doors may be forced. Should the landlord, or his agent, or both, after they have legally entered the premises, and having begun to distrain, be forcibly ejected, they may break upon the outer door, and re-enter to distrain. Should they be violently treated, or threatened with violence, they may legally call in the aid of a policeman.

An inventory of the goods distrained must be taken; the amount of rent for which they are distrained, the day on which they were distrained, and the costs. A copy of this inventory must be served upon the tenant, or must be left at the house, shop, warehouse; or be posted up on some prominent place on the premises. The goods may then be removed to any convenient place for sale, which may take place five days after.

LAVENDER.—A well-known plant. It is a pleasant and efficacious cordial, and very useful in languor, weakness of the nerves, lowness of spirits, faintings, &c.

It should be propagated by slips in March: plant them in a shady situation till they have taken root, after which they may be exposed to the sun, and when strong may be transplanted.

LAVENDER WATER.—Put in a bottle half a pint of spirit of wine, and two drachms of oil of lavender. Mix with it rose water, five ounces, orange flower water, two ounces; also two drachms of essence of musk, and six ounces of distilled water.

LAVENDER, *Compound Spirit of.*—Spirit of lavender, 1½ lb.; spirit of rosemary, 1 lb.; cinnamon, ¼ oz.; nutmeg, ¼ oz.; red sanders, 2 drachms; digest for 10 days, and then strain off. It is taken from 40 to 80 drops upon loaf sugar, in cases of lowness of spirits, &c.

LAX *in the bowels, with pain.*—Laudanum, 24 drops; spirituous cinnamon water, half a gill; if it cannot be got, use French Brandy. Take a table-spoonful at a time.—See *Bowel Complaint.*

LAXATIVE POWDER *for Horses.*—Crocus of antimony, finely levigated, nitre, cream of tartar, and flower of sulphur, of each 4 ozs. Powder and mix well together. A table-spoonful of this mixture may be given every night and morning a few times, in a mash of scalded bran, or a feed of corn moistened with water. This powder is good for horses kept on dry meat; and for stallions in the spring, as they keep the body cool and open, and cause them to cast their coat, and make his skin as bright as silk.

LEATHER, *to clean.*—Uncoloured leather may be cleaned by applying a solution of oxalic acid with a sponge. Dissolve in warm water.

LEATHER-BOTTOMED CHAIRS, *to restore the blackness of.*—Take two yolks of eggs, and the white of one. Beat well, and shake in a bottle to make them thick like oil. Dissolve in a table-spoonful of spirits of wine, lump-sugar the size of a walnut. Thicken it with ivory-black, mix with the egg for use. Lay on with a brush; after a few minutes polish with a *soft clean* brush, till dry and shining. Let it stand a day to harden.

Shoes also may be done in the same way.

LEATHER, *to join.*—Gutta percha, ½ lb.; india rubber, 2 ozs.; pitch 1 oz.; shellac, ½ oz.; boiled oil, 1 oz. Melt together, and use hot.

LEATHER, *to make waterproof.*—Dissolve gutta percha, and india rubber in wood naptha. Rub over the soles and upper leather.— Or, melt boiled linseed oil, a pint; mutton suet, 1 lb.; bees wax, ¾ lb.; resin, ½ lb. Melt all together, and apply.

LEEK AND PILCHARD PIE. —Clean and skin the white part of some large leeks; scald in milk and water, and put them in layers into a dish, and between the layers, two or three salted pilchards which have been soaked for some hours the day before. Cover the whole with a good plain crust. When the pie is taken out of the oven, lift up the side crust with a knife, and empty out all the liquor; then pour in half a pint of scalded cream.

LEGS, *Sore and Running.*—Wash them in brandy, and apply elder leaves, changing twice a-day. This will dry up all the sores, though the legs were like a honeycomb.—Tried.

Or, poultice them with rotten apples.—Tried. But take also a purge or two every week.

LEMON BISCUITS.—Beat the yolks of 10 eggs, and the whites of 5, with 4 spoonfuls of orange flower water, till they froth up, then put in 1 lb. of sifted loaf sugar; beat it one way for 40 minutes; add ½ lb. of flour with the raspings of two lemons, and the pulp of a small one; butter the tin, and bake in a quick oven carefully. Dust with sugar before placing in the oven.

LEMON BLANCMANGE.—

Isinglass, 1 part; water, 16 parts; lemon-juice, 2 parts; Lisbon wine, 8 parts. Sugar to sweeten, and a little grated lemon-peel to flavour. Clarify with an egg.

LEMON BRANDY.—Put 2 quarts of brandy to 3 quarts of water; take 2 lbs. of fine sugar, and 3 pints of milk. Pare 12 lemons thin; steep the peel in the brandy 12 hours, and squeeze the lemons upon the sugar; then put the water to it, and mix all the ingredients together. Pour the milk in boiling. Let it stand 24 hours, then strain, and bottle.

LEMON DRINK.—Water, 4 quarts; the juice of 10 lemons, loaf sugar, 2 lbs.; get the oil from the rinds by rubbing them with the sugar; mix; steep the rinds a day: then strain. *A. N.*

LEMON CAKE.—Put 3 spoonfuls of rose or orange-flower water to the whites of 10 eggs 3 ozs. of butter, a cupful of milk, and 1 lb. of white sifted sugar; beat them an hour with a whisk, and grate in the rind of a lemon. When well mixed, add the juice of half a lemon, and the yolks of ten eggs beaten smooth; stir in 1 lb. of flour; butter a pan, and bake it in a moderate oven for one hour.—Orange cakes may be made in the same way. ☞ Add a small bit of carbonate of soda to the milk, to prevent acidity.

LEMON CHEESECAKES.—Boil the peel of two large lemons; pound well, with ¼ lb. of loaf sugar, the yolks of six eggs, ½ lb. of fresh butter, and some curd beaten fine. Mix all together; lay a puff paste on the patty-pans; fill half full, and bake.

☞ Orange cheesecakes are done the same way; but the peel must be boiled in two or three waters to neutralize its bitter taste.

LEMON, *Conserve of.*—Grate the rind of a lemon into a saucer; squeeze the juice of the fruit over and mix it well together with a spoon; then boil some sugar very high, mix it in, and when of a due consistency, pour into moulds.

LEMON CREAM.—Take a pint of thick cream, and put to it the yolks of three eggs well beaten, 4 ozs. of fine sugar, and the thin rind of a lemon grated; boil; stir it till almost cold; put the juice of a lemon in a dish, or bowl, and pour the cream upon it, stirring it till quite cold. It is excellent when iced.

LEMON CREAM, *Yellow.*—Pare thin 4 lemons into a large cupful of water, and squeeze the juice on 7 ozs. of finely pounded sugar; beat the yolks of 9 eggs well; add the peels and juice beaten together for some time; then strain it into a block-tin sauce-pan; set it over a gentle fire, and stir it one way till thick, and scalding hot; but not boiling, or it will curdle. Pour it into jelly-glasses. A few lumps of sugar should be rubbed hard on the lemons before they are pared, or after, as the peel will be so thin as not to take all the essence, and the sugar will attract it, and give a better colour and flavour.

LEMON CREAM, *White.*—Is made the same as the above; only put the whites of the eggs in lieu of the yolks, whisking it well to froth.

LEMON CUSTARD.—Sherry wine, a pint; refined sugar, 1 lb.; the juice of two lemons, the rind of one pared thin, and the rind of the other boiled soft, and rubbed through a sieve; boil well. Take out the peel, and a little of the liquor; cool; pour the rest into the dish you design it for; beat four yolks and two whites of eggs; mix them with the cool liquor; strain them into the dish; stir well together; set on a slow fire to bake as a custard; when it is enough, grate the rind of a lemon over the top; brown it over with a salamander.

Another.—Beat up the yolks of 8 eggs till quite white; put to them a pint of boiling water, the rinds of two lemons grated, and the juice sweetened to taste; stir on the fire till thick enough; then add a glass of rich wine, and half a glass of brandy. Give the whole one scald, and put it into cups to be eaten cold.

LEMON DROPS.—Sifted loaf sugar, ½ lb.; squeeze 3 or 4 lemons over it; mix it well with a spoon, till it makes a thickish paste; then drop it upon writing paper about the size of a sixpence; place in a slightly warm oven to dry, and then remove from the paper.

LEMON DUMPLINGS.—Two table-spoonfuls of flour; bread crumbs, ½ lb.; beef suet, 6 ozs.; the grated rind of a large lemon; sugar, pounded, 4 ozs.; 4 eggs well beaten, and strained, and the juice of three lemons strained. Make into dumplings, and boil in a cloth one hour.

LEMON HONEY-COMB.—Sweeten the juice of a lemon to your taste, and put it in the dish that you serve it in. Mix the white of an egg that is beaten with a pint of rich cream, and a little sugar; whisk it, and as the froth rises put it on the lemon juice. Do it the day before it is to be used.

LEMON JELLY.—Clarify 2 ozs. of isinglass in 3 gills of water, add ¾ lb. of loaf sugar, and the rinds of 2½ lemons cut very thin, squeeze the juice of five lemons; strain through muslin, then stir into cool sugar and isinglass, take out the peel, boil five minutes, and when cool pour into moulds, and place in ice. In peeling lemons care should be taken not to cut below the colour.

LEMONS, *to preserve in jelly.* Cut a hole in the stalk part, the size of a shilling, and scrape out the pulp. Tie each separately in muslin, and lay in spring water two days, changing twice a day; then boil them tender on a slow fire. Keep them covered to the last. To every pound of fruit weigh two of double refined sugar, and one pint of water; boil the two latter together with the juice of the lemon to a syrup, clarify, skim well, and cool; then boil the fruit in the syrup half an hour; if not clear, do this daily till they are done.

Pare and core some green pippins, and boil in water till it tastes strong of them; don't break them; strain the water through a jelly-bag till clear; then to every pint put a pound of double-refined sugar, the peel and juice of a lemon, and boil to a strong syrup. Drain off the syrup from the fruit, and turning each with the hole upwards in a jar, pour the apple jelly over it. The bits cut out must go through the same process with the fruit. Cover with brandy paper.

LEMON JUICE, *to purify.*—Add 1 oz. of powdered charcoal to a quart of lemon juice; after standing 12 hours, filter the juice through fine muslin. It will keep good several years in a cellar, well corked in bottles, and the mucilage will fall to the bottom.

LEMON KALI.—Dry the following well; finest sugar, ½ lb.; citric acid, or tartaric acid, 4 ozs.; carbonate of soda, 6 ozs.; essence of lemon, 30 drops. Keep in a dry tightly corked bottle. A dessert-spoonful in a tumbler of water will make a pleasant beverage.

LEMON MARMALADE. — Rasp the lemons, cut out the pulp, then boil the rinds very tender, and beat fine in a marble mortar. Boil three pounds of loaf sugar in a pint of water, skim it, and add a pound of the rind; boil fast till the syrup is very thick, but stir it carefully: then put a pint of the pulp and juice, the seeds having been removed, and a pint of apple liquor; boil all gently until well jellied, which it will be in about half an hour. Put it into small pots.

Orange Marmalade may be done in the same way.

LEMON MINCE PIES. — Squeeze a large lemon, boil the outside till tender enough to beat to a mash, add to it three large apples chopped, and 4 ozs. of suet; currants, ¼ lb.; sugar, 4 ozs.; put the juice of the lemon and candied fruit, as for other pies. Make a short crust, and fill the patty pans as usual.

LEMON-PEEL CREAM.— Boil a pint of cream; when half cold, put in the yolks of 4 eggs; stir till cold; put on the fire with 4 ozs. of loaf sugar, a tea-spoonful of grated lemon-peel; stir till hot; take off the fire; when it is cold, put it into sweetmeat glasses. Lay paste-knots or lemon-peel, cut like long straws, over the tops of the glasses.

LEMON SYRUP.—Put 1½ lb. of loaf sugar to each pint of juice; add some of the peel; boil 10 minutes; then strain and cork it. It makes a fine beverage diluted, and is useful to flavour pies and puddings. *American.*

LEMON SYRUP, Common.— Citric acid, 2 ozs.; loaf sugar to syrup it; rub the sugar on 4 lemons to extract the oil. Add a wine-glassful of brandy to keep it, and also a little cinnamon. Water, sufficient for the purpose. *A. N.*

LEMON PICKLE.——They should be small, with a thick rind; rub them with flannel; slit them half down in four quarters, but not through to the pulp: fill the slits with salt hard pressed in, set them upright in a pan three days until the salt melts; turn them thrice a day in their own liquid, until tender; make enough pickle to cover them, of vinegar, the brine of the lemons, Jamaica pepper, and ginger; boil, and skim; when cold, put it to the lemons with 2 ozs. of mustard-seed, and three cloves of garlic to six lemons. Jar it, and cover closely.

LEMON PUDDING. — Beat the yolks of four eggs; add 4 ozs. of white sugar, the rind of a lemon being rubbed with some lumps of it to take the essence; then peel, and beat it in a mortar with 4 or 5 ozs. of butter warmed. Put a crust into a shallow dish, nick the edges, and put the above into it. When served, turn the pudding out of the dish.

Another.—Cut off the rind of three lemons; boil tender; pound them; and boil 1 lb. of nice biscuits in a quart of milk and cream; mix the lemon rind with them. Beat 12 yolks and 6 whites of eggs: melt ¼ lb. of fresh butter, and put in ½ lb. of sugar, and a little orange flower water. Mix all together; put it over the fire; stir till thick, and then squeeze in the juice of half a lemon. Put puff paste round the dish, and pour in the pudding. Cut candied sweetmeats, and strew them over. Bake about 45 minutes.

Another.—Blanch and beat 8 ozs. of Jordan almonds with orange flower water; add ½ lb. of butter, the yolks of 8 or 10 eggs, the juice of a large lemon, and half the rind grated; work them in a mortar till white; put puff paste in the dish; pour in the pudding, and bake half an hour.

LEMON PUFFS.—Beat and sift 1 lb. of refined sugar; put it into a bowl, with the juice of two lemons, and mix them together; beat the white of an egg to a high froth; put it into the bowl; put in 3 eggs with two rinds of lemon grated; mix it well up, and throw sugar on the buttered papers; drop on the puffs in small drops, and bake them in a moderately heated oven.

LEMON TARTS. — Pare the rinds of four lemons, and boil tender in two waters, and beat fine. Add to it 4 ozs. of blanched almonds, cut thin, 4 ozs. of lump sugar, the juice of the lemons, and a little grated peel. Simmer to a syrup. When cold, turn into a shallow tin tart dish, lined with a rich thin puff paste, and lay bars of the same over, and bake carefully.

LEMON WATER.—Put two slices of lemon, thinly pared, into a tea-pot, a little bit of the peel, and sugar, or a table-spoonful of capillaire; pour in a pint of boiling water, and stop it close two hours.

LEMON WHEY.—Pour into boiling milk as much lemon juice as will make a small quantity quite clear; dilute with hot water to an agreeable sharp acid, and sweeten as you like. *Ru.*

LEMON WINE.-Take 6 large lemons; pare off the rind thin; squeeze out the juice; steep the rind in the juice; and put to it a quart of brandy; let it stand closely covered three days; then squeeze 6 lemons more, and mix 2 quarts of spring water, and as much sugar as will sweeten the whole; boil the water, lemons, and sugar together; when cold, add a quart of sherry, the other lemons, and some brandy; mix them together; and run it through a flannel bag; let it stand two or three months. Bottle, cork well, and keep in a cool place.

LEMONADE.—Hot water, 2 quarts; 2 lemons, sliced; $\frac{1}{2}$ lb. of sugar; $\frac{1}{4}$ oz. of gum arabic. Strain through a flannel bag, and bottle off.

LEMONADE, *to be made the day before wanted,*-Pare 24 lemons thin, put 8 of the rinds into 3 quarts of hot water, and cover for four hours. Rub some fine sugar on the lemons to attract the essence, and put it into a bowl, into which squeeze the juice of the lemons. To it add $1\frac{1}{4}$ lb. of fine sugar, then put the water to the above. Some persons add boiling milk, 2 or 3 quarts, and strain; but this is optional.

LEMONADE, *concentrated.*— Take 2 lbs. of loaf sugar, break it up, and pour on it a pint of cold water; let it heat gradually, until it boils and is converted into syrup; add, while hot, 1 drachm of essence of lemon, and $\frac{1}{2}$ ounce of citric acid; a tablespoonful of this, added to a tumbler of water, makes a very pleasant drink.

LEMONADE, *Delicious Milk.* —Pour a pint of boiling water on six or eight ounces of loaf sugar, add a quarter of a pint of lemon juice, and half the quantity of good sherry wine, and a table-spoonful of brandy to keep it. Then add three quarters of a pint of cold milk, and strain the whole, to make it nice and clear.

This is an American receipt, and is much valued in that country.

LEMONADE, *like jelly.*—Pare two Seville oranges and six lemons thin, and steep them four hours in a quart of hot water. Boil $1\frac{1}{4}$ lb. of loaf sugar in three pints of water, and skim it. Add the two liquors to the juice of six China oranges, and twelve lemons; stir the whole well, and run it through a jelly-bag till clear. Then add a little orange-water, if you like the flavour, and, if wanted, more sugar. It will keep well if corked.

☞ Any of the above may be made EFFERVESCING by taking nearly half a tumbler of water, and dissolving in it 20 grains of carbonate of soda, and mixing with it the same quantity of lemonade.

LEMONADE POWDERS.—Citric acid 1 oz.; carbonate of soda, 1¼ oz.; 4 ozs. of powdered sugar. This fine dry lemonade will keep well. Powdered ginger, nutmeg, or cinnamon may be added, *ad libitum*. Put as much as you like into cold water. *Gu.*

LEMONADE, *superior*.—Pare as many lemons as you are likely to want; on the peels pour hot water, but more juice will be necessary than you need use the peels for. While infusing, boil sugar and water to a good syrup with the white of an egg whipt up; when it boils, pour a little cold water into it; set it on again, and when it boils up take off, and settle. Skim, and pour it clear from the sediment to the infusion, and the lemon juice, stir and taste it, and add as much more water as will make a very rich lemonade. Wet a jelly-bag, and squeeze it dry, then strain the liquor, which will be uncommonly fine.

LENITIVE ELECTUARY.—Senna, finely powdered, 8 ozs.; powdered coriander seed, 4 ozs.; tamarinds and prunes, of each, 1 lb.; figs, 1 lb.; mix the pulps and powders together, and with simple syrup, make into an electuary. A teaspoonful to be taken two or three times a day. It is an agreeable laxative for children, females, and delicate persons.—If a little sulphur be added, it will be a sovereign remedy for PILES.

LENT POTATOES.—Beat 4 ozs. of almonds, and 3 oz. of the bitter; blanch, and add a little orange flower water; butter, 8 ozs.; 4 eggs well beaten and strained; half a glass of raisin wine, and sugar to taste; beat all till very smooth, and grate in 3 nice biscuits, (Savoy). Make into balls with a little flour, the size of a chestnut; throw them into a stewpan of lard, and boil them in it to a yellow brown; drain; serve with sweet sauce.

LIGHTNING STROKE. —Dash cold water over the head and face, apply friction to the spine with strong liniment, and mustard poultices to the feet.

LIME LINIMENT.—Linseed or common olive oil and lime-water, equal parts, to be well shaken before using, is good for scrofulous or other sores, and still more for burns and scalds.

LIME WATER.—Put unslaked lime into a tub; cover it with pure water; stir often for one day; then strain off the water, and keep for use. It is an anti-acid tonic, kills worms, and frees the bowels from slimy and morbific matter. It promotes digestion; it is valuable in looseness, scrofula, diabetes, and whites. Mixed with a decoction of Peruvian bark, it wonderfully strengthens the debilitated, and those threatened with atrophy.

LINEAL MEASURE.
12 Inches make.. .. 1 Foot.
3 Feet, or 36 inches . 1 Yard.
2 Yards, or six feet . 1 Fathom
5½ Yds., or 16½ ft., 1 Rod, Pole, or Perch.

LINEN, *to preserve*.—Secure it from damp when you put it by; and also from insects by putting amongst it bags of lavender, roses, thyme, cedar shavings, &c.

LINIMENT, *for Burns.*—Take equal parts of Florence oil, or fresh drawn linseed oil and lime water; shake them well together in a wide bottle, so as to form a liniment. This is found to be an exceedingly proper application for recent scalds or burns. It may either be spread upon a cloth, or the parts affected may be anointed with it twice or thrice a day.

LINIMENT, *for diseases of the throat and tonsils.*—Castile soap, oil of sassafras, camphor, spirits of hartshorn, of each, 1 oz. Add cayenne pepper, 2 drachms; laudanum, ½ oz.; spirits of wine, ½ oz.

LINIMENT VOLATILE.—Spirit of hartshorn, 1 oz.; olive oil, 1½ oz.; cayenne pepper, 2 drs.; laudanum, 2 drachms; a tablespoonful of salt, and two of brandy. Shake well in a bottle. Rub the affected part with it, apply afterwards a rag saturated with it. It removes pains and swellings. It is a magic remedy.

LINIMENT, *White.*—This is made in the same manner as the white ointment, two-thirds of the wax being left out. This liniment may be applied in excoriation, where, on account of the largeness of the surface, the ointments with lead or calomel might be improper.

LINSEED, *infusion of.*—Take of linseed, two spoonfuls: liquorice root sliced, half an ounce; boiling water, three pints. Infuse by the fire for some hours, and then strain off the liquor.

If an ounce of the leaves of coltsfoot be added to the ingredients, it will then be the Pectoral Infusion. Both are emollient mucilaginous liquors, and may be taken with advantage as ordinary drink, in difficulty of making water, and in coughs and other complaints of the breast.

LINSEED TEA.—Linseed, 1 tablespoonful; liquorice root, ½ oz.; coltsfoot leaves, 1 oz.; boiling water, 3 pints. Infuse 3 hours, and strain. Add sugar, and a little lemon juice. Good for coughs, urinary disease, &c.

LIP SALVE, *Red.*—Olive oil, 4 ozs.; Alkanet root, 1 oz. Macerate with heat until the oil is well coloured; then add Spermaceti, ½ oz.; white wax, 2 ozs.; prepared suet, 3 ozs., and a little sugar. When nearly cold, stir in orange flower water, ¼ oz.; oil of lavender, ¼ drachm; otto of roses, 2 or 3 drops.

LIP SALVE, *White.*—Boil a little veal suet in salt and water; skim off the fat; mix it with 1 oz. of white wax, and ¼ oz. of spermaceti; add 3 ozs. of olive oil; melt, and when cool, add a few drops of bergamot, or otto of roses. The colour of lips may be deepened by dissolving in the mouth a cayenne lozenge occasionally.

LIPS, *chapped.*—See page 103.

LIQUID BLACKING.—Weak vinegar, 1 quart; ivory black and treacle, each 6 ozs.; vitriolic acid, and spermaceti, (or olive oil) each 1½ oz. Mix the acid and oil first, then add the other ingredients. If it does not dry quick enough on the leather, add a little more vitriol gradually till it dries quick enough. If you add too much the mixture will give a brown colour. —This is a celebrated blacking.

LIQUID JAPAN BLACKING.—Ivory black, 3 ozs.; coarse sugar, 2 ozs.; sulphuric acid, 1 oz.; muriatic acid, 1 oz.; sweet oil, and lemon acid, of each a tablespoonful, and a pint of vinegar. First mix the ivory black and sweet oil; then the lemon and sugar with a little vinegar; then add the acids, and mix well together.

LIQUID BLUE.—Dissolve extract of indigo in warm water.

LIQUID CHERRIES.—Cherries, 1 lb., to ¾ lb. of fine sugar. The cherries must be fine and ripe; cut the tails about half; put them into the sugar, and simmer five minutes; stand till next day; then add ¼ lb. of sugar to each pound of cherries, prepared as the first, and a little syrups or jelly, or red currants, or rasps. Simmer together till the syrup is glutinous.

LIQUID GLUE.—Best glue, 1 lb.; dry white lead, 4 ozs.; soft water, 1 quart; alcohol, 4 oz. Stir together when dissolved, and bottle while hot.

LIQUORICE PIPES.—Dissolve gum arabic in water with Spanish liquorice, and with the addition of sugar make into a paste. Drop, and dry them in a slow oven.

LIVER COMPLAINT.—Take 4 lbs. of Dandelion Roots, bruise and press out the juice; run it through a muslin bag, and bottle it. Of this take two table spoonfuls three or four times a day.

Drink occasionally the following decoction:—Take the bruised roots above mentioned, a small handful of Agrimony, and two ounces of Burdock Root, to three quarts of water—boil to two quarts. Of this take four half-pints a day.

LIVER, *Inflammation of.*—This disease generally begins with a sense of weight, or pain in the right side, about the false ribs. The pain often extends to the top of the right shoulder. The stomach and bowels are disordered; the appetite is impaired; the patient has sickness, often vomits bilious matter; there is a dry cough, oppressive breathing, a difficulty of lying on the right side; costiveness, emaciation, debility, hard and frequent pulse, and a sallow complexion.

The office of the liver is to secrete the bile, the origin of which is this:—the dark venous blood, passing through the liver on its way back to the heart, is there divested of its noxious matter, consisting largely of carbon, and so made fit for re-entering into the arterial circulation. A portion of the matter so separated from the blood is the *bile*, which is discharged into the duodenum, and there mixes with the digested food, and performs the important office of fitting it for absorption into the system. The bile thus mixed with the elements of nutrition is also absorbed, and it is probable that it is adapted and designed to support the processes of respiratory combustion. It is the bile that gives the colour to the fœces, which indicate a healthy flow of the bile when they are of the colour of rhubarb. When, owing to some functional derangement, the bile mixes with the blood in its circulation, it is indicated by yellowness of complexion, in jaundice, and by the symptoms previously described.

The healthy flow of bile is interrupted frequently by high living, obstructed perspiration, the drinking of wines, malt liquors, and especially ardent spirits, and dram drinking.

Dr. Graham judiciously observes; —"the term *liver complaint* is now far too indiscriminately used. It is properly applied to designate disease in the texture of the liver; but the majority of the maladies called by that name are in reality severe disorders of the digestive canal, that is, chronic affection of the stomach and intestines."

The symptoms which indicate affections of the liver, are increasing debility and emaciation, the pain and uneasiness at the right side extending to the shoulder, loss of appetite, full and hard pulse, &c. But in digestive disease, the loss of flesh is not so great, the breathing is not so laborious, and the pain is more in the region of the stomach.

Treatment.—The first thing to do is to lessen the undue determination of blood to the part by equalizing its circulation, and restoring the proper secretions. This will be effected by moderating the diet, living low, avoiding all stimulants, condiments, &c. Give the Vapour Bath, and the Sudorific Powders, to promote copious perspiration. Take gentle aperients; as, senna, manna, cream of tartar, and fennel seed. The bowels should be moved at least once a day. All *violent* purgatives are to be avoided; they must be *gentle*. In weak constitutions, a decoction of tamarinds, sweetened with manna, often answers the purpose; but if not sufficiently strong add a little senna. Mild laxative injections occasionally are of great service.

If there should be vomiting, mix supercarbonate of potash, 1 drachm, with half a pint of peppermint water; and take a table-spoonful whenever the vomiting returns. If the pain is severe, foment the side with a hot decoction of bitter herbs, as hops, &c.; or the Anodyne Fomentation; or apply the Stimulating Liniment. A poultice made of bran, or oatmeal, with a little mustard and cayenne pepper, and mixed with vinegar, and formed into a plaster or poultice, will be found to be invaluable.--A mustard plaster is also applicable, and answers better than a blister plaster, though it may be applied if the pain be obstinate; give also ten grains of the Diaphoretic Powders, for they allay pain, and promote sleep. If the sickness and irritation of the stomach continue, give an emetic, and repeat every day, if necessary.

Medicines which promote the secretion of urine have a very good effect here. (See Diuretic Drops, &c.) Or, take ½ dr. of purified nitre; or a teaspoonful of sweet spirits of nitre in gruel or balm tea three or four times a day. Continue this treatment till the symptoms are subdued.

Chronic disease of the liver arises chiefly from the induration and torpidity of the liver; therefore the object must be to correct the disordered state of the stomach and bowels, and to give tone and activity to the liver. This may be effected by the Vapour Bath, Emetics, and sponging the body with the Stimulating Liniment; by the use of the Liver Pill, or Dyspeptic Pill, &c., which see. Apply to the painful part the Irritating Plaster.

LIVER PILL.—-One ounce each of powdered blood-root, powdered mandrake, and extract of dandelion, to which add 2 drachms of powdered senna. Add a few drops of oil of spearmint, or peppermint, and form into pills. Take two or three night and morning. This pill is a *sovereign remedy* for inflammation of the liver, and for jaundice.

LIXIVIUM, *of Pearl-ashes.*—Steep ½ oz. of pearl-ashes in clear water 24 hours. Then strain off the water. This infusion is very useful in many colours, especially Brazil wood, which it will render beautiful in lustre.

LOBELIA.—An American plant, containing most valuable medical properties. It was first used with great advantage, as an emetic, by the American Indians, and was brought into notoriety by Dr. Samuel Thompson. It is emetic and stimulating, and Dr. Beech says, "from its action on the great sympathetic nerve, its effect is felt throughout the whole system. It exerts a peculiar action upon the trachea and bronchial vessels, expelling all collected mucus." It must therefore be very valuable in asthma, croup, hooping cough, and consumption. The greatest benefit from it has been found in dyspepsia, coughs, asthma, liver complaints, &c. It has relieved asthmatic subjects when on the point of suffocation by accumulated phlegm, cough, &c. Also in pneumonia of infants.

It is also a valuable sudorific; it relaxes the constricted pores of the skin, and promotes free perspiration. The leaves, seeds, and seed-vessels may be given in powder, and tincture. Dose of the powder, from a drachm, or a small teaspoonful; of the tincture, a teaspoonful.

LOBELIA POULTICE.—Linseed meal, ¼ oz.; slippery elm, 1 oz.; powdered lobelia, 1½ oz.; ginger, 1 oz.; whiskey sufficient to make it. Good for all inflamed parts, as the side in pleurisy, liver complaints, rheumatism, lumbago.

LOBELIA TINCTURE.—Put 1 oz. of the powdered plant to 1 quart of whiskey. Infuse 7 days. Dose, a teaspoonful when the cough is troublesome.

LOBELIA, *Acid Tincture of.*—Lobelia herb, 1 oz.; Cayenne, 2 drs.; Vinegar, half a pint. Boil the vinegar, and put all into a bottle, cork well for 7 or 8 days. Dose for a cough, half a teaspoonful in any pleasant vehicle. Repeat when the cough is troublesome. It will require a larger dose for asthma or croup.

LOBELIA WATER.—Lobelia leaves and capsules, or powder 1 oz.; boiling water ½ pint; brandy ¼ pint. Infuse a week.—Good for sore and inflamed eyes, erysipelas, ringworm, &c.

LOBSTERS, *buttered.*—Pick the meat out, cut it, and warm with a little weak brown gravy, nutmeg, salt, pepper, and butter, with a little flour. If done white, a little white gravy and cream.

LOBSTER, *Curry of.*—Take them from the shells, and lay into a pan, with a small piece of mace, three or four spoonfuls of veal gravy, and four of cream; rub smooth one or two teaspoonfuls of curry-powder, a teaspoonful of flour, and an ounce of butter: simmer an hour; squeeze half a lemon in, and add salt.

LOBSTER, *to pot.*—Half boil them, pick out the meat, cut it into small bits, and season with mace, white pepper, nutmeg, and salt; press close into a pot, and cover with butter, bake half an hour; put the spawn in. When cold, take the lobster out, and put it into the pots with a little of the butter. Beat other butter in a mortar with some of the spawn; then mix that coloured butter with as much as will be sufficient to cover the pots, and strain it. Cayenne may be added, if approved.—Or, take out the meat as whole as you can; split the tail and remove the gut; if the inside be not watery, add that. Season with mace, nutmeg, white pepper, salt, and a clove or two in the finest powder. Lay a little fine butter at the bottom of a pan, and the lobster smooth over it, with bay-leaves between; cover it with butter, and bake gently. When done, pour the whole on the bottom of a sieve; and with a fork lay the pieces into potting-pots, some of each sort, with the seasoning about it. When cold, pour clarified butter over, but not hot. It will be good next day; or if highly seasoned, and thick covered with butter, will keep some time.

Potted lobster may be used cold,

or as a fricassee, with a cream-sauce; it then looks very nicely, and eats excellently, especially if there is spawn.

LOBSTER, *to roast.*—When you have half boiled the lobster, take it out of the water, and while hot, rub it with butter, and lay it before the fire. Baste it with butter till it has a fine froth.

LOBSTER SAUCE.—Cut a lobster into pieces, the size of a dice; pound the spawn, a little butter, and four anchovies in a mortar, and rub them through a hair sieve; put the cut lobster into a stewpan with half a pint of gravy, and a bit of butter rolled in flour; set over a slow fire, and stir till it boils; if not thick enough, add a little flour and water, and boil again; put the spawn in and simmer it; if the spawn boils, it may spoil the colour of the sauce. Add a little lemon pickle.

LOCKED JAW, *Tetanus.*—A disease in which the muscles of the body are in a state of rigidity, with occasional spasms, and excruciating pain. The cause of this disease is injury done to the extremities of the nerves, punctured or lacerated wounds of the hands or feet, surgical operations, or the use of narcotic poisons.

The muscles of the lower jaw become hard and contracted, the mouth is closed, and the patient cannot open it; hence the name *locked jaw.* The rigidity extends to the tongue and throat, causing great difficulty in swallowing. Sometimes nearly the whole body is affected with the spasms. There is constriction of the breast, severe spasmodic pain in the stomach, shooting to the spine; the face is hideously distorted, and the breathing very laborious. It is a dangerous disease, and requires prompt skilful attention.

Treatment.—When the disease is caused by wounds, they should be cleaned, and the inflammation subdued as soon as possible. If possible foment or steam over with bitter herbs, and steep in hot soap water several times a day. Then apply a poultice of slippery elm mixed with ley or milk, and put on warm. Promote perspiration by means of the vapour bath, or place hot bricks wrapped in vinegar cloths to the feet and sides. Repeat if needful. Pour into the mouth a teaspoonful of the Antispasmodic Tincture every ten minutes until the muscles of the jaws relax to enable the patient to swallow. Give a tea made of balm and catnep. These means have often been effectual. Add more cayenne to the Antispasmodic Tincture if the rigidity does not give way. An aperient or injection will also be necessary. The latter may embrace a strong decoction of lobelia, milk, treacle, sweet oil, and a little Antispasmodic Tincture.

LOGWOOD, *an antiseptic.*—Dr. Desmartis, in a paper to the Academy of Sciences, announces that *Campeachy Logwood* (Hœmatoxylum Campeachianum) possesses the same valuable quality, and in a much higher degree, than coal, tar and plaster, or creasote, which have hitherto been esteemed as the best antiseptics. The fact was discovered by accident. Dr. Desmartis had several cancerous patients under his care, all presenting large ulcerous sores, emitting a most nauseous smell. An astringent being considered expedient, a pomatum composed of equal parts of extract of logwood and hog's lard, was applied to those sores, whereupon, to the Doctor's surprise, the fœtor disappeared completely, and the emission of pus was considerably attenuated. To complete the evidence, he suspended the use of the pomatum for a few hours only, when the offensive emanations immediately recommenced, and the purulent secretion became again abundant. Logwood causes gangrene to disappear as if by enchantment, especially that of hospitals. He has also found it efficacious in preventing or stopping erysipelas, which often occurs after amputation, or the infliction of other wounds, and is a source of constant anxiety to the surgeon. It entirely removes the putridity of ulcerous cancers, emitting characteristic effluvia, and in short, of the most fœtid sores. This substance also possesses the advantage of being capable of mixture with hœmostatic medicines, (designed to arrest spitting of blood, &c.,) such as ergotine, perchloride of iron, persulphate of iron, &c.; it may also be used as a powder and a lotion. The extract of logwood, which is much used in dyeing, and is very cheap, is only soluble in warm water.—See *Robinson's Herbal.*

LOO.——Amongst all round games Loo deservedly occupies the most prominent position; and being the most interesting, is generally played. It is a game so generally known as to require little comment; and so easily learnt, that a thorough knowledge of the game may be obtained in half an hour's play.

There are two kinds of Loo, "limited Loo," in which the person looed has to pay a certain amount as previously agreed to, and "unlimited Loo," in which the party looed pays whatever amount may be on the table at the time he was looed.

The method of playing, however, is precisely the same in both games, and is as follows:—

The whole pack of cards are used, as at whist, and rank in the same order; the deal is cut for, and when decided, the dealer pays a stake previously agreed upon: he then gives three cards (one at a time,) to each person playing; he also deals a spare hand called "miss," which the elder hand has the option of taking if his own cards do not suit him; each person looks at his cards in rotation, beginning with the elder hand and finishing with the dealer; and each in his turn may take miss (so long as she remains untaken), if his own cards do not please him.

It is optional whether you stand your own hand or not; but if you take "miss," you are compelled to stand: if there is only one player standing before him, the dealer is compelled to stand.

Laws of the Game.—1. If you hold your trumps or more in your hand, lead one; if only two players, lead the highest.

2. If you hold ace of trumps, you must lead it, but if not leader, you are not compelled to play it unless you can head the trick otherwise.

3. If you cannot follow suit, you must play a trump if you have one.

4. After taking a trick you must play a trump.

5. The cards after dealing must be taken up in rotation by the players, and no one to look at his cards until the one before him has declared whether he stands or not.

6. The dealer must not look at his cards until he has asked each player if he stands; and if there is but one player, he is forced to stand.

7. No one must play a card out of his regular turn, under penalty of being looed.

8. If the dealer makes a misdeal

he is looed, and the next player must take the deal.

9. Any one looking at "miss" is looed.

10. Any one making a revoke is looed; and even if he wins a trick, cannot claim it, but the cards must be taken up, and the hand played over again in the proper manner.

There is a kind of Loo played called five-card Loo, but it differs only from the three-card Loo in two or three points; namely, that the knave of trumps is the best card, and when held must be led as the ace; and secondly, that the dealer has the privilege of taking the turn-up card into his own hand, and discarding one from it.

LOOKING-GLASSES, to Silver.—Take a sheet of tinfoil, and spread it upon a table; then rub mercury upon it with a hare's foot till the two metals incorporate. Lay the plate of glass upon it, and load it with weights, which will have the effect of pressing out the excess of mercury that was applied to the tin-foil. In a few hours the tin-foil will adhere to the glass and convert it into a mirror. About two ounces of mercury are sufficient for covering three square feet of glass.

LOOKING-GLASSES, to Clean.—Sweep away the dirt with a soft brush, or silk handkerchief. Then sponge with a little spirit of wine, or gin and water, to remove all dust. Then dust with the finest whiting, or powder-blue. Then rub it quickly off with a cloth, and polish lightly with a silk handkerchief. The gilt frame may be cleaned with a little cotton wool.

LOTION VALUABLE.—Camphor, 5 drachms, cut into small pieces, and dissolve in half a pint of spirits of wine in a closely corked bottle; when fully dissolved, add half a pint of oxgall, and sixty drops of laudanum. Shake it well, and bottle for use.—This has been a patent medicine, and is very efficacious in the cure of fresh wounds, cuts, bruises, swellings, sores, and inflamed and pained parts.

LOZENGES.—Boil 3 lbs. of raw sugar in one pint of water, for an hour, over a slow fire; when boiled enough, it will snap like glass, by trying it in cold water; then pour it on your stone. When cold, make it into rolls, and cut it with scissors into small lumps, make them round and stamp them with a figure.

☞ Drop a little oil of peppermint into the sugar when boiled and poured upon the stone; it will give it a strong taste and smell of peppermint.

LOZENGES *for Fœtid Breath*.—Gum kino, ½ oz.; catechu, 1 oz.; white sugar, 3 ozs.; orris powder, ¾ oz. Make them into a paste with mucilage, and add a drop of neroli.

LUMBAGO.—It is a species of chronic rheumatism, which affects the muscles of the lower part of the back, causing great pain and stiffness. The patient can scarcely stir without having the most piercing pain. It may be confined to one side, or affect the loins generally. Its attacks are generally sudden, immediately after or in stooping, or rising from bed. Lumbago is connected with derangement of the stomach, of the bowels, and of the kidneys.

TREATMENT.—Take gentle aperients of Senna and Epsom Salts, with a little ginger. Drink freely of balm tea and other diluents. Great and sometimes immediate relief has been obtained by the Compound Colocynth Pill, combined with the Blue Pill. External applications are useful. Dip a flannel in hot water and apply to the affected part frequently. Or dip a flannel in hot water, and sprinkle with spirits of turpentine, and apply to the part as long as it can be endured. Or apply the Stimulating Liniment. The tincture of aconite is an excellent rubefacient; also the soap and opium liniment, with a few drops of spirits of turpentine. The diaphoretic powders are very useful. If the urine be deficient and high coloured, give 10 or 12 grains of carbonate of potassa with a teaspoonful of sweet nitre in a wineglassful of water twice a day.

LUMBAGO AND SCIATICA, *remedy for*.—Rectified oil of turpentine, 25 drops; vitriolic ether, 1 scruple; mucilage of gum arabic, 3 drs.; syrup of poppies, 1 dr.; rose-water, 1½ oz.; make into a draught; take at bed-time.

LUNCHEON CAKE.—Flour, 2 lb.; sugar, ½ lb.; currants, ½ lb.; butter, ¼ lb. beaten very fine; a few caraway seeds; nutmeg grated; milk, half a pint; half a teaspoonful of carbonate of soda; three or four eggs. Stir all together, beat them ten minutes, and bake in a tin.

LUNGS, *Inflammation of*.—Sometimes this disease affects one lobe of the lungs, and sometimes both. Males are more subject to it than females. Frequent colds, wet feet, intemperance, over exertion, and natural debility of the lungs induces this complaint.

It generally begins with cold shiverings, followed by hot fever, dull pains in the chest or side, cough, and very laborious breathing, the pulse is full and quick, the bowels are often constipated, the urine deficient, the skin dry and burning, the expectoration scanty, but is gradually increasing, and sometimes it contains blood. It is a very dangerous disease; as it may proceed with such violence as to cause an effusion of blood or lymph into the texture of the lungs, as to cause suffocation.

Treatment.—Avoid bleeding by the lancet. Dr. Beach says, "All the blood in the body must pass through the lungs, after reaching the heart, before it can be again circulated; but in this disease, they are unable to perform this double duty from the great amount which has been distributed to them. As these organs have become unduly loaded; impeding respiration, &c., the obvious indication is—instead of abstracting, or rather attempting it—to return it to its original channels, and thus remove the burden under which they labour. Bleeding will not affect this; but, on the contrary, it will so weaken or paralyze the heart, which is labouring to accomplish this object, that prostration, and often death, are the consequences."

Give sudorific medicines to produce free and copious perspiration; and for this purpose give a *vapour bath*, using an infusion of bitter herbs, as hops, camomile flowers, pennyroyal, tansy, catnep; add vinegar; cover, and infuse two or three hours. It should be repeated. If the patient cannot bear the fatigue of the bath, place hot bricks, or bottles, to the sides and feet. Give also *Sudorific Powders*, which see, until the breathing is relieved, and free perspiration induced. As soon as the patient is relieved, the bowels must be regulated by giving a gentle purge, and also an emetic; repeat, if necessary; continue the sudorific powders; as these means are calculated to unload the chest, and return the blood to its former state. Injections, where the fœces are hard, and the bowels lethargic, are of great importance, and should be given occasionally. If the cough is troublesome, give some of the *Cough Remedies*, or the *Expectorant Syrup*, or *Cough Pills*. The inhalation of the steam of bitter herbs while infusing in boiling water serves to decrease the tightness of the lungs, and to promote expectoration. This should be repeated several times a day.

Should there be much irritation, or spasmodic affection, use the *Pulmonary Syrup*. Bathe the feet occasionally in warm water. Mucilaginous drinks should be taken, as linseed, with a little lemon juice. An infusion of horehound, boneset, catnep, with slippery elm, sweetened with the finest sugar, or sugar-candy, is a very proper drink. Great attention must be paid to diet; it should be simple and easy of digestion; as arrow-root, sago, beef-tea, without or with little salt. When the inflammation is subdued, and the tongue is clean, give tonics, or the Composition Powder.

MACARONI, *dressed sweet.*—Boil 2 ozs. in a pint of milk, with a bit of lemon peel, and a good bit of cinnamon, till the pipes are swelled to their utmost size without breaking. Lay them on a custard-dish, and pour a custard over them hot. Serve cold.

MACARONI, *as usually served.*—Boil it in milk, or a weak veal broth, flavoured with salt. When tender, put it into a dish without the liquor, with bits of butter and grated cheese, and over the top grate more, and a little more butter. Put the dish into a Dutch oven a quarter of an hour, and do not let the top become hard.

Another way.—Wash it well, and simmer in half milk, and half broth of veal or mutton, till it is tender. To a spoonful of this liquor, put the yolk of an egg beaten in a spoonful of cream; just make it hot to thicken, but not boil: put it over the macaroni, and then grate fine old cheese all over, and bits of butter. Brown.

Another; Wash the macaroni, then simmer it in a little broth, with a little pounded mace and salt. When quite tender, take it out of the liquor, lay it in a dish, grate a good deal of cheese over, then cover that with bread grated fine. Warm some butter without oiling, and pour it from a boat through a little earthen colander over the crumbs; put the dish in a Dutch oven, to roast the cheese, and brown the bread of a fine colour. The bread should be in separated crumbs and look light.

MACARONI DROPS.—Pound some sweet almonds very fine, and a few bitter ones with them; add pounded sugar, and a few drops of orange flower-water, while pounding, to prevent oiliness; when done, mix with them their weight of sugar, and some whites of eggs, beaten four to each lb. of almonds and sugar; work well together; drop it upon white paper in small nuts, and bake in a gentle oven a *short* time.

MACARONI PUDDING. — Simmer 2 ozs. of the pipe sort in a pint of milk, and a bit of lemon and cinnamon, till tender; put it into a dish, with milk, two or three eggs, only one white, sugar, nutmeg, a spoonful of peach-water, and half a glass of raisin-wine. Bake with a paste round the edges.

A layer of orange marmalade, or raspberry jam, in a macaroni pudding, for change, is a great improvement; in which case omit the almond-water, or ratafia, with which you would otherwise flavour it.

MACARONI SOUP.—Boil 1 lb. of the best macaroni in a quart of good stock till tender; take out half, and put it into another stew-pot. To the remainder add more stock, and boil it till you can pulp all the macaroni through a fine sieve. To these two liquors put a pint or more of cream boiling hot, the macaroni that was first taken out, and half a pound of grated Parmesan cheese; make hot, but do not boil. Serve it with the crust of a French roll cut into bits the size of a shilling, or with nice crisp biscuits.

MACAROONS, *to make.* — Blanch 4 ozs. of almonds, and pound with four spoonfuls of orange flower-water; whisk the whites of four eggs to a froth, then mix it, and 1 lb. of sugar, sifted with the almonds to a paste; and laying a sheet of wafer-paper on a tin, put it on in different little cakes, the shape of macaroons.

MACAROON PIE, *raised.*— Raise, ornament, and bake a crust; have ready some hot macaroons, stewed, and a white fricassee of chickens, in separate stew-pans, and put them alternately on the fire; strew grated Parmesan cheese over it; put a slip of paper round the edge of the pie to prevent its burning. Brown the cheese, and serve it.

MACASSAR OIL, *to make.*— Take 3 quarts of olive oil, half a pint of spirits of wine, 3 ozs. of cinnamon powder, 2 ozs. of bergamot; put it into a large pipkin, and give it a good heat; take off the fire, and add ¼ oz. of alkanet-root, and keep it closely covered for several hours. Filter through blotting paper.

MACKEREL, *to boil.* — Rub them with vinegar; when the water boils, put them in with a little salt, and boil gently 15 minutes. Serve with fennel and parsley chopped, boiled, and put into melted butter, and gooseberry sauce.

MACKEREL, *to broil whole.*— Wash them clean, cut off their heads, and pull out their roes at the neck end. Boil them in a little water; bruise them with a spoon, beat up the yolk of an egg, a little nutmeg, a little lemon-peel cut fine, some thyme, some parsley boiled and chopped fine, a little salt and pepper, and a few crumbs of bread. Mix well together, fill the dish with them. Flour well, and broil. Serve with butter, ketchup, and walnut pickle. *Far.*

MACKEREL, *to collar.*—Gut and slit the mackerel down the belly; cut off the head; take out the bones; lay it on its back; season with mace, nutmeg, pepper, salt, and a handful of parsley shred fine; strew it over them; roll tight, and tie them separately in cloths; boil twenty minutes in vinegar, salt, and water; take out; put them into a pot; pour the liquor upon them; or the cloth will stick to the fish; when cold take the cloth off; add a little more vinegar to the pickle; keep them for use. When sent to the table, garnish with fennel and parsley, and put some of the liquor under them.

MACKEREL, *to pickle.*—Take six large mackerels, and cut them into round pieces. Take 1 oz. of beaten pepper, three nutmegs, a little mace, and a handful of salt; mix the salt and beaten spice together. Make two or three holes in each piece, and thrust the seasoning in to the holes in each piece, rub the pieces all over with the seasoning; fry them brown in oil or butter, and let them cool; put them into vinegar, and cover them with oil. They are fine eating.

MACKEREL, *to pot.*—Clean, season, and bake them in a pan with spice, bay leaves, and some butter. When cold, take out the bones; in pots lay them very close, and cover them with clarified butter.——They may be potted like lobsters. See *Lobster, potted.*

MACKEREL, *soused.* — Put together heads and tails in an earthen dish or pan. Season with chopped onions, black pepper, a pinch of allspice, and salt; add vinegar and water equally to cover the fish. Bake in the oven.—Herrings, sprats, or any other cheap fish, are done in the same manner.

MAGENTA DYE.--This splendid colouring matter may be bought of the chemists. It is first-rate for dyeing silk, ribbons, &c. Directions for use are given on each bottle.

MAGGOTS IN SHEEP, *to destroy.*—Water, 1 quart; spirit of turpentine, a table-spoonful; sublimate of mercury, as much as will lie upon a shilling; cork in a bottle, with a quill through the cork, so that the mixture may come a little at a time. Shake before using. Pour a little of the mixture upon the spot where the maggots are, and they will creep upon the top of the wool, and fall off dead. Apply afterwards a little train oil to the place.

MAGNUM BONUM PLUMS, *to preserve.*—Put the largest in a panful of water over a slow fire; keep putting them down with a spoon, till the skins will come off with a penknife; put them in a fine thin syrup, and give them a gentle boil; take off, and turn them often in the syrup, or the outside will turn brown. When cold, set them over the fire again; boil six minutes; then take off, and turn them often in the syrup till nearly cold. Take out and place on a flat china dish; strain the syrup through muslin; add the weight of the plums in fine sugar; boil, and skim well; then put in the plums; boil till they look clear; put them into jars or glasses; cover well with the syrup, or they will lose their colour; put brandy papers and a bladder over them.

MAHOGANY COLOUR, *to stain.*—1. Take 2 ozs. of dragon's blood, break it into pieces, and put it into a quart of spirits of wine; to stand in a warm place; shake often; when dissolved, it is ready for use.

2. Linseed oil, 2 pounds; alkanet, 3 ounces. Heat them together and macerate for six hours, then add resin, 2 ounces; bees' wax, 2 ounces. Boiled oil may be advantageously used instead of linseed oil.

3. Brazil-wood (ground); water sufficient; add a little alum and potash. Boil.

4. Logwood, 1 part; water, 8 parts. Make a decoction and apply it to the wood; when dry, give it two or three coats of the following varnish: Dragon's blood, 1 part; spirits of wine, 20 parts. Mix.

MAHOGANY FURNITURE, *to clean.*—Three pennyworth of alkanet root, a pint of linseed oil; two pennyworth of rose-pink; to stand in a vessel all night. Rub some of this mixture over the table or chairs, and let it stay an hour; then rub it well off with a linen cloth, and it will leave a beautiful gloss.

MAHOGANY, *to take stains out of.*—Mix 6 ozs. of spirits of salts, and ½ oz. salt of lemons together. Drop a little on the stains, and rub it with a cork till the stains disappear. Then wash off immediately with cold water.

MANDRAKE.—This plant is not so abundant in England as in America. It is a valuable plant, but requires skill and care in its application as a remedy. It is purgative, deobstruent, antibilious, anthelmintic, hydragogue, &c. It is a sure purge, superior in some diseases to jalap. It is very useful in scrofula, in bilious, dyspeptic, and venereal affections.—See *Robinson's Herbal.*

MARBLE, *to clean.*—Soap lees mixed with quick lime, pretty thick, and applied for a day, then washed off with soap and water. ——Or muriatic acid diluted with water, taking care that it be not too strong.——Or soft soap, 1 lb.; whiting, powdered, 1 lb.; soda, 1 oz.; boil together for 20 minutes; apply for 24 hours, wash off with clean water, and polish with a piece of felt, or coarse flannel.— Iron stains on marble are removed by a mixture of lemon juice and sulphuric acid; apply for a few minutes, and then rub with a soft cloth.

MARBLE, *Imitation of.*--Make a solution of alum, and of half as much of the best glue as alum. Mix with one part whiting, or rather less, and three parts of well-baked plaster of Paris. It may be coloured by first staining the water. It sets very hard.

MARBLE, *to polish.*—Mix a quantity of the strongest soap-lees with quick-lime, to the consistence of milk, and lay it on the stone, &c., for twenty-four hours, clean it afterwards with soap and water, and it will appear as new.

MARIGOLDS.—Their virtues have been lost sight of. The juice, or a strong decoction, with (or without) a very small portion of spirits of wine, is a rare application for healing lacerations, bruises, cuts, both pain and bleeding being immediately arrested. By its use in severe wounds Erysipelas is prevented. It seldom leaves a cicatrix, or mark, behind it. It has a tendency to contract the mouths of the small arteries, when directly cut across, and where they have been slit longitudinally. The tincture may be purchased of the Homœopathic Chemists; and largely diluted with water, it is a first-rate remedy.

MARIGOLDS, *to cultivate.*— Pull up all those plants, whose flowers are less double, as soon as they appear, that they may not impregnate the others with their farina. Save the seeds from the largest and most double flowers. Sow the seeds in April in places where the plants are to remain.

MARIGOLD CHEESE.—— Pound marigold petals in a mortar, and strain out the juice; put it into the milk when you put in the rennet, and stir them together; the milk being set, and the curd come, break it as gently and as equally as possible; put it into the cheese vat, and press it with a gentle weight. Manage the same as other cheeses.

MARINE GLUE.—Dissolve ½ lb. of india rubber in 3 gallons of coal naphtha. The india rubber should be first steeped in hot water, then cut into shreds with a pair of scissors, then dried, and put into the naphtha; stir till it is dissolved, and is as thick as cream. Then take one part of it and add it to two parts by weight of shellac. Melt in an iron vessel. Stir well. It has great tenacity.

MARJORAM, *to cultivate.*— The common sweet marjoram, so so much used in the culinary art, is cultivated by seeds, which are sown on a warm border at the end of March. When the plants are an inch high, transplant them into beds of rich earth; water them daily, till they have taken new root.

The plant is aromatic, and warming in cold diseases of the head and stomach. The decoction is good for diseases of the chest, asthma, bronchitis, and it removes obstructions of the liver and spleen. See *Robinson's Herbal*.

Sweet Marjoram is used for culinary purposes. It yields an essential oil, which has been applied to cancer with great benefit; and it obviates the fœtor attendant upon that cruel disease.

MARKETING READY RECKONER.

No.	2d.		2½d.		3d.		3½d.	
	s.	d.	s.	d.	s.	d.	s.	d.
2	0	4	0	5	0	6	0	7
3	0	6	0	7½	0	9	0	10½
4	0	8	0	10	1	0	1	2
5	0	10	1	0½	1	3	1	5½
6	1	0	1	3	1	6	1	9
7	1	2	1	5½	1	9	2	0½
8	1	4	1	8	2	0	2	4
9	1	6	1	10½	2	3	2	7½
10	1	8	2	1	2	6	2	11
11	1	10	2	3½	2	9	3	2½
12	2	0	2	6	3	0	3	6
13	2	2	2	8½	3	3	3	9½
14	2	4	2	11	3	6	4	1
28	4	8	5	10	7	0	8	2
56	9	4	11	8	14	0	16	4

No.	4d.		4½d.		5d.		5½d.	
	s.	d.	s.	d.	s.	d.	s.	d.
2	0	8	0	9	0	10	0	11
3	1	0	1	1½	1	3	1	4½
4	1	4	1	6	1	8	1	10
5	1	8	1	10½	2	1	2	3½
6	2	0	2	3	2	6	2	9
7	2	4	2	7½	2	11	3	2½
8	2	8	3	0	3	4	3	8
9	3	0	3	4½	3	9	4	1½
10	3	4	3	9	4	2	4	7
11	3	8	4	1½	4	7	5	0½
12	4	0	4	6	5	0	5	6
13	4	4	4	10½	5	5	5	11½
14	4	8	5	3	5	10	6	5
28	9	4	10	6	11	8	12	10
56	18	8	21	0	23	4	25	8

Market Reckoner, Continued.

No.	6d.		6½d.		7d.		7½d.	
	s.	d.	s.	d.	s.	d.	s.	d.
2	1	0	1	1	1	2	1	3
3	1	6	1	7½	1	9	1	10½
4	2	0	2	2	2	4	2	6
5	2	6	2	8½	2	11	3	1½
6	3	0	3	3	3	6	3	9
7	3	6	3	9½	4	1	4	4½
8	4	0	4	4	4	8	5	0
9	4	6	4	10½	5	3	5	7½
10	5	0	5	5	5	10	6	3
11	5	6	5	11½	6	5	6	10½
12	6	0	6	6	7	0	7	6
13	6	6	7	0½	7	7	8	1½
14	7	0	7	7	8	2	8	9
28	14	0	15	2	16	4	17	6
56	28	0	30	4	32	8	35	0

No.	8d.		9d.		10d.		11d.	
	s.	d.	s.	d.	s.	d.	s.	d.
2	1	4	1	6	1	8	1	10
3	2	0	2	3	2	6	2	9
4	2	8	3	0	3	4	3	8
5	3	4	3	9	4	2	4	7
6	4	0	4	6	5	0	5	6
7	4	8	5	3	5	10	6	5
8	5	4	6	0	6	8	7	4
9	6	0	6	9	7	6	8	3
10	6	8	7	6	8	4	9	2
11	7	4	8	3	9	2	10	1
12	8	0	9	0	10	0	11	0
13	8	8	9	9	10	10	11	11
14	9	4	10	6	11	8	12	10
28	18	8	21	0	23	4	25	8
56	37	4	42	0	46	8	51	4

MARKING INK.—Dissolve 2 drachms of lunar caustic in clean rain water; add 1 drachm of gum arabic, and 1½ oz. of common soda, or ammonia. Take the sediment, and grind it with a little citric acid, clear rain water, gum arabic, and a little black ink. It is better to damp the linen a little before writing upon it. *Gif.*

MARMALADE CREAM.—Take two table-spoonfuls of orange marmalade; add to it a quart of cream; a little, at first, for mincing the marmalade, a wine-glassful of brandy; 8 ozs. of ground loaf sugar, and the juice of a lemon; whisk it for half an hour; and drain. Serve in custard glasses.

MARMALADE, *Currant.*—Take white, or red currants; press out the juice; add lemon, orange, or raspberry juice, and fine sugar, sufficient to sweeten and candy. Boil, and skim, till it becomes a transparent mass. Marmalade may be thus made of any other kind of fruit, and candied. It is a very delicious marmalade. *A. N.*

MARMALADE, *Orange.*—Rasp the oranges, cut out the pulp, then boil the rinds very tender, and beat fine in a marble mortar. Boil three pounds of loaf-sugar in a pint of water, skim it, and add a pound of the rind; boil fast till the syrup is very thick, but stir it carefully; then put in a pint of the pulp and juice, the seeds having been removed, and a pint of apple liquor; boil all gently until well jellied, which it will be in about half an hour. Put it into small pots.

Lemon Marmalade will do in the same way; it is a very good and elegant sweetmeat.

MARMALADE, *Quince.*—Pare and quarter quinces, weigh an equal quantity of sugar; to 4 lbs. of the latter put a quart of water, boil and skim, and have ready for 4 lbs. of quinces, when tender, by the following mode: lay them into a stone jar, with a tea-cup of water at the bottom, and pack them with a little sugar strewed between; cover the jar close, and set it on a stove or cool oven, and let them soften till the colour becomes red; then pour the fruit-syrup and a quart of quince-juice into a preserving pan; boil all together till the marmalade be completed, breaking the lumps of fruit with the preserving-ladle.

This fruit is so hard, that if it be not done as above, it requires a great deal of time. Stewing quinces in a jar, and squeezing them through a cheese-cloth, is the best method of obtaining the juice to add as above: and dip the cloth in boiling water first and wring it.

MARMALADE, *Scotch,*—Take 8 lbs. of Seville oranges, pare off the skins very thin so that there shall be little white; then cut the parings into strips, put them into a pan with water to cover them, and boil for an hour; then strain them through a sieve. Next quarter the oranges, and scrape out the pulps and juice into a dish; the white skins, films and seeds must be thrown away; place the whole in a pan with 8 lbs of sugar; let the whole boil half an hour, skim, and pot for use.

It is not necessary that they should all be Seville oranges, as a few if mixed with the common sorts are sufficient to give the necessary flavour.

MARMALADE, *Transparently beautiful.*—Take 3 lbs. of bitter oranges; pare them as you would potatoes; cut the skin into fine shreds, and put them into a muslin bag; quarter all the oranges; press out the juice. Boil the pulp and shreds in three quarts of water 2½ hours, down to three pints; strain through a hair sieve. Then put six pounds of sugar to the liquid, the juice, and the shreds, the outside of two lemons grated, and the insides squeezed in; add one-pennyworth of isinglass. Simmer all together slowly for 15 or 20 minutes.

☞ The *sweet oranges* make

good marmalade, if the seeds are pulverised, and well mixed with the rest.

MARROW PUDDING.—Pour a pint of cream boiling hot on the crumbs of a penny loaf, or French roll; cut 1 lb. of beef marrow very thin; beat 4 eggs well; add a glass of brandy, with sugar and nutmeg to taste, and mix all well together. It may be either boiled or baked, 40 or 50 minutes; cut 2 ozs. of citron very thin, and stick them all over it when you dish it up.

Another way.—Blanch ½ lb. of almonds; put them in cold water all night; next day beat them in a mortar very fine, with orange or rose water. Take the crumbs of a penny loaf, and pour on the whole a pint of boiling cream; while it is cooling, beat the yolks of four eggs, and two whites, 15 minutes; a little sugar and grated nutmeg to your palate. Shred the marrow of the bones, and mix all well together, with a little candied orange cut small. Bake, &c.

MARSHMALLOW. — Decoctions of this plant are very useful where the natural mucus has been abraided from the coats of the intestines; in catarrhs from a thin rheum. It is emollient and demulcent. It is good in diseases of the urinary organs, when the urine is hot and deficient; and it is of great value in dysentery, bronchitis, &c. Two or three ozs. of the fresh roots may be boiled in 2 quarts of water, down to 1 quart; strain; add 1 oz. of gum arabic. It will be more palatable by adding liquorice-root, or raisins and sugar to sweeten it.

As an external application, it is invaluable; it subdues inflammation, and prevents gangrene, or mortification; it disperses inflammatory tumours and swellings.

It is applied by poultices, prepared by cutting the fresh root into very small pieces, bruising them fine, and boiling the pulp in sweet milk, adding slippery elm to give it proper consistence.

☞ The common roadside mallow is often used for the marshmallow, which grows in marshes near the sea. The former has not half the virtues.—See *Robinson's Herbal on this most valuable plant.*

MARSHMALLOW LOZENGES.—Pound cleaned marshmallow roots to a pulp; boil 1½ lb. of loaf sugar in 6 or 8 ozs. of rose-water to a solid consistence; add 4 ozs. of the marshmallow pulp; whisk the whole well; place it over a gentle heat, to dry up the moisture, stirring all the time; and when a good paste has formed, empty it on buttered paper; roll out, and cut into forms.

They are excellent for coughs, asthma, and even consumptions, especially if a little orris root, liquorice, or white poppy seeds powdered be added, with a little gum arabic, or gum tragacanth.

MATRIMONY, *the game of.*—Matrimony may be played by any number of persons, from five to fourteen. This game is composed of five chances, usually marked on a board or sheet of paper, in the following manner:—

Ace of diamonds turned up.

Pairs, the highest.

It must be understood that when the ace of diamonds is turned up, it takes the whole pool; but when held in hand, it ranks only as any other ace; and when it is neither turned up nor held in hand, then the king, or the next superior card in order, wins the call.

The game is generally played with counters, and the dealer may stake what he likes on each or any chance; the other players depositing each the same quantity, except one; that is, when the dealer stakes twelve, the rest lay down eleven, and so on.

After this, two cards are dealt to each; then one card is turned up to each, and if any happen to have the ace of diamonds, he sweeps all; if not turned up, all show their hands. Any holding matrimony, intrigue, &c., takes the counters on that point; and when two or three happen to have similar combinations, the eldest hand has the preference; and should any chance not be gained, it stands over to the following deal.

MATCHLESS CAKE.—As you whisk right well 5 eggs, very gradually add 8 ozs. of sifted loaf sugar; 8 ozs. of flour, dry and sifted; 6 ozs. of butter, just melted; the rinds of two small lemons, a little cinnamon, and candied lemon, or citron. Immediately before you mould the cake or cakes, incorporate ½ oz. of carbonate of soda; bake one hour in a moderate oven. Be sure to keep light by constant whisking.

MEAD, *to make.*—To 7 gallons of water, put 15 lbs. of honey; boil and skim it well; take rosemary, thyme, bay-leaves, and sweet-briar, one handful all together; boil one hour; put into a tub with a little ground malt; stir till it is lukewarm; strain, and put it into the tub again; cut a toast, and spread it over with yeast, and put it into the tub; and when the liquor is covered with yeast, put it up in a barrel; take of cloves, mace, and nutmegs, 1½ oz. of ginger sliced, 1 oz.; bruise the spice; tie it in a cloth, hang it in the vessel, stopping it up close for use.

Mead is very pleasant if cowslips and lemon are added to the above—using water, &c. in proportion.

MEAD WINE.—Soft water, 9 gallons, white currants, 3 quarts; ferment; mix honey, 15 lbs. white tartar, powdered, 1½ oz.; add balm and sweet brier, each half a handful; white brandy, ½ a gallon. This will make 9 or 10 gallons.

MEASLES, *An eruptive disease.*—It is indicated by chilliness, shivering, pain in the head, fever, sneezing, discharges from the nose, sickness, and sometimes vomiting, hoarseness, cough, heaviness of the eyes; the eyelids frequently swell so as to cause blindness, the patient complains of his throat, and a looseness often precedes the eruption. The third or fourth day an eruption, like flea-bites, appears in the face, neck, and breast, and soon after in the body and limbs; the eruption does not suppurate. But the spots soon run into one another, and form red streaks, giving to the skin an inflammatory appearance, and produce a preceptible swelling on the face. The eruption may be distinguished from the small-pox by their scarcely rising above the skin. The fever, cough, and difficulty of breathing, instead of being removed by the eruption, as in the small pox, are rather increased; but the vomiting generally ceases.

About the sixth or seventh day, and sometimes earlier, the eruption begins to fade, and gradually disappears, accompanied with a separation of the skin in the form of scales. But the other symptoms sometimes remain for a considerable time, and require care, warmth, and appropriate medicine.

In the malignant measles, the eruption appears more early, and all the symptoms, just described, in an aggravated form. The mouth and throat assume appearances. The mouth and throat appear as if they were ulcerated, and the fever is of a typhus kind, and symptoms of putrescency appear; also petichiæ, or purple, livid spots, a pain in the head and eyes, difficult respiration, no expectoration with the cough, an inflammatory affection of the lungs, feeble, but rapid pulse, delirium, and oft a violent looseness; these are very unfavourable symptoms. Such as die of the measles, generally expire about the ninth or tenth day from the first attack.—The most favourable symptoms are a moderate looseness, a moist skin, and a plentiful discharge of urine.

This disease is very infectious, often prevails epidemically, however; and the constitution that has been once under its influence is seldom, or never liable to a second attack, especially if the first attack was a mild one.

Treatment.—At the commencement of the disease, no animal food must be taken, the patient must be confined to a low spare diet, as gruel, sago, &c., and for common drink, barley-water. acidulated with lemon-juce. The bedroom should be kept moderately cool, regulating the temperature thereof by the feelings, guarding against any sudden change, and especially exposure to cold draughts.

When the attack is of a mild character, little medicine is wanted. Perhaps the less we interfere with the efforts of nature the better. It would be extreme folly to deplete the system by active treatment. In mild cases nature, a *little* assisted, generally effects a cure. But when the symptoms are of a sterner character, active means must be used. Place the feet in warm water, in which dissolve a little of carbonate of soda, two or three times a day. Give a mild emetic, (as the *Emetic Mixture*, page 155) Give also the *Aperient for Children*, page 20. Should the fever be very high, give the following *Febrifuge Mixture*;—Subcarbonate of potash, 2 drachms; purified nitre, 30 grains; camphor mixture, 6 ozs.; mix in a strong infusion of saffron. This mixture is designed to determine the eruption to the surface.——Or, the following infusion will be very effective, and it should be given as soon as possible after the emetic;—Saffron, two parts; Virginia snake-root, 1 part; infuse rapidly, or make a tea; sweeten and give warm, as much as the stomach will bear. If the eruption is slow in appearing, or only partially appears, or recedes, give the Sudorific Drops, warm milk sweetened, or strong balm tea with a little saffron infused. A bottle of hot water or a hot brick wrapped in a cloth, saturated with vinegar and water, or a vapour bath made of the decoction of bitter herbs, will be found most efficient. When the eruption is prominent, little more medicine is required. A little of the Composition Powder may be given occasionally. Sponge the body from the first, now and then, with warm ley water and a little carbonate of soda. Wash the eyes with very weak brandy and water; or with slippery elm bark and a solution of borax.

If the cough is severe, attended with impeded breathing, apply a mustard plaster to the chest, and repeat, if necessary; and give the Expectorant Syrup or Tincture, page 159; or inhale the steam of warm water, in which 30 or 40 drops of laudanum have been introduced. If the head is affected, continue to bathe the feet in warm water. Should there be much restlessness and pain, give the Diaphoretic Powder, or Decoction, page 143. From the first attack of the measles, keep the bowels regular. A voluntary looseness indicates a favourable crisis; and, if moderate, it should not be checked. When it is very severe, it should be checked by some mild astringent; as, an infusion of raspberry leaves; or an infusion of raspberry leaves and a few drops of laudanum. Should the system be much debilitated, with a tendency to putrescency, the strength should be supported with cordials, beef tea, calf's feet jelly, and an infusion of Peruvian Bark in port wine. Give also an infusion of malt with *two table-spoonfuls* of yeast to a quart of the former, in order to neutralize the putrescence indicated by purple spots, &c.

Patients recovering from the measles should not expose themselves too soon to the cold air. The food ought for some time to be light, and the drink diluting. Cooling lenitive medicines are essentially necessary after this disease, to carry off the remaining disposition to inflammatory affection of the lungs. Through every stage of the disease, the state of the lungs must be carefully regarded, for it is from the effect on them that the danger of the measles in most cases depend. It is necessary also to give tonic bitters for the recovery of the former strength, to breathe a pure air, and if the lungs will bear it, and the weather suitable, to take gentle open air exercise.

MEAT, *Observation on*.—In all kinds of provisions, the best of the kind goes the farthest; it cuts out with most advantage, and affords most nourishment. Round of beef, fillet of veal, and leg of mutton, are joints of higher price; but as they have more solid meat, they deserve the preference. But those joints which are inferior may be dressed as palatably.

In loins of meat, the long pipe that runs by the bone should be taken out, as it is apt to taint; as also the kernels of beef. Do not purchase joints bruised by the blows of the drovers.

Save shank bones of mutton to enrich gravies or soups.

When sirloins of beef, or loins of veal or mutton, come in, part of the suet may be cut off for puddings, or to clarify.

Dripping will baste any thing as well as butter; except fowls and game; and for kitchen pies, nothing else should be used.

The fat of a neck or loin of mutton makes a far lighter pudding than suet.

Frosted meat and vegetables should be soaked in *cold water* two or three hours before using.

If the weather permit, meat eats much better for hanging two or three days before it is salted.

Roast-beef bones, or shank bones of ham, make fine peas-soup; and should be boiled with the peas the day before eaten, that the fat may be taken off.

MEAT, *To keep in hot weather, &c.*—Place the meat on a wooden support, or suspend it in a close vessel, on the bottom of which some strong acetic vinegar is poured. Meat may be kept sweet a long time by thus impregnating the atmosphere with acetic acid.

A joint of meat may be preserved for several days, even in summer, by wrapping it in a clean linen cloth, previously moistened with good vinegar; hanging it up, and changing the cloth, or wringing it out afresh in vinegar, once or twice a day, if the weather be very warm.

The best meat for keeping is *mutton*, and the best joint is a leg; which, with care, if the weather be only moderately hot, in summer, will keep about a week; in winter, if the weather be open, from 2 to 4 weeks. A shoulder is the next best joint. The scrag end of a neck keeps the worst, and in warm weather it will not keep above two days; if very warm, it becomes bad the second day.

In *beef*, the ribs keep the best, even five or six days in summer, and in winter ten. The middle of the loin is the next best, and the rump the next. The round will not keep long unless salted. The brisket is the worst, and will not keep longer than two days in summer, and six days in winter.

Lamb does not keep long, and it is best to eat it soon or even the same day it is killed. The first part that turns bad of a leg of *veal*, is where the udder is skewered back. The skewer should be taken out, and both that and the part under it wiped every day, it will then keep good three or four days in hot weather.

Meat dipped into chloride of lime in a liquid state for a second will keep many days without taint; for no flies will touch it if so done. Wash the meat before cooking it.

MEAT CAKE.—According to the size, take of beef-steaks, of leg of mutton, of fillet of veal, ham and beef suet; chop all together very fine, and season with salt, fine spices, chopped parsley, green shalots, a clove of garlick, 8 yolks of eggs, half a glass of brandy, and 2 lbs. of fresh bacon, or less, cut in dice. Mix all well together. Take a stewpan, the size you intend to make the cake, and garnish it all over with thick sizes of lard; put in the minced meat, cover close, and put in the oven for four hours. When cold, take out of the stewpan and scrape the lard with a knife to make it white and even.

MEAT PIE, *of any kind*.—First fry the meat brown over a quick fire in a little drip or butter. Season with pepper and salt. Then put into a pie-dish with chopped onions, or shalots, if you like, some slices of half-cooked potatoes, a little gravy, or stock, and enough water to cause the liquid to cover the meat. Cover the dish with crust, made with 2 lbs. of flour, 6 ozs. of butter, or lard, or dripping, and water enough to knead it into a stiff paste. Bake 1½ hour.

☞ Learned chemists appear to have forgotten the important fact that, if a meat pie is made without a hole in the crust to let out certain emanations from the meat, colic, vomiting, and other symptoms of slight poisoning will occur. I have known of two instances of large parties being affected in this manner from eating meat pies that had no hole in them.—*Correspondent of the Lancet.*

MEAT AND POTATOE PUDDING.—Boil some mealy potatoes till ready to crumble to pieces; drain; mash them very smooth. Make them into a thickish batter with an egg or two, and milk, placing a layer of steaks or chops well-seasoned with salt and pepper, at the bottom of a baking dish; cover with a layer of batter, and so alternately, till the dish is full, ending with batter at the top. Butter the dish to prevent sticking or burning. Bake of a fine brown colour.

MEDICINE, *disagreeable, to take.*—Get your medicine into the mouth, do not swallow, nor open your mouth; then have a glass of water ready to take immediately after you take the medicine into the mouth. The moment it is swallowed nip the nose. This plan neutralizes the taste of the most nauseous medicine.

Chloroform mixed with medicine, even the most bitter, neutralizes the taste.

MEDICINAL TEA.—Rosemary leaves, dried, 2 ozs.; sage, 4 ozs.; rose leaves, 4 ozs.; peach leaves, 3 ozs.; hyssop, 4 ozs.; balm, 6 ozs.; male speedwell, 4 ozs.; agrimony, 6 ozs. A wineglass of these mixed herbs is sufficient to make 3 pints of infusion, which is made in the same manner as ordinary tea. All the above herbs may be used, or a selection made, but do not leave out balm and agrimony. If these herbs were imported from a distant region, they would fetch a high price, and be held in high estimation. Such tea will strengthen the stomach, and invigorate, instead of debilitating the nervous system.—See *Robinson's Herbal* on *Tea*, page 267.

MELANCHOLY.—See *Hypochondria.*

MELTED BUTTER, *to make.*—Cut 2 ozs. of butter into small bits, to melt more readily; put into the stewpan with a dessertspoonful of flour, and two tablespoonfuls of milk. When thoroughly mixed, add two tablespoonfuls of water; hold it over the fire, and shake it round every minute, all the time the same way, till it just begins to simmer; then let it stand quietly, and boil up. It should be as thick as good cream.

MENSES, *obstructed.*—Be electrified.—tried.——Or, take half a pint of strong decoction of pennyroyal every night at going to bed.——Or, boil five large heads of hemp in a pint of water to half. Strain it and drink it at going to bed, two or three nights. It seldom fails.—Tried.—*Wesley.*

MENSTRUATION. — Menstruation is a natural secretion, of a red colour, from the womb, so named from its occurring once in a month. This periodical discharge appears to be for the pupose of keeping up sanguification, or the making of blood in the body, and a determination thereof to the womb, for the purpose of gestation. In consequence of its not appearing at a proper period of life, of irregularity after it has taken place, and of its being excessive, as well as at the period of its cessation, many derangements in the system occur.

The interruption of the menstrual secretion may be considered of two kinds;—the one when it does not begin to flow at that period of life in which it usually appears, which is termed *Chlorosis*, or Green Sickness--and the other when, after it has repeatedly taken place for some time, it does, from other causes than conception, cease to return at the usual periods.

Chlorosis, or Green Sickness.—Menstruation begins from the fourteenth to the sixteenth year. But the circumstance of a female having passed the age of sixteen, does not always demand medical aid. The date of puberty varies very widely, and one female may menstruate at 12, and another at 20 years of age, without the health being impaired.

As to its *causes*, it may arise from imperfect formation of the organs concerned in the function, from the want of due force in the action of the arteries of the womb, or some preternatural resistance in their extremities; from too full habit of body, from impoverishment of the blood, and from great physical debility.

This retention produces many distressing symptoms; as, headache, flushings in the face, pain in the back and stomach, costiveness, furred tongue, failure of appetite, longing to eat chalk, lime, &c. The face loses its vivid colour, and becomes of a yellowish hue; sometimes there is bleeding from the nose and stomach; the skin becomes pale and flaccid; and the feet, and sometimes part of the body, is affected with dropsical swelling. The breathing is hurried by any quick or laborious motion of the body, which sometimes occasions palpitation and fainting. A head-ache often occurs, but more certainly pains in the back, loins, and haunches.

Treatment.--The strength of the system should be restored by exercise. Iron should be combined with some laxative medicine. If there is much pain, take the Diaphoretic Powder, page 143. Also infusions of pennyroyal, or of tansy, or blood-root, motherwort, &c. Bathe the feet occasionally in warm water, and rub well with a coarse flannel. If there is constipation, take aperient medicines; page 20 and 21. Powdered madder root has been recommended, say half a drachm to be taken three or four times a day in treacle or honey, drinking freely of pennyroyal tea. Repeat, and increase the dose, if necessary. Or it may be administered thus:—Take extract of madder, 2 drachms, muriated tincture of steel, 40 drops, bitter tincture, 2 drachms, mintwater, 8 ozs. Mix. Three tablespoonfuls to be taken three times a day.

Or, give a vapour bath of a decoction of bitter herbs.——Or in bed apply the hot brick covered with a cloth dipped in vinegar and water. Give bitter tonics. Steaming in a sitz-bath of bitter herbs till perspiration is produced, is very useful; also fomenting the abdomen, and applying herbs as a warm poultice. If the stomach is deranged, give an emetic, and a dose of mandrake, and aperients as before stated. When the menstrual flux begins, it should be promoted by the use of the hip or sitz-bath. Take the *Dyspeptic Pill*, and the *Restorative Bitters*.

Keep the feet always warm and dry; avoid a cold damp atmosphere; and when the weather permits, take plenty of open-air exercise. Let the diet be light and nourishing. Do not use any promotive medicines in retention of the menses until there is an effort or struggle of nature to effect it, which may be known by the periodical pains, pressing down upon the hips.

Painful Menstruation. — The pains are severe—in some cases extremely severe. The *remedial measures* are nearly the same as the preceding. On account of the pain, stillness, quiet of mind, and soothing remedies are rendered indispensable. Adopt the remedies prescribed for the retention of the menses; and take now and then from 10 to 20 drops of laudanum in a little Hollands gin diluted with pennyroyal tea. Let the patient lie in bed. Apply hot fomentations to the lower part of the back; and if the pain is excessive, flannels dipped in hot water, wrung out, and sprinkled with spirits of turpentine. Sponge the body well with tepid salt and water every morning, and apply friction with a flesh brush, or coarse towel. Regulate the bowels, if costive, by one of the aperients, page 20, 21. Hops boiled in vinegar, and applied to the abdomen, often give relief; so does the tincture of black cohosh, about half a teaspoonful three times a day in a little sweetened water.

Profuse Menstruation. — The flow of the menses is considered immoderate when it recurs more frequently, when it continues longer, or when, during the ordinary continuance, it is more abundant than is usual with the same person at other times. It is not, however, every *inequality* that is to be considered a disease, but only those deviations, that are *excessive* in degree, which are *permanent*, and induce a *manifest state of debility*.

When a large flow of the menses has been *preceded* by head-ache, giddiness, or difficulty of breathing, and has been ushered in by a *cold shivering*, with much pain in the back and loins, frequent pulse, heat, and thirst, it may then be considered preternaturally large; and the face becomes pale, the pulse weak, an unusual debility is felt on exercise, the breathing hurried by much motion, and the back is pained in an erect posture; the extremities are frequently cold, and in the evening the feet swell. General nervousness, with affections of the stomach, frequent faintings, and a weakness of mind, liable to strong emotion from slight causes, when suddenly presented, are also attendant symptoms.

It is produced by a preternatural determination of blood to the womb, or a plethoric state of the body, from high living, strong liquors, over-exertion, (particularly dancing,) violent passions of the mind, application of cold to the feet, frequent abortions or child-bearing, and whatever will induce great laxity, as living much in warm chambers, and especially drinking much of warm enervating liquors, such as tea and coffee.

Treatment.—Remove immediately all exciting causes of this disease. The flux must not be stopped, but moderated; avoid an erect posture, and external heat, as warm chambers, and soft beds; by using a light, cool, and unexciting diet; by obviating costiveness, as before directed; or use castor oil and lenitive electuary; the external and internal use of astringents, to constringe the vessels of the womb, as the application of cloths sprinkled with vinegar and water over the region of the womb; and three table-spoonfuls of the following mixture every three or four hours:—Red rose-leaves, $\frac{1}{2}$ oz.; infuse in a pint of boiling water, till cold; then strain; add elixir of vitriol, 60 drops, tincture of rhatany root, 1 oz. A gentle emetic may be of great service. See page 155. The Diaphoretic Powder also, is of great service in this case. An injection of cold water into the rectum may check an immoderate flow.

Obstructed Menstruation.—It is often caused by exposure to cold during the menstrual discharge, to wet feet, cold bathing, great mental fear and anxiety, &c., just before the periodical time of discharge. The obstruction injures the health, if it continues two or three periods.

Give the Composition Powder, page 119, or the Diaphoretic Powder, page 143., when the patient is in bed, and place bricks covered with vinegar and water cloths to the feet and sides, or give the Vapour Bath. Take also Peruvian bark infused in port wine. In short, use the same means as prescribed under Chlorosis. Take also the *Female Pill*, page 163.

METAL, *to clean all sorts.*——Mix ½ pint of neat's foot oil with half a gill of spirits of turpentine; scrape a little rotten stone; wet a woollen rag with the mixture; dip it into the rotten stone, and rub the metal well; wipe it off with a soft cloth; polish with dry leather, and use more of the rotten stone. As it respects steel, if it be very rusty, use a little pumice powder, or emery powder on a separate woollen rag at the first.

METAL TEA-POTS, *to clean.*——Put into them a solution of common soda, boiling hot; let it stand 12 hours near the fire, and then rub the inside with a small brush; and, if needful, put in a second solution.

MENTAL CALCULATIONS.

RULE I.

Find the Amount of the number of *yards, lbs. &c. at* one penny, and multiply it by the price: when there is a farthing with any given number of pence, (as, 2¼d. 6¼d. 10¼d.) add ¼ to what it amounts to at one penny. When there is a half-penny with any given pence, add half of the amount of what it comes to at one penny; and when 3 farthings occur, add three quarters of what it amounts to at one penny.

40 lbs. at 11d. 40 at 1d.=3s. 4d. × 11d.=£1 16s. 8d. *Ans.*

72 Gals. at 7d. per gal. 72 at 1d.=6s. ×7=£2 2s. *Ans.*

A Pipe at 10d. per gal. 126 gals.= 10s. 6d. ×10=£5 5s. *Ans.*

45 Weeks at 6d. per day. 315 days= £1 6s. 3d. ×6=£7 17s. 6d. *Ans.*

When ¼, ½, or ¾ occur in the quantity, reckon them with the yards, &c. at the rate of 1d. per yard, i. e. for a quarter of a yard reckon ¼d.: for a half a yard add ½d., &c.

32½ yards at 3d. a yard. 32½=2s. 8½d. ×3=8s. 1½d. *Ans.*

90¾ ozs. at 5d. per. oz. 90¾=7s. 6¾d. ×5=£1 17s. 9¾d. *Ans.*

60 lbs. at 8¼d. per lb. 60 at 1d.=5s. ×8¼=£2 1s. 3d. *Ans.*

111 yds. at 3¾d. 111 at 1d.=9s. 3d. × 3¾d.=£1 14s. 8¼d. *Ans.*

1200½ yds. at 6½d. 1200½d.=£5 0s. 0½d. ×6½=£32 10s. 3¼d. *Ans.*

RULE II.

To ascertain the price of any number of yards, lbs., gallons, &c., at any given shillings per lb., &c.

Ascertain the amount at one shilling, and multiply it by the price.

If 3 pence occur in the price, add one quarter of what it amounts to at a shilling; if 4 pence, add one third; if 6 pence, add half; if 9 pence, add three quarters.

If the pence in the price be not an aliquot part of a shilling, find for the shillings by this rule, and for the pence by the rule for pence, which amounts add together.

80 Gals. at 15s. per gal. 80 at 1s.=£4 ×15s.=£60. *Ans.*

With regard to fractional parts of a yard, lb., &c., when the price is shillings per yard, reckon the quarters as 3 pence, the half as 6 pence, and the three-quarters as 9 pence.

50¼ yards at 6s. per yd. 50¼ at 1s.= £2 10s. 3d. ×6=£15 1s. 6d. *Ans.*

90¾ stones at 7s. per st. 90¾=£4 10s. 9d. ×7=£31 15s. 3d. *Ans.*

100 Gallons at 6s. 6d. per gal. 100= £5 ×6½=£32 10s. *Ans.*

150 lbs. at 10s. 9d. per lb. 150=£7 10s. ×10¾=£80 12 6d. *Ans.*

60 Gallons at 8s. 4d. per gal. 60=£3 ×8⅓=£25. *Ans.*

☞ Many figures might be saved by multiplying the shillings of the price by the number of £ that the quantity amounts to at 1s., which will produce the answer in £.

MEN   MEN   253

150 Tons at 30s. 150=£7 10s. ×30= £225. *Ans.*

To calculate *cwts. qrs. lbs.*—Set down the *cwts.*, to the right put the *lbs.* contained in the *qrs.* and *lbs.*, to which add 12 *lbs.* for each *cwt.*, which will give the total number of *lbs.* If the price per *lb.* be pence, consider them as pence; if shillings, consider them as shillings.

5 cwts. 2 qrs. 20 lbs. at 6d. per lb. Thus:—5 cwts.; place after the 5 the number of the lbs. (2 qrs. and 20 lbs.) =576 lbs., to which add 5 12 lbs.= 60 lbs.+576 lbs.=636 lbs. taken as pence=£2 13s. ×6d.=£15 18s. *Ans.*

15 cwts. 3 qrs. 18 lbs. at 10½d. per lb. Number of lbs. 1782 lbs. as pence, =£7 8s. 6d ×.10½d.=£77 19s. 3d. *Ans.*

In calculating *acres, roods,* and *perches,* reckon the acres as pounds, multiply the roods by 5, the product consider as shillings, and the perches by 1¼d. (which is the price of a perch at £1 per acre) which will give the amount of the whole at £1 per acre, which multiply by the number of pounds per acre.

80 acres, 2 roods, 8 perches, at £3 10s. per acre.

£.	s.	d.
80	2	8
	5	1¼

80 11 0 × 3½=£281 18s. 6d. *Ans.*

TROY WEIGHT.—The *grs.* are to be considered as half-pence, the *dwts.* as shillings, and *ozs.* as pounds.

12 ozs. 8 dwts. 4 grs. at 6s. 8d. per oz.
6s. 8d=⅓£ £12 8 2

£4 2 8½ *Ans.*

To find the value of an ounce, the price per lb. being given.
Take the shillings as farthings, and multiply by 3 for Avoirdupois; for Troy, multiply by 4. Thus 1 oz. Avoirdupois at 4s. per lb. 4×3=12 farthings=3d. *Ans.*

The price of a pound of Avoirdupois being known, to find the price of a stone of 14 pounds.

For every penny in the price of a pound, take *one shilling* and *twopence* for the stone; thus a stone at 3d. per lb. cost 3s. 6d., at 8d. 9s. 4d. For a *farthing* in the price of a lb. reckon 3½d. in the stone; for a *half-penny,* 7d; and, for *three farthings,* 10½d.; as a stone at 9½d. per lb. comes to 10s. 6d. and 3½d. or 10s. 9½d. at 4½d., 4s. 8d. and 7d. or 5s. 3d. and at 6¾d., 7s. 10½

The price of a pound being given, to find that of a hundred-weight or 112 lbs.

For every *farthing* in the price of a pound, take twice the number of shillings, and four times the number of pence. Example: 1 cwt. at 2½d. per lb. 2½d.=10 farthings. 10 times 2=20, the shillings, 10 times 4=40, the pence, and these added, make £1 3s. 4d.

To find the value of a lb., the price per cwt. being given.—Multiply the shillings in the price by 3, and divide by 7 for the price of a pound in farthings.—

Thus, 1 lb. at 14s. per cwt. 14×3 ÷7=6 farthings=1½d. *Ans.*

From the price of a Cwt., to find that of a Ton.

For every shilling reckon a pound, for threepence, a crown, and for every half-penny over, tenpence. As, at £3 9s. 8d. a cwt., how much a ton? *Ans.* £69 and 10s. and 3s. 4d. or £69 13s. 4d.

By reversing the process, the price of a cwt. may be found from that of a ton, thus, a ton at £34 16s. 8d. how much a cwt? *Ans.* 34 shillings, 3 threepences, and 2 half-pence, or £1 14s. 10d.

When the price of *one* is known, to find that of 100.

For every *farthing* in the price of one, take *twice* as many shillings, and *once* as many pence.

Thus, 100 articles at 2¼ each, 2¼=6 farthings, 9 times 2=18s. and 9d. give 18s. 9d. *Ans.*

100 lbs. at 5¼d. per lb. 5¼d.=21 farthings, 21 times 2=42 shillings, or £2 2s. and 21d.=1s. 9d. then, £2 2s. and 1s. 9d.=£2 3s. 9d. the price of a hundred at the given rate.

To find what any number of pence per day, will amount to in a year.

Add together as many pounds, half as many pounds, and as many *fivepences* as there are pence per day, and their sum will be the answer. Examples. What does a boy who earns 3d. a day gain in a year? *Ans.* £3 and £1 10s. and 15d. or £4 11s. 3d. What will 8d. a day amount to in a year? £8 and £4 and 3s. 4d. or £12 3s. 4d. Or, take 365 days as pence=£1 10s. 5d. which multiply by the number of pence per day.

To find the amount of any number of pence per day, (Sunday excepted) for a year.

For every penny a day, take so many Guineas, Crowns, and Pence; thus, at 9d. a day.=£9 9s. and 9 crowns=£2 5s. and 9d. The sum=£11 14s. 9d.

To find the price of a Gross, the price of one article being given.— Take the pence in the price of one article as shillings, and the number of pence in these shillings will be the price of a gross in shillings.

Thus, 1 Gross at 6d. each. 6d. as 6s. reckoned as pence=72, which consider as 72s. *Ans.*

INTEREST.

At 5 per cent, multiply the principal by the months; reckon the product in Pounds sterling as pence.— Or, the Interest of £1 per month at 5 per cent. and so proportionally for any part of a pound. Find the Interest for one month, and multiply it by the number of months.

Thus, Interest of £40 for 3 months at 5 per cent.

£40 × 3 months=£120 as pence=10s. *Ans.*

Or, £40 for 1 month=3s. 4d. × 3 months=10s. *Ans.*

INTEREST AT 5 PER CENT. FOR YEARS.

The Interest of £1 per month is 1d., so the Interest of £1 for a year will be 1s.

RULE.—Multiply the principal by the years; reckon the product in pounds as shillings. Thus, £50 for 3 Years at 5 per cent. £50×3=150s. =£7 10s. *Ans.*

The Interest of £250 7s. 6d. for 10 years and 4 months.

£12 10s. 4½. for one year × 10⅓=129 7s. 2¼d. *Ans.*—7s. 6d. being the ⅜ of a £ the ⅜ of a shilling=4½d is allowed.

ANOTHER RULE.—Take the years as shillings, the months as pence, then take such part of the principal as those shillings and pence are of a £.—Thus,

Interest of £900 12s. 6d. for 5 years. ——5 years as 5s. is ¼ of a £.—Then £900 12s. 6d.÷4=£225 3s. 1½d. *Ans.*

MILE *of the various nations.*—
English Yards.

Arabian	..	..	2148
Bohemian		..	10137
Brabant	..	..	6082
Chinese illis		..	628
Danish mile		..	8244
English	..	..	1760
Do. Geographical		..	2025
Flemish	..	..	6869
French league	..		4860
French Marine	..		6075
French legal league		..	4263
German (Geo.)	..		8100
Do. mile, long		..	10126
Do. Do. short		..	6859
Hamburgh	..	..	8244
Hanover	..	..	11559
Hesse	..	..	10547
Dutch	..	..	6395
Hungarian	..	..	9113
Irish	..	..	3038
Italian	..	..	2025
Lithuanian	..	..	9784
Oldenburg	..	..	10820
Poland, short	..	..	6093
Do. long	..	..	8108
Portugal leguos	..	..	6765
Prussian mile	..	..	8461
Roman (ancient)		..	1600
Roman (modern)		..	2035
Russian verst	..	..	1167
Saxon	..	..	9905

Scotch	..	.. ..	1984
Silesian	..	.. ..	7083
Spanish legal leguas		..	4630
Do. Do.	common	..	7416
Swedish ..	..	.. ..	11704
Swiss	..	.. ..	9166
Turkey (berries)		..	1821
Westphalian mile		..	12155

MICE. See *Rats;* the same directions are applicable to *Mice.*

MILDEW, *to remove.* — Soap the linen previously wetted, and apply salt and lemon juice to both sides; or apply finely powdered pipe clay, or fullers earth, or finely powdered chalk. Expose it for several hours to the atmosphere.

MILDEW, *to remove.* — Mix soft soap with powdered starch, half as much salt, and the juice of a lemon, and lay on with a brush. Let it lay on the grass day and night till the stain is gone.——Or, take 2 ozs. of chloride of lime, pour on it a quart of boiling water, then add three quarts of cold water; steep the linen 10 or 12 hours, when every spot will be extracted.

Mix oxalic acid, citric acid, and milk together; rub into the linen; repeat as it dries; wash, and bleach on the grass.

MILK, *Chalk to detect in.*—Dilute the milk with water; the chalk if there be any, will settle to the bottom in an hour or two; put to the sediment an acid, vinegar, &c., and if effervescence takes place, it is chalk.

MILK OF ROSES, *a Cosmetic, common.*—Mix 4 ozs. of the oil of almonds with half a gallon of rose-water, and add 40 drops of the oil of tartar.

Or, take 1 lb. of Jordan almonds, 2 quarts of rose-water, 1 pint of spirits of wine, ½ oz. of oil of lavender, 1 oz. of white Windsor soap, and 2 ozs. of cream of roses. Blanch the almonds in boiling water; dry well, and pound into a paste. Pound in the soap, and mix it well with the almond paste; then add the cream of roses; mix, and add the rose-water and spirits. Strain, and add the oil of lavender gradually, and stir well. Bottle.

The *French Method.*—Mix 4 ozs. of oil of almonds, ½ oz. oil of lavender, 2 quarts of spirits of wine, and 10 ozs. of rose-water; blanch 3 lbs. of Jordan almonds; pound them with ¼ lb. of Spanish oil soap, ½ oz. of spermaceti, and half oz. of white wax. Put all into a large jar, with 2 ozs. of pearlash dissolved in 1 oz. of warm water. Shake well, and bottle.

MILK PORRIDGE.—Make a fine gruel of split grits, long boiled, or of Yorkshire oatmeal; strain, if you like; add either cold milk, or warm it with milk, as may be agreeable. Serve with toast.—See *Porridge.*

MILK PUNCH.—Take one quart of water, 3 pints of new milk, and ½ lb. of sugar, or more; boil slowly 10 minutes; take from the fire, and stir in quickly two or three well beaten eggs, mixed with a pint of cold milk. Add 4 or 5 tablespoonfuls of lemon juice, and a quart of brandy. Run it through a flannel bag. Stir it to a froth, and serve in warm glasses.

MILK SOUP.—With cinnamon boil a quart of milk, two bay leaves, and moist sugar. Put sippits in a dish; pour the milk over them; simmer over the fire till the bread is soft; beat up the yolks of two eggs with a little milk; Mix all together, and serve.

MILK, *to preserve.*—Milk often turns by an acid developed in the liquid. To prevent it, add to the milk a small portion of bi-carbonate of soda. This is not at all injurious to health; but rather aids digestion. Many of the great dairies on the continent adopt this method.

Or, scald the new milk very gently without boiling. Cream already skimmed may be kept 24 hours, if scalded without sugar; and by adding to it as much powdered lump sugar as will make it pretty sweet; it will be good two days, if kept in a cool place.

Or place a piece of newly-hammered iron, or three twelve-penny nails, in each bowl, then pour the milk upon them.

MINCED COLLOPS.—Chop beef, and mince it very small, to which add salt and pepper. Put into small jars, and pour on the top some clarified butter. When intended for use, put the clarified butter into a frying-pan, and slice some onions into the pan; fry them; add a little water to it, and then put in the mince-meat. Stew it well, and in a few minutes it will be fit to serve.

MINCE MEAT.—Good lean beef, 1 lb.; boil it 50 minutes; then chop it very fine; then take apples, currants, raisins, and suet, 1 lb. each; candied lemon, candied citron, 2 ozs. of each; and 4 ozs. of almonds. Chop each *extremely fine*; mix and add 1 lb. of sugar, and a wine-glassful and a half of brandy.

Spices and lemon juice may be added, if you like. Let it stand some hours covered before using. —This meat may be put into tartlet pans or dishes.

MINCE PIES.—Boil a neat's tongue two hours; skin it, and chop it extremely small; chop also very fine 3 lbs. of beef suet, 3 lbs. of best baking apples, 4 lbs. of clean currants, picked and well dried before the fire; 1 lb. of good raisins, stoned, and chopped very small, and 1lb. of powdered sugar; mix all together with ½ oz. each of mace and nutmeg grated; cloves and cinnamon, of each, ¼ oz., and 1 pint of brandy; make a rich puff paste. As you fill the pie, put in a little candied citron and orange, cut small.

MINCE PIES.—Clean 7 lbs. of currants, and 3½ lbs. of beef suet, chopped fine; 3½ lbs. of the lean of a sirloin of beef, minced raw; 3½ lbs of apples chopped fine; ½ lb. each of citron, lemon-peel, and orange peel, cut very small; 2 lbs. of fine sugar; 1 oz. of spice, cloves, mace, nutmegs, and cinnamon, pounded together, and sifted, the rind of 4 lemons, and 4 Seville oranges; rub all together till well mixed; mix a bottle of brandy, one of sherry, and the juice of the grated lemons and oranges together in a basin; pour half over, and press it down tight; then add the other half, at the top, to soak in by degrees; cover it close. It will keep 4 or 5 weeks. When used, sheet the dish, or tins with puff paste, and cover with the same. They will bake in ten or twelve minutes.

MINCE PIES.—Roll out puff paste to the thickness of a penny piece; lightly butter your tartlet tins; cut out from the paste round pieces, each the size of the tartlet-tins; with these pieces line the tins; put in each mince-meat; wet them round, put on the lids, making a small hole in the centre; close well at the edges; egg over lightly, and bake from 15 to 25 minutes.

Mince Meat, for the above.—Beef without skin and strings, 2 lbs.; best suet, chopped fine, free from skin, 4 lbs.; add 6 lbs. of clean dry currants; 3 lbs. chopped apples; the peel and juice of 2 lemons, half a pint of sherry, a nutmeg, ¼ oz. of cloves; ditto, mace; ditto, pimento, in finest powder; press into a deep pan or dish, and keep covered in a cool dry place.

When the pies and tarts are made, put in citron, orange, and lemon peel.

MINCE PIES, *made of eggs.*—Boil six eggs hard, shred them small; shred double the quantity of suet; then put currants washed and picked, 1 lb., or more, if the eggs are large; the peel of one lemon shred very fine, and the juice, six spoonfuls of sweet wine, mace, nutmeg, sugar, a very little salt; orange, lemon, and citron candied. Make a light paste for them.

MINCE PIES, *without meat.*—Chop fine 3 lbs. each of suet, and apples, when pared and cored; wash and dry 3 lbs. of currants; stone and chop 1 lb. of raisins; beat and sift 1½ lb. of loaf sugar; 12 ozs. of candied orange peel, and 6 ozs. of citron. Mix all well together with ¼ oz. of nutmeg, half the quantity of cinnamon, 6 or 8 cloves, and half a pint of French brandy; cover close, and keep for use.

MINT, *to cultivate.*—This is done by parting the roots in spring; or by planting cuttings in a moist soil during the summer months, and watering them several times a day till they have taken root. Plant the cuttings five inches apart.

MINT SAUCE.—Wash fresh gathered mint; pick the leaves from the stalks; mince them very fine, and put them into a sauce-boat with a tea-spoonful of sugar, and four table-spoonfuls of vinegar. It may also be made with dried mint, or with mint vinegar.

MINT VINEGAR.—Dry and pound ½ oz. of mint seed; pour upon it a quart of the best vinegar. Infuse 10 days, shaking well.

MIRANGUES.—Whisk the whites of 9 eggs to a thick froth; add the rind of 6 lemons grated fine, and a table-spoonful of sifted sugar; then lay a wet sheet of paper on a tin, and with a spoon, drop the mixture in lumps separately upon it; sift sugar over, and bake in a moderate oven, of a nice colour; then put raspberry, apricot, or any kind of jam between two bottoms; put them together, and lay them in a warm place to dry.

MOCK BRAWN.—Boil a pair of neat's feet very tender; take the meat off, and have ready the belly-piece of pork salted with salt and saltpetre for a week. Boil this almost enough; take out the bones, and roll the feet and the pork together. Then roll it very tight with a strong cloth and coarse tape. Boil it till very tender, then hang it up in the cloth till cold; after which keep it in a sousing-liquor, thus made;—Boil a quarter of a peck of wheat bran, a sprig of bay, and a sprig of rosemary, in two gallons of water, with four ounces of salt in it, for half an hour. Strain it and let it get cold.

MOCK TURTLE.—Take a calf's head with the skin on, cut it in half, and clean well; half boil it, take all the meat off in bits, break the bones of the head, and boil them in some veal and beef broth. Fry some shalot in butter, and dredge in flour to thicken the gravy; stir this into the browning, and give it one or two boils; skim it carefully, and then put in the head; put in also a pint of Madeira wine, and simmer till the meat is tender. About ten minutes before you serve, put in some basil, tarragon, chives, parsley, cayenne, pepper and salt to your taste; also two spoonfuls of mushroom-ketchup and one of soy. Squeeze the juice of a lemon into the tureen, and pour the soup upon it. Forcemeat balls, and small eggs.

MOOR GAME, *to pot.*—Pick, singe, and wash the birds; dry,

Q

and season, inside and out, pretty high, with mace, nutmeg, allspice, and salt. Pack them in as small a pot as will hold them, cover them with butter, and bake in a slow oven. When cold, take off the butter, dry them from the gravy, and put one bird into each pot, which should just fit. Add as much more butter as will cover them, but take care that it does not oil. The best way to melt it is by warming it in a basin set in a bowl of hot water.

MORELLA CHERRIES, *to preserve.*—Take full ripe cherries; take off the stalks and prick them with a pin; to every 2 lbs. of cherries, put 1½ lb. of loaf sugar; beat part of the sugar, and strew it over them; let them stand all night; dissolve the rest of the sugar in half a pint of the juice of currants; set it over a slow fire, and put in the sugared cherries, and give them a gentle scald; let stand all night again; and then give them another scald; then take them carefully out, and boil the syrup till it is thick; pour it upon the cherries; if it be too thin, boil again.

MORELLA WINE.-Free from the stalks 60 lbs of Morella cherries, and bruise them, so that the stones shall be broken. Press out the juice, and mix with 6 gallons of sherry wine, 5 lbs. of fine sugar, and 4 gallons of warm water. Powder 1 oz. each of nutmeg, cinnamon, and mace, hang them separately in small bags in the casks containing the mixture. Bung, and in a few weeks it will be a deliciously flavoured wine. Add 1 quart of French brandy.

MOTHS, *to preserve clothes from.*—Put a few cuttings of Russia leather in your trunk or wardrobe; or sprinkle a few pepper-corns, pimento-corns, or cloves in the same places.——Or, a piece of camphor in a linen bag.——Or, sheets smeared with turpentine, and well dried.

Cedar wood and tobacco leaves are very noxious to moths. It is effectual to wrap clothes in cotton or old linen saturated with a solution of camphor, and dried.——Or, mix together 12 drops of the oil of cloves, and 12 of the oil of carraway, 6 drops of the oil of lavender, a glass of whisky, and a piece of camphor. Sprinkle with it.

MOUNTAIN WINE. — Free Malaga raisins from stalks; chop them small, and put 5 lbs. to every gallon of cold spring water; infuse a fortnight, or more, stirring it occasionally; press out the liquor, and barrel it; previously fume the vessel with brimstone. Do not bung till the hissing is over. Put half a pint of French brandy to every gallon of wine.

MOUSE TRAP, *a never failing one.*—Take a piece of deal, or any kind of wood, about 6 inches broad, and 9 or 10 inches long, and put into the sides, about the middle, 2 pins, or thick pieces of round wire; then take two sticks about two feet long, and lay them on the table, or dresser, &c., with a notch cut at the end of each stick, so that about one half of the board may lie on the table, or place to which the mice resort; let the end projecting from the table be baited with cheese, &c., and when the mice run off the table to the bait, it will tip them into a vessel three fourths full of water, which must be placed directly under the projection, and they will be drowned.

MOUTH WASH.—Take ¼ oz. each of dried mint, thyme, and lemon thyme; cloves, bruised; half a nutmeg grated; pour on these ingredients ½ oz. of tincture of myrrh, and ½ oz. of spirits of wine, a cupful of water, and 12 drops of oil of peppermint. Keep in a bottle; shake up before using. Use as a gargle; it will purify the mouth from bad odours and tastes.

MUFFINS.—Take 14 lbs. of flour, 2 ozs. of salt, 4 quarts of water, and ½ a pint of yeast; beat them 20 minutes, and let them rise to the top of what you mix them in; beat them down a second time, turn them out on a bed of flour, and with a knife and spoon make them up; when the iron is hot, sift a little flour upon it, which if hot, will turn brown; lay the muffins on; when blistered on the top turn them; and when brown on the other side, they will be baked enough. Some persons, when they are half done dip them in warm milk, and bake to a pale brown. The addition of eggs is an improvement; and so is milk, i. e. 1 quart milk, and 1 quart of water, instead of the two quarts of water.

MUFFIN PUDDING.—Boil a few coriander seeds, a bit of lemon peel and sugar, in 1½ pint of milk; braize the milk over four muffins; when cold, crush them with a wooden spoon; add nearly a cupful of brandy; ½ lb. of any dried fruit, some grated nutmeg, 2 ozs. of Jordan almonds, blanched and pounded fine, and six eggs well beaten; mix well together, and boil in a basin, or bake in a dish with paste round it. It may be made plainer; or good, by substituting currants for sweet-meats.

MULLED ALE.—Boil a quart of good ale with some nutmeg, beat up six eggs and mix them with a little cold ale, then pour the hot ale to it, and return it several times to prevent it curdling; warm, and stir it sufficiently thick, add a piece of butter or a glass of brandy, and serve it with dry toast.

MULLED WINE.—Boil some spice in a little water till the flavour is gained, then add an equal quantity of port, some sugar and nutmeg; boil together, and serve with toast.

Another way.—Boil a bit of cinnamon and some grated nutmeg a few minutes, in a large cupful of water; then pour to it a pint of port wine, and add sugar to your taste; beat it up, and it will be ready. Or it may be made of good British wine.

MULLET, *red.*—It is called the Sea-Woodcock. Clean, but leave the inside, fold in oiled paper, and gently bake in a small dish. Make a sauce of the liquor that comes from the fish, with a piece of butter, a little flour, a little essence of anchovy, and a glass of sherry. Give it a boil and serve in a boat, and the fish in the paper cases.

MUMPS.—This is a disease of the salivary glands which are situated on each side of the lower jaw. It generally comes on with cold shiverings, sickness, and vomiting, pain in the head, succeeded by swelling of one or both sides of the neck, and sometimes becomes very painful, and so large as to impede the breathing, and the swallowing. It generally increases till the fourth day, and then declines.

In this complaint, little medicine is required. Give an aperient. See page 20, 21. Bathe the feet frequently in warm water. At night give the Diaphoretic Powder or Decoction, page 143. Bathe the swelling with warm water and tincture of myrrh, and thirty drops of laudanum; or apply flannels dipped in the mixture. Cover the swelling with flannel. In extreme cases, give the Vapour Bath and the Composition Powder, page 119. Should the swelling break, apply a slippery elm poultice, made with milk and water; (See Slippery Elm;) then apply the Black Salve for healing, page 65, or the Green Ointment, page 188.

MUSSELS, *to detect poisonous.*—Put a silver spoon into the vessel with the mussels, and let it continue therein while they are over the fire; when removed take out the spoon, and if it is of a bright colour, there is no poison; but if it is tinged of a black or dark hue, they are unfit for use.

MUSSEL SOUP.—Boil the mussels till they are open; take them off; put them into another stewpan; then with butter rolled in flour, some parsley, and sweet herbs, with some good gravy, let them simmer till reduced to one half; add a liaison, and serve it up hot. Before boiling, take out the moss, crabs, &c.

MUSSELS, *to stew.*—Wash and pick out moss, and boil as before; put them into a saucepan; to a quart of mussels, add half a pint of the liquor strained, two blades of mace, a piece of butter rolled in flour; let them stew; toast bread brown, and lay it round the dish; pour in the mussels, and send to table hot.

MUSHROOMS.—Every cook should be perfectly acquainted with the different sorts of things called by this name by ignorant people, as the death of many persons has been occasioned by carelessly eating the poisonous kinds.

The eatable mushrooms first appear very small, and of a round form, on a little stalk. They grow very fast, and the upper part and stalk are white. As the size increases, the under part gradually opens, and shows a fringy fur of a very fine salmon-colour, which continues more or less till the mushroom has gained some size, and then turns to a dark brown. These marks should be attended to, and likewise whether the skin can be easily parted from the edges and the middle. Those that have white or yellow fur should be carefully avoided, though many of them have the same smell (but not so strong) as the right sort.

MUSHROOMS, *to pickle.*—Buttons must be rubbed with a bit of flannel and salt; and from the larger, take out the *red* inside, for when they are black they will not do, being too old. Throw a little salt over, and put them into a stew-pan with some mace and pepper; as the liquor comes out, shake them well, and keep them over a gentle fire till all of it be dried into them again; then put as much vinegar into the pan as will cover them, give it one warm, and turn all into a glass or stone jar. They will keep two years, and are delicious.

MUSHROOMS, *to stew.*—The large buttons are best, and the small flaps while the fur is still red. Rub the large buttons with salt and a bit of flannel, cut out the fur, and take off the skin from the others. Sprinkle them with salt, and put into a stew-pan with some pepper corns; simmer slowly till done, then put a small bit of butter and flour, and two spoonfuls of cream; give them one boil, and serve with sippets of bread.

MUSHROOMS, *to dry.*—Wipe them clean, and of the large take out the brown, and peel off the skin. Lay them on paper to dry in a cool oven, and keep them in paper bags in a dry place. When used, simmer them in the gravy, and they will swell to near their former size. To simmer them in their own liquor till it dry up into them, shaking the pan, then drying on tin plates, is a good way, with spice or not, as above, before made into powder.

Tie down with bladder, and keep it in a dry place or in paper.

MUSHROOMS, *to fricassee.* — Peel and scrape the inside of the mushrooms; put them into salt and water; if buttons, rub them with flannel; take them out, and boil them with fresh salt and water; when they are tender, put in a little shred parsley, an onion stuck with cloves, (or both separately, and chopped); toss them up with a good lump of butter rolled in a little flour. You may put in three spoonfuls of thick cream, and a little nutmeg cut in pieces; but mind to take out the nutmeg and onion before serving.

MUSHROOM KETCHUP.—Take the largest broad mushrooms, break them into an earthen pan, strew salt over, and strew them now and then for three days. Then let them stand for twelve, till there is a thick scum over; strain, and boil the liquor with Jamaica and black pepper, mace, ginger, a clove or two, and some mustard seed. When cold, bottle it, and tie a bladder over the cork; in three months boil it again with some fresh spice, and it will then keep a twelvemonth.

Mushroom Ketchup, another way.—Take a stewpan full of the large-flap mushrooms, that are not worm-eaten, and the skins and fringe of those you have pickled; throw a handful of salt among them, and set them by a slow fire; they will produce a great deal of liquor, which you must strain, and put to it four ounces of shalots, two cloves of garlic, a good deal of pepper, ginger, mace, cloves, and a few bay-leaves, boil and skim very well. When cold, cork close. In two months boil it up again with a little fresh spice and a stick of horse-radish, and it will then keep for a year; which mushroom ketchup rarely does, if not boiled a second time.

MUSHROOM POWDER. — Take the thickest largest buttons; peel them, cut off the rotten end, but do not wash them; spread them separately on pewter dishes, and put in a slow oven to dry; let the liquor dry into the mushrooms, for it makes the powder stronger; continue in the oven till they can be powdered; then beat them up in a mortar, and sift them through a fine sieve, with a little cayenne pepper and pounded mace; bottle, and keep in a dry place.

MUSK JULAP.-Rub ½ drachm of musk well together with ½ oz. of sugar; gradually add simple cinnamon and peppermint water, each 2 ozs., and two drachms of volatile aromatic spirit.

In the low state of nervous fevers, hiccupping, convulsions, and other spasmodic affections, two table-spoonfuls of this julap may be taken every two or three hours.

MUSLINS, *to keep a good colour.*—Never wash muslins, or any kind of cotton goods with linen; for the latter discharges a kind of gum, and colouring matter, every time it is washed which discolours the muslin and cotton—wash them by themselves.

MUSLINS, *Uninflammable.*—Mix with starch about the same weight of carbonate of lime, commonly called Spanish white or Spanish chalk. It does not deteriorate the appearance or injure the material of the muslin.

MUSTARD. — This plant is both culinary and medicinal. As a condiment it is generally used and esteemed. As a cataplasm or poultice, it is made thus;—powdered mustard seed, 4 ozs.; vinegar, as much as is sufficient to mix it for a plaster; it is stronger by adding horse radish, scraped, 2 ozs.

It is employed as a stimulant; it often inflames the part, and raises blisters, but not so perfectly as cantharides. Sometimes they are applied to the soles of the feet, in the low state of acute diseases, for raising the pulse, and relieving the head.

The white mustard acts not only on the bowels, but also on the skin. It wonderfully strengthens the whole line of the alimentary canal, improves the appetite, the digestion, and promotes sleep, and the health generally.

When the seed is used to remove constipation, take it an hour before breakfast fasting. A small tablespoonful is sufficient.

MUSTARD, *to make.*—Mix the best Durham flour of mustard by degrees with boiling water to a proper thickness, rubbing it perfectly smooth; add a little salt, and a little tincture of cayenne, and keep it in a small jar close covered, and put only as much into the glass as will be used soon, which should be wiped daily round the edges.

MUSTARD WHEY. — Milk and water, of each, 1 pint; bruised mustard seed, 1½ oz.; boil together till the curd be separated; strain. This is a good way of giving mustard. It warms and invigorates the stomach, and promotes the secretions; it is very useful in nervous disorders, chronic rheumatism, palsy, dropsy, &c. A tea-cupful several times a day.

MUSTY CASKS, *to sweeten.* —Throw in burning coals, and then cold water. Public brewers wash their casks with lime and water, mixed nearly to the consistence of paint; remain till dry, and then wash well with water.

MUSTY FLOUR.—It may be restored by mixing with 15 lbs. of flour, 1 oz. of magnesia. Leaven and bake in the usual way. The loaves will rise well, be spongy and light, and whiter than bread made in the usual way, and have an excellent taste.

MUTTON, *to choose.*—Choose it by the fineness of its grain, good colour, and firm white fat. It is not the better for being young; if of a good breed and well fed, it is better for age; but this only holds with wether-mutton: the flesh of the ewe is paler, and the texture finer. Ram mutton is very strong-flavoured; the flesh is of a deep red, and the fat is spongy.

MUTTON, *to grill a breast of.* —Score a breast of mutton in diamonds, and rub it over with the yolk of an egg; then strew it over with a few bread crumbs, and shred parsley; put it into a Dutch oven to broil; taste it with fresh butter; pour in the dish good caper sauce, and serve.

MUTTON, *Breast of.*—Cut off the surperfluous fat, and roast and serve the meat with stewed cucumbers; or to eat cold, covered with chopped parsley. Or half boil and then grill it before the fire; in which case cover it with crumbs and herbs, and serve with caper sauce, or if boned, take off a good deal of the fat, and cover it with bread, herbs, and seasoning; then roll and boil; and serve with chopped walnuts, or with capers and butter.

MUTTON, *to collar a breast of.*—Take out the bones and gristle; then take some grated bread, a few cloves, some mace, pepper, salt, and a little lemon-peel, chopped fine; lay the meat flat; rub it over with egg, and spread the seasoning over it; add two or three anchovies, washed and boned, then roll the meat as hard as possible; bind it with coarse tape, and boil it in a cloth. Or it may be skewered, and the tape omitted, and either roasted or baked.

MUTTON, *to dress a leg of, to eat like venison.*—Take a large fat leg of mutton, cut out like a haunch of venison, as soon as it is killed; whilst warm, take out the bloody vein; stick it in several places in the under side with a sharp pointed knife; pour over it a bottle of port wine; turn it in the wine four or five times a day for five days; dry it well with a clean cloth; hang it up in the air with the thick end uppermost for five days; dry it night and morning to keep it from being damp or musty. When it is to be roasted cover with paper and paste, as you do venison. Serve with venison sauce. It will take four hours, roasting.

MUTTON, *to dress a haunch of.*—Keep it as long as it can be preserved sweet; wash it with warm milk and water, or vinegar, if necessary; wash it well, lest the outside should have a bad flavour from keeping. Put a paste of coarse flour on strong paper, and fold the haunch in; set it at a great distance from the fire, and allow proportional time for the paste; don't take it off till about thirty-five or forty minutes before serving, and then baste it continually. Bring the haunch nearer to the fire before you take off the paste, and froth it up as you would venison.

A gravy must be made of 1½ lb. of loin of old mutton, simmered in a pint of water to half, and no seasoning but salt; brown it with a little burnt sugar, and send it up in the dish but there should be a good deal of gravy in the meat; for though long at the fire, the distance and covering will prevent its roasting out. Serve with currant-jelly sauce.

MUTTON, *Leg of, boiled.*—Soak well for an hour or two in salt and water; do not use much salt. Wipe well, and boil in a floured cloth. Boil from two hours to two hours and a half. Serve with caper sauce, potatoes, mashed turnips, greens, oyster sauce, &c.

☞ To preserve the gravy in the leg, do not put it in the water till it boils; for the sudden contact with water causes a slight film over the surface, which prevents the escape of the gravy, which is abundant when carved.

MUTTON, *Leg of, to force.*—Raise the skin, and take out the lean part of the mutton; chop it very fine with one anchovy; shred a bundle of sweet herbs; grate a penny loaf, half a lemon, nutmeg, pepper and salt to your taste; make them into a force-meat, with three eggs, and a large glass of port wine; fill up the skin with the forcemeat; but leave the bone and shank in their places, and it will appear like a whole leg; lay it in an earthen dish, with a pint of port wine under it, and put it in the oven; it will take two hours and a half; when it comes out, take off all the fat; strain the gravy over the mutton; surround it with hard yolks of eggs, and pickled mushrooms. Garnish with pickles.

MUTTON, *Kebobbed.*—Take all the fat out of a loin of mutton, on the outside also if too fat, and remove the skin. Joint it at every one; mix a small nutmeg grated with a little salt and pepper, crumbs and herbs; dip the steaks into the yolks of three eggs, and sprinkle the above mixture all over them. Then place the steaks together as they were before they were cut asunder, tie them and fasten them on a small spit. Roast them at a quick fire; set a dish under, and baste them with a good piece of butter, and the gravy of the meat; but throw some more of the above seasoning over. When enough, take up, and lay it in a dish; have half a pint of good gravy ready besides that in the dish; and put into it two spoonfuls of ketchup, and rub down a tea-spoonful of flour with it; give this a boil, and pour it over the mutton, but first skim off the fat well. Mind to keep the meat hot till the gravy is quite ready.

MUTTON, *Loin of.*—Roasted; if cut lengthways as a saddle, some think it cuts better. Or for steaks, pies, or broth.

MUTTON, *a la Francois.* — Take away the fat from loin cutlets; dredge them a little with pepper on both sides, and plentifully with flour; heat in a saucepan three table-spoonfuls of water; put the cutlets in one flat layer at the bottom when the water begins to boil; throw in a little salt when they begin to stew, and a bit of butter. Let them simmer as gently as possible, the pan raised above the fire, for 1¼ hour. Turn the cutlets when half done; and put to them a little gravy, if they do not yield sufficient themselves.—It is a fine relish, very nutritious, and very suitable for invalids.

MUTTON, *Fillet of, braised.*—Take off the chump end of the loin, butter some paper, and put over it, and then a paste as for venison, roast it two hours. Do not let it be the least brown. Have ready some French beans boiled and drained on a sieve; and while the mutton is being glazed, give them one heat up in gravy, and lay them on the dish with the meat over them.

MUTTON, *Rumps and kidney to dress.*—Stew six rumps in some good mutton gravy half an hour; take up, and let them stand to cool. Clear the gravy from the fat; and put into it 4 ozs. of boiled rice, an onion stuck with cloves, till the rice is thick. Wash the rumps with yolks of eggs well beaten; and strew over them crumbs of bread, a little pepper and salt, chopped parsley, and thyme, and grated lemon-peel. fry in butter to a fine brown. While the rump is stewing, lard the kidneys with bacon, and put them to roast in a Dutch oven. When the rumps are fried, the grease must be drained before they are put on the dish, and the pan being cleared likewise from the fat, warm the rice in it. Lay the latter on the dish; the rumps put round on the rice, the narrow ends towards the middle, and the kidneys between. Garnish with hard eggs cut in half, the white being left on; or with different coloured pickles.

MUTTON SAUSAGES.-Take a pound of the rawest part of a leg of mutton that has been either roasted or boiled; chop the same very small, and season it with pepper, salt, mace, and nutmeg; add to it six ounces of beef suet, some sweet herbs, two anchovies, and a pint of oysters, all chopped very small; a quarter of a pound of grated bread, and some of the anchovy liquor, and the yolks and whites of two eggs well beaten. Put it all, when well mixed, into a little pot; and use it by rolling it into balls, or sausage-shape, and frying. If approved, a *little* shalot may be added, or garlic, which is a great improvement.

MUTTON, *Saddle of, to roast.* —Let it be well kept first. Raise the skin, and then skewer it on again; take it off a quarter of an hour before serving it, sprinkle it with some salt, baste it, and dredge it well with flour. The rump should be split, and skewered back on each side. The joint may be large or small according to the company; it is the most elegant if the latter. Being broad it requires a high and strong fire.

MUTTON, *Shoulder of, to boil with Oysters.*—Hang it some days, then salt it well for two days; bone it, and sprinkle it with pepper and a bit of mace pounded: lay some oysters over it, and roll the meat up tight and tie it. Stew it in a small quantity of water, with an onion and a few pepper-corns, till quite tender.

Have ready a little good gravy and some oysters stewed in it; thicken this with flour and butter, and pour over the mutton when the tape is taken off. The stewpan should be kept closely covered.

MUTTON, *to roll a Loin of.*— Hang the mutton till tender: bone it; and lay a seasoning of pepper, allspice, mace, nutmeg, and a few cloves, all in fine powder, over it. Next day prepare a stuffing as for hare; beat the meat and cover it with the stuffing; roll it up tight, and tie it. Half bake it in a slow oven; let it grow cold; take off the fat, and put the gravy into a stew-pan; flour the meat, and put it in likewise; stew it till almost ready; and add a glass of port wine, some ketchup, and anchovy, and a little lemon-pickle, half an hour before serving; serve it in the gravy, and with jelly-sauce. A few fresh mushrooms are a great improvement; but if to eat like hare do not use these, nor the lemon pickle.

MUTTON, *Basque of.*—Take the caul of a leg of veal; lay it in a copper dish, the size of a small punch bowl; take the lean of a leg of mutton that has been kept a week; chop it very small; take half its weight in beef marrow, the crumbs of a penny loaf, the yolks of four eggs, two anchovies, half a pint of port wine, the rind of half a lemon grated; mix it like sausage meat, and lay it in your caul in the inside of your dish; close up the caul, and bake in a quick oven; when you take out, turn the dish upside down, and turn the whole out; pour over it brown gravy, and send it up with venison sauce.

MUTTON, *French steaks of a neck of.*—Cut off most of the fat of a prime neck of mutton; cut the steaks two inches thick; make a large hole through the middle of the fleshy part of every steak with a knife, and stuff it with pepper, salt, and nutmeg mixed up with the yolk of an egg. When stuffed, wrap them in writing paper, and put them in a Dutch oven; set them before the fire to broil; they will take nearly an hour; put a little brown gravy in the dish, and serve them in the papers.

MUTTON, *Hotch Potch.*—Stew peas, lettuce, and onions, in a very little water, with a beef or ham bone. While these are doing, fry some mutton or lamb steaks seasoned, of a nice brown: three quarters of an hour before dinner put the steaks into a stew-pan, and the vegetables over them; stew them, and serve all together in a tureen.

Another.—Knuckle of veal, and scrag of mutton, stewed with vegetables as above; to both add a bit of butter rolled in flour.

MUTTON, *to hash.*—Cut thin slices of dressed mutton, fat and lean; flour them; have ready a little onion boiled in two or three spoonfuls of water; add to it a little gravy and the meat seasoned, and make it hot, but not to boil. Serve in a covered dish. Instead of onion, a clove, a spoonful of currant-jelly, and half a glass of port wine, will give an agreeable flavour of venison, if the meat be fine.

Pickled cucumber, or walnut, cut small, warm in it for change.

MUTTON, *to harrico a neck of.*—Cut the best end of a neck of mutton into chops, in single ribs; flour them, and fry them a light brown; put them into a large sauce-pan, with two quarts of water, a large carrot cut in slices, cut at the edge like wheels. When they have stewed 15 minutes, put in two turnips, cut in square slices, the white part of a head of celery, a few heads of asparagus, two cabbage lettuces fried, and cayenne to your taste; boil all together till they are tender. The gravy is not to be thickened. Put into a tureen or soup-dish.

MUTTON, *to hash.*—Cut the meat into small thin pieces; boil the bones with an onion, a few sweet herbs, a blade of mace a little whole pepper, salt, and a piece of crust toasted very crisp; boil till there is just enough for sauce; strain it and put into a saucepan with a piece of butter rolled in flour; then put in the meat; and when it is hot, it is done enough; season with pepper and salt; have ready some thin bread toasted brown, and cut three-cornerways; lay them in the dish, and pour over the hash; garnish with pickles and horse radish.

MUTTON BROTH. — Take the scrag end of a neck of mutton; chop it into small pieces; put it into a saucepan, and fill it with water; set it over the fire, and when the scum begins to rise, take it clean off, and put in a blade or two of mace, a little French barley, or a crust of white bread, to thicken it. When the mutton is boiled, so that it will shake to pieces, strain the broth through a hair sieve; skim off the fat, and serve with dry toast.

MUTTON CHOPS.—Rub the chops with pepper, salt, nutmeg, and a little parsley; roll each chop in white paper well buttered on the inside, and rolled at each end close; have some hog's lard, or beef drip, boiling in a stewpan; put in the chops, fry them of a fine brown; lay them in a dish, and garnish with fried parsley; throw some all over and serve them hot.

MUTTON COLLOPS.—Take a loin of mutton that has been well hung; and cut from the part next the leg, some collops very thin. Take out the sinew. Season the collops with salt, pepper, and mace; and strew over them shred parsley, thyme, and two or three shalots: fry them in butter till half done; add half a pint of gravy, a little juice of lemon, and a piece of butter rubbed in flour; and simmer the whole very gently five minutes. They should be served instantly, or they will be hard.

MUTTON HAM.——Choose a fine-grained leg of weather-mutton of 12 or 14 lbs. weight; cut it ham-shape, and hang two days. Then put into a stew-pan, ½ lb. of bay-salt, the same of common salt, 2 ozs. of saltpetre, and ½ lb. of coarse sugar, all in powder; mix and make it hot; rub well into the ham. Turn it in the liquor every day; at the end of four days put 2 ozs. more of common salt; in twelve days take it out, dry it, and hang it up in wood-smoke a week. To be used the same way as ordinary ham.

MUTTON PUDDING.—Season with salt, pepper, and a bit of onion; lay one layer of steaks at the bottom of the dish; and pour a batter of potatoes boiled and pressed through a colander, and mixed with milk and an egg, over them; then putting the rest of the steaks, and batter, bake it.

Batter with flour, instead of potatoes, eats well, but requires more egg, and is not so good.

MUTTON STEAKS, *to broil.*—Should be cut from the loin or neck that has been hung; if a neck the bones should not be long. They should be broiled on a clear fire, seasoned when half done, and often turned; take them up into a very hot dish, rub a bit of butter on each, and serve hot the moment they are done.

MUTTON STEAKS, *Maintenon.*—Half-fry, and stew while hot, with herbs, crumbs, and seasoning; put them in paper immediately, and finish on the gridiron. Be careful the paper does not catch; rub a bit of butter on it first to prevent that.

NAILS, *growing into the flesh.*—Cut a notch in the middle of the nail every time the nail is pared. The disposition to close the notch draws the nail up from the sides.

NAILS, *to whiten.*--Wash them with turpentine, then with soap and water, next with a solution of oxalic acid, and lastly, wash the hands well in warm water.

NANKEEN DYE.-Boil equal parts of anatto and common potash till dissolved.

NARCOTICS. —— Medicines abating pain, causing sleep, and calming irritation.

NASTURTIUMS, *to pickle.*—Get them when very young. Steep in salt and water; take them out, and put them into boiling salt and water, and boil a minute. Then pour upon them in the jar the best vinegar with what spices are most agreeable. Cover close. They will be ready in a week.

NEAT'S TONGUE, *to boil.*—"Neat" is an old Saxon word, meaning animals of the ox kind. Soak it during the previous night. Dress it; put it into cold water. It will take 4 or 5 hours. A tongue out of the pickle need not be soaked, but it will require nearly the same time. An hour before it is dished up, take it out, and blanch it; boil again till tender.

NEAT'S TONGUE, *to fricassee.*—Boil the tongue till tender; then peel and cut into slices; put them into a frying-pan with butter, and fry them brown. Pour the butter from the pan, and put in some good gravy, with sweet herbs, onion, garlic, pepper, salt, mace, and a wine-glassful of port wine. Simmer half an hour; take out the tongue; strain the gravy, and put all again into the pan with the yolks of two eggs well beaten, a little grated nutmeg, and some butter rolled in flour; shake the whole well together, simmer five minutes, and put the tongue into the dish; pour over it the sauce, and serve hot.

NEATS' TONGUE, *to fry*.—Boil till tender; cut it into slices, and season with nutmeg, cinnamon and sugar; beat up the yolk of an egg with a little lemon-juice, and rub it over the slices; make some butter boiling hot in the frying-pan, and put in the slices. When done, serve with melted butter, sugar, and sherry wine, made into a sauce.

NECK OF MUTTON, *to taste like venison*.—Perforate the neck all over with little holes, and pour a bottle of port wine over it, and let it lie in the wine two or three days; turn it often; then hang it three days in the open air, but not in the sun; often wipe down with a cloth, to prevent it becoming musty. When being roasted, baste it with the wine it was steeped in; put white paper, threefold, to keep in the fat; roast it thoroughly, and then take off the skin, and froth it nicely, and serve.

NECK OF PORK, *rolled to roast*.—Bone it; put a forcemeat of chopped sage, a very few crumbs of bread, salt, pepper, and two or three berries of allspice over the inside; then roll the meat as tightly as you can, and roast it slowly.

NECTAR.—Chopped raisins, 3 lbs.; raspberry jelly, 1 lb.; loaf sugar, 5 lbs.; two grated nutmegs, boiling water, 3 gallons. When cold, add oil of nutmeg, oil of carraway, and oil of cloves, of each, 10 drops; add 3 lemons sliced. Infuse 4 days. Strain, and add 1 quart of brandy or rum. Bottle.

NECTARINES, *to preserve*.—Peel, and cut them in two; simmer them in boiling water till they float; drain; boil in clarified sugar till they cease simmering; let them stay in till next day; drain them out, and boil the sugar to the second degree, (see *sugar*); add the fruit to it to boil a moment, and repeat the next day. Let the sugar and fruit incorporate two days before potting, and keep the pan in a warm place: the proportion of fruit and sugar is in equal quantities.

NERVES.—These are contractile bundles of white cords, whose ends are connected to the brain, and spinal marrow, and thence extending over the whole body, to receive impressions from external objects. They are in the eyes, at the root of the teeth, about the ears, in fact every where in the body, from the crown of the head to the sole of the foot. Two pairs of nerves proceed out of each side of the spine, and thence ramifying to every part of the body. They are so abundant, that we cannot touch any part of the skin with the point of a needle without coming in contact with a nerve, and a blood vessel. The great sympathetic nerve is the most important of all. It communicates with all the spinal nerves, and several of those of the brain.

NERVE POWDER.—Take 1 oz. each of scullcap, and valerian; catnep, 1 oz.; cayenne, 1 drachm; coriander seeds, ½ oz. Pulverize, and mix. Take a teaspoonful in a cupful of boiling water, leaving room for milk and sugar. Repeat according to the symptoms. This powder tranquillizes the most irritable nerves without debilitating and deadening their sensibility. It greatly strengthens the nerves.

NERVOUSNESS.—Sulphate of quinine, 1 drachm; dissolve it in 6 ounces of camphorated julap;

add of the volatile tincture of valerian, 3 drachms; tincture of Columba, ½ ounce Mix. When the nerves are irritable, attended with indigestion, flatulence, and occasional headache, this is often serviceable. Three table-spoonfuls to be taken three times a day.

NERVOUS DISORDERS; *Rev. John Wesley's Directions.*— When the nerves perform the office too languidly *a good air* is the first requisite. The patient should rise early, and, as soon as the dew is off the ground, walk; let his breakfast be mother of thyme tea, gathered in June, using half as much as we do of common tea. Or, the common garden thyme, if the former cannot be procured. When the nerves are too sensible, let the person breathe a proper air. Let him eat fresh veal, chickens, or mutton. Vegetables should be eaten sparingly; the most simple is the French bean, and the best root is the turnip. Wine should be avoided; and all sauces. Sometimes he may breakfast upon a quarter of an ounce of valerian root infused in hot water, to which he may add both cream and sugar. Tea is not proper. When the person finds an uncommon oppression, let him take a large spoonful of tincture of valerian root.

This tincture should be made thus:—Cut in pieces six ounces of wild valerian root, gathered in June, and fresh dried. Bruise it in a mortar, that the pieces may be split, but it should not be beat into powder: put this into a quart of strong sherry wine; cork the bottle and let it stand three weeks, shaking it every day; then press it out, and filter through paper.

But there is no remedy for nervous disorders of every kind, comparable to the proper and constant use of the electrical machine.

NERVOUS DROPS.—Mix 8 drops of spirits of hartshorn with 4 drops of the oil of lavender, and take in a wine-glassful of water.

NERVOUS MIXTURE.—Liquid carbonate of ammonia, ½ drachm; compound tincture of cardamom, ½ oz.; oil of lavender, 8 drops; mint water, 3 ozs.; mix. and take in two or three doses. It is invaluable.

NERVOUS PILL.—Assafœtida, extract of hops, carbonate of ammonia, of each 1 oz.; extract of valerian, 20 grains. Dissolve the first two ingredients over the fire, then take off, and add the others; mix well, and with a few drops of the oil of lavender, and a little powdered liquorice, form into pills. Dose, one or two once or twice a day.—*Valuable* in all nervous and hysterical disorders.

NERVOUS TINCTURE.—Compound tincture of bark, 2 ozs.; ammoniated tincture of valerian, 1½ ozs.; compound tincture of aloes, ½ oz. Mix. Good for general weakness, low spirits, and nervous irritability. Two teaspoonfuls twice a day.

NETTLE.—The nettles make a good rubefacient for limbs cold, benumbed, and torpid. Paralytic parts being beaten and stung with this herb, have regained their vigour, and limbs which have lost their use by rheumatism. The juice is astringent, and is good in gravelly complaints, internal hæmorrhage, and spitting of blood.

A decoction is excellent in scurvy. The decoction is valuable in cases of bloody urine. The seeds and flowers of the nettle are as good a tonic as Peruvian bark in fevers and ague. About *a drachm* given in wine. A decoction of the root is most valuable in diarrhœa and dysentery, or laxity of the bowels and bloody flux. It should be sweetened. Cancers, it has been said, have yielded to the juice of nettles, as much as four ounces having been taken in a day.—See *Robinson's Herbal.*

NETTLE BEER. — Take a peck or more of nettle tops, and 4 lbs. of malt, and boil in two gallons of water, with 2 ozs of hops; 4 ozs. of sarsaparilla, 1½ lb. of sugar, and ½ oz. of ginger; strain, and when nearly cold, add a little yeast. Bottle while in a state of fermentation. Most valuable—a pleasant beverage—and a wonderful purifier of the blood.

NETTLE RASH.—So called from its resemblance to that produced by the stinging of nettles. The skin is raised, and whitish on the top; it is attended with itching and tingling. It is a very mild disease, and seldom requires much medicine. The following remedies have been recommended:

An equal proportion of oil, vinegar, and spirit of wine, applied to the skin, will afford temporary relief for the itching. Take, at the same time, 6 grains of magnesia in a glass of lime water three times a day.——Or rub the part well with parsley.

But it is best to give the Vapour Bath of bitter decoction, and apply to the part the Stimulating Liniment, and an aperient, page 20, 21. ——Or apply tincture of lobelia and tincture of myrrh, mixed, to the skin. Sponge the body every morning in salt and water. Weak camphorated spirit is a good rubefacient in this disease. An emetic sometimes effectually dislodges the disease.

NEURALGIA, OR TIC DOLOUREUX.—Put half a drachm of sal-ammonia in an ounce of camphor water. Take a teaspoonful at a dose, and repeat the dose several times at intervals of five minutes, if the pain be not relieved at once. This medicine has generally cured.

Or, take extract of valerian, 2 ozs.; henbane, 1½ oz.; aconite, ½ oz. Mix well, and with oil of lavender, form into pills. Take one or two every four hours. It acts like a charm on neuralgia, and all nervous disorders.——Or, apply bruised horse radish to the part affected. Chloroform has recently been applied to parts affected with neuralgia. Indeed it is made a patent medicine for "Tic." A piece of lint should be soaked in it, and applied; cover it with flannel.

NEUTRALIZING MIXTURE. — Powdered rhubarb, 3 scruples; saleratus, or crude bicarbonate of potash, 3 scruples; powdered peppermint plant, 3 scruples; boiling water, ½ pint; decoction of aniseeds, ½ pint. Mix. Strain, sweeten with sugar, and add three table-spoonfuls of brandy. Take one or two table-spoonfuls as oft as the symptoms require it. For children a less dose.

Very valuable in cholera, bowel complaints of children, laxity of the bowels, flux, &c. An infallible remedy.

NIBBLE CAKES.—Make a good puff paste; roll thick; cut into lozenges about the size of the palm of the hand; brush it over with beaten yolks of eggs and strew macaroni drops powder over them, with a little powder of orange flowers, and lemon peel chopped very fine; stick bits of scalded sweet almonds in the paste pointed upwards; cover them with paper in the oven, to keep them of a palish colour.

NIGHTMARE. — The complaint always happens during disturbed sleep. It comes on with a sense of great weight on the chest, and a dreaming of something very frightful and horrible, bad persons, spectres of various shapes, wild beasts, infuriated animals in pursuit, and which the patient cannot escape, though apparently he makes or tries to make the greatest efforts to escape; he attempts to cry out, but generally in vain. The sensation is very distressing and painful. Sometimes the uneasiness continues after he awakes, so as to prevent his turning or moving in bed for some time.

Studious, and nervous people, are most subject to it; it is also caused by heavy suppers. The disease is probably produced by indigestion, and by compression of the lungs, and the consequent obstruction to the free return of blood from the brain. The disease is dangerous, and, doubtless, many have died under the attack; and their death has been attributed to apoplexy.

The remedy is to avoid all exciting causes, as too much abstruse thinking, late and heavy suppers, food difficult of digestion, cold feet, costiveness, and flatulence. To prevent the nightmare, mix together 10 grains of carbonate of soda; 3 drachms of compound tincture of cardamoms; 1 drachm of simple syrup, and 1 oz. of peppermint water. Repeat for several nights in succession; afterwards take a few drops of the *Aperient Mixture*, page 20, or the Aperient Tonic Mixture, page 21. Also a little cayenne in scullcap tea will prevent an attack. Those who are habitually subject to nightmare should not sleep in a room alone, but have some person near them, to be awakened by their moans, groans, &c.

Dr. Beach says, "It is not improbable that some of those persons who have been found dead in their beds were destroyed by it."

NIGHTSHADE, *Deadly.*—See *Robinson's Herbal*.

NIGHTSHADE, *Woody.*—See *Robinson's Herbal*.

NITRATE OF SODA.—Farmers find from one to two hundred weight per acre a good dressing for their land; and therefore this quantity may be regarded, for the present, as a safe proportion for ordinary crops. When used on a smaller scale, we are much in want of information as to its proper proportion if mixed with water. The following, however, seem to be ascertained facts:—Six ounces in four gallons of water suit lettuce and celery; one pound in twelve gallons is a safe quantity for dahlias. Strawberries are much improved by it in the proportion of one ounce to a gallon. In other cases, onions are reported to be much improved by water holding the nitrate of soda in solution in the proportion of one pound to eight gallons. Its effects are extremely active on coniferous plants, applied in a top-dressing at the rate of one hundred pounds per acre.

About its action, under favourable circumstances, there can be no doubt. Fir-trees have been changed from yellow to deep green in about a fortnight from the time of the application. We have seen similar effects upon common shrubs in a worn-out gravelly soil; and the rapidity with which the crops to which it has been applied acquired a deep green healthy colour is generally spoken of. Sometimes, however, it is stated to produce no effect. This may have been owing to the land on which it has been used already abounding in alkaline matter, so that any further addition has been useless; or it may have arisen from the nitrate having been used in a bad season of the year.—*Gardener's Chronicle.*

NITRE, *Sweet Spirit of Nitre.*—This is employed as a diuretic, antispasmodic, diaphoretic, and refrigerant in inflammatory affections. It is a good and useful diuretic in dropsies, especially in some of the mild forms of the complaint, as in dropsy following scarlatina. It is given with squills, acetate or nitrate of potash, freely diluted with barley water. As a carminative and antispasmodic it is combined with the same quantity of spirit of lavender, and is useful in relieving flatulency and sickness. As a diaphoretic or sweating draught, in febrile complaints, it should be given with twenty or thirty drops of antimonial wine, and a tea-spoonful of liquid acetate of ammonia. The usual dose of spirits of nitre is from half a tea-spoonful to two or three tea-spoonfuls diluted with water.

NITRE DROPS. — Nitre, 3 ounces; sugar, 1 pound; water to mix. Add a few drops of essence of lemon, or oil of cassia.

NITRE LOZENGES.--1. Nitrate of potash (pure), 4 parts; white sugar, 26 parts. Powder fine, and mix with mucilage. For sore throat, &c.

2. Nitre, 4 ounces; sugar, 16 ounces; and essence of lemon, 2 ounces. Mix with mucilage.

NOISE IN THE EARS.—Drop in juice of onions.

NORFOLK DUMPLINGS.—Milk, half a pint, 2 eggs, salt; make them into a thick batter with flour; roll into balls, and drop them into a pan of boiling water; from 15 to 30 minutes will boil them. Eat while hot with a little sugar, butter or treacle.

NORFOLK PUDDING PUFFS.—Mix three eggs, three table-spoonfuls of flour, half a pint of cream, and two table-spoonfuls of orange-flower or rose-water; sweeten to taste; put the batter in large deep custard cups, half full; set them in the oven; when the puff rises to the top of the cups, they are done.

NOSE, *Bleeding at the.*—See Bleeding at the Nose, page 67.

NOTTINGHAM PUDDING. --Peel six good apples; take out the cores with the point of a small knife, leaving the apples whole; fill up the place of the core with sugar; place them in a pie dish, and pour over them a nice light batter, prepared as for batter pudding. Bake an hour.

NUTMEG, *Essence of.*—Dissolve ½ oz. of the essential oil of nutmeg in ½ pint of spirit of wine. Bottle and cork well. It is very valuable to cooks and confectioners.

NUTRITIOUS DIATETIC. —Pulverize equal quantities of sago and best cocoa; mix, and stir a table-spoonful in a pint of milk, to which add a pint of boiling water. Boil for a few minutes, frequently stirring. Add sugar according to taste. It is very suitable for invalids and children.

OAK, *to stain a mahogany colour.*—Boil together Brazil wood and Roman alum; and before using it, add a little potash. A suitable varnish for wood, thus tinged, may be made by dissolving amber in oil of turpentine, mixed with a small portion of linseed oil.

OAK WAINSCOT, *to give a fine gloss to.*--If the wainscot be greasy, wash with warm beer; then boil two quarts of strong beer, bees' wax about the size of a walnut, and a table-spoonful of sugar. Apply it all over with a large brush, and when dry, rub till bright.

OATMEAL MILK. -- Mix a pint of milk and water (two-thirds

milk, and one-third water) gradually with a table-spoonful or two of oatmeal. Place in a saucepan upon a clear fire, and when it begins to rise and boil, take it off, and pour it from one basin into another to incorporate it well with the milk; return it to the pan; put on the fire, and when it is about to boil, take off, and let it stand a little to settle; when settled, pour it off into a basin, add a little salt, and let it cool. This is an excellent milk, very congenial to weak constitution, affording a good, firm nourishment, and is easy of digestion.

OATMEAL PORRIDGE. — Take nearly a quart of water, two small teaspoonfuls of salt, and when the water boils, scatter in very slowly oatmeal, and boil well. stirring all the time. Pour into basins. This is a very wholesome food—a food upon which the stalwart sons of Lancashire and Yorkshire, of the north of England, and of Scotland, lived. They *were* men and women in those days of oatmeal porridge; they were all tall, stout, handsome, lively, and captivating. This food is to be eaten chiefly with milk—take one fourth of a spoonful, dip it into the milk, causing the spoon to be full of both—or it may be eaten with butter, or sugar, or treacle.

OCTOBER BEER, *to brew the good old English way.*—The malt should be old and good, and rather coarsely ground. Take 5 quarters of malt, for 3 hogsheads of beer, and 18 lbs of hops; more if the malt be pale dried. Use soft water. The first liquor is to be boiled, adding a handful of hops to it; then before you strike it over to the malt, cool in as much liquor as will cause it not to scald the malt. With the next liquor do the same, and so to the end— but do not scald. When the malt is let-out of the mash-tub into the under tub, put to it a handful or two of hops; it will preserve it from blinking or foxing. In boiling, let the first wort boil high and quick; for the quicker the first wort is boiled, the better it is; the second boil more than the first; and the third or last more than the second.

In cooling, let into the tun leisurely, and leave behind as much sediment as possible, that the fermentation may be mild, and not fierce; for there are in all fermented liquors salt and sulphur, and we must keep those two bodies in due proportion, that the salt may not exalt itself above the sulphur —much depends upon this.

At first put but little yeast; let it work by degrees quietly; if it works too slowly, whip in the yeast several times till it is well fermented. When you cleanse do it by a tap from your tun, placed six inches from the bottom, that most of the sediment may remain, which may be thrown on the malt to mend the small beer.

When the beer is tunned, fill your vessel; let it work at the bung-hole, and have a reserve in a small cask to fill it up. Do not put any of the beer which will be under the yeast, after it has worked over into the vessels; put it in another cask, for it will not be so good as the other in the cask. When the fermentation ceases, stop it close, and let it stand till the spring; for brewing ought to be done in October, that it may settle and digest all winter.

In the spring, unstop the vent hole, and see whether the beer ferments or not; for when warm weather comes it will have another fermentation; when it is over, stop well again; let it stand till

September, and then peg it; and if you find it fine, and the hop well rotted, and of a pleasant taste for drinking, draw out a gallon of it; put to it 2 ozs. of isinglass, cut very small, to melt, stirring it often, and whisking till the isinglass is melted. Strain and put into the vessel, stirring well together; bung slightly, for this will cause a small fermentation; when that is over, stop it close, leaving only the vent hole a little stopped. Let it stand, and in about 10 days, it will be transparently fine. It will be a splendid ale for bottling, which may be done when the cask is half or two thirds drawn.

ODOURS, *Unpleasant, to remove.*—Burnt coffee is the best disinfectant, and it is very agreeable.—For water-closets, night chairs, &c. chloride of lime, and even common lime, should be used. —Or one ounce of sugar of lead, one ounce of aquafortis, in nearly one quart of water. This is effectual to cleanse utensils from bad odours.--Or charcoal powder, camphor dissolved; the articles well rinced with the composition.

OIL, *to make the hair curl.*— Olive oil, 1 lb.; oil of origanum, 1 drachm; and oil of rosemary, 1¼ drachm. Mix.

OIL, *to extract from boards.*— Make a strong ley of pearl ashes and soft water, and add as much unslaked lime as will take it up; bottle closely. Scour the part with it, using water; do it quickly.

Fullers earth, soap, and soda, mixed, form a good application, using with it sand and water.

OIL PAINTINGS, *to clean.*— Wash the picture with flannel and a weak solution of soap, or with warm beer and a little soda. When dry, apply a solution of gum tragacanth, or brown varnish.

OIL PAINTINGS, *to clean.*— If smoked, or very dirty, take stale urine, in which a little common salt is dissolved; rub them over with a woollen cloth dipped in the mixture till they are clean; then with a sponge wash them over with clean water; dry, and rub over with a clean cloth.

OIL PAINTINGS, *Varnish for.*—Use white of egg, and sugar-candy dissolved, a tea-spoonful of brandy, all most intimately mixed, first the egg alone. Varnish the pictures with it. It is better than most varnishes, as it can be washed off when the picture wants cleaning again.

OILED PAPER.—Brush sheets of paper over with "boiled oil," in which dissolve a little shellac carefully over a slow fire, and suspend them on a line until dry. Waterproof. Employed to tie over pots and jars, and to wrap up paste blacking, &c.

OIL, *of Brown Paper.*—Dip a piece of thick brown paper into the best salad oil. Set the paper on fire upon a plate and the oil that drops from it is a good remedy for burns.

OIL STAINS, *to remove.*—Apply benzoin, or magnesia to both sides of the silk, satin, or stuff; apply it moistened for two or three hours, and then brush off. Repeat if needful. Oil stains may be removed from silks, dresses, leather, paper, &c., by applying pipeclay, powdered and mixed with water to the thickness of cream; leave it on for four hours. This will not injure the best colours.

OINTMENT FOR BURNS. —Slippery elm, elder bark, scraped, yarrow tops and leaves, plantain leaves, stramonium leaves, of each 1 oz. Lard and bees' wax, sufficient to make into ointment. It is a good ointment for the Piles also.

OINTMENT, for Eruptions.— Simmer ox-marrow over the fire, add a little salt, and a tea-spoonful of brandy. Strain. When cold, rub the part affected.

OINTMENT OF LEAD.— Take of olive oil half a pint; white wax, two ounces; sugar of lead three drachms. Let the sugar of lead, reduced into a fine powder, be rubbed with some part of the oil, and added to the other ingredients, previously melted together, stirring them till quite cold. This cooling astringent ointment may be used in all cases where the intention is to dry and skin over the part, in scalding, &c.

OLD AGE, to live to.—"I am now an old man. I have seen near a century. Do you want to know how to grow old slowly and happily? I will tell you. Always eat slowly — masticate well. Get as much out-door exercise as you can. Pure air! it has lengthened my life. But avoid exposure to harsh winds, and wet weather. Go to your occupation smiling. Keep a good and kind nature, and a soft temper every where. By being good to others, you get a good name; and the happy influence upon the mind of a good name, extends itself to the body. Cultivate a good memory, and to do this you must be communicative; repeat what you have read; talk about it. Dr. Johnson's great memory was owing to his communicativeness. If you desire to be old, and comfortable with it, *do not swallow a RASP;* i. e. ardent spirits, which rasp the constitution to death. Avoid as much as possible VENERY—that your VITALITY may *hold out.*" *Dr. Muerin.*

OLDBURY PUDDING.-Beat well four eggs; flour and butter a pint basin; pour in the eggs, and fill up with new milk previously boiled, with two laurel leaves, and when cold beat them together; put a white paper over the basin; cover with a cloth, and boil twenty minutes. Serve with wine and butter sauce.—A little rice flour, or arrow-root incorporated with the milk will make it more nutritious; add the squeeze of a lemon.

OLIO OF MEAT.—Take ham, and any cold meat on hand, with a little lard; add broth, three or four onions, carrots, celery, and a green cabbage, first scalded in boiling water; boil on a slow fire till the meat is done, garnish the bottom of the dish with toasted bread, and soak it with some of the broth; put upon it the ham and meat; add broth to keep it of a thick substance.—Cold fowl, or goose, added, is a great improvement.

OLIO OF RABBITS.——Cut two rabbits into large pieces; lard them through with large pieces of bacon, seasoned with salt, pepper, and spices; put them into a stewpan with a good slice of ham, butter, sweet herbs, two cloves, a bay leaf, a little green basil, and half a clove of garlick; simmer a little; put into a larger stewpan upon slices of fillet of veal; cover with thin slices of lard; soak about half an hour over a slow fire, and add a glass of sherry; put the rabbits into the tureen; add some good gravy to the liquid; give them a boiling together; skim and sift the sauce; add a lemon squeeze, and serve it upon the meat.

OLIVE BRONZE DIP.— Nitric acid, 1 oz.; muriatic acid, 2 oz.; add titanium or palladium; when the metal is dissolved add 2 gallons of pure soft water to each pint of the solution.

OLIVE PIE.—Cut a fillet of veal in thin slices; rub them over with yolks of eggs; strew over them a few bread crumbs, shred lemon peel, with grated nutmeg, pepper and salt; roll very tight; place in a pewter dish; pour over them half a pint of good gravy made of bones; put ¼ lb. of butter over it, make a light paste, and lay it round the dish; roll the lid half an inch thick, and lay it on.

OMELETTE.—Make a batter of eggs and milk, and a very little flour; put to it chopped parsley, green onions, or chives, the latter is best, or a very small quantity of shalot, a little pepper, salt, and a scrape or two of nutmeg. Take some butter boiled in a small frying-pan, and pour the above batter into it; when one side is of a fine yellow brown, turn it and do the other. Double it when served. Some scraped lean ham, or grated tongue, put in at the first, is a very pleasant addition. Four eggs will make a pretty sized omelet; but many cooks will use eight or ten. A small proportion of flour should be used.

If the taste be approved, a *little* tarragon gives a fine flavour. A good deal of parsley should be used.

Omelet, though usually served in the course, would be much better if it was sent up after, that it might be eaten as hot as possible.

OMELETTE *of Asparagus.*—Take six eggs; beat them up with cream; boil some of the finest asparagus; when boiled, cut off all the green in small pieces, and mix them with the eggs, pepper, and salt; heat the pan; put in a slice of butter, and serve hot—on buttered toasts.

OMELETTE, *Sweet.*—Mix ten eggs with a gill of cream, ¼ lb. of butter, and syrup of nutmeg, or grated; sweeten with loaf sugar; put the whole into a frying-pan, as for a savory omelette; fry, and serve hot, with sifted sugar upon it.

ONIONS.—If you want a good crop, dig the ground deep, and manure it highly with the droppings of the hen-house. Roll the surface of the ground smooth, and scratch it with a fine rake before marking off the rows.

ONIONS.—A dry, cold, airy loft is best for store onions; do not let them lie more than two or three bulbs thick, and often look them over, and pull out bad ones. Do not remove any of the outer rind but what comes off in the handling. They keep well in ropes and hung up; the easiest way to make which is to tie them on to a hay or straw-band, which is better than a stake. This plan is useful where shelf room is scarce; but the points to observe are a cool, airy situation, warmth and moisture being more inimical to their keeping than frost.

ONIONS, *to keep.*——Let the onions be dry; heat a poker red hot, and with it singe the roots, to prevent all premature growth. Hang them in a dry cold room.

ONIONS, *to pickle.*—Take 2 quarts of the small white round onions. Scald them in very strong salt and water. Just let them boil. Strain; peel; place in jars; cover them with the best white wine vinegar. In two days pour all the vinegar off, and boil it half an hour with a teaspoonful of cayenne pepper, 1 oz. of ginger, 16 cloves, ½ oz. ground mustard, 2 ozs. of mustard seed. When cold, pour upon the onions.—Some persons prefer the vinegar boiling hot.

ONIONS, *to ragout.*—Peel a pint of young onions; then cut four large ones very small; melt some butter in a stewpan; throw in the onions, and fry them till brown; dust in flour, and shake round till thick; add salt, pepper, good gravy, and mustard; stir all together, and when pretty thick, pour into a dish, and garnish with toasted bread cut fine.

ONIONS, *to roast.*—Should be done with all the skins on. They cut well alone, with only salt and cold butter; or with roast potatoes or with beet-roots.

ONION SAUCE.—Peel the onions, and boil them tender; squeeze the water from them, then chop them, and add to them butter that has been melted, rich and smooth, as will be hereafter directed, but with a little good milk instead of water; boil it up once, and serve it for boiled rabbits, partridges, scrag, or knuckle of veal, or roast mutton. A turnip boiled with the onions makes them milder.

ONION SOUP, *Brown.*—Skin and cut round ways six large Spanish onions; fry them in butter till tender, and nicely brown; take out and drain; boil an hour in five quarts of water, stirring well; add pepper and salt; rub the crumbs of a penny loaf through a colander, and stir it well into the soup; boil two hours. Ten minutes before it is served, beat the yolks of two eggs with two spoonfuls of vinegar, and a little of the soup, pour in gradually, and stir well. Add cloves, if agreeable.

ONION SOUP, *White.*—Take 30 large onions; boil in five quarts of water, with a knuckle of veal, a blade or two of mace, and pepper; when the onions are quite soft, take up, and rub them through a hair sieve, and work ½ lb. of butter with flour in them; when the meat is boiled so as to leave the bone, strain the liquor to the onions; boil gently for half an hour; serve with a cupful of cream and a little salt; stir it well when you put in the flour and butter.

ONION STEW,—Choose five or six white onions, skin them, and first parboil them in water from 30 minutes; then chop them very fine, and boil out in milk, add butter, and gravy, or, if you like, a little cream. Do not boil too quickly. Season with salt, mace, and pepper. Thicken with a little rice flour. This kind of stew is very wholesome, and with the addition of a little chopped tender ham, not over fat, and some lean veal, it becomes a stew of first rate relish. *A. N.*

ONIONS, *to stew.*—Peel six large onions, fry gently to a fine brown, but do not blacken them; then put them into a small stew-pan with a little weak gravy, pepper and salt; cover and stew two hours gently. They should be lightly floured first.

ONIONS, *offensive breath caused by eating.*—Chew parsley, or orris root, or cloves, to neutralize the smell.——Or take 4 drops of concentrated solution of chloride of soda in a wine-glassful of water. Use fresh butter.

OPHTHALMIA, *or inflammation of the eye.*—See *Eye.* It may be caused by cold, sharp winds, intemperance, venery, dust or particles of matter in the eyes, overtaxing the eye, the result of measles, small pox, scrofula, syphilis.

Particles of iron have been removed from the eye by a magnet. Particles of sand, &c. have been removed by introducing the mucilage of slippery elm into the eye, the person lying on his back, and another injecting it into the corner or part affected, and the patient moving the eye in an opposite direction; the mucilage will wash out the particles; this is very safe, as the slippery elm has a very healing power. A hog's bristle bent semicircular, is useful to remove particles from the eye.

If the inflamatory pains are severe, foment the eye with a decoction of Stramonium leaves, simmered in spirits.—Or use a little weak mixture of laudanum and water.—A very cooling wash is made by powdering a drachm of borax, and dissolving it in a pint of boiling water.—Poultices are very good for inflammatory affections of the eyes; but *the very best of all is* SLIPPERY ELM. It should be mixed with milk and water, and applied direct to the eye, without any cloth between. During the inflammation, aperients should be given, and the Diaphoretic Powder used. See pages 159, 160, 161, for remedies for diseased eye.

OPIATE FOR THE TEETH.—Honey, 1 pound; laudanum, 8 ounces; oil of almonds, 1 ounce; essence of bergamot, 2 drachms; tincture of pelitory, 4 ounces. Mix well and strain. Apply with a piece of cotton or lint.

OPIATE, *Injection.*—Milk of assafœtida, 8 ozs,; tincture of opium, 1 drachm. This is useful in disorders of the anus attended with insufferable pain.

OPIUM, *or* LAUDANUM, *antidote to its poisonous influence.*—Immediately take the juice of lemons; or the strongest vinegar. Or sulphate of zinc, in 30 grain doses, every fifteen minutes, with plenty of warm water, is the most effectual. Opium produces great drowsiness and stupor, which must be overcome by all means; a teaspoonful of sal volatile in strong coffee is the best stimulant; repeat every half hour; do not let the patient sleep for 12 hours, for if he do, he may wake no more.

OPODELDOC.—Dissolve 1 oz. of camphor in a pint of spirit of wine; then dissolve 4 ozs. of hard white Spanish soap, scraped thin in 4 ozs. of oil of rosemary. It may be improved by adding 2 ozs. of ammonia, tincture of aconite, or opium, 1 oz., and a little oil. It is a good application for sprains, lumbago, pained limbs, weakness of joints, &c. Mixed with tincture of cantharides, or tincture of cayenne, it becomes more effectively stimulant.

ORANGE.—The orange-tree is a beautiful ever-green, a native of Asia, and cultivated in the West Indies, Europe, China, &c. The flowers are very fragrant, and have long been used as a perfume. The juice of orange is a grateful acid liquor, consisting of citric acid, syrup, extractive, and mucilage. It is of great use in febrile or inflammatory diseases, for allaying heat, quenching thirst, and promoting the salutary secretions. It is valuable in scurvy.

ORANGE BRANDY.—Pare 8 oranges very thin, and steep the peels in a quart of brandy 48 hours in a close pitcher; then take water, 3 pints; loaf sugar, ¾ lb.; boil until reduced to half the quantity; let it cool, and then mix with brandy; let it stand 14 days, and then bottle it.

ORANGE CAKES.—Take Seville oranges with good rinds quarter them, and boil in two or three waters, till tender, and the bitterness gone; dry them; take all the seeds and skins out of the pulp with a knife; shred the peels very fine, put them to the pulp; weigh them, and put rather more than their weight of fine sugar into a tossing-pan, with just sufficient water to dissolve it; boil it till it candies; then put in gradually the orange-peels and pulp; mix well; boil very gently, till it looks clear and thick; then put into flat-bottomed glasses; set them in a slow oven; when they are candied on the top, turn them

out upon glasses; cut into shapes.
ORANGE CHEESECAKES.
—*See page* 104.

ORANGE CHEESECAKES, *Crust for.*—Dry a pound of the best flour, mix with it three ounces of refined sugar; then work half a pound of butter with your hand till it comes to froth; put the flour into it by degrees, and work into it, well beaten and strained, the yolks of three and whites of two eggs. If it is too soft, put some flour and sugar to make it fit to roll. Line your patty-pans, and fill. A little above 15 minutes will bake them. Against they come out have ready some refined sugar beat up with the white of an egg, as thick as you can; ice them all over, set them in the oven to harden, and serve cold. Use fresh butter.

ORANGE CHIPS.—Cut oranges in halves, squeeze the juice through a sieve; soak the peel in water; next day boil in the same till tender, drain them, and slice the peels, put them to the juice, weigh as much sugar, and put all together into a broad earthen dish, and put over the fire at a moderate distance, often stirring till the chips candy; then set them in a cool room to dry. They will not be so under three weeks.

ORANGE COLOUR, *in silk, cotton, &c., to clean.*—If silk, clean the garment with a solution of soap; in the second liquor pearlash must be used to stay the colour. For silks the water must be handheat. If required to be more scarlet or red, the pearlash must be omitted, and a little used in the rinsing water. Remember that acids heighten the red colour, and alkalies sadden, or make it more buff.

ORANGE CREAM.—Take the juice of 4 Seville oranges, and the rind of one pared fine; put them into a tossingpan with a pint of water and 8 ozs. of sugar; beat the whites of 5 eggs; set it over the fire; stir it one way till it is thick and white; strain through a sieve; stir it till it is cold, then beat well the yolks of 5 eggs, put it in the tossingpan with cream; stir over a slow fire till it is ready to boil; put it into a basin to cool, and stir it till it is cold, then put it into jelly glasses: serve with whips and jellies. *Raf.*

ORANGE CRUMPETS.— Cream, one pint; new milk, one pint; warm it, and put in it a little rennet or citric acid; when broken, stir it gently; lay it on a cloth to drain all night, and then take the rinds of 3 oranges, boiled, as for preserving, in three different waters; pound them very fine, and mix them with the curd, and eight eggs in a mortar, a little nutmeg, the juice of a lemon or orange, and sugar to your taste; bake them in buttered tin pans. When baked, put a little wine and sugar over them.

ORANGE CUSTARDS.—Boil the rind of half a Seville orange very tender; beat it very fine in a mortar; add a spoonful of the best brandy, the juice of a Seville orange, 4 ozs. of loaf sugar, and the yolks of four eggs; beat all together ten minutes; then pour in gradually a pint of boiling cream; keep beating them till they are cold; put them into custard cups, and set them in an earthen dish of hot water; let them stand till they are set; take out, and stick preserved oranges on the top, and serve them hot or cold.

ORANGE FLOUR PASTE, *for the hands.*—Blanch 5 or 6 lbs. of bitter almonds by boiling in water; and then pound them very fine with 2 lbs. of orange flour. If the paste be too oily, add bean flour, finely sifted; but let no water enter the composition.

ORANGE FLOWER CAKES—Put four ounces of the leaves of the flowers into cold water for an hour; drain and put between napkins, and roll with a rolling-pin till they are bruised; then have ready boiled one pound of sugar to add to it in a thick syrup, give them a simmer, until the syrup adheres to the sides of the pan, drop in little cakes on a plate, and dry as before directed.

ORANGE FLOWER CANDY.—Boil in a pint of water half the white of an egg, and pour it on 2¼ lbs. of fine loaf sugar. When dissolved, place it over a clear fire; boil a few minutes; take off and let it stand a few minutes until the scum is cleared off; then boil the sugar till it is very thick; then gradually drop in 3½ ozs. of orange petals. Stir the candy till it rises into one white mass in the pan, but mind it does not burn; then pour it upon papers or into a dish. The syrup should be three parts boiled when they are added. They must be gathered on the day they are wanted for use, as they are soon discoloured by keeping.

ORANGE FOOL.—Mix the juice of six Seville oranges with six eggs well beaten, a pint of cream, a ¼ lb. of sugar, a little cinnamon and nutmeg; mix, and keep stirring over a slow fire, till it is thick; put in a small bit of butter; stir till it is cold, and dish it up.

ORANGE GINGERBREAD.—Sift 2¼ lbs of fine flour, and add to it ¾ lb. of treacle; 6 ozs. of candied orange peel, cut small; ¾ lb. of sugar; 1 oz. of ground ginger, and 1 oz. of allspice; melt ¾ lb. of butter; mix the whole well together; let it stand 12 hours; roll it out with very little flour half an inch thick; cut into pieces three inches long and two wide; mark them in the form of chequers with the back of a knife; bake a quarter of an inch apart; egg over with milk and egg; bake in a cool oven 15 minutes; when done wash over again slightly; divide the pieces with a knife, as in baking they will run together.

ORANGE JELLY.—It may be made the same as Lemon Jelly, which see. Grate the rind of two Seville and of two China oranges, and two lemons; squeeze the juice of three of each, and strain, and add to the juice a quarter of a pound of lump sugar, a quarter of a pint of water, and boil till it almost candies. Have ready a quart of isinglass jelly made with two ounces; put to it the syrup, and boil it once up; strain off the jelly, and let it stand to settle as above, before it is put into the mould.

ORANGE JUICE, *Buttered.*—Mix the juice of seven Seville oranges with four spoonfuls of rose-water, and add the whole to the yolks of eight, and whites of four eggs, well beaten; then strain the liquor to half a pound of sugar pounded, stir it over a gentle fire, and when it begins to thicken, put in about the size of a small walnut of butter, keep it over the fire a few minutes longer; then pour it into a flat dish, and serve it to eat cold.

ORANGE MARMALADE.—See *Marmalade.*

ORANGE PUDDING.—Grate the rind of a Seville orange, put to it six ounces of fresh butter, six or eight ounces of lump sugar pounded: beat them all in a mortar, and add as you do it the whole of eight eggs well beaten and strained; scrape a raw apple, and mix with the rest; put a paste at the bottom and sides of the dish, and over the orange mixture put cross bars of paste. Half an hour will bake it.

Another.—Mix of orange paste two full spoonfuls, with six eggs, four of sugar, four ounces of butter warm, and put into a shallow dish with a paste lining. Bake twenty minutes.

Another. — Rather more than two table-spoonfuls of orange paste mixed with six eggs, four ounces of sugar, and four ounces of butter melted, will make a good sized pudding, with a paste at the bottom of the dish. Bake twenty minutes.

Another.—Boil the rind of a Seville orange very soft; beat it in a marble mortar with the juice; put to it two good crisp biscuits, Naples, or any other you like, grated very fine, ½ lb. of butter, ¼ lb. of sugar, and the yolks of six eggs; mix well; lay a good paste round the edge of the dish; bake 30 minutes in a gentle oven.

ORANGE PUFFS.—Pare off the rind from Seville oranges; then rub them with salt; let them lie 24 hours in water; boil them in 4 changes of water; let the first water be salt; drain, and beat them to a pulp; bruise in the pieces of all that you have pared; sweeten well with loaf sugar, and boil it till thick; cool, and put into the paste.—Lemon puffs may be made in the same way.

ORANGE RELISH. — Cut oranges into quarters, removing the rind with a fruit knife, and adding equal quantities of brandy, madeira, or sherry, strewing a liberal allowance of finely powdered sugar over the dish.

ORANGE TART. — Squeeze, pulp, and boil two Seville oranges tender; weigh them; add double of sugar; beat both together to a paste, and then add the juice and pulp of the fruit, and the size of a walnut of fresh butter, and beat all together. Choose a very shallow dish, line it with a light puff crust, and lay the paste of orange in it. You may ice it.

Another.—Line a tart-pan with puff-paste; put into it orange marmalade that is made with apple jelly. Lay small shreds of paste on crosswise. Bake in a moderate oven.

ORANGE TONIC. — Orange peel, 1 oz.; camomile flowers, 1¼ oz., and a little ginger. Put in a pint of boiling water. Add half a wine-glassful of brandy. Take a wine-glassful at a time.

ORANGE WINE.—To 10 gallons of water add 24 lbs. of loaf sugar; beat the whites of six eggs well, and mix when the water is cold; boil an hour; skim well; then take 4 dozens of the roughest and largest Seville oranges; pare very thin; put them into a tub, and pour the liquor on boiling hot; and when cold enough, add three or four spoonfuls of good yeast, with the juice of the oranges, and ½ oz. of cochineal, beaten fine, and boiled in a pint of wine; stir all together. Ferment four days; put into the casks, and in six weeks bottle for use.

Another.——To five gallons of spring-water, put fifteen pounds of loaf sugar, and the whites of three eggs, well beaten; let it boil for a quarter of an hour, and as the scum rises, take it off; when cold, add the juice of sixty Seville oranges and five lemons; pare 10 oranges and 5 lemons as thin as possible; put them on thread, and suspend them in the barrel for two months; then take them out, and put in a pound of loaf sugar, and bung it up.

ORANGES, *to preserve, carved.* —Take the best Seville oranges;

cut the rinds with a penknife in various forms; draw out part of the peel as you cut them, and put them into salt and water, to stand three days to take out the bitter; then boil them in a large saucepan of fresh water, with salt in it, but do not cover them, or their colour will be injured; take out, and boil them ten minutes in a thin syrup, for five days successively; put into a deep jar, to stand two months, and then make a thick syrup, and just give them a boil in it; let them stand till the next day; then jar them, and cover with brandy papers; tie them down with a bladder.

Whole oranges may be preserved in the same way; but do not boil so long, and keep in a very thin syrup at first, or it will cause them to shrink and wither. Always put salt in the water for either oranges preserved, or orange chips.

ORANGES, *to preserve in jelly.* —The same as lemons preserved in jelly, page 226.

ORANGEADE.—Squeeze the juice; pour boiling water on a little of the peel, and cover close. Boil sugar and water to a thick syrup, and skim it. When all is cold, mix the juice, the infusion and the syrup, with as much more water as will make a rich sherbet; strain through a jelly-bag. Or, squeeze the juice, and strain it, and add water and capillaire.

ORANGEADE, *Effervescing.*—Make it the same as the *Ginger Beer Powders,* page 178, putting orange juice into tartaric mixture, instead of ginger.

ORGEAT.—Boil a quart of new milk with a stick of cinnamon, sweeten to your taste, and let it grow cold; then pour it by degrees to three ounces of almonds, and twenty bitter, that have been blanched and beaten, to a paste, with a little water to prevent oiling; boil all together, and stir till cold, then add half a glass of brandy.

Another way-Blanch and pound three quarters of a pound of almonds, and thirty bitter, with a spoonful of water. Stir in by degrees two pints of water, and three of milk, and strain the whole through a cloth. Dissolve half a pound of loaf sugar in a pint of water, and skim it well; mix it with the other, as likewise two spoonfuls of orange flower water, and a tea-cupful of the best brandy.

ORGEAT, *for the Sick.*—Beat 2 ozs. of almonds with a tea-spoonful of orange-flower water, and a bitter almond or two; then pour a quart of milk and water to the paste. Sweeten with sugar or capillaire. This is a fine drink for those who have a tender chest; and in the gout it is highly useful, and, with the addition of half an ounce of gum arabic, has been found to allay the pain. Half a glass of brandy may be added if thought too cooling in the latter complaints, and the glass of orgeat may be put into a basin of warm water.

OSWEGO PREPARED CORN.—It makes an excellent diet, especially for invalids and children. Simply boiled in milk and sweetened, it is excellent.

For Children the above makes the most nutritious of all food, and is invaluable.

For Invalids it is better than the best Arrow Root, and it is prepared in the same way.

For Gravy Jelly, boil in water, mix with a little strong meat gravy, and cool in a form.

For thickening Soups and Gravies it is unequaled.

OX-CHEEK, *to marinate.*—Bone the cheek; stew it with red

wine, and white wine vinegar, seasoned with salt, pepper, and sliced nutmeg; stew till tender; then take them up, and put to the liquor in which you stewed them, a quart of sherry, and sage, parsley, marjoram, thyme, a bunch of rosemary, bay leaves, whole pepper, nutmegs, and sliced ginger; boil all these together; put the cheek into the vessel, and pour the liquor upon it; lay on them some slices of lemon, and keep for use.

OX-CHEEK, *to pot.*—When you stew an ox-cheek, take some of the fleshy part, and season it well with salt and pepper, and beat it very fine in a mortar with a little clear fat skimmed off the gravy; put it close into the pots, and pour over it clarified butter.

OX-CHEEK STEW.—Soak and cleanse a fine cheek the day before; put it into a stew-pot that will cover close, with three quarts of water: simmer it after it has boiled, and been skimmed. In two hours put plenty of carrots, leeks, two turnips, a bunch of sweet herbs, some whole pepper and 4 ozs. of allspice. Skim often; when the meat is tender, take it out; cool, take off the fat, and serve the soup separate or with the meat. It should be of a fine brown, which may be done by burnt sugar; or by frying some onions brown with flour and simmering them with it. This improves the flavour of all soups and gravies of the brown kind.

If vegetables are not approved in the soup, they may be taken out, and a small roll be toasted or bread fried and added. Celery is a great addition, and should always be served. Where it is not to be got, the seed of it gives quite as good a flavour, boiled in and strained off.

Another way.—Soak half a head three hours, and clean it with plenty of water. Take the meat off the bones, and put it into a pan with a large onion, a bunch of sweet herbs, some bruised allspice, pepper, and salt.

Lay the bones on the top; pour on two or three quarts of water and cover the pan close with brown paper, or a dish that will fit close. Let it stand eight or ten hours in a slow oven; or simmer it by the side of the fire, or on a hot hearth. When done tender, put the meat into a clean pan, and let it get cold. Take the cake of fat off, and warm the head in pieces in the soup. Put what vegetables you choose.

OXFORD CAKES.—Flour, 6 lbs.; salt, about a table-spoonful; cinnamon, ½ oz.; nutmeg, ¼ oz.; cloves, 1 drachm; the same of mace, all finely beaten and sifted with the salt; add ¾ lb. of sugar; gradually work into the flour 1 lb. or more of fresh butter; it will take a long time to work it up. Then add a quart of cream, a pint of ale yeast, a gill of mountain wine, and 3 grains of ambergris, dissolved in the yolks of 8 and whites of 4 eggs, and a gill of rosewater; mix the whole with the flour, and knead them well together. Keep the paste near the fire some time; then add 1 lb. of stoned minced raisins, and 3 lbs. of clean dry currants; bake the cake in a gentle oven. Frost on the top with rose-water and the whole of an egg beaten together; sift over plenty of fine loaf sugar, and put into a slow oven to dry.

OXFORD DUMPLINGS.— Take 2 ozs. of grated bread; currants and shred suet, 4 ozs. each; two large spoonfuls of flour; a good quantity of grated lemon-peel, a bit of sugar, and a little powdered pimento. Mix with two eggs and a little milk into five dumplings, and fry of a fine yellow brown. Serve with sweet sauce.

OXFORD PUDDING.—Have 4 ozs. of bread crumbs grated, and take 4 ozs. of currants, the same of suet chopped very fine, a large spoonful of sugar, and a little nutmeg: mix all together. Take the yolks of four eggs, and make your puddings into balls, and fry them a light brown in butter. Serve with sherry or rum sauce.

OXFORD PUNCH.—Rub the rinds of four fresh lemons with loaf sugar till you have extracted a porton of the juice. Cut the peel finely off three lemons more, and two Seville oranges. Use the juice of ten lemons and six Seville oranges. Add eight glasses of calf's-foot jelly; put all into a large jug and stir well together. Put in three quarts of water boiling hot, and set the jug upon the hob for half an hour. Strain the liquor into a large bowl; pour in a bottle of capillaire, half a pint of sherry, a pint of cognac brandy, a pint and a half of old Jamaica rum, and a quart of orange shrub; stir well as you pour in the spirit. Add sugar to your taste.

OXFORD SAUSAGES.—Take 1 lb. of young pork, fat and lean, without gristle; lean veal, 1 lb.; chop all together with 1 lb. of beef suet. Add ¼ lb. of grated bread, half the peel of a lemon shred fine; a nutmeg grated; a few sage leaves chopped fine; a teaspoonful of pepper, and two of salt; some savory, thyme, and marjoram. Roll them out the size of common sausages, and fry them in fresh butter, or broil them over the fire, and send them to the table hot.

OX GALL, *prepared.*—Fresh gall, 1 pint; alum, 1 ounce. Boil until the latter is dissolved, then add fresh gall, 1 quart; salt, 1 ounce. Boil in like manner, keep both solutions in separate bottles for two or three months; pour off the clear, and mix them together; allow them to settle, and decant the pure gall for use.

OXTAIL SOUP.—Joint the tails, and let them soak for some time in warm water. Put into a gallon stew-pan 8 cloves, 2 or 3 onions; allspice and black pepper, of each ½ a drachm; cayenne pepper, 1 drachm; cover with cold water; skim as long as any scum rises; cover the pan very close, and simmer till the meat becomes tender, and will easily leave the bones. A table-spoonful of mushroom ketchup and a glass of wine will be a great improvement.

OYSTERS *au citron.*—Instead of vinegar and black pepper, squeeze fresh lemon juice over the fish, and use soluble cayenne.

OYSTERS, *Broiled.*—To broil oysters, roll them in flour or oatmeal, and as each oyster is taken from the gridiron, put a bit of butter on it. Keep hot and covered until served. Oysters ought to be eaten where they are broiled.

OYSTERS, *to escallop.*—Wash them in their own liquor; then strain the liquor, and put it to them again; put some of them into escallop shells; strew bread crumbs over them, with a little pepper, and a bit of butter; then more oysters, bread crumbs, and a bit more butter at the top; put them in a dutch-oven till they are brown.

OYSTERS, *to feed.*—Put them into water and wash them with a birch-besom till quite clean; then lay them bottom downwards into a pan, sprinkle with flour or oatmeal and salt, and cover with water. Do the same every day, and they will fatten. The water should be pretty salt.

OYSTERS, *to fry*.—Make a batter of flour, milk, and eggs, season it a very little, dip the oysters into it, and fry them a fine yellow brown. A little nutmeg should be put into the seasoning, and a few crumbs of bread into the flour.

OYSTERS, *to fry*.—Take 2 dozen large oysters; beat the yolks of two eggs; add to it a little nutmeg, a blade of mace pounded, a spoonful of flour, and a little salt; dip in the oysters, and fry them in lard a light brown; if agreeable, a little shred parsley may be added. They are a proper garnish for cod's-head, calf's head, or most made dishes.

OYSTER KETCHUP.-Beard the oysters; boil them up in their liquor; strain, and pound them in a mortar; boil the beards in spring water, and strain it to the first oyster liquor; boil the pounded oysters in the mixed liquors, with beaten mace and pepper. Some add a very little mushroom ketchup, vinegar, or lemon-juice; but the less the natural flavour is overpowered the better; only spice is necessary for its preservation. This oyster ketchup will keep perfectly good longer than oysters are ever out of season in England.

OYSTER LOAVES. — Open them, and save the liquor; wash them in it; then strain it through a sieve, and put a little of it into a tosser with a bit of good butter and flour, white pepper, a scrape of nutmeg, and a little cream. Stew them, and cut in dice; put them into rolls sold for the purpose.

OYSTER PATTIES.—Put a fine puff paste into small pattypans, and cover with paste, with a bit of bread in each; and against they are baked have ready the following to fill with, taking out the bread. Take off the beards of the oysters, cut the other parts in small bits, put them in a small tosser, with a grate of nutmeg, the least white pepper, and salt, a morsel of lemon-peel, cut so small that you can scarcely see it, a little cream, and a little of the oyster liquor. Simmer for a few minutes before you fill.

Observe to put a bit of crust into all patties, to keep them hollow while baking.

OYSTERS, *to pickle*.—Wash four dozen of the largest oysters you can get in their own liquor, wipe them dry, strain the liquor off, adding to it, a dessert-spoonful of pepper, two blades of mace, a table-spoonful of salt, if the liquor be not very salt, three of white wine, and four of vinegar.—Simmer the oysters a few minutes in the liquor, then put them in small jars and boil the pickle up, skim it, and when cold, pour over the oysters: cover close.

Another way.—Open the number you intend to pickle, put them into a saucepan with their own liquor for ten minutes, simmer them very gently; then put them into a jar, one by one, that none of the grit may stick to them, and cover them when cold with the pickle thus made. Boil the liquor with a bit of mace, lemon-peel, and black peppers, and to every hundred put two spoonfuls of the best undistilled vinegar.

They should be kept in small jars, and tied close with bladder, for the air will spoil them.

OYSTER SAUCE.—Save the liquor in opening the oysters; and boil it with the beards, a bit of mace, and lemon-peel. Throw the oysters into cold water, and drain it off. Strain the liquor, and put it into a saucepan with them, and as much butter, mixed with milk, as will make sauce enough; but first rub a little flour with it.

Put on the fire, and stir all the time; and when the butter has boiled once or twice, take them off, and keep the saucepan near the fire, but not on it; for if done too much, the oysters will be hard. Squeeze a little lemon-juice, and serve.

A little cream is a great improvement. Observe, the oysters will thin the sauce, so put butter accordingly.

OYSTER SOUP.—Take two quarts of fish stock, beat the yolks of ten hard eggs, and the hard part of two quarts of oysters, in a mortar, and add this to the stock. Simmer it all for half an hour; then strain it off, and put it and the oysters (cleared of the beards, and nicely washed) into the soup. Simmer five minutes; have ready the yolks of six raw eggs well beaten, and add them to the soup. Stir it all well one way on the side of the fire till it is thick and smooth, but do not let it boil. Serve all together.

Another.—Take 1 lb. of Skate, four flounders, or flukes, and 2 lbs. of eels; cut them in pieces; season them with mace, pepper, salt, an onion stuck with cloves, a head of celery, some parsley and sweet herbs; cover with water; simmer 1½ hour, and strain; beat the yolks of ten hard eggs, with the hard part of a pint of oysters, in a mortar; simmer all together for half an hour; have ready the yolks of six eggs well beaten, and add them to the soup; stir on the fire till it is thick and smooth, but do not let it boil.

OYSTERS, *to stew.* — Open and separate the liquor from them, then wash them from the grit; strain the liquor, and put with the oysters a bit of mace and lemon peel, and a few white peppers. Simmer them very gently, and add some cream, and a little flour and butter. Serve with sippets.

PAIN IN THE BACK.--Steep root of water-fern in water, till the water becomes thick and clammy; then rub the parts therewith morning and evening.

Or, apply a plaster, and take, daily, balsam of capivi.

Or, apply garlic and hog's lard to the feet.—*Wesley.*

PAINS IN THE HEAD AND FACE.—Take half a pint of rose-water, two tea-spoonfuls of white vinegar, and form a lotion. Apply it to the affected part three times a day. It requires fresh linen and lotion each application; this will, in two or three days, gradually take the pain away.

PAINS IN THE JOINTS.—Make a poultice of the young leaves of Rag-wort, and put on as hot as can be borne.

PAIN IN THE SIDE.-—-At bed-time apply a fresh cabbage-leaf, warmed by the fire, and bind it tightly round the body for twelve hours, or more. The first application generally gives relief; if not, apply a second leaf.

PAINTING.—The best time for painting the windows and doors of houses is autumn, or winter, if the weather be fine. Though longer in drying, it becomes harder, and therefore more durable.

PAINT.—To get rid of the smell of oil paint, plunge a handful of hay into a pale full of water, and let it stand in the room newly painted.

PAINT, *Cheap.* — Tar mixed with yellow-ochre, makes a very good paint for out-door purposes, as rails, iron fencing, &c.

PAINT, *to clean.*—Brush off the dust, and wash with strong soap and water, or soda and water, as the case may require, using a sponge or flannel. Fullers earth is also a good cleanser.

PAINT, *to remove from cloth.*—Apply spirit of turpentine with a sponge.

Grease on cloth may be removed by frequent layers of blotting paper placed over the grease spot, and pressing with a flat iron.

PAINT, *to remove spots of.*—Apply spirits of turpentine to the spot, and after a while rub the cloth as if washing, and the paint will crumble off; if not, apply the turpentine again.

PAINT, *to take away the smell of.*—Water neutralizes the smell of paint. Vessels of water placed in a newly painted room, will remove the smell, especially if impregnated with a little sulphuric acid.——Or straw and hay well saturated with water.——Or chloride of lime and water.

PAINT, *for Garden Stands.*—It may be composed of mineral green, and turpentine varnish, using a larger quantity of the varnish for the second coat, if needful. The colour may be regulated by the addition of white lead, or Prussian blue, ad libitum.

PAINTER'S COLIC; see *Colic* —This is a dangerous disease; it is attended with severe and violent pain, and paralytic symptoms, and sometimes with nausea, vomiting of acid bile, severe pains,; spasmodic pains about the region of the navel, violently shooting to each side ; it is often attended by violent spasms of the bowels with obstinate costiveness. If the disease is not arrested, it may terminate in gangrene, paralysis of the limbs, &c. It is caused by the absorption of lead into the system chiefly by respiration; hence painters, plumbers, potters, miners, and white lead workers are most subject to it.

Treatment. — To some extent the system is impregnated with lead ; the great object therefore must be to cause nature to expel the same. The nausea and the vomiting must be arrested by the *Neutralizing Mixture;* give a table-spoonful every half hour, or as often as vomiting takes place; when it ceases, give the *Aperient Electuary,* or the *Aperient Tonic Mixture,* page 20, 21, now and then. When the first symptoms appear, give an injection as follows:—Warm water, one pint, two teaspoonfuls of salt ; antispasmodic tincture, two table-spoonfuls, and a table-spoonful of slippery elm.

Apply to the stomach and region of the navel hot fomentations of a strong decoction of hops and poppy heads, a little antispasmodic tincture, and 20 or 30 drops of laudanum to a pint, Give the vapour bath daily ; and afterwards apply friction, and rub the body all over with the *Stimulating Liniment.* An emetic now and then will be of great use. The injections must be repeated until evacuations are obtained. Drink at the same time a decoction of the sudorific herbs, as balm, catnep, yarrow, peppermint, camomile, &c.

If the disease abates, discontinue gradually the use of the above remedies ; do not cease all at once, for the disease is a very insidious one, and may return. The application of dry hot salt, folded up in a bag, is a most valuable remedy. Keep it heating in the oven, and have two bags ; change as the one cools.—To remove paralysis in any part, apply frequently the *Stimulating Liniment.* The diet must be low and sparing.

PALERMO WINE.—Take to every quart of water 1 lb. of Malaga raisins ; rub, and cut the raisins small, and put them to the water, to stand ten days, stirring now and then; boil the water an hour before it is put to the raisins, and let it cool; in ten days strain the liquor, adding a little yeast with a sprig of dried wormwood. Stop close, and in two or three months bottle it, adding brandy, as much as you please.

PALPITATION OF THE HEART.—This is a very strong pulsation of the heart, sometimes only occasional, but often continual. It arises from morbid irritability of the heart; it is often purely nervous, caused, in some cases, by the disordered state of the stomach and bowels, by alcholic drinks, by excessive venery, by extreme grief, and disappointments preying upon the spirits, all tending to weaken the nervous system. It is sometimes a symptom of other diseases, as indigestion, hysteria. The beating is frequently so violent as to be heard at a considerable distance, and sometimes the effects of the increased action of the heart may be seen on the outside of the clothes. The pulse at the same time is very irregular, and often intermittent. Palpitation of the heart is not to be neglected, as it may lead to serious consequences.

The treatment of this disease is much similar to that for indigestion. The treatment must depend on the state of the body; for palpitation may be the effect of increased vitality, or fulness, or of debility and relaxation, &c. If the system be in a plethoric state, (fulness) aperients and a spare diet must be enjoined. Avoid all stimulants. In case of general debility, 20 drops of æther, with a teaspoonful of tincture of castor, in a wine-glassful of the infusion of valerian, two or three times a day. When it arises from *disease of the heart*, or of the large vessels, then avoid plethora, much bodily exertion, full meals, and excesses of every kind. The following mixture is valuable:—

Tincture of henbane, 2 ozs.; tincture of foxglove, 3 drachms; sweet spirit of nitre, ½ oz.; mix. A teaspoonful and a half to be taken two or three times a day in a glass of water.

If the action of the heart is very violent, apply a mustard plaster to the left side, or *strong hop* and *poppy head* fomentations. Two grains of hemlock powder may also be taken every seven or eight hours. After the cessation of palpitation, take tonics, sponge the breast with tepid or cold water, and gentle exercise in the open air.

PALPITATION OF THE HEART CURED BY SODA-WATER. —A lady, about forty years of age, had suffered twelve years from periodical attacks of palpitation of the heart, so violent as to shake the bed on which the patient lay. During one attack, feeling thirsty, she expressed a desire for some soda-water. No sooner had she swallowed the first draught than her palpitation left her, and recurred no more until the period of the next attack. As soon as it commenced, she sent for her medical attendant, and told him what had occurred a month previously, and requested to be allowed to try the same remedy a second time. He consented, but, wishing to ascertain which of the ingredients of the soda-water had relieved the complaint, he gave her a dose of citric acid by itself. This had no effect. He then gave her a dose of carbonate of soda, which also failed. He then mixed the powders, and gave her some ordinary soda-water, placing his hand at the same time upon her heart. The moment she swallowed the first mouthful, the palpitation ceased, and recurred no more for that time. From that period, whenever the palpitation came on, she could always stop it by this simple remedy. It appears, from the experiments made by medical men, that the carbonic acid was the active element in relieving the complaint, because, until the gas was liberated by the mixture of citric acid and the carbonate of soda, no benefit accrued.—*Journal of Health.*

PALPITATION OF THE HEART.—To 10 drops of the tincture of foxglove, add 10 drms. of camphor mixture, 1 drachm of tincture of columba, and 15 drops of sulphuric ether. Mix, and take a teaspoonful two or three times a day.

PALPITATION OF THE HEART.—Drink a pint of cold water.——Or, apply outwardly a rag dipt in vinegar.——Or, be electrified.——Or, take a decoction of mother-wort every night. *Wesley.*

PALSY, OR PARALYSIS.—It is a disease of debility, or diminished sensibility of the nerves, sometimes of the whole body. It is indicated by a suspension of motion, frequently of one side, rarely the lower extremeties from the loins; and it is sometimes confined to a muscle or nerve, as of the bladder and anus, allowing the urine and fœces to pass off involuntarily; sometimes the muscles of the tongue, causing stammering and loss of speech; sometimes of the optic nerves, producing Gutta Serena, or imperfect vision; and sometimes the nerve of the ear, causing deafness.

It is generally preceded by numbness, coldness, paleness, &c. In bad cases, where one half of the body is paralysed, the speech is much impeded, or totally lost, and convulsions often take place on the sound side. The muscles of the affected side of the face being relaxed, give those of the opposite side an appearance of being drawn up or contracted.

It may be *caused* by an apoplectic attack, any thing obstructing the flow of nervous influence from the brain into the organs of motion; hence, tumours, over distension and effusion, distortions of the spine, and thickening of the ligaments connecting the vertebræ, often give rise to it. The long-continued use of sedatives will likewise produce palsy, such as constant handling of white lead; poisonous fumes of metals or minerals; translation of morbid matter to the head; suppression of accustomed evacuations; pressure on the nerves by laxatives; fractures, wounds, or other external injuries, &c.

Treatment.—In sudden attacks, the same treatment as in apoplexy. To remove spasmodic symptoms, give the *Antispasmodic Tincture*, page 20, every hour. Betwixt give the *Stimulating Drops*, followed by herb tea. Steam the parts well with a bitter decoction of herbs; as tansy, hops, wormwood, camomile, catnep, pennyroyal, and betony, or any other bitter herbs. Pour boiling vinegar and water upon them; cover up, and let it infuse some time. Then rub the part with a stimulant, made of salt and cayenne, infused in hot vinegar.——Or, made of cayenne, whisky, and salt. Twice a day rub the spine of the back with the *Stimulating Ointment;* or apply mustard plasters; or sting the place with nettles. Electricity and dry frictions are very good. Once or twice a week give the vapour bath; and two hours after rub the whole body with the *Stim-*

ulating Liniment. Dr. Beach recommends the following injection:—cayenne pepper, 1 teaspoonful; lobelia, 2 teaspoonfuls; boiling water, 1 pint. Let it infuse; stir well, in order to get the strength out as soon as possible; sweeten with treacle; add half a pint of milk, and a gill of sweet oil. Give it warm; as much as the patient can bear; this will excite action in the bowels, and promote evacuations. Salt and water will make a very good injection.

If constipation should prevail, coarse, or brown bread, should be eaten, or aperients should be taken, page 20, 21, or a dose of castor oil; followed by the continual use of the Restorative Bitters, introducing the peroxide of iron, say ¼ oz. to a pint of the bitters. Also take a *Nervous Pill*; and occasionally the Alterative Syrup. See *Addenda.* Let the diet be simple, light, and spare. Take abundant exercise in the open air, when the weather permits.

PALSY, *Infusion for.*—Take horseradish, mustard seed bruised, of each, 4 ozs.; outer rind of orange peel, 1 oz.; infuse in two quarts of boiling water in a close vessel for 24 hours. In paralytic affections, a tea-cupful of this warm stimulant may be taken three or four times a day.

PANADA, *or bread, ar biscuit jelly.*—Set a little water on the fire; when it boils, take off, and add a glass of sherry, sugar, a little grated nutmeg and lemon-peel. At the same time grate some crumbs of bread. Put the crumbs in, and let it boil fast; when of a proper thickness to drink, take it off.

PANADA. *Another Method.*—Put to the water a bit of lemon-peel; mix the crumbs in, and when nearly boiled enough, add some lemon or orange syrup. Observe to boil all the ingredients; for if they be added afterward, the panada will break, and not jelly.

PANADA, *Chicken.*—Page 108.

PANCAKES, *General Directions for making.*—Clean the pan well before you fry the pancakes; put a little lard into it, and when hot wipe it out with a clean cloth; then put in more lard or butter, and fry the pancakes of a nice light brown, and drain them thoroughly from the fat. They should be eaten hot, and sugar strewed upon them.

PANCAKES *to make.*—A quart of milk; beat in 6 or 8 eggs, leaving half the whites out; mix, till the batter is of a fine thickness. The flour must be first mixed with a little milk; add the rest by degrees, also two spoonfuls of beaten ginger, a glass of brandy, and a little salt; stir all together; pour into the pan, (as above directed) a ladleful of batter, sufficient to make a pancake, moving the pan round, that the batter may be all over the pan; shake the pan, and when one side is enough, toss it over quickly. When both sides are done, put it upon a dish before the fire to keep hot. Sprinkle over it a little sugar.

PANCAKES, *American.*—Mix a pint of cream, five spoonfuls of fine flour, seven yolks and four whites of eggs, and a very little salt; fry them very thin in fresh butter, and between each strew sugar and cinnamon.

PANCAKES, *Common.*—Make a light batter of eggs, flour and milk. Fry in a small pan, in hot dripping or lard. Salt, nutmeg, or ginger, may be added. Sugar and lemon should be served to eat with them. If eggs are scarce, make the batter of flour, and small beer, ginger, &c., or clean snow, with flour, and a little milk.

PANCAKES, *Cream.*-Mix two eggs, well beaten, with a pint of cream, 3 ozs. of sifted sugar, 6 ozs. of flour, a teaspoonful mixed of cinnamon, nutmeg, and mace. Fry the pancakes thin with a piece of butter.

PANCAKES, *fine.* — Cream, half a pint; sherry, half a pint; the yolks of 18 eggs beaten fine, and a little salt; sugar, ½ lb.; a little ground cinnamon, mace, and nutmeg; put in as much flour as will spread thin over the pan, and fry them in fresh butter. This sort of pancake will not be crisp, but very good.

PANCAKES, *fried without butter.*—Beat six fresh eggs very well; mix, when strained, with a pint of cream, 4 ozs. of sugar, a glass of wine, half a nutmeg grated, and as much flour as will make it almost as thick as ordinary pancake batter, but not quite. Heat the frying-pan tolerably hot, wipe it with a clean cloth; pour in the batter to make thin pancakes.

PANCAKES, *Irish.*-Beat eight yolks and four whites of eggs, strain them into a pint of cream, put a grated nutmeg, and sugar to your taste; set 3 ozs. of fresh butter on the fire; stir it, and as it warms pour it to the cream, which should be warm when the eggs are put to it: then mix smooth almost half a pint of flour. Fry the pancakes very thin; the first with a bit of butter, but not the others.

PANCAKES, *pink,* &c.—Boil some beet-root till tender, and beat it fine in a mortar; add the yolks of four eggs, two spoonfuls of flour, and three of cream; sweeten, grate in half a nutmeg, and add a glassful of brandy; mix all well together, and fry the pancakes in butter; garnish them with green sweetmeats or sprigs of myrtle.

PANCAKES, *Rice.*—Boil ¼ lb. of rice to a jelly in a little water; when cold, mix it with a pint of cream, eight eggs, a bit of salt and nutmeg grated; stir in 8 ozs. of butter just warmed, and add as much flour as will make the batter thick enough. Fry in as little lard or dripping as possible.

PAPER, *to render fireproof and waterproof.*—Professor Muschamp, of Wurtemberg, advises the following :—

Take 26 ozs. of alum, and 4 ozs. of white soap, and dissolve them in a quart of water; into another vessel dissolve 2 ozs. of gum arabic, and 1 oz. of glue in the same quantity of water as the former, and add the two solutions together, which is now to be kept warm, and the paper intended to be made waterproof dipped into it, passed between rollers and dried; or without the use of rollers, the paper may be suspended until it is perfectly dripped, and then dried. The alum, soap, glue, and gum form a kind of artificial leather, which protects the surface of the paper from the action of water, and also renders it somewhat fireproof. A second immersion makes it still better.

PAPER-HANGINGS *to clean.* Rub them gently down with a crust of bread, or with stiff dough; the flock papers should not be treated this way, but brushed with a soft clothes brush.——Or, rub the paper well with a flannel cloth dipped in oatmeal.

PARAFINE, *Explosive.*—Mr. W. Herapath, of Bristol, makes the public acquainted with an easy method of proving whether parafine oil is dangerous or not. Let two or three drops be allowed to fall upon a plate or saucer, and apply to them a lighted match; if the flame spreads over the surface of the drops the oil should on no account be used, as it will under many circumstances prove explosive. The genuine paraffine or petroleum will not burn except upon a wick.

PARCHMENT GLUE.—Steep 1 lb. of parchment cuttings in a gallon of water in which has been dissolved 1 oz. of borax, and a little gum Arabic. Then strain the liquid well. Boil to the thickness required.

PARCHMENT, *to prepare for painting.*—Take 1½ yard of listing, and roll it up very tight in a circular form; then take some finely powdered white pumice stone; put the listing in it, and rub it over the parchment. This simple plan answers the best of any. If you wish it to take water colours, without sinking, choose that which is not spongy or soft, and use alum water with the colours, when you mix them for use.

PAREGORIC ELIXIR.-Take flowers of benzoin, half an ounce; opium, two drachms. Infuse in one pound of the volatile aromatic spirit, four or five days, frequently shaking the bottle; afterwards strain the elixir. It eases pain, allays tickling coughs, relieves difficult breathing, and is useful in many disorders of children, particularly the hooping cough. The dose to an adult is from fifty to sixty drops.

PARMESAN AND CAULIFLOWER.—Boil a cauliflower, drain it on a sieve, and cut the stalks so that the flower will stand upright about two inches above the dish. Put it into a stew-pan, with a little white sauce, let it stew till done enough, which will be but a few minutes; then dish it with the sauce round and put Parmesan grated over it. Brown it with a salamander.

PARKIN, *Superb.*— Oatmeal, 3 lbs.; flour, 1 lb.; butter, 1 lb.; treacle, 4 lbs.; ginger, 1 oz.; sugar, 1 lb.; 2 teaspoonfuls of carbonate of soda in a gill of beer.— The butter to be rubbed into the flour. All the ingredients to be mixed the previous evening, and baked in a moderate oven the following morning. *Do not forget to add a wineglass, or two, of the best rum.* This parkin is a luxury.

PARSNIPS, *to fricassee.*—Boil in milk till they are soft, then cut them lengthways into bits two or three inches long, and simmer in a white sauce, made of two spoonfuls of broth, a bit of mace, half a cupful of cream, a bit of butter, and some flour, pepper and salt.

PARSNIPS, *to mash.* — Boil them tender, scrape, then mash them in a stew-pan with a little cream, a good piece of butter, and pepper and salt.

PARSNIPS, *to stew.* — Boil them tender; scrape, and cut into slices; put them into a saucepan with cream enough: for sauce, a piece of butter rolled in flour, and a little salt; shake the saucepan often; when the cream boils, pour them into the dish.

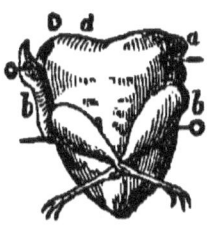

PARTRIDGES, *to choose.*—In autumn they are in season. If young, the bill is of a dark colour, and the legs yellowish; if fresh the vent will be firm; but this part will look greenish if stale; if old the bills are white, and the legs blue.

PARTRIDGE, *to boil.*—Boil quick in a good quantity of water about fifteen minutes. For sauce, take a quarter pint of cream, and a small piece of fresh butter; pour it over the birds.

PARTRIDGE, *to carve.*—The partridge is here presented as just taken from the spit; but before it is served up, the skewers must be withdrawn. It is cut up in the same manner as a fowl. The wings must be taken off in the lines *a, b,* and the merrythought, in the line *c, d.* The prime parts of a partridge are the wings, breast and merrythought, but the bird being small, the two latter are not often divided. The wing is considered the best, and the tip of it reckoned the most delicate morsel of all.

PARTRIDGE, *to dress a la braise.*—Truss the legs into the bodies of two brace of partridges; lard, and season with beaten mace, pepper, and salt; lay slices of bacon, beef, and veal, a small carrot, and onion, cut small, sweet herbs, and some whole pepper; put in the partridges with the breasts downwards; lay thin slices of beef and veal over them, and some parsley shred fine; cover, and stew 8 or 10 minutes over a slow fire; shake the pan, and pour into it a pint of boiling water; cover close, and let it stew half an hour over a quicker fire; turn out the birds; keep hot; pour into the pan a pint of thin gravy; boil till reduced to half a pint; strain, and skim off the fat. Cut a veal sweetbread small, small mushrooms, cockscombs, and fowls' livers, stewed half an hour in a pint of gravy; some artichoke buttons, and asparagus tops, blanched in warm water; then add the other gravy to this, and put in the partridges to heat; when hot, pour some sauce over them, and serve.

PARTRIDGE, *to hash.*—Cut up the partridge as for eating; slice an onion into rings; roll a little butter in flour; put them into the tossing pan, and shake it over the fire till it boils; put in the partridge with a little port wine and vinegar; and when it is thoroughly hot, lay it on the dish with sippets round it; strain the sauce over the partridge, and lay on the onion in rings.

PARTRIDGE, *to pot.*—Clean them nicely; and season with mace, allspice, white pepper, and salt, in fine powder. Rub every part well; then lay the breast downwards in a pan, and pack the birds as close as you possibly can. Put a good deal of butter on them; then cover the pan with a coarse flour paste and a paper over, tie it close, and bake. When cold, put the birds into pots, and cover with butter.

PARTRIDGE, *to roast.*—Roast them like a turkey, and when a little under roasted, dredge them with flour, and baste them with butter; let them go to table with a fine froth; put gravy sauce in the dish, and bread sauce on the table.

PARTRIDGE, *to stew.*—Truss as for roasting; stuff the craws, and lard them down each side, of the breast; roll a lump of butter in pepper, salt, and beaten mace, and put them inside; sew up the vents; dredge them well, and fry a light brown; put them into a stewpan with a quart of good gravy, a spoonful of sherry wine, the same of mushroom ketchup, a teaspoonful of lemon pickle, and a little mushroom powder, one anchovy, half a lemon, a sprig of sweet marjoram; cover the pan close, and stew half an hour; take out, and thicken the gravy; boil it a little, and pour it over the partridges, and lay round them artichoke buttons, boiled, and cut in quarters, and the yolks of four hard eggs, if agreeable.

PARTRIDGE PIE.—Pick and singe four partridges; cut off the legs at the knee; season with pepper, salt, chopped parsley, thyme, and mushrooms. Lay a veal steak and a slice of ham, at the bottom of the dish: put the partridges in, and half a pint of good broth. Put puff paste on the edge of the dish, and cover with the same; brush it over with egg, and bake an hour.

PARTRIDGE SOUP.—Take two partridges; skin them; and cut them into pieces, with three or four slices of ham, a stick of celery, and three large onions cut into slices. Fry them all in butter till brown, but take care not to burn them. Then put them into a stew-pan, with five pints of boiling water, a few pepper-corns, a shank or two of mutton, and a little salt. Stew it gently two hours; then strain it through a sieve, and put it again into a stew-pan, with some stewed celery and fried bread; when it is near boiling, skim it, pour it into a tureen, and serve it up hot.

PARSLEY, *to crisp.*—Wash it; put it into a Dutch oven, at a moderate distance from the fire, and keep turning it till crisp; lay small pieces of butter upon it, but not to make it greasy.

PARSLEY, *and other herbs to dry.*—Pick them clean from all decayed leaves. Put in a sieve; cover with blotting paper, and expose to the sun; or in a very slow oven, and turn them often; the quicker they are dried the better. Aromatic herbs, if not dried quickly, will lose much of their flavour. They may be dried also in a Dutch oven. Rub them, and pass through a sieve. Parsley thus prepared is very pleasant and useful; it breaks into parts as small as are obtained by chopping. When parsley and butter are wanted, it is only required to put a small quantity into the saucepan with the butter.

All dried herbs should be kept from the air in paper bags.

PARSLEY, *to pickle.*—Take a good quantity of curled parsley; put it into very strong salt and water; let it stand a week; put it into another strong salt and water, and let it stand another week; drain well; put it in spring water, and change it every day for three days; and scald it in hard water till it becomes green; take out, and drain dry; boil a quart of distilled vinegar a few minutes, with mace, sliced nutmeg, and two or three shalots. When it is cold, pour it on the parsley, with three slices of horse radish. Keep for use.

PARSLEY PIE.—Lay a fowl or a few bones of the scrag of veal, seasoned, into a dish; scald a colander-full of picked parsley in milk; season; and add to it the fowl or meat, with a tea-cupful of any sort of good broth, or weak gravy. When it is baked, pour into it a quarter of a pint of cream scalded, with the size of a walnut of butter, and a little flour. Shake it round to mix with the gravy already in.

Lettuces, white mustard leaves, or spinach, may be added to the parsley, and scalded before put in.

PARSLEY SAUCE.—Pound a handful of parsley, and put it into a stewpan in good cullis, sufficient for the quantity of sauce wanted; simmer it fifteen minutes, and sift it in a sieve; add some butter rolled in flour; make a liaison; and, lastly, add a lemon squeeze.

PASTE.—It is made by beating, say, half a cupful of flour in water, to the consistence of pudding batter; add half a teaspoonful of powdered alum; put it on the fire, and stir till it boils.

A little powdered corrosive sublimate will cause it to keep long, and a few drops of any of the essential oils will prevent mouldiness. The addition of a little sugar, or powdered resin, makes it more adhesive.

PASTE AND PIES, *General Directions.*—The most important thing in all kinds of pastry is the proper heat of the oven. Raised pies should have a quick oven, and well closed up, or the pie will fall in at the sides; it should not have any water put in till the minute it goes to the oven; it makes the crust sad, and may cause the pie to run. Light paste requires a moderate oven, but not too slow; it will make it sad, and a quick oven will soon burn it, and not give it time to rise. Tarts that are iced require a slow oven, or the icing will brown, and the paste not be nearly baked. This sort of tarts ought to be made of sugar paste, and rolled very thin.

PASTE FOR BIRDS.—1 lb. of unsifted flour; 2 ozs. of butter; 4 ozs. of sugar; three hard-boiled eggs, cut up very small. Put them into a sancepan, over a slow fire, and stir till it becomes crumbly. Do not let it be burned. When this is ready, put a pint of cracked hempseed to the mixture, and mix well together. When it is baking, add a pennyworth of saffron, and mix it with the rest. If kept in a dry place, it will keep for months.

Another.—Mix well together 3 lbs. of powdered or ground split-peas, 1½ lb. of fine crumbs of bread, and coarse sugar; the yolks of six eggs, and 6 ozs. of unsalted butter. Put one-third of the mixture at a time, in a frying-pan, over a gentle fire, and stir it until it is just browned. When the other two parts are thus done, and all are cold, add to the whole mass, 6 ozs. of maw seed, with 6 ozs. of good bruised hemp seed, separated from the husks. Mix all together. It is an excellent food for all singing birds.

PASTE, *to keep a year.*—Dissolve in cold water, 2 ozs. of glue, and 1 oz. of alum. Mix intimately with flour, and then boil. When nearly cool, stir in two teaspoonfuls of oil of cloves, or lavender. Make it into a pint of paste. Keep in a well covered vessel.

PASTE, *for Custards.*—Put ¼ lb. of butter in a pan of water; take 2 lbs. of flour, with as much water as will make it into a good paste; work it well; and when cooled a little, raise the custard; put a paper round the inside of them, and when they are half baked, fill them. When you make any kind of dripping paste, boil it four or five times in plenty of water to take off the strength; when you make a cold crust with suet, shred it fine; pour part of it into the flour; then make it into a paste, and roll it out as before.

PASTE, *for meat, or savoury pies.*—Sift 2 lbs of fine flour to 1½ lb. of good salt butter, which break into small pieces; rub gently together the flour and butter, and mix up with yolks of three eggs well beat up, adding nearly a pint of spring water; roll the paste out and double it in folds three times, and it is ready.

PASTE, *for Tarts.*—Take 1 lb. of fine flour; beat the white of an egg to a strong froth; mix with it as much water as will make it into a stiff paste; roll it out very thin; lay 3 ozs. of butter in thin pieces; dredge it with a little flour left for that purpose; roll it up tight; then roll it out again; do so again until all the ½ lb. of butter and flour is done; cut into square pieces, and make the tarts; it requires a quicker oven than crisp paste.

PASTE, *rich puff*.—Puffs may be made of any sort of fruit, but it should be prepared first with sugar.

Weigh an equal quantity of butter with as much fine flour as you judge necessary; mix a little of the former with the latter, and wet it with as little water as will make into a stiff paste. Roll it out, and put all the butter over it in slices, turn in the ends and roll it thin; do this twice, and touch it no more than can be avoided. The butter may be added at twice; and to those who are not accustomed to make paste it may be better to do so.

A quicker oven than for short crust.

PASTE, *less rich*.—Weigh a pound of flour, and a quarter of a pound of butter, rub them together, and mix into a paste with a little water, and an egg well beaten—of the former as little as will suffice, or the paste will be tough. Roll, and fold it three or four times.

Rub extremely fine in one pound of dried flour six ounces of butter, and a spoonful of white sugar; work up the whole into a stiff paste with as little hot water as possible.

PASTE, *without butter for family pies*.—Cut some slices of beef suet very thin; put some flour on the table; lay the suet upon it; roll it with a rolling-pin till it is quite soft; rub it very fine into some flour, and mix it with cold water. It is much better done this way than chopped, and makes a very good crust for any pie that is to be eaten hot, or for fruit puddings.

PASTILES, *for perfuming sick rooms*.—Powder and mix gum benzoin, 8 ozs.; gum storax, 4 ozs.; frankincense, 8 ozs.; fine charcoal, 1 lb. Add tincture of benzoin, 3 ozs.; essence of ambergris, 1 oz.; essence of musk, ½ oz.; 1 oz. of almond oil, and 2 ozs. of clear syrup; mix into a stiff paste, and form into pastiles of a conical form dry in the heat of the sun.

PATTIES, *to make*.—Raise them of an oval form, and bake them as for custards; cut some long narrow bits of paste, and bake them on a dusting box, but not too round as they are for handles; fill the patties, when quite hot, with the meat; set the handles across the patties; they will look like baskets; if the walls of the patties have been nicely pinched when they were raised, five will be a dish.

PATTIES, *to make fine*.—Slice turkey, lamb, with the fat, chicken, loin of veal, or sirloin of beef, parsley, thyme, and lemon-peel shred; pound it very fine; season with pepper, and salt; make a fine puff paste; roll it into thin square sheets; put the forcemeat in the middle; cover close all around, and set the paste even; just before they go into the oven, wash them over with the yolk of an egg; bake 20 minutes in a quick oven; have ready white gravy, seasoned with pepper, salt, and shalot, and thickened with cream or butter. When baked, make a hole in the top of each, and pour in some gravy, but not so as to run out.

PATTIES, *common*.—Take the kidney part of a very fat loin of veal; chop the kidney, veal, and fat, very small, all together; season with mace, pepper, and salt, to your taste; raise little patties the size of a tea-cup; fill them with the meat; put thin lids on them; bake very crisp.

PATTIES, *fried*.—Cut ½ lb. of leg of veal very small, with six oysters; put the liquor of the oysters to the crumb of a penny loaf; mix with a little salt; put into a tossing pan with ¼ lb. of butter; keep stirring for a few minutes over the fire; make a good puff paste, roll it out, and cut it into little bits the size of a crown piece, various shapes; put a little of the meat upon them, and a lid to cover; turn up the edges, to keep in the gravy; fry them in a panful of hog's lard.

PATTIES, *like mince pies.*—Chop the kidney and fat of cold veal, apple, orange, and lemon-peel candied, and fresh currants, a little wine, two or three cloves, a little brandy, and a bit of sugar. Bake as before.

PATTIES, *Savoury*.-Take 1 lb. of the cold loin of veal, or cold fowl, either boiled or roasted, and ¼ lb. of beef suet; chop them as small as possible with a little parsley; season well with nutmeg, pepper, and salt; put them in a tossing-pan, with half a pint of veal gravy; thicken the gravy with a little flour and butter, and two spoonfuls of cream, and shake them over the fire for two minutes; fill your patties.

PATTIES, *Sweet*.—Take the meat of a boiled calf's foot, two large apples, and 1 oz. of candied orange; chop them very small; grate half a nutmeg; mix them with the yolk of an egg, a spoonful of French brandy, and ¼ lb. of currants; make a good puff paste, and roll it in different shapes and fill; they may be baked or fried.

PEACH.-Dr. King, of America, says, "The dried peach, boiled or stewed with sugar, is aperient, and very wholesome for persons constipated, especially invalids. The kernels are bitter, but form a most valuable remedy. They are a great tonic for the stomach and bowels, and strengthen the digestive organs. Made into a decoction, they give strength to persons recovering from the dysentery. It may be sweetened to render it palatable. The leaves and bark are tonic, purgative, and diuretic, and are very useful in leucorrhœa, or whites, debility, and irritation of the stomach and lungs."

The flowers and kernels, say 1 oz. each, boiled, and sweetened, is a remedy for children teething, and for worms.

PEACH BLOSSOMS, *Syrup of*.—Infuse peach blossoms in hot water, sufficient to cover them; let them stand in a hot water-bath for 24 hours covered close; then strain and put in fresh flowers; infuse as before; again strain; and a third time add fresh peach blossoms to the liquor; then to every lb. of the infusion, add 2 lbs. of double refined sugar, and setting it in a hot water-bath, make a syrup.

PEACH COLOUR RIBBON, *to restore when turning red*.—Salt of potash dissolved in water; place the ribbon on a clean table, and apply the mixture with a sponge.

PEACH LEATHER.-—-This preparation is much relished by invalids, and is thus made;—Squeeze out the pulp of very ripe peaches, add a little sugar; give one boil, and spread it half an inch thick on a plate, and let it dry till quite dry and tough. Roll it in layers, with clean paper between.

PEACH MARMALADE.-The same as *Apricot Marmalade*. See page 26.

PEACH WINE.—Take 9 gallons of cold soft water; refined sugar, 13 lbs.; honey, 3 lbs.; white tartar, in fine powder, 2 ozs.; 30 or 40 peaches; then ferment without the peaches, and add a gallon of brandy. Put into the vat; and the day after, (before the peaches are put in) take the stones from them; break them and the kernels; then put them and the pulp into the vat, and proceed with the general process.

PEACH AND APRICOT WINE.—Pare and stone peaches and nectarines; slice thin, and pour upon them 1½ gallons of water, and a quart of sherry; simmer the whole gently till the fruit becomes soft; pour the liquid into another vessel containing more peaches sliced, to stand 12 hours. Strain out the whole of the liquid, and put into a cask to ferment. Add 1½ lb. of sugar to each gallon. Boil 1 oz. of cloves in a quart of sherry wine; add to the whole. To give it a peculiar flavour boil ½ oz. of mace, and ½ oz. of nutmegs in a quart of sherry, and pour it into the wine when fermenting; it should be poured in hot.

PEACHES *in Brandy.* See *Apricot,* page 26.

PEACHES, *to dry.* The same as *Apricots,* page 26.

PEACH JELLY. The same as *Apricot Jelly,* page 26.

PEACHES, *to preserve.* The same as *Apricots,* page 25.

PEARL POWDER.—Dissolve bismuth in nitro muriatic acid, and gradually add cold distilled water, and upon it a beautiful white powder will be precipitated.

PEARL WATER, *for the face.* —Put ½ lb. of the best Windsor soap, scraped very fine, into a gallon of boiling water. Stir it well for some time, and let it cool. Add a pint of rectified spirit of wine, and ½ oz. of oil of rosemary. Stir well. The Italians call this compound *Tincture of Pearls.* It is a good cosmetic, and will remove freckles.

PEARS, *Baked.*—These need not be of a fine sort; but some taste better than others, and often those that are least fit to eat raw. Wipe, but do not pare, and lay them on tin plates, and bake them in a slow oven. When enough to bear it, flatten them with a silver spoon. When done through, put them on a dish. They should be baked three or four times gently.

PEARS, *Jargonelle, to preserve.* —Pare them very thin, and simmer in thin syrup; let them lie a day or two. Make the syrup richer, and simmer again; and repeat this till they are clear; then drain, and dry them in the sun or a cool oven a very little time. They may be kept in syrup and dried as wanted, which makes them more moist and rich.

PEAR JELLY.—The large stew pears, previously stewed in the oven with a little water make good jelly. Or take jargonelle, or French pears, and boil them to a pulp; then boil gently over the fire with as much sugar as there is pulp for about twenty minutes, till it is moderately thick. Put in jars, and cover close. *Gu.*

PEARS, *Stewed.* — Pare and halve, or quarter, large pears, according to their size; throw them into water, as the skin is taken off before they are divided, to prevent their turning black. Pack them round a stew-pan, and sprinkle as much sugar over as will make them sweet, and add lemon peel, a clove or two, and some allspice cracked; cover them with water. Cover them close, and stew three or four hours; when tender, take them out, and pour the liquor over them. The stone pears may be done in the oven with sugar only.

PEAS, *green, to preserve.*—Shell, and put them into a kettle of water when it boils; give them two or three warms only, and pour them in a colander. Drain, and turn them out on a cloth, and then on another to dry perfectly. When dry, bottle them in wide-mouthed bottles; leaving only room to pour clarified mutton suet upon them an inch thick, and for the cork. Rosin it down; and keep in the cellar, or in the earth, as directed for gooseberries. When they are to be used, boil them till tender, with a bit of butter, a spoonful of sugar, and a bit of mint.

PEAS, *to boil.*—Peas should not be shelled long before they are wanted, nor boiled in much water; when the water boils, put them in, with a little salt (some add a little loaf sugar, but if they are sweet of themselves, it is superfluous); when the peas begin to dent in the middle, they are boiled enough. Strain, and put a piece of butter in the dish, and stir. A little mint should be boiled with the peas.

PEAS MUSH.—Put a quart of green peas, dried mint, and salt, into a quart of water; boil till the peas are tender; add pepper, a bit of butter rolled in flour; stir it altogether, and let it boil a few minutes; add two quarts of milk; boil 15 minutes longer; take out the mint, and serve.

PEAS PUDDING. — Put a quart of split peas into a clean cloth; allow room for them to swell; boil slowly till they are tender; if the peas are good, they will be ready in 2½ hours. Rub them through a sieve into a deep dish, adding an egg or two, 1 oz. of butter, pepper, and salt; beat them well together for 10 minutes; flour a cloth, put the pudding in, tie it tight, and boil an hour longer.

PEAS SOUP.—Soak a quart of split peas the night before, and boil them with a little carbonate of soda in sufficient water to allow them to break. Add three or four quarts of beef broth, and stew for one hour; then pass the whole through a sieve, and heat again. Season with salt and pepper. One or two small heads of celery, sliced and stewed in it, will be a great improvement.

Peas Soup may be made as above with the addition of a little bacon and veal.

PEAS SOUP, *a la creme.*—Boil with a little salt 5 lbs. of nice lean beef in 6 quarts of water. When it boils, skim, and add two carrots, three whole onions, thyme, two heads of celery, and three quarts of old green peas; boil till the meat is quite tender; strain, and rub the pulp through a hair sieve. Split the blanched part of three Cos lettuces into four quarters, and cut them an inch long, with a little mint. Then put ¼ lb. of butter into a stewpan that will hold the soup. Put the lettuce and mint into the butter, with a leek sliced thin, and a pint of green peas; stew them fifteen minutes, and shake often; then put in a little of the soup, and stew them fifteen minutes longer; then put in the soup, and as much thick cream as will make it white. Stir till it boils. Put toasted bread or French roll at the bottom of the dish, and pour the soup over it.

PEAS SOUP, *with meat.*—Take a small knuckle of veal, or 4 lbs of coarse lean beef; chop into pieces; put on the fire in 6 quarts of water. Add 1 lb. of lean bacon steeped in vinegar an hour, mace, cloves, cayenne, a little white pepper, sweet herbs, and parsley, and a crust of bread, toasted crisp; cover closely, and boil gently over a slow fire, till it is half done. Strain, and put to it a pint of green peas, lettuce, and celery, all cut small; cover closely, and stew very gently over a slow fire for two hours. In the mean time boil a pint of peas in a pint of water very tender; strain well through a coarse sieve, and pour all the pulp into the soup; boil together, and add salt.

PEAS SOUP, *White.*—To 6 quarts of water put a knuckle of veal, a large fowl, 1 lb. of lean bacon, and ½ lb. of rice, two anchovies, a few pepper-corns, onions, sweet herbs, and 3 heads of celery sliced. Stew all together till the soup is as strong as you like it; then strain through a hair sieve into a earthen pot; let it stand all night; take off the scum, and pour it off clear; add ¼ lb. of Jordan almonds, beaten fine; boil a little, and then strain. Put in a pint of cream and the yolk of an egg.

PENCIL DRAWINGS, *to fix.* Dissolve white resin in spirits of wine; lay the pencil drawing on its face upon a sheet of clean paper, and brush the back of the drawing with the solution. This penetrates through the paper, and as the spirit evaporates, the resin is deposited as a varnish on the drawing. It does not cockle the paper, which watery solutions will do; and as the brush only passes over the back of the drawing, none of the pencil marks are in any degree removed.

Pencil, or Chalk Drawings, to fix.—Immerse the drawing in a weak solution of isinglass; allowing no part of the drawing to remain without the isinglass passing over it, or it will look spotty. Drain it, by holding the drawing up by one end over a plate.

PENNYROYAL.—This plant is perennial. It flowers in August and September. It is warm, pungent, aromatic, stimulating, and diaphoretic; like spearmint, but not so agreeable. It contains a volatile oil which is obtained by distillation. The infusion is warming to the stomach, and allays sickness. It relieves spasms, hysterics, flatulency, and colic, and promotes expectoration in dry consumptive coughs. It promotes perspiration, and is most valuable in obstruction of the menses.

PENNYROYAL WATER.—Pennyroyal leaves, dry, 1½ lb.; water, from 1½ to 2 gallons. Draw off by distillation, one gallon. It is a specific remedy for female obstructions. It is good for gout, rubbing the parts with it till they are red; and if salt be added, it is good for the side in liver complaints. It is very warming to the stomach, produces perspiration, and therefore is good for coughs, asthma, &c. An infusion of the herb in hot water is nearly as good.

PEPPER POSSET; once so highly esteemed for the cure of colds, &c. Put a dozen peppercorns, or a dozen allspice, into a pint of milk, and let it simmer slowly; when it boils, pour in a gill of sherry, and let all boil till the curd becomes hard; strain off the whey, and drink it hot.

PEPPER POT.—Into 3 quarts of water, put what vegetables you like; cut them very small, and stew them with 2 lbs. of neck of mutton, and 1 lb. of picked pork, till tender. Half an hour before serving, clear a lobster, or crab, from the shell, and put it in. Season with salt and cayenne. Small suet dumplings may be boiled in the same liquid.

Instead of mutton, a fowl may be used. Pepper-pot may be made of various things. It is a proper mixture of fish, flesh, fowl, vegetables, and pulse. Boil a small quantity of rice with the whole.

PEPPER WATER, *Spirituous Jamaica.*—Take of Jamaica pepper water, half a pound; proof spirit, three gallons; water, two gallons. Distil off three gallons. This is an agreeable cordial, and may supply the use of the Aromatic Water.

PEPPERMINT, *Candied.*-Boil 3 lbs of raw sugar in a pint of water, till the sugar begins to candy round the side, then take your pan off the fire, and drop 16 drops of the oil of peppermint therein; pour it out into little round hoops made of tin; or butter a large piece of paper, and lay it on the stone with a square frame on paper; and pour the sugar on the paper, and it will become all over beautifully spotted, and then with a knife, cut it into what size or shape you please.

PEPPERMINT DROPS. — Sift finely powdered loaf sugar into lemon juice, sufficient to make it of a proper consistence; gently dry it over the fire a few minutes; take off, and add about 20 drops of oil of peppermint for every pound of sugar. Drop them from the point of a knife upon buttered paper.

Another.—Mix 1 lb. of sifted loaf sugar with the whites of 3 eggs; add 10 or 15 drops of the oil of peppermint, beat, and mix well. Drop as before directed.

PEPPERMINT, *Mentha Piperita.*—This plant is perennial. It flowers in August and September. The leaves have a strong and agreeable smell, and a pungent aromatic taste. It is stimulant, diaphoretic, antispasmodic, and anti-emetic. Its stimulating property is very volatile, producing in the mouth a peculiar sensation of coldness. It is very useful in spasms, flatulency, colic, cramps of the stomach. The oil may be taken two or three drops in a cupful of water, or cold tea.

PEPPERMINT LOZENGES —Dissolve ½ oz. of isinglass, and 1 oz. of gum arabic, in a quart of boiling water, and let it stand till cold. Grate 7 lbs. of loaf sugar, and sift it through a fine sieve; then add 50 drops of the oil of peppermint. Mix all together pretty stiff. Lay part of the sugar on a fine marble stone, roll it thin, and cut it with a tin mould of the size of the lozenges.

PEPPERMINT WATER.— Cut full grown peppermint into short lengths; fill your still with it, and put it half full of water. When it nearly boils, and the still begins to drop, if your fire be too hot, decrease the heat, to keep it from boiling over, or the water will be muddy. The slower the still drops, the water will be the clearer and stronger, but do not spend it too far; the next day bottle it; let it be uncorked a few days to take off the fire of the still.

PERCH, *to boil.*—Put them into cold water, boil them carefully and serve with melted butter and soy. Perch is a most delicate fish. They may be either fried or stewed, but in stewing they do not preserve so good a flavour.

PERCH, *to fry.*—Scale gut, and well wash; then dry them, and lay them separately on a board before the fire, after dusting some flour over them. Fry them of a fine colour with fresh dripping; Serve with crimp parsley, and plain butter.

PERCH, *to fry.*—Clean and scale them, and slit the sides in several places; marinate them about an hour in the juice of a lemon, with pepper, salt, sprigs of parsley, a clove of garlic, and a bay leaf; then drain, and roll them in flour, to fry of a good brown colour; serve with fried parsley.

PERFUME, *against moths.*—One oz. each of cinnamon, cloves, nutmegs, carraway seeds, mace, camphor, and two ounces of orris root.—Place in little bags.

PERFUME FOR GLOVES AND HANDKERCHIEFS.——Ambergris, 1 drachm; civet, 1 drachm; oil of lavender, 3 drachms; oil of bergamot, 3 drachms; camphor, ¼ oz.; spirit of wine, ½ pint. Cork and shake well for 10 days; filter, and bottle.

PERFUME, *to prevent infection.*—Take gum benjamin, storax, and galbanum, ½ oz. each; powder them with oil of myrrh, and burn them on a hot plate or shovel.

PERFUMED POWDER, *for boxes and drawers.*—Mix 1 oz. each of the following:—orris powder, coriander, cloves, cinnamon, rose leaves, lavender flowers, musk, ¼ oz.; camphor, 1 oz. Put into small bags for use.

PERMANENT INK, *for marking linen.* — Take half an ounce of vermilion, and a drachm of salt of steel; let them be levigated with linseed oil to the thickness or limpidity required for the occasion. This has not only a very good appearance, but will be found to resist the effects of acids, as well as all alkaline leys. It may be made of other colours by substituting the proper articles instead of vermilion.

PERRY.—It is made from pears in the same way as cider is made. The best pears for this purpose are such as are adapted for eating, and the redder they are the better. The pears must be quite dry.

PERSIAN MEAT CAKES. —Take the fat and sinews from the meat of a leg of mutton; beat in a marble mortar with pepper, salt, and the juice of onions, and sweet herbs. Make them all into flat cakes, and keep them pressed between two dishes for 12 hours,; then fry them with butter, and serve them with the same.

PERSPIRATION, *to restrain.* —Spring water, 2 ozs.; diluted sulphuric acid, 40 drops; compound spirits of lavender, 2 drachms; take a table-spoonful twice a day.

PERUVIAN BARK.——*See Robinson's Herbal on this valuable plant.*

PEWTER, *to clean.*—Scour it with fine calais sand in a solution of potass, or soda, with a little oil of tartar. Dry and polish with whiting.

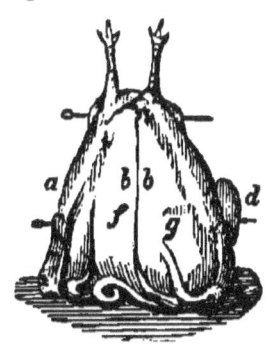

PHEASANT, *to choose.*—The cock bird is accounted best, except when the hen is with egg. If young he has short, blunt, or round spurs; but if old they are long and sharp.

PHEASANT, *to roast.*—Roast them as turkey; and serve with a fine gravy (into which put a very small bit of garlic), and bread-sauce. When cold, they may be made into excellent patties, but their flavour should not be overpowered by lemon.

PHEASANT, *to stew.*—Put it into the stewpan, with as much veal stock as will cover it; stew it till there is liquor enough left for sauce; skim, and add artichoke bottoms parboiled, beaten mace, a glass of wine, pepper and salt; thicken with a piece of butter rolled in flour, and a little lemon-juice; take up the pheasant; pour the sauce over it; put forcemeat balls into the dish, and serve it.

PICKLE, *Picallillo, or Indian Pickles.*—Lay 1 lb. of white ginger in water a night, then scrape, slice, and lay it in salt till the other ingredients are ready. Peel, slice, and salt 1 lb. of garlic three days, then put in the sun to dry. Salt and dry long pepper in the same way.

Prepare various sorts of vegetables thus: Quarter small white cabbages, salt three days, squeeze and set in the sun to dry.

Cauliflowers cut in their branches; take off the green from the radishes; cut celery in three-inch length; ditto young French beans whole, and the shoots of elder, which will look like bamboo. Apples and cucumbers, the least seedy sort; cut them in slices or quarters. All must be salted, drained, and dried in the sun, except the latter; over which pour boiling vinegar, and in 12 hours drain them, but use no salt.

Put the spice, garlic, ¼ lb. of mustard-seed, and vinegar enough for the quantity to pickle, into a stone jar, and 1 oz. of turmeric. When the vegetables are ready, put some of them into a two-quart stone jar, and pour over them one quart of boiling vinegar. Next day take out those vegetables; and when drained, put them into a large stock jar, and boiling the vinegar, pour it over more of the vegetables; let them lie a night, and do as above. Thus proceed till you have cleansed each set from dust; then to every gallon of vinegar put 2 ozs. of flour of mustard, mixing, by degrees, with a little of it boiling hot. The whole of the vinegar should be previously scalded, but left to be cold before it is put to the spice. Stop the jar tight.

This pickle will not be ready for a year; but you may make a small jar for eating in a fortnight, only by giving the cauliflower one scald in water, after salting and drying as above, but without the preparative vinegar; then pour the vinegar, that has the spice and garlick boiling hot over. If at any time it be found that the vegetables have not swelled properly, boiling the pickle, and pouring it over them hot, will plump them.

PIC-NIC BISCUITS.—Into 1 lb. of flour, work very small 2 ozs. of butter, mix well with half a salt-spoonful of the finest carbonate of soda, 2 ozs. of sugar, mix these thoroughly with the flour, and make up the paste with a few spoonfuls of milk, not more than quarter of a pint. Knead it very smooth, and roll it quarter of an inch thick, cut in rounds, 1½ inch diameter, roll it thin, prick them well, lay on tins sprinkled with flour, bake in a slow oven till they are crisp. When they are cold, put them into dry canisters. Cream instead of milk will greatly enrich them. Carraway seeds or ginger can be added at pleasure. The quantity of soda should be so small as not to taste them in the slightest; milk which is slighly sour, may be used with it.

PICTURE FRAMES, *to gild.*—The size may be made of white of egg diluted with water, or parchment boiled to a strong size; but the cheapest is the Japanner's gold size. Size the frame, and lay on the gold. When perfectly dry, burnish with an agate. Isinglass makes a good varnish.

PICTURE VARNISH.—Mastic varnish.

PIES, *Oswego*.—Line a deep plate with crust, and bake it in a quick oven; when done, fill with the Custard, (See Custard, boiled, made of Oswego, &c.,) strew the top with powdered sugar, dust it with the corn, and set it again in the oven to bake.

PIGS, *Management of, when Feeding.*—It is stated in Wade's British History, that a gentleman in Norfolk put up six pigs, of nearly equal weight, to feed at the same time, and treated them the same as to food and litter for seven weeks. Three of them were left to shift for themselves as to cleanliness; the other three were kept as clean as possible, by a man employed for the purpose, with a curry-comb and brush. The last consumed in the seven weeks fewer peas by five bushels than the other three, yet weighed more when killed by two stones and four pounds upon the average.

PIG, *to bake a.*—Lay the pig in a well-buttered dish; flour it all over; rub some butter on it, and send it to the oven; when done, take it out, rub it over with a buttered cloth, and put it into the oven again till it is dry; lay it in the dish, and cut up. Take the fat from the dish it was baked in, and some gravy will remain at the bottom; put this to a little veal gravy, with butter rolled in flour, and boil it up with the sage that comes out of the body. Serve with apple or currant sauce.

PIG, *to barbacue.*—Dress a pig of ten weeks old, as if for roasting; make a forcemeat of two anchovies, six sage leaves, and the liver of the pig, all chopped very small; put them into a mortar, with the crumbs of half a penny loaf, 4 ozs. of butter, half a teaspoonful of cayenne, and half a pint of red wine; beat all to a paste; put it into the pig's belly, and sew it up; place the pig before a brisk fire; singe it well; put port wine in the dripping pan freely, and baste it well at the time of roasting. When nearly done, take the sauce and bread, and add an anchovy chopped small, sweet herbs, half a lemon; then draw the pig. Garnish with slices of lemon. It will take four hours to roast.

PIG'S CHEEK, *to prepare for boiling.*—Cut off the snout, and clean the head; divide it, and take out the eyes and the brains; sprinkle the head with salt, and let it drain 24 hours. Salt it with common salt and saltpetre; let it lie 9 days if to be dressed without stewing with peas, but less if to be dressed with peas; and it must be washed first, and then simmer till all is tender.

PIG'S FEET AND EARS.—Clean carefully, and soak some hours, and boil them tender; then take them out; boil some vinegar and a little salt with some of the water, and when cold put it over them. When they are to be dressed, dry them, cut the feet in two, and slice the ears; fry, and serve with butter, mustard, and vinegar. They may be either done in batter, or only floured.

PIG'S FEET AND EARS, *to ragout.*—Boil them; split the feet down the middle, and cut the ears in narrow slices; dip them in butter, and fry brown; take beef gravy, a teaspoonful of lemon pickle, a table-spoonful of mushroom ketchup, one of browning, and a little salt; thicken with butter rolled in flour; put in the feet and ears, and give a gentle boil. Serve, laying the feet in the middle of the dish, and the ears round them. Garnish with curled parsley.

PIG'S FEET JELLY.—Clean the feet and ears well, and soak them a few hours; then boil them in a very small quantity of water till every bone can be taken out; throw in half a handful of chopped sage, the same of parsley, and a seasoning of chopped pepper, salt, and mace, in fine powder; simmer till the herbs are scalded, then pour all into a melon-form.   *Ru.*

PIG'S HEAD, *to collar*.—Scour the head and ears; take off the hair and snout; take out the eyes and brain; lay it into water one night; then drain, salt it well with salt and saltpetre, and let it lie five days. Boil it enough to take out the bones; then lay it on a dresser, turning the thick end of one side of the head towards the thin end of the other, to make the roll of equal size; sprinkle it with salt and white pepper, and roll it with the ears; put the pig's feet round the outside when boned, or the thin parts of two cow heels. Put it in a cloth, bind with a broad tape, and boil it till quite tender; then put a good weight upon it and take off the covering when cold.

If you want it more like brawn, salt it longer, and use more saltpetre, and add some pieces of lean pork; then cover with cow-heel, to look like the horn.

PIG'S JAW, *to boil*.—If the jaw has been dried, soak it a few hours in cold water; if pickled, wash it; make three holes in the thick part of the jaw, and all along the two sides; fill the holes with herbs; put into a clean cloth in cold water, heat slowly, and boil gently. With the herbs put salt, pepper, and a few bread crumbs.

PIG, *to roast a Suckling Pig*.—Get it when just killed; this is of great advantage. Let it be scalded. Put some sago, crumbs of bread, salt, and pepper, into the belly, and sew it up. Observe to skewer the legs back, or the under part will not be crisp. Lay it to a brisk fire till dry; then rub the pig with butter in every part. Dredge flour over it, and do not touch it again till ready to serve; scrape off the flour with a blunt knife, rub it well with a buttered cloth, and take off the head while at the fire; then take it up, cut it down the back and belly, lay it into the dish, and chop quickly the sage and bread very fine, and mix plenty of fine melted butter and a little flour. Put the sauce into the dish after the pig has been split down the back, and garnished with the ears and the two jaws. Many serves sucking pig whole. Pour the gravy into the sauce; and garnish with lemon or bread sauce and currants in a basin.

PIGEONS, *to boil*.—Wash clean; chop some parsley small; mix it with crumbs of bread, pepper, salt, and a bit of butter; stuff the pigeons, and boil 15 minutes in some mutton broth or gravy. Boil some rice soft in milk; when it begins to thicken, beat the yolks of two or three eggs, with two or three spoonfuls of cream, and a little nutmeg; mix well with a bit of butter rolled in flour.

PIGEONS, *to broil*. — After cleaning, split the backs, pepper and salt them, and broil them very nicely; pour over them either stewed or pickled mushrooms in melted butter, and serve as hot as possible.

PIGEONS, *in disguise*.—Season them with pepper and salt; make a nice puff paste; roll each pigeon in a piece of it; close them

T

well; tie them in cloths separately, and mind the paste does not break; boil them in much water 1½ hour. When they are untied, be careful they do not break; put them into a dish, and pour a little good gravy over them.

PIGEONS, *in Jelly.*—Take some of the liquor in which a knuckle of veal has been boiled; or boil a calf's foot; put the broth into a pan with a blade of mace, sweet herbs, pepper, lemon peel, a slice of lean bacon, and the pigeons. Bake them, and let them stand to be cold. Season to taste before baking. When done, take them out of the liquor, cover them close to preserve the colour; clear the jelly by boiling it with the whites of two eggs. Strain through a cloth dipped in boiling water. The fat must be perfectly removed before it be cleared. Put the jelly over and round them rough.

PIGEONS, *to jug.*—Draw the pigeons; save the livers. Put them in boiling water, and put them on the fire two minutes; take out, mince them small, bruise, and mix with a little pepper, salt, grated nutmeg, and lemon peel, shred very fine, chopped parsley, and yolks of two eggs, hard; bruise them, and put as much suet and bread as liver, pounded fine; work these together with raw eggs, and then roll it in fresh butter. Put a piece into the crops and bellies; sew up the necks and vents; dip the pigeons in water, and season with pepper, and salt, as for a pie; then put them in a jug with a piece of celery: stop them close; put the jug into cold water, and boil three hours. Then take out of the jug, and lay them in a dish; take out the celery, and put in a piece of butter rolled in flour; shake about till thick, and pour on the pigeons.

PIGEONS, *a la crapandine.*—Take three pigeons, truss the legs within, cut the flesh off the breast by sliding in the knife at the side of the leg, and running it up to the joint of the wing; turn the breast over, and flatten the body with the handle of a knife; take a stewpan large enough to contain them in the flattened state; melt a bit of butter in it; add salt and large pepper; put in the pigeons with their breasts down; turn them, and when three-fourths done, drain them and put them on the grill over a slow fire; give them a fine colour, and serve them under sauce *au pauvre homme.*

PIGEONS, *a la daube.*—Put a layer of bacon in a saucepan, one of veal, one of coarse beef, and then another of veal, about a pound of beef, and a pound of veal cut very thin; a piece of carrot, a bundle of sweet herbs, an onion, some pepper, a blade or two of mace, and a few cloves. Cover it close, and brown it over a slow fire. Put in a quart of boiling water, and when stewed till the gravy is rich, strain, and skim off the fat. Beat a pound of veal, and one of beef suet, in a mortar; an equal quantity of crumbs of bread, pepper, salt, nutmeg, beaten mace, lemon-peel, parsley cut small, and thyme. Mix them with the yolks of two eggs, fill the pigeons, and flatten the breasts; flour, and fry them in fresh butter, a little brown. Pour off the fat, and put the gravy over the pigeons. Stew them, cover close, till done. Dish them, and pour in the sauce. On each pigeon lay a bay leaf, and on the leaf a slice of bacon. Garnish with notched lemon, and serve hot.

PIGEONS, *to pot.*—Let them be quite fresh, clean them carefully, and season them with salt and pepper: lay them close in a small deep pan; for the smaller the surface, and the closer they are packed, the less butter will be wanted. Cover them with butter, then with very thick paper, tied down, and bake them. When cold, put them dry into pots that will hold two or three in each; and pour butter over them, using that which was baked as part. Observe that the butter should be pretty thick over them, if they are to be kept. If pigeons were boned, and then put in an oval form into the pot, they would lie closer, and require less butter. They may be stuffed with a fine forcemeat made with veal, bacon, &c., and then they will eat excellently. If a high flavour is approved of, add mace, allspice, and a little cayenne, before baking.

PIGEON, *to pickle.*—Bone them; turn the inside out, and lard it. Season with a little allspice, and salt, in fine powder; turn them again, and tie the neck and rump with thread. Put them into boiling water; let them boil a minute or two to plump; take them out, and dry them well; then put them boiling hot into the pickle, which must be made of equal quantities of white wine and white wine vinegar, with white pepper and allspice, sliced ginger and nutmeg, and two or three bay leaves. When it boils up, put the pigeons in. If they are small a quarter of an hour will do them; but they will take twenty minutes if large. Then take them out, wipe them, and let them cool. When the pickle is cold, take the fat off from it, and put them in again. Keep them in a *stone* jar, tied down with a bladder to keep out the air.

BACK.   PIGEON.   BREAST.

PIGEONS, *to roast.*—Take a little pepper and salt, a piece of butter, and parsley cut small; mix, and put the mixture into the bellies of the pigeons, tying the necks tight; take another string; fasten one end of it to their legs and rumps, and the other to a hanging spit, basting them with butter; when done, lay them in a dish, and they will swim with gravy.

PIGEON PIE.—Rub the pigeons with pepper and salt, inside and out; in the former put a bit of butter, and if approved, some parsley chopped with the livers, and a little of the same seasoning. Lay a beef steak at the bottom of the dish, and the birds on it; between every two a hard egg. Put a cup of water in the dish; and if you have any ham in the house, lay a bit on each pigeon; it is a great improvement to the flavour of the pie.

When ham is cut for gravy or pies, take the under part rather than the prime. Season the gizzards and the two joints of the wings, and put them in the centre of the pie; and over them a hole made in the crust, three feet nicely cleaned, to show what pie it is.

PIGEONS, *to stew.*—Take care that they are quite fresh, and carefully cropped, drawn, and washed; then soak them half an hour. In the mean time cut a hard white cabbage in slices (as if for pickling) into water; drain it, and then boil it in milk and water; drain it again, and lay some of it at the bottom of a stewpan. Put the pigeons upon it, but first season them well with pepper and salt, and cover them with the remainder of the cabbage. Add a little broth, and stew gently till the pigeons are tender; put among them two or three spoonfuls of cream, and a piece of butter and flour for thickening. After a boil or two, serve the birds in the middle, and the cabbage placed round them.

Another way.—Stew the birds in a good brown gravy, either stuffed or not; and seasoned high with spice and mushrooms fresh, and a little ketchup.

PIKE, *to bake.*—Scale it, and open as near the throat as you can, then stuff it with the following; grated bread, herbs, anchovies, oysters, suet, salt, pepper, mace, half a pint of cream, four yolks of eggs; mix all over the fire till it thickens, then put it into the fish, and sew it up; butter should be put over it in little bits; bake it. Serve sauce of gravy, butter, and anchovy.

If in serving the pike, the back and belly are slit up, and each slice gently drawn downwards, there will be fewer bones given.

PIKE, *to fricassee.*—Clean; cut into large pieces, and put them into a stewpan, with mushrooms, butter, 12 small onions, half boiled, a little parsley, green shalots, two cloves, thyme, and a bay leaf; soak all together some time; add a pint of sherry, some broth, salt, and whole pepper; boil briskly; reduce the same; take out the fagot, and make a liaison with cream, eggs, and a little nutmeg; adding a lemon squeeze, if the wine does not make it tart enough.

PIKE, *to roast a.*—Gut a large pike, and lard it with eel and bacon; then take thyme, savory, salt, mace, nutmeg, some crumbs of bread, beef suet, and parsley, all shred very fine, mix them with raw eggs, and put in the belly of the pike, sew up the belly, dissolve three anchovies in butter, to baste it with; put two laths on each side the pike, and tie it to the spit; melt butter thick, for sauce. Garnish with lemon.

PIKELETS, OR CRUMPETS —See *Crumpets,* page 134.—Take 3 lbs. of flour, two eggs, and a pint of milk; whisk the milk and the eggs well together; then add the flour, a little salt, and two tablespoonfuls of new bran; stir them well together, and let them rise; when the bakestone is hot, pour the batter upon it, either in hoops made on purpose or without; when ready to turn they will appear full of holes on the top side; turn them, and bake them a fine brown.

PILES.—An enlargement of the veins at the lower termination of the intestines, frequently causing great pain, bleeding, and difficult evacuation. The tumours are seated sometimes externally, and sometimes within the verge of the anus, for the most part attended with a discharge of blood; these are called *bleeding piles.* When no blood is discharged, they are termed *blind piles;* and, when the discharge is only serum, *white piles.*

It is most frequently caused by costiveness, by pregnancy, and a sedentary life, by strong purgatives, and by dram-drinking. The piles are sometimes the effect of relaxation and debility, and not unfrequently result from an inflammatory action in the rectum, and a diminished secretion of mucus from its inner membrane.

Treatment. — When piles are caused by constipation, and a debilitated state of the bowels, it is needful to open them, and keep them so by gentle aperients. Medicines which act moderately upon the bowels, are calculated to remove that morbid state of the liver and stomach which often causes the complaint. The patient may take sulphur, cream of tartar, confection of senna, and the lenitive electuary; but all strong purgatives must be avoided.

Mix sulphur, ½ oz.; confection of senna, 2 ozs.; saltpetre, 3 drachms; and as much syrup of orange as will give the mixture a proper consistence. About the size of a nutmeg must be taken twice or thrice a day. It is very soothing and healing to steam the parts with a sitz bath made of a strong decoction of bitter herbs; as hops, catnep, tansy, pennyroyal, and camomile flowers. Pour upon them boiling water and vinegar. Infuse some time; boil again, and let the steam approach the parts.

A cold water cloth has been found of great service. Dip a cloth into cold water; let the cloth be four-fold; apply it close, and press it to with a dry cloth: as it warms, re-dip into cold water: do this several times; then convey into the anus some pure tallow or lard, or the *Pile Ointment*, described at the end of this article. A *slippery elm poultice*, made with milk and water to a proper consistence, may also be applied. The slippery elm is both cooling and healing. Ten drops of laudanum may be added to the poultice.

When there is great constipation, an emolient injection is indicated. Take ¼ a pint of water, half a dessert-spoonful of salt, and an ounce of castor oil. Retain it as long as possible. The following injection is recommended by Dr. Simmons:—Witch hazel leaves, ½ oz.; cranesbill, ½ oz.; meadow fern burrs, 1 oz.; slippery elm, 2 drachms; mix the powders well together, and pour upon them 1½ pint of boiling water. Infuse for 4 hours, and strain it. In the morning use ½ a pint for an injection, and at night not quite so much, and retain it, if possible, all night. Repeat as often as necessary. The marshmallow ointment is also very useful.—For blind piles the tincture of lobelia is very good; so also is brandy, a little diluted, applied frequently.

It is a good plan to cleanse the anus night and morning with soft soap and water; then using tallow or the pilewort ointment, or any of the ointments for the piles. It is good to wash the anus after every evacuation. Generally speaking, the application of cold water is more effectual than warm water for fomenting, &c.; but this must be decided by the patient, as warm water in some states of the piles is very soothing.

To effect a cure, the bowels must be kept regularly open;—take Epsom salts, ½ oz.; infusion of senna, 6 drachms; tincture of senna, 3 drachms; decoction of bark, 1 oz.; spearmint water, 1 oz.; water, 4 ozs.; best manna, 3 drachms. Mix, and take from three to six table-spoonfuls every morning, or every other day. The diet should be chiefly vegetable till the disease is gone. Or, take a gentle aperient also every other night, and on the alternate night, the *Tonic Pill*, which see

When the constitution has become habituated to the disease, stimulants, as pepper and ginger, taken with the aliment often afford considerable relief.—Elecampane root, 2 ozs.; sweet fennel seed powder, 3 ozs.; black pepper powder, 1 oz.; milk of sulphur, 1 oz.; purified honey, 2 ozs.; brown sugar, and treacle, of each 1½ oz. Mix the first four ingredients; melt the honey, sugar, and treacle, and then mix all together. About the size of a nutmeg to be taken two or three times a day.—The decoction of oak bark is said to be a good remedy for piles.

"Aloes," says Dr. Buchan, "which form a principal part of the advertised pills, are frequently the cause of piles. Therefore persons subject to them should avoid all aloetic purges. An habitual costiveness is much more effectually and safely removed by a spoonful of castor oil taken occasionally in an evening."—A weak solution of sugar of lead with a little laudanum is useful when the piles are very painful.—Powdered galls and hog's lard form a good ointment.—Henbane leaves powdered and mixed with slippery elm and sweet oil, and six drops of laudanum, form a good application.—The pain is often removed by an emetic, or by taking twice a day 20 or 30 drops of balsam of capivi on loaf sugar, or in a little peppermint water.—The vapour of boiling water over leeks is useful.

PILES.—See *Lenitive Electuary*.

PILES, *bleeding.*—Lightly boil the juice of nettles with a little sugar; take 2 ozs. It seldom needs repeating.—*Wesley.*

PILES, *to cure.*—Apply warm treacle. Or, a tobacco-leaf steeped in water twenty-four hours. Or, a poultice of boiled brook-lime. It seldom fails. Or, a bruised onion, skinned, or roasted in ashes. It perfectly cures the dry piles. Or, fumigate with vinegar, wherein red hot flints have been quenched. This softens even schirrous tumours.—*Wesley.*

INWARD PILES.—Swallow a pill of pitch, fasting. One pill usually cures the bleeding piles. Or, eat a large leek, boiled. Or, take twice a-day, as much as lies on a shilling, of the thin skin of walnuts, powdered.—*Wesley.*

PILES, *Ointment for.*—Take of emolient ointment, 2 ozs.; liquid laudanum, ½ an oz. Mix these ingredients with the yolk of an egg, and work them well together.

PILEWORT OINTMENT, *improved.*—The plant, Pilewort, *(ranunculus ficaria,)* flowers in March and April. It should be gathered when in bloom, chopped extremely fine, after the roots and plant have been well washed. Boil in lard, without burning, two hours, stirring all the time. Strain while hot. Add 1 drachm of belladonna, 1 drachm each of opium and camphor, powdered. Mix, and make an ointment.

PILLAU, *Egyptian.*—Put a large fowl into a pan with chopped ham, ½ lb. of sausage meat, chopped onion, ¼ lb. of butter, a bunch of sweet herbs, a few dried mushrooms, chopped fine, pepper, and salt. Stew the fowl gently until tender, adding a little water now and then to prevent it becoming dry. Pick all the meat from the bones, and cut it into small pieces, removing the skin. Boil dryly 1 lb. of rice; mix it well with the fowl and gravy, and season it to taste. Place it at the side of the fire, or in a slow oven, half an hour before it is served that it may be properly dried. Turkey instead of fowl makes a richer dish.

PILLS, *Antibilious.*—Take of compound extract of colocynth, two scruples; extract of jalap, one scruple; calomel, one scruple; extract of scammony, one scruple; oil of cloves, ten drops. Mix and make into twenty pills. One or two is sufficient for a dose.

PILLS, *Aperient.*—Take four drachms of Castile soap, and the same quantity of soccotrine aloes, make it into pills with a sufficient quantity of syrup. Two or three may be taken when costive.

PILLS, *Aperient.*—Take four drachms of the extract of jalap, the same quantity of vitriolated tartar, and form it into pills with syrup of ginger; five of these pills is sufficient for a purge, but, to keep the body gently open, one may be taken night and morning.

PILLS, *Useful* Aperient.*—Take of compound rhubarb pill a drachm and one scruple, of powdered ipecacuanha, six grains, and of extract of hyoscyamus one scruple. Mix and beat into a mass, and divide into twenty-four pills. Take one, or two, or, if of a very costive habit, three at bed-time. For persons requiring a more powerful purge, the same formula, with ten grains of compound extract of colocynth, will form a good purgative pill. The mass receiving this addition must be divided into 30 instead of 24 pills.

PILLS *for a Bad Cough.*—Compound ipecacuanha powder, half a drachm; fresh dried squills, ten grains; sulphate of ammoniacum, ten grains; sulphate of quinine, six grains; treacle, sufficient quantity to make a mass. Divide into twelve pills; one to be taken night and morning.

PILL, *Composing.*—Take of purified opium, ten grains; Castile soap, half a drachm. Beat them together, and form the whole into twenty pills. When a quieting draught will not sit on the stomach, one, two, or three of these pills may be taken as occasion requires.

PILLS, *Female.*—Take of aloes, one drachm; calomel, one scruple. Make into twenty pills. One or two is sufficient for a dose.

PILL, *Fœtid.*—Assafœtida, half an ounce; simple syrup sufficient to form it into pills. In hysteric complaints, three or four pills may be taken twice or thrice a day; they also keep the body open; a proper quantity of rhubarb, aloes, or jalap, may occasionally be added to the above mass.

PILLS, *for Jaundice.*—Take of Castile soap, soccotrine aloes, and rhubarb, of each one drachm. Make them into pills with a sufficient quantity of syrup and mucilage. Three or four may be taken daily; and now and then a vomit of ipecacuanha.

PILL, *Purging.*—Soccotrine Aloes and Castile Soap, each 2 drachms; simple syrup sufficient to make them into pills. For keeping the body gently open, one may be taken night and morning. They are deobstruent and stomachic.

When Aloetic purges are improper, take Extract of Jalap, and Vitriolated Tartar, of each 2 drachms; Syrup of Ginger, sufficient to make them into pills. Take as above.

PILLS *for Spitting of Blood.*—Take of powdered alum five grains; powdered nutmegs, five grains; extract of gentian, two grains; mix, and divide into two pills.

PILLS, *Squill.*—Take powder of dried squills, a drachm and a half; gum ammoniac and cardamom seeds in powder, of each three drachms; simple syrup a sufficient quantity.

In dropsical and asthmatic complaints, two or three of these pills may be taken twice a day, or oftener, if the stomach will bear it.

PILLS, *Stomachic.*—Take extract of gentian, two drachms; powdered rhubarb and vitriolated tartar, of each one drachm; oil of mint, thirty drops; simple syrup a sufficient quantity.

Three or four of these pills may be taken twice a day for invigorating the stomach, and keeping the body gently open.

PILLS, *Strengthening.*—Take soft extract of bark and salt of steel, each a drachm. Make into pills.

In disorders arising from excessive debility or relaxation of the solids, as the chlorosis, or green sickness, two of these pills may be taken three times a day.

PILLS, *Vegetable Laxative.*—Take of extract of jalap, thirty grains; extract of colocynth, twenty grains; scammony, ten grains; oil of cloves, ten drops; powdered ginger, twenty grains. Make into 24 pills. Two for a dose.

PIMPLES.—They generally arise from indigestion, or some internal derangement; therefore the disease should be attacked at the root. Take the following:—Tincture of cardamoms, 1 drachm; ipecacuanha wine, and a teaspoonful of flour of sulphur, with a glass of sherry or ginger wine. Take this on going to bed; repeat it every second or third night, and keep the bowels gently open.

It is good to wash the face with warm water. Rub a sponge over old Windsor Soap, and dip in warm water and apply. Glycerine Soap is very useful.—A weak solution of sugar of lead, or sulphate of zinc, sometimes is effectual.

PINE APPLE COMPOTE.—Make a syrup with 1 lb. of sugar; peel, and cut two pine apples into slices; put them into the syrup, and boil them 12 minutes; take them out, and boil the syrup till it becomes thick; then pour it over the pine apple; when cold, it is ready for use.

PINE APPLE CREAM.—Take about 10 ozs. of pine apple jam. Put a quart of cream into another basin, with the juice of a large lemon; whisk to a strong froth; mix this with the jam, stirring well. Mix with it, at the same time, a little isinglass dissolved in a little warm milk and water.

PINE APPLE, *Jam and Jelly.*—The same as *Apple* or *Apricot Jam* and *Jelly,* which see.

PINE APPLE *Marmalade.*—Pare the pine apples. Grate them upon a dish. Then take the same weight of sugar as the pine apples weigh. Mix, and boil, skimming well. After all the scum is gone, stir the marmalade from an hour to an hour and a half. When it has boiled three quarters of an hour add a little thickly dissolved isinglass, and, if you like, a squeeze of lemon. Put into glasses, and make air-tight with brandy papers.

PINE APPLE, *Preserved.*—May be done the same as *Apple Preserve,* and *Apricot Preserve,* which see.

PINK, *Indian.*—An American plant. The root is anthelmintic, and combined with senna expels worms from the alimentary canal, especially the lumbrici, or round worms. It may be given in powder or infusion; the powder is the most efficacious. The dose for a child 3 or 4 years of age is 12 grains in powder, and 1 scruple in infusion. It has no taste.

PIPPIN PUDDING.—Coddle

six pippins in vine leaves covered with water, very gently, that the inside be done without breaking the skins. When soft, skin, and with a tea-spoon take the pulp from the core. Press it through a colander; add two spoonfuls of orange-flower water, three eggs beaten, a glass of rasin wine, a pint of scalded cream, sugar and nutmeg to taste. Lay a thin puff paste at the bottom and sides of the dish: shred very thin lemon-peel as fine as possible, and put it into the dish; likewise lemon, orange, and citron, in small slices, but not so thin as to dissolve in the baking.

PIPPIN TARTS.—Pare thin two Seville oranges; boil the peel tender, and shred it fine; pare and core twenty apples, put them in a stew-pan, and as little water as possible; when half-done add half a pound of sugar, the orange-peel and juice; boil till pretty thick. When cold, put in a shallow dish, or patty-pans lined with paste, to turn out, and be eaten cold.

PIQUET, *Game of.*—Piquet is a very scientific game, and is much played in the clubs in London and Paris. It is played by two persons, with 32 cards, all below the seven being discarded. The ace is the highest in rank, and equal to 11 points; the other cards follow in their common rotation, the court cards and the ten being equal to ten points each, and the others as many points as they have pips on them. The game consists of 101 points; the players cut for the deal, the lowest being dealer. He gives twelve cards each by two at a time, and the eight cards that remain must be placed upon the table, and are called the talon or stock. The following are the terms used at piquet:—

Capot.—This is a term used when either player makes every trick, for which he scores forty.

Cards.—Majority of tricks which reckon ten points.

Carte Blanche, means a hand without a court card in the twelve dealt, which counts ten, and takes place of every thing else.

Huitieme, eight successive cards of the same suit and counts eighteen points.

Pique, is when the elder hand has reckoned thirty in hand, and plays before the other counts one, in which case, instead of thirty points it is called sixty, adding thereto as many points as one got above thirty.

Point, the greatest number on the cards of the same suit in hand, after having taken in and reckoned by their pips scores for as many points as cards.

Quart.—Four cards in sequence of the same suit counting four points; there are five kinds of quarts; the first called quart-major, consists of ace, king, queen, and knave; the second is from the king; the third is from the queen; the fourth from the knave; and the fifth a basse-quart of quart minor, of ten, nine, eight, and seven.

Quartoze, the four aces, kings, queens, knaves, or tens, scoring fourteen points.

Quint, means five cards of the same suit in sequences, and counts fifteen points; there are four sorts of quints; a quint-major, of ace, king, queen, knave, and ten; down to knave, ten, nine, eight, and seven, which is called a quint-minor.

Repique, signifies when one of the players counts thirty or more in hand before his opponent attains one; then it is called ninety, reckoning as many above ninety as were gained above thirty.

Sixieme, or six cards of a suit in sequence, and counts for sixteen points; there are three sorts of sixiemes, viz., sixieme major from ace, sixieme from the king, and sixieme minor, from the queen.

Septieme, seven of the same suit in sequence, counting seventeen points; there are two of them, one from the ace, the other from the king.

Threes, three of any kind from aces to tens, count three.

Talon or Stock.—This is the name given to the eight cards remaining, after twelve each dealt.

Tierce, or sequences of three count three points; there are six kinds of tierces, from tierce-major, of ace, king, and queen, down to tierce-minor, of nine, eight, and seven.

In this game there are three chances, viz., the repique, the pique, and the capot, all of which may be made in one deal; for instance, suppose one player has four tierce-majors, his point good, and he elder hand, he begins by counting three for his point and twelve for his four tierce-majors, making fifteen; fourteen for the four aces, fourteen for kings, and fourteen for queens, with sixty for the repique, making in all one hundred and seventeen; thirteen in playing, make one hundred and thirty, and forty for the capot, which is one hundred and seventy.

To pique your adversary you must be elder hand; for if younger he counts one for the first card he plays, and then you having counted twenty-nine in hand, even if you then take the first trick, will not warrant you in taking sixty, but only thirty.

The Carte Blanche precedes every thing; then follow the point, the huitiemes, the septiemes, the sixiemes, the quints, the quarts, and the tierces; then the four aces, kings, queens, knaves, or tens; then the three aces, kings, queens, knaves, or tens; then the points gained in play; and lastly, the ten for winning the cards, or forty for the capot. After sorting your cards, the first thing to be considered is whether you have a Carte Blanche; if so, let your opponent discard; and then, when he is going to take in, lay your cards upon the table, counting them one after another.

The players, having examined their hands, the elder takes not more than five cards, which seem the least useful, and laying them aside, takes the same number from the talon, the younger may lay out three, and take three from the talon.

In discarding, the first intention of the most skilful players is, to gain the cards and to have the points, which most commonly engages them to keep in that suit of which they have the most cards, or that which is their strongest; for it is convenient to prefer sometimes forty-one in one suit, to forty-four in another, in which a quint is not made; sometimes even having a quint, it is more advantageous to hold the forty-one, where if one card only is taken it may make it a quint-major, gain the point or the cards, which could not have been done by holding the forty-four, at least without an extraordinary take in.

Also endeavour in laying out, to get a quartoze, each of which counts fourteen; the fourteen aces hinder the counting fourteen kings, &c., and by that authority you may count a lesser quartoze, as of tens, though your adversary may have fourteen by kings, &c.; because the stronger suit annuls the weaker; and also in want of a lesser quartoze you may count three aces, kings, queens, knaves, or tens: the same applies to the huitiemes, septiemes, sixiemes, quints, quarts, and tierces, to which the player must have regard in his discarding, so that what he takes in may make them for him.

The point being selected, the elder hand declares what it is, and asks if it is good; if his adversary has not so many, he answers, "it is good;" if he has just as many, he answers, "it is equal;" and if he has more, he answers, "it is not good;" for whoever has the point, whether elder or younger, counts it first; but if the points are equal, neither can count: it is the same when the players are equal in tierces, quarts, quints, &c.; and whoever should hold several other sequences, either of the same value or not, cannot count one.

There are no trumps at piquet, but the highest card of the same suit takes the trick. If the elder hand has the bad luck to have neither point, sequence, nor quartoze, nor any threes which are good, he must begin to count by playing that card which he thinks most proper, and continue until the adverse party wins a trick, and takes his lead.

This method must be continued till all the cards are played; and he who takes the last trick counts two; then each player counts how many tricks he has taken, and he who has most reckons the cards; but if they are equal, neither counts any thing.

MR. HOYLE'S MAXIMS FOR PLAYING PIQUET.

Play by the stage of your game, that is, when behind your adversary, play a pushing game; otherwise you ought to make twenty-seven points elder hand, and thirteen points younger hand.

Discard in hopes of winning the cards, which generally make twenty-two, or twenty; therefore don't discard for low quartoze, because the odds are against your succeeding. At the beginning of a party play to make your game, which is twenty-seven points elder hand, and thirteen younger hand.

Gaining the point generally makes ten difference; therefore when you discard, endeavour to gain it, but do not risk losing the cards.

Saving your lurch, or lurching your adversary, is so material that it is always worth risking some point to accomplish either of them.

If you have six tricks, with any winning card in your hand, play that card; you would play greatly against yourself not to do so.

The younger hand should always play upon the defensive, therefore, in order to make his thirteen points he is to carry tierces, quarts, and especially strive for the point.

It is often good play for a younger hand not to call three queens, knaves, &c.; also to sink one card of his point, which his adversary may suppose to be a guard to a king or queen.

The younger hand having the cards equally dealt him is not to take in any card, if thereby he runs the risk of losing them.

The younger hand having three aces, it is generally best to throw out the fourth suit.

The younger hand should carry guard to his queen suits in order to make points and make cards.

If the elder hand is sure to make the cards equal by playing in any particular manner, and is advanced before his adversary in the game, he should not risk them;

but if his opponent is greatly in advance, he should risk losing the cards in hopes of winning them.

If an elder hand has two aces dealt to him, it is eighteen to one that he does not take in the other two that are against him; that he does not take in one, is five to four against him, or nearly so.

LAWS OF PIQUET.

The elder hand is obliged to lay out one card at least.

If the elder hand takes in one of the three cards which belong to the younger, he loses the game.

If the elder hand, in taking his five cards, turns up one belonging to the younger hand, he is not to count any thing that hand.

If either play with thirteen cards, they cannot count any thing that deal.

Should either of the players have thirteen cards dealt, it is at the option of the elder hand to stand the deal or not: if he chooses to stand, then the person having thirteen is to discard one more than he takes in; should either have above thirteen, then a new deal must take place.

If either hand reckon more than they hold, or what they have not, they count nothing.

If the elder hand touches the stock after he has discarded, he cannot alter his discard.

If a card is faced, and it happens to be discovered either in dealing or in the stock, there must be a new deal, unless it is the bottom card.

If the younger hand takes in five cards it is the loss of the game, unless the elder has left two cards.

If the elder hand shows a point, or a quart or tierce, and asks if they are good, and afterwards forgets to reckon any of them, the other cannot reckon any of similar value.

When you are cutting, you must cut two cards at least.

If the elder hand calls a point, and does not show it, it is not to be reckoned; and the younger hand may show and reckon his point.

In the first place call your point, and if you have two points, and design to reckon the highest, you call that first, and abide by your first call.

If you play fewer than your proper number of cards, there is no penalty attached to it.

If the elder hand leaves a card, and, after he has taken in, happens to put to his discard the four cards taken in, they must remain with his discard, and he must play with eight cards.

Whoever deals twice together, and discovers it previous to seeing his cards, may compel his adversary to deal, notwithstanding he may have seen his cards.

No player can discard twice, and after he has touched the stock he is not allowed to change his discard.

When the elder hand does not take all his cards, he must specify what number he takes or leaves.

Any card that has touched the board is deemed to be played, unless in case of a revoke.

If any player names a suit and then plays a different one, the antagonist may call a suit.

The player who looks at any card belonging to the stock is liable to have a suit called.

PISMIRES, *to destroy.* - Throw gas lime upon the ant-hill, dig it well in; they will breed there no more. Gas tar might also be mixed with it. Dig it well in, and then press it down well.

PLAICE.—Sprinkle with salt, and keep 24 hours; then wash and wipe dry; wet it over with egg, and cover with crumbs of bread;

take some lard, or fine dripping, and two table-spoonfuls of vinegar, boiling hot; lay the fish in, and fry it a fine colour; drain it from the fat, and serve with fried parsley round, and anchovy sauce.

PLASTER, *Adhesive.* — Take of common plaster, half a pound; of Burgundy pitch, a quarter of a pound. Melt them together. This plaster is generally used for keeping on other dressings.

PLASTER, *Anodyne.*——See page 19.

PLASTER, *Blistering.*—Take of Venice turpentine, six ounces; yellow wax, two ounces; Spanish flies, in fine powder, three ounces; powdered mustard, one ounce. Melt the wax, and while it is warm, add to it the turpentine, taking care not to evaporate it by too much heat. After the turpentine and wax are sufficiently incorporated, sprinkle in the powders, continually stirring the mass till it be cold.

PLASTER, *Common.*—Take of common olive oil, six pints; litharge, reduced to a fine powder, 2½ lbs. Boil the litharge and oil together over a gentle fire, continually stirring them, and keeping always half a gallon of water in the vessel; after they have boiled three hours, a little of the plaster may be put into cold water, to try if it be of a proper consistence; then cool, and press the water well out of it with the hands.

This plaster is applied in slight wounds and excoriations of the skin; it keeps the part soft and warm, and defends it from the air, which is all that is necessary in such cases.

PLASTER FIGURES, *to bronze.*—For the ground, after it has been sized and rubbed down, take Persian blue, verditer, and spruce ochre. Grind them separately in water, turpentine, or oil, according to the work, and mix them in such proportion as will produce the colour desired. Then grind Dutch metal on a part of the composition; laying it with judgment on the prominent part of the figure, which produces a fine effect.

PLASTER, *Gum.*-Take of the common plaster, four pounds; of gum ammoniac and galbanum, strained, of each, half a pound. Melt them together, and add, of Venice turpentine, six ounces. This plaster is used as a digestive, and likewise for discussing indolent tumours.

PLASTER, *for the Stomach.*—Take of gum plaster, half a pound; camphorated oil, an ounce and a half; 10 drops each of the oil of mace, and mint; black pepper, or cayenne, 1 oz. Melt the plaster, and mix with it the oil; then sprinkle in the pepper, reduced to a fine powder.

This, spread upon soft leather, and applied to the region of the stomach, will be of service in flatulencies arising from hysteric and hypochondriac affections. A few drops of oil of mint, may be rubbed upon it before it is applied.

PLASTER, *Warm.*—Take of gum plaster one ounce; blistering plaster, two drachms; melt them over a gentle fire. This plaster is useful in the sciatica, and also in rheumatic pains. Should it blister, use less of the blistering paste. Renew after 8 days.

It ought, however, to be worn for some time, and to be renewed at least once a week.

PLASTIC MATERIAL *for forming various objects new.*—By Professor Purkins. Five parts of whiting are mixed with a solution of one part of glue. When the whiting is well worked up into a paste with the glue, a proportionate quantity of Venetian turpentine is added to it, by which the brittleness of the paste is destroyed. In order to prevent its clinging to the hands whilst the Venetian turpentine is being worked into the paste, a small quantity of linseed oil is added from time to time. The mass may also be coloured by kneading in any colour that may be desired. It may be pressed into shapes, and used for the production of *bas reliefs* and other figures, such as animals &c. It may also be worked by hand into models, during which operation the hands must be rubbed with linseed oil; the mass must also be kept warm during the process. When it cools and dries, which takes place in a few hours, it becomes as hard as stone, and may then be employed for the multiplication of these forms.

PLATE, *to clean.*—Wash well with soap and water; then apply a paste of whiting and sweet oil; apply it, and when dry, rub off, and polish with wash leather and dry fine whiting.

PLATE, *to make look new.*—Take 1 lb. each of unslaked lime and alum; a pint each of aqua vita, and vinegar; and two quarts of beer grounds; boil the plate in these, and they will give a beautiful gloss to the articles.

PLATE, *to take stains out of.*—Steep the plate in soap ley for 4 hours; then cover it over with whiting, wet with vinegar, so that it may stick thickly upon it; dry at the fire; rub off the whiting and pass it over with dry bran; the spots will disappear, and the plate will be very bright.

PLEURISY.—Pleurisy is inflammation of the membrane termed pleura, which covers the lungs, and lines the internal surface of the chest. It is caused by obstructed perspiration, through exposure to cold bleak winds; drinking cold liquors when the body is hot; sleeping out-doors, or on the damp ground, wet clothes, exposure to the cold air when in a state of perspiration. It may also be caused by drinking strong liquors, by the stopping of the usual evacuations, &c., &c.

The *symptoms* are shivering, pain in the head, back, stomach; sickness, and vomiting, despondency, violent pain in one or both sides, difficult breathing, high fever, thirst; the pain is greater when coughing, or when taking in a full breath; the pulse is hard, strong, and frequent.

Treatment.—In this disease the temperature of the whole body and its extremities, while the heat in the affected part is greatly augmented. Allopathists would recur to *bleeding* at once; but that system of depletion is not necessary. Common sense says, *equalize the circulation* of the blood, and this can only be done by restoring that which has been partially lost or diminished, viz., vitality or heat. See Robinson's Herbal, on *Life and Motion*, page 388; it is most valuable. The disease has been caused by cold; it must be cured by a wise application of heat. Do this at the very beginning of the disease before the patient is debilitated. Give a *vapour bath;* or bathe the feet in warm water and apply hot bricks wrapped in water and vinegar cloths while the patient is in bed. Give also an *emetic* at the same time, page 155. When the emetic has taken effect, give immediately two tablespoonfuls of the *sudorific tincture*, or half a teaspoonful of the *sudorific powders*. Continue them to keep up a gentle moisture on the skin. If they cause vomiting, never mind, for it helps to cure. At night bathe the legs up to the knees in warm water, with a little soap or soda in, for about ten minutes. Let warm herb tea be constantly drunk, as balm, hyssop, catnep, pennyroyal, &c.

Apply the *Rheumatic Liquid* to the chest or sides; or fomentations of bitter herbs, as hops, tansy, &c., to which add some cayenne tincture.

Salt, cayenne, and brandy, well simmered, and made strong, form an excellent application for pleuritic pains. These means seldom fail to arrest the disease. It may be added, if the bowels are constipated, give a gentle injection, and a gentle aperient. Let the diet be very simple, as sago gruel, arrowroot gruel, common gruel with a squeeze of lemon, &c. During the progress of the disease the *Cough Pill*, and the *Pulmonary Syrup* will be of great service. After the pleuritic symptoms are gone, take the Composition powder, and any of the tonic bitters.

PLEURISY ROOT. —— An American plant. It is expectorant, sub-tonic, astringent, diaphoretic, carminative, antispasmodic, diuretic, &c. It promotes perspiration. It is a valuable medicine for the lungs, promoting expectoration, alleviating difficult breathing in asthma, and especially in pleurisy; hence its name. It is valuable in all fevers; in colics and griping, acute pains in the stomach, and female complaints, as copious menstruation, spasms, and nervous debility. It is a specific in measles. The dose of the root in powder is from 15 to 30 grains three times a day. Nearly a cupful of the decoction may be taken nearly as often.

PLOVERS, *to choose.*—Choose those that feel hard at the vent, which shows they are fat. In other respects, choose them by the same marks as other fowls. When stale, the feet are dry. They will keep sweet a long time. There are three sorts; the grey, green, and bastard plover, or lapwing.

PLOVERS' EGGS are a nice and fashionable dish. Boil them ten minutes, and serve either hot or cold on a napkin.

PLOVERS, *to roast.*—Roast the *green* ones in the same way as woodcocks and quails, without drawing; and serve on a toast. *Grey* plovers may be either roasted or stewed with gravy, herbs, and spice.

PLUM CAKE.-Take fine flour, 1½ lb.; butter, 1½ lb.; currants, ¾ lb.; raisins well stoned and chopped, ½ lb.; sugar, 18 ozs., sifted fine; 14 eggs with half the whites. Shred the peel of a large lemon very fine, 3 ozs. each of candied orange and lemon; a teaspoonful of beaten mace, half a nutmeg grated; a tea-cupful of brandy or sherry, with a little orange flower water. Work the butter with the hand to a cream; beat the sugar well in; whisk the eggs half an hour; mix them with the sugar and butter, and put in the flour and spices. Beat the whole an hour and a half; mix in lightly the brandy, fruit, and sweet meats; put into a hoop, and bake for 2½ hours.

Another.—Flour, well dried, 2 lbs.; sugar, sifted, 1 lb.; butter, 1 lb.; nutmegs and mace, ¼ oz. each; currants, 2½ lbs.; 16 eggs; sweet almonds, ½ lb.; the same of candied lemon; half a pint of brandy, and three spoonfuls of orange flower water. Beat the butter to a cream; put in the butter and sugar. Beat the yolks half an hour, and mix with the whites. Put in the flour just before the oven is ready; mix together lightly the currants, &c. Bake two hours.

Another.—Take 4 lbs. each of dried flour, and currants, well washed and picked; sugar, 1½ lb., sifted; six oranges, lemon, and citron peels, sliced; mix all together; then beat ten eggs, the yolks and whites separately; melt 1½ lb. of butter in a pint of cream; when nearly cool, add ½ pint of ale yeast, and nearly ½ pint of sherry, and the eggs; strain the liquor to the dry ingredients; beat them well, and add ½ oz. each of cloves, mace, cinnamon, and nutmeg. Butter the pan and put it into a quick oven, two or three hours.

PLUM CAKE.—*A rich one.*—Mix well 1¾ lbs. of the best flour well dried, with ½ lb. of dry sifted loaf sugar; 1½ lb. of well cleaned and dry currants; ¼ lb. of raisins stoned and chopped, one eighth of an ounce each of clove, mace, and cinnamon, a small nutmeg grated, the peel of a lemon cut very fine, and ¼ lb of almonds. Melt 1 lb. of butter in half a pint of cream not hot; put to it half a pint of wine, a little brandy, a little rose-water, and 6 eggs, the yolks and whites beaten separately, and a quarter of a pint of yeast. Strain this gradually into the dry ingredients, beating them for an hour. Butter the pan or hoop and bake in a moderate oven for 4 hours. In putting in the batter, add plenty of candied orange, lemon, and citron peel.

If you ice the cake when nearly cold, pour the iceing over and replace it in the oven, leaving it there all night or until it becomes cold, but if the oven be warm, keep it near the front and the door open, or the colour may be spoiled; or the iceing it may be left until the next day.

PLUM CAKE, *to make little ones.*—Take 1 lb. of flour; rub into it ½ lb. of butter, and ½ lb. of sugar, a little beaten mace; beat 4 eggs well; leave out half the whites; add three spoonfuls of yeast; put to it ¼ pint of warm cream; strain them into the flour, and make it up light; set it before the fire to rise; before it is sent to the oven, put in ¾ lbs. of currants.

PLUM CAKE, *a white one.*—It is made the same as the 2nd Receipt, except beating the *whites* of the eggs well; and when mixed with the other ingredients, beating the whole for two hours.

PLUM, *Compote of.*—Green-gages are the best to preserve in syrup. They must not be quite ripe. Boil them a little in raw sugar and a little water; skim, when cooling, and reduce the syrup according to the time you intend to keep them. It is the best to prick them in several places, and scald them in boiling water until they rise on the surface; take off the fire, and let them cool in the same water; cover the pan, and put them on a slow fire, which will bring them back to their proper colour; drain them in cold water, and boil them a moment in sugar; leave them in it till next day, and boil them a little more. Prepared in this way, they will keep a long time.

POACHED EGGS.—Break an egg into a cup, and put it gently into boiling water; and when the white looks quite set, which will be in about three or four minutes, take it up with an egg sliced, and lay it on toast and butter, or spinach. Serve them hot; if fresh laid, they will poach well without breaking.

POISON, *Antidotes to.*—The treatment of cases of poisoning must vary with the nature of the poison, the quantity taken, and the peculiarities of the individual. In almost all cases, copious vomiting should be excited as soon as possible by tickling the throat, and by emetics, such especially as sulphate of zinc, or ipecacuanha with emetic tartar; the former, however, in ten-grain doses dissolved in a little warm water, and repeated every ten or fifteen minutes till it freely operates, is generally most effectual. The use of the stomach-pump should also be resorted to. The vomiting should be kept up, and the stomach washed out with bland albuminous or mucilaginous fluids, such as milk, flour and water, or thin paste, &c.; sometimes sugar and water.

The following is a short summary of the antidotes resorted to in reference to particular poisons. They should, of course, be administered as speedily as possible.

EMETIC IN CASES OF POISON. Two table-spoonfuls of made mustard in a pint of warm water; if taken immediately, this is a certain remedy, instantly producing violent vomiting. Also administer large draughts of warm milk or water, mixed with oil, melted butter, or lard.

1. *Arsenic.*—Lime water, chalk and water, and the hydrated sesqui-oxide of iron, have each been strongly recommended; the last is decidedly the best.

2. *For Mineral Acids*, or *Acetic and Oxalic Acid.*—For this form of poison, give quickly large draughts of chalk, whiting, magnesia, soap and water, about as thick as cream; followed by albuminous diluents, such as milk, and white of egg mixed with water. Or, if these cannot be procured at once, warm water; and promote vomiting by tickling the throat.

3. *Alkalies, Soda, Potash, Ammonia,* etc.—Vinegar, or any mild acid and water, or even very dilute mineral acids, such as water acidulated by them; olive oil, almond oil.

4. *Corrosive sublimate.*—White of egg and water; milk and cream; decoction of cinchona; infusion of galls.

5. *Sulphate of Copper and other poisons.*—Sugar and water; white of egg and water.

6. *Antimonial poisons.*—Warm milk, gruel, and barley-water; infusion of galls; decoction of cinchona.

7. *Nitrate of Silver.*—Copious draughts of warm salt and water.

8. *Sulphate of Zinc.*—Solution of carbonate of soda in water, with milk, and mucilaginous or farinaceous liquids.

9. *Acetate of Lead.*—Emetics, solution of sulphate of soda in water, milk, white of egg and water.

10. *Opium and its preparations.*—Emetics, strong coffee; dashing cold water upon the face and breast; preventing torpor by forced exercise.

11. *Prussic Acid.*—Ammoniacal stimulants cautiously applied to the nose; ammonia, or sal-volatile in repeated small doses of solution of chlorine in water; small doses of chloride of lime in water.

12. *Strychnia and vegetable alkaloids.*—Infusion of gall nuts; decoction of cinchona; emetics.

POKE WEED.—An American plant. It is valuable. The root is emetic, cathartic, and rather narcotic. The leaves and roots powdered, may be applied with great advantage, as a poultice in cancerous and malignant ulcer, ringworm, scrofulous abscesses, &c.

POLISHED IRONS, *to preserve from rust.*—Mix copal varnish with as much olive oil as will give it a degree of greasiness; adding thereto nearly as much spirit of turpentine as of varnish. The cast-iron work is best preserved by rubbing it with black lead, and a little turpentine in it. But when rust appears on grates, or fire-irons, apply a mixture of tripoli, with half its quantity of sulphur, intimately mixed on a slab, and applied with a piece of soft leather; or apply emery and oil.

POLISHING PASTE.—For *brass*, the best kind is two parts of soft soap mixed with four parts of rotten stone in very fine powder.

Or, eight parts of fine rotten stone powder, two parts of oxalic acid powdered, and turpentine sufficient to make them into a paste.

For *iron* emery powder and lard is used, and for pewter, powdered bath-brick and soft soap. For *wood*, spirit of turpentine and bee's wax made into a soft paste, applied with a brush and woollen rag, and afterwards polished with a dry woollen cloth and soft brush.

POLYPODY.—A valuable plant. See *Robinson's Herbal.*— It is a first-rate remedy for liver complaint, both acute and chronic; for consumption, palpitation, indigestion, eruptions, impurity of the blood, &c. When taken for cough, it produces nausea, but this departs as soon as it has caused expectoration. It is valuable in asthma, bronchitis, &c. It may be taken in infusion,—a tea-spoonful to nearly a pint of boiling water, and sweetened. Two table-spoonfuls occasionally. Begin with one table-spoonful.

POLYPUS IN THE NOSE. —Powder a lump of alum, and snuff it up frequently; then dissolve powdered alum in brandy, dip lint therein and apply it at going to bed.

POMADE.—Best lard, 4 ozs.; castor oil, 4 ozs.; white wax, 3 drachms. Melt and mix; when cool, add oil of bergamot and lavender, 15 drops of each.

POMADE.—Olive oil, 2½ ozs.; oil of almonds, ½ drachm; palm oil, 1½ drachm; white wax, ¼ oz.; lard, ¼ lb.; essence of bergamot, ½ drachm. It is first-rate for preventing baldness, and strengthening the hair.

POMADE, *Hard.*—Melt in a water-bath 3 ozs. of lard; 3 ozs. of beef marrow; 2½ ozs. of mutton suet; and 2 ozs. of white wax. Take off the fire; cool a little; then add a little *spirits of wine* to cause it to keep, and a few drops of otto of roses. Stir till nearly cold, and turn into moulds.

It may become Soft Pomade by leaving out half of the wax, the whole of the mutton suet, and doubling the beef marrow.

POMADE, *Spanish.*—Take equal parts of lemon juice and white of eggs. Beat well together, and place on a slow fire. Stir it till it is the thickness of soft pomatum. Perfume with otto of roses. It is a cosmetic that renders the complexion beautiful.

POMATUM.—Take 4 ozs. of beef marrow, melt it and strain; 4 ozs. of white wax; 1 oz. of olive oil; and 20 drops of oil of rosemary. Melt, but do not add the oil of rosemary till nearly cold. It causes the hair to grow. The more of rosemary the better.

Oils for the hair may be made by simply stirring in any of the essential oils into olive oil, oil of ben, oil of almonds, castor oil, &c. The pink and red colours are produced by boiling the oils and pouring them upon alkanet root. But it deteriorates the oils. Coloured hair oils should be avoided.

POMATUM, *Elder Flower.*—

Elder flower oil, 4 ozs.; fine mutton suet, or beef marrow, 2 ozs.; best lard, 2 ozs. Melt the suet and lard together, with as little heat as possible; then add the elder oil, and beat up the mixture till nearly cold. Any other perfume may be added before the pomatum hardens. A little eau-de-cologne makes it very agreeable, when intimately mixed.

POOR MAN'S SAUCE.—Take 5 or 6 shalots; hash them fine with a little parsley; put them into a stewpan with a little gravy and a spoonful of good vinegar, a little salt and cayenne; simmer till enough, and serve.

POPE JOAN, *Game of.*—The game of pope, or as it is sometimes called, pope joan, is somewhat similar to that of matrimony.

It is played by a number of people, who generally use a board painted for this purpose, which may be purchased at almost any toy-shop.

The eight of diamonds must first be taken from the pack, and, after arranging the deal, shuffling, &c., the dealer dresses the board, as it is called, by putting fish, counters, or other stakes, one each to ace, king, queen, knave, and game; two to matrimony, two to intrigue, and six to the nine of diamonds, styled "pope." This dressing is in some companies at the individual expense of the dealer, though in others the players contribute two stakes each towards the same. The cards are next to be dealt round equally to each player, one turned up for trump, and about six or eight left in the stock to form stops; as for example, if the ten of spades is turned up, the nine consequently becomes a stop. The four kings, and the seven of diamonds, are always fixed stops; and the dealer is the only person permitted in the course of the game to refer to the stock for information what other cards are stops in that respective deal.

If either ace, king, queen, or knave happen to be the turned-up trumps, the dealer takes whatever is deposited on that head; but when pope is turned up, the dealer is entitled to both that and the game, besides a stake for every card dealt to each player.

Unless the game is determined by pope being turned up, the eldest hand begins by playing out as many cards as possible; first the stops, then pope, if he has it, and afterwards the lowest cards of his longest suit; particularly an ace, for that can never be led through.

The other players are to follow when they can, in sequence of the same suit, until a stop occurs; and the party having the said stop thereby becomes eldest hand, and is to lead accordingly, and so on until some person parts with all his cards, by which he wins the pool, which is game, and becomes entitled besides to a stake for every card not played by the others, except from any one holding pope, which excuses him from paying; but if pope has been played previously, then the person having held it is not excused.

King and queen form what is termed matrimony; queen and knave make intrigue, when in the same hand; but neither they, nor ace, king, queen, knave, or pope, entitle the holder to the stakes deposited thereon unless played out.

No claim can be allowed after the board is dressed for the succeeding deal; but in all such cases the stakes are to remain on the board for future determination.

This game only requires a little attention to remember what stops have been made in the course of the same; as for instance, suppose a player begins by laying down the eight of clubs, then the seven in some other hand forms the stop.

Whenever clubs are led after that from any lower card, the holder may safely play it in order to clear his hand.

PORK, *to choose.*—Pinch the lean, and if young, it will break. If the rind is tough, thick, and cannot easily be impressed by the finger, it is old. A thin rind is a merit in all pork. When fresh, the flesh will be smooth and cool; if clammy, it is tainted. What is called measley pork is very unwholesome; and may be known by the fat being full of kernels, which in good pork is never the case. Pork fed at still-houses does not answer for curing any way, the fat being spongy. Dairy-fed pork is the best.

PORK, *to barbacue a leg of.*—Put down the leg to a good fire; into the dripping pan, put two bottles of port wine; baste the pork with it all the time of roasting. When enough, take up what is left in the pan; put to it two anchovies, the yolks of three eggs, boiled hard, and pounded fine, with a ¼ lb. of butter, and half a lemon, a bunch of sweet herbs, a tea-spoonful of lemon pickle, a spoonful of ketchup, and one of tarragon vinegar; boil them a few minutes; then draw the pork, and cut the skin down from the bottom of the shank in rows an inch broad; raise every other row, and roll it to the shank; strain the sauce, and pour it boiling hot.

PORK, *Chine of.*—Salt three days before cooking. Wash it well; score the skin, and roast with sage and onions finely shred. Serve with apple sauce.—The chine is often sent to the table boiled.

PORK, *to collar.*-Bone a breast or spring of pork; season it with plenty of thyme, parsley, and sage; roll it hard; put in a cloth, tie both ends, and boil it; then press it; when cold, take it out of the cloth, and keep it in its own liquor.

PORK, *as Lamb.*—Kill a young pig of four or five months old; cut up the fore-quarter for roasting as you do lamb, and truss the shank close. The other parts will make delicate pickled pork; or steaks, pies, &c.

PORK, *Leg of, to boil.*—Salt it eight or ten days; when it is to be dressed, weigh it; let it lie half an hour in cold water to make it white; allow a quarter of an hour for every pound, and half an hour over, from the time it boils up: skim it frequently. Allow water enough. Save some of it to make peas-soup. Some boil it in a cloth, floured, which gives a very delicate look. It should be small and of a fine grain.

Serve peas pudding and turnips with it.

PORK, *Leg of*, commonly called *Mock Goose*.—Parboil it, take off the skin, and then put it down to roast; baste it with butter, and make a savory powder of finely-minced, or dried and powdered sage, pepper, salt, and some bread crumbs, rubbed together through a colander; add to this a little finely-minced onion; sprinkle with this when it is almost roasted; put half a pint of made gravy into the dish, and some goose stuffing under the knuckle skin; or garnish the dish with balls of it fried or broiled.

PORK, *Loin of*.—Score it, and joint it, that the chops may separate easily; and then roast it as a loin of mutton.——Or, put it into sufficient water to cover it; simmer till almost enough; then peel off the skin, and coat it with yolk of egg and bread crumbs, and roast for 15 or 20 minutes, till it is enough done.

PORK, *to pickle*.—Cut the pork in such pieces as will lie in the pickling tub; rub each piece over with saltpetre; then take one part bay salt, and two parts common salt, and rub each piece well; lay them close in the tub, and throw salt over them.

Some use a little sal prunella, and a little sugar.

PORK PIE, *to eat cold*.—Raise a common boiled crust into either a round or oval form, which you choose, have ready the trimmings and small bits of pork cut off a sweet bone, when the hog is killed, beat it with a rolling pin, season with pepper and salt, and keep the fat and lean separate, put it in layers quite close to the top, lay on the lid, cut the edge smooth, round, and pinch it; bake in a slow soaking oven, as the meat is very solid. Observe, put no bone or water in the pork pie; the outside pieces will be hard if they are not cut small and pressed close.

PORK, *to roast a leg of*.—Choose a small leg of fine young pork; cut a slit in the knuckle with a sharp knife; and fill the space with sage and onion chopped, and a little pepper and salt. When half done, score the skin in slices, but don't cut deeper than the outer rind.

Apple sauce and potatoes should be served to eat with it.

PORK, *Rolled neck of*.—Bone it; put a forcemeat of chopped sage, a very few crumbs of bread, salt, pepper, and two or three berries of allspice over the inside; then roll the meat as tight as you can, and roast it slowly, and at a good distance at first.

PORK SAUSAGES.—Take 6 lbs of young pork, free from gristle, or fat; cut small and beat fine in a mortar. Chop 6 lbs. of beef suet very fine; pick off the leaves of a handful of sage, and shred it fine; spread the meat on a clean dresser, and shake the sage over the meat; shred the rind of a lemon very fine, and throw it, with sweet herbs, on the meat; grate two nutmegs, to which put a spoonful of pepper, and a large spoonful of salt; throw the suet over, and mix all well together. Put it down close in the pot; and when you use it, roll it up with as much egg as will make it roll smooth.

Another way.—Chop fat and lean pork together; season with

sage, pepper, and salt, and a little allspice. The hog's entrails having been well soaked, and made very clean, half fill them with the meat, or the meat may be kept in a very small pan, closely covered, and so rolled, and dusted with a very little flour before it is fried.

Another way.—Take 3 lbs. of pork, fat and lean, without skin or gristle; chop as fine as possible: season with pepper, salt, sage, rubbed fine, mix well, and put it into the skins or entrails well cleaned, or make into balls. Mix a little bread with the meat, if agreeable.

PORK, *Spring or Forehand of.*—Cut out the bone; sprinkle salt, pepper, sage dried, over the inside; but first warm a little butter to baste it, and then flour it; roll the pork tight, and tie it; then roast by a hanging-jack. About two hours will do it.

PORK STEAKS.—Cut them from a loin or neck, and of middling thickness; pepper and broil them, turning them often; when nearly done, put on salt, rub a bit of butter over, and serve the moment they are taken off the fire, a few at a time.

PORRIDGE. — See *Oatmeal Porridge.*

PORTER, *Cheap and Good.*—Linseed, 1 oz.; the same of Spanish juice and ginger; hops, 1½ oz.; malt, 1 lb.; liquorice, ½ oz.; sugar and treacle, each, 1¼ lbs. Boil with 4½ gallons of water, down to 3¼ gallons; also add a little pearl, or Iceland Moss. When cool, stir yeast into it, and let it ferment.

PORTER PLASTER, *for bruises.*—This simple remedy is nothing more than 2 quarts of porter simmered, till it is reduced to a salve.

PORT WINE.—British grape wine, or good cider, 4 gallons; recent juice of red elder berries, 1 gallon; brandy, 2 quarts; logwood, 4 ozs.; rhatany root, bruised, ¼ lb. First infuse the logwood and rhatany root in the brandy, and a gallon of the grape wine or cider, for a week; then strain off the liquor, and mix it with the other ingredients. Keep it in a cask well bunged for a month; then bottle it.

PORT WINE, *to detect Adulteration in.*—It is often adulterated with alum to make it astringent. Mix the suspected wine with lime water; to stand a day; if the wine be genuine, a number of crystals will be deposited at the bottom of the vessel. If alum be in the wine, there will be no crystals, but a slimy and muddy precipitate.—— Or, drop some solution of subcarbonate of potass into the wine; if alum be present, there will be a violet-coloured precipitate, or cloudiness, which will vanish, if a few drops of caustic potash, or of muriatic acid be added to the mixture.

PORTUGAL ONIONS, *to pickle.*—Slice them in strong salt and water for 24 hours; drain; put into a jar, and pour upon them vinegar spiced and boiled. Put a small piece of alum in the jar.

POSSET OF BARLEY.—Boil ½ lb. of French barley in 3 pints of milk; boil it till it is done enough; then put in a pint of cream, some mace, and cinnamon; sweeten with loaf sugar, and when it is just warm, pour in a pint of sherry wine, and froth it up.—A less quantity may be made.

POSSET *of ale, or beer.*—Take ½ pint of milk; put it on the fire till it just boils; pour it on cut bread in a basin; then just boil ½ pint of beer, and pour into the milk and bread. Sweeten and season as you like.

POSSET, *cold.*—Take ½ pint each of milk and cream; the juice of half a lemon, and the rind grated into it. Sweeten the cream and wine; put the latter into a basin, and pour the cream and milk into the basin, and stir them together well.

POSTAGE, *Rates of.*—From all parts of the United Kingdom, the Channel Islands, and the Isle of Man, if prepaid, and *not exceeding*—half an oz. 1d.; one oz. 2d.; 1½ oz. 3d.; 2 ozs. 4d., and so on, adding a penny for each ½ oz. No parcel will be permitted to pass through the post if more than two feet long; and in provincial Post Offices, all letters or packets must be prepaid with stamps, or be sent unpaid, as money prepayment is not permitted.——BOOK POST. —On every packet not exceeding 4 ozs. 1d.; from 4 to 8 ozs. 2d.; from 8 to 12 ozs. 3d.; from 12 ozs. to 1 lb. 4d.; from 1 lb. to 1¼ lb. 5d.; from 1¼ lb. to 1½ lb. 6d.; from 1½ lb. to 1¾ lb. 7d.; from 1¾ lb. to 2 lbs. 8d.—and 1d. for every additional ¼ lb. Every book packet must be open at the ends.

POST OFFICE SAVINGS BANKS.—By 24 Vic. cap. 14, deposits of one shilling, or of any number of shillings, will be received from any depositor at the Post Office Savings Banks, provided the deposits of such depositor in any year ending the 31st day of December do not exceed £30, and provided the total amount standing in such depositor's name in the books of the Postmaster-General do not exceed £150, exclusive of interest. Interest will be allowed at the rate of £2 10s. per cent. per annum, being at the rate of one halfpenny per calendar month for every complete pound. When the principal and interest amount to the sum of £200, all interest will cease, so long as the same funds continue £200.

A depositor in any legally established Savings Bank may transfer his account to the Post Office Savings Bank, by simply applying to the managers of the Savings Bank for a certificate of the amount of his deposits, and the amount of such certificate will be entered to his credit by the Post Office Savings Bank as so much cash. In the same way an account may be transferred from the Post Office Savings Bank to any other legally established Savings Bank.

POTAGE, *Barley.*—Take 1 lb. of pearl barley; cleanse it well from husks; put it into a quart of milk to steep, and boil it a little; when it is well boiled, put in a quart of cream, 1 oz. of salt, some mace, and cinnamon; when sufficiently thick, sweeten with loaf sugar, and serve.

POTASH, *Bicarbonate.*—In indigestion, attended with acidity, the result of disordered gastric secretion, the bicarbonate of potash is a valuable remedy, neutralizing very effectually the acid. The dose is from 10 to 20 grains given in simple solution in water, or it may be sweetened.

POTASH DROPS.—Liquor of potash, 10 drops; infusion of linseed, 1 pint; spirits of sweet nitre, ½ oz. Mix, and take two tablespoonfuls every three hours. A sure cure for the gravel.

POTASSÆ LIQUOR.—This is a solution of potash. In indigestion, acid eructations, heartburn, &c., it may be taken with great benefit. It neutralizes the acid, and counteracts the morbid tendency of the stomach to acid secretion. Dose—10 drops, gradually increased to 40. It should be greatly diluted. Take it with a bitter decoction.

POTATOES.—Much attention has been recently drawn to the fact, that the produce of potatoes may be much increased by plucking off the blossoms from the plants producing them. This important observation has been completely confirmed by M. Teller, the director of the Agricultural Society of Darmstadt. In 1839, two fields of the same size, lying side by side, and manured in the same manner, were planted with potatoes. When the plants had flowered, the blossoms were removed from those in one field, while those in the other field were left untouched. The former produced forty-seven bolls, the latter only thirty-seven bolls.—*Liebig*.

POTATOES, *to boil*.—Boil in a saucepan without lid, with only sufficient water to cover them; more would spoil them, as the potatoes contain much water, and it requires to be expelled. When the water nearly boils, pour it off, and add cold water, with a good portion of salt. The cold water sends the heat from the surface to the centre of the potatoe, and makes it mealy. Boiling with a lid on, often produces cracking.

New Potatoes should be cooked soon after having been dug; wash well, and boil.

The Irish, who boil potatoes to perfection, say they should always be boiled in their *jackets;* as peeling them for boiling is only offering a premium for water to run through the potatoe, and rendering it sad and unpalatable; they should be well washed, and put into cold water.

"Stop," says one, till I immortalize my dear old mother's receipt; —" To dress a potatoe, wash it well, but let there be no scraping. At the thickest end cut off a piece the size of a sixpence." This is the *safety-valve* by which the steam, generated in the potatoe, escapes; and such escape prevents cracking. Pour all the water off and let the skins be thoroughly dry before peeling.

POTATOES, *to escalop*.—Boil the potatoes; then beat them fine in a bowl with cream, a lump of butter and salt; put them into escalop shells; smooth the top; score them; lay thin slices of butter on the top of them; put them into a Dutch oven to brown before the fire.

POTATOE FRITTERS.—Boil two large potatoes, scrape them fine; beat four yolks and three whites of eggs, and add to the above one large spoonful of cream, another of sweet wine, a squeeze of lemon, and a little nutmeg. Beat this batter half an hour at least. It will be extremely light. Put a good quantity of fine lard in a stew-pan, and drop a spoonful of the batter at a time into it. Fry them; and serve as a sauce, a glass of white wine, the juice of a lemon, one dessert spoonful of peach-leaf or almond water, and some white sugar warmed together: not to be served in the dish.

Another way.—Slice potatoes thin, dip them in a fine batter, and fry. Serve with white sugar, sifted over them. Lemon peel, and a spoonful of orange-flower water, should be added to the batter.

POTATOES, *To fry*.—Cut them into thin slices; fry them brown, either in butter or beef gravy, or batter.

POTATOES, *to mash*.—Boil the potatoes, peel them, and break them to paste; then to 2 lbs. of them add a quarter of a pint of milk, a little salt, and 2 ozs. of butter, and stir it all well over the fire. Either serve them thus, or place them in the dish in a form, and then brown them before the fire. They may be placed in moulds, and browned. They are sometimes coated with white or yolk of egg.

POTATO PASTY.—Boil, and peel, and mash potatoes as fine as possible; mix them with salt, pepper, and a good bit of butter. Make a paste; roll it out thin like a a large puff, and put in the potatoe; fold over one half, pinching the edges. Bake in a moderate oven.

POTATO PIE.——Skin some potatoes, and cut them into slices; season them; and also some mutton, beef, pork, or veal, and a lump of butter. Put layers of them and of the meat. A few eggs boiled and chopped fine, improves it.

POTATOES IN PLENTY.— A farmer planted four potatoes in April, in two of which he inserted a bean, and a pea in each of the other two. The peas and beans produced a good crop, and the potatoes were free from disease. One of the potatoes produced 58 tubers, the second 30, the third 29, and the fourth 25.

POTATO PUDDING.—Take ½ lb. of boiled potatoes, 2 ozs. of butter, the yolks and whites of two eggs, a quarter of a pint of cream, one spoonful of white wine, a morsel of salt, the juice and rind of a lemon; beat all to froth; sugar to taste. A crust or not, as you like. Bake it. If wanted richer, put 3 ozs. more butter, sweetmeats and almonds, and another egg.

POTATO PUDDING WITH MEAT——Boil till they are fit to mash; rub through a colander, and make into a thick batter with milk, and two eggs. Then lay some seasoned steaks in a dish, then some batter; and over the last layer put the remainder of the batter. Bake a fine brown.

POTATO RIBBONS.—Cut the potatoes into slices, rather more than half an inch thick, and then pare round and round in very long ribbons. Place them in a pan of cold water, and a short time before wanted, drain them from the water. Fry them in hot lard, or good dripping, until crisp and browned; dry them on a soft cloth, pile them on a hot dish, and season with salt and cayenne.

POTATOES, *roasted under the meat.*—These are very good; they should be nicely browned. Half boil large mealy potatoes; put into a baking dish, under the meat roasting; lade the gravy upon them occasionally. They are best done in an oven.

POTATO ROLLS.—Boil three lbs. of potatoes; crush and work them with two ozs. of butter, and as much milk as will cause them to pass through a colander; take half a pint of yeast and half a pint of warm water; mix with the potatoes; pour the whole upon 5 lbs. of flour; add salt; knead it well; if too thick, put to it a little more milk and warm water; to stand before the fire an hour to rise; work it well, and make it into rolls. Bake half an hour.

POTATO ROT.—Take the apples that grow on the potato plant, when fully ripe; cut them open; take out the small seeds, and dry them; keep them till the spring; then sow them in beds, like onions; they will be small at first; plant again next season, when they will be large and good, and entirely free from disease. This requires to be done at least every fourth season. This plan has been adopted by several farmers with complete success, ever since the potato disease commenced.

POTATO YEAST.—Boil, and skin, and mash mealy potatoes. Mix hot water to make them as thin as pudding batter. Add to each lb. of potatoes 2 ozs. of treacle. When just warm, stir in for every lb. of potatoes two table-spoonfuls of yeast. Keep it warm till it has done fermenting, and in a day it will be ready for use.

POULTICE.—Take 4 ozs. of crumb of bread, a pinch of elder flowers, and camomile; boil them in equal quantities of vinegar and water.——Or, take linseed flour, and the dregs of ale or porter barrels, slightly boiled. It always keeps soft from the oiliness of the linseed, and the yeasty deposit of the malt liquor is both cooling and sweetening.

Poultices are designed to soften and relax any swelling, and allay pain and inflammation, to ripen tumours or swellings, and to cleanse inflamed and gangrenous sores, ulcers, &c. Always remove a poultice when it becomes dry; the place must be well washed in warm ley water, and a fresh poultice applied.

The best Poultice for every purpose is the *Slippery Elm Bark;* it may be made with warm milk and water, or with soap-ley. If tincture of myrrh be added, it is valuable in boils, ulcers, carbuncles, &c.

POULTICE FOR A FESTER. —Boil bread in lees of strong beer; apply the poultice in the general manner. This has saved many a limb from amputation.

POULTRY, *to feed.*—"As I suppose you keep poultry, I may tell you that it has been ascertained that if you mix with their food a sufficient quantity of egg-shells or chalk, which they eat greedily, they will then lay, *cæteris paribus,* twice or thrice as many eggs as before. A well-fed fowl is disposed to lay a vast number of eggs, but cannot do so without the material for the shells, however nourishing in other respects her food may be; indeed, a fowl fed on food and water free from carbonate of lime, and not finding any in the soil, or in the shape of mortar, which they often eat off the wall, would lay no eggs at all with the best will in the world."—*Professor Gregory.*

POUND CAKE.—Take 1 lb. each of flour, sifted loaf sugar, and currants; the rind of two lemons grated; mix all together by rubbing them between the hands; then put 1 lb. of butter into a wooden bowl; place it often before the fire, if the weather is cold; when the butter is soft, beat it up with the hand till it is like a cream; break 10 or 12 eggs into a deep pan; whisk till quite frothy; put one-third of them to the butter; and beat up till well mixed; then put in half of what is left, and mix it till it sticks to the bowl; then put in the remainder, and mix it well up; when it sticks to the bowl, it is well mixed and light; then put in the flour, &c., and mix well together. Have cake hoops, or moulds papered, and put into the oven, the heat of which must be moderate. The rind of a lemon, shred very fine, may be added.

POUND CAKE, *a good one.*— Beat a pound of butter to a cream, and mix with it the whites and yolks of eight eggs beaten apart. Have ready, warm by the fire, a pound of flour, and the same of sifted sugar, mix them, and a few cloves, a little nutmeg, and cinnamon, in fine powder together; then by degrees work the ingredients into the butter and eggs. When well beaten, add a glass of wine and some carraways. It must be beaten a full hour. Butter a pan, and bake it a full hour in a quick oven.

The above proportions, leaving out four ounces of the butter, and the same of sugar, make a less luscious cake, and to most tastes a more pleasant one.

POUND CAKE, *plain*.—Work one pound of butter with cream and one pound of sifted sugar, till it becomes quite smooth; beat up nine eggs and put them by degrees to the butter and beat altogether for twenty minutes. Then mix in lightly one pound of flour; put the whole into a hoop cased with paper, on a baking plate, and bake it for about one hour in a moderate oven. One ounce of carraway seeds added to the foregoing will make what is termed *a rich seed cake*.

POWDER, *Aperient*.—Take of the best Turkey rhubarb, cinnamon, and fine sugar, of each 2 drachms. Let the ingredients be pounded, and afterwards mixed well together.

When flatulence is accompanied with costiveness, a tea-spoonful of this powder may be taken once or twice a day, according to circumstances.

POWDER, *Carminative*.—Take of coriander seeds ½ an oz.; ginger, 1 drachm; nutmegs, ½ a drachm; fine sugar, 1½ drachm; reduce them into powder for twelve doses.

This powder is employed for expelling flatulency, arising from indigestion. It may be given in small quantities to children in their food, when troubled with gripes.

POWDER, *Saline Laxative*.—Take of soluble tartar, and cream of tartar, of each 1 drachm; purified nitre, ½ a drachm. Make them into a powder.

In fevers and other inflammatory disorders, where it is necessary to keep the body gently open, one of these cooling laxative powders may be taken in a little gruel, and repeated occasionally.

POWDER, *Steel*.—Take filings of steel, and loaf sugar, of each 2 ozs.; ginger, 2 drachms. Pound them together.

In obstructions of the menses, and other cases where steel is proper, a tea-spoonful of this powder may be taken twice a day, and washed down with wine or water.

POWDER, *Sudorific*. — Take purified nitre and vitriolated tartar, of each ½ an oz.; opium and ipecacuanha, of each 1 drachm. Mix the ingredients, and reduce them to a fine powder.

This is known by the name of Dover's powder. It is a powerful sudorific. In obstinate rheumatism and other cases where it is necessary to excite a copious sweat, this powder may be administered in the dose of a scruple, or half a drachm, accompanied with copious draughts of warm diluting liquor.

POWDER, *Worm*.—Take of tin, reduced into a fine powder, 1 oz.; Ethiop's mineral, 2 drachms. Mix well together, and divide into six doses. One of these powders may be taken in a little syrup, honey, or treacle, twice a day. Then the following anthelmintic purge will be proper:—

Powdered rhubarb, a scruple; scammony and calomel, of each 5 grains. Rub them in a mortar for one dose. For children, the above doses must be lessened according to their age. If the powder of tin be given alone, its dose may be considerably increased.

PRAWNS AND SHRIMPS.—When fresh they have a sweet flavour, are firm and stiff, and the colour is bright.—Shrimps are of the prawn kind, and may be judged by the same rules.

PRAWNS AND SHRIMPS, *to*

butter.—Take them out of the shells, and warm them with a little good gravy, a bit of butter and flour, a scrape of nutmeg, salt, and pepper; simmer a minute or two, and serve with sippets: or with a cream sauce.

PRAWNS, *Curry of.*—Take them from the shells, and lay into a pan, with a small piece of mace, three or four spoonfuls of veal gravy, and four of cream; rub smooth one or two tea-spoonfuls of curry-powder, a tea-spoonful of flour, and an ounce of butter; simmer an hour; squeeze half a lemon in, and add salt.

PREGNANCY, *a good medicine for.*—Cinnamon water, 1 oz.; tincture of rhubarb, 2 drachms; compound spirits of lavender, ½ a drachm; syrup of saffron, 1 drachm. To be taken occasionally in the middle of the day.

PRESERVES, *to keep.*—Apply the white of an egg, with a brush, to a single thickness of white tissue paper, with which cover the jars, lapping over an inch or two. It will require no tying, as it will become, when dry, inconceivably tight and strong, and impervious to the air.

PRIMROSE VINEGAR.—To 15 quarts of water put 6 lbs. of brown sugar; boil ten minutes; take off the scum; pour on it half a peck of primroses; when nearly cold, add a little fresh yeast, and let it work in a warm place all night; put it in a barrel, and when done working, close the barrel, and keep it in a warm place.

PRINTING INK, *to print linen with types.*—Dissolve one drachm of asphaltum in four drachms of oil of turpentine, then add lamp black or black lead, in fine powder, in sufficient quantity to render the ink of a proper consistence for printing with types.

PRUNES.—They abate heat, and gently relax the bowels, by lubricating the passages and softening the excrements. Hence their great use in constipation, attended with heat and irritation, which other aperients might aggravate. If not sufficiently active, they may be joined with senna, rhubarb, &c., using a little ginger as anti-flatulent. They should be stewed. The French prunes are the best.

PRUNE PUDDING.—Beat up 6 yolks of eggs and 3 whites. Take 4 spoonfuls of flour, a little salt, and some powdered ginger, in half a cupful of milk, and mix well together; add gradually nearly a quart of milk, and 1 lb. of scalded prunes. Tie it up in a cloth; boil it an hour, and pour over it melted butter.

PRUNE TART.—Give prunes a scald, take out the stones and break them; put the kernels, prunes, and sugar into a little cranberry juice; simmer, and when cold make a tart of the sweetmeat.

PUDDING, BAKED.—Three table-spoonfuls of Oswego Prepared Corn to one quart of milk. Prepare, and cook the same as Blanc Mange. After it is cool, stir up with it *thoroughly* two or three eggs well beaten, and bake half an hour. It is very good.

PUDDING, BOILED.—Three table-spoonfuls of Oswego Prepared Corn to one quart of milk. Dissolve the corn in some of the milk, and mix with it *two or three eggs, well beaten,* and a little salt. Heat the remainder of the milk to *near* boiling, add the above preparation, and boil four minutes, stirring it briskly. To be eaten warm with a sauce. It is delicious.

PUDDINGS, *in haste.*—Shred suet, and put with grated bread, a few currants, the yolks of four eggs, and the whites of two, some grated lemon peel, and ginger. Mix, and make into little balls about the size and shape of an egg, with a little flour. Boil 20 minutes.

PUDDING, *to please.*—Mix a quart of new milk with a pint of buttermilk; drain off the whey, and mix with the curd the crumb of a French roll grated, half a lemon peel grated, quarter of a pint of cream, 3 ozs of cold melted butter, the yolks of five and the whites of two eggs; sweeten the whole to taste, and bake with puff paste for half an hour.

Another.—Line a shallow dish with an inch-deep layer of several kinds of good preserves; mix together, and with them mix 3 ozs. of candied citron or orange-rind. Beat well the yolks of ten eggs, and add to them gradually ½ a lb. of sifted sugar; when well mixed, pour in gradually ½ a lb. of good clarified butter, and a little ratafia, or any other flavour. Fill the dish two-thirds with this mixture, and bake the pudding one hour in a moderate oven. Half the quantity will be sufficient for a small dish.

PUDDING, *a wholesome one.*—Put into a basin ¼ lb. of rice, 4 ozs. of coarse sugar, or treacle; 2 quarts of milk, and 2 ozs. of dripping or butter; put it cold into the oven. It will take a good while to bake, but it will be very good sclid food.

PUFF PASTE.—To 1 lb. of flour, take ¾ lb. of butter. Rub half the butter very finely into the flour, and mix it into a paste with cold water; roll out the paste; put in the remainder of the butter; roll it up, and leave it for half an hour; then roll it out for use. An egg may be beaten very fine, and mixed with the water.

PUFF, *a good light one.*—Mix two spoonfuls of flour, a little grated lemon peel, some nutmeg, half a spoonful of brandy, a little loaf sugar, and one egg; then fry it enough, but not brown; beat it in a mortar with five eggs, whites and yolks; put a quantity of lard in a frying-pan, and when quite hot, drop a dessert-spoonful of batter at a time; turn as they brown. Serve them immediately, with sweet sauce.

PUFF, *a good one.*—To a ¼ oz. of butter add 3 ozs. of Jordan Almonds with 2 ozs. of loaf sugar; pound them with a small quantity of rose water till they form a thick paste; spread the paste on buttered tins, bake in a slow oven. When cold, put a spoonful of any kind of jam in each and cover with whipped cream.

PUFF, *made of cheese.*—Strain cream curd from the whey, and beat half a pint basin of it fine in a mortar, with a spoonful and a half of flour, three eggs, but only one white, a spoonful of orange flower-water, a quarter of a nutmeg, and sugar to make pretty sweet. Lay a little of this paste, in small very round cakes on a tin plate. If the oven is hot, a quarter of an hour will bake them. Serve with pudding sauce.

PULMONARY BALSAM.—Horehound, (plant) comfrey-root, blood-root, elecampane-root, wild cherry bark, spikenard-root, penny royal, (plant) of each, 4 ozs. Pour 3 quarts of boiling water upon them; infuse for 3 hours; then heat the water again; and pour it upon the plants to infuse 5 or 6 hours. Sweeten with sugar candy.—It is very serviceable in diseases of the lungs, chronic coughs; it removes constriction of the chest, by promoting expectoration. Take half a small tea-cupful three or four times a day.

PULMONARY COM-

PLAINTS.—It is said that the tender shoots of Scotch fir, peeled and eaten fasting early in the morning in the woods, when the weather is dry, has performed many cures of pulmonary complaints among the Highlanders in Scotland.

PULMONARY SYRUP.—— Blood-root, boneset, slippery elm bark, coltsfoot, elecampane, of each 2 ozs.; white root, spikenard root, of each, 4 ozs.; comfrey-root, poplar bark, of each, 1 oz.; lobelia, horehound, snake-root, of each, ½ oz. Pour upon them 2 quarts of boiling water; stir well; add 1 lb. of treacle, and when cool, 1 quart of Hollands gin.—It is one of the best remedies for asthma, coughs, hoarseness, &c. A table-spoonful every hour; or a wine-glassful three times a day.

PUNCH, *to make.*—Take two lemons, and rub some lumps of sugar over them, till all the yellow part of the skin has been taken off. Put these lumps into a bowl, and squeeze as much lemon juice to them as is requisite to give sufficient acidity. Then add the proper quantity of sugar; mix the sugar and juice well together, to which add some boiling water, and mix till the whole be cool. Take rum and brandy, equal quantities, and mix with the above; the quantity of spirits according to taste.

PUNCH, *Royal.*—Take half a pint of brandy, a bottle of champagne, the juice of three lemons, and of two Seville oranges, and a quarter of a pint of Martinique, with nearly a quart of strong infusion of tea, and sweetened according to taste.

PUNCTUATION is the making of pauses, by points indicative of their length.

The *Comma* is written thus (,) and represents the shortest pauses in reading, and the smallest divisions in writing.

Rule 1. In general a simple sentence does not admit of any point except the period; as, True politeness has its seat in the heart.

Rule 2. The simple members of a compound sentence are separated by a comma; as, Good men are esteemed, and they are happy. He labours assiduously, and he is becoming rich.

Rule 3. When two or more words—whether nouns, adjectives, pronouns, verbs, or adverbs—are connected without the conjunction being expressed, the comma supplies the place of that word; as, My parents, brothers, and sisters were all present.—But when it is expressed, the comma is omitted; as, Cicero spoke most forcibly and fluently.

Rule 4. Absolute, relative, and, generally, all parenthetical and explanatory clauses, are separated from the other parts of a sentence by commas; as, The commander having been shot, the troops became dispirited. Paul, the chief of sinners, became the chief apostle. Christianity, though strenuously opposed by infidelity, is destined to triumph. In short, he was a great man.

Rule 5. The modifying words and phrases, *nay, however, hence, finally, in short, at least,* and the like, are usually separated by commas.

Rule 6. Words denoting the person, or object addressed, are separated by commas; as, My son, give me thine heart. John, hear what I say.

Rule 7. An emphatical repetition, requires a comma; as, Against thee, thee only, have I sinned.

Rule 8. When words are placed in opposition to each other, or with some marked variety, they require to be distinguished by a comma: as,

"Tho' deep, yet clear; tho' gentle, yet not dull;
Strong, without rage; without o'erflowing, full."

"Good men, in this frail imimperfect state, are often found, not only in union *with*, but in opposition *to*, the views and conduct of one another."

Rule 9. The words of another writer cited, but not formally introduced as a quotation, are separated by a comma; as, "I pity the man who can travel from Dan to Beersheba, and cry, 'Tis all barren."

Rule 10. A comma is often inserted where a verb is understood; as, George has acquired much property; his brother, little.

Rule 11. A comma is used between the two parts of a sentence that has its natural order inverted; as, Him that is weak in the faith, receive ye.

The *Semicolon* is written thus (;). It marks a longer pause than the comma, and separates clauses less closely connected.

Rule 1. A sentence consisting of two parts, the one containing a complete proposition, and the other added as an inference, or an explanation, the two parts are separated by a semicolon; as, My mind is sadly dejected; for I am surrounded with enemies.

Rule 2. A sentence consisting of several members, each constituting a distinct proposition, and having a dependence upon each other, or upon some common clause, they are separated by semicolons; as, Remember, weeping may endure for a night, but joy cometh in the morning; and to all true christians, it shall be a morning without clouds; for the Lord shall be their everlasting light; and the days of their mourning shall be ended.

The *Colon*, which is written thus (:) marks a longer pause than the semicolon, and is used when the sense is complete, but when there is something still behind, which tends to make the sense fuller or clearer.

Rule 1. A colon generally precedes a quotation; as, The Scriptures show the benevolence of the Deity in the words: "God is love."

Rule 2. When a sentence which consists of an enumeration of particulars, each separated from the other by a semicolon, has its sense suspended till the last clause, that clause is disjoined from the preceding by a colon; as, "If he has not been unfaithful to his king; if he has not proved a traitor to his country; if he has never given cause for such charges as have been preferred against him: why then is he afraid to confront his accusers?"

The Period, or full point, is a dot thus (.), and is used at the end of every complete sentence; that is to say, at the end of every collection of words which makes a full and complete meaning, and is not necessarily connected with other collections of words.

Besides being used to mark the completion of a sentence, the period is placed after initials, when used alone, as D. D., for Doctor of Divinity; and after abreviations, as, Lat. for Latin.

The following Grammatical signs, or marks, are used in the writing of sentences:—

Parenthesis ( ) is used to enclose a phrase to assist in elucidating the subject, or to add force to the assertions or arguments; as,

"Know then this truth (enough for man to know),
Virtue alone is happiness below."

It ought, however, to be very sparingly used. It is necessarily an interrupter; it breaks in upon the regular course of the mind: it tends to divert the attention from the main object of the sentence.

Interrogation is used when a question is asked; as, How art thou?

Exclamation or *Admiration*, denotes any sudden emotion of the mind; as, Alas! I am undone!

Apostrophe, (') or mark of elision, indicates that a letter is left out; as, lov'd for loved, don't for do not. It is used properly enough in poetry, but should never be used in prose. "It ought to be called the mark not of *elision*, but of *laziness* and *vulgarity*, except when used to denote the possessive case of Nouns."

Hyphen (-) is used to connect words or parts of words; as in teapot, water-rat.

The *Dash* marks a break in the sentence, or an abrupt turn, though it is occasionally used merely to disjoin a parenthetical clause; as, "If thou art he—but O how fallen!"

"Peter and John—for they were together — stood up before the council."

Paragraph ¶ is used to denote the beginning of a new subject.

Section (§) is sometimes used instead of the word *section*.

PUT, *Game of*—Put is usually played by two persons, with a complete pack of cards. In this game the cards rank differently from all others, the tray being the best; next the deuce, then ace, king, queen, knave, and so on in the usual order.

After cutting for deal, &c., at which the best put card wins, three cards by one at a time are given to each player; and the game is played in the following way. If the non-dealer throws up his cards he looses a point; if he plays, and the dealer does not lay down another to it, he gains a point; but should the dealer either win the same, pass it, or lay down one of equal value, forming what is called a tie, the non-dealer is still at liberty to "put," that is, play or not, and his opponent only gains a point. Then if both parties agree to go on, whoever gains all the tricks, or two out of the three, wins five points, which constitute the game. If each player obtains one trick, and the third is a tie, then neither party must be allowed to score.

Four-hand put differs only in that any two of the players give each their best card to his partner, who then lays out one of his own, and the game is then played as two-handed put.

If the dealer turns up any of his adversary's cards, another deal may be demanded, but when he shows his own, he is to abide by them.

Either party saying "I Put," must stand his cards or pay the stakes.

PUTTY, *to soften.*—Apply frequently to the putty diluted sulphuric acid, or a little nitric, or muriatic acid, and in a short time it will become so soft, as to be easily removed.

QUADRILLE, *game of.*—This game is played by four persons, and only forty cards are used, the tens, nines, eights, being discarded from the pack. The deal is made by giving each player in rotation three cards at a time, for any two rounds, and once four cards at a time, beginning with the right hand player, who is the elder hand. The following is the correct way of playing this game.

When you are the ombre, and your friend leads from a mat, play your best trump, and then lead your best trump the first opportunity.

If you hold all the trumps, keep leading them, except you have other certain winning cards.

If all the mats are not revealed by the time you have won six tricks; risk not playing for vole.

When you are the friend called, and hold only a mat, lead it, but if only a mat guarded by a small trump, lead the small one; though when the ombre is last player, lead the best trump you have.

Punto in red, or king of trumps in black, are good cards to lead, when they are your best; and should either of them succeed, then play a small trump.

When the ombre leads to disdiscover a friend, if you hold king, queen, and knave, put on the knave.

Preserve the called suit, whether friend or not.

When playing against a lone hand, never lead a king, unless you have the queen, nor change the suit, nor allow, if you can prevent it, the ombre to be the last player.

Call on the strongest suits, except you have a queen guarded: when elder hand, you have a better chance than middle hand.

A good player may succeed with a weaker hand, when either elder or younger, better than if he was middle hand.

The Rank of the Cards when not trumps.

Clubs and Spades.--King, Queen, Knave, Seven, Six, Five, Four, Three, Two.—Total 9.

Hearts and Diamonds.—King, Queen, Knave, Ace, Deuce, Three, Four, Five, Six, Seven. Total, 10.

LAWS OF THE GAME OF QUADRILLE

1. The cards are to be dealt to the right hand by threes and fours, and not differently; and the dealer is at liberty to begin either with four or with three; if a card be turned up in dealing, there must be a new deal.

2. He who deals wrong is to deal again.

3. He who has asked leave is obliged to play.

4. No one is basted for playing out of turn, but the card played may be called at any time in that deal, providing it does not cause a renounce; or either of the adversaries may demand of his partner to play any suit he thinks proper.

5. The three matadores cannot be forced by an inferior trump, but the superior forces the inferior when led by a first player.

6. A player naming trumps must abide by the same.

7. Whoever plays with eleven cards is basted.

8. If you play "sans prendre," or have matadores, they should be demanded before the next dealer has finished, or you lose the benefit.

9. Any person naming his trump without asking leave, is obliged to play "sans prendre," unless he is the younger hand, and all the rest have passed.

10. After the game is won, if the person who won the sixth trick, plays the seventh card, he is obliged to play for the vole.

11. If you have your kings dealt you are at liberty either to call a queen to one of your kings, (except the queen of trumps, or to call one of your own kings.

12. If any person separates a card from the rest, he ought to play it, if the opposite party has seen the same, unless he plays "sans prendre."

13. If the king is called, or his partner plays out of his turn, the vole is to be played for.

14. No person is to be basted for a renounce, unless the trick is turned and quitted; and if any renounce is discovered in time, should the player happen to be basted by such a renounce, all the parties are to play three cards over again.

15. Forced spadille is not obliged to play for the vole, nor make three tricks.

16. Whoever undertakes to play the vole, has the preference of playing before him who offers to play "sans prendre."

17. If agreeable to all parties, let the person have the preference of playing, who plays for the most tricks, which will prevent small games.

18. The ombre is entitled to know his king called, before he declares for the vole.

19. When six tricks are played, he who won the sixth ought to say, "I play the vole," or, "I do not play the vole," or "I ask;" and nothing else.

20. He who wins the vole is to take the double stake played for, out of the pool.

21. He who asks leave (if elder hand,) may play "sans prendre," in preference to any of the other players.

22. A player who has one or more kings, may call himself, but must win six tricks.

23. If you play the king surrendered, he must win six tricks who demands the king of any player.

24. He who has passed once (unless spadille) has no right to call afterwards; also he who has asked is obliged to play, unless somebody else plays "sans prendre."

25. If the ombre or his friend show their cards, before they have won six tricks, the adversaries may call their cards as they please.

26. Whoever asks leave, cannot play "sans prendre," unless forced.

27. You may look at all the tricks turned, when you are to lead, but not otherwise.

28. Whoever undertakes playing for the vole and does not succeed, has a right to the stakes "sans prendre," and matadores, if he has them, having won his game.

29. Any person discovering his game, is not entitled to play for the vole.

30. If there happen to be two cards of one sort, and found out before the deal is ended, the deal is void, but not otherwise.

31. Nobody is to declare how many trumps are played out.

32. He who calls and does not make three tricks, is to be basted alone, unless forced spadille.

QUAILS, *to fricassee.*—Having tossed them up in a saucepan with a little melted butter, and mushrooms, put in a slice of ham, well beaten, with salt, pepper, cloves, and savory herbs; add good gravy, and a glass of sherry; simmer over a slow fire; when almost done, thicken the ragout with a good cullis, (i. e. a good broth, strained, gellatined, &c.) or with two or three eggs, well beaten up in a little gravy.

QUAILS, *to roast.*—Roast them without drawing, and serve on toast. Butter only should be eaten with them, as gravy takes off the fine flavour. The thigh and back are the most esteemed.

QUAKING PUDDING.—Scald a quart of cream; when almost cold, put to it four eggs well beaten, a spoonful and a half of flour, some nutmegs and sugar; tie it close in a buttered cloth; boil it an hour, and turn it out with care, lest it should crack. Melted butter, a little wine and sugar.

QUASSIA.—This plant derives its name from Quassi, a negro of

Surinam: by it he cured the malignant fevers peculiar to that country. For gold he disclosed his remedy to Mr. Rolander, a Swede, who introduced it into Europe. It is now chiefly brought from the West Indies. It is much used by brewers. It is one of the most powerful of the bitter tonics, tending to the narcotic. It is a good remedy for indigestion, invigorating the digestive organs, with little excitement of the circulation, or increase of animal heat: it is very bitter, but it has no smell. Its narcotic principle, though slight, is proved by its destruction of flies. The infusion of it is made by pouring a pint of boiling water upon 2 scruples of the chips or raspings. Orange peel renders it more grateful to the stomach.

QUEEN CAKES.—Mix 1 lb. of dried flour, the same of sifted sugar, and of washed clean currants. Wash 1 lb. of butter in rose water, beat it well, then mix with it eight eggs, yolks and whites beaten separately, and put in the dry ingredients by degrees; beat the whole an hour; butter little tins, teacups, or saucers, and bake the batter in, filling only half. Sift a little fine sugar over just as you put it into the oven.

Another way.—Beat 8 ozs. of butter, and mix with two well beaten eggs, strained; mix 8 ozs. of dried flour, and the same of lump sugar, and the grated rind of a lemon; then add the whole together, and beat full half an hour with a silver spoon. Butter small patty-pans, half fill, and bake twenty minutes in a quick oven.

Another.—Take 1 lb. of flour, seven eggs, and 1 lb. of lump sugar, grated fine; beat your eggs well, then put the sugar to the eggs, beat them well together, take a ¼ lb. of butter beat to a cream, whisk up all together, then add the flour, and stir well. Do not whisk the flour in it, it will make them tough.

QUEEN'S CULLIS.—Prepare a stewpan with slices from a fillet of veal, a few bits of ham, and roots; simmer it on a slow fire, without catching at the bottom, and add some good broth—good coloured. A fowl may be added to it to increase its strength; simmer it; pound one or two breasts of fowl, with half a handful of sweet almonds, scalded, a few hard yolks of eggs, and bread crumbs soaked in broth; mix altogether in a mortar; strain, rubbing it hard with a wooden spoon; add a little cream to make it whiter.

QUEEN'S DROPS.—Soften, and work with the hand, till like cream, as directed for Queen's Cakes, ½ lb. of fresh butter; put to it 8 ozs. of sifted loaf sugar and beat them together for a minute; break in four eggs, and beat for two minutes; then lightly mix in ¾ lb. of good flour, 4 ozs. of nicely washed currants, and half a teaspoonful of powdered cinnamon. When well mixed, make it into drops the size of a walnut, upon paper on iron plates, and bake them in a hot oven.

QUICK MADE PUDDING.—Flour and suet, ½ lb. each, four eggs, ¼ pint of new milk, a little mace and nutmeg, ¼ lb. of raisins, ditto of currants; mix well, and boil three quarters of an hour with the cover of the pot on, or it will require longer.

QUICKSILVER.—Tallow will take it up;—vinegar kills it. As a medicine it is injurious. It is mercury in a peculiar state. It is poison.

QUINCE CAKES.—Mix the syrup of quinces and raspberries

together; boil and clarify them over a clear fire, skimming well; then add 1½ lb. of sugar; cause as much more to be brought to a candy height, and poured in hot; stir the whole till cold; spread it on plates, and cut it into cakes.

QUINCE JELLY.—Cut in pieces a sufficient quantity of quinces; draw off the juice by boiling them in water, in which they ought only to swim, no more. When fully done, drain and have ready clarified sugar, to which put one spoonful to two of the juice; bring the sugar to the *souffle;* add the juice, and finish. When it drops from the skimmer it is enough; take it off, and pot it.

QUINCE PUDDING.—Scald the quinces tender; pare thin; scrape off the pulp; mix with sugar very sweet, and add a little ginger and cinnamon. To a pint of cream, put 3 or 4 yolks of eggs, and stir it into the quinces till they are of a good thickness; butter a dish, pour it in, and bake it.

QUINCE SEEDS.—Of these bandoline is made—a cement for the hair; see *bandoline,* page 43. It is also used as an emollient and sheathing application to cracked lips and nipples.

QUINCE WINE.—Wipe off the fur, take out the cores of ripe quinces; bruise them and press them, adding to every gallon of juice 2½ lbs. of fine sugar; stir together till dissolved; put it in the cask, and when it has done fermenting, stop it close; let it stand six months before it is bottled; keep it two or three years, and it will be the better.

QUINCES, *red, to preserve whole.*—Core and scald six fine quinces; drain; and when cold, pare them; take their weight in sugar, and a pint of water to every lb. of sugar; boil it to a syrup, and skim; put in the quinces to stand all night; when red enough, boil them as marmalade with two basinfuls of jelly; when as soft as a straw can be run through them, put them into glasses; let the liquor boil to a jelly, then pour it over the quinces.

QUININE.—It is obtained by frequently boiling the yellow Peruvian bark *(cinchona)* in water, acidulated with sulphuric acid. It retains in a concentrated form the tonic and febrifuge properties of the Peruvian bark from which it is obtained; and as a remedy is administered to the same cases. It agrees better with an irritable stomach than the bark.

The dose is from one to five grains three or four times a day. It is valuable in ague, given during the intermission. It may be made into a pill, made with conserve of roses, or mucilage, or in liquid, as water, if previously dissolved in elixir of vitriol, or diluted sulphuric acid. It is valuable in tic doloureux, St. Vitus's dance, in mortification, bleedings in discharges attended with great debility, as diarrhœas, dysentery, obstinate ulcers, scrofula, &c.

To stop intermittent fever, take sulphate of quinine, thirty-two grains; simple syrup, one pound, mixed. A spoonful to be taken every four or six hours. For intermittents and debility, dissolve twelve grains of sulphate of quinine in half a pint of good Madeira wine, or infusion of roses, one ounce three times a day. The tincture consists of six grains of sulphate of quinine, and spirits of wine, one ounce; take a teaspoonful twice or thrice a day. From five to ten grains of quinine, taken two or three times daily, has cured tic doloureux. It has also been successful in head and toothache.

QUIN'S FISH SAUCE.—Half a pint of mushroom pickle, the same of walnut, six long anchovies, pounded, six cloves of garlick, three of them pounded; half a spoonful of cayenne pepper; put them into a bottle, and shake them well before using. It is also good with beef steaks.

QUINSY.—This disease occurs principally in spring and autumn, when vicissitudes of heat and cold are frequent. It affects especially the young and sanguine, and a disposition to it is often acquired by frequent attacks.

Symptoms.—It commences with an unusual sense of tightness in the throat, particularly on swallowing, which is often effected with difficulty and pain. On inspection, some tumefaction and redness of the fauces may be perceived, which shortly spreads over the tonsils, uvula, and soft palate, attended with a troublesome clamminess of the mouth, fever, headache, delirium, &c. In desperate cases, the tongue and tonsils are so much swollen as to prevent deglutition, and even so as to affect respiration, that the patient is often obliged to be supported in an erect posture, to prevent suffocation. The inflammation generally attacks one tonsil first, which in a day or two it sometimes leaves and affects the other, and not unfrequently quits them both suddenly, and flies to the lungs.

Causes.—It is generally caused by the external application of cold air, particular lyabout the neck. Whatever violently stimulates the fauces, in a plethoric habit, especially, as acrid food, poisons, &c., may produce it.

Treatment.—As the inflammation, from the delicate structure of the parts, soon advances to suppuration, *active* means should be speedily employed to disperse it. For this purpose the patient should take a full dose of the Aperient Mixture, and after its operation, the Saline Mixture.

One of the most effectual remedies is an *emetic*. This should be given as soon as the symptoms appear, and repeated as often as necessary. The throat should be steamed with a strong decoction of tansy, wormwood, hops, and camomile flowers, boiled in vinegar and water. Put these into a large pitcher, over which place a funnel, that the patient may inhale the steam for 15 minutes, and repeat it every two hours until the urgent symptoms are gone. Afterwards heat the herbs and bind them on the neck.

A vapour bath is also of the greatest service, benefiting the whole system, and the throat especially. Gargle the throat with a decoction of lobelia and a little gum kino. The steam of hempseed is said to be valuable in quinsey. If the patient is constipated, give an aperient. When the painful symptoms begin to subside, apply the *Rheumatic Liquid* warm to the throat, as warm and as long as the patient can bear it. Gargle the throat occasionally with a decoction of sage, hyssop, lobelia, catechu, or kino, with a little borax. Do this frequently. Repeat the aperients when necessary, and the feet bathed in warm water and soap.

Let the food, if any can be taken, be very simple. Give no spirits, no stimulants, and nothing cold. Hydropathy is very useful in quinsey. Dip a piece of cloth, in the form of a bandage, in cold water, wring it out, and wrap it round the throat, and over it a dry bandage. Repeat when hot and dry. In sore throat, black currant jelly is of great service; and so is the old plan of wrapping the stocking round the throat on going to bed. A good gargle is made of sage and vinegar, with a little *sal ammoniac*. A little sal prunel sucked is sometimes of great use.

Apply a large white-bread toast half an inch thick, dipped in brandy, to the crown of the head till it dries. Or, swallow slowly white rose water mixed with syrup of mulberries. Or, draw in as hot as you can, for ten or twelve minutes together, the fumes of red rose leaves, or camomile flowers, boiled in water and vinegar, or of a decoction of bruised hemp-seed. This speedily cures the sore throat, peripneumony, and inflammation of the uvula.—*Wesley.*

QUINSY.—Roast three or four large onions. Peel them quickly, and beat them flat with a rolling-pin. Immediately place them in a thin muslin bag that will reach from ear to ear, and about three inches deep. Apply it speedily as warm as possible to the throat. Keep it on day and night, changing it when the strength of the onions appears to be exhausted, and substituting fresh ones. Flannel must be worn round the neck after the poultice is removed.

QUINSY, *Vapour for a.*—Take powdered pepper, 1 oz.; milk, 1 quart, and boil them to 1½ pint; put the whole into a glass bottle with a small neck; let the vapour be received as hot as can be borne with the mouth open. This is about the best gargle.

QUINZE.—This game, as its name implies, is a French game of fifteen up, which are to be made in the following manner: The pack of cards must be shuffled by the players, and when they have cut for deal, which belongs to him who cuts the lowest, the dealer has the privilege of shuffling last; this being done, the adversary cuts, after which the dealer gives one card to his adversary, and one to himself: if his adversary does not like his card, he has a right to have as many more given him, one after the other; the pips of which will make fifteen, or come nearest to it; which are usually given from the top of the pack. For example; if he should draw a deuce and then a five, which make seven, he should go on again in hopes of coming nearer to fifteen; if he draws an eight, which makes just fifteen, and being elder hand, he is sure of winning the game; but if he overdraws himself, and makes above fifteen, he loses, unless the dealer does the same; in which case it is a drawn game, and they double the stakes. Thus they go on, until one of them wins the game, by standing, and being fifteen, or the nearest to it below that number.

At the end of each game the cards are shuffled, and the players cut again for deal; the elder hand always having the advantage.

This game is admired for its fairness and simplicity; depending entirely on chance, being soon decided, and not requiring that attention which most other games on the cards do.

RABBITS, *to choose.*—An *old* rabbit has very long and rough claws, and gray hairs intermixed with the wool. If *young*, the claws and wool are smooth; if *stale* it will be flexible, and the flesh will be bluish, having a kind of slime upon it; but if *fresh*, the flesh will be white and dry.

RABBIT, *an English.*—Toast a slice of bread brown on both sides; then lay it on a plate, pour a glass of port wine over it; then cut some cheese very thin, and lay it thick over the bread; put it into a Dutch oven before the fire to brown. Serve it hot.

RABBIT, *Scotch*.—Toast a piece of bread on both sides; butter it; cut a slice of cheese the size of the bread; toast it on both sides, and lay it on the bread.

RABBIT, *Welsh*.—Toast a slice of bread on both sides, and butter it; toast a slice of Cheshire cheese on one side, and lay that next the bread, and toast the other with a salamander; rub mustard over, and serve very hot, and covered.

RABBITS, *en Casserole*.—Cut them in quarters, and lard them or not; dredge them well with flour, and fry them; put them into a pipkin with a quart of common stock, a glass of sherry, pepper, salt, sweet herbs, and butter rolled in flour; cover close, and stew them half an hour, dish, and pour the same over, garnish with Seville oranges, sliced.

RABBITS, *en Matelote*.—Prepare two rabbits as for fricassee; put them with as many slices of bacon, as there are of rabbits, into a stewpan with half a pint of stock, 24 small onions, and half a bottle of mushrooms; cover with paper, and set it on a stove, to simmer an hour. Take the rabbit, and lay it on a dish; skim off the fat, and reduce the liquor nearly to a glaze; put cullis to it; give it a boil; take it from the fire, and squeeze half a lemon; add cayenne pepper, and a little sugar; pour it over the rabbit; garnish with paste.

RABBIT, *to blanch*.—Set it on the fire in a small quantity of cold water, and let it boil; then take it out, and put it into cold water for a few minutes.

RABBITS, *to boil*.—Take out the liver, and dress it separately; and to insure whiteness of flesh, let the rabbits soak for 10 minutes in tepid water. Half an hour's boiling will be sufficient for those of moderate size, more if they are larger. Smother with onion sauce, chop the liver very fine, and serve it in a sauce-boat; if you place the sauce round it, it may prevent those who dislike the flavour from partaking of the dish.

RABBITS, *to fricassee brown*.—Cut the rabbits as for eating; fry them in butter, a light brown; put them in a tossing-pan with a pint of water, a teaspoonful of lemon pickle, a large spoonful of mushroom ketchup, the same of browning, one anchovy, a slice of lemon, cayenne pepper, and salt to taste; stew them over a slow fire till they are done enough; thicken the gravy, and strain it; dish up the rabbits, and pour the gravy over them.

RABBITS, *to fricassee white*.— Cut, and put into a tossing-pan, as before, with a pint of veal gravy, a teaspoonful of lemon pickle, one anchovy, a slice of lemon, a little beaten mace, cayenne pepper, and salt; stew them over a slow fire; when they are done enough, thicken with flour and butter; strain it; then add the yolks of two eggs, mixed with a gill of cream, and a little nutmeg grated in. Do not let it boil.

RABBITS, *to florentine*.—Skin two young rabbits; but leave on the ears; take out the bones, leaving the head whole; lay them flat; make a forcemeat of a ¼ lb. of bacon, scraped; add to the bacon the crumbs of a penny loaf, a little lemon, thyme, or lemon-peel, shred fine, parsley chopped small, nutmeg, cayenne, and salt; mix them up together with an egg, and spread it over the rabbits; roll them up to the head; skewer them straight; close the ends, to keep the forcemeat in; skewer the ears back, and tie them in separate cloths, and boil half an hour. Have ready a white sauce, made of veal gravy, a little anchovy, the juice of half a lemon; take a ¼ lb. of butter, rolled in flour, so as to make the sauce pretty thick; stir while the flour is dissolving; beat the yolk of an egg; add some thick cream, nutmeg, and salt; mix it with the gravy, and simmer it a little over the fire: but do not boil. Pour over the rabbits.

RABBITS, *to pot.*—Cut up two or three young, but full grown ones, and take the leg bones off at the thigh; pack them as closely as possible in a small pan, after seasoning them with pepper, mace, cayenne, salt, and allspice, all in very fine powder. Make the top as smooth as you can. Keep out the heads and the carcases, but take off the meat about the neck. Put a good deal of butter, and bake the whole gently. Keep it two days in the pan, then shift it into small pots, adding butter. The livers also should be added, as they eat well.

RABBITS, *to roast.* — Baste them with butter, and dredge them with flour; half an hour will do them at a brisk fire; and if small, twenty minutes. Take the livers with a bunch of parsley, boil them, and chop them very fine together; melt some butter, and put half the liver and parsley into the butter; pour it into the dish, and garnish the dish with the other half; roast them of a fine light brown.

RABBIT, *to taste like a hare.*— Choose one that is young, but full grown; hang it in the skin three or four days; then skin it, and lay it, without washing, in a seasoning of black pepper and allspice in a very fine powder, a glass of port wine, and the same quantity of vinegar. Baste it occasionally for 40 hours, then stuff it and roast it as a hare, and with the same sauce. Do not wash off the liquor that it was soaked in.

RABBITS, *various modes of dressing.*—Roasted with stuffing and gravy, like hare; or without stuffing; with sauce of the liver and parsley chopped in melted butter, pepper, and salt; or larded.

Boiled, and smothered with onion sauce; the butter to be melted with milk instead of water.

Fried in joints, with dried or fried parsley. The same liversauce, this way also.

Fricasseed, as before directed for chickens.

In a pie, as chicken, with forcemeat, &c. In this way they are excellent when young.

RABBIT, *Victoria.*—Toast bread nicely on both sides, and butter. Have ready the following; nice ham, Cheshire cheese, and half boiled eggs, very finely chopped and intimately mixed together, with a little pepper and mustard; put into a Dutch oven, and place before the fire; spread it on the toast. It is delicious. Onions, if you like, may be substituted for the eggs.

RABBIT PIE.—Cut up two young rabbits; season with pepper, salt, a little mace, and nutmeg, all finely powdered, and a little cayenne; put the rabbits, slices of ham, or of bacon, forcemeat balls, and hard eggs, by turns in layers; if it is to be baked in a dish, put a little water, but none, if in a raised crust. By the time it returns from the oven, have ready a gravy of knuckle of veal, or a bit of the scrag, with some shank bones of mutton, seasoned with herbs, onions, mace, and white pepper; if it is to be eaten hot, mushrooms, &c. may be added; but not, if to be eaten cold. If it be made in a dish, put as much gravy as will fill it; but in raised crust, the gravy must be nicely strained, and then put in as cold as jelly. To make jelly clear, give it a boil with the whites of two eggs, after taking away the meat, and run it through a sieve.

RABBIT SKINS, *to cure.*— Lay the skin on a smooth board, the fur side undermost, and fasten it down with tinned tacks. Wash it over first with a solution of salt; then dissolve 2½ ozs. of alum in a pint of warm water, and with a sponge dipped in this solution, moisten the surface all over: repeat this every now and then for three days: when the skin is quite dry, take out the tacks, and rolling it loosely the long way, the hair inside, draw it quickly backwards and forwards through a large smooth ring, until it is quite soft, then roll it in the contrary way of the skin, and repeat the operation. Skins prepared thus are useful for many domestic purposes.

RABBIT SOUP.—Cut two rabbits into joints, and flour and fry them lightly; add three or four onions fried brown. Pour on these three or four quarts of boiling water, a little salt, and parsley. Add to it also good broth, and butter, or lard, three carrots, three shalots, and a pinch of cayenne; thicken with rice flour, or boiled pearl barley, a little before the soup is done; boil five hours. Put toasted bread in the tureen, and pour the soup upon it.

RADISH PODS, *to pickle.*— Make a pickle with cold spring water and bay salt, strong enough to bear an egg; put the pods in, and lay a board upon them to keep them under water; let them stand ten days; drain them in a sieve, and dry them; take as much of the best vinegar as will cover them; boil it, and put the pods in a jar with ginger, mace, cloves, and cayenne pepper; pour on the vinegar boiling hot; cover them with a cloth, doubled four times; let them stand two days; when cold, repeat three or four times. Add as much mustard seed and horse radish as you please.

RAISED CRUST, *for meat pies, fowls, &c.*—Boil water with a little fine lard, and an equal quantity of fresh dripping, or of butter, but not much of either. While hot, mix this with as much flour as you will want, making the paste as stiff as you can to be smooth, which you will make by good kneading and beating it with a rolling pin. When quite smooth, put a lump into a cloth, or under a pan, to soak till nearly cold.

Those who have not a good hand at raising crust may do thus: Roll the paste of a proper thickness, and cut out the top and bottom of the pie, then a long piece for the sides. Cement the bottom to the sides with egg, bringing the former rather further out, and pinching both together; put egg between the edges of the paste, to make it adhere at the sides. Fill your pie and put on the cover, and pinch it and the side crust together. The same mode of uniting the paste is to be observed if the sides are pressed into a tin form, in which the paste must be baked, after it shall be filled and covered; but in the latter case, the tin should be buttered, and carefully taken off when done enough; and as the form usually makes the sides of a lighter colour than is proper, the paste should be put into the oven again for a quarter of an hour. With a feather put egg over at first.

RAISED FRENCH PIE.—Raise a crust three inches high; lay in slices of veal, a few mushrooms, a few slices of ham, a cut-up chicken, more mushrooms, and a sliced sweet-bread; season with pepper, salt, and sweet herbs; cover it in, and put it in the oven; it will take about two hours in a moderate oven. When done, pour off the fat, and put six yolks of eggs boiled hard.

RAISED PIES, *Seasoning for*.—Salt, 3 lbs; white pepper, 3 ozs.; cayenne pepper, ½ oz.; cloves, 2 ozs.; allspice, 2 ozs.; and 1 oz. each of basil, thyme, marjoram, bay leaf, and nutmeg. Pound the spices and herbs by themselves, sift, and mix with the salt, and put away in a stoppered bottle.

RAISED PUFF CAKES.—Make the richest puff paste; roll it pretty thick into four or five pieces, all one size; lay one piece on a deep baking dish, upon it pour some good prepared cream, or sweetmeat; then another piece of paste, some cream, or marmalade, and so on, as many as you please; the paste to be the last, in which make a little hole, which must be filled with sweetmeat or jelly, when it is well baked; this must be done in a brisk oven, to raise the paste properly: it is done also by baking the paste first upon a baking plate, and adding the cream, jelly, or sweetmeat, when it is cold, and finishing after the same manner.

RAISIN CAKE.—One cup of flour, two cups of cream, one cup of butter, four eggs, 1 lb. of raisins, cloves, cinnamon, candied lemon, cut extremely fine, and one teaspoonful of soda.

RAISIN CAKE.—Take 1½ lb. of light dough, a tea-cupful of sugar, one of butter, three eggs, a tea-spoonful of carbonate of soda, 1 lb. of raisins, nutmeg or cinnamon to the taste; bake one hour. Let it rise before being baked.

RAISIN LOAF.—To 6 lbs. of flour, add 2½ lbs. of raisins, ½ oz. of carraway and a few coriander seeds ground, a little cinnamon or clove pepper, and half a pint of barm mixed with cold water; cut the paste with a knife very well, to make the loaf appear to be fuller of raisins. For a richer loaf, add more fruit, and rub butter in the flour and sugar; bake it a fine brown on the top.

RAISIN WINE.—To every gallon of spring-water put 8 lbs. of fresh Smyrnas in a large tub; stir it every day for a month; then press the raisins in a horse-hair bag as dry as possible; put the liquor into a cask; and when it has done hissing, pour in a bottle of the best brandy; stop it close for twelve months; then rack it off, but without the dregs; filter them through a bag of flannel of three or four folds; add the clear to the quantity, and pour one or two quarts of brandy, according to the size of the vessel. Stop it up, and at the end of three years you may either bottle it or drink it from the cask. Raisin wine would be extremely good if made rich of the fruit, and kept long, which improves the flavour greatly.

RAISIN WINE, *to make equal to Sherry.*—Wash and pick the raisins; chop them, and to every lb. add a quart of water which has been boiled and cooled. Keep the whole in a vessel for a month, frequently stirring. Then take the raisins from the cask, and closely stop the liquor in the vessel. In a month rack it into another vessel, leaving the sediment. Repeat till it becomes fine; then add to every 10 gallons, 6 lbs. of fine sugar, and 12 Seville oranges, the rinds being pared very thin, and infused in two quarts of brandy, to be added to the liquor at its last racking. Let the whole stand three months in a cask and it will be fit for bottling. It should remain in bottles twelve months. To give it the flavour of Madeira, put in, when it is in the cask, two green citrons, to remain till the wine is bottled.

RANCID BUTTER, *to cure.*—Melt it in a water-bath with powdered charcoal, and strain through flannel.

RASPBERRY.—This plant is well known. The leaves are astringent, and very useful in lax and flux. A decoction or infusion has often restrained diarrhœa when all other remedies have failed. Besides, the infusion made strong removes canker, or morbific matter from the mouth, throat, stomach, bowels, and other parts of the body. Made into a poultice, i. e. in infusion, with slippery elm, or bread, it is effectual in removing proud flesh, inflammation, &c. The infusion is a good gargle for sore mouth, &c.

RASPBERRY BRANDY.—Pick fine dry fruit, put into a stone jar, and the jar into a kettle of water, or on a hot hearth, till the juice will run; strain, and to every pint add half a lb. of sugar; give one boil and skim it; when cold, put equal quantities of juice and brandy; shake well and bottle. Some people prefer it stronger of the brandy.

RASPBERRY CAKES.—Pick out the bad raspberries that are among the fruit, weigh and boil what quantity you choose, and when mashed and the liquor is wasted, put to it sugar the weight of the fruit; mix it well off the fire till it is well dissolved, then put it on plates to dry in the sun; as soon as the top part dries, cut with the cover of a canister into small cakes, turn them on fresh plates; when dry put them in boxes with layers of paper.

RASPBERRY CREAM.—Mash the fruit gently, and let it drain; then sprinkle a little sugar over, and that will produce more juice; put it through a hair sieve to take out the seeds; then put the juice to some cream, and sweeten it; after which, if you choose to lower it with some milk, it will not curdle; which it would if put to the milk before the cream; but it is best made of raspberry-jelly, instead of jam, when the fresh fruit cannot be obtained.

Another way.—Boil 1 oz. of isinglass shavings in three pints of cream and new milk mixed, for fifteen minutes, or until the former be melted; strain it through a hair sieve, into a basin; when cool, put about half a pint of raspberry-juice or syrup to the milk and cream; stir it till well incorporated, sweeten, and add a glass of brandy; whisk it about till three parts cold. Then put it into a mould till quite cold. In summer use the fresh juice; in winter syrup of raspberries.

RASPBERRY DROPS.—Pounded loaf sugar, ¼ lb. upon a plate, and a quantity of raspberries, which must be passed through a sieve; then add the juice to the sugar, till it makes a thickish paste; dress it on fine cap paper, and place it on the stove to dry.

RASPBERRY DUMPLINGS.—Make a puff paste, and roll it out; spread raspberry jam, and make it into dumplings; boil them an hour; pour melted butter into a dish, and strew grated sugar.

RASPBERRY FRITTERS.—Grate two Naples biscuits; pour over them a glass of boiling cream; when it is almost cold, beat the yolks of four eggs to a strong froth; beat the biscuits a little; then beat both together very much. Add 2 ozs. of sugar, and as much raspberry juice as will make it a pretty pink colour, and give it a proper sharpness: drop them into a pan of boiling lard, the size of a walnut. When dished up, stick bits of citron in some, and blanched almonds, cut lengthways in others. Lay round them green and yellow sweetmeats.

RASPBERRY JAM.—Weigh equal quantities of fruit and sugar, put the former into a preserving pan, boil and break it, stir constantly, and let it boil very quickly; when most of the juice is wasted add the sugar, and simmer, skim half an hour. This way the jam is greatly superior in colour and flavour to that which is made by putting the sugar in first.—It is best to put the juice of the raspberry through a hair sieve, to keep out the seeds. Some put 1 lb. of sugar to a pint of pulp.

RASPBERRY JELLY.—Take six quarts of ripe raspberries and one of ripe currants, press out the juice and strain it, to a pint of juice add 1 lb. of loaf sugar, and finish as other jellies.

RASPBERRY PASTE.—Put any quantity of raspberries into a hair sieve; press their juice into a preserving pan, put it on the fire, and stir constantly till of a thick consistence. To each lb. of pulp, add 1 lb of loaf sugar, clarified, and boiled to the blow. Let it boil a minute or two. Pour into glasses, or upon plates. It is a delicious confectionery.

RASPBERRIES, *to preserve.*—Take raspberries that are not too ripe, and put them to their weight in sugar, with a little water. Boil softly, and do not break them; when they are clear, take them up, and boil the syrup till it be thick enough; then put them in again, and when they are cold, put them in glasses or jars.

RASPBERRY SANDWICH.—Take ½ lb. of flour, ½ lb. of sifted sugar, ¼ lb. of butter, three eggs, and 2 ozs. of ground rice; mix very well first without the flour; then add it gradually. Spread it in oblong pieces on buttered paper, about ¼ inch thick; on the first piece put a layer of raspberry preserve or jam; lay another piece of paste on the top of the preserves; then preserves again, and lastly a layer of paste. Bake in a brisk oven, and when wanted, cut like sandwiches.

RASPBERRY TART.—Roll out some thin paste, and lay it in a dish or patty-pan. Put in the raspberries, strew over them fine sugar, cover the dish with a fine crust, and bake it. When done, cut it open, and put in warm half a pint of cream, the yolks of two or three eggs well beaten, and a little sugar. Replace it in the oven for five or six minutes and serve it up.

RASPBERRY TOURTE.— The difference between tarts and *tourtes* is, that the first are always covered with paste, whilst the latter are sent to table open, or with a slight network, or trellis of paste over the fruit. Puff paste having been laid in a proper tin, pour in enough jam to fill the dish, place strings of paste across, let it brake for half an hour, but never serve it hot.

RASPBERRY VINEGAR.—Put 1 lb. of fine fruit into a bowl, and pour upon it a pint of the best vinegar; next day strain the liquor on 1 lb. of fresh raspberries; and the following day do the same, but do not squeeze the fruit, only drain the liquor as dry as you can from it; the last time pass it through a canvass, previously wet with vinegar, to prevent waste; put it into a stone jar, with 1 lb. of lump sugar to every pint of juice; stir it when melted; then put the jar into a saucepan of water. Simmer, and skim it; when cold, bottle it.

Another.—Press out the juice of 3 pints of raspberries through a hair sieve to retain the seeds; put to the juice a pint of the best vinegar; add 1 lb. of powdered loaf sugar. Let all be in a pipkin, and place it in a pan of water on the fire. Simmer 20 minutes, and filter through fine muslin. Cool, bottle and cork well. It is a very cooling beverage for thirst, colds, fevers, and inflammatory complaints. A teaspoonful or two in a tumbler of cold water. It may be made effervescing by using carbonate of soda.

RASPBERRY WATER ICE.—Ripe raspberries, 2 quarts; ripe cherries and currants, 1 lb. each; sugar, 4 lbs.; water, 1 quart, and the juice of two lemons. Crush the fruit, and pass it through a sieve; mix all together, and freeze.

RASPBERRY WINE. — To every quart of well picked raspberries put a quart of water; bruise and let them stand two days; strain off the liquor, and to every gallon put 3 lbs. of lump sugar; when dissolved put the liquor into a barrel, and when fine, which will be in about two months, bottle it, and to each bottle put a tablespoonful of brandy.

RASPBERRY or CURRANT WINE.—To every three pints of fruit carefully cleared from mouldy or bad, put one quart of water; bruise the former. In twenty-four hours strain the liquor, and put to every quart 1 lb. of good sugar. If for white currants, then you must use lump sugar. It is best to put the fruit and sugar in a large pan, and when in three or four days the scum rises, take that off before the liquor be put into the barrel.—Those who make from their own gardens may not have a sufficiency to fill the barrel at once; the wine will not hurt if made in the pan, in the above proportions, and added as the fruit ripens, and can be gathered in dry weather. Keep an account of what is put in each time.

RATAFIA.—Blanch 2 ozs. of peach and apricot kernels, bruise and put them into a bottle, and fill nearly up with brandy. Dissolve ½ lb. of white sugar-candy in a cup of cold water, and add it to the brandy after it has stood a month on the kernels, and they are strained off; then filter through paper, and bottle for use. The leaves of peach and nectarines, when the trees are cut in the spring, being distilled, are an excellent substitute for ratafia in puddings.

RATAFIA.—Nutmegs, 4 ozs.; bitter almonds, 5 lbs.; fine sugar, 4 lbs.; ambergris, 5 grains. Infuse the whole 3 days in 4 or 5 gallons of proof spirit; then filter for use. The nutmegs and bitter almonds must be bruised, and the ambergris rubbed with the sugar in a mortar, before the spirit is added.

RATAFIA CAKES. — Sweet almonds, ½ lb.; the same of bitter: blanch and beat them fine in orange, rose, or clear water, to keep them from oiling: sift 1 lb. of fine sugar, and mix it with the almonds; have ready the whites of 4 eggs: mix them lightly with the almonds and sugar; put it into a preserving pan; set it over a moderate fire, and stir it quick one way, till pretty hot; when a little cool, make it into small rolls, and cut it in thin cakes; dip your hands in flour, and shake them on it; give each a slight tap with the finger; put them on sugar papers, and sift fine sugar over them just as you put them into the oven, which should be slow.

RATAFIA CREAM. — Boil three or four laurel, peach, or nectarine leaves, in a full pint of cream; strain it; and when cold, add the yolks of three eggs beaten and strained, sugar, and a large spoonful of brandy stirred quick into it. Scald till thick, stirring it all the time.

RATAFIA DROPS.—Blanch and beat in a mortar 4 ozs. of bitter, and 2 ozs. of sweet almonds, with a little of 1 lb. of sugar sifted, and add the remainder of the sugar and the whites of two eggs, making a paste; of which put little balls, the size of a nutmeg, on waferpaper, and bake gently upon tin plates.

RATAFIA OF CHERRIES— Upon 3 lbs of ripe cherries, put a lb. of raspberries; bruise them together, and put through a sieve the next day, to mix with as much brandy and 1 lb. of sugar for each pint of liquor; you may also put the stones and kernels, pounded, into a vessel to infuse in a warm place about six weeks; strain as usual. Ratafia of currants, &c., may be made in the same manner.

RATAFIA PUDDING. —— Cream, 1 pint; the same of milk flavoured with bitter almonds, (blanched and bruised,) cinnamon, lemon peel, and two bay leaves; sugar to your taste; add a little salt. When boiled, strain it upon the crumb of two French rolls. Butter the mould, and put into it ¼ lb. of ratafia cakes. Beat up 3 eggs, and mix them with the bread and milk. Pour these ingredients into a mould, and boil an hour. Serve with wine sauce.——N. B. The ratafia cake may be divided. The above also will make two puddings.

RATS, *to destroy.*—Mix powdered nux vomica, with oatmeal, crumbs of cheese, and a quantity of lard. For a few nights omit the nux vomica till they become familiar with the other food.——Or, add, instead of nux vomica, powdered phosphorus. Mix with a piece of wood, that the rats may not scent your hands. Place it beyond the reach of other animals. The addition of a little oil of amber attracts the rats.——Or, cut cork into very fine bits, and fry them with lard and cheese crumbs. When cold, add oil of amber to entice them.-—Or, take oil of amber, ox-gall, and powdered phosphorus, in equal parts, add oatmeal sufficient to form a paste, which make into little balls, and lay them near the places visited by rats. Surround the balls with vessels full of water. The smell of the oil attracts the rats; they greedily devour the balls, which make them thirsty, and they kill themselves with drinking the water.

The asphodel is useful in driving away rats and mice, which have such an antipathy to this plant, that if their holes be stopped up with it they will rather die than pass.

It is a good thing to put gas tar in the runs and holes of rats. When once daubed with it they will come no more.

Feed them well for a week with fresh oatmeal, every day; but never touch it with your hand; put it into a dish pressed down that you may see what quantity they have eaten. Then mix another lot, with 4 drops of oil of aniseed, or oil of rhodium; feed with this two or three days more. Then give the following mixture:—To 4 ozs. of dry oatmeal, scented with 6 drops of oil of aniseed, add ½ oz. of carbonated barytes, or nux vomica in powder, sifted through muslin. Mix this intimately with the scented oatmeal; then lay it upon the slate, or, leave it 24 hours for the rats to eat. This kills them. Keep the mixture from dogs, cats, or other animals, and from children.

RAZOR, *to sharpen*.—The simplest method of sharpening a razor is to put it for half an hour in water to which has been added one twentieth of its weight of muriatic or sulphuric acid, and after a few hours set it on a hone. The acid acts as a whetstone, by corroding the whole surface uniformly, so that nothing further than a smooth polish is necessary.

RAZOR, *to smooth*.—Pass the razor on the inside of your hand, first warming it before the fire. Or use the strap of a soldier's knapsack, or calf leather, on which some fine black lead has been rubbed and consolidated to a slight surface.

RAZOR STROP AND PASTE.—It may be made of rough calf leather, two or three inches broad, or of the strap of a soldier's knapsack. Upon it spread powdered oxalic acid and candle snuffs, with a little tallow.——Or spread upon it crocus martis and fine tallow.——Or, emery ground as fine as possible, mixed with spermaceti or fine tallow.——Or, glue, half ounce; treacle, quarter ounce; steep the glue in water to soften it, and then boil both together for a few minutes, add crocus martis, or fine emery powder, and then spread on the leather. When you use it apply first a drop or two of sweet oil.

RECEIPTS.—Always keep your receipts above six years. It is generally supposed that it is sufficient to keep receipts for six years; this is not so: the period for bringing an action on a simple contract debt being limited by an Act of Parliament, which is called the Statute of Limitations, to six years from the time the debt is due; and it may happen that the action may be commenced some time previous to the expiration of the six years, without the party who is sued having any knowledge of it, so that it is unsafe to destroy receipts immediately on the expiration of the six years; you should keep them for six years and a half.

RED CABBAGE, *to pickle*.—Slice it into a colander, and sprinkle each layer with salt; let it drain two days, then put it into a jar, with boiling vinegar enough to cover it, and put in a few slices of beet-root. Observe to choose the purple red-cabbage. Those who like the flavour of spice will boil some pepper-corns, mustard-seed, or other spice, *whole*, with the vinegar. Cauliflower in branches, and thrown in after being salted, will colour a beautiful red.

RED FIRE.—Forty parts of dry nitrate of strontian, thirteen parts of finely-powdered sulphur, five parts of chlorate of potash, and four parts of sulphuret of antimony. The chlorate of potash and sulphuret of antimony should be powdered separately in a mortar, then mixed on paper, after which add to the other ingredients previously powdered and mixed.

RED HERRINGS, *to dress.*—Choose those that are large and moist; cut them open and pour some boiling small beer over them to soak half an hour; drain them dry, and make them just hot through before the fire; rub some cold butter over them. Egg sauce, or buttered eggs, or mashed potatoes should be served up with them.

REGISTRATION OF BIRTHS.—An infant should be registered within six weeks after birth. No fee is payable; but after 42 days a fee of 7s. 6d. is chargeable.

REGISTRATION OF DEATHS.—Notice should be given of deaths to the district registrar. Let this be done early, that the undertaker may have a certificate to give the minister who performs the funeral service.

RED CEMENT.—Black resin, five parts; yellow wax, one part. Melt, and stir in gradually red ochre, or Venetia red in fine dry powder. This cement must be melted before using, and also the glass, china, &c. must be made hot before it is applied.

RED INK.—The finest Brazil wood, 6 ozs.; cochineal powdered, 1 oz.; alum, ½ oz.; best vinegar, 1 pint; water, a cupful. Boil slowly in a brass pan for one hour. Put the cochineal in when three-fourths boiled. Add 1 oz. of gum arabic.

RENNET, *for curdling cheese, to prepare.*—Take the stomach of a calf as soon as it is killed, and scour inside and out with salt, after it is cleared of the curd always found in it. Let it drain a few hours; then sew it up with two good handfuls of salt in it, or stretch it on a stick well salted, or keep it in the salt wet, and soak a bit, which will do over and over again by adding fresh water.

RESIN OINTMENT.—Yellow wax, 3 ozs.; white resin, 6 ozs.; hog's lard, 8 ozs. Melt together slowly, stirring till it is intimately mixed. It is very good for burns and scalds, for dressing blisters, when a discharge must be kept up for a few days; it has a stimulating influence.

RESPIRATION.—It is not every person that knows how to breathe. Our artificial modes of living, sedentary habits, cramped attitudes, the constraint of clothing, weaken and compress the respiratory organs, and hinder their development. The breath is shortened, and life is shortened in consequence. Animals breathe with the whole body. Well-developed persons in full health breathe in the same way. The vivifying air goes to the bottom of the lungs, and the entire system seems to swell and undulate, and sink again at the flow and ebb of the aërial tide; but the seamstress over her sewing, the editor over his desk, the sloth who sits on a curve of his spinal column, the young lady whose waist is compassed by the smallest possible girdle, use only the top of the lungs in respiration, wearing out that portion of them, while the lower portion is left to decay for want of proper exercise. Consumption is most commonly the result of imperfect respiration; and many other evils point back to the same cause. The throat becomes diseased, and the voice weak and hollow, so that utterance is painful to both speaker and hearer. Let every person who reads this, watch himself, and see whether respiration is deep and full, or shallow and short. If the latter, this is what he must do: correct his attitudes, always sitting erect; loosen his clothing, so that there will be plenty of play for the lower muscles used in the process of breathing; and regularly each day exercise those muscles by filling his lungs and expanding his chest, especially in the depths of it, by muscular discipline of the shoulders and arms, by reading and talking with the lungs well filled, and by making the respiration at all times as long and deep as possible.

RESTORATIVE WINE BITTERS.—Quassia, ¼ oz.; golden seal, 2 drachms; bitter-root, 2 drachms; cayenne pepper, 2 drachms; whitewood bark, 2 drachms. Bruise all, and add 1 pint of Hollands gin, and 2 quarts of wine. A less quantity may be made. Dose, a table-spoonful or two twice a day. Remarkably useful in indigestion.

Another, by Dr. Thompson of America.—Balmony bark, 1 part; poplar bark, 5 parts. Boil in water sufficient to strain from 1 lb. 2½ gallons of water, to which add— sugar, 3½ lbs.; nerve powder, 2½ ozs.; while hot, strain and add— best Malaga wine, 3½ gallons; tincture of meadow-fern, 1 quart; prickly ash seeds, 1 quart.—A less quantity may be made. Dose, from half to a wine-glassful twice a day.—These bitters are *priceless.* They are sure to correct the bile, and create an appetite, by giving tone to the digestive powers, and may be freely used, both as a restorative, and as a preventive of disease.

RHENISH WINE.—To every gallon of the juice of apple, soon as it comes from the press, add 2 lbs. of loaf sugar; boil as long as any scum arises; strain through a sieve, and let it cool. Add some good yeast, and stir it well. Let it stand in the tub for two or three weeks, or till the head begins to flatten: skim off the head, draw it clear off, and tun it. In 10 or 12 months rack it off, and fine it with isinglass. Add a pint of brandy to every three gallons. This wine will be found very superior.

RHEUMATISM. — This disease commonly occurs in autumn and spring, and seldom in winter or summer, unless the vicissitudes of heat and cold be sudden and frequent. In a plethoric habit, or when attended with fever or super-irritation, it is called *acute* or *inflammatory rheumatism;* and when with sub-irritation, *chronic rheumatism.*

Acute Rheumatism.—Its symptoms are fever, with pain, swellings, and redness of the joints, as the knees, hips, ancles, shoulders, elbows, wrists, &c. The *fever* rarely continues violent more than *fourteen* days, although sometimes the *pain* keeps shifting from one joint to another for some weeks. The pain and sometimes the fever are much increased in the evening, and the former, during night, is often acute. As the pains become fixed the fever generally abates.

It is caused by exposure to cold, when the body is unusually warm, or by its *partial* application, or from a *continuance* of cold, as wet clothes, &c.

Treatment.—In the first place, clear the stomach and bowels by aperients and emetics. If the skin is hot and dry, sponge the body all over with warm water and carbonate of soda, or common soda. If the skin is not very hot and dry, give the vapour bath of bitter herbs. Dry well, and apply the *Stimulating Liniment.* Repeat every day. From ten to thirty drops of colchicum or meadow saffron may be given two or three times a day, in a wine-glass half

w

full of the camphorated mixture. The Diaphoretic Powder is very useful in this disease; also an aperient of senna, manna, and cream of tartar, in solution. Use the Rheumatic liquid, except in case of great debility. In such cases, the *camphorated spirit*, combined with *tincture of aconite* and *oil of hemlock*. This is an excellent rubefacient. Apply it two or three times a-day. It always reduces the swelling and mitigates the pain. The *Alterative Syrup* is very effectual in the cure of rheumatism.

Chronic Rheumatism.—This sometimes succeeds the acute. It is not so painful, but it abides longer. The period of acute rheumatism seldom exceeds 40 days; after which, if the pain continue, it may be pronounced *chronic*. The joints most surrounded by muscles, and the parts most required for bodily exertion, as the hip and the loins, are commonly the seats of this complaint. When it affects the hip joint, it is called *Sciatica*, and when situated in the loins, *Lumbago*.

Treatment.—Keep the evacuations and secretions regular, as directed under acute rheumatism. Take the Diaphoretic Powder constantly on going to bed. Apply to the body the Rheumatic Liquid. Take the following:—

The sarsaparilla root, sliced and bruised, 6 ozs.; sassafras, shavings of guiac wood, liquorice root, of each 1 oz.; mezereon, 3 drachms; distilled water, 10 pints. Macerate for 6 hours; then boil down to 5 pints; adding the mezereon and sassafras a few minutes before taking off. Strain for use. A pint nearly should be taken every day.

Alkalies are very useful. Take ½ oz. of bicarbonate of soda, and put it into a pint of pure water. Dose,—a table-spoonful two or three times a-day. The vapour bath is also very serviceable, after which rub the body well with the *Stimulating Liniment*. It is a good thing to envelop the joints in carded cotton, covered with oiled silk, or gutta percha sheeting: this acts as a vapour bath, by excluding the air. White mustard seed taken inwardly may be tried; also, a decoction of Peruvian bark, sassafras, and gum guiac. Bitters and mild purgatives render great benefit. Friction by the flesh brush, electricity, or galvanism, should be tried. The warm baths of Buxton and Matlock are of essential service. The Miscellaneous remedies are invaluable.

RHEUMATISM.—To those who dwell in damp districts, or damp houses, and are hence subject to rheumatism, coughs, colds, &c., the free use of *Lemon Juice*, (when strained, and where it does not disagree with the stomach) is a most effectual preventive as well as a remedy. I have found the regular use of a wine-glassful or two a day so to strengthen a very delicate constitution, liable to cold on the slightest occasions, that in a short time it defied not only damp, but every inclemency, and all exposure.

A Correspondent of the *Medical Circular* vouches for the relief he has experienced in the liberal use of *lime (fresh lemon) juice*, while labouring under the paroxysms of rheumatism. By repeated indulgence in the above simple acid, for the space of three days, avoiding all stimulating liquids, the most confirmed rheumatism will, he says relax, and the tone of the muscular and nervous system will be restored to its usual character. The fact was first established by the circumstance of the Jews being, as a general body, scarcely ever affected with the above disease, and this particular exemption from the malady under consideration, as affecting the disciples of the Hebrew persuasion, was, and has been, attributed to the very free indulgence which the above people exercise in their dietary consumption of lemon juice.

When lemon juice disagrees, either of the two following formulæ may be substituted:—Lemon juice (strained or filtered) and treacle, equal parts; powdered sugar candy, sufficient; mix intimately,—a table-spoonful three or four times a day.

Or, take powdered rhubarb, 2 drachms; acetate of potash, 1 oz.; guaiacum, 1 drachm; sulphur 2 ozs.; 1 nutmeg, grated very fine; treacle, 1 lb. Mix, and take two tea-spoonfuls night and morning.

The seat of rheumatism is in the muscles — electro-galvanism must be used; it is generally the best plan to begin with currents of the weakest power, and gradually to increase their strength so long as the application causes no pain. Dumb bells should be used above all, every day; they should never exceed in weight 1 lb. for ladies and 4 lbs. for men. Silk is the best non-conductor of cold we have, and it is affirmed that those of the fair sex who wear tight fitting sleeves to their silk dresses are not subject to rheumatism; males should wear thick silk sleeves to all their waistcoats; they can be easily taken off, and tacked or sewn on to another vest; besides the above precautions, flannel must be worn summer and winter by day, "but never by night," next the skin: at night a small flannel spencer or jacket should be worn over the night dress.

Tailors and milliners have much to answer for in introducing such modern inventions as the wide sleeves, and in like manner "the apology of a bonnet;" this last, the cause of tic doloreux, rheumatism, &c.

RHEUMATISM.—To prevent, wear washed wool under the feet. To cure, use the cold bath with rubbing and sweating.—— Or, apply warm steams.——Or, rub in warm treacle, and apply to the part brown paper smeared therewith; change it in twelve hours.——Or, drink half a pint of tar-water morning and evening.——Or steep six or seven cloves of garlic in half a pint of white wine: drink it lying down. It sweats, and frequently cures at once.——Or, mix flour of brimstone with honey, in equal quantities, take three teaspoonfuls at night, two in the morning, and one afterwards, morning and evening, till cured. This succeeds oftener than any remedy I have found.— *Wesley.*

RHEUMATISM. — Extract of Sarsaparilla, 1 ounce. Triturate in a pint of boiling water. Dissolve 2 drachms of Iodine of Potass; and begin with small doses twice or thrice a day. Very valuable.

The application of wheat, bran, or oatmeal poultice, diluted with muriatic acid water, or the tincture of lobelia water, has often been known to give relief.

RHEUMATISM.-Take a large handful of buckbean, four ounces of white mustard seeds, and one of lignum vitæ, or wood of life, to two quarts of water; boil to three pints. Dose—three tea-cupfuls a day. Use also the following *Liniment.* Take of sal volatile, three ounces; oil, one ounce, camphor, quarter of an ounce, laudanum, one ounce. Rub the part affected with this liniment three times a day.

RHEUMATISM, *Embrocation*

for, and for *Lumbago* or *Strains*— ½ oz. spirits of turpentine, ½ oz. of strongest camphorated spirit, 1 raw egg, half pint of best vinegar. Well mix the whole, and keep it closely corked. To be rubbed in three or four times a day. For rheumatism in the head, or face-ache, rub all over the back of the head and neck, as well as the part which is the immediate seat of pain.

RHEUMATISM, *Embrocation for.*—Olive oil, 2 ozs.; water of ammonia, 2 drachms; oil of rosemary, 10 drops; oil of cloves, 5 drops. Mix, and keep tightly corked.

RHEUMATIC DECOCTION —Virginian snake root, 1 drachm; sarsaparilla in powder, 6 drachms; burdock seed, 2 drachms; poke root, 2 drachms; wine-pine bark, 2 drachms; cayenne pepper, ¼ drachm. Powder them, and add 3 quarts of water. Boil down to 2 quarts. A cupful two or three times a day. It is most valuable in chronic rheumatism.

RHEUMATIC DROPS.—Extract of sarsaparilla, 2 drachms; gum camphor, ¼ drachm; laudanum, 1 scruple; spirit of wine, 1 oz. Mix and macerate 24 hours. Take from 20 to 50 drops three times a day.

RHEUMATIC GOUT, *Draught for.*—Camphorated mixture, seven drachms; infusion of rhubarb, five drachms; tincture of henbane, half a drachm; subcarbonate of potass, ten grains. Mix for a draught; take two or three a day, particularly the last thing at night.—It is a most excellent remedy.

RHEUMATIC LINIMENT.- Take sassafras oil, 2 ozs.; tincture of prickly ash, 1 oz.; tincture of cayenne, 1 oz.; hemlock oil, 1 oz. Mix, and rub well in. A few applications will relieve, if not cure.

Another.—Tincture of cayenne, oil of turpentine, olive oil, hemlock oil, gum camphor, sassafras oil, tincture of prickly ash, of each, 1 oz.; *powdered* capsicum, or cayenne, 1 oz.; spirit of wine, 2 quarts; vinegar, 1 quart; ammonia, 1 quart; add 2 ozs. of gum camphor. Mix; put in a vessel, and stir occasionally till mixed and dissolved. This is a magic liniment, soon giving ease in rheumatic pains, gout, neuralgia, sprains, &c., &c. It is worth much gold. It seldom or never fails.

RHEUMATIC LIQUID.— Sarsaparilla, powdered, 2 ozs.; cayenne pepper, 1 oz.; gum myrrh, ½ oz.; brandy, or Hollands gin, 2 quarts. Let it stand a few days. A teaspoonful in tea, or water sweetened. This is excellent for rheumatism, gout, &c.

RHEUMATIC LIQUID, *for External application.* See RHEUMATISM, *Embrocation for.*——Or, RHEUMATIC LINIMENT. —— Or, RHEUMATIC PAINS, *in the bones and joints.*

RHEUMATIC MIXTURE.— Saltpetre, sulphur, powdered mustard, Turkey rhubarb, sarsaparilla powder, of each, ½ oz.; powdered gum guiacum, ¼ oz. Mix. Take a teaspoonful every other night for three nights; then omit three nights, in a wine-glassful of cold water.

RHEUMATIC PAINS, *in the bones and joints.*—Take opodeldoc, one ounce; tincture of cantharides, three drachms; spirits of sal ammoniac, three drachms; rectified oil of amber, three drachms. This forms a liniment, wherewith frequently to rub the painful part. Wrap up in fine, soft flannel, and keep warm.

Or, take friar's balsam and tincture of myrrh, of each, one ounce;

spirits of turpentine, two ounces, and good old strong ale dregs, three ounces; mix all of them well together, and bathe the afflicted part with the same.

Or, take a raw egg well beaten, half a pint of brandy; 1½ oz. of turpentine; ½ oz. of spirits of wine, and 1 oz. of camphor; and a table spoonful of salt. Put them into a wine bottle, and shake well. This liniment is to be well rubbed on the affected parts three or four times a day. It has often effected a cure in a few days.

RHEUMATIC PILL.—Gum guiacum, ½ drachm; compound powder of ipecacuanha, ½ drachm; confection of opium, 10 grains; mix, and divide into 20 pills. Take two on going to bed.

RHEUMATIC POWDER.— Ipecacuanha powder, and purified opium, of each, 1 part; sulphate of potass, 8 parts; triturate them together to a fine powder. Be very careful to reduce the opium, and intimately mix with the rest. This powder is recommended by Dr. Dover as an effectual remedy for rheumatism. The dose is from two to five grains, repeated. Avoid much drinking after taking it, or it might act as an emetic.

RHUBARB.—It is a mild purgative, operating without violence and irritation. It is a suitable aperient for females and children. It is astringent, and increases the tone of the stomach and intestines, and is very useful in diarrhœa, and disorders proceeding from laxity. It is given chiefly in powder, and operates more powerfully as a purgative in this form than any other. The dose for an adult is about a scruple, or rather more.

RHUBARB, *Compound Pills of.*—Rhubarb, in powder, 1 oz.; socotrine aloes, 6 drachms; myrrh, ½ oz.; oil of peppermint, ½ a drachm; make into a mass with syrup of orange peel. This is a gentle aperient. Four may be taken night and morning.

RHUBARB PIE.—Strip off the skin of the tender stalks of the plant; stew till soft, and sweeten; add a little ginger, and grated lemon peel; put it into a baking dish, and cover with paste. Clip two or three holes in the top, to allow evaporation.

RHUBARB POWDER, *for Diarrhœa.*—Powdered rhubarb, and columba, of each, 3 grains. To be taken every three hours.—— Or, take a bolus of 3 grains of powder; opiate confection, 6 grains. To be taken every four hours.

RHUBARB TARTS.—Take rhubarb stalks which grow in the garden, peel them, and cut them into small pieces. Then do in every respect as in making a gooseberry tart.

RHUBARB, *Tincture of.*—— Rhubarb, two ounces and a half; lesser cardamom seeds, half an ounce; brandy, two pints; digest for a week, and strain.——Or, infuse the above ingredients in a pint of Lisbon wine, adding to it two ounces of proof spirits. If an ounce of gentian root and a drachm of Virginia snake root be added, it will make the bitter tincture of rhubarb. All these tinctures are stomachics and corroborants, as well as purgatives. In weakness of the stomach, indigestion, laxity of the intestines, fluxes, and colicky complaints, they are of great service. The dose is from half a spoonful to three or four spoonfuls or more.

RHUBARB WINE, *(beverage)* —Take the stems of full grown rhubarb, and bruise them in a mortar to a pulp. Put the pulp into a tub, and to every 10 lbs. weight of the stems, add two gallons of cold spring water. Infuse for 4 days, stirring oft. Then press the pulp and strain off the liquor. Put the liquor into a tub, and to every gallon of the liquor add 2 lbs. of fine sugar, stirring till the sugar is dissolved. Let it stand 3 or 4 days till the fermentation stops. Skim it well; put it into a cask, but do not stop it, as it will ferment again. When the fermentation ceases, add more loaf sugar to sweeten it, and stop it close. In two months it will be fit to bottle. Add a little brandy. It improves with age.

RHUBARB WINE, *(medicinal.)*—Sliced rhubarb, 2½ ozs.; lesser cardamon seeds, bruised and husked, ½ oz.; saffron, 2 drachms; sherry wine, 1 pint; proof spirit, half a pint. Digest for 10 days, and strain.

RICE, *buttered.*—Wash and pick some rice, drain, and put it with some new milk, just enough to swell it, over the fire; when tender, pour off the milk, and add a bit of butter, a little sugar, and pounded cinnamon. Shake it, do not burn, and serve.

RICE, *to eat with curry.*—Wash and strain the rice; just cover it with boiling water; add salt; stir well, and boil quickly. When sufficiently swelled, drain off the water, and pour the rice on the shallow end of a sieve. Put it before a fire till it separates and dries. Serve without sauce.

RICE CAKE.—Ground rice and sifted white sugar, of each, 8 ozs.; essence of almonds, 8 drops; five eggs beaten well; the rind of a lemon grated, a little nutmeg, or cinnamon, and 2 ozs. of butter. Mix all well together. Bake as a whole cake, or drop upon a buttered tin. Put upon the top buttered white paper.

RICE CAUDLE.—When the water boils, pour into it ground rice mixed with a little cold water; when of a proper consistence, add sugar, lemon-peel, and cinnamon, and a glass of brandy to a quart. Boil all smooth.

Another.—Soak some Carolina rice in water an hour, strain it, and put two spoonfuls of the rice into a pint and a quarter of milk; simmer till it will pulp through a sieve, then put the pulp and milk into a saucepan, with a bruised clove and a bit of white sugar. Simmer ten minutes; if too thick, add a spoonful or two of milk, and serve with a thin toast.

RICE CHEESECAKES.—See page 104.

RICE CUSTARDS.—Boil 3 pints of new milk with a bit of lemon-peel, cinnamon, and 3 bay leaves; sweeten: then mix a large spoonful of rice flour into a cup of cold milk, very smooth; mix it with the yolks of 4 eggs well beaten. Take a basin of the boiling milk, and mix with the cold that has the rice in it; add the remainder of the boiling milk; stir it one way till it boils; pour immediately into a pan; stir till cool, and add a spoonful of brandy, or orange-flower water.

RICE FLUMMERY.—Boil with a pint of new milk, a bit of lemon-peel, and cinnamon; mix with a little cold milk, as much rice-flour as will make the whole of a good consistence, sweeten, and add a spoonful of peach-water, or a bitter almond beaten; boil it, observing it does not burn; pour it into a shape or pint-basin, taking out the spice. When cold, turn the flummery into a dish, and serve with cream, milk, or custard round; or put a tea-cupful of cream into half a pint of new milk, a glass of white wine, half a lemon squeezed, and sugar.

RICE-GLUE, or CEMENT.—Mix rice-flour with water, the same as in making paste, (See Paste) and gently simmer over the fire till it boils. It is used in making ornaments, and for joining paper and cardboard.

RICE MILK.—Put 1 lb. of Carolina rice into a pan with 2 ozs. of butter, two quarts of water, a bit of cinnamon or lemon-peel, and salt; boil very gently until the rice is soft; about one hour and a quarter; then add three pints of milk and an egg well beaten; stir it over the fire ten minutes longer, and sweeten it with a little honey or sugar, and it will produce an excellent meal for five or six persons.

RICE MILK, *ground.*—Boil one spoonful of ground-rice, rubbed down smooth, with three half-pints of milk, a bit of cinnamon, lemon-peel, and nutmeg. Sweeten when nearly done.

RICE PANCAKES.—Cream, 1 quart; ground rice, 3 or 4 spoonfuls; stir it on a slow fire till of a proper thickness; stir in ½ lb. of butter and a nutmeg grated; then pour it out into an earthen pan; when cold, stir in four spoonfuls of flour, a little salt, some sugar, nine eggs well beaten, and, if you like, the squeeze of a lemon.

RICE PASTE *for fruits, &c.*—Boil ¼ lb. of ground rice in the smallest quantity of water, strain from it all the moisture; beat ½ oz. of butter and one egg well, and it will form an excellent paste for tarts, &c.

RICE PUDDING, *baked.*—Swell the rice with a little milk in the oven or over the fire; then add milk, egg, sugar, allspice, and lemon peel. Bake in a deep dish.

RICE PUDDING, *to boil.*—Boil ¼ lb. of rice; take it up, and stir in ¼ lb. of butter, or milk and cream; grate nutmeg and sugar according to taste; tie it up tight, and boil it another hour; when done, pour melted butter over it. Currants may be added, if you like.

RICE PUDDING, *plain.*—Wash and pick some rice; throw among it some pimento finely pounded, but not much; tie the rice in a cloth and leave plenty of room for it to swell. When done, eat it with butter and sugar, or milk. Put lemon peel if you please.

It is very good without spice, and eaten with salt and butter.

Another.—Put into a very deep pan half a pound of rice washed and picked; two ounces of butter, four ounces of sugar, a few allspice pounded, and two quarts of milk. Less butter will do, or some suet. Bake in a slow oven.

RICE PUDDING, *a rich one.*—Boil ½ lb. of rice in water, with a bit of salt, till quite tender; drain it dry; mix it with the yolks and whites of four eggs, a quarter of a pint of cream, with 2 ozs. of fresh butter melted in the latter; 4 ozs. of beef suet or marrow, or veal suet taken from a fillet of veal, finely shred, ¾ lb. of currants, two spoonfuls of brandy, one of peach-water, or ratafia, nutmeg, and a grated lemon peel. When well mixed, put a paste round the edge, and fill the dish. Slices of candied orange, lemon, and citron, if approved. Bake in a moderate oven.

RICE PUDDING, *with fruit.*—Swell the rice with a very little milk over the fire; then mix fruit of any kind with it (currants, gooseberries, scalded, pared, and quartered apples, raisins, or black currants): put one egg into the rice to bind it; boil it well, and serve with sugar.

RICE SMALL PUDDINGS.—Wash two large spoonfuls of rice, and simmer it with half a pint of milk till thick, then put the size of an egg of butter, and near half a pint of thick cream, and give it one boil. When cold, mix four yolks and two whites of eggs well beaten, sugar and nutmeg to taste; and add grated lemon and a little cinnamon.

Butter little cups, and fill three parts full, putting at the bottom some orange or citron. Bake three quarters of an hour in a slowish oven. Serve the moment before to be eaten, with sweet sauce in the dish, or a boat.

RICE WHITE POT.—Boil 1 lb. of rice in 2 quarts of new milk, till it is tender and thick; beat it in a mortar with ¼ lb. of sweet almonds blanched; then boil two quarts of cream, with a few crumbs of white bread, and a little mace. Mix all together with 8 eggs, a little rose water, and sweeten to your taste. Cut some candied orange, and citron peels, thin, and lay it in when in the oven—a *slow* oven.

RICE AND APPLE, *Soufle of.*—Blanch Carolina rice; strain, and boil it in milk with lemon-peel, and a bit of cinnamon. Boil till the rice is dry. Cool, and raise a rim three inches high round the dish, having egged the dish, where it is put, to make it stick: then egg the rice all over; fill the dish half way up with a marmalade of apples; beat the whites of 4 eggs to a fine froth, and put them over the marmalade; sift fine sugar over it, and put it in the oven.

RICE AND WHEAT BREAD.—Simmer 1 lb. of rice in two quarts of water till it becomes perfectly soft; when it is of a proper warmth mix it extremely well with 4 lbs. of flour, and yeast and salt as for other bread; of yeast about four large spoonfuls; knead it extremely well; then set it to rise before the fire. Some of the flour should be reserved to make up the loaves. If the rice should require more water, it must be added, as some rice swells more than others.

RING GOLD.-Melt together of Spanish copper six pennyweights and twelve grains; fine silver, three pennyweights and sixteen grains to one ounce, five pennyweights of gold coin. This is worth about £3 per ounce.

RING WORMS. — Dissolve borax in water, and apply till it produces redness, and a painful sensation. Discontinue a day or two, and ultimately it will effect a cure.

RING WORM.——Wash the head with soft soap every morning, and apply this lotion every night; —one drachm of sub-carbonate of soda, dissolved in half a pint of vinegar.

RING WORMS.—Apply rotten apples, or pounded garlic.—— Or, rub them with the juice of house-leek. —— Or, wash them with Hungary-water camphorated. ——Or twice a-day with oil of sweet almonds and oil of tartar mixed.—*Wesley.*

RING WORMS.—To one part of sulphuric acid, add 16 to 20 parts of water. Use a brush or feather, and apply it to the parts night and morning. A few dressings will generally cure. If the solution is too strong, dilute it with more water; and if the irritation is excessive, rub on a little oil or other softening applicant; but always avoid soap.

Dr. Chapelle adopts the following plan:—The hairs are to be cut short, the creamy fluid let out of the pustules, and the crusts removed by linseed poultices. The denuded surface is then to be covered with a thin layer of oil of naphtha, over which a flannel compress is to be placed, the whole being secured by an oil silk cap. The application is to be renewed twice a day; first well washing the parts with soap and water; the surface of the scalp is to be carefully searched, in order to detect any small favous pustules that may have appeared. These must be pricked with a pin, the matter removed, and the surface covered with the oil. This evolution of pustules is successive, so that the hair must be kept short in the vicinity, that their advent may be watched. This application secures the rapid abortion of the pustules; but when the scalp is too tender to bear it, it should be mixed with other less irritating oils of which empyrheumatic oil of juniper is one of the best.

ROLLS, *Excellent*—Warm 1 oz. of butter in half a pint of milk, put it to a spoonful and a half of yeast of small beer, and a little salt. Put 2 lbs. of flour into a pan, and mix in the above. Let it rise an hour; knead it well; make into seven rolls, and bake in a quick oven.

If made in cakes three inches thick, sliced and buttered, they resemble Sally Lunns as made at Bath.

The foregoing receipt, with the addition of a little saffron boiled in half a tea-cupful of milk, makes them remarkably good.

ROMAN CEMENT.—Roman Cement, M. Berthier says, consists of common chalk and clay—one part clay, and two and a half parts of chalk, set almost instantly.

Another.—Mix a bushel of slaked lime with 3½ lbs of green copperas, half a bushel of fine gravel sand, and 15 gallons of water. Dissolve the copperas in hot water, and stir frequently. It must be mixed the same day it is used.

ROOMS, *to fumigate for sick persons.*—Put a table-spoonful of salt in a *glass* cup, and add, at four different times, a dessert spoonful of vitriolic acid. The vapour will come in contact with the malignant miasmata, and destroy them.

ROOMS, *to take the smell of paint from.*—Place vessels of water combined with a little vitriolic acid in a newly painted room; it will absorb the effluvia in three days.

ROSES.—Put some powdered charcoal around the roots of your roses. It will improve their colour.

ROSES, *Cream of.*—Oil of sweet almonds, 1 lb.; spermaceti and white wax, of each 1 oz.; rose water, 1 pint, Malta rose or neroli essence. Put the oil, spermaceti, and wax into a well-glazed pipkin, over a clear fire, and when melted, pour in the rose water gradually, beating till the compound becomes like pomatum. Add the essences, and pot the mixture; cover well with bladder.

ROSES, *Infusion of.*—Take of red roses dried, ½ an oz.; boiling water, a quart; oil of vitriol, ½ a drachm; loaf sugar, 1 oz. Infuse the roses in the water for 4 hours, in an unglazed earthen vessel; then pour in the acid, strain the liquor, and add to it the sugar.

In an excessive flow of the menses, vomiting of blood, and other hæmorrhages, a tea-cupful of this gentle astringent infusion may be taken every three or four hours. It likewise makes an exceedingly good gargle.

ROSE CAKE.—Boil 2 lbs. of sugar in a tea-cupful of water, over a slow fire, until you perceive it begins to candy on the sides of the pan, or has reached the degree of blown; take off, and add 12 drops of the oil or otto of roses. Colour with prepared cochineal. Mix all together, and pour into small tin hoops, any shape you like. Or, pour it upon buttered paper in a tin, and dry in the oven. While rather soft, cut into shapes.

ROSE LOTION *for the eyes.* —Vitriolated zinc, 10 grains; distilled vinegar, 2 drachms; rose water, 14 drachms; make into a wash for the eyes, and apply frequently with a rag. When the eyelids are tumified, this performs a cure. Even rose water alone strengthens the eyes, and its smell is fragrant and reviving.

ROSE LEAVES, *to preserve.*— Gather them when dry; press them into a jar well sprinkled with brandy for future use. Some pack them with common salt only. *Hu.*

ROSE LOZENGES.——Boil gently 2 lbs. of sugar in a cupful of water until it begins to candy, or till it is blown; take off, and add 2 ozs. of gum arabic dissolved; then add 15 drops of the oil or otto of roses; roll out, and make into lozenges. Colour as you please. A little powdered starch, or olive oil, scented, will prevent them from sticking. Dry well. *Gu.*

ROSE WATER.-Damask Rose leaves, 6 lbs.; water sufficient to prevent burning; distil off a gallon. These leaves retain their odour if preserved as above directed

ROSEMARY.—See *Robinson's Herbal.* The *Spirit of Rosemary* is a good external application for strains and bruises. It is said to have cured a queen of Hungary of a paralytic affection. For headache, 4 drops of the oil are given in a dessert-spoonful of the spirit in a glass of water. It is good for hysterics.

ROSEMARY, *to cultivate.*—It is propagated by slips or cuttings in the spring, in a bed of light earth. When they are rooted, transplant them. The best season is in August; if they are planted later, they seldom live through winter, therefore if not transplanted at this time, they should be left till the following March, which is a very good time for removing them; if the season be showery, they take root immediately. *Hu.*

ROSEMARY POMATUM.— Melt equal parts of beef marrow, spermaceti, and olive oil. When nearly cool, add 15 drops of oil of rosemary. If not stiff enough, add a little white wax, or beef suet. *Gu.*

ROUGE.—Make a decoction of best Brazil wood, powdered, and best vinegar. Boil half an hour; strain, and replace on the fire. Dissolve ¼ lb. of alum, in a pint of best vinegar. Mix the two liquids and stir well with a wooden spatula. The scum which arises, on being carefully taken off, and gradually dried, will make a beautiful and harmless rouge, or carmine.

ROUGE ET NOIR, *Game of.*—This game is much in vogue on the continent. It takes its name of red and black, not from the cards, but from the colours marked on the green cloth with which the table is covered.

All the terms used in this game are French; nevertheless to be better understood by the general reader, we shall give them in English as well.

The game is played in the following manner:—

The tailleur and croupier sit opposite to each other, at each side of the table, with a basket, for the purpose of receiving the cards of every coup after dealing, placed on the middle of the table, just between them. The tailleur then passes round six packs of cards, to be shuffled, and mixed confusedly together by all the company.

He then shuffles them himself, putting all the end cards into various parts of the entire lot, until he comes to an honor of any kind, which being placed upright at the end, is offered to a punter or player, who puts the same into any part of the pack he thinks proper: the tailleur then separates the pack just at that part, and lays that portion of the card that was below the honor uppermost, and, taking therefrom a handful of cards, places a weight upon the remainder, and commences to deal: he takes afterwards the other portions from the heap under the weight, as they are wanted, until the whole are dealt.

He looks at the first card, and puts it face downwards: a red card and a black card are then placed back to back, and that one which is of the same colour with the first card he looked at, is placed uppermost in a conspicuous manner: these two cards that are placed back to back, are turned over each deal, if necessary, so that that card may be uppermost whose colour is the same as the turn-up card in each succeeding coup.

When the stakes are deposited, the tailleur cries "Noir" (black), and turning up the top card, places each succeeding card in a row, until the number of points of those turned up shall exceed thirty; whatever number that may happen to be he declares, at "trente et une" (one and thirty;) if above that number, he merely says, "deux, trois, quatre, cinq, six, sept, huit, neuf" (two, three, four, five, six, seven, eight, nine,) if it reaches forty, he says quarante.

Another parcel of the cards is then dealt out for Rouge, or red, until he comes to thirty-one, or the number nearest to it; and whichever colour comes nearest to that number wins the stakes; this the tailleur declares by saying "rouge gagne" (red wins) or "rouge perd" (red loses).

These two parcels, one for each colour, make coup.

When the same number is dealt and turned up for each, the tailleur says "apres," (after), which forms "un refait" (a doublet), by which neither party loses, except it is "un refait trente et une," then the tailleur wins half the stakes punted on each colour, which half the punters may either pay or have their stakes moved into the middle semicircles of the colour, they then choose on the table called "la premiere prison," (the first prison), to be determined by the next event whether they lose all or are set at liberty; but if what is called "un refait second trente et une" (a second doublet of one and thirty) should happen in the next succeeding deal, the punters lose half of their remaining moiety, or three-fourths of the stake they put down at first, and are removed into the smallest semicircle named "la seconde prison" (the second prison), and the next coup determines whether the punter loses all, or is to be removed again into the first prison.

At this game the banker cannot refuse any stake that does not exceed his funds; which the punter declares by saying "Je vais la Banque" (I aim at the bank.) Bankers most generally furnish punters with slips of card-paper ruled in columns, each marked N. or R. on the top, on which accounts are kept by pricking with a pin. Some bankers give up the profit of "un refait" during the first deal.

ROYAL FRITTERS.—Milk, 1 quart; put it into a saucepan, and as the milk boils up, pour in a pint of sherry. Boil up and take off for six minutes. Skim off all the curd, and put it into a basin. Beat it well up with six eggs; season with nutmeg, and beat it up with a whisk; add flour to make it as thick as batter; add fine sugar, and fry quick.

RUE, GARDEN.—It is very serviceable for approaching blindness, caused by disease of the optic nerve. It is a great disinfectant. In sprains, injury of the joints, rheumatic paralysis of the joints, in bed sores, even if broken and ulcerated, it is of immense service. It is best to buy the Tincture of the Homœopathic chemists. See *Robinson's Herbal.*

RUM SHRUB.—Rum, 1 pint; orange and lemon juice, of each a wine-glassful; orange and lemon peel, ¼ oz.; sugar, 1 oz.; dissolve in 1½ pint of water. A little tartaric acid may be added to give it acidity.

RUSKS.—Beat seven eggs well, and mix with ½ a pint of new milk, in which have been melted 4 ozs. of butter; add to it a ¼ lb. of yeast, and 3 ozs. of sugar, and put them by degrees into as much flour as will make a very light paste, like a batter; let it rise before the fire half an hour; then add some more flour, to make it a little stiffer. Work it well, and divide it into small loaves or cakes, about 5 or 6 inches wide, and flatten them. When baked and cold, slice them the thickness of rusks, and put them in the oven to brown a little.

Note.—The cakes, when first baked, eat deliciously buttered for tea; or, with carraways to eat cold.

RUST, *to remove from iron.*—Pound glass to a fine powder: having nailed some strong woollen cloth upon a board, lay upon it a strong coat of gum-water, and sift thereon some of the powdered glass: let it dry; repeat this operation three times, and, when the last covering of powdered glass is dry, you may easily rub off the rust from iron with the cloth thus prepared.

RUST, *to prevent.*—Lard, free from salt, 1 lb.; camphor, 1 oz.; black lead powder, and dragon's blood, finely powdered, of each, 2 drachms; melt the same on a slow fire, until it is dissolved, and let it cool for use.

If rusty iron be rubbed with a mixture of boiled oil and red lead, on a warm day, or in a warm room, it will restrain the rusting process.

SACHETS, *perfumed.* — Make ornamented bags, or packets, and insert cotton wool, and the following scents, as you please, viz:—orris root, 2 ozs.; calamus, 1 oz.; cloves, 2 drachms; dry bergamot, 1 oz.; benzoin, 4 drachms; reduce to impalpable powder, and mix intimately.

Or, dried rose leaves, 8 ozs.; cloves, 4 drachms; nutmegs, 4 drachms.

Or, orris root, 6 ozs.; dry orange flowers, and rose leaves, 16 ozs.; storax, 2 ozs.; dry bergamot, 1 oz. Powder well, and sieve. Sprinkle over the whole a few drops of oil of bergamot, and otto of roses. Keep close.

SACK CREAM.—Boil a pint of raw cream, the yolk of an egg well beaten, two or three spoonfuls of white wine, sugar, and lemon peel; stir it over a gentle fire till it be as thick as rich cream, and afterwards till cold; then serve it in glasses, with long pieces of dry toast.

SACK MEAD.—To every gallon of water put 4 lbs. of honey, and boil it three quarters of an hour, taking care to skim it. To every gallon add 1 oz. of hops; then boil it half an hour, and let it stand till next day; put it into your cask, and to thirteen gallons of the liquor, add a quart of brandy. Let it be lightly stopped till the fermentation is over, and then stop it very close. If you make a large cask, keep it a year in cask.

SAGE CHEESE.—Bruise the tops of young red sage in a mortar, with some leaves of spinach, and squeeze the juice; mix it with the rennet in the milk, more or less according as you like for colour and taste. When the curd is come, break it gently, and put it in with the skimmer, till it is pressed two inches above the vat. Press it eight or ten hours. Salt it, and turn every day.

SAGE AND ONION SAUCE.—Chop fine 2 ozs. of onion, and 1 oz. of green sage leaves; put them into a pan with a small cupful of water; simmer gently 10 minutes; then put in a teaspoonful of pepper, and some salt, and 1 oz. of fine bread crumbs; mix well together; then pour to it a ¼ pint of broth, or melted butter; stir and simmer a few minutes longer.

SAGO.—To prevent the earthly taste, soak it in cold water an hour; pour that off, and wash it well; then add more, and simmer gently till the berries are clear, with lemon peel and spice, if approved. Add wine and sugar, and boil all up together.

SAGO MILK.—Clean it well, and boil it slowly and wholly with new milk. It swells so much, that a small quantity will be sufficient for a quart, and when done it will be diminished to about a pint. It requires no sugar or flavouring.

SAGO PUDDING.——Boil a pint and a half of new milk, with four spoonfuls of sago nicely washed and picked, lemon-peel, cinnamon, and nutmeg: sweeten to taste; then mix four eggs, put a paste round the dish, and bake slowly.

Another.—Boil 4 ozs. of sago in water a few minutes; strain, and add milk, and boil till tender. Boil lemon peel and cinnamon in a little milk, and strain it to the sago. Put the whole into a basin; break 8 eggs; mix it well together, and sweeten with moist sugar; add a glass of brandy, and some nutmeg; put puff paste round the rim of the dish, and butter the bottom. Bake three quarters of an hour.

SALINE JULEP.—Dissolve two drachms of salt of tartar in three ounces of fresh lemon juice, strained; when the effervescence is over, add of mint-water and common water, each two ounces; of simple syrup, one ounce. This removes sickness at the stomach, relieves vomiting, promotes perspiration, and may be of some service in fevers especially of the inflammatory kind.

SALINE LAXATIVE POWDER.—Take of soluble tartar and cream of tartar, each 1 drachm; purified nitre, ½ drachm; make into a powder. In fevers, and other inflammatory disorders, where it is necessaay to keep the body gently open; one of these cooling laxative powders may be taken in a little gruel and repeated occasionally.

SALINE MIXTURE.—Take of crystallized acid of lemon, one drachm, or fresh lemon juice, an ounce and a half; salt of wormwood, one drachm; white sugar, three drachms; pure water, twelve ounces; essence of peppermint, thirty drops. Mix. A teacupful to be taken often in inflammatory fevers and sore throat.

SALISBURY CAKES.—To three pounds of flour, add one pound of moist sugar, to be mixed into paste with half a pint of water, and to be baked in an oven.

SALLY LUNN'S *Tea Cakes.*
——These cakes are made as follows:—Put into a pan one pint of warm milk and a quarter of a pint of thick small beer yeast, with flour sufficient to make a batter; cover it, and let it stand about two hours; then add 2 ozs. of lump sugar dissolved in a quarter of a pint of warm milk (or four eggs) and a ¼ lb. of butter rubbed into the flour; then make a dough as for French rolls; let it stand half an hour. Then make up the cakes, and put them on tins, and when they have stood to rise, bake them in a quick oven. Care should be taken never to put the yeast to the water or milk too hot or too cold; in summer it should be lukewarm, and in winter a little warmer, and in very cold weather warmer still.

SALMAGUNDY is a beautiful small dish, if in nice shape, and if the colour of the ingredients are varied. For this purpose chop separately the white part of cold chicken or veal, yolks of eggs boiled hard, the whites of eggs; parsley, half a dozen anchovies, beet-root, red pickled cabbage, ham, and grated tongue, or any thing well flavoured, and of a good colour. Some people like a small proportion of onion, but it may be better omitted. A saucer, large tea-cup, or any other base, must be put into a small dish; then make rows round it wide at bottom, and growing smaller towards the top; choosing such of the ingredients for each row as will most vary the colours. At the top a little sprig of curled parsley may be stuck in; or without any thing on the dish, the salmagundy may be laid in rows, or put into the half-whites of eggs, which may be made to stand upright by cutting off a bit at the round end. In the latter case, each half-egg has but one ingredient. Butter and parsley may be put as garnish between.

SALMON, *to choose.*—If new, the flesh is of a fine red (the gills particularly), the scales bright, and the whole fish stiff. When just killed, there is a whiteness between the flakes, which gives great firmness; by keeping, this melts down, and the fish is more rich. The Thames salmon bears the highest price; that caught in the Severn is next in goodness, and is even preferred by some. Small heads, and thick in the neck, are best.

SALMON, *to boil.*——Clean it carefully, boil it gently with salt and a little horse radish; take it out of the water as soon as done. Let the water be warm if the fish be split. If underdone it is very unwholesome. Serve with shrimp, lobster, or anchovy sauce, and fennel and butter.

SALMON, *to broil.*—Cut slices an inch thick, and season with pepper and salt; lay each slice in half a sheet of white paper well buttered, twist the ends of the paper, and broil the slices over a slow fire six or eight minutes. Serve in the paper with anchovy-sauce.

SALMON, *collared.*--Split such a part of the fish as may be sufficient to make a handsome roll, wash and wipe it, and having mixed salt, white pepper, pounded mace, and Jamaica pepper, in quantity to season it very high, rub it inside and out well. Then roll it tight and bandage it, put as much water and one third vinegar as will cover it, with bay-leaves, salt, and both sorts of pepper. Cover close, and simmer till done enough. Drain and boil quick the liquor, and put on when cold. Serve with fennel. It is an elegant dish, and extremely good.

SALMON, *dried.*—Pull some into flakes; have ready some eggs boiled hard, and chopped large; put both into half a pint of thin cream, and two or three ounces of butter rubbed with a tea-spoonful of flour; skim it and stir it till boiling hot; make a wall of mashed potatoes round the inner edge of a dish, and pour the above into it.

SALMON, *to dry.*——Cut the fish down, take out the inside and roe. Rub the whole with common salt after scaling it; let it hang 24 hours to drain. Pound three or four ounces of saltpetre, according to the size of the fish; 2 ozs. of bay-salt, and 2 ozs. of coarse sugar; rub these, when mixed well, into the salmon, and lay it on a large dish or tray two days, then rub it with common salt, and in 24 hours more it will be fit to dry; wipe it well after draining. Hang it either in a wood chimney, or in a dry place; keeping it open with two small sticks.

Dried salmon is eaten broiled in paper, and only just warmed through; egg-sauce and mashed potatoes with it; or it may be boiled, especially the bit next the head.

SALMON, *to marinate.*—Cut the salmon in slices; take off the skin, and take out the middle bone; cut each slice asunder; put into a saucepan and season with salt, pepper, 6 cloves, a sliced onion, some whole chives, a little sweet basil, parsley, and a bay leaf; then squeeze in the juice of three lemons, or use vinegar. Let the salmon lie in the marinade for two hours; take it out; dry with a cloth; dredge with flour, and fry brown in clarified butter; then lay a clean napkin in a dish; lay the slices upon it; garnish with fried parsley.

SALMON, *to pickle.*—Boil as before directed, take the fish out, and boil the liquor with bay-leaves, peppercorns, and salt; add vinegar, when cold, and pour it over the fish.

Another way.——After scaling and cleaning, split the salmon, and divide into such pieces as you choose; lay it in the kettle to fill the bottom, and as much water as will cover it; to three quarts put a pint of vinegar, a handful of salt, twelve bay-leaves, six blades of mace, and ¼ oz. of black pepper. When the salmon is boiled enough, drain it and put it on a clean cloth, then put more salmon into the kettle, and pour the liquor upon it, and so on till all is done. After this, if the pickle be not smartly flavoured with the vinegar and salt, add more, and boil it quick three quarters of an hour. When all is cold, pack the fish in something deep, and let there be enough of pickle to plentifully cover. Preserve it from the air. The liquor must be drained from the fish, and occasionally boiled and skimmed.

SALMON, *to pot.*——Take a large piece, scale and wipe, but do not wash it; salt very well; let it lie till the salt is melted and drained from it, then season with beaten mace, cloves, and whole pepper; lay in a few bay-leaves, put it close into a pan, cover it with butter, and bake it; when well done, drain it from the gravy, put it into the pots to keep, and when cold, cover it with clarified butter.

In this manner you may do any firm fish.

SALMON PIE.—Clean and scrape well a piece of fresh salmon; season it with salt, mace, and nutmeg; put a piece of butter at the bottom of the dish, and lay in the salmon; melt butter in proportion to the size of the pie; boil a lobster; pick out all the flesh, and chop it small; bruise the body, and mix it well with the butter; pour it over the salmon; make a good crust; put on the lid, and bake it well.

SALT, *to prepare for the table.*—Dry it in a Dutch oven before the fire. Then place it upon clean, smooth, stiff paper, and roll it with a rolling-pin.

SALT, *to save manure.*—Dissolve common salt in water; sprinkle the same over the manure heap, and the volatile parts of the ammonia will become fixed salts, from their having united with the muriatic acid of the common salt, and the soda thus liberated from the salt will quickly absorb carbonic acid, forming carbonate of soda; thus you will retain with your manure the ammonia that would otherwise fly away, and you have also a new and important agent introduced, viz., the carbonate of soda, which is a powerful solvent of all vegetable fibre.

SALT COD, *to dress.*—Soak the cod all night in 2 parts water, and 1 part vinegar. Boil, and break into flakes on the dish; pour over it boiled parsnips, beaten in a mortar, and then boil up with cream, and a large piece of butter rolled in a bit of flour. It may be served with egg-sauce instead of parsnip, or boiled and served without flaking with the usual sauce.

All *Salt Fish* may be done in a similar way. Pour egg-sauce over it, or parsnips, boiled and beaten fine with butter and cream.

SALTS OF LEMONS.—Take equal parts of cream of tartar and citric acid, powdered very fine, and mix together. This forms the salts of lemons as sold at the druggist's shops in small oval boxes at 1s. each, printed directions for using which may be had of any druggist.

SALVE, *family.*——Take the root of yellow dock and dandelion, equal parts; add a good proportion of celandine and plaintain. Extract the juices by steeping or pressing. Strain carefully and simmer the liquid with sweet cream, or fresh butter and mutton tallow, or you may take sweet oil and mutton tallow. Simmer together until no appearance of the liquid remains. Before it is quite cold, put it into boxes as you may desire. This is one of the most soothing and healing preparations for burns, scalds, cuts, and sores of every description that can be produced.

SALVE, *for all wounds.*—Take 1 lb. of hog's lard, 3 ozs. of white lead, 3 ozs. of red lead, 3 ozs. of bees' wax, 2 ozs. of black rosin, and 4 ozs. of common turpentine; all these ingredients must be put together in a pan, and boil three quarters of an hour; the turpentine to be put in just before it is done enough, and give it a gentle boil afterwards. This is an excellent cure for burns, sores, or ulcers, as it first draws, then heals afterward; it is excellent for all wounds.

SAMPHIRE.—Put green samphire in a pan, throw salt over it, and cover with spring water. After laying 24 hours, put into a jar with a handful of salt, and cover it with the best vinegar. Put over a gentle fire in a saucepan till it is just crisp and green; do not let it be soft, for it would then be spoiled. Put into pickling jars, and cover close.

SANDARAC VARNISH, *for cut-paper works, dressing boxes, &c.*--Gum sandarac, 6 ozs.; gum elemi, 4 ozs.; spirits of wine, 2 lbs. The soft resins must be pounded with the dry bodies; the camphor is to be added in pieces.

SANDWICH.——Butter and

grated cheese, equal portions, with a little mustard; beat them in a mortar into one mass; spread this mixture upon slices of bread; then put on slices of ham, or any kind of meat; cover with another piece of bread, the size of the first. Add salt if necessary.

SARAGOSSA WINE, *or English Sack.*—To every quart of water, put a sprig of rue, and to every gallon a handful of fennel root; boil half an hour; strain off, and to every gallon of liquor, put 3 lbs. of honey; boil it two hours, and skim well; pour it into the cask for a year, then bottle it.

SARSAPARILLA.-This plant is a native of America. It has a mild, bitterish, and glutinous taste, not at all disagreeable. It is healing, pectoral, sudorific, stimulant, diaphoretic, cordial. An infusion or decoction is good for all diseases of the blood, for scrofula, swellings, chronic rheumatism, local pains, and cutaneous affections. As a pectoral, it may be used in syrups, cordials, decoctions, &c., and has been found useful in coughs, catarrhs, languor, debility, &c.

For decoction, 3 ozs. of the root should be used for making a quart of the decoction; bruise the root, and pour upon it 3 pints of boiling water; let it stand a night, then boil down to a quart, and strain. A little liquorice root, or cinnamon, or sassafras, may be added to the decoction before it is taken from the fire; or, a little cinnamon water may be added after straining.

SARSAPARILLA, *Decoction of.*--Take fresh sarsaparilla root, sliced and bruised 2 ozs.; shavings of guaiacum wood, 1 oz. Boil over a slow fire in 3 quarts of water, to one, adding, towards the end, ¼ an oz. of sassafras wood, and 3 drachms of liquorice. Strain the decoction. Take from half a pint to a quart per day.

This decoction strengthens the stomach, and restores fresh vigour to habits emaciated by the venereal disease. It may also be taken in the rheumatism, and cutaneous disorders proceeding from foulness of the blood. It may be taken from a half to two quarts in a day.

SATIN AND SILKS, *to clean.*—French chalk must first be strewed over them, and then well brushed off with a hard brush. Should the satin not be sufficiently cleansed by the first dusting, it may be done a second time, and it will clean and beautify the satin. The more it is brushed the better.

SAUCE, *a la Cruster, for fish.*—Thicken a quarter of a pound of butter with flour, and brown it; then put to it a pound of the best anchovies cut small, six blades of pounded mace, ten cloves, forty berries of black pepper and allspice, a few small onions, a faggot of sweet herbs, (namely—savoury, thyme, basil, and knotted marjoram,) and a little parsley and sliced horse-radish; on these pour half a pint of the best sherry, and a pint and a half of strong gravy. Simmer all gently for twenty minutes, then strain it through a sieve, and bottle it for use: the way of using it is, to boil some of it in the butter while melting.

SAUCE *a la Maitre d' Hotel.*—Put a piece of butter into a saucepan with some hashed parsley, some tarragon leaves, one or two leaves of balm, with salt, lemon, or a glass of verjuice; mix the whole with a wooden spoon, until they are well incorporated.

SAUCE *a la Matelote.*—Put into a saucepan a ladleful of reduced cullis, or broth; put in small onions, which have been fried in butter, with some dressed mushrooms, and artichoke bottoms. When ready to serve, put in but-

x

ter the size of a walnut, shake it well, in order to mix it, without breaking the ingredients.

SAUCE, *a la Nonpareille.*—Cut some ham into dices, with the same weight of mushrooms or truffles; put them into a stewpan, with a bit of butter, upon a slow fire, and simmer 15 minutes. If the sauce is to be white, put three skimming spoonfuls of white cullis. If brown, add half a glass of port wine, and seasoning; put in the whites of hard eggs, and mushrooms, in the same quantity as the ham and truffles, and cut in the same way; also, lobsters' tails, and spawn, if there be any; finish with a bit of butter.

SAUCE, *Excelsior.*—Put into a saucepan a wineglassful of vinegar, some garlic, shalots, a laurel leaf, thyme, and pepper. Put on the fire till reduced to half the quantity. Add to it some gravy or soup. Pass it through a sieve; rub some butter into a little flour, and add it to the sauce, with finely chopped herbs. Excellent for cutlets, or warmed slices of meat, &c.

SAUCE, *Grande.*—Chop two shalots very fine, and a small bunch of parsley. Beat up the yolks of two or three eggs, and add Florence oil till the mixture is pretty thick. Add two tea-spoonfuls of the best vinegar, a small one of salt, and one of soluble cayenne, and then mix all with the shalots and parsley.

SAUCE, *Italienne.*—Cut twelve dices of ham, and put it into a stewpan, with a handful of mushrooms well minced, and a sliced lemon, from which the peel and seeds must be taken; add a spoonful of hashed shalot, washed and dried in a cloth, half a bay-leaf, two cloves, and a gill of oil; put them all upon the fire; when nearly ready, take out the lemon, and put in a spoonful of minced parsley, a spoonful of *Espagnole*, a glass of good white wine, without reducing it, and a little pepper; reduce, skim, take out the ham, and when it has obtained its point, take it off.

SAUCE, *Lemon, for boiled Fowls.*—Put the peel of a small lemon, cut very thin, into a pint of sweet rich cream, with a sprig of lemon-thyme, and ten white pepper-corns. Simmer gently, till it tastes well of the lemon; then strain it, and thicken it with a quarter of a pound of butter, and a dessert-spoonful of flour rubbed in it. Boil it up; then pour the juice of the lemon strained into it, stirring it well. Dish the chickens, and then mix a little white gravy, quite hot, with the cream, but don't boil them together, and salt to your taste.

SAUCE, *Menhold.*—Put into a stewpan a bit of butter broken in pieces; shake over it a little flour, and add a little milk or cream; season it with parsley, young onions, a small bay-leaf, mushrooms, and shalots; put it on the fire and stir often; pass it through a sieve; put it on the fire with some parsley and a little pepper.

SAUCE, *Poivrade.*—Cut twelve small dices of ham, and put them into a stewpan, with a little bit of butter, five or six branches of parsley, two or three young onions cut in two, a clove of garlic, a bay-leaf, a little sweet basil, thyme, and two cloves; put them together upon a quick fire; when they are well done, put in a little fine pepper, a large spoonful of vinegar, and four spoonfuls of cullis or broth, not reduced; shake and boil it, draw it to the edge of the stove, and let it simmer three quarters of an hour; skim, and pass it through a sieve or colander.

SAUCE, *Ramolade.*—Put into a very nice tin saucepan a pint of fine port wine, a gill of mountain, half a pint of fine walnut ketchup, 12 anchovies, and the liquor that belongs to them, a gill of walnut pickle, the rind and juice of a large lemon, four or five shalots, some cayenne to taste, 3 ozs. of scraped horse-radish, 3 blades of mace, and 2 tea-spoonfuls of made mustard; boil it all gently till the rawness goes off; then put it into small bottles for use. Cork them very close, and seal the top.

SAUCE, *Robart, for Rumps or Steaks.*—Put a piece of butter, the size of an egg, into a saucepan, set it over the fire, and when browning throw in a handful of sliced onions, cut small; fry them brown, but don't let them burn; add half a spoonful of flour, shake the onions in it, and give it another fry: then put four spoonfuls of gravy, and some pepper and salt, and boil it gently ten minutes; skim off the fat; add a tea-spoonful of made mustard, a spoonful of vinegar, and juice of half a lemon; boil it all, and pour it round the steaks. They should be of a fine yellow brown, and garnished with fried parsley and lemon.

SAUCE *for any kind of fish.* —Take a little of the water that drains from the fish; add an equal quantity of veal gravy; boil them together, and put it into a saucepan, with an onion, an anchovy, a spoonful of ketchup, and a glass of sherry; thicken with butter rolled in flour, and a spoonful of cream.

SAUCE *for Carp or boiled Turkey.*—Rub ½ lb. of butter with a tea-spoonful of flour, put to it a *little* water, melt it, and add near a quarter of a pint of thick cream, and half an anchovy chopped fine, not washed; set it over the fire, and as it boils up, add a large spoonful of real India soy. If that does not give it a fine colour, add a little more. Turn it into the sauce-tureen, and put some salt and half a lemon; stir well to hinder from curdling.

SAUCE *for cold Partridges, Moor-game, &c.*—Pound four anchovies, and two cloves of garlic, in a mortar: add oil and vinegar to the taste. Mince the meat, and put the sauce to it as wanted.

SAUCE *for Ducks.*—Serve a rich gravy in the dish; cut the breast into slices, but don't take them off; cut a lemon, and put pepper and salt on it; then squeeze it on the breast, and pour a spoonful of gravy over before you help.

SAUCE *for Fowl of any sort.* —Boil some veal gravy, pepper, salt, the juice of a Seville orange and a lemon, and a quarter as much of port wine, as of gravy: pour it into the dish or a boat.

SAUCE *for hot or cold roast beef.*—Grate, or scrape very fine, some horse-radish, a little made mustard, some pounded white sugar, and four large spoonfuls of vinegar. Serve in a saucer.

SAUCE *for Salmon.*—Boil a bunch of fennel and parsley; chop them small, and put into it some good melted butter. Gravy sauce should be served with it:—put a little brown gravy into a saucepan, with one anchovy, a tea-spoonful of lemon pickle, a table-spoonful of walnut pickle, two spoonfuls of the water in which the fish was boiled, a stick of horse-radish, a little browning, and salt; boil them four minutes; thicken with flour and a good lump of butter, and strain through a hair sieve.

SAUCE *for Savoury Pies.*—— Take some gravy, one anchovy, a sprig of sweet herbs, an onion, and a little mushroom liquor; boil it a little, and thicken it with burnt butter, or a bit of butter rolled in flour; add a little port wine, and open the pie, and put it in. It will serve for lamb, mutton, veal, or beef pies.

SAUCE *for a Turkey.*—Open some oysters into a basin, and wash them in their own liquor; save the liquor, and as soon as settled, pour into a saucepan; add a little white gravy, a tea-spoonful of lemon pickle; thicken with flour and butter; boil it three or four minutes; add a spoonful of thick cream, and then the oysters; shake them over the fire till they are hot, but do not let them boil.

SAUCE *for Wild Fowl.*—Simmer a tea-cupful of port wine, the same quantity of good meat-gravy, a little shalot, a little pepper, salt, a grate of nutmeg, and a bit of mace, for ten minutes; put in a bit of butter and flour, give it all one boil, and pour it through the birds. In general they are not stuffed as tame, but may be done so if liked.

SAUSAGES, *to eat cold.*—Season fat and lean pork with some salt, saltpetre, pepper, and allspice, all in fine powder, and rub into the meat; the third day cut it small, and mix with it some shred shalot, or garlic, sage very fine; a little bread, if you like. Fill prepared skins or gut with this stuffing; tie up the ends, and hang to smoke, like hams; but first wrap it in a fold or two of old muslin. It must be highly dried. Some eat it without boiling; but it is best boiled. Tie the skin in different places; each link to be about 8 or 9 inches long.

SAUSAGES, *Francois, smoked.* Mince what quantity of fresh pork will be necessary; mix with it equal to a quarter of lard, salt, and fine spices; fill the puddings and tie them; hang them in the smoke for three days; then cook them in broth or soup for three hours, with salt, a clove of garlic, thyme, bay, basil, parsley, and young onions; when cold, serve upon a napkin.

SAUSAGE ROLLS.——Take nice pork chops, more lean than fat, but free from gristle; chop it very fine, and season it well with pepper, salt, and spices, sage, or basil; use a little water, or beer, or port wine, in chopping the meat, or a little soaked bread. Roll out some paste in square pieces, lay a roll of meat in the centre lengthways; fold them so as to form long puffs, and wash them with egg before they are baked.

SAUSAGES, *Spadbury's Oxford.*—Chop a pound and a half of pork, and the same of veal, cleared of skin and sinews; and three quarters of a pound of beef suet; mince and mix them; steep the crumb of a penny loaf in water, and mix it with the meat, with also a little dried sage, pepper, and salt.

SAVINE OINTMENT.-Take fresh savine leaves, bruised, $\frac{1}{2}$ lb.; pure lard, 2 lbs.; yellow wax, $\frac{1}{4}$ lb. Boil the leaves in the lard until they are crisp; press through a filter; add the wax to the filtered lard, and melt them together. This is an excellent issue ointment, being, in many respects, peferable to that of cantharides. It is mixed with equal parts of blistering ointment in order to keep up a discharge.

SAVOURY JELLY.—Spread some slices of lean veal and ham on the bottom of a stew-pan, with a carrot or turnip, or two or three onions; cover it, and let it simmer on a slow fire till it is sufficiently brown; put to it a quart of good broth, whole pepper, mace, a very little isinglass, and salt to your taste; boil ten minutes: strain, and skim off all the fat; add the whites of three eggs; run it through a jelly bag several times.

SAVOURY JELLY, *for cold meats.*—Boil beef and mutton to a stiff jelly; season it with a little pepper and salt, a blade or two of mace, and an onion; then beat the whites of four eggs; put them to the jelly, and beat it a little; then run it through a jelly bag, and when clear, pour it on your meat or fowls.

SAVOURY JELLY, *to put over cold pies.*—Make it of a small bare knuckle of leg or shoulder of veal, or a piece of scrag of that, or mutton; or if the pie be of fowl or rabbit, the carcases, necks and heads, added to any piece of meat, will be sufficient, observing to give consistency by cow-heel or shanks of mutton. Put the meat, a slice of lean ham or bacon, a faggot of different herbs, two blades of mace, an onion or two, a small bit of lemon peel, and a tea-spoonful of Jamaica pepper bruised, and the same of whole pepper, and three pints of water, in a stew-pot that shuts very close. As soon as it boils skim it well, and let it simmer very slowly till quite strong; strain it, and when cold take off the fat with a spoon first, and then to remove every particle of grease, lay a clean piece of cap or blotting paper on it. When cold, if not clear, boil it a few minutes with the whites of two eggs, (but don't add the sediment,) and pour it through a nice sieve, with a napkin in it, which has been dipped in boiling water, to prevent waste.

SAVOURY RICE.——Wash and pick some rice, stew it very gently in a small quantity of veal, or rich mutton broth, with an onion, a blade of mace, pepper and salt. When swelled, but not boiled to a mash, dry it on the shallow end of a sieve before the fire, and either serve it dry, or put it in the middle of a dish, and pour the gravy round, having heated it.

SCALDS AND BURNS.——Bathe the part with heated vinegar by means of a rag, and then cover with a liniment made of one part of oil of turpentine, and two parts of yellow basilicon. It will smart at first, but gradually and soon abate, and the wound feel comparatively easy; the dressing then may be changed for sugar of lead ointment, or the common liniment of lime water and oil, equal parts. The blisters, if any, may be opened with a needle; if the skin has been removed, the treatment is the same, since equal relief is experienced.

A solution of Epsom salts has been recommended for scalds and burns. Dissolve Epsom salts in a little spirits of wine, and add water. Apply cloths saturated in it. —See *Burns.*

SCALD HEAD.—This affects the heads of children chiefly. The scabby eruptions at the roots of the hair are very disagreeable. It is a very obstinate and infectious disease. First, cut off all the hair, and wash the head night and morning with warm soap suds, and afterwards bathe with tincture of blood-root. Then apply the brown ointment, as described in the 83*rd page,* once a day. Give the patient sulphur and cream of tartar in treacle, so as slightly to open the bowels. A poultice of dock roots is very useful.

SCALD HEAD.——Anoint it with Barbadoes tar.—Or, apply daily white wine vinegar.

If wood soot is mixed with fresh butter into an ointment, and the head anointed with it every day, it will generally cure it at the beginning; but when it is become very bad, a plaster should be made of gall dried to the consistence of salve, and spread upon linen. This should be applied all over the parts affected, and continued on four or five days; then it should be taken off and the head dressed with soot ointment as before. After the cure, give two or three gentle purges.

If a proper regard was paid to cleanliness in the head and apparel of children, the scald head would be seldom seen.—*Wesley*.

SCALLOPED COLD CHICKEN.—Mince the meat very small, and set it over the fire, with a scrape of nutmeg, a little pepper and salt, and a little cream, for a few minutes. Put it into the scallop shells, and fill them with crumbs of bread, over which put some bits of butter, and brown them before the fire. Veal and ham eat well done the same way, and lightly covered with crumbs of bread, or they may be put on in little heaps.

SCARLATINA, or *Scarlet Fever*.—It derives its name from the colour of its eruptions. It is a disease of infancy, and seldom attacks adults. It never attacks the same person twice. It begins with chilliness and shiverings, languor, and depression of spirits, a dry skin, and pains in the head; and soon the whole skin becomes covered with specks, or minute inflammations, larger and redder than those of the measles. In two or three days, they disappear, succeeded by scalings of the scarf skin, like bran dispersed over the body, which fall off and appear again two or three times successively. This disease is sometimes of a more malignant type, tending towards putrefaction. It is attended with severe sore throat; the uvula, and all the back part of the throat are very red, painful, and swollen, and the swallowing much impeded, or rendered nearly impossible. It is often attended with delirium, the spots become black; the disease becomes dangerous. Scarlatina is infectious.

Treatment.—If the disease is of a mild character, little more is required than to observe a cold diet, and to avoid cold air, and cold drinks. If the body be costive, give an aperient; see pages 20, 21. If the fever be high, give the *Saline Mixture*, which see. Take a small cupful at a time. Barley water, acidulated with tamarinds, or lemon-juice affords a good beverage. Give also the Sudorific Powder. Emetics will be useful as soon as the disease begins. The Emetic Powder should not be neglected. Bathe the feet in warm water, and give saffron tea. Drink balm tea frequently.

Scarlet fever is caused by some morbific matter taken into the circulation by the lungs; and the increased action in the system is a healthy effort of nature to expel such morbific matter. Nature therefore must be assisted; or if her efforts are too great, she must be restrained. It is not always necessary to give the Emetic Powder; but if there be soreness of the throat, and much phlegm, hindering the breathing, the powder will have a good effect, abating the febrile symptoms, curing the disease, or rendering the attack light. Mr. Stephens asserts that he gave the following mixture in 400 cases, after they had assumed the most alarming appearance, the majority of which it cured; viz.—Cayenne, a table-spoonful; common salt, 1½ teaspoonful. Beat into a paste; pour upon it a pint of boiling water; to stand an hour; then add half a pint of good vinegar. A tablespoonful of the mixture every hour. Do not neglect to give an aperient that will cleanse the stomach and bowels. Castor oil, and salts and senna, or senna and manna, are appropriate purgatives.

It is very good to bathe the surface with warm soft water, to which has been added a little ley. Some have recommended ablutions of cold water; but they should not be adopted except where the heat of the skin is great, and where perspiration is absent. It often moderates the subsequent symptoms.— But no dangerous reaction takes place from tepid as from cold water, nor will any danger whatever result from it, as it is a most valuable auxiliary, and the use of it cannot be too highly recommended. If the throat be sore, and the swallowing difficult, foment it with the Rheumatic Liquid. Gargle, as in Sore Throat. The Diaphoretic Powder will have an anodyne influence, and should not be neglected.

Should the disease assume the malignant type, give immediately the vapour bath of bitter decoction, and emetics, and doses of the cayenne and salt mixture, as just mentioned; it may be made a little stronger. If putrid symptoms appear, give yeast mixed with honey and milk. Also gargle with it; and apply yeast poultices to eruptions run into a sore. Let the room in which the patient is confined be well ventilated, and of a proper temperature; but keep away cold air from him by all means.

In the beginning of the disease, the diet should be light and easy of digestion. Diluents should be freely taken, as balm tea, barley gruel, &c., with a squeeze of lemon in them. If there is debility, let the food be nutritious, as beef tea, jellies, arrow-root, sago, rice milk, and a little wine. During recovery avoid exposure to cold; keep the skin clean by tepid ablutions, and occasionally bathe the feet in warm water at bed-time. Apply friction to the whole body as much as the patient can bear. Give the tonic bitters, also the Composition Powder.

Bella donna has been found to render persons unsusceptible of the fever, in places where it is raging. It is to be given in extract,—the twentieth part of a grain morning and evening.

SCARLATINA & MEASLES —Dr. Witt states that sesquicarbonate of ammonia is an antidote to scarlatina and measles. "The dose in these complaints varies from 3 to 10 grains, according to the age of the patient, given at longer or shorter intervals, according to the mildness or severity of the attack. The suitable dose dissolved in as small a quantity of cold water as will admit of its being swallowed with as many grains of loaf sugar, merely to make it palatable, is all that is required. Any admixture with other medicines, as salines, bark, &c., and all acidulous drinks, are to be avoided. The preliminary treatment is also simple; from half a grain of calomel, for children, to five grains for adults, should be placed on the tongue and swallowed. About an hour after, the first dose of the ammonia is to be given, and repeated every three or four hours, as long as the disorder takes the favourable course. If the disorder increases in violence, the medicine must be given every two hours, or every hour, or sometimes even more frequently, till the graver symptoms are subdued. This medicine has been found to possess similar powers over diphtheria."

SCIATICA, *a form of neuralgia.*

—It derives its name from the pain taking the course of the sciatic nerve down to the hip and thigh. It is often connected with rheumatism and gout, and most of the remedies for those diseases are applicable to sciatica.—The vapour bath is very serviceable. Rub also with the Rheumatic Liquid, or the tincture of aconite. Galvanism applied is also good. Also, an embrocation composed of one part of turpentine, two of soap and opium liniment, and one of tincture of cayenne. A hot bran poultice sprinkled with laudanum often gives ease. Take an aperient, if necessary. Avoid all alcoholic drinks, and take light nourishing food. Sciatica often occurs in persons of broken constitution; tonic medicines are appropriate to them, as quinine and iron, or the bitters, which see.

SCORBUTIC BLOTCHES.—Put a few handfuls of water cresses bruised, to half a pint of milk. Simmer over a slow fire until they assume a green colour; bathe the parts affected with this liquid, and rub it in by the fire. Then rub with simple ointment.

SCORBUTIC GUMS. — Take bole ammoniac, 2 drachms; myrrh, 1 drachm; roche alum, ½ drachm; claret, better than ½ pint. Boil over a gentle fire. Strain. Wash the mouth with it several times a day.

SCORBUTIC GUMS.—Wash them daily with the decoction of the Peruvian bark, adding a little tincture of rosemary, with a solution of myrrh.

SCOTCH COLLOPS.——Cut veal into thin bits about three inches over, and rather round; beat with a rolling-pin, and grate a little nutmeg over them; dip into the yolk of an egg; and fry them in a little butter of a fine brown; pour the butter off; and have ready warm to pour upon them half a pint of gravy, a little bit of butter rubbed into a little flour, a yolk of egg, two large spoonfuls of cream, and a bit of salt. Don't boil the sauce but stir it till of a fine thickness to serve with the collops.

Another.—Cut slices from a fillet of mutton, or veal. Sprinkle with flour, and brown them with butter in the frying-pan. Place in the stew-pan, and cover with gravy, weak broth, or water; simmer gently ten or twelve minutes, then add lemon juice, ketchup, mace, pepper, and salt. Put the sauce or liquor in the frying-pan, and thicken with flour, which pour over the collops, and garnish with curled slices of ham or bacon.

SCOTCH COLLOPS, *brown.* —Brown the butter before the collops are put in; fry them over a quick fire; turn and keep in a fine froth; when they are a light brown, put them into the pot, and fry them. Pour all the gravy into a tossing-pan, with half a pint of gravy made of the bones, and bits from which the collops have been cut, two teaspoonfuls of lemon pickle, a table-spoonful of ketchup, the same of browning, half a lemon, a little anchovy, cayenne, and salt to your taste; thicken with flour and butter. Boil five or six minutes; then put in the collops, and shake them over the fire. When they have simmered a little, take them out, lay in the dish. Strain the gravy and pour it hot upon them.

SCOTCH LEEK SOUP.——Put the water that has boiled a leg of mutton into a stew-pot, with a quantity of chopped leeks, and pepper, and salt; simmer them an hour; then mix some oatmeal with a little cold water quite smooth, pour it into the soup, set it on a slow part of the fire, and let it simmer gently; but take care it does not burn to the bottom.

SCOTCH MUTTON BROTH —Soak a neck of mutton in water for an hour; cut off the scrag, and put it into a stew-pot with two quarts of water. As soon as it boils, skim it well, and then simmer it an hour and a half; then take the best end of the mutton, cut it into pieces (two bones in each), take some of the fat off, and put as many as you think proper: skim the moment the fresh meat boils up, and every quarter of an hour afterwards. Have ready four or five carrots, the same number of turnips, and three onions, all cut, but not small, and put them in soon enough to get quite tender: add four large spoonfuls of Scotch barley, first wetted with cold water. The meat should stew three hours. Salt to taste, and serve all together. Twenty minutes before serving put in some chopped parsley. It is an excellent winter dish.

SCOURING BALLS.——Dry fullers earth moistened with the juice of lemons; add a small quantity of pearl ashes, and a little soft soap; knead the whole well together into a thick elastic paste; form it into small balls, and dry them in the sun. When used, moisten the spot on the clothes with water; then rub it with the ball, and let the spot dry in the sun. When washed with pure water the spot will disappear.

SCRATCHES.—Do not neglect them. Wash them in cold water; close them as much as you can, and cover with diachylon plaster. If there is inflammation, apply a bread poultice, or one of slippery elm.

SCROFULA. —— The Latins termed this disease scrofula, from *scrofa*, a hog, because it has been observed in swine. It is called the *King's Evil*, because Edward the confessor, and other succeeding kings, both of England and France, pretended to cure it by the touch. Queen Anne, in 1807, by proclamation invited her scrofulous subjects to the royal touch.

The disease is well known, and requires little description. It is generally seen in the glands of the neck, in the ligaments of the joints, and even in the substance of the bones. The glands of the mesentery are often tumefied, and accumulation takes place in the substance of the lungs, forming tubercles.

Treatment.—This must depend on the state of the constitution, and the structure of the parts affected, &c. When the lungs are the seat of the mischief, it produces *Pulmonary Consumption;* when it exists in the ligament of a joint, it is called *White Swelling.* The general health should be regarded, and means adopted to establish it. To invigorate and strengthen the absorbent system, cold bathing, and the sea air has been very beneficial; and the mineral waters have not been useless, though they are not a specific. All these means, however, do not apply to scrofula in the lungs. Administer the vapour bath of bitter decoction; give tonics, and an emetic occasionally; rub the tumours freely with the stimulating liniment night and morning; and the body with salt and water every morning.

If the tumours are much inflamed, apply a poultice of bran and slippery elm bark. Linseed meal and slippery elm are very good. Apply cold, and renew when dry. The poultice is almost sovereign when the tumours burst, if it is mixed with the pulverized bark of the root of bay-berry, and a little sweet oil. First, cleanse the tumour well with soap and water; then apply the poultice. The extract of clover is very good for this purpose. It is made by boiling down the flour in water, and evaporating the liquid.

Iodine has been highly recommended by many English and French physicians, as a specific remedy for scrofula; and, for the very favourable results I have witnessed, in a great variety of cases, I am disposed to consider it to possess antiscrofulous properties. The best preparation is the spirituous solution termed the Tincture of Iodine, which may be administered twice a day, in the dose of three to fifteen drops, in a wine-glassful of a decoction of marsh-mallow roots, or of Peruvian bark, if the patient be in a debilitated stage.

"Devonport's Syrup of iodide of quinine and iron is a ternary compound of marked efficacy, in cases of scrofula, and of bloodlessness, *(anæmia.)* It is borne well by the stomach, and not possessing the nauseous qualities of its constituents, is admirably adapted for children."—*Dr. Graham.*

The scrofulous patient must have a nourishing diet, plenty of exercise, and abundance of fresh pure air.

SCROFULA, OR KING'S EVIL.—Take as much cream of tartar as lies on a shilling every morning and evening.—Or, drink for six weeks half a pint of strong decoction of devil's bit.——Or, make a leaf of dried burdock into a pint of tea; take half a pint twice a day for four months. I have known this cure hundreds.—*Wesley.*

SCURVY.—This disease arises from a depraved state of the blood, which induces general debility, and a corruption of all the fluids. It is characterized by extreme diminution of vitality, such as a very pale and bloated complexion, spongy gums, livid spots on the skin, offensive breath, swelling of the legs, foul ulcers, fœtid urine, weakness, &c.

This disease arises from the want of fresh provisions, and a due quantity of vegetables; probably assisted by the prevalency of cold and moisture, and also such other causes as depress the nervous energy, as indolence, confinement, neglect of cleanliness, much labour and fatigue, sadness, despondency, &c. A preternatural saline state of the fluids is assigned by Dr. Cullen as its proximate cause. The reason that salted meat is so productive of scurvy is, because it is drained of its nutritious juices, which run off in brine, its fibres being at the same time hardened, and rendered more difficult of digestion.

Treatment.—Abstain from salt as much as possible. A diet of fresh vegetables, and a beverage strongly impregnated with the juice of lemons, oranges, and the sub-acid fruits, are more efficacious in the cure of this disease than the most powerful anti-scorbutic medicines. The essences of malt and spruce have likewise been found of great service, probably from the quantity of fixed air they contain. When lemon or orange-juice cannot be obtained, nitre dissolved in vinegar, in the proportion of an oz. of the former to a quart of the latter, has been found to afford the best substitute; water acidulated with the nitric acid, is, perhaps, not less efficacious: from 1 to 2 ozs. or more of the former may be given three or four times in the course of the day; and of the latter, a quantity containing about 15 or 20 drops of the nitric acid may be taken every five or six hours. The vitriolic acid, the Peruvian bark, and the red sulphate of iron, are likewise very valuable remedies in the far advanced stage of this disease.

The vapour bath of bitter decoction is very appropriate. A decoction of sassafras and sarsaparilla is very useful—to be taken freely; add the juice of lemon. Steam affected parts with a decoction of bitter herbs. Let the diet be vegetable, consisting chiefly of milk. Emetics are sometimes necessary; tonics always.

SCURVY.—Take 2 ozs. each of field daisies and dandelion roots. Boil in 3 quarts of water down to 1 quart. Take a tea-cupful night and morning.

SCURVY.—John Wesley says, "Live on turnips for a month.

Or, take tar-water, morning and evening, for three months.

Or, 3 spoonfuls of nettle-juice every morning.

Or, decoction of burdock. Boil 3 ozs. of the dried root in 2 quarts of water to 3 pints. Take ½ a pint daily. A decoction of the leaves (boiling 1 leaf 4 minutes in a quart of water), has the same effect.

Or, take a cupful of the juice of goose grass in a morning, fasting, for a month; it is frequently called hariff, or cleavers. I have known many persons cured by it.

Or, pound into a pulp, of Seville oranges, sliced, rind and all, and powder sugar, equal quantities. Take a tea-spoonful three or four times a day.

Or, squeeze the juice of half a Seville orange into a pint of milk over the fire. Sweeten the whey with loaf sugar, and drink it every morning new milk warm. To make any whey, milk should be skimmed after it is boiled.

Or, pour 3 quarts of boiling water on a quart of ground malt; stir them well, and let the mixture stand close covered for four hours; strain it off, and use this as common drink: in hot weather brew this fresh every day. It will hardly fail.

Or, take morning and evening a spoonful or two of lemon juice and sugar. It is a precious remedy, and well tried.

Water and garden cresses, mustard, and juice of scurvy grass help in a cold scurvy.

When there is a continual salt taste in the mouth, take a pint of lime-water morning and evening."

SCURVY *in the Gums.*—Make a strong infusion of sage, and dissolve in it a little alum. By means of a cloth apply it to the gums. Burnt alum, mixed with honey, and the juice of celandine, is very good for scorbutic gums, and it *whitens the teeth.*

SEA KALE.—Trim and wash it, and tie it in bundles. Boil it well in equal parts of milk and water. It can scarcely be boiled too much. Drain, and serve on toast.

SEALING-WAX.—The base of sealing-wax is the best resin, 3 parts; shellac, 2 parts; Venice turpentine, 1 part. Colour with vermilion for the best. Melt the varnish first, and then add the colouring matter.—For black, use the best lamp black.--Other colours may be made by varying the pigments, using Venetian red, red lead, or bole; or mixing vermilion with Venetian red.

SEALING - WAX, *Blue.*—— Shellac, 2 parts; smalts, 1 part; yellow resin, 2 parts. Powder, and mix carefully with heat.

SEA-SICKNESS.—In all ordinary occasions, if in dread of sickness, lie down on the back at least a quarter of an hour before the vessel starts. No other position will do. Let the head, body, and back become, as it were, part of the vessel, participating in its motion without any muscular effort. This precaution is often of itself sufficient. It will be of little use to assume this position after the sickness has commenced. It must be beforehand. At Naples I met a gentleman about to embark, who said he could not describe the agony he endured in the best weather. I told him to go to his berth while the vessel was still at anchor; to lie on his back and shut his eyes, and on no account to turn on his side. He took my advice, and next morning when we cast anchor at Cevita Vecchia, he joyfully told me that, for the first time in his life, he had passed through a voyage without being sick. If the sickness comes on, neither eat food, nor drink soup, &c. The stomach, once it begins to go, will neither be equal to solid or fluid food, and, as the shortest means of getting rid of it, sends it back as it came; but drink plenty of plain water, iced if you can get it: when after some time you begin to feel that you can swallow, then take a little champagne and water, or soup with cayenne pepper, and you will soon feel comfortable.—*Dr. Corrigan.*

SEA-SICKNESS.—Take camphorated spirit, sal volatile, and Hoffman's ether, a few drops, mixed in a small quantity of water, or upon a small lump of sugar. This often relieves when other prescriptions fail. The Neutralizing Mixture is a good preventive. So is a tea-spoonful of bicarbonate of soda in half a pint of water. Take an aperient before a voyage.

One of the best means of counteracting the tendency to sea-sickness, is the assumption of the horizontal position. A little chloroform has lately been suggested as a good remedy,--5 to 10 drops on a piece of lump sugar.

SEED CAKES.—Mix 8 lbs. of flour with ½ lb of sugar, ¼ oz. of allspice, and a little ginger. Melt ¾ lb. of butter with ½ a pint of milk; when just warm, add ¼ of a pint of yeast, and work up to a good dough. Let it stand before the fire a few minutes before it goes to the oven, add seeds or currants, and bake an hour and a half.

SEED CAKES, *Common.*—To 6 lbs. of flour add 1 lb. of butter, ½ a lb. of sugar, and 1 oz. of carraway seeds, mixed up with milk, and baked in a pretty hot oven.

SEED SOWING.—A correspondent of the *Gardeners' Chronicle* says, "all flat seeds should be sown sideways, for if laid flat on the soil they are apt to rot; and if this misfortune does not befall them they never germinate so readily as those placed sideways. This accounts for so many failures amongst gourds, melons, cucumbers, &c.

SEIDLITZ POWDER, *in one paper.*—One part of bicarbonate of soda, and two parts of bitartrate of soda. Each must be dried before they are mixed. Half a tea-spoonful dissolved in a tumbler of spring water, and drunk quickly is an excellent thing for those who are thirsty in the morning.

SENEKA, *Decoction of.*—Take of seneka rattle-snake root, 1 oz.; water, 1½ pint. Boil down to one pint, and strain. It is very useful in dropsy, pleurisy, rheumatism, and disorders of the skin. Take an ounce or two three times a day.

SENNA.--The leaves are a very useful purgative, operating mildly yet effectually; yet they are apt to gripe; but this may be prevented by adding to the senna some aromatic substance, as ginger, cinnamon, &c. It is best to infuse it the night before taking it in warm (not boiling) water. The taste may be neutralized by mixing it with black tea, milk, and sugar.

Alexandria senna is the best. It is chiefly given in the form of infusion. Take of senna leaves, 1½ oz.; ginger, 1 drachm; warm water, 1 pint. Pour the water on as above directed. Add ½ lb. of prunes, stewed separately, if you like.

SENNA, *another infusion of.*—Take of tamarinds, 1 oz.; senna, and crystals of tartar, each 2 drachms. Infuse 5 hours in a pint of hot water; strain, and add an oz. or two of the aromatic tincture. Persons easily purged, may leave out the tamarinds or the crystals of tartar. This is an agreeable cooling purge. A teacupful may be given every half hour till it operates.

SENNA, *compound tincture of.*—Take of senna, 1 oz.; jalap, coriander seeds, and cream of tartar, of each ½ an oz. Infuse them in a pint and a half of French brandy for a week, then strain the tincture and add to it 4 ozs. of fine sugar. This is an agreeable purge, and answers all the purposes of the Elixir Salutis and of Daffy's Elixir. The dose is from 1 to 2 or 3 ozs.

SENNA, *Electuary of.*—Senna leaves, finely powdered, 4 ozs.; pulp of French prunes, 1 lb.; pulp of tamarinds, 2 ozs.; treacle, 1½ pint; essential oil of carraway, 2 drachms. Boil the pulps in the syrup to the thickness of honey; add the powder, and, when the mixture cools, the oil. Mix all well.

SHALOTS, *to pickle.*—The same as onions.

SHALOT SAUCE.—Peel and cut small 5 or 6 shalots; put them into a saucepan, with 2 spoonfuls of white wine, or sherry, 2 of water, and 2 of vinegar. Give them a boil up, and pour them into a dish, with a little pepper and salt.

SHAVING OIL.—Soft soap, 3 lbs.; rectified spirits of wine, 2 quarts.

SHEEP-DIPPING WASH.—White arsenic, powdered, ½ lb.; soft soap, 4½ lbs. Beat these for a quarter of an hour, or until the arsenic is dissolved, in five gallons of water. Add this to the water sufficient to dip 50 sheep.

SHELFORD PUDDING.—Mix ¾ lb. of currants or raisins, 1 lb. of suet, 1 lb. of flour, 6 eggs, a little good milk, some lemon-peel, a little salt. Boil it in a melon shape six hours.

SHERBET.—A species of negus, without wine. It is good to allay thirst. It is made as under:

1. Take 9 Seville oranges, and 3 lemons; grate off the yellow rinds, and put the raspings into a gallon of water, and 3 lbs. of the finest sugar; boil to a candy. Take off the fire, and put into the juice the pulp of the above, and stir till it is almost cold. Put into bottles for use.

2. Pare 4 large lemons, and boil the peels in 6 quarts of water, and a little bruised ginger. Boil 15 minutes; then add 3 lbs. of sugar; and when it is cold, put in the juice of the lemon, and strain.

3. Take 12 quarts of water, and 6 lbs. of Malaga raisins; slice 6 lemons into it, with 1 lb. of fine sugar; put them all together into an earthen pan; stir three times a day for 3 days. Take them out and drain in a flannel bag. Bottle, but do not fill the bottles too full, lest they burst. It will be ready in a fortnight.

SHERBET, *Persian.*—Loaf

sugar, finely powdered, 1 lb.; tartaric acid, 4 ozs.; carbonate of soda, 4 ozs.; add 3 tea-spoonfuls of essence of lemon, or according to your taste. Mix very well, and then bottle and cork well. When used, put 2 teaspoonfuls in a glass tumbler of spring water, stir briskly, and drink while in a state of effervescence.

SHERRY, *British.*—Put ½ a bushel of good pale malt into a tub, and pour upon it 4 gallons of boiling water; stir well, cover the vessel, and infuse four hours. Strain through a hair sieve. Add pure water, 7 gallons; white sugar, 16 lbs.; boil together gently for three quarters of an hour, constantly skimming it. Pour it into a clean tub, and dissolve in it 4 lbs. of sugar candy, powdered; ferment with yeast for three or four days. When poured off clear into a sweet cask, add 5 lbs. of the best raisins, bruised and stoned. Stir once or twice a day. Slightly bung for 2 days, and add 3 or 4 quarts of French brandy. Bung closely. In three months bottle for use.

SHINGLES.——Called *herpes, tetters, salt rheum,* &c. It is a disease of the skin; an inveterate eruption on different parts of the body, usually the hands, and sometimes it appears in distinct clusters round or near the waist, surrounding one half of the trunk of the body, like a belt, generally towards the right side. It is a species of ringworm or tetter.

The eruptions or vesicles which appear break and discharge a thin corrosive fluid which causes much irritation or itching.

Treatment.——Keep the body open by the black draught, and seidlitz powder; administer tonics in the decoction of sarsaparilla. Give also a vapour bath of bitter decoction, and afterwards, rub the body with the stimulating liniment. If there is much fever, give five grains of the carbonate and nitrate of potash two or three times a day. Celandine ointment is very good; when the itching is very troublesome, apply it to the affected parts.

Dr. Beach recommends a wash to be made of celandine and whiskey; infuse a table-spoonful of the former in the latter; wash often, and then apply the *Brown Ointment.* Should the vesicles form or run into a bone, apply a poultice of slippery elm, and a little cream. The tincture of bloodroot, and tincture of myrrh, make a good wash. Apply as before the Brown Ointment. The tepid water cloth is a good application to allay itching. The warm baths should often be taken.

SHOES AND BOOTS, *to make waterproof.*—Melt 5 ozs. of spermaceti in a pipkin or other earthen vessel, over a slow fire; add 2 ozs. of cut india-rubber; add a little wood naphtha. Dissolve, and add 2 ozs. of hog's lard, 8 ozs. of tallow, and 4 ozs. of amber varnish. Mix. Apply to the shoes or boots a few times.

SHORTNESS OF BREATH.—Take of vitriolated spirits of ether, one ounce, and of camphor twelve grains. Make a solution, of which take a teaspoonful during the paroxysm. This is usually found to afford instantaneous relief in difficult breathing, depending on internal disease, and other causes, where the patient, from a quick and very laborious breathing, is obliged to be in an erect posture.

Or, take a quarter of an ounce of powder of elecampane root, half an ounce of powder of liquorice, as much flower of brimstone and powder of aniseed, and two ounces of sugar-candy powdered. Make all into pills, with a sufficient quantity of tar; take four large pills when going to rest. This is an incomparable medicine for an asthma.

SHRIMPS, *to choose*.—When fresh they have a sweet flavour, are firm and stiff, and the colour is bright.—Shrimps are of the prawn kind, and may be judged by the same rules.

SHRIMPS, *to butter*.——Take them out of the shells; and warm them with a little good gravy, a bit of butter and flour, a scrape of nutmeg, salt, and pepper; simmer a minute or two and serve with sippets; or with a cream sauce instead of brown.

SHRIMPS, *to pot*.——When boiled, take them out of the skins, and season them with salt, white pepper, and a very little mace and cloves. Press them into a pot, set it in the oven ten minutes, and when cold, cover with butter.

SHRIMP PIE.—Pick a quart of shrimps; if they are very salt, season them with only mace and a clove or two. Mince two or three anchovies; mix these with the spice, and then season the shrimps. Put some butter at the bottom of the dish, and over the shrimps, with a glass of sharp sherry wine. The paste must be light and thin. They do not take long baking.

SHRIMP SAUCE.—Pick the shrimps, and put them into a stewpan with a little gravy. When hot, pour in some melted butter and some anchovy sauce; add a little lemon pickle, and a trifle of cayenne.

SHRUB, *Brandy*.—Take 8 ozs. of citric acid, 1 gallon of porter, 4 gallons of raisin wine, 2 quarts of orange flower water, 5 gallons of good brandy, 6 gallons of water; this will produce 16 gallons. Dissolve the citric acid in the water; then add the brandy; next, mix the raisin wine, porter, and orange flower water, and in a week or 10 days it will be ready for drinking.

SHRUB, *Rum*.—Leave out of the above the brandy and porter, and add one gallon more of raisin wine, 6 lbs. of honey, and 5 or 6 gallons of good rum. Add lemons if you like. Less quantities may be made.

SHRUB, *Lemonade*.—Take the juice of 10 lemons, 4 ozs. of the juice of barberries, 2 ozs. of loaf sugar, and 1 pint of sherry wine, a pint of brandy, and a quart of water. Mix with water as you like.

SHRUB, *White Currant*.-Strip the fruit, and prepare in a jar as for jelly; strain the juice, of which put two quarts to one gallon of rum, and two pounds of lump-sugar; strain through a jelly-bag.

SICK ROOMS, *Cautions in visiting*.—Never enter a sick room in a state of perspiration, for as soon as the body becomes cold, it may absorb the infection or disease.—Do not visit a sick person with an empty stomach, as it disposes the system more readily to receive infection.—In a sick room, stand where the air passes from the door or window to the bed of the diseased. When poisonous vapour is much diluted with fresh air, it is not noxious.—The windows of a sick room, small and confined, should not be closed; if the wind is cold, nearly close the curtains of the bed.—Remove all dirty cloths, clothes, and discharges, as soon as possible.—Let the visitor have about his person camphor, &c.—After leaving an infectious room, a person should continue in the open air some time before he enters his own dwelling.

SILK, *to clean*.—Steep first in cold water, and wash in a hot lather made of soft soap. Then to renovate the colours, rinse in clean warm water. For blue and purple, use a little soda or pearlash. For crimson, maroon, scarlet, or bright yellow, add half a tea-spoonful of sulphuric acid; but never use the acid for brown, fawn, or orange. For olive green add a little verdigris; and for light green, Persian berry and indigo. For carnation, pink, or rose, add a little lemon juice. Roll in a coarse cloth and wring.

SILK, BLACK, *to clean.*—Steep a few hours in cold water. Then put a quarter of a pint of the *Black Reviver* in half a gallon of water, and a cupful of ox-gall. Make hot, and sponge the silk. Dry, and smooth with an iron. (See *Black Reviver*.)

Rusty black silk may be cleaned in the same way. Some persons clean black silk by rubbing it with a flannel dipped in gin.

SILK, *stained.*—We often find that lemon-juice, vinegar, oil of vitriol, and other sharp corrosives, stain dyed garments. Sometimes by adding a little pearlash to a soap lather, and passing the silks through these, the faded colour will be restored. Pearlash and warm water will sometimes do alone, but it is the most efficacious method to use the soap lather and pearlash together.

SILK, *to remove grease from.*—Take French chalk, finely scraped, and put it on the grease-spot, holding it near the fire, or over a warm iron reversed, or on a water-plate in which is boiling water. This will cause the grease to melt, and the French chalk will absorb it, and it may then be brushed or rubbed off. If any grease remains, proceed as before, until it is all extracted. The French chalk is a fine soluble powder of a dry absorbent quality, acting upon silks as Fuller's earth does upon woollens.

SILKS, *to renovate.*—Sponge faded silks with warm water, soap, and bran. Then rub them with a dry cloth on a dresser or table; next, iron them on the *inside* with a smoothing iron. Old black silks may be renovated by sponging with spirits. Iron on the right side, but with thin paper on the silk.

SILVER PLATE, *to clean.*—Dissolve alum in a strong ley; skim it carefully, and mix it up with soap, and wash the silver with it, using a linen rag. Then, when dry, rub with wash-leather and impalpable whiting.

SIRLOIN OF BEEF.—See *Beef*.

SKATE, *to choose.*—If good, they are very white and thick. If too fresh they eat tough, but must not be kept above two days.

SKATE, *to boil.*—Clean well, and cut into long narrow pieces; put into boiling water with a little salt in it. Boil 15 minutes, and take it out; and after adding a little vinegar to the water, boil again till enough. When taken up, drain. Serve while hot, and pour over it cockle, shrimp, or muscle sauce. Lay over it oyster patties. Garnish with horse-radish.

SKATE, *to crimp.*—Cut into long strips, crossways. Boil them quickly for about 10 minutes. Drain, and serve hot, with butter and anchovy.

SKATE, *to fricassee.*—Prepare it the same as soles and flounders; put into a saucepan; to every lb. of fish put a quarter of a pint of water, a little beaten mace, and a grated nutmeg, sweet herbs, and salt; cover close, and boil 15 minutes. Take out the herbs, and put in a pint of cream, a piece of butter rolled in flour, and a glass of sherry. Shake the pan all the time till the fricassee be thick and smooth. Garnish with lemon.

SKATE SOUP.—Make it of the stock for fish-soup, with an oz. of vermicelli boiled in it, a little before it is served. Then add ½ a pint of cream, beaten with the yolks of two eggs. Stir it near but not on the fire. Serve it with a small French roll made hot in a Dutch oven, and then soaked in the soup an hour.

SKIN, *to cleanse from dark spots or flesh worms.*——The best way is to squeeze them out; or wash the skin with milk and flowers of sulphur well mixed. Apply elder-flower ointment at night. An infusion of horse-radish in milk is very useful.

SKIN, *to clear a tanned.*—Wash with a solution of carbonate of soda and a little lemon juice; then with fuller's earth water, or the juice of unripe grapes.

SKIN, *to dye it olive.*——Mix walnut juice with an infusion of anotta; only a small quantity of the latter. Dip paper in to ascertain the tint.

SKIN, *to preserve in persons confined to bed.*—Apply the white of an egg, well beaten, and mixed with spirits of wine.

SKITTLES.—The game of skittles is a favourite amusement in many parts of England, and is too well known to require description in these pages; we shall merely give a few instructions for young players, and the laws by which the game is governed.

Bowling.—Let the player hold the bowl in his right hand, with the bias side from him, with his left foot advanced before the right, which must be at the mark, his body bending towards the frame, but in an easy position; then with an equal motion, throw the bowl along the board with sufficient strength to reach the frame; he should endeavour to hit with the bowl the left-hand side of the first pin, in accomplishing which he will be tolerably certain of bringing down four or five every time the first pin is hit in that manner.

He must take care not to aim at the first pin in a straight direction, but cause the bowl to form a curve, by which it will lose something of its force, and strike the pins with a greater certainty of success.

Tipping.—When the learner is going to tip he should hold the smaller circumference, or opposite side of the bias in the palm of his hand, grasping it very strong with his fingers, as few can be tipped when the bowl is loosely held; he must place his left foot quite clear of the frame between the first and ninth pin, and his right foot behind him in an easy position, and in such direction that he may with ease hit his pins in the manner following:

He must strike his first or second pin in the middle or largest part, and in the same motion and instant of time, deliver his bowl at the fourth pin.

Striking them in this manner generally has the following effect: hitting the first pin not quite full, forces it against the middle or fifth pin from thence to the seventh, and will frequently rebound to the eighth without any roll.

The second pin if struck well will knock down the third, and the fourth or bowl pin will strike the sixth, the ninth is often brought down by some of the rolling pins.

When the learner is to tip for four upon game he should choose the pins No. 8, 7, and 4, placing his left foot by the side of the frame, with his toe nearly in a line with the bottom of the seventh

Y

pin, and right foot behind him, he must strike the three side pins at one motion, at the same time throwing the bowl at the pin No. 4.

To tip for five, let him place his left foot a little to the left of the pin number nine, and his other foot behind; he should strike the ninth pin to hit the seventh, the fifth the fourth, and the bowl must knock down the sixth.

When six are wanted, which number is generally thought most difficult to get, place the left foot in a line with the opposite angle of the frame, and the other foot behind at a good distance; strike the eighth pin full in the middle which will hit the seventh and sixth, and with the same motion, hit the middle pin against the third, and the bowl will hit the fourth, by which means the player will lay the sixth fairly down, and if not struck hard, without danger of rolling, especially if they are tipped down hill, to do which he must make his sixth his first pin.

The proper proportion of a skittle is fifteen inches round, in the largest part, and twelve inches high.

The bowl should be eighteen inches in circumference; and each angle of the frame for the pins 3 feet 4 inches.

Laws and Rules.-1. The bowler must stand at the mark with one foot, and from thence deliver his ball fairly out of his hand, which should run upon the board fixed for that purpose before it arrives at the frame; for if the bowler does not cause his bowl to run along the board, or touch in some part, he loses the benefit of bowling.

2. If the bowler throws the bowl so as to cause it to run double, as it is commonly called, and any one of the opposite party calls out a foul blow; if it has not reached the pins the player must bowl again; but if it arrived at the frame, before the opposite party called out foul, whatever number is bowled down must be scored.

3. If a bowl runs clearly through the frame, and knocks down any number of pins, and is stopped in its return back again by one of the opposite party, one additional pin must be allowed the person who bowled at the time.

4. If a bowl passes through the frame, and on its return strikes a standing pin, and then a rolling or live pin, as it is called, runs against the falling pin, that shall be deemed fair, because the live pin hits the other pin last.

5. If a live pin rolls against a standing pin, and the bowl comes on its return against the falling pin before it is down, that is deemed an unfair pin, because the bowl struck it last.

6. If the bowl runs through the frame, and knocks at the head board, though it may have bowled down many pins, none are allowed.

7. If the bowl runs through, or on the outside of the frame, and knocks, and then runs round the other side of the frame, without crossing any part of it or touching any of the live pins, the bowler must stand to take his tip with one foot upon the spot where the bowl stopped; and in tipping from such place, he must not strike the ground with the bowl before it hits the pins, if he does he loses all he may knock down.

8. If in tipping the bowl is caught or stopped by one of the opposite party, who in so doing stops or impedes a live pin, he loses one, because he prevented the tipper from receiving the benefit which might have arisen from a live pin.

9. If an apponent takes up the bowl in order to prevent it running amongst the pins, and it slips out of his hand and hits any of the pins, he loses one.

10. If a person tipping, gives a sweep round with his hand and brings down any pin with his hand or sleeve, it is unfair; he loses one.

11. Care should be taken in tipping not to jump into the frame immediately after, as in this case the player is not allowed any of the pins he tips.

If the player bowls and tips for a limited number, at the close of the game, and throws down more than are wanted, he must go for nine.

13. In all grounds where these rules are observed, a disinterested person is generally appointed to score the game; and should any dispute occur where the case varies from any here mentioned, his decision is to be taken, and considered final.

SKYROCKETS, *Composition for.*—1. If under 1 inch bore, nitre, 15 parts; charcoal, 6 parts; sulphur, 4 parts; meal powder, 3 parts; steel filings, 5 parts. Mix.

2. If over 1 and under 2 inches, nitre, 16 parts; charcoal, 8 parts; sulphur, 4 parts; steel filings, 5 parts. Mix.

3. If three quarter inch or under, nitre, 16 parts; charcoal, 4 parts; sulphur, 3 parts; cast-iron borings, 4 parts. Mix.

4. If over 1 inch and under 2 inches bore, nitre, 16 parts; charcoal, 4 parts; sulphur, 4 parts; iron borings, 5 parts. Mix.

5. If under three quarter inch bore, nitre, 16 parts; charcoal, 7 parts; sulphur, 4 parts; gunpowder, 1 part. Mix.

6. If over three quarters and under one and a half inch bore, nitre, 16 parts; charcoal, 8 parts; sulphur, 4 parts. Mix.

7. If larger, nitre, 16 parts; charcoal, 9 parts; sulphur, 4 parts. Mix.

SLEEP.—-Dr. Marshall Hall gives the following observations on sleep:—

That early rising may be beneficial, it is necessary that we should retire early, and on rising be properly employed.

Every person should be allowed to have his sleep out; otherwise the duties of the day cannot be properly performed, and will be slighted even by the most conscientious.

To children, young persons, students, persons of sedentary occupations, and invalids, the fullest sleep that the system will take, without artificial means, is the very balm of life.

Never wake up children, or the sick and infirm, of a morning—it is barbarity; let them wake of themselves. Do not hurry up the young and healthy; and it is not well even for adults, if they have passed an unusually fatiguing day, to jump out of bed the moment they wake up. It is best to remain in bed, without going to sleep again till the sense of weariness gradually passes away.

At ten o'clock at night, when possible, all the year round, the old, the middle-aged, and the young should be in bed; and then the early rising will take care of itself, with the invaluable accompaniment of *a fully rested body and a renovated mind.*

SLEEPLESSNESS.-—-Avoid previous mental excitement by listening to startling accounts, reading romances, putting yourself in passion, &c.—Avoid heavy suppers. To sleep well all night—let your supper be light.—Go to bed early.

—It is a good thing when a person is sleepless, to rise and apply friction to the limbs with a flesh brush, or a coarse towel.

SLIPPERY ELM BARK.—This tree, *ulmus fulva*, is a native of America. The powdered bark is now extensively sold and used in that country. It is used as an article of diet for invalids, on account of its soothing and nutritious properties. Milk thickened with it makes excellent food for infants, for dyspeptic and consumptive patients; it subdues inflammation, and agreeably calms the system.

According to the celebrated Dr. Beach, it is "demulcent, pectoral, diuretic, deobstruent, emollient, and refrigerant, useful in all bowel complaints, in scurvy, cutaneous eruptions, &c. In the form of a poultice, it is an admirable remedy (far exceeding any other known production in the world) for ulcers, tumours, swellings, wounds, chilblains, burns, scalds, skin diseases, erysipelas, obstinate ulcers, scabs, &c.; and in sore mouth, or thrush, &c., used as a wash." It quickly allays inflammation, promotes resolution and suppuration. The tea is much used by the Indian women to procure easy labour. In point of utility, it is of far more value than its weight in gold. It has rapidly come into use as an invaluable *medical* agent.

As an ingredient in injections, it is most valuable, healing, soothing, and preventing any painful sensations. It may be obtained at the vendors of botanic medicines.

SLUGS AND SNAILS, *to protect trees from*.—If the trees are planted against a wall, brush over the wall gas tar. Or, mix common tar and pitch, horse hair, an abundance of salt, and apply it to the wall in a band about 3 to 5 inches wide; and draw a circle round each tree of the same mixture.

SMALL POX.—This dreadful disease is very infectious, attended with inflammatory fever, assuming sometimes a typhoid character, attended with nausea and vomiting, and upon the pressure of the stomach, with much pain. The constitution that has been once really under its influence is rarely liable to a second attack. When the pustules are separate from each other, it is termed *distinct*; and when they run together, it is denominated *confluent*.

The first symptoms are shivering pains in the head, back, and loins, redness of the eyes, fever, thirst, nausea, loss of appetite; and in some cases, a few hours before the eruption, children are affected with convulsions. The eruption appears about the *fourth* day of the *fever*, first on the face, and afterwards on the neck, breast, and body. The pustules gradually enlarge, and proceed to maturation which is completed about the *eleventh* day after their first appearance, when the inflammation and swelling abate, the eruption beginning to dry and scale off, and about the fifteenth day it entirely disappears. The confluent sort is attended with more violent symptoms than the distinct, but observes the same period of termination. Dr. Beach says, "The effluvia is very offensive; and I have seen worms, or maggots crawling in the flesh; and yet the patient has recovered." This disease generally terminates favourably under judicious treatment, unless the subject of it is intemperate, in which case it proves very dangerous, or fatal.

Treatment.—The great object is to assist nature to expel the morbific or poisonous matter from the system. If the patient has much vomiting, give 10 or 12 grains of bicarbonate of potash in balm tea twice or thrice a day. The bowels must be opened by gentle aperients, (page 20, 21) attention must be given to the skin, and medicine given to produce a gentle determination to the surface. Take an infusion of saffron and catnep, or balm and hyssop, with 10 drops of elixir of vitriol; this will aid nature to drive out the eruption, by producing a moisture of the skin. It should be repeated several times. Bathe the feet twice a day in warm ley water, and wash the body with the same liquid warm; do not neglect this if the fever is high. If there is pain in the head apply a mustard poultice to the soles of the feet in addition to bathing the feet and legs in warm water. Apply to the head cloths dipped in vinegar and water, or whiskey and warm water. Let the room of the patient be well ventilated, and often sprinkle it with vinegar and water; do not cover him up close. Give warm diluents, as balm, spearmint, pennyroyal, catnep, &c.; any of these will do. If the throat be sore, administer the remedies under *Sore Throat*. Sage tea, a little vinegar, and a little borax, form a good gargle. The expectorant tincture is very useful.

If the debility is great, and the strength gradually sinking, give tonics, as quinine dissolved in elixir of vitriol; 10 or 12 drops in balm tea three or four times a day. If there is considerable irritation, give 8 or 10 drops of laudanum in the *Saline Draught*, which see. Or, give from 5 to 10 grains of the *Diaphoretic Powder*, page 143. Sudorifics are also very serviceable, especially when the pustules are flabby, and not well filled.

If the symptoms become unfavourable, as the striking in of the eruption, great fever, and delirium, black tongue, &c., the danger is very great. In such case, give immediately the vapour bath of bitter decoction, and an emetic; then give a decoction of saffron and Virginia snakeroot with a teaspoonful or two of sweet spirit of nitre. Give also the Sudorific Powder, and at intervals the Seidlitz Powder. Sponge the surface of the body with warm water If there is any tendency to putrescency in the fluids, give a wineglassful of yeast several times a day.

Dr. Anthony Thompson says, "The sulphuric acid combined with wine is the only remedy on which we can rely in the confluent small pox, when the pustules are filled with a bloody sanies, and the urine is coloured by broken-down particles of blood."

Camphor is valuable in this disease.

To prevent the pustules from affecting the eyes, cold water cloths should be continually applied.

While the fever continues high, the diet should be mild and rather spare, as barley gruel, sago gruel, beef tea without salt.

When the pustules begin to maturate, the patient may be permitted gradually to take to his usual diet; and if the crop be considerable, and the strength of the patient much reduced, provided he be free from fever, a little port wine, diluted with water, may likewise be allowed after dinner.

SMALL POX.—The *Sarracenia Purpurea*, or Indian Cup, a native plant of Nova Scotia, the specific used by the Indians against the small pox, bids fair to realise the expectations entertained by medical men of its efficacy. In a letter addressed to the *American Medical Times*, Dr. Frederick W.

sary to clean them. Dry them in a cloth, then lightly flour them, but shake it off. Dip them into plenty of egg, then into breadcrumbs, grated fine, and plunge them into a good pan of *boiling* lard; let them continue gently boiling, and a few minutes will make them a bright yellow-brown. Take care not to take off the light roughness of the crumbs, or their beauty will be lost.

SMELTS, *to pickle.*——Clean and wash them; beat very fine, pepper, nutmeg, mace, saltpetre, and salt; put the smelts in a row in a jar; between every layer of smelts, strew the seasoning with 4 or 5 bay leaves. Then boil some port wine, and pour on a sufficient quantity to cover them. When cold, close the jar, and keep for use.

SMELTS, *Eperlans a la Anglaise.*—Put 2 spoonfuls of oil into a stewpan; salt, and pepper; the half of a lemon cut in pieces; having taken off the skin and seeds, with 2 glasses of sherry wine; let this seasoning boil a quarter of an hour; put in the smelts; let them cool; drain, and pour over them the following sauce :—put a small clove of garlic into boiling water to *blanch ;* bruise it with the blade of a knife, and put it into a stewpan with parsley and small onions hashed, and 2 glasses of Champagne; let it boil five minutes; put in a pat of butter, rubbed in flour; and another pat without flour, salt, and pepper; thicken the sauce, and add the juice of a lemon.

SMOKY CHIMNEYS.—Certain chimneys draw well ordinarly, but are subject to violent fits of smoking in certain winds, and generally in boisterous weather, blowing both flame and smoke into the room to an intolerable extent. For this particular class of nuisance I have for many years past adopted a very cheap and permanent remedy, which has never failed. Instead of a common chimney-pot, I fix, in the like manner, a 9-inch drain-pipe, two feet long, socket downwards, which gives it a firm seat; and on this I fix another like drain-pipe, having two 4-inch double junctions, inserted obliquely into the 9-inch pipe. When the wind blows, it rushes into these lateral openings, which, having a turn upwards, direct its blast against the downward current from the top of the pot. The fixing should be in cement, and you have a cheap chimney-top, which will neither perish nor blow off. I use nothing but drain-pipes for chimney-pots, which, as well as being cheaper and stronger than any thing else, admit of a second and third story being added to them if the draught be dull, or the branch pipe top as I have described, if subject to downward gusts. For kitchen flues, 12-inch pipes are safer.—T. E. in the *Builder.*

To increase the draught in the chimney, some persons make a hole in the hearthstone, providing there is a room below, and cover it with a ventilator to protect it from cinders and ashes.

Or, inflate a large ox's bladder, and tie it by the neck to the middle of a stick, and place it across a chimney, two feet from the top, or at the foot of the chimney-pot. The buoyancy of the air keeps the bladder continually in a circular motion, and thereby prevents the rush of air into the funnel from descending so low as the fire-place.

SNIPES, *to dress in surtout.*—Make a forcemeat of veal and beef suet, pounded with crumbs of bread; add beaten mace, pepper, salt, parsley, and sweet herbs, mixed with the yolk of an egg; lay some of this round the dish; put in the birds drawn and half-roasted. Chop the trail, and put it all over the dish. Put some small mushrooms, a sweetbread, and artichoke bottoms, cut small, into some good gravy; stew all together, and beat up the yolks of 2 eggs in a spoonful of sherry; stir all together one way. When thick take it off, and when cold pour it into the surtout. Put the yolk of a few hard eggs here and there. Season with beaten mace, pepper, and salt; cover with the forcemeat; colour with the yolks of eggs, and send to the oven for half an hour.

SNIPES, *to roast*.——Do not draw them. Spit them; flour them, and baste with butter. Toast a slice of bread brown; place it in the dish under the birds for the trail to drop on. When they are enough, take up, and lay them on the toast; put good gravy in the dish. Serve with butter, and garnish with orange or lemon.

SNIPE PIE.—Bone 4 snipes, and truss them. Put in their insides finely chopped bacon, or other forcemeat; put them in the dish with the breast downwards, and put forcemeat balls around them. Add gravy made of butter, and chopped veal and ham, parsley, pepper, and shalots. Cover with nice puff paste; close it well to keep in the gravy. When nearly done, pour in more gravy, and a little sherry wine. Bake two or three hours. *A. N.*

SNOWBALLS.—Pare six baking apples, and take out the cores; fill the holes with orange marmalade. Make a little good hot paste, and roll the apples in it; make the crust of an equal thickness, and put them into a dripping pan; bake in a moderate oven. When you take them out, make icing for them the same way as for plum cake, and ice them all over with it, a quarter of an inch thick. Place them a good distance from the fire till they are hardened, but do not let them brown. Put one in the middle of a china dish, and the other five round it. Garnish with flowers.

Another.—Swell rice in milk, and strain it off, and having pared and cored apples, put the rice round them, tying each up in a cloth. Put a bit of lemon-peel, a clove, or cinnamon in each, and boil them well.

SNOW RICE CREAM.—Put into a pan 5 ozs. of ground rice, 3 ozs. of loaf sugar, eight drops of essence of almonds, 3 oz. of fresh or salt butter. Add a quart of new milk. Boil twenty minutes, until smooth. Pour into a mould previously greased with butter. Turn it out when quite cold, and serve with preserves round it.

SNUFFLES.—-A troublesome complaint, to infants especially. The mucous membrane of the nose, through the taking of cold, being much swollen, the child is no longer able to breathe through its nose, as it was accustomed to do, but is compelled to breathe through the mouth. The difficult breathings are attended by a peculiar snuffling noise, which, in sleep, becomes a regular loud snore. It often interferes with its sucking at the breast; as soon as it seizes the nipple a threatening suffocation compels it to desist.

While this complaint lasts the child may be partially fed with the spoon; give it a very mild purgative; bathe its legs frequently in warm water. Rub the nose with tallow, and apply a slippery elm poultice mixed with cream.

SOAP, *Chemical*.——Powdered Fullers earth, 1 oz.; just moisten with Spirits of Turpentine; add Salt of Tartar, 1 oz.; best Potass, 1 oz.; work the whole into a paste with a little Soap. It is excellent for removing grease spots.

SODA CAKE.—Rub ½ lb. of good butter into 1 lb. of dry flour, and work it very small. Mix well with these ¼ lb. of sifted sugar; add a cupful of boiling milk, and three eggs well beaten; also ½ lb. of currants, grated nutmeg, and fresh lemon rind. Mix all well and lightly together; and just before you mould it, stir in a teaspoonful of carbonate of soda. Bake an hour or more.

SODA WATER POWDERS. —Soda water is prepared from powder just like ginger beer, (see *Ginger Beer*), except that instead of the two powders, there mentioned, these two are used, viz.—for one glass, 30 grains of carbonate of soda; for the other glass, 25 grains of tartaric or citric acid.

SOLDER.—Two parts of lead and one part of tin; its goodness is tried by melting it, and pouring the size of a crown piece upon the table, and, if it be good, there will arise little bright stars in it. Apply resin when this solder is used.

SOLDERING.—Tin Plate Workers, and Plumbers solder with an alloy, comprising about one part tin, and two parts lead. *Pewter* contains about the same, adding three parts of bismuth.— *Brass, iron,* and *copper* are soldered with an alloy of zinc and copper, called spelter.—Zinc and lead are soldered with lead and tin, not quite equal parts, lead preponderating.—*Hard solder* consists of two parts copper, and tin one part. —*Soft Solder*, two parts tin, and lead one part.

SOLES, *to choose.*——If good, they are thick and firm, the belly of a fine cream colour: if they incline to a bluish colour, and are flabby, it is evident that they are not fresh. They are in perfection about Midsummer. *Run.*

SOLES, *a la Horley.*——After cleaning the soles cut them entirely open by the back from head to tail; cut each into four nice fillets, and steep them in lemon juice, salt, parsley, and sliced onions; shake them in this seasoning, where they ought to remain nearly an hour; when ready to serve, drain, flour, and fry them; they must be firm and of a good colour; dish, and serve under them an *Italienne* or *tomate* sauce.

SOLES, *a la Portugeese.*—Take one large, or two small; if large, cut the fish in two; if small, they need only be split. The bones being taken out, put the fish into a pan with a bit of butter and some lemon juice, give a fry, then lay the fish on a dish, and spread a force-meat over each piece, and roll it round, fastening the roll with a few small skewers. Lay the rolls into a small earthen pan, beat an egg and wet them, then strew crumbs over; and put the remainder of egg, with a little meat gravy, a spoonful of caper sauce, an anchovy chopped fine, and some parsley into the bottom of the pan; cover it close, and bake it till the fish are done enough in a slow oven. Then place the rolls in the dish for serving, and cover it to keep them hot till the gravy baked is skimmed; if not enough, a little fresh, flavoured as above, must be prepared and added to it.

SOLES, *to boil.*—Skin and gut two soles; wash, and lay them in vinegar, salt and water for two hours; then put them into a stew-pan with a pint of sherry, sweet herbs, onion, and cloves, pepper, and salt. Cover them, and when done enough, put in the dish; strain the liquor, thicken it with butter and flour; pour the sauce over. Garnish with horse radish and with lemon.

SOLES, *broiled*.—Take two or three soles, divide them from the back bone, and take off the head, fins, and tail. Sprinkle the inside with salt, roll them up tight from the tail end upwards, and fasten with small skewers. If large or middling, put half a fish in each roll; small do not answer. Dip them into yolks of eggs, and cover them with crumbs. Do the egg over them again, and then put more crumbs; and fry them a beautiful colour in lard, or do them in the oven.

SOLES, *to fricassee*.—Cut the flesh from the bones; cut it longways, and then across, so that each fish may make 8 pieces; put the bones (and head if you like) into a stew-pan with a pint of water, sweet herbs, onion, pepper, mace, salt, a crust of bread, and a little lemon peel; cover, and boil till half wasted. Strain, and put it into the stew-pan with the fish; add half a pint of sherry, a little chopped parsley, a few cut mushrooms, grated nutmeg, and a piece of butter rolled in flour. Place over a slow fire, and shake till the fish are enough.

SOLES, *to fry*.—Take what soles are necessary; gut and skin them; cut them down the back; draw the blade of the knife along the fins to separate the flesh; when ready to serve dip them in milk; shake a little flour over, and fry them over a good fire; when done and of a fine colour drain them upon a clean cloth; dish upon a napkin; send whole lemons to the table with them.

SOLES, *to fry*.—Dip them in egg, after having cleaned them,
and cover with fine crumbs of bread. Set on a frying-pan that is just large enough, and put into it a good quantity of fresh lard or dripping; boil, and immediately slip the fish into it; do them of a fine brown.

SOLES, *stewed*.——Scald and clean, take care of the roe, &c., lay the fish in a stew-pan, with a rich beef gravy, an onion, eight cloves, a dessert-spoonful of Jamaica pepper, the same of black, a fourth part of the quantity of gravy or port (cyder may do); simmer close covered: when nearly done add two anchovies chopped fine, a dessert-spoonful of made mustard, and some fine walnut ketchup, a bit of butter rolled in flour, shake it, and let the gravy boil a few minutes. Serve with sippets of fried bread, the roe fried, and a good deal of horse radish and lemon. *Carp may be stewed the same way.*

SOLES *to souse*.—Cut the soles on the white side; but not too deep; boil them well in sherry wine, and a little water, and vinegar; season with salt, ginger, cloves, mace; let the liquid just cover them; when it boils, put in the soles, and winter savory, sweet marjoram, sage, thyme, sliced onions, or shalots; when they are boiled enough, set them by to cool. *Hu.*

SOLE PIE.—Split some soles from the bone, and cut the fins close; season with a mixture of salt, pepper, a little nutmeg and pounded mace, and put them in layers, with oysters. They eat excellently. A pair of middling sized ones will do, and half a hundred of oysters. Put in the dish the oyster liquor, two or three spoonfuls of broth, and some butter. When the pie comes home, pour in a cupful of thick cream.

SORE THROAT.——The old

nurse's remedy is good, "Put your stocking round your neck going to bed." But I have found a piece of *new* flannel quite as beneficial, if put warm round the neck. The following gargle is useful either for ulcerated or common sore throat. Make a strong solution of alum to every half pint of which add two table-spoonfuls of port wine; gargle the throat several times a day. In ulcerated sore throats, it is safest to have the ulcers touched with caustic immediately on their appearance.——Or, gargle with a mixture of yeast and milk, and take a wine-glassful of good yeast once or twice a day. Sage and vinegar are generally recommended for a gargle. It is best to add a little salt, and from 15 to 30 drops of laudanum.——Or, apply a cold water cloth, wringed out, to the throat, covered with a dry flannel.

In the first stages of the disease, a mild emetic will be useful. In bed apply to the throat a bag of hops saturated with hot vinegar and a little salt, or camomile flowers moistened with hot vinegar, and 20 or 30 drops of laudanum,—The remedies under *Quinsy* are appropriate here. Apply to the feet and sides hot bricks covered with vinegar cloths. If constipated, take an aperient, and afterwards the Composition Powder.

SORE THROAT.-Five spoonfuls of the syrup of elderberry, mix with one spoonful of honey, and as much powdered sal prunella as will lie on a shilling. Take a teaspoonful frequently.

SORREL, *to stew.*—Wash the sorrel, and put it into a silver vessel, or stone jar, with no more water than hangs to the leaves. Simmer it as slow as you can, and when done enough, put a bit of butter, and beat it well.

SOUFFLE *of Apple and Rice.* —Blanch Carolina rice, strain it, and set it to boil in milk, with lemon-peel, and a bit of cinnamon. Let it boil till the rice is dry, then cool it, and raise a rim three inches high round the dish; having egged the dish, where it is put to make it stick well. Then egg the rice all over. Fill the dish half way up with a marmalade of apples; have ready the whites of four eggs beaten to a fine froth, and put them over the marmalade; then sift fine sugar over it, and set it in the oven, which should be warm enough to give it a beautiful colour.

SOUP, *a la Jardinere..*—Take some carrots and turnips; cut them an inch long and thickness of a penny piece, with a little parsley root. Boil gently in some good stock, till quite tender, with leeks and two heads of celery tied together; these must be taken out when serving the soup. Boil tender 12 onions whole; season with salt and pepper.

SOUP, *a la Reine.*—Take the breasts of three fowls, skewer them, put over them a thin slice of lard, cover them with paper, and put them upon the spit or into a stewpan, which must be covered with slices of ham, veal, and an onion, with two or three pared carrots and a bunch of seasoned parsley; cover it lightly with thin slices of lard, and afterwards with two or three rounds of buttered paper, that they may not take any colour; put in two or three spoonfuls of *consomme;* make them boil upon the fire, or put them into an oven; let them cook twenty minutes; take them up and let them cool; strain the soup through a gauze search, make a panade with it, hash the breasts very fine, put them in a mortar, and pound them with twenty sweet and two bitter almonds; pound all together, afterwards take it out and mix it with the *consomme* made of the carcases of the three fowls from which the breasts were taken; run it through a search.

SOUP, *a la sap.*—Boil ½ lb. of grated potatoes, 1 lb. of beef sliced thin, a pint of grey peas, an onion, and 3 ozs. of rice, in six pints of water to five, strain it through a colander, then pulp the peas to it, and turn it into a saucepan again, with two heads of celery sliced. Stew it tender, and add pepper and salt, and when you serve, add also fried bread.

SOUP AND BOUILLE.—Stew a brisket of beef with some turnips, celery, leeks, and onions, all finely cut. Put the pieces of beef into the pot first, then the roots, and half a pint of beef gravy, with a few cloves. Simmer for an hour. Add more beef gravy, and boil gently for half an hour.

SOUP, *Consomme.*—Take a proper tinned pot; heat it lightly and wipe it well; put in a shank and a piece of a buttock of beef, a knuckle of veal, a fowl, an old rabbit, or two old partridges, and about six pints of stock; reduce it upon a quick fire till it becomes a jelly, then add more stock, boil it on a quick fire and skim it; season it with three turnips, three carrots, three onions, one stuck with two or three cloves, a bunch of leeks, and celery; then put it on the side of the grate, and let it simmer till it is done enough: when the different meats of which it is composed are sufficiently cooked, they ought to be taken out, as they may be dressed for successive tables; when ready take off the fat, put it through a gauze search or a linen cloth, first wet and wrung.

SOUP, *Cressy.*—According to the season, have all sorts of vegetables picked and washed with care, such as carrots, turnips, celery, onions, &c., in small quantity; boil them a quarter of an hour; put them into a stew-pan with a large piece of butter, and some slices of ham; set them upon a slow fire till they are enough; drain and pound them in a mortar, and add the liquor in which they were boiled; rub them through a search to make a *puree;* let it boil, and leave it to cook two hours; skim well; have ready a *mitonnage*, as before directed, and serve the cressy upon it.

SOUP, *good and cheap.*—Lean beef, 1 lb., cut into small pieces; half a pint of split peas; 2 ozs. of rice, or Scotch barley; 5 potatoes, sliced; 3 onions, cut in quarters; pepper and salt to taste. Tie the peppercorns in a bag; put these into a gallon and a pint of water. Put into the oven for 3½ hours. It will waste 1 pint in the oven, but more in boiling.

SOUP, *Grand Bouillon.*—To prepare a great dinner, it is necessary that a sufficient quantity of stock for soups and sauces should be ready, for which purpose put into a large pot a piece of the breast or rump of beef, with the dressings of any other sort of meat; veal, mutton, lamb, with the bones, neck, and feet of the poultry and game, that may be prepared for removes. Put the pot upon a moderate fire, not quite filled with water, and skim it carefully; throw into it a little cold water every time you skim it, till it becomes perfectly limpid; for upon this stock depends the beauty of your soups and sauces; season it with salt, two turnips, six carrots, six onions, one of which is to be stuck with three cloves and a bunch of leeks, and let the whole simmer slowly. When the piece of meat is cooked, or nearly so, if it is to be served, put it into a stewpan, and pour over it a little of the top of the stock; wet and wring a cloth, and run the stock through, which will then be in readiness to make soups, sauces, &c.

SOUP, *Grand Consomme.*—Put into a pot two knuckles of veal, a piece of a leg of beef, a fowl, or an old cock, a rabbit, or two old partridges; add a ladleful of soup, and stir it well; when it comes to a jelly, put in a sufficient quantity of stock, and see that it is clear; let it boil, skimming and refreshing it with water; season it as the above; you may add, if you like, a clove of garlic; let it then boil slowly or simmer four or five hours: put it through a towel, and use it for mixing in sauces, or clear soups.

SOUP, *Julienne.*—Take some carrots and turnips, and turn them riband-like; a few heads of celery, some leeks and onions, and cut them in lozenges, boil them till they are cooked, then put them into clear gravy soup. Brown thickening.—N.B. You may, in summer time, add green peas, asparagus tops, French beans, some lettuce or sorrel.

SOUP, *Maigre.*—Melt ½ lb. of butter in a stewpan, shake it round and throw in six middling onions, sliced. Shake the pan well for 2 or 3 minutes, then put in 5 heads of celery, 2 handfuls of spinach, 2 cabbage-lettuces, cut small, and some parsley, Shake the pan well for 10 minutes, then put in 2 quarts of water, some crusts of bread, a tea-spoonful of beaten pepper, 3 or 4 blades of mace; add a large spoonful of white beet leaves, cut small.

Boil gently an hour. Just before serving beat in two yolks of eggs, and a spoonful of vinegar.

SOUP, *Mitonnage.*——Take a household loaf and rasp it lightly, cut out the crumb without breaking it, which will answer for frying to garnish spinach dishes or soups, or for a charlotte or a panade; round the crusts handsomely, and let them simmer a few minutes; before serving, put any vegetables on them, and pour over an empotage: serve it as hot as possible.

SOUP, *Portable.*—Boil one or two knuckles of veal, one or two shins of beef, and 3 lbs. of beef, in as much water only as will cover them. Take the marrow out of the bones, put any sort of spice you like, and three large onions. When the meat is done to rags strain it off, and put it into a *very* cold place. When cold, take off the cake of fat (which will make crusts for servants' pies); put the soup into a double-bottomed tin saucepan, and set it on a pretty quick fire, but do not let it burn. It must boil fast and uncovered, and be stirred constantly for eight hours. Put into a pan, and let it stand in a cold place a day, then pour it into a round soup chinadish, and set the dish into a stewpan of boiling water on a stove, and let it boil, and be now and then stirred, till the soup is thick and ropy—then it is enough. Pour it into the little round part at the bottom of cups or basons turned upside-down to form cakes, and when cold turn them out on flannel to dry. Keep them in tin canisters. When they are to be used, melt them in boiling water, and if you wish the flavour of herbs, or any thing else, boil it first, strain off the water, and melt the soup in it.

This is very convenient in the country, or at sea, where fresh meat is not always at hand, as by this means a basin of soup may be made in five minutes.

SOUP, *Royal.*—Take a scrag or knuckle of veal, slices of undressed gammon of bacon, onions, mace, and a small quantity of water; simmer till very strong, and lower it with a good beef broth made the day before, and stewed till the meat is done to rags. Add cream, vermicelli, almonds, and a roll.

SOUPS, *various.*—Good soups may be made from fried meats, where the fat and gravy are added to the boiled barley; and for that purpose, fat beef steaks, pork steaks, mutton chops, &c. should be preferred, as containing more of the nutritious principle. When nearly done frying, add a little water, which will produce a gravy to be added to the barley broth; a little wheat flour should be dredged in also; a quantity of onions, cut small, should also be fried with the fat, which gives the soup a fine flavour, assisted by seasonings, &c.

Soups may be made from broiled meats. While the fat beef steak is doing before the fire, or mutton chop, &c., save the drippings on a dish, in which a little flour, oatmeal, with cut onions, &c., are put.

SOUP, *White Blond de Veau.*—Butter the bottom of a saucepan, and put into it some slices of ham, four or five pounds of a leg of veal, two or three carrots, and as many onions; wet them with a ladleful of *grand bouillon*, make it sweat over a slow fire, and reduce it to jelly; when it is of a fine yellow tint, take it off the fire, prick the meat with the point of a knife to let the juice flow; cover, and let it sweat another quarter of an hour, and then put in a sufficient quantity of *grand bouillon:* season it with parsley and small onions, a clove of garlic stuck with a clove; boil and skim, and put it to simmer on the edge of the grate, and when enough, skim it, run it throgh a cloth, and make use of it for empotage, or rice or vermicelli soup, and even sauces.

SOUSE, *for Brawn.*—Boil a quarter of a peck of wheat bran, a sprig of bay, and a sprig of rosemary, in two gallons of water, with 4 ozs. of salt in it, for half an hour. Strain it, and let it get cold.

SPANISH CREAM.——Dissolve in ½ pint of rose-water, 1 oz. of isinglass cut small; run it through a hair sieve; add the yolks of three or four eggs, beaten and mixed with half a pint of cream, and two sorrel leaves. Pour it into a deep dish, sweeten with loaf sugar powdered. Stir it till cold, and put it into moulds. Lay rings round in different coloured sweetmeats. Add, if you like, a little sherry, and a lump or two of sugar, rubbed well upon the rind of a lemon to extract the flavour.

SPANISH FLIES, *Tincture of.*—Take finely powdered Spanish flies, 2 ozs.; spirits of wine, 1 pint. Infuse for two or three days, and strain. This tincture is an acid stimulant for external use. It is good to apply to chilblains, for chafed skin, frostbites, &c.

SPANISH INFUSION, *for colds, coughs, &c.*-Spanish juice, cut into small pieces, 1 oz.; salts of tartar, 3 drachms. Infuse in a quart of boiling water for a night: to the strained liquor, add 1½ ozs. of the syrup of poppies. Take three or four times a day.

SPAR BASKET.—Procure a small common wire basket, and cover the wire with different coloured worsted, the brightest you can obtain; suspend this in a vessel so that it may not touch the bottom or sides by two or three inches. Then take as much boiling water as will cover it, having previously dissolved as much alum in the water as it will take up. Pour this over the basket, and in twelve hours you may take it out: it will be covered with masses of splendid coloured crystals, glittering with all the colours of the rainbow.

SPARE-RIB OF PORK, *to roast.*—About 9 lbs. will take 2½ hours roasting. Baste well to prevent the skin burning.

SPASMS.—Oil of red lavender, 1 part; sal-volatile, 1 part; oil of peppermint, 2 parts. Mix, and take 10 or 12 drops in half a wineglassful of lukewarm or cold water. If the first dose is not efficacious, repeat.

SPASMS, *Certain cure for.*—Take threepennyworth of balsam of sulphur, and the same quantity of the oil of aniseed; put these together, and let them stand in a warm place for 24 hours. Then take twopennyworth of the spirits of wine, and twopennyworth of spirits of turpentine; put these together, and let them stand as above; then mix the whole well together. Take 7 or 8 drops on a piece of loaf sugar, when the pain is on; it will give instant relief.

SPEARMINT WATER, *to distil.*—Take of spearmint leaves, any quantity, and three times the quantity of water; distil as long as the liquor which comes over has a considerable taste, or smell of the mint.——Or, take spearmint leaves, dried, 1½ lb., and as much water as is sufficient to prevent burning. Distil one gallon.

SPECIFICS.—Medicines curing a disease by an unknown mode of action.

SPECULATION, *Game of.*—This is a lively round game, very often introduced into parties, as allowing scope for conversation and laughter. Almost any number may play at it; in fact, the more the merrier.

A complete pack of cards is used, bearing the same value as at whist, with fish or counters, on which a certain value is fixed; the highest trump in each deal wins the pool.

After determining the deal, the dealer puts six fish into the pool, and the other players four each; next three cards are given to each by one at a time, and another turned up for trumps.

The cards must not be looked at except in this manner: the eldest hand shows his top card, which if a trump, the company may speculate or bid for; he that bids highest getting it and paying for it, provided the price offered is satisfactory to the seller of that trump.

After this is settled, or if the first card does not prove a trump, then the next eldest shows his top card, and so on; the company speculate as they please on each trump turned up, till all are discovered, when the possessor of the highest trump, whether by purchase or otherwise, gains the pool.

To play this game well, little more is requisite than recollecting what superiors of that particular suit have appeared in the preceding deals, and calculating the probability of the trump offered proving the highest in the deal.

When no high trump has been discovered, it is often customary to purchase cards on speculation, before they are shewn; more particularly when but few are left to be turned up.

When a party turns up a trump he ought to be allowed time to sell it to the best advantage, before another card is turned up. It is advisable to sell any low trump if you can, particularly if there are many players. When a card is purchased, the buyer places it on his other cards immediately before him, and does not turn up any more until a better trump appears in some other hand.

In some companies it is usual for all who turn up a knave to put a fish into the pool. The game may also be varied, as is frequently done, by dealing a spare hand, which must not be looked at till all the rest have been shown; and if it contains the best trump, the pool remains for the next deal, in addition to the usual contribution of every player.

SPERMACETI OINTMENT —Take of olive oil, one pint; white wax and spermaceti, of each three ounces. Melt them with a gentle heat, and briskly stir together till quite cold. If two drachms of camphor previously rubbed with a small quantity of oil, be added to the above, it will make the White Camphorated Ointment.

SPICED BEEF.-Take a round of an ox, or young heifer, from 20 to 40 lbs. Cut it neatly, so that the thin flank end can wrap nearly round. Take from 2 to 4 ozs. of saltpetre, and 1 oz of coarse sugar, and two handfuls of common salt. Mix them well together; rub it all over. The next day salt it well as for boiling. Let it lie from two to three weeks, turning it every two or three days. Take out of the pickle, and wipe it dry. Then take cloves, mace, well powdered, a spoonful of gravy, and rub it well into the beef. Roll it up as tightly as possible; skewer it, and tie it up tight. Pour in the liquor till the meat is quite saturated, in which state it must be kept.

To keep the beef a long time, once in two months boil the pickle, and clear off the scum. Put in when boiled 2 ozs. of sugar, and ½ oz. of common salt. When taken out of pickle, dry well, and put in paper bags, and hang them in a dry place.

SPICE CAKE.—Take 3 lbs. of flour, 2 lbs. of butter, 1½ lb. of sugar, 1 lb. of currants, and a few seeds; mix all together with milk; observe that the butter and sugar must be rubbed into the flour, and then made into round cakes of any size, and nipped on the edges, then baked in a pretty hot oven, with its door open while you bake.

SPINACH *to dress.*—Spinach requires great care in washing and picking it. When that is done, throw it into a sauce-pan that will just hold it, sprinkle it with a little salt, and cover close. The pan must be set on the fire, and well shaken. When done, beat the spinach well with a small bit of butter; it looks well if pressed into a tin mould in the form of a large leaf, which is sold at the tin shops. A spoonful of cream is an improvement.

SPINACH AND EGGS.-When the spinach is boiled, it must be squeezed dry, chopped very fine, and put into a stew-pan, with a little butter, cream, pepper, and salt. Dish the spinach, and then put in the eggs to poach; trim the ragged parts of the whites, and put them on the spinach.

SPINACH SOUP.—Shred two handfuls of spinach, a turnip, two onions, a head of celery, two carrots, and a little thyme and parsley, put all into a stew-pot, with a bit of butter the size of a walnut, and a pint of broth, or the water in which meat has been boiled; stew till the vegetables are quite tender, work them through a coarse cloth or sieve with a spoon, then to the pulp of the vegetables and liquor, put a quart of fresh water, pepper, and salt, and boil all together. Have ready some suet-dumplings, the size of a walnut; and before you put the soup into the tureen, put them all into it. The suet must not be shred too fine.

SPIRITS of MINDERERUS.—Take volatile sal ammoniac, any quantity. Pour on it gradually distilled vinegar till the effervescence ceases. This medicine is useful in promoting a discharge by the skin and urinary passages. It is also a good external application in strains and bruises. When intended to raise a sweat, half an ounce of it in a cup of warm gruel, may be given to the patient in bed every hour till it has the desired effect.

SPIRIT VARNISH.—Strong alcohol, 32 parts; pure mastic, 4 parts; sandarach, 3 parts; clear Venice turpentine, 2 parts; coarsely powdered glass, 4 parts. Dissolve.

SPITTING OF BLOOD.—In cases of spitting of blood, it is often difficult to determine whether it proceeds from the internal surface of the mouth, from the fauces, from the stomach, or from the lungs. When the blood is of a florid or frothy appearance, and brought up with more or less coughing, preceded by rigours, a short tickling cough, a saltish taste, anxiety, and tightness across the chest, its source is the lungs. The blood proceeding from the lungs is usually of a florid colour, and mixed with a little frothy mucous only. It may be distinguished from bleeding from the stomach, by its being raised by hacking or coughing, and by its florid and frothy appearance; that from the stomach is vomited in considerable quantities, and is of a dark colour.

What is strictly meant by *spitting of blood*, is when the blood is discharged from a ruptured vessel in the lungs, which is technically termed *Hæmoptysis*. It occurs generally from the age of 16 to 35. It is often an hereditary disease, which implies a peculiar and faulty conformation. It happens to persons who discover the smallest capacity of the lungs, by the narrowness of the chest, and by the prominency of their shoulders, an evidence of difficult respiration. It occurs in persons of a slender delicate make; to persons of much sensibility and irritability, and whose bodies are of a delicate texture. It arises sometimes from the stoppage of the menstrual flux, from plethora, and violent exercise of the lungs.

One great cause of hæmoptysis is, the deposition of scrofulous matter in the substance of the lungs, forming tubercles. The blood-vessels being partially distended by the pressure of tubercles, are easily ruptured by cough, or bodily exertion.

Treatment.—Moderate the discharge of blood by avoiding whatever tends to irritate the body and increase the action of the heart. A low diet should be strictly observed, and external heat and bodily exercise avoided; the air of the room should be cool, and the drink (which should consist chiefly of barley-water, acidulated with lemon-juice) taken cold, and the patient not suffered to exert his voice. After the operation of a little gentle aperient medicine, as lenitive electuary, or an infusion of senna, with a little cream of tartar dissolved in it, take 10 drops of laudanum, and 10 drops of elixir of vitriol in half a cupful of cold water. If there is no cough, the laudanum may be omitted.

A little salt and water given will often check spitting of blood, when it comes on. Put the feet in warm water, and give as above, the elixir of vitriol, &c. Give also ipecacuanha powder in small doses, of from one to two grains every four hours.

Emetics have been given in this disease with advantage by Dr. Robinson, and still more lately by Dr. Stoll, of Vienna, who observes, that in discharges of blood from the lungs, ipecacuanha powder often acts like a charm, seeming to close the open vessels sooner and more effectually than any other remedy. The good effects of this remedy are probably the consequence of the compression the lungs undergo during vomiting, from the action of the diaphragm and expiratory muscles.

The recurrence of hæmoptysis should be prevented by invigorating the lungs and purifying the blood, and by the use of cooling and astringent medicines. Keep in the mouth a little alum, or saltpetre. The patient should participate very freely of acidulous fruits; as, roasted apples, oranges, lemons, &c. Alcoholic drinks should be strictly forbidden. A decoction of bark with lemon juice or a few drops of elixir of vitriol, is of great service.

When the symptoms are severe, give 8 or 10 drops of the tincture of digitalis, or a drachm of nitre dissolved in cold water, and afterwards a compound of ipecacuanha and Glauber's salt. In extreme cases, give from 10 to 20 drops of elixir of vitriol every two hours; or give the vapour bath, and an injection, and place hot bricks to the feet in bed. Sugar of lead, 2 grains; opium, $\frac{1}{4}$ of a grain, made into a pill with a little honey, or treacle and liquorice powder, may be given every five hours. The temporary application of cloths dipped in cold water to the genitals will check spitting of blood. Ice is still better. Mustard plasters applied to the legs and feet have been recommended, and found beneficial.

The diet must be light and easy of digestion. The patient must avoid much speaking, and all muscular exertion, and all cold and damp.

SPITTING OF BLOOD.—Take a tea-cupful of stewed prunes at lying down for two or three nights.—Or, two tea-spoonfuls of nettle-juice every morning, and a large cup of decoction of nettles at night, for a week.—Or, 3 spoonfuls of sage-juice in a little honey. —Or, half a tea-spoonful of Barbadoes tar, on a piece of lump sugar at night. It commonly cures at once.——Infusion of red roses, 5 ozs.; syrup of poppy, $\frac{1}{2}$ oz.; diluted sulphuric acid, 20 drops. Mix. Two tea-spoonfuls three or four times a day.—*Wesley.*

SPONGE BISCUITS.—Beat the yolks of ten eggs half an hour. Add 1½ lb. of sugar sifted, and whisk it well till it rises in bubbles. Then beat the whites to a strong froth, and whisk them well with the sugar and yolks. Beat in 14 ozs. of flour, with the rinds of two lemons grated. Sprinkle sugar upon them. Bake in moulds, in a hot oven, but do not close it. Bake half an hour. *Far.*

SPONGE CAKE.—Weigh 10 eggs, and their weight in very fine sugar, and that of 6 in flour; beat the yolks with the flour, and the whites alone, to a very stiff froth; then by degrees mix the whites and the flour with the other ingredients, and beat them well half an hour. Bake an hour.

Another, without butter.—Dry

1 lb. of flour, and 1¼ lb. of sugar; beat 7 eggs, yolks and whites apart; grate a lemon, and, with a spoonful of brandy, beat the whole together with your hand for an hour.. Bake in a buttered pan. Sweetmeats may be added

Another.——Beat 12 eggs to a froth; dissolve a little volatile salts in half a pint of hot water, and let it cool; mix them together, and beat them for 10 minutes; then add 1 lb. of grated loaf sugar, and nearly 1 lb. of fine flour; beat them well together, add a few seeds, and bake in a hot oven. Rub some of the pieces of sugar on the rind of a lemon to give it a flavour.

SPRAIN.—Take of camphorated spirit, common vinegar, spirits of turpentine, of each, 1 oz.

SPRAIN.—Hold the part in very cold water for two hours.—— Or, apply cloths dipt therein, four times doubled, for two hours, changing them as they grow warm. ——Or, bathe in good crab verjuice.——Or, boil bran in wine vinegar to a poultice. Apply this warm, and renew it once in twelve hours.——Or, mix a little turpentine with flour and the yolk of an egg, and apply it as a plaster. This cures in a desperate case.

Weakness remaining after a sprain is cured by fomenting the part daily with beef brine. Suppose the ancle sprained:—1st. Foment it with warm vinegar four or five times every four hours. 2nd. Stand, if you can, three or four minutes at a time on both your feet, and frequently move the sprained foot. Sometimes also while sitting with your foot on a low stool, move it to and fro. 3rd. Let it be gently rubbed with a warm hand at least thrice a-day. 4th. Two hours after every application of the vinegar, let it be just wetted with spirits of wine, and then gently rubbed.—*Wesley.*

SPRAINS.——Take a few globules of Rhus Toxicodendron, and apply to the sprained part this Rhus liniment for about 10 minutes, and repeat twice a day for three days. The Rhus is sold by the Homœopathic chemists.

SPRAINS *of the Muscles of the Back.*—Take of Canada turpentine, ½ oz; soap liniment, 6 ozs., and one-pennyworth of laudanum. Mix, and rub well in before a hot fire.

SPRATS, *to broil.*—Sprats are very good and nutritious food; but to be enjoyed they must be eaten in the room in which they are cooked; they admit of few removes, on account of becoming cold so soon.

When cleaned, they should be fastened in rows by a skewer run through the head, and then broiled; dredge with flour, and place on a gridiron over a nice clear fire for 4 or 5 minutes. Grease the gridiron. Or, they may be done in a Dutch oven.

SPRATS, *to bake.*—Rub them with salt and pepper; put into a deep dish; cover with vinegar and port wine; cover and place in the oven all night. Cochineal liquor gives them a rich colour. They keep well. *Far.*

SQUILL MIXTURE.—Take of simple cinnamon-water, 5 ozs.; vinegar of squills, 1 oz.; syrup of marsh-mallows, 1½ oz. Mix them. This mixture, by promoting expectoration and the secretion of urine, proves serviceable in asthmatic and dropsical habits. A table-spoonful at a time.

STAINS on LINEN, *to remove.*—Apply benzoin; or salt of wormwood, diluted with water; or hold the article over the flames of brimstone; or wash with soap and potass.

STALE BEER, *to restore.*—To about a quart of stale beer, put ½ a tea-spoonful of salt of wormwood; this will restore the beer, and make it sparkle when poured into a glass like bottled porter.

"STAMMERING," *Dr. Turner* says, "is caused by attempts to speak with empty lungs. In singing, the lungs are kept well inflated, and there is no stuttering. The method of cure is to require the patient to keep his lungs well filled; to draw frequent and long breaths, to speak loudly, and to pause on the instant of finding embarrasment in his speech, taking a long inspiration before he goes on again. I cured one of the worst cases I ever knew on this principle."

STAMMERING.—Frequently read aloud with the teeth closed, and tap with the finger at every syllable pronounced.

STEAM JOINTS, *Red Putty for.*—Stiff white lead worked well in red lead powder.

STEEL POWDER.—Take filings of steel and loaf sugar, of each, 2 ozs.; ginger, 2 drachms. Pound them together. In obstructions of the menses, and for strengthening the constitution, this powder is valuable. Take a tea-spoonful twice a day.

STEEL, *to preserve from rust.*—Rub it well with a little sweet oil and Bath brick; wipe it very dry; warm the article at the fire, and rub it over with virgin wax.

STEW.—In a jar of cold water put a shin of beef; put in salt, a few cloves, pepper, onions, celery, savoury herbs, &c. Put it into a slow oven the night before, and simmer till noon. Serve with toasted bread.

STIMULATING FOMENTATION.--Cayenne pepper, 3 ozs.; mustard seed, just bruised, 2 ozs.; whiskey, 2 quarts. Simmer all together a few minutes. Excellent external application in cholera, paralysis, palsy, rheumatism, &c. A less quantity may be made.

STIMULATING LINIMENT.—Cayenne, 1½ oz.; salt, 1 table-spoonful; spirits of wine, 2 ozs.; camphor, ½ oz.; spirits of turpentine, ¼ pint. Bottle, and shake now and then during 1 day. Then add ½ a pint of vinegar.—It is excellent for sponging the body in cases of pain, debility, inflammation, rheumatism, gout, sore throat, numbness, neuralgia, &c.

STINGS OF BEES.—Rub the place with the newly-pressed juice of the honeysuckle.——Or, wet it with extract of lead, (the *liquor plumbi* of the shops) and keep a rag soaked in the extract on the puncture a short time. Hartshorn, spirits of wine, or a solution of sal-ammoniac, are sometimes effectually used.

STITCH *in the side.*——Apply treacle spread on brown paper.

STOCK, *for Fish Soups.*-Take 1 lb. of skate, 4 or 5 flounders, and 2 lbs. of eels. Clean them well, and cut them into pieces; cover them with water, and season them with mace, pepper, salt, and an onion stuck with cloves, a head of celery, two parsley roots sliced, and a bunch of sweet herbs. Simmer an hour and a half, closely covered, and then strain it off for use. If for brown soup, first fry the fish brown in butter, and then do as above. It will not keep more than two or three days.

STOCK, *for Gravy Soup.*——Take 20 lbs. of coarse lean beef, cut into small pieces, and put into a pot, with water to cover it. Skim well. Add pot herbs to give it the desired flavour. Season with salt and ground pepper; simmer till the meat becomes tender; skim well, and strain.

Or, put a knuckle of veal, 1 lb. of lean beef, and 1 lb. of the lean of gammon of bacon, all sliced, into a stew-pan, with onions, turnips, celery, and two quarts of water. Stew the meat tender, but do not let it brown. It will serve either for soup, or brown, or white gravy; if for brown, put some of the browning in, and boil it a few minutes.

STOMACHICS.—Medicines, stimulating and warming the stomach.

STOMACHIC CORDIAL.—Ginger, 1 drachm; tincture of cardamoms, 2 drachms; compound tincture of senna, 3 drachms.

STOMACHIC WINE.—Powdered Peruvian bark, 1 oz.; cardamom seeds, and orange peel bruised, each 2 drachms. Infuse in a bottle of Port wine for five or six days. Strain off the wine. This is a good tonic for the stomach and intestines; it is also a preventive of intermittent fever. It gives tone and vigour to the system after recovering from disease.

STOMACHIC DRAUGHT.—Quassia shavings, 2 drachms; boiling water, 1 pint. Let it remain in a close vessel till cold. Strain. Add to the liquor, tincture of cardamom, 2 ozs.; compound spirits of lavender, 4 drachms; rhubarb in powder, 1 scruple. Take three table-spoonfuls an hour before dinner to create an appetite.

STOMACHIC ELIXIR, *Dr. Stoughton's.*—Pare off the thin yellow rinds of 6 large Seville oranges, and put them in a quart bottle with 1 oz. of gentian root, scraped and sliced, and $\frac{1}{2}$ a drachm of cochineal. Pour over these ingredients a pint of brandy; shake the bottle well several times during that and the following day; let it stand two days more to settle, and clear it off into bottles for use.

Take one or two tea-spoonfuls morning and afternoon, in a glass of wine or in a cup of tea. This elegant preparation is a most valuable tonic.

Another.—Gentian root, 2 ozs.; bitter oranges sliced, 1 oz.; Virginia snake root, $\frac{1}{2}$ oz. Bruise, and infuse for four days in 1 pint of brandy; then add a pint of water. A wine-glassful to be taken occasionally. Good for flatulency, indigestion, want of appetite, &c.

STONE.—Stone is an accumulation of particles of gravel which unite and form a hard mass, or stone; and they enlarge by successive layers of gravel until they become very large and difficult to remove.

The symptoms are itching at the extremity of the glans of the penis, an increased desire to make water, with more or less pain in making it; even when the bladder is emptied, the pain continues; sometimes there is difficulty in retaining the water; and at other times the flow of it is liable to stop suddenly. The irritation caused by the presence of a stone often produces remote symptoms, as pain in the back and lower limbs.

Treatment.—Give the diuretic medicines described pages 145, 146. See also *Gravel,* page 185. Drink strong pennyroyal tea; or a decoction of burdock, dandelion, white carrot, and parsley roots. Drink half a cupful several times a day. Flannels dipped in the Stimulating Liniment, combined with tincture of cayenne, with 30 drops of laudanum, may be applied externally to the region of pain. It is said that a gill of red onion juice and a pint of horsemint tea, drank morning and evening, but not together, will cause a change, and probably dissolve the stone. The following pills may be taken with great benefit:—Parsley seeds, powdered, ¼ oz.; castile soap, 1 oz.; oil of juniper, 30 drops; solidified copaiba, 1 oz. Form into pills. Take two per day. Drink at the same time a solution of saleratus.

Many persons have been benefited by a decoction of the wild carrot. Injections, and the vapour bath are very useful. When the patient finds it difficult to make water, let him lie on his back for a while, by which the stone may be thrown to the posterior part of the body, and enable him to make water by turning on one or the other side. The diuretic pills should be taken frequently.

Dr. Morris, of Canada, has found that an injection of castor oil has great effect in relieving sufferings caused by a stone in the bladder, and as the pain and irritation from this cause are often very great, we recommend it to the notice of those labouring under the affliction. Dr. Morris, being afflicted with the stone, tried the experiment on his own person.

"I first rid myself of the contents of my bladder; then with a large syringe I injected through a small leaden tube, reaching to the sphincter, 2 ozs. of cold drawn castor oil, and I cannot express my feelings caused by the change which took place upon its introduction, for it seemed as if a new lower half had been given me. The relief continuing, I went to bed, and can safely say, that I had not known, for sometime previous, the pleasure of a sound and uninterrupted sleep. Latterly I never awoke without a wish to make water, and the morning following was the first expectation to it. When I did obey the call, I took care, finding that the oil came last, to leave as much within the bladder as I could.

After this the bladder was constantly supplied with 2 or 3 ozs. of castor oil, and under this treatment every symptom of irritation vanished, and during two months no one symptom re-appeared to remind him of the existence of the calculous concretion.

STONE.—Beat onions into a pulp and apply them as a poultice to the back, or to the groin. It gives speedy ease in the most racking pain.——Or, take morning and evening a tea-spoonful of onions, calcined in a fire shovel into white ashes, in sherry wine. An oz. will often dissolve the stone.——Or, drink largely of water impregnated with fixed air. Those who have not a convenient apparatus, may substitute the following method: Dissolve 16 grains of salt of tartar in 6 spoonfuls of water, to which add as much water acidulated with oil of vitriol as will neutralise the salt. They are to be gradually mixed with each other, so as to prevent the effervescence or dissipation of the fixed air as much as possible.——Or, boil an oz. of common thistle-root, and 4 drachms of liquorice in a pint of water. Drink of it every morning.——Or, take a decoction, or juice, or syrup of ground ivy, morning and evening. —*Wesley.*

STONE-WORK. *to preserve.* —Give one coating of a saturated solution of carbonate of potash, and another coat of muriate of lime (or chloride of calcium).

STOVES, *the bright bars of, to polish.*—Clear from dirt, and then dip a piece of hat felt or cloth, into a composition of soft soap and emery; polish with fine glass paper, or rotten stone.

STRANGURY. — A frequent disposition to make water, attended with smarting pain, heat, difficulty in voiding it: and a great sensation of fulness in the bladder. Give plentiful draughts of warm liquid, as barley-water, infusion of linseed, or of gum arabic, with a little nitre dissolved in it. At the same time, apply warm fomentations to the lower part of the belly, and copious emollient and opiate injections are to be administered; as gruel, half a pint, sweet oil, 1 oz., and laudanum, 12 drops.

STRAWBERRIES.——They have many valuable medical properties. They are diaphoretic, diuretic, diluent, cooling, pectoral, of great benefit to the lungs. In fevers, on account of their refrigerant properties, they are very useful. Persons afflicted with gravel, scurvy, gout, and consumption, may be greatly benefited by them. They cure chilblains; the water is used in France as a wash for that purpose.

STRAWBERRIES, *to preserve whole.*—Take equal weights of the fruit and refined sugar, lay the former in a large dish, and sprinkle half the sugar in fine powder over, give a gentle shake to the dish that the sugar may touch the whole of the fruit; next day make a thin syrup with the remainder of the sugar, and instead of water allow one pint of red currant juice to every pound of strawberries; in this simmer them until sufficiently jellied. Choose the largest scarlets, or others when not dead ripe.

STRAWBERRIES, *to preserve in wine.*—Put a quantity of the finest large strawberries into a gooseberry-bottle, and strew in three large spoonfuls of fine sugar; fill up with Madeira wine or fine sherry.

STRAWBERRY SHERBET. —Take 1 lb. of fine strawberries, and crush them in a mortar; add to them 3 pints of water. Pour this into a basin with 2 small lemons sliced, and 2 table-spoonfuls of orange-flower water, to remain 4 hours. Put 1½ lb. of loaf sugar into another basin; cover it with a cloth, through which pour the strawberry juice to drain through; gather up the cloth, and press out all the juice. When the sugar is dissolved, strain again. Put it to be iced, or add a wine-glassful of brandy.

STRAW BONNETS, *to clean.* —First brush them with soap and water; then with a solution of oxalic acid.

Bleaching.—If they want bleaching, proceed thus:—Get a deep box air-tight, if possible; place at the bottom a stone, on the stone a flat piece of iron red hot, or a pan of charcoal, on which scatter powdered brimstone; close the lid, and let the bonnets remain a night. There should be hooks in the box, on which to hang the bonnets.

STRICTURE OF THE RECTUM.—It often proceeds from costiveness, and hardened fœces, which lacerate the parts in passing down the rectum; also by drastic purges, piles, &c. The rectum becomes partially or nearly closed by tumours or scirrhus, which renders evacuation very painful, except the fœces are in a very liquid state.

Treatment.—Eat chiefly bread made of unsifted flour; and small doses, twice or thrice a day, of the best Turkey rhubarb and magnesia; this aperient has no injurious effect; the same may be said of castor oil; they do not tend to constipation after promoting evacuation.

The rectum may be dilated by the half of a small tallow candle, dipped in sweet oil; or by means of a bougie, sold by chemists. They should be inserted from 10 to 20 minutes. Occasionally take an injection of slippery elm bark and castor oil; retain it as long as possible.

Let the diet be mild, cooling, and easy of digestion; and, if you value ease and comfort, avoid the use of all intoxicating drinks—the great creators of piles, strictures, and diseases of the liver and heart.

STURGEON, *to boil.*—Water, 2 quarts; vinegar, 1 pint; a stick of horseradish; a little lemon peel, salt, pepper, a bay leaf. In this boil the fish; when the flesh is ready to leave the bones, take it up; melt ½ lb. of butter; add an anchovy, some mace, a few shrimps, good mushroom ketchup, and lemon juice; when it boils, put in the dish; serve with the sauce; garnish with fried oysters, horseradish, and lemon. *Hu.*

STURGEON, *to broil.*—Cut slices, rub beaten eggs over them, and sprinkle them with crumbs of bread, parsley, pepper, and salt; wrap them in white paper, and broil gently. Use for sauce, butter, anchovy, and soy.

STURGEON, *to dress fresh.*—Cut slices, rub egg over them, then sprinkle with crumbs of bread, parsley, pepper, salt; fold them in paper, and broil gently.

Sauce; butter, anchovy, and soy.

STURGEON, *to roast.*—Put a piece of butter, rolled in flour, into a stew-pan with four cloves, a bunch of sweet herbs, two onions, some pepper and salt, half a pint of water, and a glass of vinegar. Set it over the fire till hot; then let it become lukewarm, and steep the fish in it an hour or two. Butter a paper well, tie it round, and roast it without letting the spit run through. Serve with sorrel and anchovy sauce.

ST. VITUS'S DANCE.—This is a convulsive disease, principally attacking children from 10 to 16 years of age. It is indicated by a twitching and convulsive action of the muscles of the body, and by lameness or unsteadiness of one of the legs, which the patient draws after him like an idiot. Then it affects the hand on the same side; so that if a glass of liquor be put into his hand to drink, before he can get it to his mouth, he uses a great number of odd gestures, on account of the hand being drawn different ways by the convulsive action of the muscles, so that he cannot carry it in a straight line. The will of the patient seems often to yield to these convulsive motions as to a propensity. After continuing some weeks, the intellectual operations of the brain are weakened. Females are most subject to this disease.

This disease arises from an increased irritability of the nervous system, which is often produced by some derangement of the stomach, bowels, and nerves; sometimes by worms, violent passions, fright, or violent mental emotions, &c. In females, it probably arises from the same causes which produce hysterics.

Treatment--The irritation of the cerebral system (brain and nerves) being generally symptomatic of a disordered state of the digestive organs, or kept up by irritation in the stomach or bowels, the cure must be commenced by a purgative. Do not allow the bowels to be constipated. If the stomach is deranged, give an emetic. (See *Emetic.*) This will evacuate and cleanse the stomach, give it tone, and benefit the nervous system. Repeat, if necessary. The diet must be very plain. The vapour bath of bitter decoction is of immense service. Rub the body frequently with the Stimulating Liniment. When symptoms of improvement are manifest, give Peruvian bark in port wine, adding water if too strong; or give the Restorative Wine Bitters, adding a ¼ oz. of the red oxide of iron. Give the aperients now and then, especially the *Dyspeptic Pill*, page 150. The subcarbonate of iron, 2 drachms for a dose, is a most valuable remedy. It may be given in a little syrup, beer, or porter.

Dr. Reece says, "When the symptoms are abated, cold bathing every morning, if it does not alarm the mind, will prove of great advantage; and with the use of the muriated tincture of steel, in the dose of 10 or 15 drops, in a glass of cold valerian and camomile tea, will probably complete the cure: if the patient have not sufficient resolution to go into the cold bath, cold water may be applied every morning to the head.

The diet should be regulated according to the strength of the patient: if plethoric, a low diet should be observed, and wine and stimulants avoided; on the contrary, if the body be much debilitated, a nutritious diet should be employed; but even in this case, wine and stimulants should be allowed with great caution."

STYE.—It is a small boil which projects from the eyelid, much inflamed, and very painful. Apply a poultice of linseed meal, or bread and milk, and take at the same time an aperient. If the stye is ripe, puncture it, and then apply spermaceti ointment.

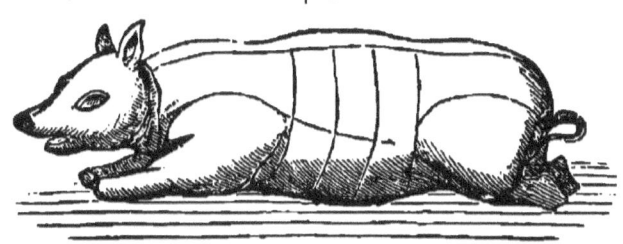

SUCKING PIG, *to roast.*—— Get it when just killed: this is of great advantage. Let it be scalded. Put some sage, crumbs of bread, salt, and pepper, into the belly, and sew it up. Observe to skewer the legs back, or the under part will not crisp. Lay it to a brisk fire till dry; then rub the pig with butter in every part. Dredge flour over it; scrape off the flour with a blunt knife, rub it well with a buttered cloth, and take off the head while at the fire. Then take it up, cut it down the back and belly, lay it into the dish, and chop quickly the sage and bread very fine, and mix plenty of fine melted butter and a little flour. Put the sauce into the dish after the pig has been split down the back, and garnished with the ears and the two jaws. Many now serve a sucking pig whole. Pour the gravy into the sauce; and garnish with lemon or bread sauce and currants.

SUCKING PIG, *baked.*—Prepare in the same way as for roasting, and rub it over with white of egg, which has been slightly beaten. Baste it well with butter.

SUCCEDANEUM *for filling Decayed Teeth.*--Tinfoil and quicksilver. Melt together in a convenient vessel, and take a small quantity, knead it in the palm of the hand, and apply it directly.

SUDORIFICS. —— Medicines causing much perspiration.

SUDORIFIC, OR FEVER POWDER.—Crawley root, 1 oz.; lobelia herb, ½ oz.; pleurisy root, 1 oz.; skunk cabbage, ½ oz. Powder, and mix them together. Dose, from a quarter to half a tea-spoonful every one hour and a half till perspiration is produced. It may be given in balm or common tea. In fevers, inflammations, influenza, and colds, this powder is invaluable. It subdues irritation, corrects the pulse, improves respiration, and promotes sound natural sleep. It is sure, if properly administered, to arrest a fever. Keep it in a bottle, well corked.

SUET DUMPLINGS.—Shred 1 lb. of suet; mix with 1¼ lb. of flour, 2 eggs beaten separately, a little salt, and as little milk as will make it. Make it into two small balls. Boil 20 minutes. The fat of loins or necks of mutton finely shred makes a more delicate dumpling than suet.

SUET PUDDING.—Take six spoonfuls of flour, 1 lb. of suet, shred small, 4 eggs, a spoonful of beaten ginger, a spoonful of salt, and a quart of milk. Mix the eggs and flour with a pint of milk very thick, and with the seasoning, mix in the rest of the milk with the suet. Boil two hours.

SUGAR, *to clarify.*—Put the whites of two eggs in four pints of water; froth the water by whipping it with a whisk; put into a proper pan a loaf of sugar of 12 or 14 lbs., broken in pieces; wet it, and make it fall by adding two-thirds of the water in which the egg has been mixed; set it upon the fire; take care when it rises; throw in a little cold water, and take it off, to let it fall and throw up the scum; in five or six minutes put it again on the fire, and continue to skim it as it rises, throwing in a little water sufficient to keep it from flying over: when it is very pure it will rise no more; take it off, and pass it through a wet bag or napkin. The first degree is the short thread; for which it must again be put upon the fire; let it boil, till dipping the finger into it, and pressing it against the thumb, which on opening forms a thread and breaks, and runs back into a drop upon the finger.

SUGAR, *to clear all kinds of.*—Take a little gum arabic, and a little isinglass dissolved in hot water; pour it when dissolved in your sugar, when it is boiling, and it will clear all the sediment to the top of the pan, which you must skim off as soon as it rises.—Loaf sugar may be cleared with the white of an egg, isinglass, or gum arabic. A little of each will do.

SUGAR BOILING.——When you boil loaf sugar, to about 3 lbs. add a table-spoonful of vinegar; it prevents it from going too hard and glassy while you are making it up.

You may make birds, &c. of all kinds, out of a loaf sugar, when boiled and pulled till white as snow.

Loaf sugar also, when boiled, by pulling it very well, rolling it into long rolls and twisted a little, will make rock, which is commonly called snowy rock, or snow.

Sugar when boiled may be made into small balls, called bull's eyes.

You may twist, roll, and cut it into any shape you choose.

A marble stone must be provided to make your paste on, also to pour your sugar on when boiled. —In purchasing all your articles, be careful to have them good and genuine.

SUGAR CAKE.—Half a lb. of butter, 1 lb. of flour, 3 eggs, milk enough to form a dough. Beat the butter and sugar together. Whisk the eggs light, and add them; then stir in the milk and flour alternately, so as to form a dough. Cut in cakes, and bake in a moderate oven.

SUGAR GINGERBREAD.— Butter, 12 ozs.; sugar, finely powdered, 8 ozs.; ground ginger, 1 table-spoonful, and a little cinnamon and nutmeg; beat these up to a foam; beat well 4 eggs, and mix them with the other. Add a cupful of cream, a table-spoonful of saleratus, or bicarbonate of potass, dissolved in hot water. Stir in fine flour as long as it can be worked, and knead thoroughly. Roll into thin cakes; bake in a quick oven.

SUGAR LOAF, *to make.*— Take 6 lbs. of raw sugar, a little bullock's blood and water, boil it, and skim till it is clear, and till it comes to a candy round the edges of the pan; then pour it into a mould in the shape of a sugar loaf. Make strong lime water, and when the sugar is cold in the mould, pour the water over it.

SUGAR PASTE.—For 1 lb. of flour, take a ¼ lb. of sugar, as much butter, a little salt, water, and an egg. This paste may serve for any second course dish.

SUGAR PUFFS.—Beat up the whites of ten eggs, till they rise to a high froth; put them into a mortar, with as much double refined sugar as will make it thick; rub it well round the mortar; add a few carraway seeds, and take a sheet of wafer cake, and lay it on as broad as a sixpence, and high. Put into a moderate oven for 15 minutes, and they will look white.

SULPHUR OINTMENT.— Take of hog's lard prepared, four ounces; flour of sulphur, an ounce and a half; crude sal ammoniac, two drachms; essence of lemon, ten or twelve drops. Make them into an ointment. This ointment rubbed upon the parts affected will generally cure the itch. It is both the safest and best application for that purpose, and when made in this way, has no disagreeable smell.

SWEATING DROPS.—Take of camphor, saffron, ipecacuanha, opium, Virginian snake root, of each ½ oz.; Hollands gin, 1½ pint. Infuse 2 or 3 days. A wonderfully efficacious cure for fever and ague, after suitable evacuants. Dr. Beach says, "I find this the best medicine for fever and ague of any with which I am acquainted. In two cases this tincture removed the paroxysms where other remedies failed; one patient had been under homœopathic treatment for many months.

SWEETMEAT PUDDING.— Cover the dish with a plain puff paste; then take candied orange, or lemon peel, and citron, of each 1 oz.; slice them thin, and lay them all over the bottom of the dish. Beat up 8 yolks of eggs, and 2 whites, and put to them ½ lb. of sugar, and ½ lb. of melted butter. Mix all well together; put it on the sweetmeats, and bake it in a moderate oven an hour.

SWELLINGS, *Poultice for.*— Take of barley-meal, or oatmeal, 6 ozs.; fresh leaves of Hemlock, bruised, 2 ozs.; vinegar, a sufficient quantity; boil together a few minutes. It is very useful in reducing swelling of nearly every kind.

SWISS PUDDING.—Butter a basin. Take bread crumbs, add a little sugar; then dissolve 1 oz. of butter; chop a few apples fine, and mix. Bake half an hour.

SYLLABUB.—Put a pint and a half of port or white wine into a bowl, nutmeg grated, and a good deal of sugar, then milk into it near two quarts of milk, frothed up. If the wine be not rather sharp, it will require more for the quantity of milk.—In Devonshire, clouted cream is put on the top, and pounded cinnamon and sugar.

SYLLABUBS, *Durable.*—Mix a quart of thick raw cream, one pound of refined sugar, a pint and a half of fine raisin wine in a deep pan; put to it the grated peel and the juice of three lemons. Beat, or whisk it one way half an hour; then put it on a sieve with a bit of thin muslin laid smooth in the shallow end till next day. Put it in glasses. It will keep good, in a cool place, ten days.

SYMPATHETIC INK.—Dissolve bismuth in nitrous acid. When the writing is exposed to the vapour of sulphur, it will become quite black.—-Make a weak solution of galls; write with it. To make it visible, moisten with a weak solution of copperas.—Write with a solution of copperas; moisten the paper with a solution of prussiate of potass, and it will appear blue.——Sulphate of copper (blue vitriol) and sal ammoniac, equal parts, dissolved in water, write colourless, turn yellow when heated.—— Onion juice, like the last.—-Solution of salt or saltpetre, shows when heated.—-Write with starch water—a weak solution of iodine will make it visible.

SYRUP, *Simple.*—Refined sugar, 15 parts; water, 8 parts. Dissolve by a gentle heat. Boil a little to form a syrup. Simple syrup should have neither flavour nor colour. Syrup is easily clarified by beating to a froth the white of an egg, with 3 or 4 ozs. of water, mixing it with the syrup, and boiling the mixture for a few seconds, until the albumen coagulates, and forms a scum, which may be easily taken off, or separated by filtration.

TAPE WORMS. See *Worms.*

TAPIOCA JELLY.——Wash well two large spoonfuls of large tapioca; soak it in 1½ pint of water for four hours; stew it gently in the same water till it is clear. Let it cool, and use it either with or without a little new milk.

TAPIOCA PUDDING.—Put ¼ lb. of tapioca into a saucepan of cold water; when it boils, strain it to a pint of new milk; boil till it soaks up all the milk, and put it out to cool. Beat the yolks of four eggs, and the whites of two, a table-spoonful of brandy, sugar, nutmeg, and 2 ozs. of butter. Mix all together; put a puff paste round the dish, and send it to the oven. It is very good boiled with melted butter, wine, and sugar.

TAR.—It is beneficial in bronchitis and other affections of the chest. *Tar water* is made by digesting 2 ozs. of tar in three pints of water for four days. It is good for hoarseness; it clears the lungs, and facilitates public speaking.

TARTAR, *to remove from the teeth.*—Brush the teeth often up and down, not horizontally, with soap, then with salt. Eating fruit or oat-cake, cleanses the teeth greatly. In using the tooth brush the friction ought never to cause the gums to bleed.

TARTS, *Paste for.*—See page 295.

TART, *Almond.*—Bleach some almonds, beat them fine in a mortar, with a little sherry and sugar in the proportion of 1 lb. to 1 lb. of almonds; add grated bread, nutmeg, cream, and the juice of spinach for a colouring. Bake it gently, and thicken it with candied orange or citron.

TART, *Apple.*——Prepare puff paste, and put in apple preserves, or apple jelly; add lemon-peel without pith.

TART, *Orange.*—Line a tart pan with thin puff paste; put into it orange marmalade made with apple jelly; lay bars of paste, and bake in a moderate oven.

TARTS, *Transparent.*—Take 1 lb. of flour, beat an egg till thin, then melt ¾ lb. of clarified fresh butter to mix with the egg, and when cool, pour the whole into the flour, and form the paste. Roll it thin, make up the tarts, put in the oven, wet them over with a little water, and grate on sugar.

TARTLETS.—Sheet the tartlet pans with puff paste; put any kind of sweetmeat; cross bar, and put them into the oven to bake; when done, put them on paper to soak the butter from the paste.

TEA AND COFFEE, *Substitute for.*—Take a small handful of agrimony, one handful of blackberry leaves, and a few raspberry leaves, and a small quantity of balm or mint, according to taste; put it into a jug that will hold three pints, then pour on boiling hot water, infuse five minutes, then sweeten. For a change, you may use Avens in the same way as agrimony.

TEA CAKES.—Take 3 lbs. of flour, 5 ozs. of sugar, 6 ozs. of butter, rubbed into the flour, and a tea-cupful of new balm; set them to rise with milk and water; then mix them, to stand half an hour; make them up, roll them thin, and lay them on tins to rise; bake them a fine brown in a hot oven; when they are baked, rub a little butter over them.

TEA CAKES.—Rub fine 4 ozs. of butter into 8 ozs. of flour; mix 8 ozs. of currants, and six of fine sugar, two yolks and one white of egg, and a spoonful of brandy; roll what size you like; beat the other white of egg, and wash over them. Dust sugar upon them, or not.

TEA CAKES, *Small.*—Put a ¼ lb. of butter into 1 lb. of flour; mix ¼ lb. of sifted loaf sugar, and wet it with water; when made up divide into two equal parts; put 1 oz. of carraway seeds to one piece, to have two sorts. Rub the paste out very thin, and cut it out with a small round cutter; butter a baking sheet, and dust it with flour; lay the cakes on, and bake in a slow oven till of a light brown.

TEAL.—— This delicate bird should be dressed with the utmost care. They should be served up with the gravy in them, and put to a quick fire or oven. A few minutes will be sufficient. Serve with a rich gravy, or shalot sauce.

TEETH, *decayed to fill.*—If it has a cavaty, steep a little gutta percha in boiling water; then place sufficient in the cavity, press it down well, till it is level with the other teeth. Cool it by holding cold water a few minutes on the same side, and it will harden. ☞ Wipe the cavity as dry as possible previous to the insertion.

The fluid mastic cement of the shop will fill a cavity, and it allays the toothache immediately.—See *Teeth, hollow.*

TEETH, *hollow, to fill.*—See *Succedaneum.*—Or, take a drachm of gutta percha, softened by hot water, worked up with catechu powder and tannic acid, of each half a drachm, and with a drop of essential oil. For use, a morsel is to be softened over the flame of a spirit lamp, introduced while warm into the cavity of the tooth, and adapted properly. The mass becomes hard, and after several months exhibits no decomposition.

TEETH, *Loose, to fasten.*—Dissolve ½ oz. of myrrh in half a pint of port wine, and 2 ozs. of oil of almonds. Mix, and wash the mouth every morning.—Chew a little catechu, or kino, or alum occasionally.

TENCH, *to fry.*—Scale, gut and well wash. Dry them, and lay them separately on a board before the fire, after dusting some flour over them. Fry them with fresh dripping to a fine colour. Serve with crimp parsley, and plain butter. ☞ *Tench may be cooked the same as Trout*, which see.

TESTICLES, *Cancer in.*—The same treatment as in *Cancer*, which see.

TESTICLES, *Inflammation of.* The part is much pained and swollen, the pain extending along the spermatic cord; there are symptomatic pains in the loins, &c.

Adopt a recumbent posture. Suspend the part by means of a bag truss. Foment with refrigerants, washes, and apply poultices, and the stramonium ointment, or ointment made of burnt sponge, which is made by burning sponge in a close vessel; powder it, mix with lard, and apply it. Poultices of bread and milk, softened with oil may be applied when the patient is in bed. The discutient ointment applied will be of great use. The stramonium poultice is highly recommended.

The food must be light, and the drink diluting. Wine, spirits, and beer must be avoided. Aperients should be occasionally given, and the general health established.

THOMPSON'S HOT DROPS —Gum myrrh, 2 ozs.; cayenne pepper, 1½ drachm; spirit of wine, 1 pint. Put in a bottle, and shake several times a day for a week. Take from a teaspoonful in a little warm tea. These drops remove pain, and prevent mortification, internally and externally. It is a fine remedy for rheumatism. It will relieve the headache by taking a dose, bathing the head with it, and snuffing it up the nose. It is good for bruises, sprains, swollen joints, and old sores, &c., &c.

THRUSH.—An affection peculiar to young children, during the period of teething. It is an affection of the mucous membrane of the mouth. It appears in small white ulcers upon the tongue, gums, and around the mouth. If not mild it may extend to the whole of the alimentary canal, from the mouth down to the anus, attended with flatulency, purgings, &c. In this severe form it often terminates fatally. Sometimes the inside of the mouth becomes so raw and sore, as to make it painful to take nourishment. Elderly people, and persons with debilitated constitutions, are liable to this complaint.

Attention should be paid to the state of the general system, especially to the stomach and bowels. An emetic is often of great service. Give also a gentle aperient. Small doses of magnesia, and the use of lime water will be of great service in removing the acid from the stomach and bowels. The Neutralizing Mixture diluted may be given till the bowels are acted upon. Make a decoction of sage and hyssop, add a little borax, and wash the affected parts with it. Let it be sweetened. A solution of burnt alum has been recommended; or apply it pulverised.

THUNDER STORMS.—During those storms, avoid trees, and elevated objects of every kind. If the flash is instantly followed by thunder, it indicates that the electric fluid is very near, and then a recumbent position is best.—— Avoid rivers and ponds, because water is a conductor, and persons in boats are very likely to be struck by the lightning.——Avoid the chimney, for the iron about the grate, the soot, and the rarified air are all conductors.——Do not sit near an open window, because a draught of humid air is a good conductor. In bed we are comparatively safe, for the feathers and blankets are bad conductors, and we are, to a great extent, insulated in such situations.

TIC DOLOUREUX.—Take ½ a pint of rose-water, add 3 teaspoonfuls of white vinegar, to form a lotion. Apply it to the part affected 4 or 5 times a day. It requires fresh linen and lotion each application : this will in 2 or 3 days gradually take away the pain. Quinine, either in pills or as a draught, is also efficacious in removing these pains.—— *Quinine Draught.*—Sulphate of quinine, 2 grains; diluted sulphuric acid, 2 drops; spirit of nutmegs, 1 drachm; distilled water, 10 drachms. Mix. A wine-glassful to be taken daily at mid-day.

Cleanse the stomach and bowels by an emetic and an aperient. Give the *Restorative Wine Bitters*, to which add a liittle of the subcarbonate of iron. If constipated, take the *Dyspeptic Pill.* Cold water cloths applied form no mean remedy: also the *Rheumatic Liquid*, which see

If the pain is very severe, apply the *Stimulating Liniment*, and afterwards a poultice made of hops, powdered valerian, and a little tincture of cayenne. I have found extract of henbane, in the dose of 3 grains, formed into a pill, given three times a day, to afford great relief.

Where there is much irritation of the nerves of the face, particular attention must be paid to the state of the digestive organs; for nothing tends more to keep up nervous irritability than *indigestion.* See *Indigestion.* The extract of belladonna is a good preventive taken previous to the attack. Take one grain. Repeat, if necessary. Chloroform is now used for Tic. It should be advised by a skilful chemist.

Or, pour a pint of boiling water on 1 oz. of valerian root, and ¼ oz. of cassia. Infuse 24 hours. Take a wine-glassful three times a day, between meals, with a tea-spoonful of powdered Peruvian bark in each glass. Take no tea, coffee, ale, porter, or acids, but a light, nourishing diet; and keep the bowels regular with a little Turkey rhubarb.

TIN COVERS, *to clean.*—— Mix the finest whiting with the least drop of sweet oil; rub well, and wipe clean ; then dust some dry whiting over, and rub bright with dry leather.

TINCTURE OF LOBELIA.— See page 233. Take 4 ozs. of the dried plant, water, and spirits of wine, of each, 1 pint; sulphuric ether, 1 oz. ; spirits of nitric ether, ½ a pint. Macerate in a dark place one or two weeks. Strain. Begin with one or two drops at a time. It is excellent for asthma, and asthmatic or spasmodic cough. It is good in hooping cough, chronic bronchitis, croup, &c.

TINNING.—Plates or vessels of brass or copper, boiled with a solution of stannate of potassa mixed with turnings of tin, become, in the coarse of a few minutes, covered with a firmly attached layer of pure tin. A similar effect is produced by boiling the articles with tin filings and caustic alkali, or cream of tartar. In the above way, chemical vessels made of copper or brass may be easily and perfectly tinned.

Tinning Process.—The articles to be tinned are first covered with diluted sulphuric acid, and when quite cleaned in warm water, are dipped in a solution of muriatic acid, copper, and zinc, and then plunged into a tin bath, to which a small quantity of zinc has been added. When the tinning is finished, the articles are taken out and plunged into boiling water. The operation is completed by placing them in a very warm sand bath. This process softens iron.

TINNING COPPER.—First clean the copper with sandstone; then heat and rub it over with sal-ammoniac. The tin, mixed with powdered resin, is then placed on the copper, which is made so hot as to melt the tin, and to allow of its being spread over the surface, with a bit of tow.

TOAST AND CHEESE.—Cut a slice of bread half an inch thick; toast it slightly on both sides, so as just to brown it. Cut a slice of good Cheshire cheese an inch thick; place upon the toasted bread in a cheese toaster to toast. Season with salt, pepper, and mustard.— Or, the cheese may be mixed with butter, yolk of egg, well mixed, browned in a Dutch oven spread upon toast.

TOAST AND WATER.—Take a thin slice of bread, and toast it on both sides, until it is browned all over, not burnt; put it into a jug, and pour water over it from the tea kettle. Let the water be in a boiling state. Cover the jug and let it cool.

TOBACCO, *British Herb.*— This is made of coltsfoot and plantain leaves, with a smaller portion of sage, thyme, eyebright, rosemary, wood betony, and yarrow.

TOFFY.—Butter, 2½ ozs.; sugar, 1 lb.; melt and stir over the fire till it comes to the crackled degree. The addition of a little lemon juice greatly improves it. Some add ginger. A nice toffy may be made as above, not boiled so much, by the addition of well strained jelly, as apricot, currant, raspberry, strawberry, &c.

Everton Toffy requires more butter. Some mix with the above Toffy blanched Almonds.

TOFFY.—To 1 lb. of raw sugar add 2 ozs. of butter. When boiled to the crackled degree, grain it, and pour it out in square tins, either oiled or buttered.

TOLU LOZENGES.——*They are good for Coughs.*—Powdered sugar, 5 ozs.; cream of tartar ½ oz.; tincture of balsam of tolu, 1½ drachm. Mix well, and form into lozenges with 10 drops of laudanum, and a solution of gum arabic.

TOMATO SAUCE.—Take 12 tomatoes, very red and ripe; take off the stalks, take out the seeds, and press out the water. Put the expressed tomatoes into a stewpan with 1½ oz. of butter, a bay leaf, and a little thyme; put it upon a moderate fire; stir it into a pulp; put into it a good cullis, or the top of broth, which will be better. Rub it through a search, and put it into a stewpan with two spoonfuls of cullis; put in a little salt and cayenne.

Another.—Proceed as above with the seeds and water. Put them into a stewpan, with salt and cayenne, and three table-spoonfuls of beef gravy. Set them on a slow stove for an hour, or till properly melted. Strain, and add a little good stock, and simmer a few minutes.

TOMATOES, *stewed.*—Pour boiling water over 12 peeled tomatoes; cut them into a stew-pan, with bread crumbs, salt, pepper, butter, and a cooked onion. Simmer long. Add eggs before done.

TONGUE, *to boil.*——If the tongue be a dry one, steep in water all night. Boil it three hours. If you prefer it hot, stick it with cloves. Clear off the scum, and add savoury herbs when it has boiled two hours; but this is optional. Rub it over with the yolk of an egg; strew over it bread crumbs; baste it with butter; set it before the fire till it is of a light brown. When you dish it up, pour a little brown gravy, or port wine sauce mixed the same way as for venison. Lay slices of currant jelly round it.

TONGUE, *to eat cold.*—Season with common salt and saltpetre, brown sugar, a little bay-salt, pepper, cloves, mace, and allspice, in fine powder, for a fortnight; then take away the pickle, put the tongue into a small pan, and lay some butter on it; cover it with brown crust, and bake slowly till so tender that a straw would go through it.

The thin part of tongues, when hung up to dry, grates like hung beef, and also makes a fine addition to the flavour of omelets.

TONGUE, *to pickle for boiling.*—Cut off the root, but leave a little of the kernel and fat. Sprinkle some salt, and let it drain from the slime till next day: then for each tongue mix a large spoonful of common salt, the same of coarse sugar, and about half as much of saltpetre; rub it well in, and do so every day. In a week add another heaped spoonful of salt. If rubbed every day, a tongue will be ready in a fortnight; but if only turned in the pickle daily, it will keep four or five weeks without being too salt.

When it is to be dressed, boil it till extremely tender; allow five hours; and if done sooner, it is easily kept hot. The longer kept after drying the higher it will be: if hard, it may require soaking three or four hours.

Another way.—Clean as above: for two tongues allow an ounce of saltpetre, and an ounce of salts of prunella; rub them well. In two days, after well rubbing, cover them with common salt, turn them every day for three weeks, then dry them, and rub over them bran, and smoke them. In ten days they will be fit to eat. Keep in a cool dry place.

TONGUE, *to pot.*——Rub the tongue with 1 oz. of saltpetre, and 4 ozs. of brown sugar; let it lie 2 days; then boil it till it is quite tender. Take off the skin and side bits; then cut the tongue in very thin slices, and beat it well, with 1 lb. of butter, mace, pepper, and salt to taste. Then pot, and pour over it clarified butter. *Hu.*

TONGUES, *to salt.*——Scrape the tongue, and dry clean with a cloth; salt with common salt, and ½ oz. of saltpetre to every tongue; lay them in a deep pot, and turn them every day for 9 days. Salt them again, and let them lie 6 days longer. Take up; dry; flour them, and hang up.

TONGUE, *to stew.*——Salt a tongue with saltpetre and common salt for a week, turning it every day. Boil it tender enough to peel; when done, stew it in a moderately strong gravy; season with soy, mushroom ketchup, cayenne, pounded cloves, and salt if necessary.

Serve with truffles, morels, and mushrooms. In both this receipt and the last, the roots must be taken off the tongues before salting, but some fat left.

TONICS.--Medicines strengthening the system in general.

TONIC BITTERS.—See page 61. The following herbs are for tonic bitters. They may be *infused* or *decocted*. They increase the tone or contractility of all the muscular fibre, and thereby strengthen the whole body. They drive away fever, increase the appetite, expel worms, &c.—*White Poplar bark, Golden Seal, Gum Myrrh, Tansy, Dandelion Root, Balmony, Hops, Centaury, Bogbean, Gentian, Barberry Bark, Columba, Unicorn Root, Wormwood, Quassia, Camomile Flowers.*

TONIC PILL.--Extract of gentian, 2 scruples; sulphate of iron, 16 grains; sulphate of quinine, 10 grains. Mix, and form into pills. Take one pill three times a day.

TONIC TINCTURE.—Peruvian bark, bruised, 1½ oz.; orange peel, bruised, 1 oz.; brandy, or proof spirit, 1 pint. Infuse ten days; shake the bottle every day. Pour off the liquor, and strain. Take a tea-spoonful in a wineglassful of water twice a day, when you feel languid.

TOOTHACHE REMEDIES. —The following are good:—

1. Oil of cloves, ½ drachm; laudanum, 2 drachms; powdered alum, 1 drachm; spirits of nitre, 2 drachms; chloroform, ½ drachm. Mix. Apply with lint.

2. A mixture of two parts of the liquid ammonia of commerce, with one of some simple tincture, (tincture of Benjamin, &c.) is a good remedy for toothache. A piece of lint dropped into this mixture and introduced into the carious tooth, when the nerve is immediately cauterised, and the pain stopped.

3. Saturate a little cotton wool with oil of cloves, and put it to the tooth.—The oil of cloves might be kept ready in a bottle. It would be more efficacious if mixed with camphor, and two or three drops of chloroform.——Or creosote, one part; spirits of wine, ten parts; mix, and apply.

4. Sometimes diluted ammonia relieves the toothache. Also a mixture of camphor, laudanum, oil of cloves, and chloroform. Mix well.—Or keep in the mouth warm water and salt, with one-fourth of laudanum.

5. Take of alum, in powder, two drachms; spirits of nitre, seven drachms. Mix, and apply it to the teeth.

6. Take 3 spoonfuls of brandy, adding to it 1 drachm of camphor, with 30 or 40 drops of laudanum. Drop a little on some lint. Apply it to the affected tooth and gum. A little tincture of cayenne would be an improvement.

7. Be electrified through the teeth.——Or apply to the aching tooth an artificial magnet.——Or lay roasted parings of turnips, as hot as may be, behind the ear.—— Or, lay a clove of garlic on the tooth.——Or keep the feet in warm water, and rub them well with bran just before bed time.

8. Alum reduced to an impalpable powder, three drachms; nitrous spirit of ether, 1 scruple; mix; and apply to the tooth.—— Or, take of compound tincture of Benjamin, and Battley's solution of opium, of each, one drachm. Mix. A little dropped on cotton, and applied to the hollow, and the gum of a decayed tooth, will afford effectual relief.

9. Take of tincture of cayenne, oil of cloves, and oil of summer savory, equal parts; put into three table-spoonfuls of spirit of wine. Add six drops of chloroform. Apply to the affected tooth and gums. Apply to the face at the same time a flannel bag of hops and camomile flowers saturated with hot vinegar, and thirty drops of laudanum.

10. Warm water and salt kept in the mouth for some time, and renewed, is a good remedy.

TOOTHACHE, *to prevent.*—Wash the mouth with cold water every morning, and rince them after every meal.——Or, rub the teeth often with tobacco ashes.—*Wesley.*

TOOTH POWDERS. — The following are recommended:—

1. Take ½ oz. of powdered gum myrrh, 1 oz. of powdered bark, 2 drachms of cream of tartar, 1 drachm of bole ammoniac, mix in a mortar. A constant use of this powder will cause the teeth to obtain a beautiful whiteness, and preserve them from decaying, and prevent the toothache.

2. Peruvian bark, charcoal, armenian bole, of each, ½ oz.; powdered cinnamon, and bicarbonate of soda, of each, ¼ oz.; oil of cinnamon, 4 drops. Mix.

3. One, *to cure a bad breath.*—Cream of tartar and chalk, each ½ oz.; myrrh, powdered charcoal, 2 drachms; powdered orris root, ½ a drachm; powdered Peruvian bark, 2 drachms. Mix well together.—Rubbing the gums with salt occasionally destroys the animalcula which probably cause decay and aching of the teeth.

4. Pounded charcoal very fine, 2 ozs.; Peruvian bark, 1 oz.; camphor, ½ oz.

5. Prepared chalk, orris root, and charcoal, powdered, equal parts.

6. Coffees newly ground fine, mixed with charcoal, is a first rate powder. Scent as you like.

7. Powdered cuttle-fish, 8 ozs.; powdered charcoal, 2 ozs.; burnt alum, 1 oz.; powdered myrrh, 1 oz. Mix.

TOOTH WASHES.—Tincture of myrrh, diluted with water, and camphorated spirits.—— Or, a solution of borax and camphorated spirit combined.

TRACING PAPER.—Use Canada balsam dissolved in spirits of wine, and a little turpentine. Apply with a soft brush, or sponge, and hang up to dry. The best tissue paper should be used.

TREACLE BEER.—Take 4 lbs. of treacle, 2 ozs. of hops, and ½ oz. of ginger bruised. Pour upon the same 4 gallons of boiling water. Ferment with a small cupful of yeast.

TREACLE PARKIN.—Oatmeal, 4 lbs.; flour, 1 lb.; butter, 1 lb.; treacle, 4 lbs.; sugar, 1 lb.; ginger, 1¼ oz.; sweet pepper, 1 oz.; carraway seeds, 1 oz.; carbonate of soda, 3 teaspoonfuls. Add half a cupful of cream, which with the treacle, sugar, and butter, must be well rubbed into the meal and flour. Warm the treacle and sugar in the oven, and mix well.—See *Parkin.*

TREACLE POSSET.—Boil a small basinful of milk, and put in treacle sufficient to curdle it. Drink it on retiring to bed. It generally cures a severe cold by producing profuse perspiration, and dispelling the fever of the patient. *Gu.*

TREACLE PUDDING.—Make the paste as for other boiled puddings, adding treacle, and small raisins, (or without,) according to taste. Boil in a cloth three hours. Serve with sweetened melted butter.

TRIFLE, *to make.*—Lay macaroons and ratafia drops over the bottom of your dish, and pour in as much raisin wine as they will suck up; then pour on them cold rich custard and some rice flour. It must stand two or three inches thick; on that put a layer of raspberry-jam, and cover the whole with a very high whip made the day before, of rich cream, the whites of two well beaten eggs, sugar, lemon-peel, and raisin wine.

TRIPE, *to fricassee.*—Cut into small square pieces. Put them into the stewpan with as much sherry as will cover them, with pepper, ginger, a blade of mace, sweet herbs, and an onion. Stew 15 minutes. Take out the herbs and onion, and put in a little shred parsley, the juice of a small lemon, half an anchovy cut small, a gill of cream, and a little butter, or yolk of an egg. Garnish with lemon.

TRIPE, *to fry.*—Cut the tripe into small square pieces ; dip them in yolks of eggs, and fry them in good dripping, till nicely brown ; take out, and drain, and serve with plain melted butter.

TROUT, *a-la-Genevoise.*-Clean the fish well; put it into the stew-pan, adding half champagne and half sherry wine. Season it with pepper, salt, an onion, a few cloves stuck in it, and a small bunch of parsley and thyme ; put in it a crust of French bread ; set it on a quick fire. When done, take the bread out, bruise it, and thicken the sauce ; add flour and a little butter, and boil up. Lay the fish on the dish, and pour the sauce over it. Serve it with sliced lemon and fried bread.

TROUT, *to broil.*—Wash, dry, tie it, to cause it to keep its shape; melt butter, add salt, and cover the trout with it. Broil it gradually in a Dutch oven, or in a common oven. Cut small an anchovy, and chop some capers. Melt some butter with a little flour, pepper, salt, nutmeg, and half a spoonful of vinegar. Pour it over the trout, and serve it hot.

TROUT, *to fry.*—Do them the same as Graylings. See page 187.

TROUT, *to pot.*—The same as *Lobsters*, which see.

TROUT, *Stewed.*—Wash two middle-sized trout clean, and wipe them dry, lay them in a stew-pan with half an onion cut in thin slices, a little parsley, two cloves, one blade of mace, two bay leaves, a little thyme, salt and pepper to taste, a pint of stock, and a glass of port wine ; simmer gently for thirty minutes, take it out, strain the gravy, thicken with butter and flour, and stir it over a sharp fire for five minutes; pour over the trout and serve.

TRUE LOVERS' KNOTS.— Roll out a piece of puff paste into a thin sheet, cut it into pieces three or four inches square, fold each corner over into the centre, and cut a piece out from each side, leaving it in the form of a true lover's knot; put them on a tin, and bake them in a moderate oven ; when they are done, place some jam or preserve on each point, and some in the centre.

TUMOURS, *Cure of.*—To remove tumours, Dr. Simpson, of Edinburgh, introduces a hollow acupuncture needle, or very fine trocar, into their tissue, and injects in a few drops of some irritant liquid, such as a solution of chloride of zinc, perchloride of iron, or creosote. The effect has been to destroy the vitality of the tumours so treated, and they have been separated. We have seen a similar plan adopted in Paris by M. Maisonneuve. He had slender stylets, made of a paste composed of flour, water, and chloride of zinc. These are baked. A puncture is made in the tumour, the caustic stylet is inserted, broken off, and left. We saw several malignant tumours treated in this manner, and some cases in which a healthy granulating surface was left, after the separation of tumours which had been destroyed in this manner.

TURBOT, *Fillets of.*—After having skimmed and boned the fish, divide into square pieces the remains of cold turbot and lobster sauce; brush them over with egg, sprinkle with bread crumbs mixed with a little minced parsley and seasoning. Lay the fillets in a baking-dish, with sufficient butter to baste with. Bake for ¼ hour, and moisten them well with the butter. Put a little lemon-juice and grated nutmeg to the cold lobster sauce; make it hot, and pour over the fish, which must be well drained from the butter. Garnish with parsley and cut lemon.

TURBOT, *to boil.*—Set the fish in cold water sufficient to cover it completely, throw a handful of salt and a glass of vinegar into it, and let it gradually boil: be very careful that there fall no blacks: but skim it well, and preserve the beauty of the colour.

Serve it garnished with a complete fringe of curled parsley, lemon and horse-radish.

The sauce must be the finest lobster, and anchovy, and plain butter, served plentifully in separate tureens.

TURBOT, *to fry.*—Cut the turbot across, as if it were ribbed. Flour it, and put it into a large frying-pan, with lard to cover it. Fry till brown; drain. Clean the pan, and pour into it sherry wine, almost enough to cover it, anchovy, salt, nutmeg, and a little ginger. Stew the fish in it till half the liquor is wasted. Take out the fish, and put into the pan a piece of butter rolled in flour, and some minced lemon. Simmer till of a proper thickness. Lay in a dish rubbed with shalot. Pour the hot sauce over it, and serve.

TURKEY, *to carve.*—A turkey roasted or boiled is trussed and sent

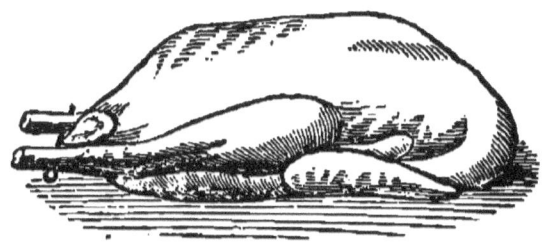

to the table like a fowl, and cut up like a pheasant. The best parts are the white ones, the breast, wings, and neck bones. The neck is taken away, and the hollow part under the breast stuffed with forcemeat, which is to be cut into thin slices, from the rump to the neck, and a slice given with each piece of Turkey.

TURKEY, *to boil.*——Make a stuffing of bread, herbs, salt, pepper, nutmeg, lemon-peel, a few oysters or anchovy, a bit of butter, some suet, and an egg: put this into the crop, fasten up the skin and boil the turkey in a floured cloth to make it very white. Have ready oyster-sauce made with butter, a little cream, and a spoonful of soy, if approved, and pour it over the bird; or liver and lemon-sauce. Hen-birds are best for boiling, and should be young.

TURKEY, *a la Daube.*——Cut the turkey down the back, just enough to bone it. Stuff it with nice forcemeat, made of bread crumbs, and oysters chopped fine, pepper, salt, shalots, thyme, parsley, and butter. Fill, and sew it up. Tie it in a clean cloth, and boil it very white. Serve it with oyster sauce, made good. Or take the bones with a piece of veal, mutton, and bacon, and make a rich gravy, seasoned with pepper, salt, mace, and shalots. Strain, and stew the turkey in it, after it has been half boiled half an hour. Dish it up in the gravy, after it is well skimmed, strained, and thickened with a few mushrooms stewed white, or stewed palates, forcemeat balls, and pieces of lemon, fried oysters, &c.

TURKEY, *to hash.*—Take off the legs; cut the thighs in two pieces; cut off the pinions and breast in large pieces. Take off the skin, or it will give the gravy a greasy taste. Stew with a pint of gravy, a teaspoonful of lemon-pickle, the end of a lemon, and a little mace; boil the turkey seven minutes. Put it on your dish; thicken the gravy with flour and butter. Mix the yolks of two eggs with a spoonful of thick cream; put it on the gravy; shake it over the fire till it is hot, but do not let it boil. Strain, and pour it over the turkey. Lay sippets round, and garnish with lemon and parsley.

TURKEY, *to roast.*—— The sinews of the legs should be drawn whichever way it is dressed. The head should be twisted under the wing; and in drawing it, take care not to tear the liver, nor let the gall touch it.

Put a stuffing of sausage-meat; or, if sausages are to be served in the dish, a bread stuffing. As this makes a large addition to the size of the bird, observe that the heat of the fire is constantly to that part; for the breast is often not done enough. A little strip of paper should be put on the bone to hinder it from scorching while the other parts roast. Baste well and froth it up. Serve with gravy in the dish, and plenty of bread-sauce in a sauce-tureen. Add a few crumbs, and a beaten egg to the stuffing of sausage-meat.

TURKEY PATTIES, *to make.* —Mince some of the white part, and, with grated lemon, nutmeg, salt, a very little white pepper, cream, and a bit of butter warmed, fill the patties.

TURKEY, *pulled.*—Divide the meat of the breast by pulling instead of cutting; then warm it in a spoonful or two of white gravy, and a little cream, grated nutmeg, salt, and a little flour and butter; don't boil it. The leg should be seasoned, scored, and broiled, and put into the dish with the above round it. Cold chicken does as well.

TURNIPS, *to mash.*——Boil them very tender. Strain till no water is left. Place in a saucepan over a gentle fire, and stir well a few minutes. Do not let them burn. Add a little cream, or milk, or both, salt, butter, and pepper. Add a table-spoonful of fine sugar. Stir and simmer five minutes longer.

TURNIP PIE.—Season mutton chops with salt and pepper, reserving the ends of the neck bones to lay over the turnips, which must be cut into small dice, and put on the steaks. Put two or three good spoonfuls of milk in. You may add sliced onion. Cover with a crust.

TURNIP SOUP.—Take off a knuckle of veal all the meat that can be made into cutlets, &c., and set the rest on to stew with an onion, a bunch of herbs, a blade of mace, and five pints of water; close it on a slow fire five hours. Strain it, and set it by till next day; then take the fat and sediment from it, and simmer it with turnips cut into small dice till tender; season with salt and pepper. Before serving, rub down half a spoonful of flour with half a pint of good cream, and the size of a walnut of butter. Simmer a small roll in the soup till wet through, and serve this with it. It should be as thick as middling cream.

TWELFTH CAKE.—Flour, butter, sifted loaf sugar, of each, 2 lbs.; 18 eggs; currants, 4 lbs.; almonds, blanched and chopped, ½ lb.; citron, ½ lb.; candied orange and lemon-peel, cut into thin slices, 1 lb.; a large nutmeg grated; ground allspice, ½ oz.; ground cinnamon, mace, ginger, and corriander, ¼ oz. each, and a gill of brandy.

Put the butter into a stew-pan, and work it into a smooth cream with the hand, and mix it with the sugar and spice for some time; break in the eggs by degrees, and beat 20 minutes. Stir in the brandy, then the flour, and work it a little; add the fruit, sweetmeats, and almonds, and mix all together lightly. Have ready a hoop, cased with paper on a baking plate; put in the mixture; smooth it on the top with the hand dipped in milk. Put the plate upon another elevated a little, to prevent the bottom from colouring too much. Bake it in a slow oven four hours or more, and when nearly cold, spread the ice over it.

TWIST, *to make.*—Put 6 lbs. of loaf sugar into a pan with 1½ pint of water, boil it gradually for half an hour; when it is boiled enough it will snap like glass, by putting the tube of a pipe into the pan, and then into water; after which pour it out on a smooth stone till cold; then take a part of that, and pull it on a long nail till it becomes very white; then lap it over the other which is on the stone; and make it up either for twist, or cut it in short lengths.

TWIST, *Common.*—Boil 3 lbs. of raw sugar in a pint of water over a slow fire; skim it not; when boiled enough, pour it on a stone; take a part of it and pull it like wax, and it will turn white, twist it over the other, and roll it small; then cut it into lengths of twist. Put a few drops of the oil of peppermint into the sugar when boiled and poured upon the stone, to flavour it.

TWIST, *Paradise.*—Boil 3 lbs. of loaf sugar in half a pint of water, for half an hour; put in it a little gum water to clear it and a table-spoonful of vinegar, which will cause it to give you more time to make it up; pull one part of it and lap it over the other; cut it into twist, roll and streak it with red and white.

TYPHUS FEVER.——From the Greek *tuphos, stupor.* It is generally indicated by certain well-marked symptoms. It is characterised by great lethargy, prostration of muscular power, and sometimes delirium.

It commences with pain in the head, slight shiverings, vomiting, debility, sighing, loss of appetite, oppressive breathing, great mental anxiety and depression, uneasiness in the back; the pulse is quick and small, dry tongue, with a brown or black crust; urine pale, then high-coloured with a bad smell, evacuations black and offensive, breath hot and offensive. The delirium becomes more constant, and at length changes to a stupor. An eruption of livid spots sometimes appears. Great purging, cold clammy perspiration, and hiccup, precede its fatal termination.

The favourable termination of typhus is indicated by a gradual decrease of those symptoms; by the disappearance of stupor in the face of the patient, and his increasing attention to things around him; the pulse becomes moderated, the heat of the skin natural, the tongue becomes clean, &c.

Treatment.—If there is nausea, oppression, and sickness, give an emetic; and if the patient is chilly, give the *Vapour Bath*, and then the Sudorific Powder to promote perspiration, which will give much ease, and dislodge from the fauces phlegm, and other morbific matter endangering suffocation. *Observe* an emetic in the first stages of typhus is of the utmost importance, and at any time before prostration commences. It has been known to restrain the disease instantly, and in many cases to mitigate the symptoms.

If the patient is constipated, aperients must be given. But if there is a tendency to diarrhœa, they must be omitted, or be administered sparingly; a small dose of rhubarb and magnesia may act as a corrective, or a single teaspoonful of castor oil.

Dr. Beach says, "In typhus, the brain and the system generally, are thrown into an unhealthy state, by an accumulation of acrid and vitiated bile, and matter collected in the stomach and first passages, caused by an inactive and torpid state of the liver. Delirium, great heat, and prostration of strength, take place from this cause. The sympathy existing between these organs is surprising; if one is healthy so is another; if one is in a morbid condition, those that sympathize with it are also diseased. Hence the very great importance of exciting a healthy state of the stomach, liver, and the whole alimentary canal. Aperients are admirably calculated to fulfil this indication. They cleanse and stimulate at the same time; and although a patient may be very weak, he will gain strength under the administration of repeated purgatives. They may be given in moderate doses, in protracted cases, every other day. Persons in a very low or distressed state of typhus fever will soon assume a more healthy appearance after the administration of purgatives. The combination of a tonic, as a solution of quinine, with purgatives, would render them more beneficial.

A Scotch physician observes,— "By oft sponging the surface of the body with cold water and vinegar, and the application of cold to the head, and bathing the feet in warm water, the discomfort and headache of the patient may be mitigated. Pain in the belly, or tenderness, in typhoid fever is best met by the use of warm fomentations."

Where there is great sensibility and swelling of the abdomen, showing an inflammatory state of the intestines, and where the stomach rejects medicine, the use of injections is indicated.

The saline mixture should be given in a state of effervescence; or a table-spoonful of yeast twice a day. Fixed air affords as much relief as any medicine, and has, in some instances, proved an effectual remedy, not by counteracting putrescency, but by cooling the body, abating thirst, and diminishing the morbid irritability of the system.

Let the patient drink balm and pennyroyal tea, and take the Diaphoretic Powder; for no medicines stand higher than those which produce perspiration; though too much sweating must not be promoted, as debility may follow. A mere moisture of the skin through the disease, must be maintained. In thirst give a teaspoonful of spirits of nitre in a weak decoction of Peruvian bark. The juice of houseleek and sugar is an excellent febrifuge. See *Houseleek*. Frequently wash the body with cold or tepid, or warm water and vinegar. The salutary effects are often soon visible. Rub the body well with the flannel and liquid.

Great attention must be paid to cleanliness. The patient's face, breast, neck, &c., must be often washed, his linen often changed; there must be good ventilation, and plentiful fumigation. Sprinkle the room with vinegar, camphorated spirits, or chloride of lime. Acidulous fruits should be given, as grapes, oranges, lemons, &c. If the throat is sore, give the appropriate gargles. Should the patient sink in the advanced stages, give port wine diluted with the same quantity of water. Give a wine-glassful several times a day. ——Or a little *weak* brandy, ammonia, and water, mixed warm. If the feet are cold, put to them a bottle of hot water, wrapped in a vinegar and water cloth, and rub the surface of the body with the Stimulating Liniment. If signs of putrescency appear, give yeast in a little wine, adding two teaspoonfuls of fresh powdered charcoal, and a little solution of quinine. Bottled porter may also be given. Let the patient be supported by beef-tea, gruel, &c. Should one part of the body be heated more than another, apply to the heated part a poultice of hops and vinegar, with a little tincture of cayenne.

In diarrhœa, lime water is a suitable remedy; when more severe, chalk mixture with a little laudanum may be substituted; when blood appears, more decided astringent remedies are needed, as gallic acid, or acetate of lead. In typhus fever, bed sores, by long lying, are formed. Wash the skin with rum or other spirit to prevent this. If broken, apply a healing plaster, or a poultice made of slippery elm and butter.

ULCER.—An ulcer is an injury done to the flesh from which issues matter, or some kind of discharge, with more or less pain and inflammation.

The *common ulcer* should be kept clean and cool, and protected from the atmosphere, especially in frosty or cold weather. It should be washed now and then with warm soap-water. Put upon it a little lint, wet occasionally with salt and water, and put over it the Black Salve. Perhaps the best dressings are the saturnine cerate, described hereafter. Poultices made of the oak bark, sumach bark, may be used alternately.

Sometimes ulcers are very irritable, tender, and painful. They discharge a thin acrid fluid. They should be steamed every night with a bitter decoction, and occasionally washed with an infusion of camomile flowers, or a strong decoction of wild cherry bark, with a little spirit. Poultice with slippery elm, mixed with a strong decoction of poplar bark, and a trifle of salt. Repeat, as required.

If the ulcer or ulcers are indolent, steam as before, and apply the Cancer Plaster, with only a trifle of the white vitriol mixed with it; or, sprinkle the ulcer with powdered blood-root.

Sometimes ulcers become very much inflamed, and assume a livid colour; they are covered with small vesicles or blisters, as in mortification. Wash the ulcer with tincture of myrrh, and apply a poultice made of charcoal, yeast, slippery elm, ginger, and a minute portion of tincture of cayenne. Bear it as long as possible. Then apply the saturnine cerate.

The following is recommended by Dr. Beach:—Take sweet clover tops and stalks, burdock leaves, and parsley, a handful of each; get the strength out by boiling; strain, and add 1 lb. of rosin, and ¼ lb. of fresh butter; simmer until of a proper consistence.

A cold water cloth constantly applied is a good remedy. Put a little cerate on the ulcer previously.

Attend to the general health, by cleansing the stomach and bowels, and then giving tonics.

Saturnine Cerate.——Powdered acetate of lead, 2 drachms; white wax, 2 ozs.; olive oil, half a pint. Melt the wax in the oil, and add gradually the acetate of lead, separately rubbed down with a portion of the oil reserved for that purpose.

ULCER.—Dry and powder a walnut leaf, and strew it on, and lay another walnut leaf on that.— Or, boil walnut-tree leaves in water with a little sugar. Apply a cloth dipped in this, changing it once in two days. This has done wonders.

——Or, foment morning and evening with a decoction of walnut-tree leaves, and bind the leaves on. This has cured foul bones; yea, and a leprosy. Foment morning and evening with a decoction of mint; then sprinkle on it finely-powdered rue.——Or, burn to ashes, but not too long, the stalks on which the red coleworts grow. Make a plaster of this and fresh butter. Change it once a day. ——Or apply a poultice of boiled parsnips. This will cure even when the bone is foul.—*Wesley.*

ULCERATED GUMS.—Dilute elixir of vitriol, so as to make it slightly acid, and wash the mouth frequently with it.——Or wash with diluted tincture of myrrh.

ULCEROUS SORES.——See *Logwood.*

URINE, *Involuntary.*—It proceeds from weakness of the urinary organs caused by the great use of tea and coffee, ardent spirits, &c. It is often an attendant of advanced life, especially when the habits have been irregular. It sometimes results from paralysis. It is a very troublesome complaint.

"If the patient can endure it, use the cold bath. Or, take a teaspoonful of powdered agrimony in a little water morning and evening. Or a quarter of a pint of alum posset every night."—*Wesley.*

Make a decoction of bayberry bark, hemlock bark, wild cherry tree bark. Bruise them. Take a wine-glassful at a time. Use at the same time the *Diuretic Drops.* Take occasionally 6 or 7 drops of laudanum in a little water. Abstain from tea and coffee, or reduce the quantity taken. Ardent spirits must be abandoned, and all liquids sparingly taken.

When it is occasioned by stone or gravel, it requires the same treatment as recommended for the latter disease. When it is the consequence of morbid irritation of the bladder, prostrate gland, or disease in the urethra, the tincture of Buchu leaves in the dose of two tea-spoonful, two or three times a-day, in a large wine-glassful of the decoction of Marshmallow Root, is a very valuable remedy.

If incontinence of urine proceeds from paralysis, a blister must be applied to the upper part of the sacrum. Or rub the region of the bladder with tincture of cayenne, or with the antispasmodic tincture, page 20. Give also an injection of antispasmodic tincture, 1 tablespoonful; warm water, ½ pint; slippery elm, 2 teaspoonfuls. This course of treatment is applicable when the disease arises from nervous debility. Dr. Beach recommends the use of the tincture of cantharides in doses from 10 to 20 drops three times a day in half a cupful of linseed tea. Linseed tea is an appropriate drink; add sometimes 5 or 6 drops of laudanum.

If it proceeds from obstructed perspiration, the secretion should be restored; use the Sudorific Powder, or the vapour bath. Incontinence of urine may be benefited by bathing the body every morning with salt and water; and afterwards rubbing with the Stimulating Liniment.

URINE, *Hot and Scalding.*—It may arise from various causes, from inflammation of the kidneys, uterus, alcoholic drinks, luxurious diet, excessive venery, &c.

Take the juice of ground-ivy in linseed tea, with a little sweet spirits of nitre. Drink cooling and mucilaginous drinks. Let the diet be light and spare. Buttermilk is very appropriate. See *Diuretic Drops;* for this complaint they are effectual.

URINE, *Bloody.*—" Take twice a day copious draughts of infusion of yarrow."—*Wesley.*

It generally indicates some other disease. Give small doses of a solution of gum kino, and gum arabic, and alum, to which add from 8 to 16 drops of laudanum. The *Diuretic Drops* may be given half a teaspoonful at a time two or three times a day.

When blood is discharged with the urine in a plethoric habit, the use of an aperient medicine is necessary (See Castor Oil.) The saline purgatives are in this case inadmissible, on account of their rendering the urine more irritating. The diet should be low, unless the patient be much reduced, or the discharge of blood be the consequence of ulceration of the kidneys or bladder. In all cases, stimulants, as pepper, salt, &c. should be avoided.

When it is occasioned by the *mechanical* action of a stone in the bladder, or gravel in the kidneys or ureters, it will require the treatment recommended for those complaints. When ulceration is the cause (which is known from its being attended with a discharge of matter), the essential oil of turpentine, in the dose of twelve drops, in marsh-mallow root tea, has generally a very happy effect. The buchu leaves with gum-arabic, in these affections, have also proved particularly serviceable, as the following: Take of infusion of the buchu leaves, eight ounces; Tincture of ditto, six drachms; mucilage of gum arabic, 3 ounces. Three table-spoonfuls of this mixture may be taken three times a day.

URINE, *Suppression of.*—It may proceed from gravel. See *Gravel.* "Drink largely of warm lemonade.—Or, take a scruple of nitre every two hours.—Or, a spoonful of lemon-juice sweetened with syrups of violets."—*Wesley.*

Immerse the feet in warm water and soap, and drink parsley root tea. Take half pint of spearmint tea, to which add 3 teaspoonfuls of sweet spirits of nitre, and a wineglassful of Hollands gin. Sweeten it with sugar or honey. Repeat, if necessary. If the disease is obstinate, steam with the vapour bath, or put the patient into a warm bath. Apply the tincture of cayenne over the bladder; and then a poultice of hops, if there is much pain. Or, give an injection of lobelia herb; slippery elm bark, and valerian; balm water, a small cupful. Infuse 15 minutes. Take at the same time the Diuretic Drops in penny-royal tea. An aperient may be useful. Parsley tea, spirits of mint, sweet spirits of nitre, and a little camphorated spirit, all combined, have often effected a cure.

The *Diuretic Drops, Urinary Decoction*, and infusions of spearmint, are very efficient. Also decoctions or infusions of white poplar bark, dandelion root, linseed, queen of the meadow, cleavers, sweet shrub, juniper berries, uva ursi, commonly called bearberry coolwort.

URINARY DECOCTION.—Cleavers, queen of the meadow, marsh-mallows, juniper berries, of each 2 ozs. Boil in 4 quarts of water down to 1 quart. Dose, a small cupful a day.

USQUEBAUGH.—This liquor is in high repute in Ireland. Take best brandy, 1 gallon; raisins stoned, 1 lb.; cinnamon, cloves, nutmeg, and cardamoms, each, 1 oz., crushed in a mortar; saffron, ½ oz.; the rind of a Seville orange, and brown sugar candy, 1 lb. Shake well every day for 14 days. Some add 1 quart of water, and 1 quart of whiskey.

UVULA, *Relaxation of*.—This is the pendulous body which hangs down from the middle of the soft palate, at the top of the throat. It is subject to be relaxed; to hang down too far; and by its contact with the epiglottis, and the root of the tongue, it causes cough, retching; and very much interferes with the voice in speaking, especially publicly.

Keep a small portion of gum catechu or gum kino in the mouth; alum also is good. Or, with a camel hair pencil touch the uvula occasionally with a solution of nitrate of silver. If such remedies ultimately fail, then excision must take place. Before that the most astringent gargles should be tried.

VACCINATION ACT.—It is imperative by law that parents should have every child vaccinated within three calandar months after birth, either by the appointed public vaccinator, or by a legally qualified practitioner. If other than the parents are left in charge of the child, the vaccination must then be within four months of birth. If the child be not taken in eight days after vaccination to be examined by the medical practitioner in order to ascertain the result of the operation, parties not complying incur a penalty not exceeding 20s. The registrars of each district are required to send notices to the parents or guardians of children, whose births they have registered, stating also the names and addresses of the public vaccinators, and the hours of attendance.

VALERIAN.—See *Robinson's Herbal*. Valerian is a medicine of great use in nervous disorders, hysteria, lowness of spirits, restlessness, and diseases of the bladder, &c. The common dose is from a scruple to a drachm, in powder; and in infusion from one to two drachms. Its unpleasant flavour may be neutralized by the addition of mace.

VAPOUR BATH.—Sit naked upon a chair; place the legs upon a stool. Place a vessel under the chair. Throw a large blanket around the patient and the chair; pin it under his chin, and make it tight all round. The vessel is to contain the liquid, hot water, or decoction of bitter herbs, or otherwise medicated. Heat a couple of bricks nearly red hot, and put one of them into the vessel under the chair. Then pour about 3 pints of boiling water into the vessel, with a gill of strong vinegar. Be careful not to pour it upon the brick, but down the sides of the vessel. Close up, and the patient will soon be immersed in vapour. Change the brick when cool. If the patient be too hot, lift up the blanket a little to admit the cold air, which will lower the temperature. During the bath, drink freely of balm, catnep, or pennyroyal tea. When out, dry well, and apply friction, with a flesh brush, or with rough towels dipped in vinegar and water.

The benefits arising from the vapour bath are immense.

VARNISH, *for Furniture.*—Melt one part of virgin white wax in eight parts of oil of petroleum, lay a slight coat of this mixture, while warm, on the wood, with a badger's brush, and after a little time polish it with a woollen cloth.

VARNISH, *for Straw Hats.*—Mix the best ivory black, shellac, and spirits of wine, or turpentine. Apply it before the fire with a soft sponge or brush. Some persons instead of the above dissolve black sealing wax in spirits of wine.

VARNISH FOR VIOLINS.—Spirits of wine, one quart; mastic three ounces, and ¼ pint of turpentine; put together in a vessel, and keep in a very warm place, frequently stirring or shaking it, till all is dissolved. Then strain.—This varnish may be used for furniture.

VARNISH, *for Wood Patterns.*—Shellac, ¼ lb.; spirit of wine, 1½ pint. Put into a bottle, and when wanted for use, mix with a little lamp black, the thickness of cream, and varnish the pattern, rubbing it into the grain of the wood, until friction produces a polish. This varnish makes a smooth surface on the pattern, rendering it easy to draw from the sand, and it fills up all pores in the wood, by which a cleaner and smoother casting is produced.

VEAL, *to choose.*—The flesh of a bull-calf is firmest, but not so white. The fillet of the cow-calf is generally preferred for the udder. The whitest is not the most juicy, having been made so by frequent bleeding, and having had whitening to lick. Choose the meat of which the kidney is well covered with white thick fat. If the bloody vein in the shoulder looks blue, or of a bright red, it is newly killed; but any other colour shows it stale. The other parts should be dry and white; if clammy or spotted, the meat is stale and bad.

The kidney turns first in the loin, and the suet will not then be firm.

VEAL, *a la daube.*—Cut off the chump end of the loin; take out the edge-bone; stuff the hollow with good forcemeat, tie it up tight, and lay it in a stew-pan with the bone you took out, a little fagot of herbs, an anchovy, two blades of mace, a few white peppers, and a pint of good veal broth. Cover the veal with slices of fat bacon, and lay a sheet of white paper over it. Cover the pan close, simmer it two hours, then take out the bacon, and glaze the veal.—Serve it on mushrooms; or with sorrel-sauce, or what else you please.

VEAL BROTH.—Stew a small knuckle in about three quarts of water, two ounces of rice, a little salt, and a blade of mace, till the liquor is half wasted away.

Another.—Knuckle of veal, two turnips, two carrots, two heads of celery, and six onions; stew them in a gallon of water till reduced to one half; add a lump of butter rolled in flour, with a little cayenne, and salt; strain, and add a gill of cream; 2 ozs. of vermicelli may be added with good effect.

VEAL CAKE.—Boil six or eight eggs hard; cut the yolks in two, and lay some of the pieces in the bottom of the pot: shake in a little chopped parsley, some slices of veal and ham, then add eggs again; shaking in after each some chopped parsley, with pepper and salt, till the pot is full. Then put in water enough to cover it, and lay on it about an ounce of butter; tie it over with a double paper, and bake it about an hour. Then press it close together with a spoon, and let it stand till cold.

It may be put into a small mould; and then it will turn out beautifully for a supper or side dish.

VEAL COLLOPS.—Cut long thin collops; beat them well; and lay on them a bit of thin bacon of the same size, and spread forcemeat on that, seasoned high, and also a little garlic and Cayenne. Roll them up tight, about the size of two fingers, but not more than two or three inches long; put a very small skewer to fasten each firmly; rub egg over; fry them of a fine brown, and pour a rich brown gravy over.

VEAL COLLOPS, *to dress quick.*—Cut them as thin as paper with a very sharp knife, and in small bits. Throw the skin, and any odd bits of veal, into a little water, with a dust of pepper and salt; set them on the fire while you beat the collops; and dip them into a seasoning of herbs, bread, pepper, salt, and a scrape of nutmeg, but first wet them in egg. Then put a bit of butter into a frying-pan, and give the collops a very quick fry; for as they are so thin, two minutes will do them on both sides; put them into a hot dish before the fire; then strain and thicken the gravy, give it a boil in the frying-pan, and pour it over the collops. A little ketchup is an improvement.

VEAL CUTLETS, *in Crust.*—Make a marinade with melted butter or lard, mushrooms, shalots, half a clove of garlic, pepper, and salt; simmer the cutlets in this about half an hour; then wrap them in puff paste, with all the seasoning; put them in a deep dish; bake them in an oven, and baste with yolks of eggs; make a hole in the middle, into which pour a clear sauce.

VEAL CUTLETS, *Maintenon.*—Cut slices about three quarters of an inch thick, beat them with a rolling-pin, and wet them on both sides with egg; dip them into a seasoning of bread-crumbs, parsley, thyme, knotted marjoram, pepper, salt, and a little nutmeg grated; then put them into papers folded over, and broil them; and serve in a boat of melted-butter, with a little mushroom-ketchup.

VEAL CUTLETS.—Another way.—Prepare as above, and fry them; lay them into a dish, and keep them hot; dredge a little flour, and put a bit of butter into the pan; brown it, then pour some boiling water into it, and boil quick: season with pepper, salt, and ketchup, and pour over them.

Another way.-Prepare as before, and dress the cutlets in a Dutch-oven; pour over them melted butter and mushrooms.

VEAL, *Fillet of.*—Veal requires a good bright fire for roasting. Before cooking, stuff with a forcemeat, composed of 2 ozs. of finely-powdered bread crumbs, half a lemon-peel chopped fine, half a teaspoonful of salt, and the same quantity of mixed mace and Cayenne pepper, powdered, parsley, and some sweet herbs; break an egg, and mix all well together. Baste your joint with fresh butter, and send it to table well browned. A nice bit of bacon should be served with the fillet of veal, unless ham is provided.

VEAL, *Fricandeau of.*—Cut a large piece from the fat side of the leg, about nine inches long, and half as thick and broad; beat it with the rolling-pin; take off the skin, and trim off the rough edges. Lard the top and sides; and cover it with fat bacon, and then with white paper. Lay it into the stewpan with any pieces of undressed veal or mutton, four onions, a carrot sliced, a faggot of sweet herbs, four blades of mace, four bay-leaves, a pint of good veal or mutton broth, and four or five ounces of lean ham or gammon. Cover the pan close, and let it stew slowly three hours; then take up the meat, remove all the fat from the gravy, and boil it quick to a glaze. Keep the fricandeau quite hot, and then glaze it; and serve with the remainder of the glaze in the dish, and sorrel-sauce in a sauce-tureen.

Another.—With a sharp knife cut the lean part of a large neck from the best end, scooping it from the bones the length of your hand, and prepare it the same way as in the last receipt: three or four bones only will be necessary, and they will make the gravy; but if the prime part of the leg is cut off, it spoils the whole.

VEAL GRAVY.—Put in the stewpan bits of lard, then a few thin slices of ham, a few bits of butter, then slices of fillet of veal, sliced onions, carrots, parsnips, celery, a few cloves, upon the meat, and two spoonfuls of broth; set it on the fire till the veal throws out its juice; then put it on a stronger fire till the meat catches to the bottom of the pan, and is brought to a proper colour; then add a sufficient quantity of light broth, and simmer it upon a slow fire till the meat is well done. A little thyme and mushrooms may be added. Skim and sift it clear for use.

VEAL HAM, *to make.*—Cut a leg of veal like a ham. Mix a pint of bay salt, 2 ozs. of saltpetre, and 1 lb. of common salt, with 1 oz. of cinnamon and juniper berries, and rub the ham with it. Lay it in a hollow tray with its face downwards; baste it every day with the pickle for a fortnight, and hang it in wood smoke for another fortnight. It may be either boiled or roasted.

VEAL, *Haricot of.*—Take the best end of a small neck; cut the bones short, but leave it whole: then put it into a stewpan just covered with brown gravy; and when it is nearly done, have ready a pint of boiled peas, six cucumbers pared and sliced, and two cabbage-lettuces cut into quarters, all stewed in a little good broth: put them to the veal, and let them simmer ten minutes. When the veal is in the dish, pour the sauce and vegetables over it, and lay the latter with forcemeat balls round it.

VEAL, *Knuckle of, to stew.*—As few people are fond of boiled veal, it may be well to leave the knuckle small, and take off some cutlets or collops before it is dressed; but as the knuckle will keep longer than the fillet, it is best not to cut off slices till wanted. Break the bones, to make it take less room; wash it well; and put it into a saucepan with three onions, a blade of mace or two, and a few pepper-corns; cover it with water, and simmer till quite ready. In the meantime some macaroni should be boiled with it if approved, or rice, or a little rice-flour, to give it a small degree of thickness; but don't put too much. Before it is served, add half-a-pint of milk and cream, and let it come up either with or without the meat.

Or fry the knuckle with sliced onions and butter to a good brown; and have ready peas, lettuces, onion, and a cucumber or two, stewed in a small quantity of water an hour: then add these to the veal; and stew it till the meat is tender enough to eat, but not overdone. Throw in pepper, salt and a bit of shred mint, and serve altogether.

VEAL, *Leg of, to roast.*—Let the fillet be cut large or small as best suits the number of your company. Take out the bone, fill the space with a fine stuffing, and let it be skewered quite round; and send the large side uppermost. When half-roasted, if not before, put a paper over the fat; and take care to allow a sufficient time, and put it a good distance from the fire, as the meat is very solid; serve with melted butter poured over it. —You may pot some of it.

VEAL, *Neck of.*—Cut off the scrag to boil, and cover it with onion-sauce. It should be boiled in milk and water. Parsley and butter may be served with it, instead of onion sauce.

Or it may be stewed with whole rice, small onions, and pepper-corns, with a very little water.

Or boiled and eaten with bacon and greens.

The best end may be either roasted, broiled as steaks, or made into pies.

VEAL, *Neck of a la braise.*—Lard the best end with bacon rolled in parsley chopped fine, salt, pepper, and nutmeg; put it into a tosser, and cover it with water. Put to it the scrag end, a little lean bacon or ham, an onion, two carrots, two heads of celery, and about a glass of Madeira wine.

Stew it quick two hours, or till it is tender, but not too much. Strain off the liquor; mix a little flour and butter in a stew-pan till brown, and lay the veal in this, the upper side to the bottom of the pan. Let it be over the fire till it gets coloured; then lay it into the dish, stir some of the liquor in and boil up, skim it nicely and squeeze orange or lemon-juice into it.

VEAL OLIVES.—Cut long thin collops, beat them, lay on them thin slices of fat bacon, and over these a layer of forcemeat seasoned high, with some shred shalot and Cayenne. Roll them tight, about the size of two fingers, but not more than two or three inches long; fasten them round with a small skewer, rub egg over them, and fry of a light brown. Serve

BB

with brown gravy, in which boil some mushrooms, pickled or fresh. Garnish with balls fried.

VEAL PATTIES.—— Mince some veal that is not quite done with a little parsley, lemon-peel, a scrape of nutmeg, and a bit of salt; add a little cream and gravy just to moisten the meat; and add a little ham. Do not warm it till the patties are baked.

VEAL PIE.——Take some of the middle, or scrag, of a small neck; season it; and either put to it, or not, a few slices of lean bacon or ham. If it is wanted of a high relish, add mace, cayenne, and nutmeg, to the salt and pepper; and also forcemeat and eggs; and if you choose, add truffles, morels, mushrooms, sweet-breads, cut into small bits, and cocks'-combs blanched, if liked. Have a rich gravy ready, to pour in after baking.—It will be very good without any of the latter additions.

VEAL PIE, *common.*—Cut a breast of veal into pieces; season with pepper and salt, and lay them in the dish. Boil hard six or eight yolks of eggs, and put them into different places in the pie; pour in as much water as will nearly fill the dish; put on the lid, and bake.—*Lamb Pie* may be done the same way.

VEAL PIE, *a rich one.*—Cut steaks from a neck or breast of veal; season them with pepper, salt, nutmeg, and very little clove in powder. Slice two sweetbreads, and season them in the same manner. Lay a puff paste on the ledge of the dish; then put the meat, yolks of hard eggs, the sweetbreads, and some oysters up to the top of the dish. Lay over the whole some very thin slices of ham, and fill up the dish with water, cover, and when it is taken out of the oven, pour in at the top, through a funnel, a few spoonfuls of good veal gravy, and some cream to fill up; but first boil it up with a tea-spoonful of flour. Truffles, &c., if approved.

VEAL, *or Chicken and Parsley* PIE.—Cut some slices from the leg or neck of veal; if the leg, from about the knuckle. Season them with salt; scald some parsley that is picked from the stems, and squeeze it dry; cut a little, and lay it at the bottom of the dish; then put the meat, and so on, in layers. Fill the dish with new milk, but not so high as to touch the crust. Cover it; and when baked, pour out a little of the milk, and put in half a pint of good scalded cream.

Chicken may be cut up skinned, and made in the same way.

VEAL SAUSAGES. — Chop equal quantities of lean veal and fat bacon, a handful of sage, a little salt, pepper, and a few anchovies. Beat all in a mortar; and when used, roll and fry it, and serve with fried sippets, or on stewed vegetables, or on white collops.

VEAL, *Shoulder of.*—Cut off the knuckle for a stew or gravy. Roast the other part with stuffing; you may lard it. Serve with melted butter.

The blade-bone, with a good deal of meat left on, eats extremely well with mushroom or oyster-sauce, or mushroom ketchup in butter.

VEAL STOCK.—Boil, in two quarts of water, for four hours, 4 lbs. of veal; knuckle, neck, or breast; the weight of meat to be reckoned without the bones; put into the saucepan an onion and a carrot, with a tea-spoonful of salt; strain, and take the fat off when cold.

VEAL, *to mince.*—Cut cold veal

as fine as possible, but do not chop it.—Put to it a very little lemon-peel shred, two grates of nutmeg, some salt, and four or five spoonfuls of either a little weak broth, milk, or water; simmer these gently with the meat, but take care not to let it boil; and add a bit of butter rubbed in flour. Put sippets of thin toasted bread, cut into a three-cornered shape, round the dish. Poached eggs may be served with it.

VEAL, *to pot.*——Cold fillet makes the finest potted veal; or you may do it as follows:—

Season a large slice of the fillet before it is dressed, with some mace, pepper-corns, and two or three cloves; lay it close into a potting-pan that will just hold it, fill it up with water, and bake it three hours; then pound it quite small in a mortar, and add salt to taste; put a little gravy that was baked to it in pounding, if to be eaten soon; otherwise only a little butter just melted. When done, cover it over with butter.

VEAL, or CHICKEN, *to pot.*—Pound some cold veal or white of chicken, seasoned as directed in the last article, and put layers of it with layers of ham pounded or rather shred; press each down and cover with butter.

VEAL, *to stew a breast of.*—Stew it gently till tender in some stock, a glass of sherry, some sweet herbs, as marjorum, lemon thyme, onions, mace, cloves, pepper, salt, and a few mushrooms. When done, strain, and skim the sauce. Garnish with forcemeat balls.

VEGETABLE CAUSTIC.—Burn oak or beech wood to ashes. Make a ley from them, and simmer it till it becomes rather thicker than cream; the evaporation may be continued in the sun. Spread on leather when used. It is valuable in cancers, fistulas, scrofulous and indolent ulcers, where there is proud flesh.

VEGETABLES, *to dress.*——Vegetables should be carefully cleaned from insects, and nicely washed. Boil them in plenty of water, and drain them the moment they are done enough. If overboiled, they lose their beauty and crispness. Bad cooks sometimes dress them with meat; which is wrong, except carrots with boiling beef.

VEGETABLES, *to boil green.*—Be sure the water boils when you put them in. Make them boil very fast. Don't cover, but watch them; and if the water has not slackened, you may be sure they are done when they begin to sink. Then take them out immediately or the colour will change. Hard water, especially if chalybeate, spoils the colour of such vegetables as should be green.

To boil them green in hard water, put a teaspoonful of salt of wormwood into the water when it boils, before the vegetables are put in.

VEGETABLE MARROW, *To boil or stew.*—This excellent vegetable may be boiled as asparagus. When boiled, divide it lengthways into two, and serve it upon a toast accompanied by melted butter; or when nearly boiled, divide it as above, and stew gently in gravy like cucumbers. Care should be taken to choose young ones not exceeding six inches in length.

VEGETABLE PIE.——Scald and blanch some broad beans: cut young carrots, turnips, artichoke-bottoms, mushrooms, peas, onions, lettuce, parsley, or any of them you have; make the whole into a nice stew with some good veal gravy. Bake a crust over a dish, with a little lining round the edge, and a cup turned up to keep it from sinking. When baked, open the lid and pour in the stew.

VEGETABLE SOUP.—Pare and slice five or six cucumbers; and add to these as many cos lettuces, a sprig or two of mint, two or three onions, some pepper, and salt, a pint and a half of young peas, and a little parsley. Put these, with ½ lb. of fresh butter, into a sauce-pan, to stew in their own liquor, near a gentle fire, half an hour; then pour two quarts of boiling water to the vegetables, and stew them two hours; rub down a little flour into a tea-cupful of water, boil it with the rest twenty minutes, and serve it.

VEILS, *Black Lace, to clean.*—Pass through a warm liquor of bullock's gall and water; after which rinse in cold water, then cleanse for stiffening, and finish as follows:—Take glue, about the size of a bean, pour boiling water upon it, and, when dissolved, pass the veil through it, then clap it between your hands. Starch and dry.

VEILS, *White Lace, to clean.*—Boil the veil gently for 15 minutes in solution of white soap, put into a basin holding warm water and soap, and keep gently squeezing it till it is clean, and then rinse it from the soap. Then take a vessel of cold water, into which put a drop or two of chemic, or liquid blue; rinse the veil in it, and then starch and dry.

VELVET CREAM.—Dissolve ½ oz. of isinglass in a cupful of sherry wine, one pint of cream, the juice of a large lemon. Sweeten the cream as you like, and when the isinglass is dissolved, put in the juice to the cream, then pour the wine to that. Stir it frequently until it begins to thicken, and pour into a mould.

VELVET, *to raise the plush of.*—Make a clean brick hot, place upon it a wet cloth, and hold the velvet over it, and the steam will raise the plush. A basin of boiling water placed underneath will answer the same purpose.

VENICE TURPENTINE OINTMENT.—Venice Turpentine, 2 ozs.; tar, 1 oz.; butter 4 ozs. Simmer until they are well mixed. This is very good for scald head, ringworm, &c. First wash the head well with soap and water, and then apply the ointment.

VENISON, *to choose.*—If the fat be clear, bright, and thick, and the cleft part smooth and close, it is young; but if the cleft is wide and tough, it is old. To judge of its sweetness, run a very sharp narrow knife into the shoulder or haunch, and you will know by the scent. Few people like it, when it has much of the *haut gout.*

VENISON, *to dress.*—A haunch of buck will take three hours and a half roasting; doe, only three hours and a quarter. Venison should be rather over than under-done.

Spread a sheet of white paper with butter, and put it over the fat, first sprinkling it with salt; lay a coarse paste on strong paper, and cover the haunch; tie it with fine packthread, and set it at a distance from the fire. Baste it often; ten minutes before serving take off the paper, put nearer the fire, and baste with butter and flour to make it froth up well.

Gravy for it should be put into a boat, and not into the dish; made thus: Cut off the fat from 2 or 3 lbs. of a loin of old mutton, and set it in steaks, on a gridiron just to brown one side; put them into a saucepan with a quart of water; for an hour simmer gently; uncover and stew till the gravy is reduced to a pint. Season with only salt.

Currant-jelly must be served in a boat.

Formerly pap-sauce was eaten with venison; which, as some still like it, it may be necessary to direct. Grate white bread, and boil it with port wine, water, and a large stick of cinnamon; and when quite smooth, take out the cinnamon, and add sugar. Claret may be used for it.

Make the jelly-sauce thus. Beat some currant-jelly and a spoonful or two of port wine, and set it over the fire till melted. Where jelly runs short put more wine, and a few lumps of sugar, to the jelly, and melt as above. Serve with French beans.

VENISON, *to carve.*—1. The

Haunch.——2. The Neck.——3. The Shoulder.——4. The Breast.

VENISON, *to fry.*—Cut the meat into slices, and make a gravy of the bones; fry it of a light brown, and keep it hot before the fire; put butter rolled in flour into the pan, and stir it till thick and brown; add ½ lb. of loaf sugar powdered, with the gravy made from the bones, and some port wine. Let it be as thick as cream; squeeze in a lemon; warm the venison in it; put it in the dish, and pour the sauce over it.

VENISON, *Haunch of, to roast.* —The haunch of a doe will require 15 minutes less than a buck. Venison should always be rather under than over done. Place the haunch on the spit; lay over it a large sheet of paper, and then a thin common paste, with a paper over that; tie it fast to keep the paper from dropping off. If the haunch be large, it will take four hours to roast it. When done, take off the paper and paste; dredge it well with flour, and baste it with butter. When it is of a light brown, dish it with brown gravy, or currant jelly sauce.

VENISON, *to hash.*—It should be warmed with its own gravy, or some without seasoning, as before: and only warmed through, not boiled. If there is no fat left, cut some slices of mutton-fat, set it on the fire with a little port wine and sugar, simmer till dry, then put to the ash, and it will eat as well as the fat of the venison. Garnish with currant jelly.

VENISON, *to stew a Shoulder of*.—Let the meat hang till it is fit to dress; take out the bone, beat the meat with a rolling-pin, lay some slices of mutton-fat, that have lain a few hours in a little port wine, among it, and sprinkle ground pepper and allspice over it; roll it up tight, and tie it. Set in a stew-pan with some mutton or beef gravy not strong, half a pint of port wine; pepper and allspice. Simmer it, closely covered, as slowly as you can, for three or four hours. When tender, take off the tape, and set the meat in a dish; strain the gravy over it; serve with currant-jelly sauce.

VERMICELLI CREAM.— Boil some vermicelli in milk until it becomes a marmalade; cool, and then mix it with a pint of cream, macaroni drops, orange flowers, and lemon peel, all chopped fine, with a little ground cinnamon, five eggs well beaten, and sugar to taste. Pour it upon the table dish. Bake it in a slow oven.

VERMICELLI PUDDING.— Boil 4 ozs. of vermicelli in a pint of new milk till soft, with a stick or two of cinnamon. Then put in half a pint of thick cream, $\frac{1}{4}$ lb. of butter, the same of sugar, and the yolks of 4 eggs. Bake without paste in an earthern dish.

Another.—Simmer 2 ozs. of vermicelli in a cupful of milk till tender; flavour it with a stick or two of cinnamon, or other spice. Beat up 3 eggs, 1 oz. of sugar, half a pint of milk and a glass of wine. Add to the vermicelli. Bake in a slow oven. *A. N.*

VERMICELLI SOUP.—Boil tender $\frac{1}{2}$ lb. of vermicelli in a quart of rich gravy; take half of it out, and to it add more gravy; boil till the vermicelli can be pulped through a sieve. To both put a pint of boiling cream, a little salt, and $\frac{1}{4}$ lb. of Parmesan cheese. Serve with rasped bread. Add two or three eggs, if you like. *Gu.*

Brown Vermicelli Soup is made in the same manner, leaving out the eggs and cream, and adding one quart of strong beef gravy.

VERMIN *in Childrens' heads, to destroy.*—Take 1 oz. each of vinegar and stavesacre, $\frac{1}{2}$ oz. of honey, do. sulphur, and 2 ozs. of sweet oil. Make into a liniment, and rub the head with it.

VESSELS, *to purify.*——All kinds of glass vessels and other utensils may be purified from smells of every kind, by rinsing them out well with charcoal powdered after the grosser impurities have been scoured off by sand and pearl-ash.

VINEGAR, *balsamic.* — Take the best vinegar, a handful of lavender leaves and flowers, some hyssop, balm, thyme, savory, a handful of salt, and two heads of garlic; infuse these in the vinegar three weeks. It is a good remedy for wounds, spasms, sprains, &c. By rubbing the hands and temples with it, and putting a little in the mouth, a person may go into foul air with safety.

VINEGAR, *from malt.*—For 5 gallons of malt liquor, mix $\frac{1}{4}$ oz. each of cream of tartar, bay salt, and alum, well powdered, with a gallon of the liquid boiling hot, and poured the instant it is dissolved, and while it is hot, into the cask. Cover the bung-hole with stiff brown paper, and in a few days you will find it a very fine vinegar.

Or, to every gallon of water, put 1 lb. of coarse sugar. Boil the mixture and skim. When it is cool as beer when fermented, put to it a warm toast rubbed over with yeast; let it ferment 24 hours. Put it into a cask in a very *warm* place, or where the sun may shine upon it. In three months it will be fit for use.

VINEGAR OF ROSES.—Take of red roses, half a pound; strong vinegar, half a gallon. Infuse in a close vessel for several weeks, in a gentle heat, afterwards strain off the liquor. Used as an embrocation for head-ache, &c.

VIOLET LOZENGES.—Orris powder, 1 ounce; gum arabic, 1 ounce; white sugar, 2 pounds. Make into a thick paste with the following: cochineal, 1 drachm; water, 1 quart. Macerate two days.

VIRGIN WHITE WAX.—White wax, 3 parts; cake stearine, 2 parts; mucilage, 1 part. Melt and stir well; when nearly cold, form into cakes as before.

VOICE, *to improve.*—See *Tar.*

VOLATILE LINIMENT.—Mix together equal portions of spirit of hartshorn and sweet oil. It is the domestic Liniment for sore throat, pained limbs, stiff and aching joints, &c.—The addition of oil of hemlock, or laudanum and tincture of cayenne, will be a great improvement.

VOMITING.—It is generally preceded by the sensation of nausea and sickness, and a disposition to faint. Endeavour to ascertain the particular condition on which it depends. If it arises from some irritating substance in the stomach, as bile, then the stomach should be thoroughly cleansed. Take a beer-glassful of warm water, and about one hour afterwards an effervescing draught, in which drop a very little tincture of cayenne.—

The Neutralizing Mixture is an appropriate remedy; also the Black Draught, or one of the aperients, page 20, 21.—A mustard poultice over the stomach, and ten drops of laudanum in a little brandy and water, tend to settle the stomach.

VOMITING BLOOD. — The escape of blood by vomiting is carefully to be distinguished from the expectoration of blood from the lungs. If from the stomach, the blood will be dark and clotted, and mixed with the contents of the stomach. The blood from the lungs is a bright red, often frothy and mixed with mucus. It is generally preceded by chilliness, nausea, heaviness, and pain at the stomach. It is followed by great weakness, and from that the danger chiefly arises.

The patient should be placed in bed immediately, and be perfectly quiet. Place the feet and hands in warm water, and apply mustard plasters to the calves of the legs. The following draught may be very serviceable:—

Infusion of roses, 12 drachms; diluted sulphuric acid, 10 drops; syrup of roses, 1 drachm; tincture of opium, 10 drops. Mix.——Or, take acetate of lead, 3 grains; purified opium, 1 grain; extract of hemlock, 10 grains. Make 3 pills, one to be taken twice a day; drink after them iced lemon-juice and water, or vinegar and water. Use the vapour bath, if the person is cold and chilly, and afterwards apply hot bricks saturated in vinegar and water to the feet and sides. If there be constipation, give aperients, pages 20, 21; or a mild injection.

Sometimes the vomiting of blood proceeds from the retention of the menses. See *Menses, retention of.*

VULNERARIES.—Medicines healing wounds.

WAFER CAKES.—Rub 1 lb. of sifted sugar into 3 lbs. of fine dried flour, 1 lb. of butter, and 1 oz. of carraway seeds. Make it into a paste with three quarters of a pint of boiling new milk; roll very thin, and form as you like. Make it full of holes, and bake.

WAGES TABLE.

Yr.	Pr. Month			Pr. Week			Pr. Dy	
£.	£.	s.	d.	£.	s.	d.	s.	d.
1	0	1	8	0	0	4¾	0	0¾
2	0	3	4	0	0	9¼	0	1¼
3	0	5	0	0	1	1¾	0	2
4	0	6	8	0	1	6½	0	2¾
5	0	8	4	0	1	11	0	3¼
6	0	10	0	0	2	3½	0	4
7	0	11	8	0	2	8¼	0	4½
8	0	13	4	0	3	0¾	0	5¼
9	0	15	0	0	3	5½	0	6
10	0	16	8	0	3	10	0	6½
11	0	18	4	0	4	2¾	0	7¼
12	1	0	0	0	4	7¼	0	8
13	1	1	8	0	4	11¾	0	8¼
14	1	3	4	0	5	4¼	0	9¼
15	1	5	0	0	5	9	0	10
16	1	6	8	0	6	1¾	0	10½
17	1	8	4	0	6	6¼	0	11¼
18	1	10	0	0	6	10¾	0	11¾
19	1	11	8	0	7	3½	1	0½
20	1	13	4	0	7	8	1	1¼
30	2	10	0	0	11	6	1	7¾
40	3	6	8	0	15	4	2	2¼
50	4	3	4	0	19	2	2	9
60	5	0	0	1	3	0¼	3	3¼
70	5	16	8	1	6	10¼	3	10
80	6	13	4	1	10	8¼	4	4½
90	7	10	0	1	14	6¼	4	11½
100	8	6	8	1	18	4½	5	5¾

WALNUT KETCHUP.—Put any quantity of soft green walnuts into jars with cold strong vinegar. Tie them close for a year. Then take them out, and for every gallon of liquor, put two heads of garlic. ½ lb. of anchovies, a quart of port wine, and 1 oz. each of mace, cloves, long, black, and Jamaica pepper, and ginger. Boil all together till ths liquor is reduced to half. Bottle for use. It is good in fish sauce, or stewed beef. The longer it is kept, the better it is.

WALNUT KETCHUP, *very fine.*—Boil a gallon of the expressed juice of green tender walnuts, and skim it well; then put in 2 lbs. of anchovies, bones and liquor, 2 lbs. shalots, 1 oz. each of cloves, mace, pepper, and one clove of garlic. Let all simmer till the shalots sink; then put the liquor into a pan till cold; bottle and divide the spice to each. Cork closely, and tie a bladder over. It will keep twenty years, but is not good the first. Be very careful to express the juice at home; for it is rarely unadulterated, if bought.

WALNUTS, *to pickle.*—When a pin will go into them, put a brine of salt and water boiled, and strong enough to bear an egg, being quite cold first. Let them soak six days; then change the brine, let them stand six more; then drain, and pour over them in the jar a pickle of the best vinegar, with plenty of pepper, pimento, ginger, mace, cloves, mustard-seed, and horse raddish; all boiled together, but cold. To every hundred of walnuts put six spoonfuls of mustard-seed, and two or three heads of garlick or shalot, but the latter is least strong. In this way they will be good for several years, if closely covered. They will not be fit to eat under six months. This pickle makes good ketchup.

WARM PLASTER.——Gum plaster, 1 oz.; blistering plaster, 2 drachms. Melt over a gentle fire. This plaster is useful in sciatica, and in rheumatic pains; renew once a week. Should it blister the part, use less blistering plaster, and add a little camphor.

WARTS.—These may be cured by daily touching the top of the wart with the pure Tincture of the *Rhus Toxicodendron*, or Poison Oak, which grows in North America. It is sold by the Homœopathic Chemists. The application should be continued for a few weeks.

Or touch them frequently with blue vitriol, or nitric acid, or chloride of zinc.—A bit of impure potass, moistened, should be applied to the warts, a few minutes, so as to leave a whitish paste upon them; put over it a sticking plaster for a week. Repeat, if needed.

WARTS.—Rub them daily with a radish. Or, with juice of marigold flowers: it will hardly fail. Or, water in which sal-ammoniac is dissolved. Or, apply bruised purslain as a poultice, changing it twice a-day. It cures it in seven or eight days.—*Wesley.*

Or, steep in vinegar and salt the rind of a lemon, and apply it to the wart, first the outer side, and then the inner; keep on for two hours, and change.

Or rub the wart now and then with elixir of vitriol; apply with a bit of wood.

WASH *for Cleansing and Preventing the Hair from falling off.*—Take three handfuls of rosemary leaves, a small lump of common soda, and 1½ drachm of camphor. Put in a jug, with a quart of boiling water, and cover closely, to keep the steam in. Let it stand for twelve hours, then strain it, and add a wine-glassful of rum. This will keep good for six months in bottles well corked, and a piece of camphor in each. If the hair falls off much, the wash ought to be applied to the roots, with a piece of sponge, every other day.

WASH *for a blotched face.*—Rose-water, 3 ozs., sulphate of zinc, 1 drachm. Mix. Wet the face with it, gently dry it, and then touch it over with cold cream, which also dry gently off.

WASH, *for the arm-pits after sweating.*—One quart of spring water; tincture of myrrh, 1 oz.; sulphate of zinc, ½ oz. Mix, and sponge.

WASHING, *made easy.*—One of the best bleaching and emolient agents in washing either the person or clothing, is common refined borax. Dissolve in hot water, half a pound to ten gallons; a great saving in soap is effected by its use. The borax should be pulverized first. It may be procured in the form of crystals at any druggist's; it will not injure the most delicate fabric; and laces or other fine tissues may be washed in a solution of borax with advantage to colour, &c.

WASHING, *ready and effectual mode of.*—Dissolve 1 lb. of soap in 3 quarts of boiling water, the night before washing. Beginning to wash, put the soap into the dolly tub, add 8 table-spoonfuls of spirits of turpentine, and 6 ditto of hartshorn. Pour upon the above 8 gallons of boiling water. Have the clothes ready assorted; begin with the fine ones. Dolly each lot about five minutes, wash them in hot water in another dolly-tub, if you have it; next in blue water.—When the water is getting cool, put it into the boiler to boil kitchen towels, or any greasy things.

N. B.—The quicker the washing is done the better. As soon as one lot is taken out of the dolly tub, put another in whilst the others are being rinsed.

A little pipe-clay dissolved in the water employed in washing linen cleans the dirtiest linen entirely, with about one half the labour, and saving full one half of soap.

WASPS *and* FLIES *to destroy.*—Dip a feather in a little sweet oil, and touch them with it between their wings; this renders their breathing impossible.

WATER *for Low Spirits.*-Coriander seeds and aniseeds, of each 1½ oz,; valerian 1½ oz.; cardamoms, bruised, 2 ozs.; saffron, 1 oz.; carraway seeds, 2 ozs.; cinnamon, 3 ozs. Simmer half an hour in a quart of water, to which add 4 ozs. of sugar candy. Cool. Then add a quart of port wine, and a quart of brandy. Cork well in bottles. Through all the operation cover close.

WATER, *to purify.*—Put into it powdered charcoal, then filter through a compressed sponge, and it will become perfectly sweet, however impure previously.

Water may be filtered and purified by means of a deep flowerpot, with a compressed sponge in the hole at the bottom. Put over the sponge an inch thick of pebbles, next an inch of coarse sand, next a layer of charcoal, and over again pebbles. The water will filter pure and clear through the hole into another vessel.

WATER, *to purify.*—A large spoonful of pulverised alum sprinkled into a hogshead of water (the water stirred round at the time) will after the lapse of a few hours, so purify it, that it will be found to possess nearly the freshness and clearness of finest spring water. A pailful containing four gallons may be purified by a single spoonful; or a mixture of one part chalk and two of alum will be still better.

WATER, *to soften.*—Wood ashes form a good lye for softening water, but care must be taken that they should be all wood.

WATER, *hard to make soft.*—Boil it, and expose it to the atmosphere. Add a little carbonate of soda.

WATER BRASH.—A discharge of thin watery fluid from the stomach upwards to the mouth. It generally arises from weakness of the stomach, indigestion, &c. Persons affected with diseases of the chest, and persons of debilitated constitution, are much subject to it.

Take from 4 to 8 grains of the white oxide of bismuth. Give an aperient pill to keep the bowels open, and give bitters freely. Take nourishing diet, and be frequently in the open air. Take now and then some of the Neutralizing Mixture diluted. A little brandy bitters, and effervescing draughts are beneficial. Use friction with the flesh brush. If the patient is consumptive, then most gentle means must be used, and chiefly in reference to the disease which is the cause of water brash.

WATER CEMENT.—This will *harden under water.*—Mix 4 parts of grey clay, 6 of oxide of manganese, and 90 of good limestone reduced to fine powder. Calcine the whole to expel the carbonic acid. Work into the consistence of a soft paste with 60 parts of washed sand. If a lump of this cement be thrown into water, it will harden immediately.

WATER-CRESSES. — Medicinally it acts as a gentle stimulant and diuretic. The expressed juice which contains the peculiar taste and pungency of the herb, may be taken in doses of one or two ounces. Eat the plant also at meals. It is famous for purifying the blood, and the cure of scurvy.

WATER GRUEL, *to make.*—Boil a table-spoonful of oatmeal in a quart of water for one hour, or till it is fine and smooth. Take off the fire, and let it settle; then pour it into a china bowl and add sugar, sherry, and nutmeg to your taste.

WATER PIPES, *to manage in winter.*—In frost cover the water pipes with hay, or straw bands.

WATERPROOF BOOT SOLES.—If hot tar and rosin be applied to boot soles, it will make them waterproof. Apply it with a piece of old flannel, or cloth, and dry it in by the fire. The operation may be repeated two or three times during the winter, if necessary. It makes the surface of the leather quite hard, so that it wears longer. Oil or grease softens the sole, and does not keep the water out.

WATERPROOFING, *for Boots and Shoes.*—Linseed oil, 1 pint; oil of turpentine, or naptha, ¼ pint; yellow wax, ¼ lb.; burgundy pitch, ¼ lb. Melt together with a gentle heat. For use, rub into the leather before the fire.

WATERPROOFING SHOES —Melt bees' wax and mutton suet, and when you take from the fire, add a tea-spoonful of turpentine. ——Or, India rubber and gutta percha, dissolved in good naphtha. ——Or, yellow wax, 4 ozs; rosin, 4 ozs.; linseed oil, 1 pint; oil of turpentine, a quarter of a pint. Melt over a *slow fire*, and when melted, take from the fire, and add the turpentine, and stir well. Remember that it is very inflammable. When required for use, melt and apply.

WATERPROOF CLOTH.— Apply to the calico or linen two coats of boiled oil, a little rosin or burgundy pitch, and a small quantity of turpentine. Hang up to dry.

WATERPROOF CLOTH.— To one ounce of melted white wax add one quart of spirits of turpentine; when thoroughly mixed and cold, dip the cloth in it and hang it up to dry.

WATERPROOF COMPOSITION.—Mix gas tar, common oil, and slaked lime, and use as paint, applying three or four coats. Petroleum oil, and Norway tar might also be employed with advantage.

WAX, *Black, to make.*—Take two ounces of bees' wax, half an ounce of burgundy pitch, and melt them together, then add one ounce and a half of ivory black, ground very fine and dried.

WEAK EYES.——Wash frequently in cold water, or in a decoction of the plant, eye-bright. ——Or, dissolve 4 grains of sugar of lead and crude sal-ammoniac, in 8 ozs. of water, to which add a few drops of laudanum. Bathe the eyes with it three or four times a day.——Or bathe the eyes frequently in salt and water, or in weak brandy, salt, and water.

WEIGHTS, *Average.*—

		lbs.
1 Peck of Potatoes	=	20
1 " of White Turnips..	"	16
1 " of Swede Turnips..	"	18
1 " of Onions	"	16
1 " of Broad Beans ..	"	10
1 " of Kidney Beans ..	"	9
1 " of Green Peas ..	"	9
1 " of Apples	"	16
1 " of Pears..	"	18
1 " of Gooseberries ..	"	16
1 " of Plums, Damsons, and all Stone Fruit ..	"	18

WEIGHT OF ENGLISH GOLD AND SILVER COINS.

	dwt.	gr.	
Sovereign	5	3¼	
Half Sovereign ..	2	13½	
Crown	18	4	4-11
Half Crown ..	9	2	2-11
Florin	7	6	6-11
Shilling	3	15	3-11
Sixpence.. ..	1	19	7-11

WEEDS AND WORMS, to destroy.—Sprinkle the walks with salt, and then water it. Observe not to throw the salt upon the box edging.

WELSH PUDDING.—Melt ½ lb. of butter gently; beat it with the yolks of eight, and whites of four eggs; mix in 6 ozs. of loaf sugar, and the rind of a lemon grated. Put a paste into a dish for turning out, and pour the above in, and bake it.

WELSH RABBIT, or RAREBIT.—See page 343.

WEN, to cure.—Take a limestone and slake it in soap lees; then mix it with a little soap. Spread it as a plaster, and apply it to the wen, and often anoint it with the lees in which the lime was slaked. It will sink and destroy the wen.

WHIPPED CREAM.—To one quart of good cream, put a few drops of bergamot water, a little orange flower water, and ¼ lb. of sugar. When it is dissolved, whip the cream to a froth, and take it up with a skimmer; drain on a sieve, and if for icing, let it settle half an hour before you put it into cups or glasses. Use that which drops into the dish under the sieve, to make it froth the better, adding two whites of eggs. Coloured powdered sugar may, if you like, be sprinkled at the top of each.

WHITE GLOVES, to dye a good purple.—Boil 4 ozs. of logwood, and 2 ozs. of roche alum, in 3 pints of soft water till half wasted. Strain and cool. Then with a brush rub the gloves over, and when dry, repeat it. When dry, rub off the loose dye with a coarse cloth; beat up the white of an egg, and with a sponge rub it over the leather.

WHITE SAUCE.—See Sauce.

WHITE SOUP.—— Take a knuckle of veal, a fowl, and a shank of ham; put them into a pan with 6 quarts of water; add ½ lb. of rice, two anchovies, some peppercorns, sweet herbs, two onions, and a head of celery; stew the whole till strong enough, and strain. The next day skim it carefully, and pour it into a stewpan; put in ½ lb. of sweet almonds beaten fine; boil 15 minutes, and strain.

WHITE SOUP,—Take a scrag of mutton, a knuckle of veal after cutting off as much meat as will make collops, two shank-bones of mutton, and ¼ lb. of fine lean bacon, sweet herbs, lemon-peel, three onions, three blades of mace, and a dessert-spoonful of white pepper; boil all in three quarts of water, till the meat falls to pieces. Next day take off the fat, clear the jelly from the sediment, and put it into a sauce-pan. If macaroni is used, add it soon enough to get tender, after soaking in cold water. Vermicelli may be added after the thickening, as it requires less time to do. Have ready the following: —Blanch ¼ lb. of sweet almonds, and beat them to a paste, with a spoonful of water to prevent their oiling; mince a large slice of dressed veal or chicken, and beat with it a piece of stale white bread; add a pint of thick cream, a bit of fresh lemon-peel, and a blade of mace, in the finest powder. Boil it a few minutes; add to it a pint of soup, and strain and pulp it through a coarse sieve: put this thickening to the rest, and boil for half an hour.

WHITES, or, Leucorrhœa, (Fluor Albus,)—This disease is peculiar to females. It is indicated by a morbid secretion of mucous from the passage leading to the womb, termed vagina. It varies. in appearance, consistence, and quantity, in different persons.

Women of delicate constitution, debilitated by hard labours, miscarriages, grief, poor living, and of an erysipelatous habit, generally termed scorbutic, are most subject to it, and in them it proves very obstinate.

It is the effect both of relaxation and inflammatory excitement.

Treatment. — When it arises from relaxation, the Tonic Pills, will generally succeed in effecting a cure. Cold bathing or the local application of cold water, is a good remedy for this disease, and should be used every morning, provided the patient be free from cough or difficulty of breathing, and not subject to a determination of blood to the brain.

If the discharge continue after the employment of these means, an astringent lotion may be used; as the following:—Take of pomegranate-rind, bruised, 3 drachms; boil in a quart of water to a pint and a half; then strain, and add alum, a drachm and a half. To be injected by means of a female syringe.

Give an emetic and a vapour bath occasionally. If the stools are of a pale clay or very dark colour, or the patient be subject to erysipelas, or eruption of the skin, take a little rhubarb and magnesia every other night for about ten days.

When fluor albus occurs in a person of a robust and sanguine habit, it may be considered of an inflammatory nature; in which case, instead of tonic medicines above recommended, the patient should take every other morning, 2 drachms of Epsom salt, and 10 grains of nitre powder, with 15 of gum-arabic powder, in a glass of barley-water three times a day; which, with a low diet, free from all kinds of stimulants,) will succeed in curing it. To these remedies, the application of cold water, will be a powerful auxiliary.

When the discharge is of an *ichorous* nature, and of a *dark* or *yellowish* colour, and attended with *pain* in the region of the womb, or with irritation, burning heat, difficulty or heat of urine, troublesome itching, a sense of bearing down, and a frequent inclination to evacuate; pains on the approach, or during the time of menstruation; and particularly if pieces of coagulated blood (generally termed clots) are discharged; some *organic* disease of the womb may be suspected, especially if they occur about the time of the cessation of the menstrual discharge.

The buchu leaves are a good remedy for this disease, and in many cases of long standing, the tincture, in the dose of two teaspoonfuls in a wine-glass of the decoction of marshmallow root, has succeeded in curing the disease, and improving the general health. In obstinate cases it may be given in an infusion of the leaves, in lieu of the decoction of marshmallow root.

The diet must depend on the general health of the patient. If she be weakly, and of a delicate constitution, it should be nourishing and easy of digestion, such as blanc mange, and the vegetable and animal jellies, with a small portion of meat; a little good Port or Sherry may also be allowed, but water should be adopted in lieu of malt liquor: but if the complaint be attended with much irritation or pain on making water, it will be advisable to avoid pepper and much salt, but not otherwise.

Mr. Wesley recommends the following:—Live chastely: feed sparingly: use exercise constantly: sleep moderately, but never lying on your back. Take eight grains of jalap every eight days. This usually cures in five weeks.

Or, make Venice turpentine, flour, and fine sugar, equal quantities, into small pills. Take three or four of these morning and evening. This also cures most pains in the back. Or, take yellow resin, powdered, 1 oz.; conserve of roses, ½ oz.; powdered rhubarb, 3 drms.; syrup, a sufficient quantity to make an electuary. Take a large teaspoonful of this twice a day, in a cup of comfrey-root tea.

WHITE SWELLING.—This is a very painful disease; it more frequently affects the knee than any other joint; sometimes the hip, ancle, and elbow. At first a severe pain is felt penetrating the joint, or only one particular part of the joint. The least motion aggravates the pain. It soon begins to swell considerably, and suppuration takes place. Matter is discharged from several openings or ulcers, the bones are affected; and if the disease is not arrested, the life of the patient is endangered.

Treatment. Avoid the old system of treatment by the allopathic doctors, by mercury, blistering, setons, amputation, &c. Attend to the stomach and bowels, giving an emetic, and an aperient, if needed; to be followed by bitter tonics occasionally, giving the *alterative syrup*, (see Addenda) diluted when first taken; or a decoction of sarsaparilla, sassafras, guiacum, queen's delight, unicorn root, cleavers. prickly ash berries, of each 1 oz. Simmer in a covered pan with twe quarts of water down to three pints. Sweeten. A dessert spoonful three or four times a day. Steam the part with bitter herbs, and now and then give the Vapour Bath to the whole body. After steaming the affected part, rub the limb with the Rheumatic Liquid.

Dr. Beach recommends the following;—" Oil of hemlock; oil of sassafras, gum camphor, tincture of opium, ½ oz. each, and a pint of spirit of wine. When dissolved and properly mixed, bathe the part with it frequently."—Then apply an oatmeal and bran poultice, mixed with a little finely powdered charcoal, salt and cayenne pepper. If the pain is great, sprinkle on the poultice, ½ oz. of laudanum. Keep it on as long as possible, and then steam.

WHITE SWELLING. — The pain arising from white swellings, and other similar swellings, may be instantly eased thus:—Take the white of an egg, and beat it up with two table-spoonfuls of spring water; rub the part affected frequently, but gently with the finger.

WHITE SWELLINGS. —— Hold the part half an hour every morning under a pump or cock. This cures all pains in the joints. It seldom fails.—Tried.——Or, pour on it daily a stream of warm water.——Or, a stream of cold water one day, and warm the next, and so on by turns. Use these remedies at first, if possible. It is likewise proper to intermix gentle purges to prevent a relapse.—— Or, boiled nettles.—*Wesley.*

WHITINGS, *to choose.*—The firmness of the body and fins is to be looked to, as in herrings; their high season is during the first three months of the year, but they may be had a great part of it.

WHITINGS, *to fry.*—Wash and gut; skin them, and turn their tails into their mouths, to lie round. Season with salt and pepper; steep them in vinegar; flour them, and dip them in butter; then fry them

WHITLOW.—This is an inflammation of the fingers, thumb, or hand, and is very painful. It is often situated at the root of the nail. The pain is attended with throbbing, swelling, and inflammation. It gradually progresses to suppuration.

Steam the whole hand with bitter herbs for 30 or 40 minutes; bathe it frequently in strong hot ley water. The steaming must not be dispensed with. Apply a poultice of linseed and slippery elm, with a little salt and brandy. The formation of matter is indicated by a small white spot in the centre of the swelling. When this appears, open it with the point of a large needle or probe, that the matter may escape. Repeat if necessary. If proud flesh appears, apply the vegetable caustic or chloride of potass, diluted. A poultice of powdered hops is very effectual to relieve pain. Attend to the general health, by giving aperients, tonics, and nutritious cooling diet.

WHITLOW.—Cut a hole in a lemon, and wear it on the finger like a thimble; the whitlow must be encased in the lemon.—See *Felon.*

WILD DUCKS, *Widgeon, &c.*—They should be taken up with the gravy in. Baste them with butter, and sprinkle a little salt before they are taken up; put a good gravy under them, and serve with shalot-sauce.

WILD FOWL, *to roast.*—The flavour is best preserved without stuffing. Put pepper, salt, and a piece of butter into each.

Wild fowl require much less dressing than tame; they should be served of a fine colour, and well frothed up. A rich brown gravy should be sent in the dish; and when the breast is cut into slices, before taking off the bone, a squeeze of lemon, pepper and salt, is a great improvement to the flavour.

To take off the fishy taste which wild fowl sometimes have, put an onion, salt, and hot water, into the dripping-pan, and baste them for the first ten minutes with this; then take away the pan, and baste constantly with butter.

WIND IN THE STOMACH.—See *Flatulency.*—Take oil of juniper, tincture of myrrh, lavender water, sweet nitre, equal quantity of each: shake them in a bottle. Dose:—One teaspoonful in a cup of cold water. The above is a dose for an adult.——Or, take a large handful of feverfew, and cummin seeds and ginger, 1 oz. of each to three quarts of water; boil to three pints. Add a little tincture of cayenne. Dose—three or four wine-glassfuls a day.

WINDSOR PUDDING-Shred ¼ lb. of suet very fine; grate into it ½ lb. of French roll, a little nutmeg, and the rind of a lemon; add ½ lb. of chopped apples; ¼ lb. of currants; ¼ lb. of good reisins, stoned, and chopped, a glass of rich sweet wine, and five eggs beaten, with a little salt. Mix all thoroughly together, and boil it in a basin, or mould for three hours. Sift fine sugar over it when sent to table, and pour wine sauce into the dish.

WINDSOR SOAP is merely the best white soap melted, and scented with oil of carraway, and put into moulds.

WINE, *English White.*—Boil 40 lbs. of sugar in 14 gallons of water, twenty minutes, taking the scum as it rises. Put it into a tub, and when nearly cold put in 8 lbs. of raisins chopped; and when cold, add two gallons of strong ale, when the ale is ready to tun. Let it stand three days, stirring it well every day. Then put it into the cask with a pint of brandy, a pound of sugar candy, and an ounce of isinglass. It may be bottled in eight months.

WINE, *to make astringent.*—Mix a little alum with the wine; or gum kino, catechu, or rhatany.

WINE, *rich and pleasant.*—Take new cider from the press, mix it with as much honey as will support an egg, boil gently fifteen minutes, but not in an iron, brass, or copper pot. Skim it well; when cool let it be turned, but don't quite fill. In the March following bottle it, and it will be fit to drink in six weeks; but will be less sweet if kept longer in the cask. You will have a rich and strong wine, and it will keep well. This will serve for any culinary purpose for which sack, or sweet wine is directed.

Honey is a fine ingredient to assist, and render palatable new crabbed austere cider.

WINE BISCUITS.—Take the yolks of 6 eggs, and the whites of 5; beat with orange flower water till they come to a froth; then add sifted sugar, 1 lb.; rice flour, ½ lb.; the raspings and pulp of a lemon, with a few carraway seeds. Dust with sugar.

WINE WHEY.—Put half a pint of new milk on the fire; the moment it boils up, pour in as much sound raisin wine as will completely turn it, and it looks clear; let it boil up, then set the sauce-pan aside till the curd subsides, and do not stir it. Pour the whey off, and add to it half a pint of boiling water, and a bit of white sugar. Thus you will have a whey perfectly cleared of milky particles, and as weak as you choose to make it.

WOOD, *to bronze.*—Cover with a coating of thin glue. When dry, coat it again with white of egg and water; do not put much on. Then apply the bronze with a hare's foot, or dust from a small fine muslin bag.

WOOD, *to coat.*—The Germans have recently adopted the following method:—The ingredients are 40 parts of chalk, 40 of rosin, 4 of linseed oil, to be melted together in an iron pot. One part of native oxide of copper, and one of sulphuric acid are then to be added, when the composition is ready for use. It is applied hot to the wood with a brush in the same way as paint, and the varnish becomes as hard as stone when dry.

WOOD, *to preserve.*—Gas tar, rosin, or pitch, and lime, boiled well together, and applied to wood exposed to the weather, form a good preservative. Apply two or three coats, and on the last dash fine sand to give it the appearance of stone, and to make it durable.

Gas tar, turpentine, and a little nitric acid make a good paint for iron.

WOOD, *to resemble mahogany.*—Take two ounces of dragon's blood, (gum tragacanth) break it into pieces, and dissolve in a quart of spirits of wine, to which add a little soda; let it stand in a warm place and shake it frequently; when dissolved, it is fit for use.

Or take four ounces of logwood, and half a pound of madder; boil in a gallon of water, adding a little pearl-ash, and 1 oz. of walnut peeling. Apply while hot.

WOODCOCK, *Snipe, &c.*—Clean well, and stuff with mealy potatoes, well washed, and seasoned with butter, salt, pepper, and a little cream, or new milk; cut off the pinions at the first joint; fasten the legs close to the ribs, turn the head backward, between the legs and the body. Do them before a bright fire, or in the oven; dredge them with flour, and baste often with butter melted in hot water.

WOODCOCKS, *Snipes*, and *Quails* keep good several days. Roast them without drawing, and serve on toast. Butter only should be eaten with them, as gravy takes off the fine flavour. The thigh and back are esteemed the most.

WOODWORK, *to preserve*.— Boiled oil and finely powdered charcoal, mix to the consistence of a paint, and give the wood two or three coats with this composition. ——Or, mix 5 lbs. of chloride of zinc with 25 gallons of water. This, if the wood be steeped in it, will prevent the dry rot.

WOOLLEN CLOTH, *to remove oil spots from*.—Apply moistened pipe-clay, or fullers earth. When dry, brush off. If needful, repeat, heating the place by holding it to the fire, or applying carefully a hot iron. Lemon juice or pearlash, in solution, used to moisten the pipe clay or fullers earth, would render it more effectual.

WORMS.—The worms found in the human body are mostly the *ascarides*, the thread worm, infesting the lower intestine, causing much itching and irritation about the anus. The *teres*, or long round worm, generally seated in the small intestines, and stomach.

The symptoms denoting the existence of worms are common to the different species, viz. indigestion, with a variable appetite: foul tongue; offensive breath; hard, full, and tense belly, with occasional gripings and pains about the navel; heat and itching sensation in the rectum and about the anus; the eyes heavy and dull; itching of the nose; short dry cough; grinding of the teeth; and starting during sleep, attended often with a slow fever.

The indications of cure are, first, to clear the stomach and intestines of redundant slime, and afterwards to strengthen the stomach and bowels, so as to destroy the disposition to their generation.

Give an emetic once or twice a week, in order to rid the stomach of impurities, slime, and morbific matter, the cause of worms. Attend to the state of the bowels, for they are often irregular through worms. A dose of the Composition Powder given night and morning, and bitter tonics during the day will be of essential service. This should be continued a week or two.

Lime-water being capable of dissolving the mucus in which the worms breed, may be taken; a teacupful two or three times a day—less for a child. Take with it the Tonic Mixture, or bitters. It is very effectual in relieving children.

The following infusion is valuable:—Best senna, Carolina pinkroot, manna, worm-seed, rhubarb; of each ½ oz. Bruise them, and infuse for two or three hours in boiling water. Sweeten with treacle. Give to a child six years old from three table-spoonfuls a day.

Sweets should be avoided. Salt and water taken in the morning will expel worms, especially the seat worms. It may be made by dissolving a table-spoonful of salt in half a pint of water. It may also form an injection to bring away the ascarides. — Camphor is another remedy. Dissolve 10 grains in a little spirit of wine, and add it now and then to the tonic bitters.

Various Remedies for the cure of Worms :—

Take an ounce of tin, finely powdered, and two drachms of Ethiop's mineral, mixed together; divide it into six powders, and take one of them, in a little syrup, twice a day: when they are used work them off with a little rhubarb. Or,

Jalap, quarter of an ounce; powdered rhubarb, quarter of an ounce; gamboge, two drachms; syrup of bear's-foot, sufficient to make it into a paste; then make it into ordinary sized lozenges. Dose:— For a child three years old, half a lozenge; six years, one lozenge; and so on, according to years. Or,

Spirits of turpentine, in doses of from 8 drops to a teaspoonful, in gruel sweetened.——Or,

Cowhage mixed with treacle. Give a child a teaspoonful fasting for 3 or 4 mornings successively—an adult a table-spoonful. Then give a purge.

Powdered rust of iron is a good vermifuge. It expels the worms and strengthens the constitution. To a child six years old from 10 to 40 grains may be given. An adult may take from a ¼ oz. It may be given in treacle or in beer. Dr. Rush says, "Of all the worm medicines that I have given I know none more safe and certain than this simple preparation of iron." It should always be followed by an aperient.

The common male fern-root is a certain remedy for the *tape*-worm. Two or three drachms of the powdered root to be taken in the morning, no supper having been taken the night before. It generally sickens a little. A brisk purgative is to be given a few hours after, which sometimes brings off the worm entire; if not, the same course must be followed at due intervals. For the success of this remedy, the root should be *recently* gathered; as after being kept long in the shops, its activity is diminished or destroyed.

WORMS.—Take two tea-spoonfuls of brandy, sweetened with loaf sugar, every morning. Or, a spoonful of the juice of lemons.

Or, take two tea-spoonfuls of worm-seed mixed with treacle, for six mornings. Or, one, two, or three drachms of powdered fern-root boiled in mead. This kills both the flat and round worms. Repeat the medicine from time to time.—*Wesley.*

WORM FEVER.—Boil a handful of rue and wormwood in water: forment the belly with the decoction, and apply the boiled herbs as a poultice; repeat the application night and morning. This frequently brings away worms from children who will take no internal medicine, and is likewise serviceable if the fever be of the putrid kind.—*Wesley.*

WORM SEEDS.—The seeds of this American plant form a powerful vermifuge. It speedily expels round and other worms from the intestines. The seeds are given in substance from 10 drains, or half a drachm, finely powdered, strewed on bread and butter, or made into an electuary with honey or treacle. After using some days, give an aperient, and the tonic bitters.

In America they use the oil also. Five to ten drops of the oil mixed with sugar, are a common dose for a child. Or, from 12 drops for an adult.

WORM SYRUP.—Senna, Carolina pink, of each 1 oz.; peach leaves, male fern, of each ½ oz.; kousso 1½ oz. Powder, and add a cupful of pure water, near boiling; shake up in a bottle for a day; then add a cupful of spirit of wine. Shake up several times a day for a week, keeping the bottle in a warm place. Then add another cupful of hot water in which has previously been infused half a teaspoonful of cayenne pepper.—This recipe is valuable, it will cause all kinds of worms to flee before it.—Dose, for a child six years old a teaspoonful four times a day. It may be given in well sweetened coffee.

WORMWOOD.-See *Robinson's Herbal*. It is a valuable plant, but very bitter, It is used in stomach complaints, promoting digestion and appetite by its stimulating and tonic properties. It strengthens the membranes of the intestines. It is often given in intermittent fevers successfully, and it is a powerful expellant of worms; hence its name.

The dose of the *powder* is from one scruple to a drachm. The infusion is made by adding ½ oz. of powder to a pint of water.

WOUNDS.—See *Bruises*.

WOUNDS.—Apply juice or powder of yarrow. Or, bind leaves of ground-ivy upon it. Or, wood-betony bruised. This quickly heals even cut veins and sinews, and draws out thorns or splinters.—*Wesley*.

WOUNDS, *to prevent from mortifying*.—Sprinkle sugar upon them, or powdered blood-root.

WOUNDS, *Putrid*.——Wash them morning and evening with warm decoction of agrimony. If they heal too soon, and a matter gathers underneath, apply a poultice of the leaves pounded, changing them once a-day till well.

Or, apply a carrot poultice; but if a gangrene comes on, apply a wheat flour poultice (after it has been by the fire till it begins to ferment) nearly cold. It will not fail.

WOUNDS, *to staunch the bleeding of*.—Where it can be done, take a bandage, handkerchief, or garter, and put it round the limb betwixt the wound and the heart, and tie it tight. It will answer the purpose of a tourniquet, and stop the bleeding till effectual relief can be given. In many cases, it might save life.

Or take a pledget of lint, and form it into a little ball, and press it upon the mouth of any bleeding vein or artery. Apply lint and small compresses saturated with salt and water, and bind them on the wound, to suppress the bleeding.

In dressing, bring the lips of the wound together, and keep them so by means of adhesive plaster, compresses, and a bandage. Wounds thus dressed may heal without suppuration. Frequently wet the dressings with diluted brandy and salt. Let the dressings remain two or three days. If suppuration takes place, remove the adhesive plaster, &c., and apply a bread poultice, or the slippery elm bark poultice; afterwards apply the salve or plaster. In case of proud flesh appearing, sprinkle sugar, or powdered bloodroot upon the wound; or apply as a lotion of the *diluted* solution of chloride of soda, or of chloride of lime—that is, in proportion of 1 oz. of the solution to a pint of water.—Or use a few grains of the vegetable caustic.

YARROW.—This plant is well known. The infusion taken inwardly, and applied outwardly as a wash, is good for piles, and sores. It is excellent for flux, looseness, and nervous melancholy. The powder is recommended for colic, ague, whites; and it is very useful in colds. It restrains the involuntary discharge of urine in children.—See *Robinson's Herbal*.

YEAST, *to make*.-Thicken two quarts of water, with fine flour about three spoonfuls, boil half an hour, sweeten with near half a pound of brown sugar; when near cold, put into it four spoonfuls of fresh yeast in a jug, shake it well together, and let it stand one day to ferment near the fire, without being covered. There will be a thin liquor on the top, which must be poured off; shake the remainder and cork it up for use. Take always four spoonfuls of the old to ferment the next quantity, keeping it always in succession.

A half-peck loaf will require about a gill.

Another way.—Boil one pound of potatoes to a mash; when half cold, add a cupful of yeast, and mix it well. It will be ready for use in two or three hours, and keeps well.

Use double the quantity of this to what you do of beer-yeast.

To take off the bitter of yeast, put bran into a sieve, and pour it through, having first mixed a little warm water with it.

YEAST, *for home made bread.* —Boil a handful of hops half an hour in 3 pints of water. Pour half, *boiling*, through a sieve, upon a cup of flour, mix, and add the rest of the hop water; a spoonful of salt, half a cup of treacle, and *when warm*, a cup of yeast.

YEAST DUMPLINGS. —— Make a very light dough with yeast, as for bread; use milk if you like, instead of water, add salt. Let it rise an hour before the fire; twenty minutes before you are to serve, have ready a pan of boiling water. Make the dough into balls; put them in, and boil 20 minutes. Stick a fork into one, and if it come out clear, it is enough. Do not cut them, but tear them apart at the top, or they will become heavy. Eat while hot, with treacle or sugar, preserve, &c.

YEAST POULTICE.—Yeast, 1 gill; milk, 1 pint; slippery elm bark sufficient to make a poultice. Sprinkle over with very finely powdered charcoal, and blood-root. Mix, and form a poultice. It is cooling and adapted to arrest gangrene or mortification. It is very appropriate to most sores and ulcers, especially offensive sores.

YELLOW DOCK.—See *Robinson's Herbal.*—This plant is well known. The leaves are boiled and eaten. It is moderately astringent, and rather purgative. It is very appropriate to scrofulous complaints. In bilious complaints, internal heat, hectic fever, palpitation of the heart, piles, cutaneous eruptions, &c., it is most valuable.

The root may be given in decoction. A poultice of it is very good to discuss all indolent swellings. Made into an ointment, it is good for tetter, ringworm, &c.

YELLOW FEVER. —— The first stage usually begins with weariness, chilly fits, faintness, giddiness, flushing of the face, redness of the eyes, pain in the eye-balls, forehead, back, great weakness, anxiety, thirst, and lethargy. The urine is high coloured, deficient, and turbid. The tongue is covered with a dark fur; the perspiration is irregular, interrupted, and lessened; the bile is secreted in unusual quantities, and speedily ejected from the stomach. The skin is very dry, hot, and hard. The eyes, face, and breast become *yellow.*

This stage of the disease lasts about 48 hours. The symptoms begin to abate, by which the patient is flattered; but returning aggravated symptoms soon undeceive him. He becomes very debilitated; putrefaction takes place; large patches of livid spots appear on different parts of the body; the tongue becomes dry and black; black fur on the teeth, and oft blood from the mouth, nose, nostrils, &c. The whole body often exhibits a livid yellow.

The *causes* may be contagion, the use of ardent spirits, marbleizing the liver, destroying digestion, &c. It may be caused by cold, wet feet and clothes, obstructed perspiration, &c.

Treatment. — The first object must be to excite action in the stomach, bowels, liver, and skin. Give an emetic; clear the bowels by a brisk purgative. Give the diaphoretic powder, and place the patient in the vapour bath, regulating the heat according to the strength of the patient. While in the bath let the patient drink balm, pennyroyal, or catnep tea. When he comes out of the bath, place him in a warm bed, well covered with blankets to produce perspiration. If he perspires, gradually lessen the covering.

If vomiting prevails, give the neutralizing mixture, a tablespoonful every half hour till the vomiting ceases. If the stomach be very irritable, give with the neutralizing mixture a drachm of Epsom salts to each dose, in a little tea; if the vomiting does not abate, preserve with the medicine, and apply mustard plasters to the stomach and feet twice a day. Do not neglect aperients; for it is of the highest importance to promote the natural evacuations.

Attend also to the skin. If dry, hot, and parched, give an infusion of boneset, to be drunk freely, to promote perspiration. If this should fail, give the Sudorific Powder, or the Sweating Drops till perspiration shall take place. Should they cause too much sickness, give lemonade or cream of tartar water. In the West Indies they effect a cure by drinking an infusion of boneset, by using the warm or vapour bath, and bathing the body with lemon juice and water, or warm vinegar and water.

YELLOW FLUMMERY. — Take 2 ozs. of isinglass; beat it; put it into a bowl, and pour a pint of boiling water upon it; cover it till cold, and add a pint of sherry; the juice of two lemons with the rind of one, and the yolks of 8 eggs. Beat well; sweeten; put it into a pan, and when it boils, strain it through an iron sieve. When nearly cold, put it into cups and moulds.

YELLOW INK.—This ink is useful in drawing and making pen and ink sketches; it is prepared thus:—Take Persian berry liquor, 1½ oz.; alum, ½ oz.; rain-water, as required, gum arabic, ½ oz. Boil the whole together ten minutes; then strain through fine muslin; when cold, it is fit for use.

YELLOW WAX.—Yellow resin, 1 lb.; Burgundy pitch, 1½ oz.; bees wax, 1½ oz; mutton tallow, 1½ oz. Melt all together; then add camphor, 2½ drachms; olive oil, a tablespoonful; sassafras oil, 2 drachms; best rum, 2 tablespoonfuls. Mix well, and pour into a vessel of water, and knead it till it is cold. It acts as a good sticking plaster. It is useful in cuts, ulcers, sores, &c. It is very good for rheumatism; and would be a sovereign remedy by the addition of ½ oz. of cayenne, and ½ oz. of opium.

YORKSHIRE CAKES.—See page 92.

YORKSHIRE PUDDING.— Mix five spoonfuls of flour with a quart of milk, and three eggs well beaten. Butter the pan. When brown by baking under the meat, turn the other side upwards, and brown that. It should be made in a square pan, and cut into pieces to come to table. Set it over a chafing-dish, and stir it well.

FAMILY DYEING RECEIPTS.

☞ THE NEWEST MODES.

BLACK for WORSTED or WOOLLEN.—Water, 3 gallons; bichromate of potass, ¾ oz. Boil the goods in this 40 minutes; then wash in cold water. Then take 3 gallons of water, add 9 ozs. of logwood, 3 ozs. of fustic, and one or two drops of D. O. V. or Double Oil of Vitriol; boil the goods 40 minutes, and wash out in cold water. This will dye from 1 to 2 lbs. of cloth, or a lady's dress, if of a dark colour, as brown, claret, &c.

☞ All coloured dresses with cotton warps should be previously steeped one hour in sumach liquor; and then saddened in 3 gallons of clean water, with one cupful of nitrate of iron for 30 minutes, then it must be well washed and dyed as first stated.

BLACK for SILK.—Dye the same as Black for Worsted; but previously steep the silk in the following liquor. Scald 4 ozs. of logwood, and ¼ oz. of turmeric in a pint of boiling water. Then add 7 pints of cold water. Steep 30 or 40 minutes; take out, and add 1 oz. of sulphate of iron, (or copperas) dissolved in hot water; steep the silk 30 minutes longer.

BROWN for WORSTED or WOOL.—Water, 3 gallons, bichromate of potass, ¾ oz. Boil the goods in this 40 minutes. Wash out in cold water. Then take water, 3 gallons, 6 ozs. of peachwood, and 2 ozs. of turmeric. Boil the goods in this 40 minutes. Wash out.

IMPERIAL BLUE for SILK, WOOL, and WORSTED.—Water, 1 gallon; sulphuric acid, a wine-glassful; Imperial Blue, 1 tablespoonful, or more, according to the shade required. Put in the silk, worsted, or wool, and boil 10 minutes. Wash in a weak solution of soap lather.

SKY BLUE, for WORSTED and WOOLLEN.—Water, 1 gallon; sulphuric acid, a wine-glassful; glauber salts, or crystals, two table-spoonfuls; liquid extract of indigo, a teaspoonful; boil the goods about 15 minutes. Rinse in cold water.

CLARET for WOOL or WORSTED.—*A short way of dyeing the same.*—Water, 3 gallons; cudbear, 12 ozs.; logwood, 4 ozs.; old fustic, 4 ozs.; alum, ½ oz. Boil the goods in it one hour. Wash. This will dye from 1 to 2 lbs. of material.

CRIMSON for WORSTED or WOOL.—Water, 3 gllons; paste Cochineal, 1 oz.; cream of tartar, 1 oz.; nitrate of tin, a wine-glassful. Boil your goods in this one hour. Wash out in cold water. Then in another vessel with 3 gallons of warm water, a cupful of ammonia, the whole well mixed. Put in the goods, and work well 15 minutes. For a bluer shade, add more ammonia. Then wash out.

FAWN DRAB for SILK.—Hot water, 1 gallon; Annotta liquor, a wine-glassful; 2 ozs. each of sumach and fustic. Add copperas liquor, according to the required shade. Wash out.

It is best to have the copperas liquor in another vessel.

☞ A *Dark Drab* may be obtained by using a little archil, and extract of Indigo.

FLESH COLOUR, *for dyeing* SILK.—Boiling water, 1 gallon; put in one ounce of white soap, and one ounce of pearlash. Mix well; then add a cupful of Annotta liquor. Put the silk through several times, and proportion the liquor till you obtain the required shade.

A *Salmon colour* may be obtained by first passing through the above liquor, and then through diluted muriate of Tin.

MAGENTA *for* SILK, WOOL, *or* WORSTED.—Water, 1 gallon, heated up to 180 degrees; add Magenta Liqour, 1 tablespoonful; stir it well up. This will dye a broad ribbon 4 yards long; or a pair of small stockings. To dye a larger quantity of material, add more Magenta Liquor and water. The shade of colour may be easily regulated by using more or less. Magenta Pink may be obtained by increased dilution.

MAUVE, *for* SILK, WOOL, *or* WORSTED.—Water, 1 gallon; add one tablespoonful of sulphuric acid; then heat to boiling point. For a very *light Mauve*, add one teaspoonful of imperial Violet Liquor; boil the same amount of material, as stated under Magenta, about 10 minutes. Rinse in cold water. If the colour be too deep, use a little soap in rinsing, using warm water.

A *violet colour* may be produced by using a tablespoonful of Violet Liquor instead of a teaspoonful.

PEA-GREEN, *for* SILK. — To one quart of water, put half a teaspoonful of Picric Acid, and rather more than half a wineglassful of sulphuric acid, and a teaspoonful of paste extract of indigo; boil about five minutes; then add water to cool it down to blood heat, or 100 degrees. Put in the silk, and work it about 20 minutes. The shade may be varied by adding more or less of the Picric Acid, or extract of indigo; if more of either be added, boil separately in a little water, and add to the previous liquor.

PEA-GREEN *for* WORSTED.—Use the same materials as the aforesaid; but boil all the time in 1 gallon of water for about 20 or 30 minutes.

☞ A DARKER GREEN may be obtained by using a larger quantity of material.

PLUM COLOUR *for* WORSTED, SILK, *or* COTTON.—Water, 1 gallon; sulphuric acid, a teaspoonful; glauber salts, or common Dyer's crystals, 2 tablespoonfuls; violet liquor, a tablespoonful; magenta liquor, half a tablespoonful. Boil the article (silk, wool, or worsted,) about ten minutes.

☞ Cotton should be dyed the above colours separately, and by first running them through weak Gall Liquor, and weak double muriate of tin. Then wash well, and work in the aforesaid liquor, according to colour and shade. The liquor should be cold for *Cotton*.

SCARLET *on* WORSTED *or* WOOL.—Water, 3 gallons, 2 ozs. of dry cochineal, 1 oz. of cream of tartar, nitrate of tin, a wine-glassful; boil the goods 1 hour. To give the goods a yellower hue, and a little young fustic. Wash out as before.

YELLOW, *for Dyeing* SILK, —Proceed the same in Dyeing as *Pea Green*, omitting the extract of indigo, and using oxalic tin instead of sulphuric acid.

THE COLD WATER CURE.

The Cold Water treatment is that which nature has placed in the power of all her creatures; and without water taken inwardly and applied outwardly, there can be no health. Nature has no secrets in giving man life; she has implanted within him the knowledge of that which is to support and render pleasant that life. "I leave behind me," said a celebrated physician, on his death-bed, "*two great physicians, diet and water.*"

Water is the great dissolvent in nature. If the primary ducts be obstructed, water dilutes, attenuates, divides, and scatters the impurities contained in them; and these are afterwards ejected by the stomach and intestines. If disease be settled in the blood, and the morbific matter deposited in the different organs of the animal economy, nothing is so effectual as water to dilute the thickened and blunt the acute; to revivify that which languishes, extinguish that which burns, and to open again all the passages by which injurious humours can escape.

Cold water creates a sudorific process causing perspiration, without wearying the organic system. It is supported by copious draughts of cold water, which quench the thirst, moisten and refresh the blood, replace the lost juices, and maintain the tone of the muscles.

The drinking of cold water, and its application to the body by various processes, convey the morbid humours to the skin, whence they exude in eruptions, boils, and abscesses. These eruptions, constituting the crisis of the complaint, are the certain sign of a perfect cure. After the unwholesome juices are driven out and replaced by wholesome ones, then follow the restoration of the digestive powers, and the freeing of all the organs by the dissolving of all obstructions; the vital and animal functions are re-established in their former harmony; and thus nothing then remains but health, a treasure which can only be preserved by continuing the system by which it has been obtained.

Some will ask, Is the cold water treatment applicable to all descriptions of disease? We answer, that its application must be of advantage in the large number of acute and chronic diseases. There are cases, however, wherein some essential organ having become defective, art can do no more than prolong existence and alleviate suffering. Among such exceptions are consumption, organic diseases of the heart, of the lungs, of the large vessels, dropsy, &c. Yet all these cases, and others deemed incurable, by the moderate judicious use of some of the cold water applications, will ensure relief and palliation of pain.

Again, will the cold-water treatment produce a radical cure? What is to be understood by the word radical? If it means the final extirpation from the system the cause of disease, and the relief of the patient from pain, then, the cure by the cold water method is *radical!* But if to be radical, a cure is sought which is to prevent a return of the disease, in cases of parties exposing themselves to the same influences which originated the disease, then neither this nor any other means of treatment will produce such an effect.

As to danger from the cold water treatment there can be no active mode of treatment more innocent, with reference to its present or future effects, if applied with judgment; but if not, it may be followed by very dangerous consequences.

The water used must be cold and fresh, and *soft;* that is, it must have the quality of dissolving, and therefore must be cold, and without any mineral properties. To prove its fitness, linen cloth washed in it must become white, and vegetables dressed in it must be tender.

The SWEATING PROCESS is the most disagreeable part of the treatment; but it is the most important, and the benefits derived from it compensate for the unpleasantness of its duration.

The patient is enclosed, naked, in a large coarse blanket, the legs extended, and the arms kept close to the body; the blanket is then wound round it, as tight as possible, turning it well under at the feet; over this is placed, and well tucked in a small feather bed, sometimes two; and then a sheet and a counterpane are spread over all; thus, the patient resembles a mummy. Sometimes when perspiration is difficult, the head, except the face, is covered. Perspiration begins in about 45 minutes, and then the irritation goes off. The patient should lie perspiring at least one hour. The windows in the room must be opened, and a glass of cold water given every half hour, to refresh the patient, and promote perspiration. If there is headache, a damp cloth may be wrapped round the head. This process does not weaken the patient; he loses neither weight nor strength, but improves in personal appearance, even under several processes.

The necessary duration of the process may be known by profuse perspiration on the patient's face. The person should be washed well in warm or tepid water. The sweating process must be used with great care, and the constitution of the patient must be considered. M. Priessnitz, of Silesia, practised and recommended the cold bath immediately afterwards. 'Strange as it may appear to many,' says Dr. Graham, 'I consider the determination towards the skin, induced by the perspiring blankets, to be a great advantage, prior to the use of the cold bath; because the internal organs are thereby relieved, and the shock has quite a different effect on them from what it would have if they were not first soothed, and the skin relieved.'

By this process internal diseases are often brought to the surface, and pass away; the nervous system is wonderfully strengthened; and skin diseases are annihilated. The sweating contains morbid matter. M. Priessnitz justly remarks,—

Covered and swaddled with clothes, in our darkness we do not see that if the corrupt and dirty matter from daily insensible perspiration, or from sensible sweating, is not carefully cleared from the skin by washing, it must increase and attach itself to the skin, close the pores, and obstruct the excretion so indispensable to health, and must inevitably, from such evil tendency, at last produce disease. We relax and debilitate the skin, by dressing so warmly during the day, and sleeping on feather beds at night, or by washing ourselves with warm water.

The COLD BATH.—Do not bathe soon after walking. During the bathing immerse the head several times in cold water. Keep in motion during the time. Priessnitz advises his patients to avoid the second sensation of cold, which is a sort of fever, by leaving the bath before it is felt, that they may avoid a too powerful re-action, provoked by a great subtraction of heat. Take a glass or two of water immediately after the bath.

The DOUCHE BATH is very efficacious in extracting the morbid humours from all the parts they have seized upon for years. In long continual complaints the douche is a most powerful remedial agent. It removes the weakness of the skin, and strengthens it. It renders the body hardy, and fortifies it to endure all changes of the air. It powerfully excites the muscular and nervous systems. The Douche Bath is a stream of falling water as thick as the wrist, and permitted to fall on the diseased parts of the body, which it benefits and strengthens. The water should fall from 12 to 18 feet.

The EYE BATH is a glass instrument made to fit the eye, so as to apply cold water, the eye being opened at the same time.

The FINGER BATH is used for Whitlows, &c. Place the finger in a glass of water, four times a-day for a quarter of an hour each time; and the elbow in water twice a-day, and put on a heating bandage above the elbow, to draw the inflammation from the hand.

The FOOT BATH is used when the doctors would order warm baths. Thus headaches, toothaches, eye-inflammation, and a flow of blood to the head, are always relieved by the foot-bath, with the addition of wet bandages on the parts affected. But the foot-tub should not contain more than from two to four inches depth of water, just enough to cover the foot, not the ancles; for toothache an inch is enough, and the time from 15 to 30 minutes. For sprains the water must be up to the ancles. The water to be changed as soon as it feels warm. Afterwards apply friction, or walk out, to restore the warmth. Dr. Graham says, "I can recommend the foot-bath, with confidence, in determination of blood to the head, in headache, in affections of the eyes, and in habitual coldness of the feet."

The HEAD BATH is a vessel with a few inches of water for bathing the back part of the head, to cure its rheumatic pains, common headaches, rheumatic inflammation of the eyes, deafness, loss of appetite, delirium tremens, giddiness of the head, and to prevent apoplexy. It often causes bad morbific matter to exude from behind the ears.

The SITZ or SITTING BATH is a small shallow tub 18 inches in diameter, with water 3 or 4 inches deep, in which the patient sits, with his feet on the ground, for 15 minutes or more, twice or thrice per day. It wonderfully strengthens the nerves, draws down humours from the head and chest, relieves flatulency, and has the most important results to those who lead a sedentary life. Use only 3 or 4 inches of water, as a larger quantity would remain cold, and perhaps cause congestion to the upper extremities; a wet bandage to the head will, however, prevent any congestion. Rub the abdomen as much as possible, while in the bath, with the wet hand. *It is a most valuable bath.* It is a remedy of great power in weak bowels, piles, congestion in the liver, chlorosis, and other female complaints; its value is little known.

COOLING BANDAGES. — These are mostly used in inflammation, congestion of blood, headache, rheumatism, &c., and should always be accompanied by the sitz baths. Linen is first wetted in cold water, doubled in several folds, and placed on the parts affected; renew them as they get warm.

STIMULATING BANDAGES.—— They are dipped in cold water, then well wrung out, then appled to the part affected so as to exclude the external air; to effect this, an outside bandage is placed over the first, which retains and throws back the moisture. Heat is thus generated, and has an exciting and dissolving property, which stimulates perspiration, and draws out the vicious humours. For throat and chest complaints, they are worn one round the neck, and one on the chest, at night; for weak and inflamed eyes, one is worn at the back of the head or neck at night; for weak digestion and cases of debility, one round the waist, all day; and for gout and rheumatism, the legs are wrapped in them night and morning. The *umschlag*, or *stimulating bandage*, is always used for wounds, bruises, and diseased parts, and for pain in any particular region of the body. Its alleviating power is most surprising.

The bandage for the waist is a towel, three yards long, and one foot wide; of this one-third is dry, and two-thirds wetted. The wet part is placed on the belly, the dry covers it. It is made tight round the body. It is a cure for intestine congestion, for constipation of the bowels, relaxation, colics, and for gripes. It rallies the powers of the stomach, increases its heat, and by assisting digestion, enables the system to form better juices. Gout, rheumatism, enlargement of the bones, abscesses, chronic inflammation, cancers, caries, and syphilitic ulcers, demand the application of these bandages; for they relieve pain when all other remedies fail.

The WET SHEET.—All diseases of the skin, as ringworms, small pox, measles, and scarlet fever, may be cured by the *wet sheet*. Do not start at this, for it is consonant with reason. It soothes the patient, promotes the eruption, and in fevers it produces salutary perspiration.

Spread a blanket on a bed, then on it a *wet sheet*, well wrung out; wrap the patient close up in it, except his face; wind the blanket round the body, already cased in the sheet; then add plenty of blankets, tuck them well in, and the necessary perspiration will soon be generated. To stop fever, change the sheet every hour or half hour. "In desperate cases," says a medical writer, "we have known this done fifty times in little more than 24 hours, and perseverance in this treatment ends infallibly in success."

When the fever has abated, the patient is placed in a bath of tepid water (about 64° Fahrenheit,) for a quarter of an hour; during which time two persons must rub him briskly with the hand, water being taken up from the bath occasionally, and poured over his head and shoulders. The wet sheet, or bandage, is not unpleasant long; the patient gets warm almost directly;

but we must not regard inconvenience or unpleasantness for a cure. Are drugs, blisters, and leeches pleasant? But the application of cold water, in any way, relieves the skin, excites it, and disencumbers it of obstructions which close the orifices of the pores, a reaction of the whole system ensues, a heat being created on the surface, 40 or 50 degrees above the usual temperature of the body. The body imbibes a portion of the water, which in conjunction with the heat newly caused, softens and dissolves the morbid humours, and assists in their exudation by the pores of the skin.

ABLUTIONS.—Where persons are very weak, washing and rubbing the body must be done, in place of the bath or douche; and water may be poured over the heads of feverish patients, and rubbed on the shoulders and parts affected. If the patient be too weak to allow of this rubbing, a wet sheet is thrown over him, on which the friction is applied. This is of great advantage in weak cases and young children. The ablutions are an essential, agreeable, and valuable portion of the cold water system. In trifling complaints, gout in its infancy, nervous irritability, or in weakness in the skin, ablutions, accompanied by drinking abundantly cold water is very often sufficient to establish health. Ablutions should be performed in the morning immediately in getting out of bed, before the body has become chilled, and the patient must afterwards take exercise in the open air. Fatigued persons may try the wet sheet and the rubbing, and they will speedily find the benefit of it. To use the wet sheet as an ablution, the patient stands up, and the servant flings it over his head and body; rub the body well for five minutes, then take off the wet sheet, and put on a dry one. This is a certain relief for fatigue and over-exertion.

COLD WATER DRINKING.—The best time both for drinking cold water and exercise is before breakfast. Then they both produce their *best* effects; but the only general rule prescribed by Priessnitz is to drink cold water as much, and at all times, as it can be done without inconvenience. Water may be drunk after breakfast, but the stomach must not be over-charged. At dinner also a few glasses may be taken to moisten the food; after that the stomach must be left to itself; and after the lapse of a few hours, we may go on drinking cold water until supper time. It may be taken after supper, but not so as to disturb the rest. Exercise, which is in itself a part of the curative process, excites the beneficial action of the water, and promotes the cure. *The water* should be fresh from the spring, and as cold as possible. Stoppers must be kept in the bottles and decanters which hold it, as the water then will preserve its coldness and freshness much longer.

ADVICE. — Immediately on rising in the morning, rince the mouth, and wash the teeth with cold water, then drink two or three glasses of spring water; after this, the whole body, especially the head, must be washed. If a thickness in the throat be felt, gargle well, and rub the outside of the throat three or four times a-day, with a cold wet hand; keep the water in the mouth until it becomes warm, then repeat it. This method is recommended for clearing and strengthening the throat.

Splendidly Illustrated with 130 Engravings of various Plants.
The Best, Most Simple, and Practical Work on British and Foreign Herbs ever published.

Price, 2s. 6d. Plain.   Coloured Plates, 3s. 6d.
OR SENT POST FREE FOR 4 STAMPS EXTRA.

ROBINSON'S
NEW FAMILY HERBAL:

Comprising a Description of British and Foreign Plants, and their Medical Virtues; founded on the Works of the best English and American Writers on the Medical Properties of Herbs. Directions for Gathering Leaves, Flowers, Seeds, Roots, Barks; and for making Juices, Syrup, Preserves, Oils, Electuaries, Conserves, Ointments, Poultices, Pills, Decoctions, &c., to which is added, The Botanic Family Physician, with complete Directions for the use of the various Herbs. General Directions for curing or Preventing Disease. Valuable Receipts, and Remarks on Diet, Clothing, Bathing, Air, Exercise, &c., Nursing the Sick, Hints in Emergencies, Nutrition of Grain, Flesh, Animal and Vegetable Food, Fruits, &c. Definition of Terms, and other important matter.

☞ *This part has already been found by the afflicted, to be more valuable than gold.*

EXTRACT FROM THE PREFACE.

The *government of Herbs by the sun, moon, and planets*, has been exploded by modern science; and is now regarded as absurd in the extreme. Botanical knowledge has been greatly extended, and some Medical Men and Herbalists have very ably written upon it. The properties of Herbs are now better understood than in the days of Culpeper, and others.

In preparing this Work, I have rejected the Astrological government of Herbs, such as, for instance, Culpeper's laughable description of Wormwood. I have consulted the works of Hill, Woodville, Don, Thornton, and especially some of the *great American Herbalists.*

☞ Respecting this Work, a Gentleman writes, "I thank Mr. Robinson for publishing his very valuable Herbal, and especially for appending to it, *The Botanic Family Physician*, which contains lucid and appropriate Directions for the cure and prevention of disease. The Botanico-Medico System I prefer to the Allopathic, the Homœopathic, and to all other systems whatever. I prefer it, on account of the great benefit I have received from it, and I do feel grateful for having purchased Robinson's invaluable Herbal. Why, it is only the price of one bottle of Allopathic medicine, and this ought to induce the sale of it, which, I learn, is very extensive. I deem it a rare Family Book, and it will save pounds on pounds in the ordinary Allopathic Advice and Physic."—*C. M., Manchester*, 1865.

WAKEFIELD: W. NICHOLSON AND SONS.

NICHOLSON'S ARITHMETIC

SIMPLIFIED AND IMPROVED BY THE ADDITION OF

SHORT RECKONINGS, MENTAL CALCULATIONS, AND A CONCISE SYSTEM OF BOOK-KEEPING.

In this work the obscure rules of other Arithmetics have been exchanged for **PLAIN** and **SIMPLE** directions which a child may understand, and the unscientific methods of working have been abandoned for those which accord with Arithmetical science.

MENTAL CALCULATIONS,

so very important in business, have been incorporated. OBJECT-TEACHING, or teaching by sight, (the best and most effective of all teaching) forms a prominent part in the first part of the book, and in Fractions ; and a

SYSTEM OF BOOK-KEEPING

has also been appended.

*** It is surprising with what tenacity some Schoolmasters cling to old usages. Disregarding all modern discoveries and improvements, they would employ the very same Educational Works by which they were taught in their childhood, although those works have been superseded by others infinitely superior. In these days of rapid intellectual development, bearing some resemblance to Railways, Electric Telegraphs, &c., Schoolmasters, Parents, and Guardians of Youth, must abandon their prejudices, and espouse those Educational Works which modern science offers them as decided improvements, or they will subject themselves to the suspicion of incompetency for teaching.

The Publishers of this **ARITHMETIC**, had, at the first, to contend with such absurd prejudices; but, thanks to the discernment of the more intelligent Preceptors, and to the good sense of the Public, this work now commands an extensive sale, and bids fair to supplant the antiquated Editions. IMPROVEMENT AND PROGRESS ARE IRRESISTIBLE. Price 1s. By Post 1s. 2d.

(Side text: IMPORTANT TO YOUNG MEN AND YOUNG WOMEN — WHO WISH TO IMPROVE THEMSELVES.)

KEY to NICHOLSON'S ARITHMETIC,

SIMPLIFIED AND IMPROVED.   PRICE ONLY ONE SHILLING.

☞ The lowness of the Price of this Key is a new feature ! ! Keys having always been charged from 3s. to 5s. each.

GRAY'S ARITHMETIC.—Containing Rules for working the SLIDING RULE, MENSURATION, AND MENTAL CALCULATION.
☞ *This is a most valuable Arithmetic ; it is a complete book of Arithmetical Science; and for lowness of price is unparalleled.*
Cloth, 6d.

Published by W. NICHOLSON & SONS, Wakefield.

Price 1s.   By Post 1s. 2d.

The Easiest, Cheapest, and Most Comprehensive Grammar of the Age.

THE GRAMMAR

OF THE

ENGLISH LANGUAGE MADE EASY:

With Exercises Adapted to every Part.

ALSO, ENGLISH, LATIN, AND GREEK

PREFIXES AND AFFIXES,

AND

DERIVATION,

EXHIBITING NEARLY 10,000 WORDS,

Derived from the Anglo-Saxon, Latin, Greek, and French Languages.

BY W. NICHOLSON.

Schoolmasters, and Teachers, whether Public or Private, would be benefitted by this Grammar—it is a Student's book—and is eminently calculated to make an efficient teacher.

Young Persons, male or female, would reap great mental advantage by studying this Grammar. It would teach them not only to speak and write correctly; but by the study of Derivation they would obtain a copious knowledge and command of Language. Derivation is eminently adapted to produce such a result.

☞ The attention of YOUNG MEN is especially called to these advantages.

Though this Grammar may be called a *Student's Book*, yet it is so very simple in its Definitions, Rules, and Exercises, that it is *the* Grammar for Children.

Even to adults whose education is imperfect, this Grammar offers very great facilities for improvement.

LONDON: SIMPKIN, MARSHALL, & CO., AND W. TEGG.

Reciters & Penny Readings.

Published by W. Nicholson & Sons, Wakefield.
(LATE OF HALIFAX.)

THE EXCELSIOR RECITER:
Comprising Sentimental, Pathetic, Witty and Humourous Pieces, Speeches, Narrations, &c., for Recitation at Evening Parties, Social, Temperance and Band of Hope Meetings. By Professor Duncan, Lecturer on Elocution. Price 1s. 6d. By Book Post 3d. extra.

PENNY READINGS and RECITATIONS;
In Prose and Verse, of most Interesting and Instructive Subjects, Scientific, Historical, Witty, and Humorous. Adapted for Evening parties and Various Social Gatherings. By Professor Duncan. First Series.   1s. 6d.

PENNY READINGS and RECITATIONS.
Second Series. 1s. 6d.

THE CHOICE RECITER;
For Evening Orations, and Beautiful and Humorous Readings for the entertainment of Social Temperance and other Popular Gatherings. By Professor Duncan. 1s.

THE TEMPERANCE ORATOR;
Comprising Speeches, Readings, Dialogues, and Illustrations of the Evils of Intemperance, &c., in Prose & Verse. By Professor Duncan. 1s.

Recitations from SHAKESPERE, and other Popular Authors. By Professor Duncan. 6d.

THE RECITER FOR THE MILLIONS;
Consisting of Entertaining, Comic, and Humorous Pieces, in Prose and Poetry, many of which are original. By Professor Duncan. Cloth 9d. Stiff Covers 6d.

THE SABBATH SCHOOL RECITER,
Adapted for Anniversaries, Tea Parties, Band of Hope Meetings, Social Gatherings, &c. Price 1s. Bound, can also be had in 2 Parts, each complete at 6d.

Catalogues may be had on Application.

www.ingramcontent.com/pod-product-compliance
Lightning Source LLC
Chambersburg PA
CBHW031956300426
44117CB00008B/786